REGIONAL AND METROPOLITAN
GROWTH AND DECLINE
IN THE UNITED STATES

REGIONAL AND METROPOLITAN GROWTH AND DECLINE IN THE UNITED STATES

William H. Frey
and
Alden Speare, Jr.

for the
National Committee for Research
on the 1980 Census

RUSSELL SAGE FOUNDATION / NEW YORK

The Russell Sage Foundation

Library of Congress Cataloging-in-Publication Data

Frey, William H.
  Regional and metropolitan growth and decline in the United States
  William H. Frey, Alden Speare, Jr.
    p. cm. — (The population of the United States in the 1980s)
  Bibliography: p.
  Includes index.
  ISBN 0-87154-293-5
    1. Metropolitan areas—United States. 2. Metropolitan areas—United States—
Population. 3. Cities and town—United States—Growth. I. Speare, Alden.
II. Title. III. Series.
HT334.U5F68 1988   88-6727
307.7'6'0973—dc19   CIP

Cover and text design: HUGUETTE FRANCO

10 9 8 7 6 5 4 3 2

The National Committee for Research on the 1980 Census

The committee is sponsored by the Social Science Research Council, the Russell Sage Foundation, and the Alfred P. Sloan Foundation, in collaboration with the U.S. Bureau of the Census. The opinions, findings, and conclusions or recommendations expressed in the monographs supported by the committee are those of the author(s) and do not necessarily reflect the views of the committee or its sponsors.

Foreword

Regional and Metropolitan Growth and Decline in the United States is
one of an ambitious series of volumes aimed at converting the vast statistical yield of the 1980 census into authoritative analyses of major
changes and trends in American life. This series, "The Population of the
United States in the 1980s," represents an important episode in social
science research and revives a long tradition of independent census
analysis. First in 1930, and then again in 1950 and 1960, teams of social
scientists worked with the U.S. Bureau of the Census to investigate
significant social, economic, and demographic developments revealed
by the decennial censuses. These census projects produced three landmark series of studies, providing a firm foundation and setting a high
standard for our present undertaking.

There is, in fact, more than a theoretical continuity between those
earlier census projects and the present one. Like those previous efforts,
this new census project has benefited from close cooperation between
the Census Bureau and a distinguished, interdisciplinary group of scholars. Like the 1950 and 1960 research projects, research on the 1980 census was initiated by the Social Science Research Council and the Russell Sage Foundation. In deciding once again to promote a coordinated
program of census analysis, Russell Sage and the Council were mindful
not only of the severe budgetary restrictions imposed on the Census
Bureau's own publishing and dissemination activities in the 1980s, but
also of the extraordinary changes that have occurred in so many dimensions of American life over the past two decades.

The studies constituting "The Population of the United States in
the 1980s" were planned, commissioned, and monitored by the National Committee for Research on the 1980 Census, a special committee
appointed by the Social Science Research Council and sponsored by the
Council, the Russell Sage Foundation, and the Alfred P. Sloan Foundation, with the collaboration of the U.S. Bureau of the Census. This com-

mittee includes leading social scientists from a broad range of fields—demography, economics, education, geography, history, political science, sociology, and statistics. It has been the committee's task to select the main topics for research, obtain highly qualified specialists to carry out that research, and provide the structure necessary to facilitate coordination among researchers and with the Census Bureau.

The topics treated in this series span virtually all the major features of American society—ethnic groups (blacks, Hispanics, foreign-born); spatial dimensions (migration, neighborhoods, housing, regional and metropolitan growth and decline); and status groups (income levels, families and households, women). Authors were encouraged to draw not only on the 1980 census but also on previous censuses and on subsequent national data. Each individual research project was assigned a special advisory panel made up of one committee member, one member nominated by the Census Bureau, one nominated by the National Science Foundation, and one or two other experts. These advisory panels were responsible for project liaison and review and for recommendations to the National Committee regarding the readiness of each manuscript for publication. With the final approval of the chairman of the National Committee, each report was released to the Russell Sage Foundation for publication and distribution.

The debts of gratitude incurred by a project of such scope and organizational complexity are necessarily large and numerous. The committee must thank, first, its sponsors—the Social Science Research Council, the Russell Sage Foundation, and the Alfred P. Sloan Foundation. The long-range vision and day-to-day persistence of these organizations and individuals sustained this research program over many years. The active and willing cooperation of the Bureau of the Census was clearly invaluable at all stages of this project, and the extra commitment of time and effort made by Bureau economist James R. Wetzel must be singled out for special recognition. A special tribute is also due to David L. Sills of the Social Science Research Council, staff member of the committee, whose organizational, administrative, and diplomatic skills kept this complicated project running smoothly.

The committee also wishes to thank those organizations that contributed additional funding to the 1980 census report—the Ford Foundation and its deputy vice president, Louis Winnick, the National Science Foundation, the National Institute on Aging, and the National Institute of Child Health and Human Development. Their support of the research program in general and of several particular studies is gratefully acknowledged.

The ultimate goal of the National Committee and its sponsors has been to produce a definitive, accurate, and comprehensive picture of the U.S. population in the 1980s, a picture that would be primarily descriptive but also enriched by a historical perspective and a sense of the challenges for the future inherent in the trends of today. We hope our readers will agree that the present volume takes a significant step toward achieving that goal.

CHARLES F. WESTOFF

Chairman and Executive Director
National Committee for Research
on the 1980 Census

Acknowledgments

The preparation of this book was facilitated by the Russell Sage Foundation through the National Committee on the 1980 Census, which provided support to the authors at The University of Michigan and Brown University. In addition, Alden Speare worked on the monograph while on sabbatical leave from Brown University at the Bureau of the Census during 1984–1985. While at the Bureau, he received partial salary and research support from the Center for Demographic Studies. Further support at Michigan was provided to William H. Frey by the Center for Population Research, NICHD grant No. HD17168. Special tabulations from the 1980 census were provided by the U.S. Bureau of the Census, and a wide range of computer-readable census data was made available by the Inter-university Consortium for Political and Social Research in Ann Arbor.

The authors wish to acknowledge the helpful comments they received from the advisory panel members, John D. Kasarda (chair), Sidney Goldstein, and John F. Long; as well as from Charles F. Westoff, chairman and executive director of the National Committee for Research on the 1980 Census. They are also grateful to Richard L. Forstall for his valuable critiques of several of the chapters and to the authors of other books in this series for their reactions and cooperation.

The preparation of this book represents the product of many individual efforts. The authors are grateful for the assistance of Priscilla Lewis and her staff at the Russell Sage Foundation, who are responsible for the final copyediting and processing of the entire manuscript. At Brown University, Michael P. Guest, Jean Lynch, Mary Speare, and Joan Winter assisted in the preparation and analyses of data. At the Bureau of the Census, Michael Fortier assisted with data processing; and at The University of Michigan, Anne Croisier and Kelvin Pollard assisted with the data analysis, Kathleen Duke assisted with copyediting, and Ingrid Naaman assisted in the typing and preparation of the manuscript. Finally, the authors wish to express a particular debt of gratitude for the computer programming efforts of Cathy Sun of The University of Michigan Population Studies Center, who single-handedly made order out of the vast array of census data for different time periods, geographic areas, and boundary definitions that were placed at her disposal. The rich geographic detail and consistent time series that appear in the various tables and figures in this monograph would not have been possible without her efforts.

This monograph represents a joint effort wherein both authors contributed to each chapter. Nevertheless, each author bore primary responsibility for one of the book's two major parts. Alden Speare took the lead in drafting the chapters for Part One (3, 4, 5, and 6), which pertain to regional and metropolitanwide growth and decline. William H. Frey took the lead in drafting the Part Two chapters (7, 8, 9, 10, and 11) pertaining to city–suburb redistribution within large metropolitan areas. In this examination of various aspects of regional, metropolitan, and city growth and decline in the United States, the authors have attempted to provide an authoritative description of post–1970 trends that is possible only with the rich area-based data at their disposal. It is hoped that these analyses provide fresh insights to scholars, practitioners, and general readers who seek a thorough understanding of the fundamental population redistribution shifts that have been occurring in the United States since 1970.

WILLIAM H. FREY
The University of Michigan

ALDEN SPEARE, JR.
Brown University

Contents

List of Tables

List of Appendix Tables

List of Figures

OVERVIEW

1

INTRODUCTION

Charting Post-1970 Redistribution Changes

PRIOR to 1970 the patterns of growth and decline across the nation's regions and metropolitan areas could be characterized, fairly accurately, as a redistribution that favored the West region over the Northeast, Midwest, and South, that favored the large metropolis over smaller-sized metropolitan areas, and that favored urban communities over rural ones. This characterization did not apply to all areas, but it constitutes a relatively apt description of the broad redistribution tendencies that dominated the nation's growth and decline patterns over most of its recent history. Redistribution patterns within the nation's largest and oldest metropolitan areas had also become well established. The selective suburbanization that had begun to emerge in the early decades of this century became greatly accelerated during the immediate post–World War II period. As a consequence, many central cities sustained significant population declines over the 1950s and 1960s, and their population compositions became sharply differentiated from their surrounding suburbs with regard to race, socioeconomic status, and family characteristics.

During the post-1970 period—even before the 1980 census was taken—decidedly different redistribution tendencies became evident across the nation's regions, metropolitan areas, and central cities, and gained the attention of demographers, popular commentators, and academic scholars, alike. The most dramatic of these new patterns—those that appeared to reverse longstanding redistribution tendencies—grabbed the largest headlines and were subject to the greatest commentary. As a consequence, a large literature began to appear on "the decline of the Northern metropolis," "the rise of the sunbelt city," the emergence of a "rural renaissance," and a middle-class "white return" to old depopulating northern cities.[1]

This renewed interest in the nation's redistribution patterns has brought to light a variety of reasons why longstanding redistribution tendencies might be expected to take on new directions.[2] Some of these are related to economic influences specific to the 1970s—such as the energy crisis and the mid-decade recession. Others emphasize longer-term economic transformations that will continue to restructure the relative economic pushes and pulls of the nation's regions and metropolitan areas. Still other long-term effects are associated with continued technological improvements in transportation and communication that provide for more flexible, multilocational production organizations, a more widespread distribution of consumer goods, and a more dispersed overall settlement pattern.

New nationwide demographic developments that emerged during the 1970s also may have served to alter the country's internal redistribution tendencies. These include:

1. A significant rise in the number of so-called footloose population segments, with primarily non-wage incomes (such as the retired elderly), whose residential preferences are unconstrained by the unavailability of employment.

2. A rise in the number of low-wage immigrants—particularly from Mexico—who locate, to a large degree, in selected Southwest metropolitan areas.

3. The advancement of the large baby-boom cohorts into both the housing and labor markets.

---

[1]A sampling of this literature appears in Benjamin Chinitz, ed., *The Declining Northeast: Demographic and Economic Analyses* (New York: Praeger Publishers, 1978); David C. Perry and Alfred J. Watkins, eds., *The Rise of the Sunbelt Cities* (Beverly Hills, CA: Sage Publications, Inc., 1977); Peter A. Morrison and Judith P. Wheeler, "Rural Renaissance in America? The Revival of Population Growth in Remote Areas," *Population Bulletin* 31, no. 3 (Washington, DC: Population Reference Bureau Inc., 1976), p. 26; and Shirley B. Laska and Daphne Spain, eds., *Back to the Cities: Issues in Neighborhood Renovation* (New York: Pergamon Press, Inc., 1980).

[2]See, for example, Royce Hanson, ed., *Rethinking Urban Policy: Urban Development in an Advanced Economy* (Washington, DC: National Academy Press, 1983); Manuel Castells, ed., *High Technology, Space and Society* (Beverly Hills, CA: Sage Publications, Inc., 1985); David L. Brown and John M. Wardwell, eds., *New Directions in Urban–Rural Migration* (New York: Academic Press, 1980); Katharine L. Bradbury, Anthony Downs, and Kenneth A. Small, *Urban Decline and the Future of American Cities* (Washington, DC: The Brookings Institution, 1982); and Paul E. Peterson, ed., *The New Urban Reality* (Washington, DC: The Brookings Institution, 1985).

The potential impact of these cohorts on intrametropolitan redistribution, in particular, has been speculated upon by commentators who noticed that these cohorts were not only large in magnitude, but differed from earlier cohorts in fertility levels, household living arrangements, and (among women) their labor force participation patterns in ways that could alter longstanding residential preferences.[3] Moreover, baby-boom cohort blacks, in comparison to their predecessor cohorts, had achieved greater educational and economic gains and were in a position to encounter less discrimination in suburban housing markets.

Hence, a variety of socioeconomic and demographic factors have been put forth as possible explanations for the redistribution reversals that appeared to emerge in the post-1970 period. Still, most observers were relatively handicapped in their attempts to account for these new redistribution tendencies *as they were occurring* because they did not yet have at their disposal the rich characteristic-laden area data that can be obtained only from the decennial census. Between censuses and until the most recent census results are processed and distributed, information on subnational population characteristics is limited to broad geographic areas, ascertained from sample surveys of the national population. Information for most individual metropolitan areas and nonmetropolitan counties is limited to postcensal estimates of those areas' total populations.[4] Although these data sources were sensitive enough to monitor the major dimensions of the post-1970 redistribution reversals, they were not appropriate to provide a detailed account of the overall pervasiveness of these shifts, or analyses of their determinants and selective redistribution tendencies—which required the area-based summary data from the 1980 census.

The present volume affords us the opportunity to take a more in-depth view of the post-1970 redistribution changes as they affect popu-

[3]Larry H. Long, "Back to the Countryside and Back to the City in the Same Decade," in Shirley B. Laska and Daphne Spain, eds., *Back to the Cities: Issues in Neighborhood Renovation* (New York: Pergamon Press, Inc., 1980), pp. 61–76; William Alonso, "The Population Factor and Urban Structure," in Arthur P. Solomon, ed., *The Prospective City: Economy, Population, Energy and Environmental Developments* (Cambridge, MA: The MIT Press, 1980); and William H. Frey, "Lifecourse Migration of Metropolitan Whites and Blacks and the Structure of Demographic Change in Large Central Cities," *American Sociological Review*, vol. 49 (December 1984):803–827.

[4]The main source of postcensal information on population characteristics is obtained from the U.S. Census Bureau's *Current Population Survey*, Annual Demographic Supplement (undertaken in March of each year). However, the survey's main utility lies with its provision of nationwide population characteristics. Its relatively small sample of approximately 68,000 households does not permit reliable estimates of population characteristics at the individual metropolitan area level, except for the largest metropolitan areas. The Census Bureau's postcensal population estimates series (series P-25 in the Census Bureau's *Current Population Reports*) does provide estimates of the total populations for counties and county subareas during postcensal years. However, these estimates do not provide information on population characteristics and are subject to the assumptions and limitations of the estimation methodology.

lation shifts across the nation's regions and metropolitan areas, as well as between the central cities and suburbs of the nation's largest metropolitan areas. In so doing, we are able to take advantage of the full complement of area-based 1980 census data, along with data from the 1950, 1960, and 1970 censuses, and the more limited area population estimates that have become available since the 1980 census was taken.[5] Our main objective is to interpret the redistribution patterns of the 1970s and early 1980s in light of the changing social and economic contexts for redistribution that emerged during this period, taking cognizance of the major explanations and theories that have been offered to account for these new patterns. We conclude in the volume's final chapter that the 1970s can be regarded as a transition decade in the recent history of United States population redistribution. This conclusion is based on the collective results of the monograph's individual chapters, which review various aspects of the new redistribution tendencies.

Our evaluation of United States redistribution patterns divides logically into two distinct parts. Part One, comprising Chapters 3 through 6, pertains to redistribution across regions and metropolitan areas. This portion of the monograph provides an overview of the new regional and metropolitan area redistribution patterns by evaluating the pervasiveness of the post-1970 redistribution reversals, as well as shifts in the demographic components of change that underlie them. It seeks to explain post-1970 shifts through empirical analyses which incorporate elements of theories that have been proposed to account for the new redistribution patterns. Finally, this part of the monograph examines the impact of 1970–1980 growth and decline on population and household subgroups in various areas, and undertakes a separate examination of redistribution patterns, determinants, and consequences for the nation's black population.

Part Two of this monograph, consisting of Chapters 7 through 11, evaluates post-1970 shifts in central city–suburban redistribution within the nation's largest 39 metropolitan areas. This part of the study also documents aggregate population changes for central cities and suburbs along with their underlying demographic components. However, it devotes most attention to shifts in the racial and socioeconomic selectivities that have become associated with post-1970 suburbaniza-

---

[5]The present analysis employs the 1980 PUMS Sample "A" and "B" files and the 1980 STF 3C files which became available for the entire United States in 1983. It also employs a specially prepared nationwide extract of the STF 4B files which was advanced to us by the Census Bureau in 1984. Complete bibliographic citations for these files are listed in Appendix 7.

tion, and their impacts on the central city. Most of the 1970s city revival literature emphasized the significance of black suburbanization, a
white central city "gentrification," and the general slowing down of the
strong race- and class-selective suburbanization that generated the
city–suburb disparities of the late 1960s. This portion of the monograph
provides a careful evaluation of selective post-1970 city–suburb redistribution tendencies with the aid of rich area-based summary data from
the 1970 and 1980 decennial censuses. It evaluates the extent to which
the 1970s' shifts in racial segregation, the decline of full-family households, and the rise of the so-called service city have effected beneficial
demographic changes in large central cities. It also examines to what
degree the metropolitan area's less select population subgroups have become less city-concentrated during this period.

The final chapter of this volume ties together this study's major
results and underlying perspectives. In it we review what appear to be
the most important influences on redistribution in the post-1970 period
and go on to speculate about future redistribution tendencies that could
emerge across the nation's regions, metropolitan areas, and large central
cities.

The remainder of the present chapter introduces topics and issues
that are taken up in each of the two major sections of this study. This is
followed, in Chapter 2, by a discussion of the metropolitan area and
central city units that are employed in the analyses, and the concepts
and definitions upon which they are based. Finally, in this chapter we
provide a list of previous census monographs and other significant studies of population redistribution within the United States which serve as
references for earlier periods.

Growth and Decline Between Metropolitan Areas

Our analysis of growth and decline follows in the tradition of earlier census monographs on internal population redistribution patterns,
by focusing on the metropolitan area as the basic analysis unit.[6]
Although the urbanization process has become increasingly diffuse over
time, the metropolitan area still constitutes a relatively independent

---

[6]While earlier census monographs employed different metropolitan area definitions
in accordance with Census Bureau practices and other considerations, the general concept
of a large central city node surrounded by a socially and economically integrated territorial
hinterland forms the basis for these various metropolitan area definitions. A selected list
of previous census monographs and reference volumes on this topic is given in the final
section of this chapter.

functional unit which can be thought of as containing a population that both lives and works in the same area and obtains most of the goods and services that are needed for daily life from the area.[7] Metropolitan areas exchange goods and services with other metropolitan areas, with nonmetropolitan areas, and through international trade. Their growth can be viewed as tied to their competitive position in the exchange of goods and services with other areas. In Part One of the monograph, we evaluate redistribution patterns across metropolitan areas, both within and across the nation's major geographic regions, in order to evaluate the scope, determinants, and consequences of the aforementioned post-1970 reversals.

Components of Growth

Metropolitan area population growth can be broken down into the following demographic components: natural increase (births minus deaths), net internal migration and international migration that occurs within fixed area boundaries, and into growth associated with metropolitan territory changes—the expansion of existing areas, or the addition of new ones. There has been some disagreement about the exact contributions to metropolitan and nonmetropolitan growth during the 1970s that could be attributable to changes in the criteria for defining metropolitan areas during the decade.[8] Unless considerable care is taken to separate growth within constant boundaries from growth due to the addition of new metropolitan territory, results can be confusing.

One reason that metropolitan growth slowed down within fixed boundaries was related to the decline in the rate of natural increase. The total fertility levels of approximately 1.8 children per woman, as registered in the late 1970s, contrast markedly with late 1950s' levels of around 3.8 children per woman.[9] Fertility varied considerably from one part of the United States to another. Part of the variation in growth rates for individual metropolitan areas can be attributed to variations in birthrates.

Most of the variation in growth rates among metropolitan areas, however, is attributable to migration—both within the United States and from foreign countries. Although in earlier decades migration-induced metropolitan growth had come largely from nonmetropolitan

[7]See Amos H. Hawley, "Urbanization as Process," David Street and Associates, eds., *Handbook of Contemporary Urban Life* (New York: Jossey Bass Publishers, 1978), pp. 3–26.

[8]Calvin L. Beale, "Poughkeepsie's Complaint or Defining Metropolitan Areas," *American Demographics* (January 1984):28–48.

[9]U.S. Bureau of the Census, *Statistical Abstract*, 1985.

areas, much of the migration to growing metropolitan areas in the 1970s came from other metropolitan areas—often in other regions. Some metropolitan areas contain large military bases, and their growth depends more on decisions of the Department of Defense than on economic factors. It is important to identify these areas and treat them separately in the analysis.

International migration also accounted for variation in metropolitan growth over this period. During the 1970s, 5.6 million immigrants entered the United States and approximately 94 percent of these went to metropolitan areas.[10] Did these immigrants go to the same areas that attracted internal migrants, or did they locate in areas near their point of entry, or in those that already had concentrations of persons from their country of origin? This question and others relating to components of growth are addressed in Chapter 3.

Determinants of Growth

Most theories of regional or metropolitan growth focus on migration because it accounts for most of the intermetropolitan variation in growth rates. From an individual perspective, the migrant can be seen as attracted to places that have employment opportunities and relatively high wages.[11] Yet, some migrants are also attracted to areas for amenity-related reasons—a good climate, recreational opportunities, and relatively low costs of living. At first glance, the 1970s would appear to be a period when the latter reasons for moving were more important than the former because migration was directed toward lower wage areas, with warmer climates. While these amenity-related reasons are likely to be important for the migration of more footloose population segments—that of older persons to Florida—this explanation appears to be more questionable for younger persons in the labor force, as is shown in Chapter 4.

An alternative approach to the study of metropolitan growth focuses on the structure of employment in an area and how national changes in employment affect areas differently.[12] Although the 1970s

[10]Calculated from U.S. Bureau of the Census, "Characteristics of the Population," Chapter C: General Social and Economic Characteristics, *1980 Census of Population,* U.S. Summary, table 99. (Census figures include both legal and illegal immigrants.)

[11]Such models are reviewed in R. Paul Shaw, *Migration Theory and Fact,* Bibliography Series No. 5 (Philadelphia, PA: Regional Science Institute, 1975), pp. 53–103; Michael Greenwood, "Research in Internal Migration in the United States: A Survey," *Journal of Economic Literature* 3:2 (June 1975): 397–433.

[12]Thierry J. Noyelle and Thomas M. Stanback, Jr., *The Economic Transformation of American Cities* (Totowa, NJ: Rowman & Allanheld Publishers, 1984); and Sternlieb and Hughes, eds., *Post-Industrial America: Metropolitan Decline and Inter-Regional Job Shifts* (New Brunswick, NJ: Rutgers University, Center for Urban Policy Research, 1975).

was a period of relative decline in manufacturing, there was growth in service employment. Thus, it is not surprising to find "deindustrialization"-related population declines in areas that had a high degree of specialization in manufacturing, and to find growth in areas that specialized in high-level services. However, this is not always the case, and there are some offsetting trends that confuse this picture. The second part of Chapter 4 examines the extent to which initial industrial specialization is responsible for metropolitan area growth during the decade.

If migrants move to areas with job opportunities, one can question what determines the location of such job opportunities. One possibility is that migrants follow capital and that the answer lies in the factors that determine the location of investments in businesses.[13] Proponents of this theory point out that international competition and declines in transportation and communication costs encouraged investors during the 1970s to seek areas with relatively low wages. Although this theory is consistent with the observed 1970s' migration to low-wage areas, it does not readily explain why migrants were willing to move to these areas. Part of the answer may lie in the fact that some of these migrants did not come from higher-wage areas in the United States, but were immigrants from Mexico and other lower-wage countries. Among those who came from other parts of the United States, many were new entrants to the labor force who may have been primarily motivated by job opportunities rather than average income levels. These arguments are tested with data from the 1970s and early 1980s in the final part of Chapter 4.

Consequences of Growth and Decline

It is generally believed that growth is beneficial and decline is detrimental to an area. The benefits of growth include both those related to greater population size and those related to rates of growth. Greater size may result in economies of scale that benefit consumers and producers alike. Large areas provide the opportunity for certain services and forms of entertainment which can only be supported by populations above some minimum size. However, scale effects are not all positive. Increased size implies greater population density, higher costs due to competition for space, and greater potential for air pollution, water pollution, and traffic congestion.

---

[13]Gordon L. Clark, *Interregional Migration, National Policy and Social Justice* (Totowa, NJ: Rowman & Allanheld Publishers, 1983).

Apart from size, growth is usually associated with increased demand for labor and increased wages. Although residents can expect to benefit from greater employment and income opportunities, they also must face increased competition for available housing and, at least temporarily, increases in costs for those goods and services for which the growth in supply lags behind the growth in demand.

Because of the selective nature of migration, most areas of net in-migration receive young adults who are better educated than average, while areas of net outmigration lose such persons. This means that the quality of the labor force of growing areas improves—making them more attractive for further investment, while the reverse is the case in declining areas. To what extent has this actually happened during the 1970s? How have the population compositions of growing and declining areas changed? To what extent have changes in elderly migration altered selected areas' age compositions? These are questions that will be addressed in Chapter 5.

Blacks and other minorities have tended to display post-1970 interregional and metropolitan redistribution shifts that follow those for the population as a whole. Nevertheless, significant "gaps" still exist. For example, blacks have not moved out of declining metropolitan areas as rapidly as whites have—leading to an increased concentration of blacks in these areas. How have blacks in these metropolitan areas fared in terms of employment, income, and housing? To what extent have they been "left behind" by the regional and metropolitan restructuring of growth in the United States? Chapter 6 will examine, specifically, the changing redistribution of the black population, its determinants, and the consequences that metropolitan growth or decline holds for blacks residing in different parts of the country.

City–Suburb Redistribution within Metropolitan Areas

In Part Two of the monograph, the focus shifts to the *intrametropolitan redistribution process* between central cities and suburbs within each of the nation's 39 largest metropolitan areas. The familiar list of maladies—eroding tax bases, declining services, and high unemployment levels—that had begun to affect America's oldest and largest central cities when the 1970 census was taken reflect, in large measure, demographic developments of the immediate postwar years. In the 1945–1970 period, the city–suburb redistribution process was shaped significantly by:

1. A massive metropolitanward migration of southern rural blacks and their continued confinement to segregated city residences.

2. A sharp rise in the level of family formation and childbearing and an accompanying proliferation of low-density suburbs.

3. A shift of the American work force toward industries and occupations that had become less dependent on central locations.

These developments spawned well-known race- and status-selective redistribution patterns that relegated high concentrations of unemployable, dependent, and minority populations within the political city boundaries, and further isolated the city and its residents from the broader metropolitan area.

A number of societal developments have been set in motion since 1970 which suggest that these well-ingrained patterns of race-selective migration, household formation, and employment location—which had shaped the redistribution during most of the post–World War II era—may be taking on distinctly new directions. First, blacks achieved significant gains in economic status since the immediate postwar decades and, as a consequence of extensive civil rights legislation in the 1960s, encountered considerably less discrimination in suburban housing markets. Second, a greater career orientation among women and changing living arrangements among members of the postwar born cohorts, as they reached adulthood, led to increases in the number of small, childless, and dual-earner households—household types which have, in the past, valued central locations. Third, the realization grew that, even though old industrial cities can no longer dominate in a post-industrial society, they can serve as specialized service and administrative centers employing a significant share of the metropolitan areas' professional and white collar work force. Some cities are becoming national or even international decision centers, with the proliferation of corporate mergers and multinational corporate linkages. Although these new developments are generally perceived, the absence of specific details has left unclear their implications for the future viability of declining central cities.

Part Two of this monograph provides a portrait of how these societalwide developments are affecting the internal redistribution processes in our largest metropolitan areas, to gauge how sharply they differ from the metropolitan redistribution processes that characterized the immediate postwar period, and to suggest the consequences these redistribution processes imply for the cities' future demographic structures. The portrait we paint will update—with detailed 1980 census results—the demographic conditions of America's "problem" cities—old declining industrial cities within the nation's heartland and along its Northeastern seaboard.

The chapters in Part Two also focus on the city–suburb redistribution processes in the country's large, fast-growing metropolitan areas. When the 1970 census was taken, these Sunbelt growth centers were still something of a novelty, and their internal redistribution patterns were subject to much less analytic scrutiny than those of the nation's older urban centers. However, the large, growing metropolitan areas in the South and West regions are among the nation's most economically dynamic and vital urban centers. Because of their varied growth histories and economic bases, their relatively low-density settlement patterns, and the influx of new ethnic and immigrant groups into their borders, city–suburb redistribution patterns within these present-day metropolitan growth centers diverge markedly from their predecessors. The analyses in Part Two will examine internal redistribution patterns for these areas, as well.

Central City–Suburb Population Change

Chapter 7 sets the stage for the analysis of central city–suburb redistribution in the five chapters devoted to this topic. It introduces a metropolitan area typology that facilitates these analyses and also employs this typology to evaluate the demographic components of city–suburb redistribution within the metropolitan areas focused upon in Part Two. These 39 metropolitan areas represent the nation's largest—those with 1980 populations that exceed 1 million. Some of them contain the nation's most fiscally distressed and depopulated large central cities while others surround some of the greatest sunbelt growth centers.

Given this diversity across metropolitan areas, a six-category typology is developed which sorts these areas into classes with common development histories, in order to facilitate the analysis of post-1970 change in the city–suburb redistribution processes. The typology is also used to compare the influences that post-1970 societalwide changes in race relations, household preferences, and workplace location impose on the city–suburb redistribution processes within distinctly different types of metropolitan areas.

An important aspect of this typology lies in its identification of declining metropolitan areas since *metropolitanwide* decline is a fairly recent phenomenon in areas that surround large, depopulating central cities. Our analysis in the Part Two chapters pays particular attention to the 1970s' city–suburb redistribution tendencies within the 13 metropolitan areas we have identified as "North-Declining." Each of these areas is located in the North, surrounds older central cities, and has exhibited sharp city–suburb growth and population composition disparities during the 1950s and 1960s. Hence, post-1970 internal redistribution patterns of these areas—within the context of metropolitanwide decline—are of considerable interest. The remaining 26 large nondeclining metropolitan areas are classed according to their regional location, and the age of their central cities under the categories: North–Old, South–Old, West–Old, South–Young, and West–Young. These categories also represent different development and growth contexts which condition intrametropolitan city–suburb redistribution patterns in ways that are explained in Chapter 7.

The analyses in Chapter 7 employ this typology to evaluate total central city and suburb population changes over the 1950–1980 period, as well as contributions to these changes associated with city annexation, net migration and natural increase, and specific migration streams. Significant 1970s' shifts over the previous two decades are emphasized and post-1980 population estimates are presented. These analyses, therefore, form a backdrop for the examination of suburban selectivity shifts undertaken in Chapters 8 through 11.

Race and Status Dimensions of City–Suburb Redistribution

Chapter 8 evaluates post-1970 changes in racial selectivity associated with the city–suburb redistribution process—in light of societalwide developments that could lead to an alteration of longstanding trends. The significant economic and civil rights gains achieved by the black population may well serve to increase their levels of residential integration between central cities and suburbs and across neighborhoods. The greater career orientation taken on by more metropolitan whites in the 1970s may make city locations more attractive to them. Chapter 8 examines 1970s' shifts in black and nonblack suburbanization and neighborhood segregation patterns in order to examine if, in fact, such redistribution changes have occurred, what their magnitudes were, and how pervasive they were across different types of metropolitan areas. The chapter also evaluates the city–suburb and neighborhood segregation patterns of two newly growing minorities in many American cities—Hispanic- and Asian-Americans—and contrasts their patterns with those of blacks. Chapter 9 extends this analysis of race-selective redistribution shifts by contrasting the income, education, and occupation selectivity of post-1970 suburbanization with that which operated in the 1950s and 1960s. Does black suburbanization in the 1970s cut across all status categories of blacks? Has nonblack suburban selectivity become more moderated since the immediate postwar decades? Are Hispanic- and Asian-Americans more likely to reside in the suburbs as their incomes rise? These questions are taken up in Chapter 9.

Household and Family Dimensions of City–Suburb Redistribution

Chapter 10 considers how emerging trends toward smaller, childless, and dual-earner households might have altered the strong suburbanization pattern that was shaped by the predominantly family-oriented households in the 1950s and 1960s. The potential for a white middle class "return to the city" was seen to depend upon the magnitude of increases in smaller nontraditional households and the tendency for these households to form in or to select central locations. Chapter 10 examines the redistribution implications of both shifts and also considers the impact of the large baby-boom cohorts that passed into their household formation ages during the 1970s. Another aspect of the post-1970 rise in nontraditional households concerns the increased number of poverty households—both black and nonblack—that have been created over this period. Chapter 10 examines the extent to which nontraditional and traditional poverty households have either suburbanized or continued to concentrate in the city since the 1970 census was taken.

Worker and Workplace Dimensions of City–Suburb Redistribution

Chapter 11 investigates how post-1970 shifts in residences and workplaces have altered the mismatches between job locations and worker residential locations that emerged in earlier decades—when manufacturing and blue collar employment moved suburbanward at the same time that white collar employment opportunities concentrated in the central city. Major residential responses to these relocations—greater city commuting among suburban white collar residents, increased suburbanward movement among city blue collar residents, and high levels of unemployment among city blue collar minorities—served to aggravate the fiscal plight of cities and the economic circumstances of their minority and nonmobile residents. This chapter evaluates whether the post-1970s' trends—toward greater black suburbanization and toward the increasing development of central cities as both workplaces and residences for professionals—are helping to reduce job–

worker mismatches observed in the 1960s. It also examines the extent to which the central city's role as a dominant node of employment concentration is becoming reduced—in light of the emergence of more suburban employment nodes and the increased reliance on private transportation among metropolitan area commuters.

Units of Analysis and Data

The metropolitan areas and their component central cities and suburbs, which are the units of analysis for this study, are based on those defined in the censuses of 1950 to 1980, with minor exceptions. The initial definitions of these units were derived from concepts of urban sociology, geography, and human ecology, which date from the first half of this century. As new forms of urban settlement evolved, there have been periodic revisions in the definitions of what constitutes metropolitan areas and central cities. Since many of our findings are, to some degree, dependent upon the definitions of these units, we devote the next chapter to discussing the concept of a metropolitan area, the evolution of the official definitions of these areas since 1950, and the specific choice of units for this study.

The data utilized in this volume are drawn primarily from the U.S. Population Censuses of 1950, 1960, 1970, and 1980, as well as from postcensal population estimates prepared by the U.S. Bureau of the Census. Because of the emphasis given to documenting redistribution between the 1970 and 1980 censuses, the data draw heavily from area-based computer files available with both of these censuses. These include the 1980 Summary Tape Files (STFs), 3C and 4B, and tabulations from the 1980 Public Use Microdata Sample (PUMS) "A" and "B" files—from the 1980 census; and the 1970 Fourth Count Summary File and other special tabulations—from the 1970 census. Trend analyses over the four censuses, 1950 through 1980, were drawn from computer file versions of the U.S. Census Bureau's *1983 County and City Data Book,* and from computer files which consolidate the data that appear in U.S. Census Bureau county and city data books published between 1947 and 1977. Complete bibliographic citations for these sources can be found in Appendix F.

Reference Volumes for Earlier Periods

This volume represents the most recent in a series of census monographs and reference works which document trends and characteristics associated with metropolitan area and central city–suburb population redistribution within the United States. We present below a selected list of these earlier works which have adopted a nationwide focus and also provide a comprehensive statistical and descriptive overview of change across metropolitan area units or across central cities and suburbs within metropolitan areas. These volumes are classed by the most recent census year for which they provide data:

1970 **Mills, Sara Mazie,** ed. "Population, Distribution and Policy." *Commission Research Reports,* vol. 5. U.S. Commission on Population Growth and the American Future. Washington, DC: U.S. Government Printing Office, 1972.

1960 **Taeuber, Irene B.,** and **Conrad Taeuber** *People of the United States in the Twentieth Century.* A 1960 Census monograph. Washington, DC: U.S. Government Printing Office, 1971.
Pickard, Jerome P. *Dimensions of Metropolitanism.* Research Monograph 14. Washington, DC: Urban Land Institute, 1967.

1950 **Shryock, Henry S., Jr.** *Population Mobility Within the United States.* Chicago, IL: Community and Family Studies Center, 1964.
Hawley, Amos H. *The Changing Shape of Metropolitan America: Deconcentration Since 1920.* Glencoe, IL: The Free Press, 1956.
Duncan, Otis Dudley, and **Albert J. Reiss** *Social Characteristics of Urban and Rural Communities, 1950.* A 1950 Census monograph. New York: John Wiley and Sons, Inc., 1956.
Bogue, Donald J. *Population Growth Within Standard Metropolitan Areas, 1900–1950.* Washington, DC: Housing and Home Finance Agency, 1953.

1940 **Thompson, Warren S.** *The Growth of Metropolitan Districts in the United States: 1900–1940.* U.S. Bureau of the Census. Washington, DC: U.S. Government Printing Office, 1948.
Bogue, Donald J., Henry S. Shryock, Jr., and **Siegfried A. Hoermann** *Subregional Migration in the United States, 1935–40: Volume 1. Streams of Migration between Subregions.* Scripps Foundation Studies in Population Distribution, no. 5. Oxford, OH: Scripps Foundation, Miami University, 1957.

2

METROPOLITAN AREAS
AS UNITS OF ANALYSIS

E XPERTS have never agreed upon how to draw the line between urban and rural or between metropolitan and nonmetropolitan. [1]
Writers in the first half of this century saw the metropolis as a
center that organized the economic activity of a large hinterland. [2] The
core was a central city through which all goods that entered or left the
region passed. Some of these cities were primarily central places that
served agricultural regions. [3] However, most of the major cities of the
United States that had large populations by 1900 were located at break
points between land and water transportation. [4] With the increase in
manufacturing during the nineteenth century, several cities developed
which owed their growth more to the growth of manufacturing than to
the growth of commerce. However, the location and structure of these

[1] For discussions of urban and rural definitions, see O.D.Duncan and A. J. Reiss, Jr.,
Social Characteristics of Urban and Rural Communities (New York: The Free Press,
1956); Sidney Goldstein and David F. Sly, *Basic Data Needed for the Study of Urbanization* (Liège, Belgium: IUSSP, 1974); and Jack P. Gibbs, ed., *Urban Research Methods* (New
York: D. Van Nostrand Co., 1961).
[2] This literature is reviewed in O.D. Duncan, et al., *Metropolis and Region* (Baltimore: Johns Hopkins Press, 1960).
[3] Central place theory was developed by Losch and Christaller to explain the development of towns in areas of uniform geography. Christaller's work is summarized by Edward
Ullman, "A Theory of Location for Cities," *American Journal of Sociology* 46 (1941):
853–864; and August Losch, *The Theory of Location*, translated by William H. Woglom
(New Haven: Yale University Press, 1954).

cities was not much different from that of the commercial cities because they had to receive shipments of raw materials and export finished products; thus, they needed to be near major transportation routes.

Cities of the nineteenth century were limited in physical size because most of the work force had to walk to work, and most of the intracity flow of parts and goods among businesses was transported by foot or horse cart. With the introduction of the streetcar in the second half of the century, cities slowly expanded by adding residential suburbs on their peripheries. This also enabled some manufacturers who required cheaper land to move further from the center, although they still had to locate along transport lines, which gave them easy access to their suppliers.

The development of automobiles, trucks, and buses in the twentieth century made it possible for businesses to locate further from the center and in areas where there were no rail lines. Motor transportation began to replace other modes of transportation following World War I, resulting not only in increased suburbanization of residences but also in the suburbanization of many places of work.[5] Gradually, as we have moved through the twentieth century, our need for concentration of activities in an urban center decreased. According to Amos Hawley, "The city has been stripped of most of its unique functions and lingers on as a political anachronism."[6] Although many would differ with the suggestion that central cities will soon disappear, most would agree that the central city is no longer essential to the economic functioning of a metropolitan area.

As suburbanization spreads further and further into the countryside, and as some large suburban concentrations develop without clear centers, it becomes increasingly difficult to separate what is urban from what is rural and what is metropolitan from what is not. Clearly the "urban way of life" which Louis Wirth described is now enjoyed by most of the American population.[7] By the year 2000, both farmer and nonfarm worker may spend large parts of their days pushing buttons on computerized control panels or repairing broken machinery, and they may live in adjacent homes.

[4]Charles Horton Cooley, "The Theory of Transportation" (1894), reprinted in *Sociological Theory and Social Research* (New York: Henry Holt & Co., 1930). Prior to 1890 all cities of over 100,000 were located along the sea, or a navigable river or lake, according to Duncan, et al., *Metropolis and Region* (Baltimore: Johns Hopkins Press, 1960), p. 24.

[5]Gary A. Tobin, "Suburbanization and the Development of Motor Transportation: Transportation Technology and the Suburbanization Process," in Barry Schwartz, *The Changing Face of the Suburbs* (Chicago: University of Chicago Press, 1976), pp. 95–111.

[6]Amos H. Hawley, "Population Density and the City," *Demography* 9:4 (1972): 528.

[7]Louis Wirth, "Urbanism as a Way of Life," *American Journal of Sociology* 44 (1938): 1–24.

Fortunately, the present study deals with the past and not the future. For the period up to 1980, it can still be argued that the concept of metropolitan area as consisting of one or more sizable central cities and their surrounding suburbs can still be applied to most parts of the country. Given the large investment in business and residential structures in existing areas, most of these areas are likely to remain for many more years.

For the purposes of this study, there are three criteria that a definition of the metropolitan area should meet if metropolitan areas are to serve as the basic units of analysis:

1. Metropolitan areas should include all large concentrations of cities and their suburbs.

2. The metropolitan area should be delineated in terms of existing geographical units for which census data are tabulated—and which do not change much over time—so that it is possible to assemble data for the beginning and end of a decade using the same territory.

3. These areas ought to approximate labor market areas since they contain both the place of residence and place of work for most of their population.

Although not perfect, the official definition of Standard Metropolitan Statistical Areas fits all of these criteria. Urbanized areas, while more closely approximating the actual areas of population concentration which include cities and suburbs, are less useful for analysis because they are not constructed from geographical units for which data are published, and it is extremely difficult to analyze change within constant boundaries.

Standard Metropolitan Statistical Areas (SMSAs)

The SMSAs, which are used in census publications, are designated by the U.S. Office of Management and Budget. Since 1949 the general concept of SMSAs has been one of a large population nucleus together with adjacent communities that have a high degree of integration with the nucleus.[8] For all of the United States, except New England, SMSAs

[8]For a more detailed description of SMA and SMSA definitions, see Office of Management and Budget, *Standard Metropolitan Statistical Areas, 1975;* "Official Standards Followed in Establishing Metropolitan Statistical Areas," *Federal Register,* Jan. 3, 1980, part 6. Also see the definitions in *The Number of Inhabitants,* U.S. Summary volumes for each census from 1950 through 1970 and Federal Committee on Standard Metropolitan Statistical Areas, Office of Management and Budget, "The Metropolitan Statistical Area Classification, 1980 Official Standards and Related Documents," 1983. (These documents were published in *Statistical Reporter,* in December 1979 and August 1980.)

have been defined in terms of counties or county equivalents. There are two advantages to defining metropolitan areas in terms of counties. First, the county is the smallest geographical unit for which many types of data are tabulated. Second, there have been very few changes in county boundaries over time; thus, it is relatively easy to study metropolitan change over time using constant boundaries.[9]

For all of the censuses between 1950 and 1980, SMSAs have been defined as including a densely settled urban core with a population of at least 50,000, the rest of the county in which most of this core was located, and any contiguous counties which met both the criteria of metropolitan character and the criteria of integration with the core. When they were initially defined in 1949, these areas were called Standard Metropolitan Areas (SMAs), and each had to have a central city with a population of at least 50,000. In 1958, when the term Standard Metropolitan Statistical Area was adopted, these criteria were revised so that two contiguous cities with a combined population of 50,000 could qualify as the nucleus of a metropolitan area, providing that the smaller had at least a population of 15,000. In 1980 the concept of urban core was again enlarged to include census-defined Urbanized Areas of at least 50,000. When the core consists of an Urbanized Area without a central city of at least 50,000, the entire metropolitan area must have 100,000 population (except in New England where this minimum is 75,000).

Although most of the Urbanized Areas consisted of central cities and surrounding places with densities of at least 1,000 persons per square mile, there were some exceptions. Even though these revised criteria were not fully implemented until 1983, after the publication of the 1980 census, they were used in defining 36 new SMSAs, which are included in the 1980 census tabulations. Although many of these new areas would have qualified as SMSAs in 1980 under the earlier definitions due to growth during the 1970s, some became SMSAs only because of the revision in the criteria.

Since 1949 adjacent counties have been added if they met the criteria of metropolitan character and social and economic integration. In the 1950 census a county met the criteria of metropolitan character if at least one-half of its population lived in minor civil divisions with a

---

[9]Most of the changes in boundaries since 1950 have been in the states of Virginia and Alaska. In Virginia cities are treated as independent county level units and whenever a new city is designated, a new unit is created. To deal with this problem, we have combined most cities with the counties from which they originated. In Alaska there are no counties and the state is divided into census districts for purpose of enumeration, but these have not remained constant over time. We have regrouped them to provide larger districts which are roughly comparable over time, paying particular attention to Anchorage, the only metropolitan area.

density of 150 or more persons per square mile, and less than one-third of its workers were engaged in agriculture. It met the criteria of integration if at least 15 percent of its resident workers worked in the central city's county, or 25 percent of the people working in the county commuted from the central county.[10] As a result of the declining proportion of the labor force in agriculture, the criteria of metropolitan character were modified in 1958 to require that at least 75 percent of the population of a contiguous county be employed in nonagricultural activity before the county could qualify for addition to a metropolitan area. In 1980 the requirement that contiguous areas have a minimum proportion employed in nonagriculture was dropped. By that time, only about 7 percent of the nonmetropolitan labor force was engaged in agriculture, so that there were few counties in the United States which did not meet the nonagricultural requirement.

According to the 1975 criteria, which were used in defining most of the SMSAs for the 1980 Census, a county could qualify for inclusion in an SMSA if it had at least 75 percent of its resident labor force employed in nonagricultural activities, if at least 15 percent of its workers commuted to central counties, and if it met two of the following three criteria for metropolitan character:

1. At least 25 percent of the population was urban.
2. The county had an increase of at least 15 percent between the last two censuses.
3. The county had a density of at least 50 persons per square mile.[11]

This enabled several relatively low-density counties to be added to metropolitan areas.

In 1980 the criteria of metropolitan character were combined with the criteria of integration to provide a sliding scale whereby a county could qualify for inclusion either because it had high density or a high level of commuting to the core. For example, an adjacent county in which 50 percent of the workers commute to the core could be added with a density of as low as 25 persons per square mile, whereas a county

[10]In addition to these criteria, counties could also qualify for inclusion in SMSAs, based on the number of nonagricultural workers and certain other criteria that affected only a few areas. See the 1950, 1960, and 1970 census volumes for the full set of criteria.

[11]Counties could also qualify for inclusion without meeting the criteria for metropolitan character if they had 75 percent of their workers in nonagricultural jobs and 30 percent commuting to the central city. Counties with less than 15 percent commuting to the central county could qualify if they had 15 percent commuting from the central county or a sum of 20 percent commuting in both directions. See Office of Management and Budget, *Standard Metropolitan Statistical Areas, 1975.*

with only 15 percent commuters needed a density of 50 persons per square mile and other evidence of metropolitan character. However, these criteria were not applied until 1983.

From the beginning, slightly different criteria have been used to define metropolitan areas in New England. Because the cities and towns in New England have more political significance than the counties, they were used as the building blocks for SMAs and later for SMSAs. The result is that most New England SMSAs are smaller in land area than those in the rest of the United States, and some New England counties contain two or more metropolitan areas. Because some data are collected only at the county level, New England County Metropolitan Areas (NECMAs) were defined during the 1970s to provide an alternative unit of analysis. We feel that these NECMAs are more similar to the SMSAs in the rest of the United States than the official New England SMSAs, and we will use NECMAs in our analysis. For earlier censuses, when there was no official definition of NECMAs, we have created NECMAs that contain the counties of the core cities and adjacent counties for which at least one-half of the population lives within officially defined SMSAs.[12]

Since commuting data require considerable time to compile, the SMSA criteria that the U.S. Bureau of the Census has used in the publication of decennial census data have been based on earlier commuting data than those collected in the census. In most cases the boundaries of 1980 SMSAs reflect 1970 commuting patterns, although 1980 populations were taken into account in defining new areas for 1980. In effect, this means that the SMSAs which are defined for a particular census are based on a combination of measures from the beginning and the end of the preceding decade. As such, the SMSA definitions at the end of a decade are more suitable units for studying change within constant boundaries than those at the beginning of the decade, which are based on commuting data which are 20 years old by the end of the decade.

The distribution of metropolitan areas throughout the United States, according to the official 1980 definition, is shown in Figure 2.1. A considerable proportion of the land area is metropolitan, and this is particularly true in the northeastern part of the country.

The growth of metropolitan areas as officially defined and as

---

[12]An alternative would have been to use the Metropolitan State Economic Areas for 1950 through 1970. A comparison of our NECMAs and the Metropolitan SEAs in 1960 showed that they were identical with the exception of Lewiston, ME, and New London, CT, which had become SMSAs between 1950 and 1960, but had not been recognized as Metropolitan SEAs. See U.S. Bureau of the Census, *U.S. Census of Population 1960, Selected Area Reports, State Economic Areas,* final report PC(3)-1A, 1963.

FIGURE 2.1

Standard Metropolitan Statistical Areas, 1980,
as Defined by the Office of Management and Budget, June 1981

SOURCE: U.S. Bureau of the Census, *State and Metropolitan Area Data Book*, 1982, pp. xii-xiii.

FIGURE 2.1 *(continued)*

TABLE 2.1

Number and Population of Metropolitan Areas at Each Census

Census Date	Official Definition		As Defined in this Study	
	Number of Areas	Population (millions)	Number of Areas	Population (millions)
1950*	169	84.9	165	85.9
1960	212	112.9	203	114.4
1970	243	139.4	231	141.4
1980	318	169.4	304	170.5

SOURCES: U.S. Bureau of the Census, U.S. Summary, Number of Inhabitants, 1950: table 26; 1960: table 31; 1970: table 32.

U.S. Bureau of the Census, "Standard Metropolitan Statistical Areas and Standard Consolidated Statistical Areas: 1980," 1980 Census of Population, Supplementary Reports PC80-S1-15.

*Includes Honolulu, to provide continuity over time.

defined for this monograph are shown in Table 2.1. Between 1950 and 1980 the number of metropolitan areas and the total population in metropolitan areas have nearly doubled. This growth is depicted on the map of Texas where the counties that were added to metropolitan areas or which became new areas are designated for each decade from 1950 to 1980 (see Figure 2.2).

The use of NECMAs in place of New England SMSAs adds about 1 million to the metropolitan total for each year, but decreases the number of areas because some NECMAs contain more than one SMSA. An extreme example is Fairfield County, Connecticut, which contains the four SMSAs of Bridgeport, Danbury, Norwalk, and Stamford, plus nonmetropolitan territory. In 1960 and 1970 we have also added Somerset and Middlesex Counties in New Jersey to the metropolitan population to provide consistency with 1950 and 1980.[13]

Consolidated Metropolitan Areas

In several parts of the country the Urbanized Areas surrounding major cities have grown together, so that it is hard to determine where one metropolitan area begins and another ends. The area between Boston and Washington has long been described as one of nearly continu-

[13]In 1960 and 1970 Somerset County, NJ, was added to the Newark SMSA, and Middlesex County, NJ, was added as the New Brunswick SMSA, which it became officially in November 1971.

FIGURE 2.2

Metropolitan Areas in Texas, 1950–1980

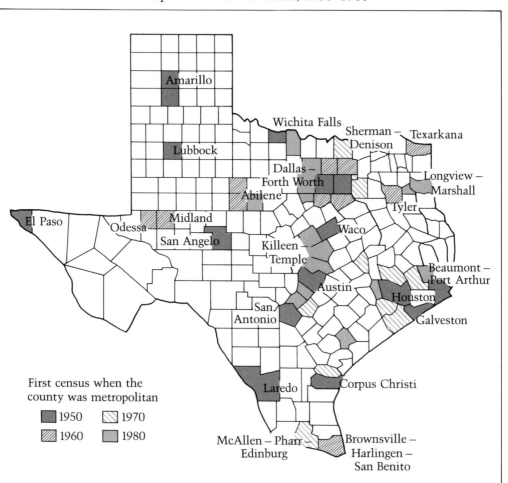

First census when the
county was metropolitan

■ 1950   ▨ 1970
▧ 1960   ▤ 1980

ous urbanization.[14] More recently, several other large urban clusters
have been identified such as "Cleveburgh," which contains the area surrounding and between Cleveland and Pittsburgh; and the "Lower Great
Lakes," which includes the area from Toledo through Detroit and Chicago to beyond Milwaukee.[15] Although the rules for defining metropoli-

[14]Jean Gottman, *Megalopolis–The Urbanized Northeastern Seaboard of the United
States* (Cambridge, MA: The MIT Press, 1961).
[15]" 'Strip Cities' Still Gobbling Up Land, People," *U.S. News and World Report* (Oct.
3, 1983): 54–56.

tan areas provide for the combination of two central cities which are within 20 miles of one another into the same metropolitan area, unless there are good reasons for not doing so, additional rules are needed to deal with situations where there are several cities with adjacent Urbanized Areas. Often, local political pressure has resulted in the division into two or more SMSAs of areas that meet the criteria for integration into a single area. For example, the New York–Northeastern New Jersey area, which was one large metropolitan SMSA in the 1950 census publications, was divided into nine SMSAs by 1980.[16]

In all parts of the country, improvements in highways have made it easier for people to commute longer distances, and metropolitan areas which were once quite separate have become more closely tied to one another. Occasionally, as in the case of Dallas and Fort Worth, these areas have merged into a single SMSA. However, in other cases, such as Ann Arbor and Detroit and Houston and Galveston, they have remained separate.

In the 1960 census the concept of Standard Consolidated Area (SCA) was introduced to provide an alternative aggregate unit which included two or more adjacent SMSAs that were closely integrated. In 1960 there were only two SCAs, New York–Northeastern New Jersey and Chicago–Northwestern Indiana. In 1975 definite criteria of size and integration were established, and the name was changed to Standard Consolidated Statistical Areas (SCSAs).[17] In 1980 there were 16 SCSAs consisting of 48 SMSAs. All of these SCSAs had at least 1 million people in 1980.

The establishment of SCSAs gives the analyst a choice of units to use. In ranking metropolitan areas by size, the SCSA seems more accurately to represent the total size of metropolitan areas such as New York than does the more restricted New York SMSA. However, the SMSAs are better units for studying processes of change such as suburbanization because they are more likely to contain only a single central city and its suburbs. Also, since local governments play an important role in determining the directions of change in an area, two nearby cities which logically fit within a single consolidated area may experience different patterns of growth or decline. Another consideration is that the coding of metropolitan migration in the Public Use Microdata Samples, which are major data sources for this study, was in terms of

[16]In our analysis, we have combined the Nassau–Suffolk and New York SMSAs and have included Bergen County, NJ, with Paterson as it was in 1970.

[17]For the 1980 census, SCSAs were defined as (a) having a combined population of at least 1 million; (b) at least 60 percent of the population of each included SMSA had to be urban; and (c) the sum of the workers commuting between two included SMSAs had to equal 15 percent of the employed workers residing in the smaller SMSA (or 10 percent if urbanized areas were shared).

SMSAs rather than CMSAs. We shall therefore use SMSAs as the basic unit of analysis in this monograph, except where we rank areas by size.

1983 Revision of Criteria

In June 1983 the Office of Management and Budget announced revised definitions of the metropolitan areas that were based on the 1980 criteria and the commuting flows measured in the 1980 census. These areas were renamed Metropolitan Statistical Areas (MSAs).[18] Metropolitan areas with over one million population that contained two or more counties were divided into two or more Primary Metropolitan Statistical Areas (PMSAs) if local opinion supported such a division. The original metropolitan area was known as a Consolidated Metropolitan Statistical Area (CMSA) and the components were called Primary Metropolitan Statistical Areas (PMSAs). The 1983 revision resulted in 253 MSAs which were not part of larger units plus 19 CMSAs which contained a total of 60 PMSAs.[19] Fifty-one counties lost metropolitan status while 61 others gained that status. This reclassification resulted in only a small change in the 1980 population classified as metropolitan (from 170.5 to 172.1 million).[20] The differences between the 1983 MSA definitions and the 1980 SMSA definitions for some of the measures used in this monograph are discussed in Appendix A.

Criticisms of the SMSA Concept

From the beginning, both the criteria for defining metropolitan areas and the application of these criteria to specific cases have been sharply criticized. On one side, those who feel that a metropolitan area should be a relatively autonomous economic area have pointed out that most officially defined metropolitan areas are underbounded in terms of including all of the population that depends upon the area for such ser-

---

[18]The criteria for these areas were set forth in "The Metropolitan Statistical Area Classification, 1980." Also see Richard L. Forstall and Maria E. Gonzalez, "Twenty Questions—What You Should Know About the New Metropolitan Areas," *American Demographics* (April 1984): 22–31, 42–43.

[19]These counts and those in the rest of the paragraph are based on using NECMAs in New England rather than MSAs. According to the 1983 classification, there were 15 MSAs, three CMSAs, and 17 PMSAs in New England. These are replaced here by 16 NECMAs. Fifteen of the NECMAs are at the level of MSAs and one, Fairfield County, CT, is a PMSA. In 1984 two CMSAs, Kansas City and St. Louis, were changed to MSAs by Acts of Congress and two new MSAs, Naples, FL, and Santa Fe, NM, were created.

[20]Using the 1983 classification, the excess of the population of NECMAs over the New England MSAs and PMSAs was only about 350,000. Personal communication from Richard Forstall.

vices as public utilities, retail shopping, medicine, education, and other personal services.[21] Alternative areas such as Berry's "urban fields" tend to be considerably larger on the average, although there is much variability.[22]

On the other side are those who associate metropolitan character with size, density, and the performance of certain "metropolitan" functions. These critics feel that the concept has been stretched to allow more and more marginal areas to qualify for federal programs targeted for metropolitan areas. Most notable among these critics is Calvin Beale who has pointed out that the new metropolitan areas, which were designated in the B 1970s through 1981 (the basis for the 1980 census tabulations), lack many of the facilities that might be expected of a metropolitan area, such as a television station, a Sunday newspaper, local bus service, a four-year college, and specialized hospital services.[23] Forty-six out of the 58 areas added during this period lacked central cities of 50,000 and nine did not even have a central city of 25,000.

Although Beale's criticism applies to many of the newer SMSAs that he cites, some of the new SMSAs represent a newer form of metropolitan settlement—one based more on suburbs than central cities. An example of this newer form of settlement is the Long Branch–Asbury Park SMSA in New Jersey. The largest central city, Long Branch, has only 29,819 people and the two central cities together have only 46,834, but the total area has a population of 503,173 within 472 square miles, or a density in excess of 1,000 persons per square mile. Another example is Bradenton, Florida, which has a central city of only 30,170, but a total population of 148,442 which is 89 percent urban.

Part of Beale's criticism deals with the application of the SMSA criteria rather than the criteria themselves. Rosenwaike found numerous deviations from the official criteria among the 1960 SMSAs.[24] He observed that some of the SMSAs that had met the minimum-size criterion by combining two central cities did so with cities that were not contiguous. He also found that 13 out of the 102 counties that were added to SMSAs did not meet the criterion of integration because fewer than 15 percent of their workers commuted to the county containing

[21]Allan G. Feldt, "The Metropolitan Area Concept: An Examination of the 1950 SMAs," *Journal of the American Statistical Association* 60 (1965): 617–636.

[22]Brian J. L. Berry, Peter G. Goheen, and Harold Goldstein, "Metropolitan Area Definitions: A Re-Evaluation of Concept and Statistical Practices," U.S. Bureau of the Census, Working Paper, 1968. Reprinted in Brian J. L. Berry and Frank E. Horton, *Geographic Perspectives on Urban Systems* (Englewood Cliffs, NJ: Prentice-Hall Inc., 1970).

[23]Calvin L. Beale, "Poughkeepsie's Complaint or Defining Metropolitan Areas," *American Demographics* (January 1984): 28–48.

[24]Ira Rosenwaike, "A Critical Examination of the Designation of Standard Metropolitan Statistical Areas," *Social Forces* 48:3 (1970): 322–333.

the central city. However, he noted that there were an additional 78 counties that did meet these criteria which were not part of the SMSAs. One-half of these adjacent counties were added when SMSAs were revised in 1963. Most of the others did not meet the criterion of "metropolitan character," which was primarily based on the concentration of population within a densely settled area of the county.

To what extent do these criticisms diminish the utility of SMSAs as units of analysis? One way to answer this question is to look at how much the population of metropolitan areas would change if adjustments were made to take account of specific criticisms. Forstall and Fulton calculated that the 19 counties that did not meet the commuting criterion for inclusion in 1970 contained only 1 million people, or less than 1 percent of the total metropolitan population. [25] With respect to the question of overbounding of metropolitan areas, they estimated that dropping outlying counties that had less than 50 people per square mile and less than 250,000 total population would only reduce the total metropolitan population in 1970 by 1.8 million.

Metropolitan areas with less than 100,000 population accounted for only 2.2 million people, or about 1.3 percent of the total metropolitan population in 1980. Those that were under 200,000 and lacked a central city or cities of 50,000 accounted for 6.9 million, or 4 percent of the 1980 metropolitan population. The eight SMSAs with populations over 200,000 that lack central cities of 50,000 contain another 2.4 million people, but there is more agreement that these should be metropolitan because they contain relatively large Urbanized Areas.

Another way of looking at the effect of changes in the criteria for defining SMSAs is to apply the 1980 criteria to earlier censuses. Using these criteria, Forstall estimated that there would have been about 26 additional areas in 1950, 28 more in 1960, and 38 more in 1970. [26] Because most of these areas are small, they do not add a great deal to the total metropolitan population—only about 3 million persons in 1950 and 5.6 million in 1970.

SMSAs are not perfect, either in the correspondence between official criteria and theoretical notions of what should be classified as metropolitan, or in the application of these criteria, but the deviations are not large in terms of the proportion of the United States population that is affected. Many of the problems can be minimized by using constant boundaries for studying change over time so that changes in definition are not confused with changes in the variables of interest. In

[25]Richard L. Forstall and Philip N. Fulton, "The Official SCSA/SMSA Definition: Concept and Practice," *Statistical Reporter* (October 1976): 1–11.

[26]Richard L. Forstall, "Is America Becoming More Metropolitan?" *American Demographics* 3:11 (December 1981): 18–22.

addition, since most of the controversy about metropolitan areas relates to the smallest areas, much of our analysis will focus on the larger SMSAs.

Central Cities and Suburbs

The second part of the monograph analyzes the redistribution of population, households, and employment between central cities and their surrounding suburbs in large metropolitan areas. The central city–suburb distinction has long constituted a focal point in the study of intrametropolitan redistribution processes. The central city constitutes a crude approximation to the functional nucleus of the metropolitan area which, according to urban scholars, contains those institutions that administer and coordinate the "diverse activities" of the lesser cities, villages, and intervening areas that comprise the metropolitan area's hinterland.[27]

As the official definition of an SMSA has changed over time, the definition of a central city has also changed. In 1950 the largest city in each metropolitan area was designated as a central city, and any additional cities were so designated if they had a population of 25,000 or more and were at least one-third that of the largest city.[28] When the requirement for the metropolitan core was modified in 1960 to allow two adjacent cities with a total of 50,000 to qualify (providing the smaller had at least 15,000), both of such cities were considered central cities.[29] Also in 1960 a provision was made that any city of 250,000 or more would be a central city, regardless of what proportion of the largest city's population it had.

In 1980 a new standard was adopted whereby cities with populations between 15,000 and 25,000, which had at least one-third the population of the largest central city in the SMSA, had also to meet two commuting criteria. These cities had to have at least 40 percent of the workers who were resident in the city working in the city, and have at least 75 local jobs per 100 working residents.[30] Also, any city with at least 100,000 persons working within its boundary was designated as a central city.

[27]Amos H. Hawley, "Urbanization as Process," in David Street and Associates, eds., *Handbook of Urban Life* (San Francisco: Jossey Bass Publishers, 1978), pp. 3–26.
[28]U.S. Bureau of the Census, *1950 Census of Population*, Number of Inhabitants (Washington, DC: U.S. Government Printing Office, 1952), pp. 27–28.
[29]U.S. Bureau of the Census, *1960 Census of Population*, Number of Inhabitants (Washington, DC: U.S. Government Printing Office, 1961), pp. xxxi-xxxiii.
[30]U.S. Bureau of the Census, *State and Metropolitan Area Data Book, 1982* (Washington, DC: U.S. Government Printing Office, 1982), p. xviii.

The central cities, which are designated by the Office of Management and Budget and used in tabulations by the U.S. Bureau of the Census, are only approximations to the concept of a "functional nucleus." Many of the older metropolitan areas, such as Boston, Buffalo, Hartford, Newark, Paterson, and Pittsburgh, have central cities with relatively small land areas that have not changed since 1950. In these areas the central city is probably much smaller than the functional nucleus. However, several other central cities, such as Dallas, Houston, Indianapolis, Kansas City, Phoenix, and San Diego, have relatively large land areas that have grown in the past 30 years, which contain territory likely to be classified as suburban under a functional classification.[31]

A major problem with the use of existing political boundaries for classifying central cities is the variation across states in laws and practices with regard to annexation. In some states annexation runs ahead of growth at the periphery of central cities, whereas in others there is virtually no recognition of the territorial expansion of the core. Between 1970 and 1979 the U.S. Bureau of the Census recorded 61,356 annexations and 1,026 detachments for a net change of 8,309 square miles of territory of municipalities, of which 2,718 square miles were added to cities with over 50,000 population.[32] Most of the annexation occurred in a few states, with California, Florida, Illinois, and Texas accounting for 40 percent of the total. There was very little annexation in the New England and Mid-Atlantic states.

Annexations often occur because residents outside a city want services, such as piped water and police and fire protection. Yet racial balance, voting balance, and economic factors may enter into decisions to annex.[33] However, strong suburbs have developed in many older metropolitan areas, which provide the service needs of their residents and which resist attempts at annexation on the part of the central cities. In newer areas in the South and West, central cities tend not to be "hemmed-in" by incorporated suburbs and thus have much more freedom to annex.

Despite the many limitations of central cities as surrogates for the cores of metropolitan areas, they will be used as the basis for the intrametropolitan analysis in this monograph for two reasons. First, much of the data of interest are not available for alternative definitions of

[31]We are indebted to Richard Forstall of the U.S. Bureau of the Census for pointing out many of these problems with the definitions of central cities to us.

[32]U.S. Bureau of the Census, *Boundary and Annexation Survey 1970–79*, Report GE-30-4 (Washington, DC: U.S. Government Printing Office, 1980), pp. 1–9.

[33]Joel Miller, "Annexation: The Outer Limits of City Growth," *American Demographics* (November 1984): 31–35. An interesting case study of annexation in Houston can be found in Robert D. Thomas, "Metropolitan Structural Development: The Territorial Imperative," *Publius* 14 (1984):83–115.

metropolitan cores because the U.S. Bureau of the Census has utilized the basic distinction between central cities and suburbs, which they refer to as "balance of the SMSA," for many of their tabulations and for coding of geography on the Public Use Microdata Samples from which users can make their own tabulations.

Even if data were available for alternative metropolitan core areas, central cities would still be of interest from a more pragmatic standpoint because they represent, by and large, the independent political jurisdictions that bear primary responsibility for collecting revenue from, and providing services for, their resident populations. Hence, irrespective of their functional and symbolic roles, the quality of services that a metropolitan area's central city can maintain and its level of taxation have implications for movements into and out of its boundaries.

Definition of Units Used in this Study

The metropolitan area and central city units of analysis that are used in this study follow closely from those used in decennial census publications. With few exceptions, the metropolitan area units outside of New England are identical to those used in the official census publications for the corresponding dates: 1950, 1960, 1970, or 1980. The exceptions have to do with the definition of the New York SMSA and the related areas of Nassau–Suffolk, Paterson, Newark, and New Brunswick. First, Nassau and Suffolk Counties in New York, which had been part of the New York SMSA from 1950 to 1970 and which were separated from New York in 1972 and designated as the Nassau–Suffolk SMSA, will not be treated as a separate metropolitan area in 1980 because no central city was designated. Instead, these counties will be combined with the New York SMSA, as they were in 1970 and earlier years. Second, Bergen County, New Jersey, which was transferred to New York in 1973 from the Paterson–Clifton–Passaic area, will be kept with the Paterson–Clifton–Passaic area in 1980 to maintain continuity with earlier censuses. These changes do not affect the total metropolitan population in 1980 or the central cities. However, they do result in Paterson–Clifton–Passaic being included in the list of areas over 1 million and Nassau–Suffolk being removed from that list.

The only other exception to the use of official definitions outside New England relates to the counties of Middlesex and Somerset in New Jersey. These counties had been part of the New York–Northeastern New Jersey SMSA in 1950, but not part of any metropolitan area in 1960 and 1970. In 1980 Middlesex County was the New Brunswick

SMSA and Somerset was part of the Newark area. In order to maintain continuity between 1950 and 1980, we have treated these areas as metropolitan in 1960 and 1970 and classified them according to the 1980 definition.

In New England we used the NECMAs instead of SMSAs. In 1980 our New England units are identical to the NECMAs defined in census publications. Since NECMAs were not defined for earlier censuses, we followed the rule of including the county that contained each of the New England SMSAs and any additional counties where a majority of the population was metropolitan. The NECMAs that we have defined correspond to the metropolitan State Economic Areas for 1950, 1960, and 1970, with two exceptions. For all three years, we have included Plymouth County, Massachusetts, which contains the city of Brockton, with Boston, although it is treated as a separate State Economic Area in all three censuses. This does not alter the total metropolitan population, but treats Brockton as part of Boston, which is consistent with the 1980 definition of the Boston NECMA. Second, in 1960 and 1970 we define a Lewiston–Auburn, Maine, NECMA containing Androscoggin County, although there was no metropolitan SEA for that area in those years.[34]

In order to construct measures for metropolitan areas with constant boundaries over a decade, we began by building a county file with all of the necessary measures. The data sources for this file are listed in Appendix F. We then constructed separate metropolitan area files for each decade, using the metropolitan area definitions at the end of the decade and aggregating the data for all of the counties within each of the metropolitan areas.

The intrametropolitan analysis is limited to the 39 metropolitan areas over 1 million in 1980. With the exceptions of New York, Paterson, and Nassau–Suffolk, which are described above, these areas are identical to those in the 1980 census. The central cities are the same as those listed in the 1980 census publications. In Hartford and Boston, where NECMAs are used, the central cities are Hartford and Boston.

Unlike the trend analysis for entire metropolitan areas, the intrametropolitan analysis will employ constant metropolitan area boundaries and central city definitions throughout the period of analysis. This

---

[34]Not all metropolitan areas were designated as Metropolitan State Economic Areas. In order to be a Metropolitan State Economic Area, an SMSA had to have a central city of 50,000 and a total population of 100,000. U.S. Bureau of the Census, *U.S. Census of Population: 1960. Selected Area Reports. State Economic Areas*, final report PC(3)-1A (Washington, DC: U.S. Government Printing Office, 1963), pp. ix-x. Lewiston–Auburn, ME, did not meet either of these criteria.

means that the same boundaries will be used for the 39 metropolitan areas from 1950 to 1984. The reason for using consistent boundaries in this part of the analysis relates to the emphasis on subgroup selectivity and changes in central city and suburban population compositions. In this case, comparisons over time would be distorted by changing metropolitan area boundaries.

PART ONE

3

COMPONENTS OF METROPOLITAN GROWTH AND DECLINE

Overview of Metropolitan Growth in the Twentieth Century

T HE TWENTIETH CENTURY has seen the rapid growth and spread of metropolitan areas throughout the United States. At the beginning of the century, less than one-third of the population lived in metropolitan areas and only five of these areas had populations over 1 million. By 1980 three-quarters of the population lived within metropolitan areas and there were 39 areas with populations over 1 million. Both the number of metropolitan areas and the size of these areas increased over the century, although there are signs that the larger areas had reached their maximum size by 1970 and that future metropolitan growth may be concentrated in smaller areas.

The growth of the metropolitan population and its share of the national population is detailed in Table 3.1. For the period prior to 1950 we have used Bogue's estimates, which he obtained by applying 1950 criteria to each census from 1900 to 1940.[1] Since metropolitan growth

[1]Donald J. Bogue, *Population Growth in Standard Metropolitan Areas 1900–1950* (Washington, DC: Housing and Home Finance Agency, 1953). Bogue used counties in New England, which is consistent with our practice. For each decade prior to 1950, he counted as metropolitan all counties of metropolitan areas that had a central city over 50,000 and a total population of at least 100,000. Although the minimum total size of 100,000 was not part of the official 1950 definition, only five metropolitan areas with a total population of 372,700 were excluded in 1940 due to this limitation, and the number was even smaller in earlier years. Even though the U.S. Bureau of the Census did define Metropolitan Districts for the censuses from 1910 to 1940, these included only the larger areas and the suburbs closest to these areas and were not comparable with the metropolitan areas defined for the 1950 census. These Metropolitan Districts are described in the summary volumes for the censuses from 1910 to 1940.

TABLE 3.1

Growth of Total and Metropolitan Population of United States and Percentage Metropolitan by Decade, 1900 to 1980

Year	Total Population (millions)	Percent Growth in Population During Previous Decade	Population Metropolitan Areas (millions)	Percent Growth for Metropolitan Areas		Percent of U.S. Population in Metropolitan Areas	Number of SMSA/ NECMA
				Overall	w/in Constant Boundaries		
1900	76.0	—	24.1	—	—	31.7	52
1910	92.0	21.0	34.5	43.2	32.6	37.5	71
1920	105.7	14.9	46.1	33.4	25.2	43.6	94
1930	122.8	16.1	61.0	32.4	27.0	49.7	115
1940	131.7	7.2	67.1	10.0	8.3	51.0	125
1950	151.3	14.9	85.9	28.0	21.8	56.8	162
1960	179.3	18.5	114.4	33.2	26.5	63.8	203
1970	203.3	13.4	141.4	23.6	16.8	69.6	231
1980	226.6	11.4	170.5	20.5	10.3	75.3	304
1984	236.2	4.2	178.0	4.4	4.4	75.4	304

NOTES:
1. 1900 to 1940 based on coterminous U.S. 1950 to 1984 figures include Alaska and Hawaii.
2. Metropolitan areas refer to SMAs (1950) or SMSAs (1960–1984), as defined at the time of the census, with exceptions noted in Chapter 2. NECMAs are used in New England.
3. Data for 1900 to 1950 taken from Donald Bogue, *Population Growth in Standard Metropolitan Areas 1900–1950* (Washington, DC: Housing and Home Finance Agency, 1953) pp. 11, 13. Data for 1960 to 1980 were obtained from the *County and City Data Book*. Data for 1984 were obtained from *Current Population Reports*, Series P-26, no. 84-52-C.
4. Growth within constant boundaries was calculated using end of decade boundaries as defined for census publications, except for 1984 when 1980 boundaries were used.

is due both to growth of existing areas and the expansion of territory classified as metropolitan, we have also shown the percentage growth of metropolitan areas for each decade using constant boundaries as defined at the end of each decade. End of decade boundaries are preferable to beginning of decade boundaries because growth occurring at the periphery of metropolitan areas and growth of new metropolitan areas are included in the growth within constant boundaries. Because of lags in redefining metropolitan areas, which were discussed in Chapter 2, it is safe to assume that the end of decade boundaries more nearly represent the metropolitan areas during the decade than do the beginning of period boundaries.

Up until 1930 the metropolitan areas grew much more rapidly than nonmetropolitan areas, even when growth was measured within constant boundaries. This was a period of rapid rural to urban migration, and the major cities also received most of the immigrants from abroad, who contributed significantly to total growth. The Depression and restrictive legislation greatly reduced immigration in the 1930s, and the rate of metropolitan growth slowed considerably during that decade, although it still exceeded the rate of national growth. The upsurge of economic activity during World War II and thereafter resulted in the resumption of rapid metropolitan growth from 1940 to 1960.

By the 1960s much of the metropolitan growth was the result of outward expansion of metropolitan areas and new areas achieving metropolitan status. While metropolitan areas as a whole grew by 24 percent, the growth within constant boundaries was only 17 percent, and the difference between metropolitan and total growth was not as great as it had been in earlier decades.

In the 1970s the rate of metropolitan growth within constant boundaries was less than the rate of total growth, which meant that nonmetropolitan areas grew more rapidly than metropolitan areas for the first time in the century. This so-called nonmetropolitan turnaround is clearly depicted in Figure 3.1. During the 1950s metropolitan areas grew at three to four times the rate of growth of nonmetropolitan areas. In the 1960s the rate of growth of metropolitan areas declined with the decline in the natural increase of the population, while the rate of growth of nonmetropolitan areas remained the same as it had been in the preceding decade. In the 1970s metropolitan growth continued to decline with the further decline in natural increase, but nonmetropolitan growth increased to a rate that more than doubled that of the two previous decades and exceeded that of metropolitan areas.

The nonmetropolitan turnaround of the 1970s attracted considerable attention from reporters and scholars alike and led to speculation that the United States had reached a level of affluence where people

FIGURE 3.1

Average Annual Rates of Metropolitan and Nonmetropolitan Growth by Decade

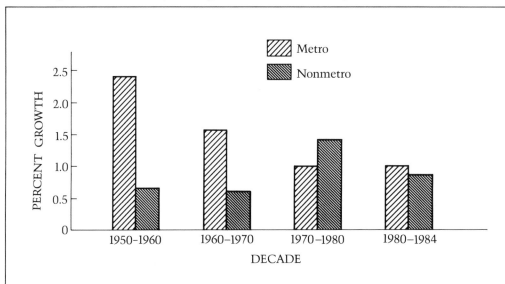

could afford to live where they pleased.[2] This view was supported by studies of residential preferences conducted in the 1970s, which showed that a majority of people preferred to live in either small cities (under 50,000), or rural areas.[3]

However, the turnaround appears to have been short-lived because estimates for population growth from 1980 to 1984 show that metropolitan areas grew at a slightly higher rate than nonmetropolitan areas. A more detailed examination of these trends is presented in Appendix A, which discusses the effect of changing definitions on conclusions about the turnaround. Although metropolitan growth rates appear higher when more recent definitions of "metropolitan" are used, the turnaround of the 1970s is evident under all alternative definitions, and the

[2]An excellent discussion of many factors associated with the 1970s turnaround can be found in John Wardwell, "Toward a Theory of Urban–Rural Migration in the Developed World," in David L. Brown and John M. Wardwell, eds., *New Directions in Urban–Rural Migration: The Population Turnaround in Rural America* (New York: Academic Press, 1980), pp. 71–114.

[3]*The Gallup Opinion Index,* report 57 (Princeton, NJ: Gallup International, 1970); Glenn V. Fuguitt and James J. Zuiches, "Residential Preferences and Population Distribution," *Demography* 12:3 (August 1975):491–504; Gordon F. De Jong and Kenneth G. Keppel, "Urban Migrants to the Countryside," Bulletin 825, Agricultural Experiment Station, Pennsylvania State University (June 1979).

end of the turnaround is clear when either the 1980 or more recent definitions are used.

The South did not experience the turnaround in the 1970s, and the continued strong growth of southern metropolitan areas in the 1980s is the main reason for higher national rates of metropolitan than non-metropolitan growth for 1980–1984. The data from the 1980s suggest that there may be little difference between metropolitan and nonmetropolitan growth for the nation as a whole in the future.

Territorial Expansion of Metropolitan Areas

During the decade of the nonmetropolitan turnaround, there was considerable growth in the metropolitan population due to re-classification of territory, and the proportion of population living in areas classified as metropolitan increased from 69.6 to 75.3 percent. This has resulted in considerable debate about the extent of the actual turnaround and the interpretation of the turnaround. On the side of the proponents of the turnaround, it is argued that most of the newly created metropolitan areas would not have qualified if earlier criteria had been rigidly applied.[4] Supporting this argument are data that show that nonmetropolitan areas grew more rapidly than metropolitan areas, regardless of which definitions are used as long as growth is measured within constant boundaries.[5]

Critics of the view that there was a turnaround in metropolitan growth have pointed out that deconcentration of metropolitan areas has taken place throughout this century and that the outward expansion of metropolitan areas and creation of new areas are valid components of metropolitan growth. Forstall argues that "the very success of non-metropolitan areas in attracting people from neighboring metropolitan areas sometimes resulted in the formation of new metropolitan areas and the consequent loss to the nonmetropolitan category."[6] While residential preference studies demonstrate preferences for nonmetropol-itan areas, they also show that most people stating this preference prefer to be within 30 miles of·a metropolitan area.[7] This suggests that

[4]Calvin L. Beale, "Poughkeepsie's Complaint or Defining Metropolitan Areas," *American Demographics* (January 1986): 28–48.

[5]Using 1970 SMSA definitions, metropolitan areas grew by 8.8 percent compared to 17.3 percent for nonmetropolitan areas between 1970 and 1980. Using 1980 boundaries, these percentages were 10.3 and 15.1, respectively.

[6]Richard L. Forstall, "Is America Becoming More Metropolitan," *American Demo-graphics* 3:11 (December 1981): 22.

[7]Glenn V. Fuguitt and James J. Zuiches, "Residential Preferences and Population Dis-tribution."

people may really be expressing a preference to move further from the central cities while continuing to enjoy the facilities provided by metropolitan areas. L. Long and D. De Are found that nonmetropolitan growth was greater in counties adjacent to metropolitan areas than in nonadjacent counties.[8] J. Long observed that nonmetropolitan counties with a relatively high proportion of commuters to metropolitan areas grew more rapidly than other nonmetropolitan counties.[9]

A more detailed examination of the relationship between the total growth of metropolitan areas and the territorial expansion of metropolitan areas is provided in Table 3.2, where total growth has been divided into the components of (1) the population added by enlarging existing SMSAs through the addition of counties; (2) the population of newly defined SMSAs; and (3) growth within constant boundaries. Because the added counties and the new SMSAs are assumed to have been added at the beginning of the decade during which they were defined, all growth in the added counties and the new SMSAs is treated as part of the growth within fixed boundaries.

Between 1950 and 1980 there was a marked decline in the proportion of metropolitan growth that occurred within constant metropolitan area boundaries. This proportion fell from 84 percent in the 1950s to 55 percent in the 1970s. In the 1950s added counties and new areas accounted for only 16 percent of the growth. This follows a pattern of concentration of growth in existing, larger metropolitan areas which Berry and Kasarda documented for the first half of the century.[10] The proportion of growth due to new areas and added counties increased somewhat in the 1960s and rose to 45 percent for the 1970s. Most of this increase in the 1970s was caused by new areas which accounted for almost one-third of total growth.

There is no doubt that some of the new metropolitan areas came into being because the criteria for qualifying for SMSA status were revised in 1980 to allow areas with smaller cities to qualify. (This problem was discussed in Chapter 2.) The impact of the change in criteria can be roughly estimated by using Forstall's estimate that the 1970 metropolitan population would have been about 5.6 million greater had 1980 criteria been in effect then.[11] This is approximately 19 percent of

[8]Larry Long and Diane De Are, "Repopulating the Countryside: A 1980 Census Trend," *Science* 217 (September 17, 1982): 1111–1116.

[9]John F. Long, *Population Deconcentration in the United States,* U.S. Bureau of the Census, Special Demographic Analyses, CDS-81-5 (November 1981): 20–23.

[10]Brian J. L. Berry and John D. Kasarda, *Contemporary Urban Ecology* (New York: Macmillan Publishers, 1977), pp. 165–172. Their figures for 1950 to 1970 are not precisely comparable to ours because they used boundaries defined by commuting data rather than those in the official census publications.

[11]Richard L. Forstall, "Is America Becoming More Metropolitan," p. 20.

TABLE 3.2

Sources of Metropolitan Change, 1950–1980

Decade	Total Increase	Added Counties	New Areas	Growth in Constant Boundaries
POPULATION IN MILLIONS				
1950–1960	28.5	1.3	3.2	23.9
1960–1970	27.0	3.6	3.0	20.4
1970–1980	29.1	3.7	9.5	15.9
PERCENTAGE OF TOTAL				
1950–1960	100.0	4.7	11.3	84.0
1960–1970	100.0	13.4	11.2	75.4
1970–1980	100.0	12.6	32.6	54.7

NOTES:
1. See Table 3.1 for sources of data.
2. The total increase is the difference between the metropolitan population at the end of the decade and the beginning of the decade, as shown in Table 3.1.
3. The populations for added counties and new areas are those at the beginning of the decade. Growth in these areas during the decade is included in the last column.

the total metropolitan change between 1970 and 1980 and, if this were removed from the total, the proportion of metropolitan growth which is due to new areas declines from 33 to about 17 percent. Even with such an adjustment, new areas accounted for a larger proportion of total growth in the 1970s than in earlier decades. Furthermore, if this adjustment is made to the total amount of growth, the proportion of growth which is accounted for by added counties rises to about 16 percent, making this a more significant component than in previous decades. Thus, even when adjustments are made for changing definitions, the 1970s was a period when metropolitan growth shifted more in the direction of outward expansion and the multiplication of points of concentration than had been true in preceding decades.

Regional Variation in Metropolitan Growth

The twentieth century has also seen a dramatic shift in the location of metropolitan areas within the United States. In 1900 most of the major cities were located in the Northeast region and the eastern part of the Midwest—from Ohio to Wisconsin. Of the 11 areas with populations over 500,000, eight, including all of those over 1 million in size, were located in the Northeast region or the East North Central division, and two others, Baltimore and St. Louis, were located just outside this area (see Figure 3.2). San Francisco was the only metropolitan area with over 500,000 population that was located well outside the northeastern quarter of the nation. Several of the major metropolitan areas in 1980 were only small towns in 1900. Miami had a population of only 4,955, and the combined populations of Dallas, Houston, Los Angeles, and San Diego were less than that of the Providence, Rhode Island, metropolitan area.

The concentration of metropolitan areas in the Northeast was due in part to the concentration of total population in this region. However, there were significant regional differences in the level of metropolitanization as well. In 1900, when less than one-third of the population of the United States lived in metropolitan areas, almost 65 percent of the population in the Northeast was within metropolitan areas.[12] In contrast, 26 percent of the population of the Midwest, 28 percent of the population of the West, and less than 10 percent of the population of the South lived in metropolitan areas.

During the first half of the century there was a continual westward movement of the population. By 1950 the proportion of the metropolitan population that was west of the Mississippi had doubled and there were 41 metropolitan areas between the river and the Pacific coast. However, this period also witnessed substantial metropolitan growth in the eastern part of the Midwest, led by a sixfold increase in the population of Detroit. In 1950 the Northeast and Midwest regions still contained most of the metropolitan areas over 1 million, although two western areas, Los Angeles and San Francisco, and two southern areas, Baltimore and Washington, had grown to over 1 million (see Figure 3.2).

Between 1950 and 1980 the West continued to grow, but there was a gradual shift in the East away from the northeastern areas toward southern areas. While the number of areas in the Northeast increased from 36 to 49, the number in the South doubled from 59 to 119, with the largest number of new areas appearing in the South Atlantic states. By 1980 a majority (21 out of 39) of the metropolitan areas over 1 million were located in the South or the West (see Figure 3.2).

The regional shift in urbanization can also be seen in the rankings of the top 20 metropolitan areas (Table 3.3). In 1900 this list was dominated by areas in the Northeast region and the East North Central division. If the boundaries of these regions are stretched a little to include the adjacent areas of Minneapolis and St. Louis in the West North Central division and Baltimore and Washington to the South region, then

---

[12]Estimates for metropolitan areas in 1900 are based on Donald J. Bogue, *Population Growth in Standard Metropolitan Areas 1900–1950.*

FIGURE 3.2
Locations of Large Metropolitan Areas in 1900, 1950, and 1980
(census divisions are shown on maps for reference)

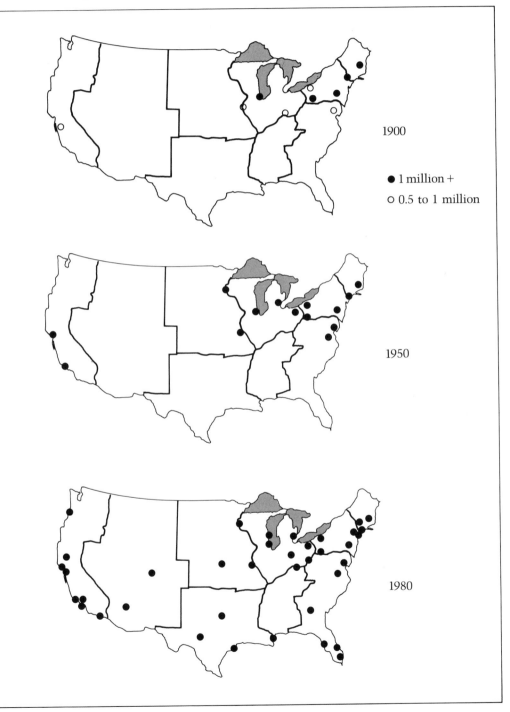

1900

● 1 million +
○ 0.5 to 1 million

1950

1980

TABLE 3.3
Largest 20 Metropolitan Areas in 1900, 1950, and 1980

Rank	1900	Population in Millions	1950	Population in Millions	1980	Population in Millions
1	New York–NE New Jersey	5.0	New York–NE New Jersey	12.9	New York–Newark–SCSA	16.1
2	Chicago	2.1	Chicago	5.5	Los Angeles–SCSA	11.5
3	Philadelphia	1.9	Los Angeles	4.4	Chicago–Gary–SCSA	7.9
4	Boston*	1.7	Philadelphia	3.7	Philadelphia–SCSA	5.5
5	Pittsburgh	1.1	Detroit	3.0	San Francisco–SCSA	5.2
6	St. Louis	0.8	Boston*	2.4	Detroit–Ann Arbor SCSA	4.6
7	Baltimore	0.6	San Francisco–Oakland	2.2	Boston–*	3.7
8	San Francisco–Oakland	0.5	Pittsburgh	2.2	Houston–Galveston SCSA	3.1
9	Cincinnati	0.5	St. Louis	1.7	Washington, DC	3.1
10	Buffalo	0.5	Cleveland	1.5	Dallas–Ft. Worth	3.0
11	Cleveland	0.5	Washington, DC	1.5	Cleveland–Akron–SCSA	2.6
12	Minneapolis–St. Paul	0.5	Baltimore	1.3	Miami–Ft. Lauderdale SCSA	2.6
13	Detroit	0.4	Minneapolis–St. Paul	1.1	St. Louis	2.4
14	Washington, DC	0.4	Buffalo	1.1	Pittsburgh	2.3
15	Providence*	0.4	Cincinnati	0.9	Baltimore	2.2
16	Worcester*	0.4	Milwaukee	0.9	Minneapolis–St. Paul	2.1
17	Albany–Schenectady–Troy	0.3	Kansas City	0.8	Seattle–Tacoma SCSA	2.1
18	Milwaukee	0.3	Houston	0.8	Atlanta	2.0
19	New Orleans	0.3	Providence*	0.7	San Diego	1.9
20	Kansas City	0.3	Portland, OR	0.7	Cincinnati–Hamilton SCSA	1.7

SOURCE: 1900 and 1950 data obtained from Donald Bogue, *Population Growth in Standard Metropolitan Statistical Areas 1900–1950*. 1980 based on 1980 census counts for SCSAs and SMSAs.

NOTES: Populations in 1900 are based on 1950 boundaries. A '–' at the end of a name means there are other cities in the title which are not shown.

*New England County Metropolitan Area

only San Francisco and New Orleans lie outside this area. By 1950 the list had changed considerably. Two northeastern areas had dropped off the list and six others had fallen in rank substantially. Three new areas outside the North had climbed onto the list: Los Angeles, Houston, and Portland. Los Angeles's growth was most phenomenal, raising it to third place in 1950. Only one northern city, Detroit, improved its ranking substantially.

By 1980 several other northern areas had fallen from the list and there had been declines in remaining ones. Los Angeles had moved into second place and two new western areas, Seattle–Tacoma and San Diego, and three southern areas, Dallas–Fort Worth, Miami–Fort Lauderdale, and Atlanta, had made it onto the list. Although none of the officially defined northern SMSAs improved its ranking, Washington, which is near the North–South boundary, did move up significantly as a result of the expansion of the federal government.

The data in Table 3.4 summarize the growth in metropolitan areas by census division between 1950 and 1984. In the three decades prior to 1980, growth was greatest in the Mountain division, which had only 1.5 million people in metropolitan areas in 1950, but over 7 million in 1980. Although this area is still characterized by vast mountain ranges and deserts with very low population densities, there are now substantial metropolitan areas, such as Denver, Las Vegas, Phoenix, and Salt Lake City, as well as several smaller but growing areas, such as Albuquerque, Billings, and Casper. The metropolitan areas in the South Atlantic, West South Central, and Pacific divisions grew more rapidly than the total metropolitan population in each of the four periods. Among these divisions, the metropolitan areas in the Pacific division grew most rapidly in the fifties and sixties, although those in the West South Central division, which includes Texas, grew fastest in the seventies and eighties.

Throughout the 1950–1984 period, the lowest metropolitan growth was found among the northern census divisions. In the 1950s the metropolitan areas of New England and the Mid Atlantic had the lowest growth rates. In the 1960s all four northern divisions, as well as the East South Central division, had rates below average. Since 1970 the growth in the northern divisions has been very low, the Mid Atlantic division lost population in the 1970s, and the East North Central division lost population between 1980 and 1984. It appears that although metropolitan growth for the country slowed from the 1950s to the 1970s and 1980s, it slowed down much more in the North than in the rest of the nation. If these trends continue, each decade will see a larger and larger proportion of the metropolitan population located in the South and West.

TABLE 3.4

Percentage Growth of Metropolitan Areas by Decade and Census Division, 1950–1984

Region and Division	1950–1960	1960–1970	1970–1980	1980–1984
NORTHEAST	13.7	9.6	−1.5	1.1
New England	13.0	12.8	2.6	1.6
Mid Atlantic	14.0	8.7	−2.7	0.9
MIDWEST	23.5	13.0	2.6	0.4
East North Central	23.4	12.7	2.0	−0.3
West North Central	23.8	13.8	5.0	2.7
SOUTH	36.2	22.0	21.5	8.0
South Atlantic	39.7	25.9	20.7	7.4
East South Central	22.6	11.6	14.4	2.8
West South Central	38.1	21.3	26.4	11.4
WEST	48.5	28.5	22.6	8.2
Mountain	63.9	34.6	41.4	11.4
Pacific	45.8	27.3	18.6	7.4
Total	26.5	16.8	10.3	4.4
Average Annual Rate	2.38	1.57	0.99	1.03

NOTES:
1. Based on SMSAs and NECMAs as defined at the end of each decade.
2. Region and division boundaries were adjusted for SMSAs that crossed division boundaries so that the entire SMSA was within the division containing the largest of its central cities.
3. Average annual rate calculated using: $P2 = P1(1 + r)^t$, where $P1$ and $P2$ are the populations at the beginning and end of the period, respectively, r is the average annual growth rate, and t is the number of years.

Components of Growth Within Fixed Boundaries

Population growth within any area with fixed boundaries is the sum of natural increase and net migration where net migration is defined as the difference between the number of people moving into the area and the number of people moving out of the area; natural increase is the difference between births and deaths. Since either or both components can be negative, growth may be negative.

Throughout this century the birthrate has exceeded the death rate in both the nation as a whole and within metropolitan areas. The post–World War II baby boom lasted into the mid-1960s, resulting in a natural increase for the nation of 16.5 percent for the 1950s and 11.3 percent for the 1960s. In the 1970s the decline in the birthrate reduced the rate of natural increase to only 6.5 percent for the decade.

TABLE 3.5

Components of Change of Metropolitan Areas, 1950–1980,
as a Percentage of Population at Beginning of Decade
(using constant end of decade boundaries for each decade)

Decade	Total Growth	Natural Increase	Total Net Migration	Internal Migration	Net Immigration	Change in Enumeration
1950–1960	26.5	17.0	9.5	7.2	2.3	0.0
1960–1970	16.8	12.2	4.6	2.4	2.2	0.0
1970–1980	10.3	7.0	1.6	−1.8	3.4	1.7
1980–1984	4.4	3.2	1.2			
Percentage Distribution of Total Growth						
1950–1960	100.0	64.2	35.8	27.2	8.7	0.0
1960–1970	100.0	72.6	27.4	14.3	13.1	0.0
1970–1980	100.0	68.0	15.5	−17.5	33.0	16.5
1980–1984	100.0	72.7	27.3			

NOTES:
1. For 1960–1970 and 1970–1980, foreign immigrants are those counted in the census. For 1950–1960, immigrants are estimated from data from the immigration service.
2. Natural increase for 1960–1970 and 1970–1980 is calculated from births and deaths by county provided by John Long, U.S. Bureau of the Census. For 1950–1960, net migration as reported in the *County and City Data Book* was subtracted from total growth to obtain natural increase. For 1980–1984, natural increase was obtained from "1984 Population Estimates by County with Components of Change" machine-readable data file, U.S. Bureau of the Census, 1986.
3. Net internal migration is estimated as a residual. This includes net immigration from Puerto Rico and other outlying areas.
4. Increased enumeration is estimated from data provided by Jeff Passel, Charles Cowan, and Robert Fay. No estimate was made for 1950–1960 or 1960–1970.

Since 1950 natural increase has been the major component in metropolitan growth within constant boundaries. Table 3.5 shows the total metropolitan growth for each decade within fixed boundaries divided into three components of natural increase, net internal migration, and immigration from abroad. For 1970–1980, a fourth component is added to represent that part of the population increase thought to be due to differences in the level of enumeration between 1970 and 1980. Although there may have been differences in enumeration in earlier decades, they were probably not as great as that between 1970 and 1980, and no regional estimates are available for earlier decades.[13]

[13]Passel and Robinson have prepared revised estimates of underenumeration which take account of illegal immigrants who were enumerated in censuses, emigration, and migration of Puerto Ricans and foreign students. These show overall rates of underenumeration of 4.4 percent for 1950, 3.3 percent for 1960, 2.8 percent for 1970, and 1.0 percent for 1980. Jeffrey S. Passel and J. Gregory Robinson, "Revised Demographic Estimates of the Coverage of the Population by Age, Sex, and Race in the 1980 Census," U. S. Bureau of the Census, memorandum, April 8, 1985.

The table shows that natural increase accounted for over two-thirds of the total increase in each decade. While natural increase has declined over the 34-year period, so has internal migration to metropolitan areas. In the 1950s net migration accounted for a 9.5 percent growth in the metropolitan population. In the 1960s the growth due to net migration was less than one-half this amount, and in the 1970s it was only about 1.6 percent. Net migration to metropolitan areas in the 1970s would have been negative, because of the net internal flow to nonmetropolitan areas, had it not been for substantial immigration from foreign countries. Although net migration was slightly higher for the first part of the 1980s, the general trends for the 1980s do not look very different from those of the 1970s.

Regional Variations in Natural Increase

Natural increase varied considerably among metropolitan areas in different parts of the country (see Table 3.6). In each decade the rates of natural increase were lowest in the two divisions of the Northeast, and in the 1970s natural increase in these areas was less than 4 percent for the 10-year period. Natural increase was highest in the West South Central and Mountain divisions, which had rates in excess of 25 percent in the 1950s and in excess of 10 percent in the 1970s. The other divisions had intermediate values that were close to the national averages for each decade. Data from the first four years of the 1980s indicate that the rates of natural increase for the 1980s are very similar to those of the 1970s.

In all four decades, natural increase has been higher in metropolitan areas than in nonmetropolitan areas. This difference was most pronounced in the 1960s when natural increase was about 25 percent higher in metropolitan than in nonmetropolitan areas. The higher rate of natural increase in metropolitan areas is accounted for primarily by the younger age structure of these areas compared to nonmetropolitan areas. This results in substantially lower crude death rates in metropolitan areas. For example, for the 1970–1980 decade, the average annual death rate was 8.6 (per 1,000 population) in metropolitan areas compared to 10.2 in nonmetropolitan areas. Although age structure also has some effect on birthrates, the difference in the proportion of women in the childbearing years between metropolitan and nonmetropolitan areas is not great enough to alter the negative relationship between metropolitan residence and fertility. For the decade of the seventies, metropolitan areas had an average annual birthrate of 15.2 (per 1,000 population) compared to 15.9 for nonmetropolitan areas. Since the difference in birthrates is smaller than the difference in death rates, metropolitan areas have higher rates of natural increase despite their lower fertility.

TABLE 3.6

*Natural Increase by Decade and Census Division
for Metropolitan Areas, 1950–1984
(as percentage of initial population)*

Region and Division	1950–1960	1960–1970	1970–1980	1980–1984
NORTHEAST	12.3	9.0	3.9	1.7
New England	12.4	9.7	3.9	1.8
Mid Atlantic	12.3	8.8	3.9	1.7
MIDWEST	18.5	12.6	7.2	3.2
East North Central	18.4	12.4	7.2	3.0
West North Central	18.7	13.0	7.4	3.6
SOUTH	20.7	14.5	8.5	3.6
South Atlantic	17.7	13.7	6.7	2.6
East South Central	20.1	13.0	8.2	3.0
West South Central	25.3	16.2	11.7	5.4
WEST	20.0	14.0	9.0	4.5
Mountain	27.2	17.5	13.6	5.5
Pacific	18.7	13.3	8.0	4.2
Total	17.0	12.2	7.0	3.2
Average Annual Rate	1.58	1.15	0.68	0.75

NOTES:
1. Based on SMSAs and NECMAs as defined at the end of each decade.
2. Region and division boundaries were adjusted for SMSAs that crossed division boundaries so that the entire SMSA was within the division containing the largest of its central cities.
3. The average annual rate was calculated from the formula $P1 + B - D = P1(1 + r)^t$, where $P1$ is the population at the beginning of the period, B and D are the births and deaths during the period, r is the rate of annual growth, and t is the number of years.

Regional Variations in Net Migration

Throughout the 1950–1984 period, the metropolitan areas of the West region gained significant numbers of migrants, while those of the Northeast region lost migrants. During the 1950s the West region added 28.5 percent to its metropolitan population through migration. While this declined to 14.4 percent in the 1960s and 12.8 percent in the 1970s, net migration in the West remained higher than in any other region up to 1980. In each decade metropolitan areas in the Mountain division grew more rapidly than those in the Pacific division and this difference was most pronounced during the 1970s. During the 1980–1984 period,

53

the estimated rate of net migration for the West declined further and fell below the rate for the South for the first time.

The South gained from net migration during each of the four decades. In the first two decades the migration was greatest to metropolitan areas in the South Atlantic states, but in the 1970s and 1980s it was slightly higher to areas in the West South Central states. Throughout this period the East South Central states (Alabama, Mississippi, Tennessee, and Kentucky) had very low rates of net migration compared to the rest of the South. In two decades, the 1960s and the 1980s, these states lost more migrants than they gained.

TABLE 3.7

Net Migration as a Percentage of Population at Beginning of Decade for Metropolitan Areas by Census Division

Region and Division	1950–1960	1960–1970	1970–1980	1980–1984
NORTHEAST	1.4	.7	− 6.4	− .7
New England	.5	3.1	− 2.6	− .2
Mid Atlantic	1.7	− .1	− 7.6	− .8
MIDWEST	5.0	.4	− 5.6	− 2.8
East North Central	5.0	.3	− 6.2	− 3.4
West North Central	5.1	.8	− 3.5	− .9
SOUTH	15.5	7.5	9.2	4.4
South Atlantic	21.9	12.2	10.2	4.7
East South Central	2.5	− 1.4	2.3	− .3
West South Central	12.8	5.0	11.0	6.0
WEST	28.5	14.4	12.8	3.7
Mountain	36.7	17.1	27.5	5.9
Pacific	27.1	13.9	9.8	3.2
Total	9.5	4.6	1.6	1.2
Average Annual Rate	.80	.41	.31	.28

NOTES:
1. Based on SMSAs and NECMAs as defined at the end of each decade.
2. Region and division boundaries were adjusted for SMSAs that crossed division boundaries so that the entire SMSA was within the division containing the largest of its central cities.
3. The average annual rate is the difference between the annual growth rate (Table 3.4) and the annual rate of natural increase (Table 3.6).
4. Percentages in Tables 3.6 and 3.7 do not add to those shown in Table 3.4 for 1970–1980 because of adjustment for differences in levels of enumeration.

Metropolitan areas in the northern states grew from net migration from nonmetropolitan areas and abroad during the 1950s, but at much lower rates than the southern and western areas. Net migration in the Midwest averaged 5 percent, while that in the Northeast was below 2 percent. In the 1960s net migration was close to zero in all northern divisions except New England, which had a modest 3 percent growth from migration. In the 1970s and 1980s all four northern divisions had net outmigration, with the greatest losses occurring in the Mid Atlantic states during the 1970s and the East North Central states in the 1980s.

Migration Between Regions 1975–1980

The net internal migration that benefited metropolitan areas in the South and the West was primarily due to the difference between migrants moving to areas in these regions from other regions and migrants leaving these areas for other regions. The migration streams that give rise to these differences can be constructed from the question on place of residence five years ago, which was asked in the censuses between 1960 and 1980. In all three periods there was net movement away from the Northeast and Midwest regions and net movement toward the West (see Table 3.8). The Northeast sent more migrants to metropolitan areas in each of the other regions than it received from these regions and the West gained from exchanges with each of the other regions.[14] These flows remained relatively constant between 1955–1960 and 1965–1970, but increased during 1975–1980.

The flows involving the Midwest and South were not as stable over time. During the 1950s the South had net outmigration, with the major loss being in the exchange with the West, although the South also had a small net loss in its exchange with the Midwest. The 1965–1970 period saw a slight reversal in flows between the Midwest and the South resulting in a small net outmigration for the southern areas as a whole.

---

[14]The data refer to migrants who were living in metropolitan areas at the time of each census. Their place of residence five years prior to the census could have been either a metropolitan or a nonmetropolitan area. A more complete tabulation of the data distinguishing metropolitan and nonmetropolitan type of residence five years prior to the census is not available in the published census tables. However, such a table was published for 1975–1980 from the March 1980 Current Population Survey. See "Geographical Mobility: March 1975 to March 1980," *Current Population Reports*, series P-20, no. 368 (Washington, DC: U.S. Government Printing Office, 1981). For 1960 the data are tabulated by urban versus rural rather than metropolitan versus nonmetropolitan. Approximately 79 percent of the urban population was metropolitan in that year.

TABLE 3.8

Interregional Metropolitan Migration, 1955–1960, 1965–1970, and 1975–1980
(in thousands)

Region of Residence, 1955	Region of Residence in 1960				Total Out-migrants
	Northeast	Midwest	South	West	
INTERREGIONAL MIGRANTS TO URBAN AREAS 1955–1960*					
Northeast		292	654	384	1,330
Midwest	240		727	944	1,911
South	452	750		685	1,887
West	122	271	356		749
Total Inmigrants	814	1,313	1,737	2,013	5,877
Net Migrants	−516	−598	−150	1,264	0

Region of Residence, 1965	Region of Residence in 1970				Total Out-migrants
	Northeast	Midwest	South	West	
INTERREGIONAL MIGRANTS TO METROPOLITAN AREAS 1965–1970					
Northeast		356	794	422	1,572
Midwest	299		803	813	1,915
South	483	735		693	1,911
West	182	352	546		1,080
Total Inmigrants	964	1,443	2,143	1,928	6,478
Net Migrants	−608	−472	232	848	0

Region of Residence, 1975	Region of Residence in 1980				Total Out-migrants
	Northeast	Midwest	South	West	
INTERREGIONAL MIGRANTS TO METROPOLITAN AREAS 1975–1980					
Northeast		385	1,524	701	2,610
Midwest	297		1,394	1,064	2,755
South	538	760		893	2,191
West	208	405	802		1,415
Total Inmigrants	1,043	1,550	3,720	2,658	8,971
Net Migrants	−1,567	−1,205	1,529	1,243	0

SOURCES: "Mobility for States and State Economic Areas," Census of Population 1960, PC(2) 2B, table 14; "Mobility for States and the Nation," Census of Population 1970, PC(2)-2B, table 42; "General Social and Economic Characteristics," Census of Population 1980, vol. C, U.S. Summary, table 196.

*For 1955–1960, migration was not tabulated by metropolitan areas and urban areas are used instead.

In the 1975–1980 period, the South received substantially more migrants from the Northeast and Midwest and came close to breaking even in its exchange with the West. The result was a substantial net inmigration to southern metropolitan areas from other regions. This trend appears to have increased in the first half of the 1980s, with larger net flows from the Midwest to the South than in previous periods and correspondingly smaller net flows from the Northeast and Midwest to the West.[15] The two northern regions have also switched places in the 1980s with net outmigration from the Midwest exceeding that from the Northeast for the first time.

Although the census tabulations do not distinguish whether the place of origin was metropolitan or not, this distinction is available for interregional migration between 1975 and 1980 as measured by the March 1980 Current Population Survey.[16] These data indicate that 956,000 out of 3,598,000 migrants from the North to metropolitan areas in the South and West originated in nonmetropolitan areas. Offsetting these were 897,000 migrants from metropolitan to nonmetropolitan areas among those moving between the same regions. Since these numbers differ by less than the sampling error, we can conclude that interregional migration does not result in a significant net shift between metropolitan and nonmetropolitan areas. In fact, these same data show that most of the net movement from metropolitan to nonmetropolitan areas occurred within regions.[17]

Although space does not permit displaying the flows between the nine census divisions, there are a few departures from the regional trends that are worthy of comment. All four northern divisions had net outmigration, but the losses were greatest in the Mid Atlantic and East North Central divisions. These divisions sent large numbers of migrants to the South Atlantic, West South Central, and the two western divisions. Most of the net migration to these two divisions went to metropolitan areas in Florida and Texas. The East South Central division received far less migration than the other two southern divisions, although it was not that different from the remainder of the South, if Florida and Texas are excluded. In the West the metropolitan areas in the Mountain states grew more rapidly than those in the Pacific division.

---

[15]Based on special tabulations of Current Population Survey tapes reported in John D. Kasarda, Michael D. Irwin, and Holly L. Hughes, "Demographic and Economic Shifts in the Sunbelt," presented at the Sunbelt Research Conference, Miami, November 3–6, 1985.

[16]U.S. Bureau of the Census, "Geographical Mobility: March 1975 to March 1980," *Current Population Reports*, series P- 20, no. 368. The Current Population Survey differs from the census in excluding mobility of military and college students who are not in households and in using 1970 definitions of metropolitan areas rather than 1980 definitions.

[17]Among all interregional migrants in the 1980 CPS, 1,908,000 moved from nonmetropolitan to metropolitan areas whereas 1,866,000 moved from metropolitan to nonmetropolitan areas. In contrast, among intercounty movers within regions, 4,084,000 moved from nonmetropolitan to metropolitan areas compared to 5,471,000 making the reverse move. "Geographical Mobility: March 1975 to March 1980," *Current Population Reports*, series P-20, no. 368, 1981, tables 3, 39, and 42.

The composition of some of these major migration streams is illustrated in Table 3.9, based on tabulations from the Public Use Microdata Sample of the 1980 Census for selected metropolitan areas, which are either major sources of migration or major destinations. The areas of New York, Philadelphia, Detroit, and St. Louis are representative of larger northern areas that had substantial losses from net outmigration during the 1970s. In the five-year period from 1975 to 1980, these four metropolitan areas lost 2,809,200 outmigrants, but received only 1,466,400 inmigrants from other parts of the United States. Over one-half of these outmigrants left the region for metropolitan areas in the South and West.

Only about 15 percent of those leaving these northern SMSAs moved to nonmetropolitan areas but, with the exception of St. Louis, they were more likely to move to nonmetropolitan areas in the South and West than to nonmetropolitan areas in the northern regions. There

TABLE 3.9

Origins of Internal Migrants to Selected Growing SMSAs and Destinations of Migrants from Selected Declining SMSAs

| | Type of Area of Origin (percentage distribution) | | | | |
| | North | | South or West | | |
Growing SMSAs	Metropolitan	Nonmetro-politan	Metropolitan	Nonmetro-politan	Total
Denver–Boulder	29.3	11.5	46.1	13.1	100.0
Houston	25.9	6.2	52.3	15.7	100.0
San Diego	25.3	5.8	58.7	10.2	100.0
Tampa–St. Petersburg	51.0	10.3	29.3	9.3	100.0
Total	31.9	8.0	47.8	12.3	100.0

| | Type of Area of Destination (percentage distribution) | | | | |
| | North | | South or West | | |
Declining SMSAs	Metropolitan	Nonmetro-politan	Metropolitan	Nonmetro-politan	Total
Detroit	23.6	4.0	58.2	14.2	100.0
New York	30.7	5.2	57.7	6.3	100.0
Philadelphia	29.4	6.7	52.9	11.0	100.0
St. Louis	23.1	13.2	54.3	9.4	100.0
Total	28.5	6.1	56.5	8.8	100.0

SOURCE: Based on special tabulation of place of residence 1975 versus place of residence in 1980, from the Public Use Microdata Sample 1980 (sample "B").

was very little movement to adjacent nonmetropolitan areas—in contrast to the overall finding that most metropolitan to nonmetropolitan movement occurred within regions. Movers out of New York, who stayed in the Northeast, went primarily to other metropolitan areas within the New York–Northern New Jersey Consolidated Area or to other major metropolitan areas, such as Boston, Chicago, or Philadelphia. Only 2 percent of the total outmigrants from New York went to nonmetropolitan areas in the adjacent states of Connecticut, New Jersey, or New York.

In contrast to the pattern for outmigrants, who tended to leave the region, the majority of inmigrants to three of the four selected growing SMSAs shown in Table 3.9 came from the South or West regions. Only Tampa–St. Petersburg received a majority of its migrants from the northern region. In the South and West there was far more circulation of migrants among metropolitan areas within the same region than there was in the Northeast and Midwest.

Southern and western SMSAs received about one-fifth of their migrants from nonmetropolitan areas and, with the exception of Tampa–St. Petersburg, the majority of these nonmetropolitan migrants came from the South or West. Much of this migration, however, was offset by metropolitan to nonmetropolitan migration within the same regions.

Another source of growth is migration from abroad, which is not included in Table 3.9. The four growing SMSAs in this table received an additional 233,100 migrants from abroad between 1975 and 1980.[18] Most of these were foreign-born immigrants, although some were United States citizens who had been abroad in 1975 serving in the armed forces, or for other reasons. The migrants from abroad accounted for 11.7 percent of the total inmigrants to these four SMSAs. The importance of immigration as a source of metropolitan growth will be discussed in greater detail in a later section.

The Changing Relationship Between Size and Growth

During the four decades covered by this study, the relationship between size and growth has changed from favoring intermediate and large-sized areas to one favoring small areas (see Table 3.10). The shift toward an inverse relationship between size and growth, combined with an overall decline in the rate of metropolitan growth, resulted in nega-

---

[18]Unfortunately, no data exist on migration from outmigration areas to destinations outside the United States, but it is reasonable to assume that these flows are small compared to the total outmigration from these areas.

TABLE 3.10

Metropolitan Growth by Size and Region for Each Decade

Size Group	Percentage Growth for Decade				
	Northeast	Midwest	South	West	Total
1950–1960					
Under 250,000	13.1	22.4	31.8	31.4	26.9
250–999,999	13.0	25.7	37.3	53.7	33.8
1 million +	14.0	23.0	37.8	52.7	21.2
Total	13.7	23.5	36.2	48.5	26.5
1960–1970					
Under 250,000	9.7	13.2	11.9	27.5	14.0
250–999,999	11.3	13.8	19.2	31.5	17.4
1 million +	9.0	12.5	31.2	27.6	17.0
Total	9.6	13.0	21.9	28.5	16.8
1970–1980					
Under 250,000	7.0	7.2	21.0	38.6	17.1
250–999,999	3.9	4.4	19.7	30.3	13.4
1 million +	− 4.5	0.7	23.6	18.4	7.2
Total	− 1.5	2.6	21.5	22.6	10.3
1980–1984					
Under 250,000	0.8	0.6	6.9	9.2	4.6
250–999,999	1.9	− 0.1	7.4	9.1	4.7
1 million +	0.6	0.5	9.2	7.9	4.2
Total	1.1	0.4	8.0	8.2	4.4

NOTE: Growth is measured within constant end of decade boundaries. Regional boundaries adjusted to include entire SMSA within region with largest central city. Size based on SMSAs not SCSAs.

tive or very slow rates of growth for many of the major metropolitan areas.

Part of the shift in growth by size is caused by the movement away from the Northeast and Midwest regions, which contain most of the largest cities, to regions with smaller average metropolitan size. However, the pattern is observed within most regions. In the two northern regions, growth was fairly evenly divided among size groups for the first two decades, but has a strong negative relationship to size in the 1970s. Between 1980 and 1984, there was little growth in metropolitan areas of the Northeast and Midwest and relatively little variation by size of area.

In the South growth in all four decades has been greatest for areas over 1 million. This effect is most pronounced for the 1960s. In the first decade the growth of southern metropolitan areas of intermediate size is almost equal to that of the large areas, while large areas have a much higher average growth rate for the second decade. Between the first decade and the second decade several southern cities shifted from the intermediate category to the million-plus category as a result of their rapid growth, and much of the change in growth rates by size between those two decades can be accounted for by these shifts. Since 1970 the differences in growth rates between larger and smaller areas of the South have diminished, but still favor the larger metropolitan areas.

Western metropolitan areas display the greatest change in the relationship between size and growth over time. In the first decade the large and intermediate SMSAs in the West grew significantly faster than those under 250,000. In the middle decade there is almost no variation in growth rates by size, while in the last two decades there is a clear negative relationship between size and growth.

Examples of rapidly growing areas in the West include: Fort Collins, Colorado; Olympia, Washington; Reno, Nevada; Provo, Utah; Richland, Washington; Boise City, Idaho; and Santa Cruz, California. With the exception of Richland, Washington, all of these continued to grow at more than double the national metropolitan growth rate for the 1980–1984 period. Most of these areas were well separated from larger metropolitan areas and could be considered to be centers of regional growth. All of these areas grew by more than 50 percent between 1970 and 1980. A few had grown at this rate in previous decades, but most had not.

Although the two northern regions had the same negative relationship between growth and metropolitan size as the West, few metropolitan areas in these regions had growth rates comparable to those of southern and western areas. There were only four midwestern metropolitan areas with growth rates of over 20 percent for 1970–1980, Bismarck, North Dakota; Columbia, Missouri; St. Cloud, Minnesota; and Springfield, Missouri. All of these were small areas located in the western part of the Midwest (the West North Central division). In the Northeast, there were only two areas with rapid growth, Portsmouth, New Hampshire, and Manchester, New Hampshire—both intermediate size areas. All six of these northern areas continued to grow more rapidly than the national metropolitan average during 1980–1984.

Although the growth trends of some of the smaller metropolitan areas appear to be unique in the 1970s, there is considerable continuity in the growth patterns of larger metropolitan areas over the 34-year period. Table 3.11 shows the growth rates for the ten most rapidly growing areas and the ten biggest losers among areas of over 250,000 for each decade. Five areas, Fort Lauderdale–Hollywood, Las Vegas, West Palm Beach, Orlando, and Phoenix, appear among the top ten gainers for three

TABLE 3.11

Ten Biggest Gainers and Losers in Each Decade Among Metropolitan Areas Over 250,000 at End of Decade

Rank	1950–1960	Percent	1960–1970	Percent	1970–1980	Percent[a]	1980–1984	Percent
				Biggest Gainers				
1	Fort Lauderdale–	298	Las Vegas	115	Las Vegas	70	Fort Myers–	23
2	Orlando	125	Anaheim–Santa Ana–	102	West Palm Beach	65	Melbourne–	21
3	San Jose	121	Oxnard–Ventura	90	Fort Lauderdale–	64	Austin	20
4	Phoenix	100	Fort Lauderdale	86	McAllen–Pharr–	56	West Palm Beach–	20
5	Miami	89	San Jose	66	Phoenix	55	McAllen–Pharr–	19
6	Tampa–St. Peters	89	Santa Barbara	56	Orlando	55	Orlando	18
7	Tucson	88	West Palm Beach	53	Daytona Beach	53	Riverside–San B.	16
8	San Diego	86	Phoenix	46	Tucson	51	Daytona Beach	16
9	Sacramento	81	San Bernardino–	41	Austin	49	Las Vegas	16
10	Albuquerque	80	Houston	40	Santa Rosa	46	Houston	15
				Biggest Losers				
1	Wilkes Barre–Haz.	−12	Johnstown, PA	−6	Jersey City	−6	Duluth–Superior	−5
2	Jersey City	−6	Duluth–Superior	−4	Buffalo	−4	Detroit	−4
3	Johnstown, PA	−4	Wilkes-Barre–Haz.	−1	Cleveland	−1	Flint	−4
4	Huntington–Ashland	4	Jersey City	−1	New York	−1	Eugene–Springfield	−3
5	New Bedford–Fall River	4	Huntington–Ashland	0	Utica–Rome	0	Buffalo	−3
6	Providence–Pawtucket	5	Pittsburgh	0	Pittsburgh	0	Peoria	−3
7	Charleston, WV	6	Wichita	2	Paterson–Clifton–	2	Youngstown–	−3
8	Worcester	7	Birmingham	3	Newark, NJ	3	Pittsburgh	−2
9	Reading, PA	8	Utica–Rome	3	Akron	3	Johnstown	−2
10	Pittsburgh	9	South Bend	3	Dayton	3	Gary–Hammond–	−2

NOTES: Growth is measured within constant end of decade boundaries as a percentage of the beginning of decade population. '–'indicates that other city names are included in the title, but are not shown here.

[a]The percentage growth for 1970–1980 is not adjusted for changes in census enumeration.

of the four decades. Throughout this 34-year period, all of the leading growth areas were located in the South and the West and in only six states: Florida, Texas, New Mexico, Arizona, Nevada, and California.

Over the 34-year period there has been some shift in growth patterns. California, which had three areas among the top ten growth centers in 1950–1960 and five in 1960–1970, had only one area on the list for each of the last two decades. Since 1970 growth has become focused more on areas in Texas and Florida.

The list of the biggest losers in each decade, which includes areas that lost population and those that grew much more slowly than average, is almost completely composed of areas in the Northeast and eastern part of the Midwest—an area frequently described as the old manufacturing belt. The three exceptions to this rule are: Charleston, West Virginia, for 1950–1960 and Birmingham, Alabama, and Wichita, Kansas, for 1960–1970.[19] Pittsburgh, Pennsylvania, is the only area to make the list in all four decades. Two others, Jersey City, New Jersey, and Johnstown, Pennsylvania, make the list of losers in three of the decades.

Over time, there is a significant shift in the size of areas experiencing the greatest losses. For the first two decades all of the losing metropolitan areas except Pittsburgh had populations of less than 1 million. However, for 1970–1980, nine of the losers either had populations of over 1 million or were included in Standard Consolidated Statistical Areas with populations of over 1 million. The only exception was Utica–Rome, New York. In the most recent period, larger metropolitan areas have fared somewhat better and only four of them appear among the areas with the greatest losses. The most recent period also shows that although all of the losers are still in the old "manufacturing belt," there is a westward shift so that seven of the ten top losers for 1980–1984 are in the Midwest, whereas in 1970–1980, seven out of ten were in the Northeast.

Growth of the Civilian and Military Populations

Several of the metropolitan areas contain large military bases, and changes in the number of personnel stationed at these bases are more a function of the defense needs of the nation than they are of factors associated with the local economy or amenities offered by the area. It is thus appropriate to consider migration of the military as a separate

---

[19]Huntington–Ashland, which includes parts of Ohio, Kentucky, and West Virginia, is not counted as an exception since it is partly within the East North Central division.

component of growth. John Long observed that 11.6 percent of interstate migration between 1965 and 1970 was comprised of persons who were in the military in either 1965 or 1970 or both times.[20] In this section we shall try to determine the impact that the military has had on metropolitan growth during the 1960 to 1980 period.

In order to estimate the contribution of the military to net migration for each area, we have assumed that all of the change in the armed forces population of each area is due to migration into and out of the area. It is safe to assume that natural increase is not significant because people are not born into the armed forces, and death rates at bases within the United States are very low because of the young age distribution. It is also reasonable to assume that most entrants into the armed forces come from outside the metropolitan area.[21] However, some of those leaving the military may chose to remain in the metropolitan area. These persons would be counted as both military outmigrants from the area and civilian inmigrants to the area under these assumptions.[22]

Separating the military from the civilian net migration does not change the regional pattern of migration very much (see Table 3.12). During the 1970s the number of persons in the armed forces who were based in the United States declined from about 1.8 to 1.4 million.[23] Within metropolitan areas, the number of armed forces personnel declined by about 290,000—equivalent to 0.2 percent of the total metropolitan population in 1970.[24] This proportion was highest in the South Atlantic division, which lost 0.4 percent of its population due to cuts in military personnel. The only division where metropolitan areas gained from military changes during the 1970s was the East South Central division, but this gain was very small. The overall effect of removing

[20]John F. Long, "The Effects of College and Military Populations on Models of Interstate Migration," *Socio-Economic Planning Science* 17 (1983): 281–290. Miller had observed that 20 percent of the male interstate migration from 1955 to 1960 was armed forces migration. See Ann R. Miller, "Note on Some Problems in Interpreting Migration Data from the 1960 Census of Population," *Demography* 6 (1969): 13–16.

[21]Only 9.8 percent of the persons in the armed forces in 1970 were living in the same county in 1965 based on data from the U.S. Bureau of the Census, *United States Census of Population 1970, Characteristics of the Population*, U.S. Summary, table 48. The proportion who were living in the same metropolitan area would be somewhat higher since some of those living in different counties in 1965 may have moved to a different county within the same metropolitan area.

[22]Among those serving in the armed forces in 1965, 30.2 percent were living in the same county in 1970. Since this is higher than the percent of persons in the armed forces who were living in the same county in 1965, it suggests that some people leaving the military tend to remain in the same area. *United States Census of Population 1970, Characteristics of the Population*, U.S. Summary, table 47.

[23]U.S. Bureau of the Census, *Statistical Abstract of the United States 1981* (Washington, DC: U.S. Government Printing Office, 1981): 363–364.

[24]Many military personnel also have dependents, so the actual effect of military movements is somewhat greater than estimated here.

TABLE 3.12

Estimates of Civilian and Armed Forces Net Migration for
Metropolitan Areas by Census Division, 1970–1980

Region and Census Division	Net Migration as a Percentage of 1970 Population		
	Total	Armed Forces	Civilian
NORTHEAST	−6.4	−0.1	−6.2
New England	−2.6	−0.2	−2.4
Mid Atlantic	−7.6	−0.1	7.4
MIDWEST	−5.6	−0.1	−5.5
East North Central	−6.2	−0.1	−6.2
West North Central	−3.5	−0.1	−3.4
SOUTH	9.2	−0.3	9.5
South Atlantic	10.2	−0.4	10.7
East South Central	2.3	0.1	2.3
West South Central	11.0	−0.1	11.1
WEST	12.8	−0.3	13.2
Mountain	27.5	−0.1	27.6
Pacific	9.8	−0.3	10.1
Total	1.6	−0.2	1.8

NOTES:
1. Based on SMSAs and NECMAs as defined at the end of each decade.
2. Region and division boundaries were adjusted for SMSAs that crossed division boundaries so that the entire SMSA was within the division containing the largest of its central cities.
3. Armed forces net migration is assumed to equal the change in the armed forces between 1970 and 1980.

the military is that civilian rates for the 1970s are very similar to the total rates, but slightly lower in outmigration areas and slightly higher in inmigration areas.

Military movements have had little effect on the regional redistribution of population, but they have been significant for a few metropolitan areas with relatively large proportions of their population in the armed forces. Table 3.13 shows changes in military and civilians for all metropolitan areas in which 20 percent or more of the labor force was employed in the armed forces in 1970.[25] Most of the 11 metropolitan

[25]In addition to the areas shown in Table 3.13, there were five areas that became metropolitan between 1970 and 1980 and had over 20 percent of employed persons in the armed forces. These were: Anchorage, AK; Clarksville–Hopkinsville, TN; Fort Walton Beach, FL; Jacksonville, NC; and Killeen–Temple, TX.

TABLE 3.13

Civilian and Armed Forces Net Migration
for Metropolitan Areas with Significant Armed Forces Employment, 1960–1980

		Net Migration as Percent of Population at Beginning of Decade					
Metropolitan Area	Percent Air Forces Employment 1970	1960–1970			1970–1980		
		Total	Armed Forces	Civilian	Total	Armed Forces	Civilian
Anchorage	24.1				15.2	−1.6	16.8
Biloxi–Gulfport, MS	25.2	−8.2	−0.4	−7.8	3.6	−1.7	5.3
Clarksville, TN	34.6				7.0	3.3	3.6
Col. Springs	33.2	42.3	33.1	9.2	15.0	−2.9	17.9
Columbus, GA	29.5	−10.3	13.7	−24.0	−14.1	−2.5	−11.6
El Paso, TX	14.3	−9.2	−6.6	−2.6	10.2	0.5	9.7
Fayetteville, NC	50.7	14.4	31.6	−17.2	−5.3	−2.5	−2.8
Ft. Walton Beach, FL	35.5				5.0	−0.1	5.1
Honolulu	17.7	3.6	1.1	2.5	4.6	1.4	3.2
Jacksonville, NC	67.6				−16.6	−1.5	−15.1
Killen–Temple, TX	48.7				7.3	3.4	3.9
Lawton, OK	50.2	−4.9	11.2	−16.1	−17.2	−5.7	−11.4
Newport News, VA	19.1	10.6	9.7	0.9	−4.7	−1.5	−3.2
Norfolk–Virginia Beach–, VA	27.0	0.3	7.1	−6.8	−3.9	−1.2	−2.7
Petersburg–, VA	21.9	4.2	21.9	−17.7	−11.0	−4.0	−7.0
Salinas–Seaside–, CA	28.1	8.2	0.9	7.3	3.7	−4.0	7.7
San Diego	23.3	16.3	5.9	10.5	27.3	−0.9	28.2
Tacoma, WA	24.1	14.4	12.2	2.3	7.7	−3.1	10.8
Wichita Falls, TX	22.0	−15.8	3.2	−19.0	−10.6	−2.9	−7.7

NOTES:
1. Armed forces net migration is assumed to equal the change in the armed forces between beginning and end of each deacde.
2. Table includes all metropolitan areas with 20 percent or more of employed persons in armed forces i 1960, 1970, or 1980.
3. Net migration for 1960–1970 is not shown for those areas that became metropolitan only after 1970.

areas shown in the table had significant proportions of their net migration attributable to changes in the military.

Between 1960 and 1970, 10 of the 11 areas experienced growth in the number of armed forces in the area. This growth amounted to 13.2 percent of the total population for Colorado Springs, Colorado, the home of the Air Force Academy, and 12.8 percent in Fayetteville, North Carolina. Although it would seem reasonable that civilian migration might follow armed forces migration because some of the military have dependents and because they create a demand for local goods and services, this occurred in only five of the ten areas experiencing growth in armed forces during the 1960s. It is possible that the expansion of military bases caused displacement of civilian population in some of these areas.[26]

During the 1970s all of the areas that had high proportions of armed forces at the beginning of the decade experienced a decline, which is consistent with the national decline in military personnel after the Vietnam War. However, this decline was matched by outmigration of civilians in only about one-half of the areas. Clearly, civilian and military migration are not strongly related, and one might draw misleading conclusions about migration for areas that have large proportions of armed forces if these two types of migration are not separated.

The Role of Immigration from Abroad

Immigration was a very important component in urban growth in the early part of this century. Between 1900 and 1910 almost 10 million persons immigrated to the United States, and the majority of these went to metropolitan areas in the Northeast, Midwest, and the West.[27] These immigrants provided labor for construction and for the rapidly growing manufacturing plants. In cities such as Boston and New York, over one-third of the population in 1910 was foreign-born.

Immigration was virtually cut off during World War I, but resumed in the 1920s, leading to concern about the impact on national character. In a series of laws passed by Congress between 1921 and 1928, immigration from Eastern Hemisphere countries was severely restricted by the imposition of national quotas. As a result of these quotas and the Depression of the 1930s, during which time some earlier immigrants returned to their countries of origin, there was very little net immigration to the United States between 1929 and 1940. Immigration was also impeded during the early 1940s because of World War II. From 1945 to 1967 immigration was still restricted by national origin quotas, but exceptions were made for refugees from some Communist countries. Immigration increased from 1 million persons in the 1940s to 2.5 million persons in the 1950s.

In 1965 a new immigration bill was passed which went into effect in July 1968. It equalized quotas among countries in the Eastern Hemi-

---

[26]An alternative possibility is that there was local recruitment into the armed forces. These recruits would have been counted as civilian outmigrants in Table 3.13. However, it is unlikely that there was much of this because most of these areas have relatively small civilian populations, and over 90 percent of persons entering the military nationally come from different counties.

[27]Historical statistics on immigration were obtained from decennial census reports and from Irene B. Taeuber and Conrad Taeuber, *People of the United States in the 20th Century*, A Census Monograph (Washington, DC: U.S. Government Printing Office, 1971).

sphere while continuing to allow immigration from the Western Hemisphere. In the first two years after these new rules went into effect, immigration increased by about 25 percent. This change in quotas resulted in a significant change in the origins of immigrants, with much higher proportions coming from Asia.

In addition, migration from the Western Hemisphere became a much more significant part of total immigration after 1950. While Western Hemisphere immigration had not been subject to as much formal restriction as Eastern Hemisphere immigration, it had not been a very large part of total immigration up to 1950. However, high rates of natural increase in Latin America and much more rapid economic growth in the United States made immigration considerably more attractive after 1950. Many entered under the more lenient rules for Western Hemisphere immigrants, and large numbers of Cubans were admitted under special legislation following the Cuban Revolution. Mexicans and other Latin Americans who could not obtain visas found it easy to cross the border illegally.

The Asian and Latin American immigrants were not only ethnically different from the earlier European immigrants, but they also arrived at different points of entry in the United States. Most Asians arrived in Honolulu, Los Angeles, or San Francisco, while Cubans went to Miami and Mexicans to cities in states along the Mexican border. New York, which had been the primary port of entry of earlier immigrants, continued to be an important destination for immigrants from Europe and parts of the Caribbean. However, it received a smaller percentage of the total immigration to the United States. Since many immigrants remain in or near their point of entry, this change in points of entry has had a significant impact on the distribution of immigrants within the United States. This impact can be seen in the variation in growth due to immigration among metropolitan areas.

The growth of a metropolitan area's population due to immigration can be roughly approximated from the number of foreign-born persons in a census who report that they arrived in the United States during the previous ten years. This information was obtained in both the 1970 and 1980 censuses. This is only an approximate measure of net migration from outside the United States since no adjustment has been made for emigration or for the return of persons born in the United States who had been living abroad.[28] These figures also include only those illegal immigrants who were enumerated in the censuses, and it seems likely that illegals had relatively high rates of underenumeration.[29] Overall, we should consider these estimates of immigration to be lower than the actual numbers, but if the extent of underestimation does not vary greatly by division of the country, they should serve to indicate geographical variations in the contribution of immigration to growth.

In 1960 only about 5 percent of the population were foreign-born, and they were relatively old since most had come prior to 1930. Despite their long time in the United States, the foreign-born were highly concentrated in metropolitan areas, with 84 percent within SMSAs compared to 63 percent of the total population. The 2.9 million immigrants who arrived between 1960 and 1970 were even more highly concentrated in metropolitan areas. Ninety-two percent of these immigrants resided in metropolitan areas when they were enumerated in the 1970 census. Similarly, among the 5.6 million foreign-born who were enumerated in the 1980 census and who reported that they had arrived between 1970 and 1980, 94 percent were residing in metropolitan areas.

The contribution of immigration to metropolitan growth varied considerably from one part of the country to another, ranging from 0.3 percent for the East South Central states from 1960–1970 to 8.1 percent for the Pacific division from 1970–1980 (see Table 3.14). During the 1960s immigration more than compensated for internal net outmigration in the two northern regions, resulting in small but positive rates of total net migration. However, during the 1970s the internal outmigration from these regions was much greater and, despite higher rates of immigration than the previous decade, immigrants replaced only one-third of the outmigration from the Northeast and less than one-quarter of the net outmigration from the Midwest. The impact of immigration was particularly strong in the Pacific states where immigration doubled from the 1960s to the 1970s while internal migration declined significantly. As a result, immigration accounted for most of

[28]Emigration from the United States is not counted by the Immigration and Naturalization Service and can be estimated only indirectly. In making current population estimates for 1981, the U.S. Bureau of the Census assumed an annual emigration of 36,000 (see U.S. Bureau of the Census, "Preliminary Estimates of the Population of the United States by Age, Sex, and Race 1970 to 1981," *Current Population Reports*, series P-25, no. 917 (Washington, DC: U.S. Government Printing Office, 1982). However, Warren and Peck estimated that 521,000 of the foreign-born persons who were enumerated in the 1960 Census emigrated between 1960 and 1970, which implies a higher rate of emigration. Robert Warren and Jennifer Marks Peck, "Foreign-Born Emigration from the United States: 1960 to 1970," *Demography* 17:1 (1980): 71–84. Even higher figures are given in Robert Warren and Ellen Percy Kraly, "The Elusive Exodus, Emigration from the United States," *Population Trends and Public Policy*, no. 8, Population Reference Bureau, 1985. More recently the U.S. Bureau of the Census has increased the estimate of emigration used in making population estimates to 160,000. U.S. Bureau of the Census, "Estimates of the Population of the United States by Age, Sex, and Race: 1980 to 1985," *Current Population Reports*, series P-20, no. 985 (April 1986): 7–8.

[29]Briggs reviews several studies with estimates ranging from under 1 million illegals to over 6 million. Vernon Briggs, Jr., "Methods of Analysis of Illegal Immigration into the United States," *International Migration Review* 18 (Fall 1984):623–641. Passel and Robinson estimated that about 2 million illegals were enumerated in the 1980 census, but that there may have been 3 or 4 million present in the United States at that time. Jeffrey S. Passel and J. Gregory Robinson, "Revised Demographic Estimates of the Coverage of the Population by Age, Sex, and Race in the 1980 Census."

TABLE 3.14

*Estimates of Total Net Migration, Immigration, and Internal Net Migration
for Metropolitan Areas by Census Division, 1960–1980*

Region and Census Division	1960–1970			1970–1980		
	Total Net Migration	Immigration	Internal Migration	Total Net Migration	Immigration	Internal Migration
NORTHEAST	0.7	2.7	−2.0	−6.4	3.2	−9.6
New England	3.1	2.4	0.7	−2.6	2.4	−5.0
Mid Atlantic	−0.1	2.8	−2.9	−7.6	3.5	−11.1
MIDWEST	0.4	1.1	−0.7	−5.6	1.6	−7.2
East North Central	0.3	1.2	−1.0	−6.2	1.7	−8.0
West North Central	0.8	0.5	0.3	−3.5	1.0	−4.5
SOUTH	7.5	1.7	5.8	9.2	2.6	6.6
South Atlantic	12.2	2.5	9.6	10.2	2.7	7.5
East South Central	−1.4	0.3	−1.7	2.3	0.7	1.7
West South Central	5.0	1.2	3.8	11.0	3.5	7.5
WEST	14.4	3.6	10.8	12.8	7.1	5.7
Mountain	17.1	1.3	15.8	27.5	2.7	24.7
Pacific	13.9	4.1	9.9	9.8	8.1	1.7
Total	4.6	2.2	2.5	1.6	3.4	−1.8

NOTES:
1. Based on SMSAs and NECMAs as defined at the end of each decade.
2. Region and division boundaries were adjusted for SMSAs that crossed division boundaries so that the entire SMSA was within the division containing the largest of its central cities.
3. Immigration is assumed to equal the number of foreign-born who said that they moved to the U.S between 1970 and 1980.

the growth from net migration in the 1970s and was equal to natural increase in its contribution to total growth.

A few metropolitan areas, most of which were ports of entry for immigrants or close to these ports, experienced substantial growth from immigration. First among these was Miami, which was the main port of entry for migrants from Cuba and some other Latin American countries. Immigration added 21 percent to Miami's population in the 1960s and another 16 percent in the 1970s. The second largest percentage gain was observed in Los Angeles, which received one out of six immigrants to the United States during the 1970s. However, during both decades Los Angeles had net outmigration of internal migrants, and in the 1970s it would have lost population had it not been for immigration. Jersey City also experienced high rates of immigration in both decades at the same time that it had net outmigration of internal migrants. On the other hand, Anaheim and Oxnard, California, attracted large numbers of both immigrants and internal migrants, relative to their populations. Four areas in Texas: Brownsville, El Paso, Laredo, and McAllen, all experienced immigration with internal outmigration during the 1960s, but a change to positive or near-zero internal net migration for the 1970s while immigration increased considerably.

Immigration also played a significant, if proportionally smaller, role in several of the older northern metropolitan areas, such as New York, Chicago, Boston, Newark, and Detroit, where immigration helped to reduce the losses from internal outmigration. For example, during the 1960s New York received about 526,000 immigrants, which almost replaced the internal migration loss of 557,000. In the 1970s, when internal net outmigration was heavier, immigration compensated for about one-third of the loss from net internal migration.

TABLE 3.15

Metropolitan Areas That Received Significant Immigration from Abroad During 1960–1970 or 1970–1980

Metropolitan Area	1960–1970			1970–1980		
	Total	Immigrants	Internal	Total	Immigrants	Internal
	Net Migration as Percent of Beginning of Decade Population					
Anaheim–Santa Ana–Garden Grove, CA	78.6	5.0	73.6	24.8	9.7	15.2
Brownsville-Harlingen–San Benito, TX	−29.6	4.2	−33.7	21.7	13.2	8.5
El Paso, TX	−9.2	6.6	−15.8	10.2	12.0	−1.8
Honolulu, HI	3.6	4.4	−0.8	4.6	9.6	−5.0
Jersey City, NJ	−7.6	8.4	−16.0	−12.6	9.7	−22.3
Laredo, TX	−14.8	5.7	−20.5	8.9	10.8	−1.9
Los Angeles–Long Beach, CA	4.5	5.5	−1.0	−2.6	13.5	−16.1
McAllen–Pharr–Edinburg, TX	−23.7	3.9	−27.6	25.5	13.7	11.8
Miami, FL	27.3	21.2	6.1	21.9	16.2	5.7
Oxnard–Simi Valley–Ventura, CA	67.1	6.4	60.8	27.0	8.0	19.0
Salinas–Seaside–Monterey, CA	8.2	4.4	3.9	3.7	10.7	−7.0
San Diego, CA	7.0	4.9	2.1	27.3	8.2	19.1

NOTES:
1. Based on SMSAs as defined for census at end of decade.
2. Immigration is assumed to equal the number of foreign-born who said that they moved to the U.S. during the decade.
3. Includes all SMSAs that grew by 8.0 percent or more from immigration during 1960–1970 or 1970–1980.

Conclusion

Metropolitan growth in the United States in the twentieth century has been a combination of growth in established cities and their suburbs and the establishment of new areas. Since 1970 the growth has been concentrated primarily in the newer metropolitan areas and in the establishment of new areas. Older areas, particularly those in the North, either experienced population loss or very slow growth, while newer areas in the South and West grew rapidly. The southern and western areas benefited from both higher rates of natural increase and higher net migration than did the northern areas. Many West Coast areas and southern areas close to the Mexican border have also had significant growth from foreign immigration, and these immigrants have also contributed to the higher than average rates of natural increase in these areas.

With the slowing of growth of established metropolitan areas in the 1970s, there was a reversal in the earlier pattern of concentration of growth in intermediate and large size areas. In the 1970s areas of less than 250,000 grew much more rapidly than did larger areas; Las Vegas and West Palm Beach led the list. In contrast, some of the largest metropolitan areas, such as Cleveland, New York, and Pittsburgh, were among the areas experiencing the largest percentage losses. Some of these, such as New York, might have experienced even greater losses had they not received considerable immigration from abroad. During this decade the rate of metropolitan growth was slower than the rate of nonmetropolitan growth, which can be seen as another part of the overall picture of population deconcentration.

Population estimates for the first few years of the 1980s indicate that the regional shifts in metropolitan growth are continuing with even greater focus on the South as the major region of metropolitan growth. Some of the major northeastern areas which had suffered losses in the 1970s, such as New York, Philadelphia, and Boston, registered small gains in the 1980s, while some of the major midwestern areas, such as Detroit and Cleveland, continued to lose population. However, the trend toward population deconcentration was considerably slowed. There were smaller differences in growth rates among areas of different sizes, and metropolitan growth exceeded nonmetropolitan growth by a small amount. In the next chapter we shall examine some of the factors responsible for the growth and decline of metropolitan areas during this and earlier periods.

4

DETERMINANTS
OF METROPOLITAN GROWTH

IN THE previous chapter we saw that there were great differences in the rates of growth of metropolitan areas. At one extreme, Las Vegas, West Palm Beach, and Fort Lauderdale grew by more than 60 percent during the 1970s; at the other extreme, Jersey City, Buffalo, and Cleveland lost an average of 8 percent of their populations. What accounts for this variation in rates of growth? Why do some metropolitan areas grow while others decline? These are questions that have been explored by several writers. However, when explanations which seemed plausible prior to 1970 do not explain changes occurring in the 1970s, alternative explanations must be sought. In this chapter we shall review some of the alternative theories of regional or metropolitan growth and evaluate their explanatory power.

Although total metropolitan growth is a combination of net migration, natural increase, and reclassification of territory, we are mainly concerned with the first of these. Problems of reclassification are avoided by studying growth within constant boundaries. Natural increase, while a major source of metropolitan growth, does not account for a large part of the variation in growth rates. Part of the variation in natural increase is due to the effect of migration on the age structure.[1]

---

[1] The part of natural increase, which is not related to net migration, results mainly from regional variations in fertility. Since the causes of these variations are likely to be quite different from the causes of net migration, they are best left to a monograph on fertility.

In the preceding two decades, migration accounted for 93 percent of the variation in metropolitan growth rates. Thus, if we are able to explain net migration, we will have explained most of metropolitan growth.

The explanation of metropolitan migration has been addressed at two different levels. The first focuses on the migrants and their motives for moving, whereas the second focuses on businesses and governments as the major decision makers. Because of this difference, we shall refer to the models that focus on the factors that influence the decisions of migrants as micro-models, and those that focus on factors affecting the decisions of businesses, governments, and other aggregate level responses as macro-models, even though most of the data used for both models are aggregated to the level of metropolitan areas.

Micro-Level Models of Metropolitan Migration

Much of the literature on intermetropolitan migration is based on the "human capital" theory of migration. As originally expounded by Sjaastad, this theory states that a person will move if the benefits from moving exceed the costs of moving.[2] In the migration of labor force participants, the main benefit is income, while the main cost is the dollar cost of moving. Sjaastad tested this model using interstate migration from 1955–1960 and found that migration was positively related to income at the destination.[3] Similar results were obtained in studies from the 1950s and 1960s.[4] Whether measured by net migration or gross flows between areas, migration was found to be in the direction of higher average incomes and lower levels of unemployment.

The positive relationship between income in 1960 and net migration from 1960–1970 is demonstrated in Figure 4.1. Although there is little variation in migration among metropolitan areas in the middle income categories, net migration was very low for those metropolitan areas in the lowest income category and was several times higher in the highest income category. In general, the results were stronger for the North and South regions than for the West (see panel 1, Table 4.1).

[2]Larry A. Sjaastad, "The Costs and Returns of Human Migration," *Journal of Political Economy* 70 (1962):80–93.

[3]Larry A. Sjaastad, "The Relationship between Migration and Income in the United States," *Papers and Proceedings of the Regional Science Association* 6 (1960):37–64.

[4]Ira S. Lowry, *Migration and Metropolitan Growth: Two Analytical Models* (San Francisco: Chandler Publishing Co., 1966); Michael J. Greenwood, "Research on Internal Migration in the United States: A Survey," *Journal of Economic Literature* 3:2 (1975):397–433; Philip E. Graves, "A Life Cycle Empirical Analysis of Migration and Climate, by Race," *Journal of Urban Economics* 6 (1979):135–147; and Michael J. Greenwood, *Migration and Economic Growth in the United States* (New York: Academic Press, 1981).

Nevertheless, the results for 1960–1970 generally supported the hypothesis of the micro theory which is that migration is in the direction of higher incomes.

However, during the 1970s migrants moved away from higher income areas toward lower income areas, as is clearly shown in Figure 4.1. The highest migration rates are for areas with average household incomes below $11,000 in 1970, which contained about 55 percent of the metropolitan population in 1970. The average migration rate for areas with incomes over $11,000 was negative. While the negative relationship between income and migration can be observed for all regions of the United States, this relationship is much stronger in the North and South than in the West (see panel 2, Table 4.1). The negative relationship between income and migration became much weaker in the 1980s, as indicated by estimates from the 1980–1984 period. Furthermore, the negative relationship was observed in only the North and West during the 1980s, and there was a weak positive relationship for the South (see panel 3, Table 4.1).

In both the 1960s and the 1970s, inmigration areas tended to experience more growth in income than outmigration areas. During the 1960s

FIGURE 4.1

Net Migration by Average Income Level of Metropolitan Area

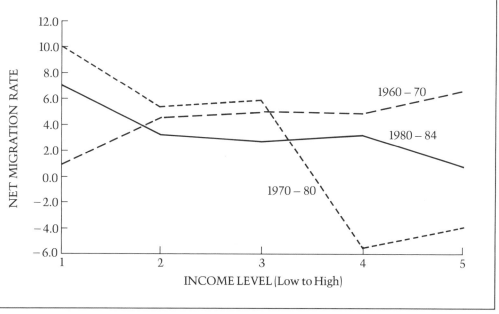

TABLE 4.1

*Net Migration by Average Income Level of Metropolitan Areas by Region
(average annual rate of net migration per 1,000 persons)*

Mean Household Income	North	South	West	Total
NET MIGRATION 1960–1970 (PER 1,000 PERSONS IN 1960)				
1960 Income				
Less than $6,000	−3.2	1.6	11.5	0.9
$6,000 to $6,599	−1.4	10.1	11.7	4.6
$6,600 to $7,249	0.7	13.0	17.3	5.0
$7,250 to $7,899	1.2	—	11.9	4.9
$7,900 or more	2.0	17.1	23.9	6.7
NET MIGRATION 1970–1980 (PER 1,000 PERSONS IN 1970)				
1970 Income				
Less than $9,000	2.2	10.6	18.0	10.1
$9,000 to $9,999	−2.7	6.2	22.6	5.4
$10,000 to $10,999	−4.7	13.4	19.9	5.9
$11,000 to $11,999	−8.7	0.2	1.6	−5.6
$12,000 or more	−7.2	−7.2	14.9	−3.9
NET MIGRATION 1980–1984 (PER 1,000 PERSONS IN 1980)				
1980 Income				
Less than $18,000	−2.8	10.8	15.9	7.0
$18,000 to $19,999	−3.7	6.7	5.5	3.2
$20,000 to $21,999	−3.0	11.4	14.9	2.7
$22,000 to $23,999	−5.0	12.9	6.6	3.2
$24,000 or more	−6.2	12.1	5.8	0.8

SOURCE: Based on residual estimates of net migration calculated by methods described in Chapter 4 and mean household income for SMSAs and NECMAs from 1960, 1970, and 1980 censuses. SMSAs and NECMAs are defined at the end of the decade, except for 1980–1984 when 1980 definitions are used. Results are weighted by the population at the beginning of the decade.

the relationship between income and migration was stronger at the end of the decade, although during the 1970s the relationship became weaker at the end of the decade. This suggests that migrants who moved to areas with lower average incomes than their areas of origin may have recouped some of the loss by the end of the decade. However, the fact that they moved to lower income areas, when human capital theory would suggest that income at the destination needs to be sufficiently higher than that at the origin to offset moving costs, is puzzling.[5]

[5]It is possible that the migrants differed sufficiently from the total population that they could have received gains in income while moving from high-income to low-income areas, since individual outcomes are not always the same as aggregate outcomes. We shall return to this question near the end of the chapter.

One possible interpretation of these results is that growing affluence of the United States population has resulted in a willingness of many migrants to trade income for other amenities.[6] Several studies using data from the 1960s reported positive relationships between net migration and temperature.[7] This relationship was much stronger for whites than for blacks, which could be taken as supporting the argument that the more affluent are willing to give up income for other amenities while the less affluent are influenced primarily by economic opportunities. However, it may be that temperature is merely a proxy for region or some other variable, and that the regional differences in opportunities for blacks and whites can explain the different relationship between migration and temperature for these two races.

In order to explore the potential relationship between migration and various amenities, we begin by examining migration rates by temperature (see Figure 4.2). For all three decades, the overall relationship between net migration and temperature is positive, but not entirely linear. Areas with average January temperatures below 30 degrees show no consistent relationship between migration and temperature. For 1970–1980 the coldest areas have positive rates of net migration, while those with temperatures from 10 to 40 degrees have negative rates. However, for 1960–1970 the coldest areas have the greatest out-migration and for 1980–1984 they have close to the greatest rate of out-migration. Above 30 degrees, rates of migration increase with temperature in all three decades, with the largest increase for areas with January temperatures above 60 degrees. These areas include Honolulu and ten areas in the southern part of Florida. Honolulu's migration rate was the lowest for this group of metropolitan areas. Except for Orlando, which is the site of the large Disney World entertainment complex, all of the other areas had unusually high proportions of elderly persons (65+) and those near retirement (55 to 64) among their inmigration streams. The elderly appear to have been particularly attracted to the warm climate of Florida. However, there were many warm areas with high in-migra-

[6]Richard J. Cebula and Richard K. Vedder, "A Note on Migration, Economic Opportunity and the Quality of Life," *Journal of Regional Science* 13:2 (1973):205–211; and Joe E. Stevens, "The Demand for Public Goods as a Factor in the Nonmetropolitan Migration Turnaround," in David L. Brown and John N. Wardwell, eds., *New Directions in Urban–Rural Migration: The Population Turnaround in Rural America* (New York: Academic Press, 1981), pp. 115–135.

[7]Philip E. Graves, "A Reexamination of Migration, Economic Opportunity, and the Quality of Life," *Journal of Regional Science* 16 (1976):107–112; Philip E. Graves, "A Life Cycle Empirical Analysis of Migration and Climate, by Race," *Journal of Urban Economics* 6 (1979):135–147; Michael J. Greenwood and Patrick J. Gormely, "A Comparison of the Determinants of White and Nonwhite Interstate Migration," *Demography* 8 (1971):141–155; and Kenneth E. Hinze, *Causal Factors in the Net Migration Flow to Metropolitan Areas of the United States 1960–70* (Chicago: Community and Family Study Center, University of Chicago, 1977).

FIGURE 4.2

Net Migration Rate by Mean January Temperature

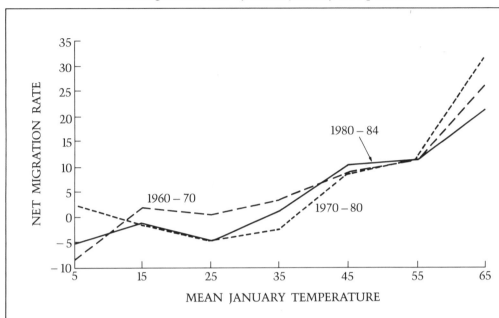

tion rates in California, Texas, and Arizona, which attracted large numbers of migrants in the labor-force ages.

Further examination of the relationship between temperature and migration within regions provides additional puzzling findings (see Table 4.2). Although a strong positive relationship can be observed for the South during all three decades, the other two regions have inconsistent results. In fact, during the decade of the 1970s when the arguments about the influence of amenities on migration seemed most salient, there was a negative relationship between migration and temperature in the North, and essentially no relationship in the West. Much of the overall relationship between temperature and migration is due to migration from the North to the other two regions; regional factors other than temperature may have been the cause of most of this migration.

In addition to temperature, several other amenity variables were used to study net migration in the 1960s. Cebula and Vedder found a positive association between migration and the number of physicians per capita, but only weak relationships between migration and crime rates or air pollution.[8] Hinze included population density, on the assumption that people would prefer to avoid the congestion and social problems associated with higher densities.[9] However, density did not have a significant relationship to net migration once economic conditions and temperature were controlled.

A micro-level model of determinants of net migration for metropolitan areas for 1960–1970, 1970–1980, and 1980–1984 is shown in Table 4.3. Two economic determinants are included—the mean household income and the unemployment rate at the beginning of the decade. Two amenity variables are also included—the mean January temperature and the population density measured on a log scale.

Results for all metropolitan areas, as defined at the end of each decade, show a clear change in the relationship between income and migration between decades.[10] For the 1960s, migration is positively associated with household income and negatively associated with unemployment, as expected (see column *a* of Table 4.3). However, for the 1970s and 1980s, neither of these variables has the expected relationship.

In column *b* of Table 4.3, the two variables representing noneconomic amenities are added to the equation. These variables have the expected relationships in all three decades. Temperature has a positive effect on net migration and density has a negative effect. The effect of temperature becomes stronger over time, while density becomes weaker. These results suggest that amenities may have played a role in influencing total migration during recent periods. Furthermore, when

[8]Richard J. Cebula and Richard K. Vedder, "A Note on Migration, Economic Opportunity, and the Quality of Life," *Journal of Regional Science* 13:2 (1973):205–211. Also see: Ben-chieh Liu, "Differential Net Migration Rates and the Quality of Life," *Review of Economics and Statistics* 57:3 (1975):329–337. Liu constructed several indexes of quality of life, which were related to net interstate migration, but most of his component variables are not available for metropolitan areas. In another study, Porell used several measures of quality of life, including crime and air pollution, to study streams between metropolitan areas from 1965–1970 and found that most of these were not significant when economic factors were also included, although temperature, rainfall, and an index summarizing outdoor recreational facilities were significant. Frank W. Porell, "Intermetropolitan Migration and Quality of Life," *Journal of Regional Science* 22 (1982):137–158.

[9]Kenneth E. Hinze, *Causal Factors in the Net Migration Flow to Metropolitan Areas of the United States 1960–1970*, p. 14.

[10]In this table and the following ones, standardized regression coefficients are shown rather than unstandardized ones because this makes it easier to compare effects of variables, which are measured on different scales. Conventional levels of statistical significance are shown, based on the assumption that the metropolitan areas constitute a random sample. Since the metropolitan areas represent the entire universe, there is no sampling error and, if there were no other errors, all results would be significant. Since the effects of measurement errors are unknown, the statistical tests provide a rough guide to the strength of relationships, which may aid in distinguishing strong relationships from weak ones.

TABLE 4.2

Net Migration by January Temperature by Region for Metropolitan Areas (average annual rate per 1,000 persons)

Mean January Temperature	North	South	West	Tota
NET MIGRATION 1960–1970				
Less than 10 degrees	−8.3	—	—	−8.
10 to 19.9 degrees	1.9	—	−7.0	1.
20 to 29.9 degrees	0.2	—	3.7	.
30 to 39.9 degrees	1.1	5.5	14.5	3.
40 to 49.9 degrees	—	5.8	13.2	8.
50 to 59.9 degrees	—	3.0	15.4	11.
60 degrees or more	—	30.0	3.5	26.
NET MIGRATION 1970–1980				
Less than 10 degrees	2.3	—	—	2.
10 to 19.9 degrees	−1.8	—	3.9	−1.
20 to 29.9 degrees	−5.6	−3.6	14.9	−4.
30 to 39.9 degrees	−9.1	.4	16.8	−2.
40 to 49.9 degrees	—	6.9	11.1	8
50 to 59.9 degrees	—	12.3	11.2	11
60 degrees or more	—	34.5	4.5	31.
NET MIGRATION 1980–1984				
Less than 10 degrees	−5.1	—	—	−5
10 to 19.9 degrees	−2.2	—	29.2	−1.
20 to 29.9 degrees	−5.5	−4.7	6.0	−5
30 to 39.9 degrees	−1.1	2.5	5.9	1
40 to 49.9 degrees	—	11.0	9.4	10
50 to 59.9 degrees	—	13.6	9.7	11
60 degrees or more	—	23.8	−.6	21

SOURCE: Based on residual estimates of net migration calculated by methods described in Chapter The mean January temperature is the mean for 1941–1970 for the central city as reported in the *Coun and City Data Book,* 1977. SMSAs and NECMAs are defined at the end of the decade, except 1980–1984 when 1980 definitions are used. Results are weighted by the population at the beginning the decade.

density and temperature are added to the equations, the coefficients for income are positive for all three decades and the coefficients for unemployment are either negative or close to zero. Thus, migrants appear to be responding rationally to differences in income and unemployment among places with comparable amenities, although the effects are rather weak for the 1970s.

The micro-model that is tested in Table 4.3 assumes that migrants are in the labor force, or are members of households where the employment opportunities and earnings of some members are considerations in the decision to move. This assumption does not hold for two groups of

TABLE 4.3

Regression Coefficients for Micro-Level Determinants of Net Migration
for Metropolitan Areas, 1960–1970, 1970–1980, and 1980–1984
(standardized regression coefficients)

Independent Variables	All Areas		Excluding Retirement and Military Areas		
	a	b	c	d	e
	1960–1970				
Mean Household Income 1960	.228*	.400*	.466*	.326*	.217*
Percent Unemployed 1960	−.148*	−.163*	−.167*	−.164*	−.235*
Density 1960 (log scale)		−.153*	−.192*	−.288*	−.131
Mean January Temperature		.396*	.330*		
Climate Rating†				.362*	.221*
Region: South					.049
West					.314*
R Squared	.095	.260	.269	.284	.336
Number of SMSAs/NECMAs	231	231	215	215	215
	1970–1980				
Mean Household Income 1970	−.192*	.188*	.301*	.120	.007
Percent Unemployed 1970	.117*	.022	.168*	.158*	−.145*
Density 1970 (log scale)		−.396*	−.543*	−.541*	−.259*
Mean January Temperature		.525*	.446*		
Climate Rating†				.248*	−.062
Region: South					.242*
West					.743*
R Squared	.056	.365	.416	.291	.519
Number of SMSAs/NECMAs	304	.304	277	277	277
	1980–1984				
Mean Household Income 1980	−.095	.140*	.088	−.049	−.056
Percent Unemployed 1980	.396*	−.255*	−.300*	−.441*	−.362*
Density 1980 (log scale)		−.212*	−.223*	−.245*	−.002
Mean January Temperature		.578*	.551*		
Climate Rating†				.225*	−.060
Region: South					.393*
West					.491*
R Squared	.148	.470	.486	.244	.413
Number of SMSAs/NECMAs	304	304	277	277	277

NOTE: Includes all SMSAs or NECMAs defined at end of decade, except retirement areas in southern Florida, or areas with 20 percent or more of labor force in armed forces.

*Would be statistically significant at p = .05 level if this were a random sample.
†From *Places Rated Almanac*, Rand McNally, 1985.

migrants, the elderly and those in the armed forces.[11] The elderly derive most of their income from social security, pensions, and other sources of fixed income, and are less concerned about wages and employment opportunities than younger persons. They have been attracted to warmer climates because of problems with health and getting about, which increase with age and are exacerbated by cold weather. Earlier migration streams to Florida, Arizona, and California helped to establish retirement areas in these states. During the 1970s and early 1980s an increasing number of elderly persons moved to these areas.

The migration of the armed forces, at least in the aggregate, is determined by military policies. Although these have tended to favor warmer climates in recent years because of lower maintenance costs and the need to train soldiers for warfare in warm places, such as Vietnam and Central America, we cannot assume that the migration of armed forces personnel to these places is motivated by any preference for climate on their part.

In order to remove the effect of these two migration streams from the analysis, we excluded areas with relatively large proportions of elderly migrants (these were all in Southern and Central Florida). We also excluded areas with large military bases, defined by having more than 20 percent of the total labor force employed in the armed forces.[12] These exclusions, which amounted to 17 areas for the 1960s and 28 areas for the 1970s and 1980s, reduced the total variance in net migration by 15 percent for 1960–1970, 31 percent for 1970–1980, and 29 percent for 1980–1984.[13]

[11]Another significant group of migrants who are not in the labor force are college students. However, many college towns are also sites for high-technology industries, and it is not possible to separate the migrants to these industries from the students. In fact, some of the students may work in these industries when they graduate, which means that their migration to the area may be influenced by income and employment prospects even though they went first to get an education.

[12]It would have been better to focus the study on the migration of the labor force, rather than excluding areas that had large proportions of elderly or armed forces personnel. However, estimates of labor force migration were not available for metropolitan areas for entire decades. Such estimates are available for the periods from 1955–1960, 1965–1970, and 1975–1980. One study that uses these data is Michael Greenwood, *Migration and Economic Growth in the United States.* Several other studies are reviewed by Charles F. Mueller, *The Economics of Labor Migration–A Behavioral Analysis* (New York, Academic Press, 1982), pp. 7–70.

[13]Areas that became SMSAs after 1970 are indicated with an asterisk. The Florida retirement areas excluded from the analysis are: Bradenton,* Daytona Beach,* Fort Lauderdale–Hollywood, Fort Myers–Cape Coral,* Lakeland–Winter Haven,* Melbourne–Titusville–Cocoa,* Miami, Ocala,* Sarasota,* Tampa–St. Petersburg, and West Palm Beach–Boca Raton. Areas that were excluded because 20 percent or more of the labor force were in the armed forces are: Anchorage, AK;* Biloxi–Gulfport, MS; Clarksville–Hopkinsville, TN;* Colorado Springs, CO; Columbus, GA; Fayetteville, NC; Fort Walton Beach, FL;* Jacksonville, NC;* Killeen–Temple, TX;* Lawton, OK; Norfolk–Virginia Beach, VA–NC; Petersburg–Col. Heights, VA; Salinas–Seaside–Monterey, CA; San Diego, CA; Tacoma, WA; and Wichita Falls, TX.

The exclusion of metropolitan areas with high concentrations of military personnel or retirees reduces the effect of temperature in all three periods and increases the effect of income for 1960–1970 and 1970–1980. There are also slight increases in the magnitude of the negative coefficients for unemployment in 1960–1970 and 1980–1984. These findings are in line with our expectations that labor force migration should be more responsive to income and employment opportunities and less responsive to temperature than the movement of the elderly and the military. However, there are two exceptions where the results do not agree with expectations. For 1970–1980 migration has a positive relationship to unemployment, and for 1980–1984 the relationship between migration and income is weakened when the retirement and military areas are removed from the analysis.

The other "amenity" variable, density, increases in strength when the retirement and military areas are removed, which suggests that those moving from high-density to low-density areas were predominantly persons in the civilian labor force or their dependents. This is consistent with the shift in growth toward smaller places during the 1970s, which was observed in Chapter 3.

For all three decades there is an increase in explained variance (R Squared), which indicates that the model fits better when the military and elderly are excluded. In order to focus on factors associated with the migration of the civilian labor force, we shall continue to exclude the military and retirement areas from the rest of our analysis.

The removal of retirement and military areas makes a slight improvement in the model, in terms of its ability to fit the data, but it does not fully answer the question of why temperature has such a strong effect on migration during this period. Since 1970 the effect of temperature is stronger than that of either income or unemployment. However, the interpretation that migrants are giving priority to climate in picking a destination is at odds with the findings of Long and Hansen that only 5 percent of the interstate migrants from 1973 to 1976 gave climate as their main reason for moving, compared to 64 percent who gave employment-related reasons.[14] Furthermore, if climate were an important factor, it would seem reasonable to assume that migrants would want to avoid both places with very cold winters and those with very hot summers and that the January temperature alone should not be an adequate measure of climate.

A more comprehensive measure of climate was constructed by the *Places Rated Almanac*, which takes into account the number of ex-

---

[14]Larry H. Long and Kristin A. Hansen, "Reasons for Interstate Migration," *Current Population Reports*, series P-23, no. 81 (Washington, DC: Bureau of the Census, 1979).

tremely hot or cold days and the humidity.[15] Their climate index assumes that most people prefer a mild climate throughout the year. Starting with a base of 1,000 points, they deduct points in proportion to the number of heating and cooling degree days. They also deduct additional points for very cold (below 32 degrees) or very hot days (above 90 degrees). According to their ratings, San Francisco, Oakland, and San Diego, have the best climates, and the three metropolitan areas in North Dakota have the worst. The growing California areas, such as Anaheim, Oxnard–Simi Valley–Ventura, Riverside–San Bernardino, and San Diego, all had mild summers, as well as mild winters, and rated high on the climate index of the *Places Rated Almanac*. Climate is, therefore, a plausible explanation for migration to these areas. Phoenix and Tucson, Arizona, had intermediate climate ratings, but climate could be an attraction to these areas if greater weight were given to dryness. However, the growing areas in Texas included places such as Houston, Brownsville, and McAllen–Pharr–Edinburg, which were given poor ratings in the *Places Rated Almanac*. Climate does not appear to be a very plausible reason for movement to these areas. This index has a slightly stronger correlation with migration than does temperature for 1960–1970, but has much weaker coefficients for the more recent time periods (see column *d* of Table 4.3). It appears that January temperature is measuring something more than simply a preference for climate.

In the last column we have added dummy variables for region, using the North as the omitted reference category. Cebula had used a dummy variable for the West region to represent quality-of-life factors not correlated with temperature.[16] Although this interpretation of the variable is questionable, the regional dummy variables will pick up the effects of any omitted variables that are associated with both region and migration and, as such, will provide a test for the adequacy of the model. If all of the relevant factors are included and the same model applies to all regions, the coefficients for the dummy variables should be close to zero.

Unfortunately, the micro-model that we have used here does not adequately account for all of the regional variation in migration for any of the three time periods. In all three periods, there is a substantial coefficient for the West region, and for the latter two periods there are sizable coefficients for the South as well. This suggests that there are other factors that influence migration beyond income, unemployment, density, and climate.

[15]Richard Boyer and David Savageau, *Places Rated Almanac* (Chicago: Rand McNally, 1985).

[16]Richard J. Cebula, *Geographic Living-Cost Differentials* (Lexington, MA: Lexington Books, 1983).

The addition of the regional dummy variables has a major impact on the effects of the two "amenity" variables. The effect of density is substantially reduced and the effect of climate becomes slightly negative for the 1970–1980 and 1980–1984 periods. This suggests that the correlation between temperature and net migration may be a spurious one, due to other factors that correlate with both temperature and migration, and not due to preferences for climate.

Attempts to include other amenity variables in the regression equation failed to turn up any substantial effects. Measures of the crime rate, air pollution, and a dummy variable for coastal areas indicate that all had standardized regression coefficients of less than .14, and none would have been statistically significant if this were a random sample.

Adjusting for Cost of Living

The micro-model of metropolitan migration can be refined by adding an adjustment for differences in costs of living among metropolitan areas. In attempting to explain the relationship between migration and temperature, Greenwood and Gormely point out that warmer areas tend to have lower living costs and that this may be a reason for movement to these areas.[17] Cebula analyzed net migration estimates for the period from 1970–1980 as a function of living costs, using the 36 SMSAs for which the Bureau of Labor Statistics calculates cost of living indices.[18] He showed that living costs had a significant negative effect on net migration when income and unemployment were controlled.

Since no comprehensive measure of living costs is available for all metropolitan areas, we constructed a measure based only on housing costs as estimated from rent, housing values at the beginning of the decade, and local electricity costs. It was expected that housing costs would have a negative effect on migration, but the opposite was observed for all three periods (see columns *a*, *c*, and *e* of Table 4.4). Furthermore, the addition of housing costs to the equation causes the coefficient for income to become negative for the 1970–1980 period. Income in 1970 is highly correlated with housing costs (.87), and there appears to be a problem of multicollinearity when both are included in the model. An alternative approach, in which average housing costs were subtracted from mean income to create a net income measure, is shown

[17]Michael Greenwood and Patrick Gormely, "A Comparison of the Determinants of White and Nonwhite Interstate Migration."

[18]Richard J. Cebula, *Geographic Living-Cost Differentials;* and Izraeli Odeh and Ah-Loh Lin, "Recent Evidence on the Effect of Real Earnings on Net Migration," *Regional Studies* 18 (1984): 113–120.

TABLE 4.4

Regressions Including Cost-of-Living Measures for Metropolitan Areas,
1960–1970, 1970–1980, and 1980–1984 (standardized regression coefficients)

Independent Variables	1960–1970		1970–1980		1980–1984	
	a	b	c	d	e	f
Household Income	.209		−.242*		−.013	
Housing Costs	.311*		.629*		.135	
Household Income Net of Housing Costs†		.424*		.233*		.055
Percent Unemployed	−.174*	−.175*	.123*	.170*	−.302*	−.309*
Density (log scale)	−.228*	−.160*	−.601*	−.494*	−.238*	−.204*
Mean January Temperature	.312*	.329*	.360*	.438*	.514*	.553*
R Squared	.291	.248	.498	.397	.492	.483
Number of SMSAs/NECMAs	215	215	277	277	277	277

NOTE: Includes all SMSAs or NECMAs defined at end of decade, except retirement areas in southern Florida, or areas with 20 percent or more of labor force in armed forces. All independent variables are defined as of the beginning of each decade.

*Would be statistically significant at p = .05 level if this were a random sample.
†Adjusted for housing costs by subtracting average housing costs in area from the mean income.

in columns *b*, *d*, and *f* of Table 4.4. The coefficients for this variable are positive for all three periods, indicating that migration is the direction of higher incomes net of housing costs. However, the coefficients for net income for 1970–1980 and 1980–1984 are not very large, and the explained variances for this model for all three periods are somewhat less than the corresponding R-Squared values in Table 4.3, indicating that net income explains less of the differences in net migration than does total income.

Why are these results different than those obtained by Cebula for the 36 SMSAs for which cost-of-living indexes are available? Are the differences due to the fact that housing costs measure only one component of cost-of-living differences, to differences in the period of study (1970–1980 versus 1970–1978), to differences in the other variables included in the regression equation, or to the representativeness of the 36 SMSAs? The regressions shown in Table 4.5 attempt to answer some of these questions. The first regression includes the same variables that Cebula used, with the exception of the dummy variable for the West region. Cost of living has the expected negative relationship to migration, which is consistent with Cebula's findings, although the effects of income and unemployment are not as strong as in Cebula's equation. When density and temperature are added to the equation, as shown in the second column of Table 4.5, the effect of cost of living becomes

TABLE 4.5

Regressions Including Cost-of-Living Measures for Metropolitan Areas,
1960–1970, 1970–1980, and 1980–1984
(standardized regression coefficients)

Independent Variables	a	b	c
Household Income	−.151	−.025	−.153
Cost of Living Index	−.601*	−.104	
Housing Costs			.189
Percent Unemployed	−.104	−.269*	−.283*
Density (log scale)		−.456*	−.589*
Mean January Temperature		.545*	.548*
R Squared	.511	.720	.726
Number of SMSAs/NECMAs	36	36	36

SOURCE: U.S. Bureau of Labor Statistics, "Three Budgets for an Urban Family of Four Persons," Supplement to Bulletin 1570-5 (1971): Intermediate budget.

NOTE: Includes all SMSAs or NECMAs with cost-of-living indexes for 1970 except: Anchorage, Honolulu, Orlando, and San Diego.

*Would be statistically significant at p = .05 level if this were a random sample.

much weaker but remains negative. Thus, part of the difference between our results and Cebula's is due to the inclusion of the two amenity variables in our model. Because cost of living is positively correlated with density and negatively correlated with temperature, it is difficult to separate the effects of these variables with this type of analysis. However, if cost of living were the main reason for the relationships between density and migration and temperature and migration, we would expect it to have the strongest coefficient among these three variables, but that is not the case. Thus, part of the difference in results can be accounted for by the inclusion of these amenity variables in our model.

When housing costs are substituted for cost of living, the effect is positive, but not statistically significant. Although housing costs have a correlation of .71 with cost of living for these 36 areas, they clearly do not measure all of the relevant cost differences among metropolitan areas. However, the results for the equation, including housing costs for these 36 areas, are very different from those that we obtained with the same variables for all 277 areas in Table 4.4. This suggests that the 36 areas are not very representative of all metropolitan areas. The 36 areas tend to be larger, older, and more densely populated than the average of all metropolitan areas, and do not include many of the southern and western areas, which experienced rapid growth during the 1970s. The means for housing costs and income for these areas are almost one standard deviation above the means for all areas. Thus, we have theoretical reasons for expecting differences in cost of living among metropolitan areas to be important in the choices of destination made by migrants, but we are unable to find strong support for this in the data.

In summary, individual level models of migration, which assume that migration is motivated by higher income, lower unemployment, lower costs of living and amenities, such as climate, do not provide a wholly adequate explanation for migration during the 1970s and 1980s. As we have seen, attempts to refine measures of income and amenities to get closer to the factors that we believe to be important to the decisions of migrants have generally lead to weaker rather than stronger results.

While migration during the 1970s and 1980s does not always have the expected relationship to income and climate, it is strongly related to the growth in employment. The correlation between migration and employment growth was .92 for 1970–1980 and .93 for 1960–1970. Although migration and employment growth have reciprocal effects on one another, Greenwood and Hunt demonstrate that the effect of employment growth on migration is stronger than the reverse effect.[19] This suggests that migration in the 1970s and 1980s may be more a response to jobs than to income and that one ought to look at factors responsible for the changing location of jobs to explain migration. This issue will be explored in the next two sections.

Growth of Metropolitan Areas by Functional Types

The second approach to the study of metropolitan growth has its roots in human ecology.[20] The micro-models focused on the individual migrants and ignored the forces that give rise to changing opportunities within different metropolitan areas, but human ecology ignores the individuals and emphasizes how environment, technology, and social organization affect population growth. Central to this approach is the view that growth during a particular period depends upon the organizational structure of an area and how it relates to changes in technology and environment. The organization of an area is viewed as closely re-

[19]Michael Greenwood and Gary L. Hunt, "Migration and Interregional Employment Redistribution in the U.S.," *American Economic Review* (December 1984): 957–969.

[20]An excellent review of this literature can be found in Franklin D. Wilson, "Urban Ecology: Urbanization and Systems of Cities," in *Annual Review of Sociology* 10 (1984): 283–307.

lated to the key function or functions of an area. Metropolitan areas differ in functions because of differences in their environments, their position in the network of trade routes, and historical reasons. For example, Washington is a center of government, New York is primarily a commercial center, and Detroit is known as the center of automobile manufacturing.

Although the general framework of human ecology is a broad one, most of the studies growing out of this tradition have emphasized changes in environment or in technology as the major forces which affect population distributions. For example, Sly showed how environmental change and technology resulted in changes in the organization of southern agriculture, which in turn resulted in black outmigration from the rural South during the period from 1940 to 1960.[21] South and Poston use an ecological framework to show how shifts in relative demand for goods and services between 1950 and 1970 favored growth in the South.[22]

However, a somewhat different school of thought has approached these problems by focusing on broader societal trends which affect population distribution, such as the changing structure of capitalism in the United States and the increasing importance of international trade and investment, and how these factors interact with changing technology to bring about a restructuring of regional industries. Bluestone and Harrison, for example, view the plant closings and work force reductions in northern manufacturing during the 1970s as due, in part, to a shift of investment to foreign countries and Sunbelt areas where labor was cheaper.[23] Castells argues that the transition from traditional manufacturing to information processing and related development of high technology industries has favored newer metropolitan areas and led to the decline of older metropolitan areas, which had heavy concentrations of traditional manufacturing.[24]

Several scholars have developed functional classification schemes for metropolitan areas. Some of these try to distinguish regional metro-

[21]David F. Sly, "Migration and the Ecological Complex," *American Sociological Review* 37 (1972):615–628.

[22]S. J. South and D. L. Poston, Jr., "The U.S. Metropolitan System: Regional Change 1950–70," *Urban Affairs Quarterly* 18 (1982):187–206.

[23]Barry Bluestone and Bennett Harrison, *The Deindustrialization of America* (New York: Basic Books, 1982).

[24]Manuel Castells, "High Technology, Economic Restructuring, and the Urban–Regional Process in the United States," in Manuel Castells, ed., *High Technology, Space and Society* (Beverly Hills: Sage Publications, 1985), pp. 11–40. L. Sawyers and W. Tabb, eds., *Sunbelt/Snowbelt Urban Development and Regional Restructuring* (New York: Oxford University Press, 1974).

politan areas from national areas.[25] Others simply try to identify the major functions.[26] One of the most straightforward of these is the scheme developed by Stanback and Knight, using the distribution of employment by industry for each area in 1960.[27] They found that about one-half of the areas could be classified as either nodal or manufacturing areas. The nodal areas were defined as regional centers for transportation, communication, and wholesale trade, as well as related financial and business services. In studying growth in the 1960s they argued that the nodal areas were better prospects for new growth than the manufacturing areas because they provided a more general infrastructure and more amenities.

In addition to these two main types of areas, Stanback and Knight identified special-purpose areas, which served as resorts, medical and educational centers, or centers of government. Finally, they listed areas as "mixed" which did not fit any of the other five categories. Among the mixed areas, about one-half were subclassified as having "nodal character." These were areas that met three of their criteria for being nodal instead of the four that they required to classify an area as nodal.[28]

Between 1950 and 1980, the industrial structure of the United States underwent considerable change, as can be seen in Table 4.6. Although the proportion of the labor force employed in the primary sector, which includes agriculture, fishing, forestry, and mining, continued to decline during each decade, this shift involved only a small fraction of the labor force in the last decade. The major change during this period was the slowing of growth of the manufacturing sector and its decline in terms of relative share of production and employment. The percentage employed in manufacturing reached a peak of 27.5 percent in 1960 and then declined to only 22.1 percent in 1980. Since 1950 there

[25]Otis Dudley Duncan et al., *Metropolis and Region* (Baltimore, MD: The John Hopkins Press, 1960).

[26]These classifications schemes are reviewed by Maurice H. Yeates and Barry J. Garner, *The North American City* (New York: Harper and Row, Publishers, 1971). Examples of these schemes are: Chauncy D. Harris, "A Functional Classification of Cities in the U.S.," *The Geographical Review* 33 (1943):86–99 and H. J. Nelson, "A Service Classification of American Cities," *Economic Geography* 31 (1955):189–210. An alternative approach using factor analysis and many variables appears in Brian J. L. Berry and John D. Kasarda, *Contemporary Urban Ecology* (New York: Macmillan, 1977).

[27]Thomas M. Stanback, Jr., and Richard Knight, *The Metropolitan Community* (New York: Columbia University Press, 1970), chap. 6.

[28]Stanback and Knight classified an area as a nodal center if it ranked in the top quartile of all areas in at least four of the following six business or consumer service categories: transportation, wholesale, communication, finance (includes insurance and real estate), business/repair services, and other retail (not food, dairy or eating/drinking) places.

TABLE 4.6

Employed Persons by Industrial Group, 1950–1980

Industrial Group	Percentage Distribution			
	1950	1960	1970	1980
Primary (Agriculture and Mining)	14.1	7.9	4.4	4.0
Manufacturing	25.9	27.5	25.3	22.1
Nodal Services*	18.4	19.2	22.1	24.3
Medical and Educational Services	6.6	9.4	13.2	15.7
Personal and Entertainment Services	7.0	6.8	5.3	4.1
Government and Military	5.4	6.8	7.0	6.8
Retail, Construction, Utilities	22.6	22.4	22.7	23.0
Total	100.0	100.0	100.0	100.0

SOURCES: Censuses of 1960, 1970, and 1980, *Characteristics of the Population: U.S. Summary.*

*Includes transportation, communication, postal service, wholesale, finance, insurance and real estate, business and repair services, and other professional services.

have been substantial increases in parts of the service sector. Nodal services, as defined by Stanback and Knight, increased from 18 to 24 percent of employment. Medical and educational services grew from under 7 percent of employment to over 15 percent. These shifts have favored some metropolitan areas and not others.

A simple hypothesis would be that metropolitan areas that specialized in industries that were growing would gain in employment relative to those that were not so specialized. This hypothesis has been exhaustively studied using a form of analysis known as "shiftshare" analysis. In a major study by Edgar Dunn, covering the period from 1940 to 1970, it was found that industrial composition of an area accounted for only a part of its growth, and that a considerable proportion of growth was due to competitive effects between areas.[29] An analysis by Kasarda, Irwin, and Hughes for 1974–1982, produced similar results.[30] We should, therefore, expect that functional specialization will account for only part of the variation in growth among metropolitan areas.

In developing a functional classification of metropolitan areas for the 1970s, we have followed Stanback and Knight's scheme, but have modified the classification rules to take account of the changes in the

[29]Edgar S. Dunn, Jr., *The Development of the U.S. Urban System* (Washington, DC: Resources for the Future, Inc., 1983), 2 vols.
[30]John D. Kasarda, Michael D. Irwin, and Holly L. Hughes, "Demographic and Economic Shifts in the Sunbelt," paper presented at the Sunbelt Research Conference, Miami, November 3–6, 1985.

United States industrial structure between 1960 and 1970.[31] For example, while they required that an area have at least 32 percent of its employment in manufacturing to classify it as a manufacturing area, we reduced that level to 30 percent, in line with the national decline in the proportion of the labor force employed in manufacturing. We simplified the criteria for nodal areas to a single sum of the percentages employed in all of the nodal-type industries and reduced the cutoff slightly to allow more areas to qualify. The criteria are shown in the note to Table 4.7. There were relatively few cases that qualified for two or more functional types. These were classified in the group where they had the largest percentage relative to the minimum required for that group.

Stanback and Knight's prediction that nodal areas should do better than manufacturing areas is borne out by the employment growth and net migration rates for 1970–1980 (see Table 4.7). Manufacturing areas, as a group, had the lowest growth in employment and had net outmigration amounting to slightly over 5 percent of their population. In contrast, nodal areas had about double the rate of employment growth of manufacturing areas and gained about 2 percent from net migration. Although the average gain from migration in nodal areas was modest, this average comprised very different regional migration rates. Nodal areas in the North, and New York in particular, experienced significant losses while nodal areas in the South and West had gains of 11 and 9 percent, respectively. Nodal areas with above-average net migration included Atlanta, Dallas, Denver, Houston, Phoenix, Portland (Oregon), and San Jose.

The biggest employment and migration gains, however, were in the resort areas, the medical and educational centers, and the mixed areas. Some of the most rapidly growing medical and educational centers were: Austin and Bryan–College Station, Texas; Gainesville and Tallahassee, Florida; and Fort Collins, Colorado, all sites of major state universities. The growth of the medical and educational centers reflects the increasing national employment in these industries, but shifting industrial employment cannot explain the growth of resort and mixed areas. Resort areas are characterized by relatively high employment in personal and entertainment services, a category that declined in terms

---

[31]The Stanback and Knight classification scheme was updated in a later work by Noyelle and Stanback, covering the period from 1959 to 1976. Thierry J. Noyelle and Thomas M. Stanback, Jr., *The Economic Transformation of American Cities* (New York: Rowman and Allenheld, 1984). In this book they used cluster analysis to group SMSAs into groups with similar industrial location quotients. Since they used only 140 SMSAs, we could not utilize this classification for our analysis. However, most of their classifications of these 140 areas agreed with ours.

TABLE 4.7

Employment Growth and Net Migration, 1970–1980,
by Functional Type of Metropolitan Area and Region

Functional Type[a]	Region			Total	Number of SMSAs
	North	South	West		
EMPLOYMENT GROWTH (PERCENT)					
Nodal	11.5	43.9	41.6	27.7	101
Manufacturing	12.0	24.4	—	13.3	99
Government/Military	—	28.5	46.7	34.8	36
Medical/Educational	30.2	61.0	65.2	47.1	24
Resort	26.1	88.6	102.8	86.0	9
Mixed	28.8	34.4	59.7	43.7	35
Total	12.4	40.0	45.4	26.0	304
NET MIGRATION (PER 1,000 POPULATION)					
Nodal	−66.8	109.9	90.1	19.6	101
Manufacturing	−60.0	14.7	—	−51.9	99
Government/Military	—	−17.0	175.1	50.2	36
Medical/Educational	10.5	221.2	257.0	127.0	24
Resort	93.0	630.6	558.8	569.5	9
Mixed	31.5	65.7	258.7	138.4	35
Total	−60.1	92.1	128.4	16.2	304

[a]Functional types were defined as follows:

Nodal = 20 percent or more of total employment in transport, communications, wholesale, finance, business and repair, or other professional services.
Manufacturing = 30 percent or more of employment in manufacturing.
Government/Military = 20 percent or more of employment in public administration or armed forces.
Medical/Educational = 20 percent or more of employment in medical, educational, or related services.
Resort = 10 percent or more of employment in personal or entertainment services.
Mixed = Areas not qualifying for any of the above.

of its national share of employment between 1970 and 1980. Six of the nine resort areas are in Florida.[32] Their growth is largely explained by elderly migration to these areas and the demand for retail trade and a variety of services needed to support this population. More than one-quarter of the net migrants to these Florida resort areas between 1975–1980 were aged 65 and over in 1980. Many of the younger migrants were working in retail trade, local services, or construction, to serve the growing population of these areas.

[32]The resort areas in Florida are Daytona Beach, Fort Lauderdale, Fort Myers–Cape Coral, Ocala, Sarasota, and West Palm Beach. Although Miami qualified as a resort area, it also qualified as a nodal center and was given the latter classification. Other resort areas are Atlantic City, Las Vegas, and Reno.

Mixed areas tended to be relatively small (the average size was 195,000 in 1970). The most rapidly growing among these were: Bradenton, Florida; Medford, Oregon; and Santa Cruz, California—all small areas with central cities of less than 50,000. These areas fell just short of the required percentage of employment to be classified as nodal.

Although manufacturing areas lost migrants during the 1970s, several authors have attributed this to the decline of the older "smoke stack" industries, such as steel and textiles.[33] As these older industries have declined, there has been growth in "high-tech" industries, such as computers, communications equipment, aerospace, medical and dental instruments, and supplies.[34] Tomaskovic-Devey and Miller have pointed out that there is no agreement on the definition of high-technology industries, and that growth varies considerably with the definition used.[35] Using the percentage of employees in 1970 who were college graduates as an indicator, we classified manufacturing industries as either "high-tech" or "low-tech".[36] The effects of technology on the growth of manufacturing areas is shown in Table 4.8.

For the total set of manufacturing areas and for those in the North, there was no consistent relationship between either growth of employment or net migration from 1970 to 1980 and the proportion of employment in high-technology industries. In the North the expected positive relationship between technology and growth is observed for employment, but not for migration. Such a difference between employment growth and net migration could occur if low-technology areas had older age distributions and slower growth of the indigenous labor force than high-technology areas.

In the South there was a negative relationship, with the most employment growth and migration found in the areas with the least amount of high-technology industries. These were smaller metropolitan areas in South Carolina, North Carolina, Tennessee, and Virginia, which benefited from the relocation from the North of textiles, apparel, and related industries between 1970 and 1980. These industries suffered

[33]John Cremeans et al., "Structural Change in the U.S. Economy: 1979–87 High Technology versus Smokestack Industries," in U.S. Department of Commerce, *1984 U.S. Industrial Outlook* (Washington, DC: U.S. Government Printing Office, 1984), pp. 39–45; and Bluestone and Harrison, *Deindustrialization.*
[34]John Cremeans et al., "Structural Change in the U.S. Economy," p. 41.
[35]Donald Tomaskovic-Devey and S. M. Miller, "Recapitalization: The Basic Urban Policy of the 1980s," in Norman I. Fainstein and Susan S. Fainstein, eds., *Urban Policy Under Capitalism*, Urban Affairs Annual Reviews 22 (Beverly Hills: Sage Publications, 1982), pp. 23–42.
[36]Industries were classified as high-tech if 8 percent or more of their work force were college graduates in 1970. This classification was somewhat crude as 1970 Census Summary Tape File 4, which provided the data on industries for each county, presented only 12 industrial groups within manufacturing.

TABLE 4.8

*Net Migration, 1970–1980, for Manufacturing Areas
by Percentage High-Technology Manufacturing and Region**
(net migration per 1,000 population in 1970)

Percentage High-Technology	Region		Total
	North	South	
EMPLOYMENT GROWTH (PERCENT)			
Less than 30%	9.2	27.4	16.1
30 to 50%	12.7	22.9	13.3
50 to 70%	11.2	21.5	11.9
70% or more	15.9	23.8	17.0
Total	12.0	24.4	13.3
NET MIGRATION (PER 1,000 POPULATION)			
Less than 30%	−49.9	50.1	−11.8
30 to 50%	−49.8	25.5	−45.9
50 to 70%	−72.8	−20.3	−69.0
70% or more	−40.9	−28.5	−39.2
Total	−60.0	14.7	−51.9

NOTE: High-technology industries were defined as including: machinery (except electric), electric machinery, transportation equipment (except motor vehicles), instruments and other durables, printing and publishing, and chemicals and allied industries.

*There are no metropolitan areas classified as manufacturing within the West region.

from increased foreign competition during the decade, and national employment in textiles and apparel declined by about 9 percent. These industries responded, as they had done since the 1930s, by relocating in areas with lower wages. For example, in 1970, the average wage of textile workers in North Carolina and South Carolina was 60 to 85 percent of that in Massachusetts and New York.[37] As a consequence, employment in textiles and apparel grew significantly in these southern areas during the 1970s, despite a national decline in these industries.

What appears to have happened during the 1960s and 1970s is that the traditional advantages of the large northern manufacturing metropolitan areas have declined as costs of transportation declined. Other locational considerations, such as the costs of land and labor, have be-

[37]The largest difference was for male workers in "Apparel and Other Fabricated Textile Products" and the lowest difference was for females in "Yarn, Thread, and Fabric Mills," U.S. Bureau of the Census, *1970 Census of Population, Characteristics of the Population*, tables 188 and 189 (State Volumes: Massachusetts, New York, North Carolina, and South Carolina).

come more important and have favored smaller metropolitan areas outside the North.[38] In addition, much of the growing service sector had to be located within the market areas being served.

Macro-Models of Metropolitan Migration

Viewing net migration as a response to employment growth, which in turn is a function of decisions on the location of firms, we have developed a macro-level model of migration, which emphasizes those factors likely to influence these decisions. Because of the limited data available, the variables in this model are not entirely distinct from the micro-level model, which was tested above. However, the theoretical interpretation of these variables is different.

The macro-model includes variables that relate to the availability and costs of labor, and costs of land and operation. Labor costs are represented by the average earnings of unskilled workers in the metropolitan area in 1970. Most firms require both unskilled workers and more highly skilled workers, including managers and professionals. Unskilled workers are most likely to be recruited locally, and local wages for these workers should have an effect on location decisions. To measure this effect, we have included the average earnings of laborers in the model.

In addition to the current costs of labor, businesses are concerned with the prospects for future wages and their ability to control the process of wage negotiations. Cebula argued that employers should be attracted to states with right-to-work laws because such laws make it more difficult for unions to become established and to shut down production through strikes.[39] We have, therefore, included a dummy variable for metropolitan areas that are located in states with right-to-work laws.

During the period of study, immigration was a major source of unskilled workers; the largest number of these came from Mexico. This gave an advantage to areas close to the Mexican border, and we have

[38]Factors involved in industrial location decisions are discussed in Michael J. Webber, *Industrial Location* (Beverly Hills: Sage Publications, 1984) and Eva Mueller and James N. Morgan, "Location Decisions of Manufacturers," *American Economic Review*, Papers and Proceedings 502 (1962): 204–217. A recent study by Moomaw demonstrates that large metropolitan areas have lost many of their advantages of scale and have the disadvantage of higher wages compared to smaller areas. Ronald L. Moomaw, "Firm Location and City Size: Reduced Productivity Advantages as a Factor in the Decline of Manufacturing in Urban Areas," *Journal of Urban Economics* 17 (1985): 73–89.

[39]Richard Cebula, *Geographic Living-Cost Differentials.*

represented this by a dummy variable for those metropolitan areas within about 400 miles of the Mexican border.[40]

Although managers and professionals are often recruited from other areas, they were in shorter supply than unskilled workers during this period; areas that had relatively good supplies of persons qualified for such positions had an advantage. The local availability of persons qualified for managerial or professional positions is measured by the proportion of the population over age 25 who have college degrees. Areas with more college graduates ought to also contain more entrepreneurs capable of starting new businesses.

In addition to labor costs and availability, businesses are concerned with the costs of land, transportation, and other costs. It can be argued that, since the 1960s, these costs have shifted in favor of lower-density metropolitan areas, as the costs of transportation over long distances have decreased and cost advantages of purchasing materials in large metropolitan areas have declined. However, the land costs and costs of coping with congestion in the older, denser metropolitan areas have continued. In balance, these areas have become relatively more expensive sites for businesses than the newer, lower-density metropolitan areas. In order to measure this effect, we have included population density in the model. Because the density of metropolitan areas varies from less than 100 persons per square mile in SMSAs covering large amounts of area, such as Riverside–San Bernardino and Casper, Wyoming, to more than 6,000 persons per square mile in New York, and because it is unreasonable to expect the same range in amenities associated with density, we have used the logarithm of density.

We argued earlier that the industrial structure of an area should have some impact on its development. In particular, we showed that areas that were diversified in transportation, communication, and business services had an advantage over areas that were specialized in manufacturing. Following this argument, we have included the proportion of the beginning of decade employment that was in manufacturing, on the assumption that a high proportion in manufacturing was a disadvantage for a metropolitan area.

Table 4.9 presents two sets of results for each decade. The first set of regressions, which are shown in columns *a, c,* and *e,* include only the six macro-model variables discussed above. The second set of results,

[40]The dividing point of 400 miles was chosen after examining the relationship between distance and the proportion of immigrants in the 1980 population of metropolitan areas. It represents a reasonable day's journey by public transportation, which is an important consideration for those immigrants who wish to maintain ties to their places of origin.

TABLE 4.9

Regression Coefficients for Macro-Level Determinants of Net Migration
for Metropolitan Areas, 1960–1970, 1970–1980, and 1980–1984
(standardized regression coefficients)

Independent Variables	1960–1970		1970–1980		1980–1984	
	a	b	c	d	e	f
Unskilled Earnings†	.391*	.424*	.134	−.061	.073	.125
Log of Density	−.111	−.150	−.369*	−.278*	−.045	−.138
Near Mexico	.175*	.013	.237*	.036	.399*	.277
Percent College Graduates‡			.126*	.134*	.040	.101
Right to Work Law	−.074	−.078	.052	.080	.256*	.109
Percent Manufacturing	−.139	.015	−.253*	−.028	−.273*	−.162
Mean January Temperature		.335*		.256*		.349
Region: South		−.020		−.081		.054
West		.164		.432		−.008
R Squared	.191	.288	.380	.572	.453	.538
Number of SMSAs (or NECMAs)	215	215	277	277	277	277

NOTE: All independent variables are defined at beginning of the decade. Includes all SMSAs or NECMA
as defined at end of decade, except for retirement areas in southern Florida, and areas with more than ?
percent of labor force in armed forces.

*Would be statistically significant at p = .05 level if this were a random sample.
†For 1960–1970 and 1980–1984; earnings in 1960 were not available and per capita income was use
instead.
‡Not available for 1960.

shown in columns *b, d,* and *f,* also include temperature and the two regional dummy variables in order to test the extent to which the macro-model has been able to explain differences in net migration between regions and among areas differing in temperature.

Focusing on the first set of results, we see that the macro-model does not provide a fully satisfactory explanation for variations in net migration among metropolitan areas. Although most of the regression coefficients have the expected signs, some do not, and many of the coefficients are not very large.

Among the four indicators of costs and availability of labor, the only variable with a consistently significant relationship for all three periods is proximity to Mexico. This has the predicted positive relationship, and the effect appears to increase over time. The proportion of college graduates has the expected positive relationship to net migration, but is significant only for the 1970–1980 period.

Earnings of unskilled workers did not have the anticipated negative relationship to migration in any of the three periods. For 1960–1970 there was a significant positive relationship, which was similar to the findings for household income in the micro-model. For 1970–1980 earnings of unskilled workers have a negative correlation with net migration, but when other variables are controlled, the relationship becomes positive, but not statistically significant. For 1980–1984 neither the correlation nor the regression coefficient for earnings are significant. These results suggest that low labor costs for indigenous workers were not, in themselves, a major factor in attracting businesses and creating new jobs which in turn attracted migrants.

The fourth labor variable, the existence of right-to-work laws, had very little effect on migration during the 1960s and 1970s, once other factors were controlled. These findings for 1970–1980 differ from those of Cebula, who found that right-to-work laws had a significant effect on net migration for 36 SMSAs between 1970–1978.[41] However, the existence of right-to-work laws had the expected positive effect during the 1980s, suggesting that it has become a more important consideration in the location of employment opportunities.

Density, which is interpreted here as indicating costs of land and congestion, has the expected negative relationship to migration and its effect is strongest for 1970–1980. Percent in manufacturing, which indicates the conduciveness of the industrial structure to growth in a post-industrial society, also has the expected negative relationship. Its relationship to migration becomes stronger over time, which is consistent with the declining importance of manufacturing in the total economy.

In columns *b*, *d*, and *f*, the January temperature and regional dummies were added to test whether our model has adequately explained the effects of temperature and region on migration. In all three decades, the increase in the explained variance is significant, indicating that the macro-model fails to provide an adequate explanation for variations in migration among metropolitan areas. The coefficient for temperature is significant for all three periods, and the dummy variable for the West region has a relatively large and significant coefficient for the 1970–1980 period. Although the coefficients for temperature are significant, for 1970–1980 and 1980–1984, they are not as strong as they were in the micro-level model (Table 4.3).

Because temperature is correlated with proximity to the Mexican border and negatively correlated with earnings, the effects of these two

---

[41]Richard Cebula, *Geographic Living-Cost Differentials*. We pointed out earlier that the 36 SMSAs used by Cebula were not representative of all SMSAs. In addition, our regression equation includes density, percent in manufacturing, percent college graduates, and proximity to Mexico, which he did not include.

variables are reduced when temperature is added. Overall, this analysis supports the argument that at least part of the relationship between temperature and net migration is a "spurious" relationship due to the relationship of temperature to factors, such as proximity to Mexico and labor costs that have stronger theoretical justification.

The explained variance for the equations without temperature and the regional dummies is a modest 19 percent for the first decade, 38 percent for the second decade, and 45 percent for the period from 1980–1984. These proportions are no better than those shown in Table 4.3 for the micro-model of migration. However, when temperature and the regional dummies are added, the explained variance is higher than that for the comparable micro-models for 1970–1980 and 1980–1984, which provides some suppport for the argument that migration during this period was primarily a response to a restructuring of the economy, which changed the location of job opportunities.[42]

The failure of the macro-model to provide a better fit to the migration data may be due to various inadequacies in the variables included in the model and the way in which it is applied. First, there are likely to be other variables that account for local variations in economic growth, which have not been included here. One of the factors, which is frequently mentioned, is taxes.[43] However, when a measure of local taxes was added to the regression for the 1970–1980 period, it had no significant effect on migration.[44] One of the problems with measuring

---

[42]The R-Squared values for the full equations in Tables 4.3 and 4.9 cannot be directly compared because climate is used in Table 4.3 and temperature in Table 4.9. The comparable values for the micro- and macro-models when both contain temperature and the regional dummy variables are as follows:

	micro-model	macro-model
1960–1970	.354	.288
1970–1980	.552	.572
1980–1984	.506	.538

These figures show that the micro-model fits the data better for 1960–1970, but the macro-model fits better in the latter two periods.

[43]Weinstein and Firestine cite taxes as one of the factors considered by firms in making location decisions. Bernard L. Weinstein and Robert E. Firestine, *Regional Growth and Decline in the United States* (New York: Praeger, 1978). Newman found that corporative tax-rate differentials between states had an impact on the redistribution of industry for 1957–1973. Robert J. Newman, "Industry Migration and Growth in the South," *Review of Economics and Statistics* 65 (1983):76–86. Althaus and Schachter found that progressive state taxes and taxes supporting welfare programs had a negative effect on migration, but that high levels of general services, which were supported by taxes, attracted migrants. Paul H. Althaus and Joseph Schachter, "Interstate Migration and the New Federalism," *Social Science Quarterly* 64 (1983):35–45.

[44]Local taxes were obtained from the 1977 census of governments, as reported in the U.S. Bureau of the Census, *State and Metropolitan Area Data Book 1982*. They refer to total local government tax collections per capita.

the effect of taxes on business location decisions is that states and municipalities often make tax concessions, or agree to provide roads and other infrastructure to meet the specific needs of industries that they are trying to attract to the area. These arrangements are not reflected in the average tax rates used for analysis.

A second consideration is the length of the time period used in the analysis. We have adopted the strategy of measuring the independent variables at the beginning of a period and then observing net migration during the period. This strategy assumes that the independent variables remain relatively constant during that time. The longer the period, the less likely it is that this assumption will remain valid. Although we do not know the length of the lags involved, ten years is probably too long a period of time for this type of analysis. The fact that the explained variance is highest for the 1980–1984 period suggests that a shorter period may be more appropriate. Unfortunately, many of the independent variables can only be obtained from census data and are thus not available for shorter intervals.

Finally, the continued strength of the dummy for the West region raises the question about whether the determinants of economic growth and migration are the same in all regions. Only a small part of the total migration between metropolitan areas flows between regions of the United States; it seems possible that economic growth and migration within different regions may be responding to somewhat different factors.

To explore this question, separate regressions were run for each region for the 1970–1980 period (see Table 4.10). The results show that there are differences in the determinants of migration in each of the three regions. The regressions for the North and South both display the expected relationships between migration and density and migration and unskilled earnings. However, they differ in the effect of manufacturing, college graduates, and right-to-work laws. Manufacturing appears to be a detriment to migration in the North, where levels of manufacturing are relatively high, but a positive factor in the South, where manufacturing levels are low. The proportion of college graduates, which is in general much lower in the South, has a substantial effect on migration in the South, but no relation in the North, where college graduates are more abundant. Right-to-work laws explain little variance in migration within the South because most southern states have such laws. The unexpected negative relationship between right-to-work laws in the North and migration appears to be spurious because only four northern states (Iowa, Kansas, Nebraska, and North Dakota) had such laws, and metropolitan areas in these states did not grow because of other factors.

TABLE 4.10

Regression Results for Net Migration, 1970–1980, for Metropolitan Areas by Region (standardized regression coefficients)

Independent Variables	Region			
	North	South	West	Total
Unskilled Earnings	−.286*	−.222*	.162	.134
Log of Density	−.277*	−.240*	−.423*	−.369
Near Mexico		.219*	.106	.237
Percent College Graduates	−.032	.397*	.135	.126
Right-to-Work Law	−.191*	.044	.245	.052
Percent Manufacturing	−.249*	.049	.070	−.253
R Squared	.337	.422	.203	.380
Number of SMSAs (or NECMAs)	133	97	47	277

See NOTE for Table 4.9.

*Would be statistically significant at p = .05 level if this were a random sample.

The macro-model fits the North and the South better than it does the West. The coefficient for the earnings of unskilled workers has a positive, but not significant, sign in the West. Proximity to Mexico has a much weaker effect in the West than in the South. The main factor of importance in explaining migration in the West is density, which has the expected negative relationship. Although densities in the West are lower than in other regions, some of the denser areas, such as Los Angeles and San Francisco, had by 1970 experienced relatively high land costs. This may explain why they grew much more slowly during the 1970s than in earlier decades.

Table 4.11 supports the arguments, which were made in developing the macro-level models, that the determinants of net migration were essentially the same as the determinants of employment growth. On the whole, the coefficients in Table 4.11 are very similar to those in Table 4.10. However, there are some differences. Proximity to Mexico has more effect on employment growth than it does on net migration. The percentage who are college graduates has a stronger effect on employment growth in the North and West and overall than it had on net migration. While the effect of college graduates on employment growth is relatively strong in the South, it is not as strong as its effect on net migration.

The overall negative effect of manufacturing on employment is stronger than it is on migration, which is consistent with the observation of Bluestone and Harrison that many of the workers who lose jobs

TABLE 4.11

Regression Results for Employment Growth, 1970–1980, for Metropolitan Areas by Region (standardized regression coefficients)

Independent Variables	Region			
	North	South	West	Total
Unskilled Earnings	−.128	−.291*	.117	.067
Log of Density	−.288*	−.097	−.396*	−.288*
Near Mexico		.346*	.151	.279*
Percent College Graduates	.163	.257*	.328*	.163*
Right-to-Work Law	.098	−.079	.302*	.094
Percent Manufacturing	−.251*	−.179	.062	−.343*
R Squared	.438	.402	.292	.526
Number of SMSAs (or NECMAs)	133	97	47	277

See NOTE for Table 4.9.

*Would be statistically significant at p = .05 level if this were a random sample.

when plants close choose not to move out of these areas even at the risk of unemployment.[45]

In separate regressions, which are not shown here, the effect of temperature within each region was also investigated. In general, temperature did not add very much to the explained variance. It had a significant effect only in the South, indicating that much of its effect was in explaining migration between regions rather than within regions. Temperature had a much weaker overall effect on employment growth than on migration. In the North region temperature had a negative effect on employment growth, indicating that cooler areas did better than milder areas. However, in the South the effect of temperature on growth was stronger than on migration, suggesting that part of the expansion of employment in the warmest areas came from increased labor force participation of the local populations of these areas.

In summary, the regional tests of the macro-model have strengthened the argument that migration to warmer areas in the United States, with the exception of migration to retirement communities in Florida, is primarily related to economic growth. Changes in industrial structure and in agglomeration economies during the past two decades appear to have increased the relative advantages of southern metropolitan areas as sites for new or relocating businesses. However, to complete the argument that this economic growth led to net migration, it is

[45]Bluestone and Harrison, *Deindustrialization.*

necessary to demonstrate that the migrants who left northern metropolitan areas for southern areas were able to benefit economically from these moves, even though the southern areas had lower average income levels than the northern ones.

Using the 1980 Public Use Microdata Sample, we selected outmigrants from four large metropolitan areas in the North which had experienced substantial outmigration during the 1970s, and inmigrants into three southern areas which had experienced high levels of inmigration. We found that the migrants were not typical of the populations at either the place of origin or the place of destination. A substantial proportion of the migrants from northern metropolitan areas to southern areas were young persons who had not been employed in 1975. One-third of the outmigrants from New York, Philadelphia, Detroit, and Saint Louis, who went to southern metropolitan areas, entered the labor force between 1975 and 1980. Similarly, 37 percent of the employed inmigrants to Atlanta, Denver, and Houston had not worked in 1975. For migrants who were not employed in 1975, a plausible argument can be made that they moved in order to find a job, and that if no comparable job were available in their place of origin, the average earnings in the place of origin was not relevant to their decision.

A comparison of earnings of outmigrants from the four selected northern metropolitan areas with published means for earnings of 1980 residents of these areas indicates that, on the average, male migrants earned about as much at the destination as residents of the same age at the origin, while female migrants earned slightly less (see Table 4.12). However, when the earnings of residents at the places of origin are adjusted for the higher costs of living in these areas, migrants' earnings were higher in six of the eight comparisons. The conclusion is that most migrants from northern SMSAs to southern SMSAs gained in real earnings, and their moves can therefore be explained in terms of economic factors.

Conclusion

In this chapter we have explored different theories of regional change in an attempt to explain variations in growth rates among metropolitan areas. We have focused primarily on net migration because this is the component of population growth that accounts for most of the variation among areas; it is also more responsive to changes in social and economic conditions than are fertility and mortality. The 1970s present a challenge to theories of regional growth because the positive relationship between net migration and income, which had been

TABLE 4.12

Age Standardized Earnings of Migrants from Four Northern SMSAs
to Southern SMSAs and Residents of These Northern SMSAs, 1979

	Annual Earnings in Dollars		
	Mean Earnings of Migrants	Mean Earnings of Residents	Real Earnings of Residents
MALES			
New York	18,456	18,170	14,959
Philadelphia	17,598	18,692	17,164
Detroit	19,167	22,086	20,884
St. Louis	22,597	19,141	18,845
FEMALES			
New York	9,014	10,618	8,742
Philadelphia	8,446	8,799	8,080
Detroit	8,567	9,795	9,261
St. Louis	8,680	8,516	8,385

NOTE: Migrants' earnings were tabulated from the Public Use Microdata Sample "B." These refer to migrants who moved between 1975 and 1980. Residents' earnings were obtained from the 1980 Census, vol. D, table 237. Migrants and residents are standardized on average age distribution of migrants to all four SMSAs. Real earnings = earnings divided by ratio of cost-of-living index for the SMSA and average index for southern SMSAs in 1979.

observed in most studies of preceding decades, was reversed, and there was net migration from high to low income areas.

We first attempted to explain variations in net migration rates among metropolitan areas in terms of conventional micro-economic models, which were based on the assumption that migrants moved to places where they expected to be able to improve their material well-being. Following previous studies, we modeled migration as a function of average income, unemployment, and various amenity variables, at the beginning of the decade. We also added measures of living costs because many of the low-income areas of destination were also low-cost areas, and migrants may have responded to differences in actual purchasing power rather than differences in nominal income. Although income had the expected positive effect during the 1960–1970 period, it had no significant effect on migration during the 1970–1980 and 1980–1984 periods, and the coefficient was negative in some of the regressions. However, the expected negative relationship between unemployment and migration was observed, suggesting that migrants in the 1970s were motivated more by job opportunities than by income. This suggestion was supported by the observation that a large proportion of the migrants between 1975 and 1980 had not been employed in 1975; they had either entered the labor force since 1975 or been unemployed at that time.

Another puzzling finding of the 1970s was that there was a relatively strong correlation between growth and temperature, and this relationship remained when income, unemployment, costs, and other factors were controlled. Others had interpreted this result as an indication of increasing concern for nonmonetary amenities among migrants, and this explanation seemed to apply primarily to elderly migrants to metropolitan areas in southern and central parts of Florida. However, the removal of these areas from the analysis did not remove the relationship between migration and temperature. The interpretation that migrants of labor force ages were giving up income for climate was questioned, however, by the use of a more refined measure of climate, which gave the highest ratings to places with mild climates, such as Southern California, but penalized both the cold northern areas and the southern areas with high heat and humidity. This measure showed a much weaker relationship to migration than did temperature, leaving open the question of why migrants were moving to areas with high temperatures.

Another indicator of amenities, the population density of the area, showed the expected relationship to migration. Migrants during the 1970s moved away from the more congested high-density areas and toward low-density areas. However, it is hard to be sure that density is an indicator of amenities and not some other factors, such as lower costs.

The second approach was to explore further the relationship between migration and changes in job opportunities by examining changes in the industrial structure in the United States and the extent to which these changes favored particular regions and types of metropolitan areas. The relative decline of manufacturing clearly affected employment in many northern metropolitan areas, which were highly specialized in manufacturing. In addition, the shift of the economy toward services seemed to favor those metropolitan areas that were relatively more specialized in wholesale trade, transportation, and business services. However, these changes explain only part of the variation in growth among metropolitan areas. Despite the relative decline in manufacturing, some southern and western areas, which had not been highly specialized in manufacturing, gained from the relocation of manufacturing firms in these areas. Other areas, which had been specialized in manufacturing, were able to expand in service employment. The biggest employment gains were observed in resort areas, areas specializing in education and medical services, and smaller areas that were not specialized in any industry. Thus, industrial shifts in the economy provided only part of the explanation for metropolitan growth.

The final part of the analysis involved a reformulation of the model for determinants of net migration in terms of macro factors responsible for employment growth. Some of these factors had also been used in the micro-model, but were reinterpreted in terms of their effects on location decisions of businesses. For example, density was reinterpreted as reflecting the cost of land and other costs associated with greater congestion.

The results of testing the macro-model showed that employment growth and migration were greater in areas that had lower wages for unskilled labor and in areas close to Mexico, where there was an abundant supply of immigrant labor. Despite the low average incomes in these areas, migrants from higher-wage northern areas were found to have experienced somewhat higher incomes in real terms (when adjusted for the lower costs in these areas) than residents of the same age in their areas of origin. Thus, migration to these areas conforms to microeconomic assumptions, even though this was not apparent from the study of aggregate relationships. The reason for this is that migrants were younger than the working populations at the places of origin and, thus, could not expect to earn average incomes in these areas; but in the areas of destination, they often received above-average incomes.

When the macro-model was applied separately to each region, the expected relationships were generally observed in the North and the South, but somewhat different relationships were observed in the West. It would appear that the West has a somewhat separate economic structure and that it is isolated to a greater extent from the other regions than the North and South are isolated from each other. If this is true, it would explain the continuation through the 1970s of higher economic growth and migration in the West, despite higher costs of labor and other factors. However, by the early 1980s the growth of the West had slowed and the analysis indicates the West had become similar to the other regions.

5

CONSEQUENCES
OF GROWTH AND DECLINE

I N THE previous two chapters we have seen that there are great variations in the rates of growth of metropolitan areas. While the populations of some areas grew by more than 50 percent in a decade, other
areas experienced population decline. In this chapter we shall examine
some of the consequences and correlates of growth or decline for these
areas.

Although there is a general belief among urban and regional
planners that areas benefit from growth, there is little direct evidence to
this effect. Growth brings obvious rewards to those persons involved in
construction and related businesses, which provide facilities for the
growing population; the absence of growth may lead to unemployment
in these industries. Growth may also be seen as beneficial to local
officials seeking to expand their staffs as they increase their tax base; it
provides the means of increasing the budget for public administration.
However, the impact on the rest of the population is not so clear.

Growth can affect an area in at least three ways. First, by changing
the size of the community, growth (or decline) has a long-run effect on
the scale of activities in that community. Some goods, such as consumer durables and certain business services, may become cheaper because of economies of scale, while other items, such as the price of
land, may become more expensive because of increased competition for
limited local resources. This increased scale can also lead to increased
congestion and air and water pollution.

Second, growth (or decline) is likely to lead to a temporary disequilibrium between the supply and demand of certain goods and services. Where population growth is driven by economic growth, there are likely to be increased employment opportunities for local residents in the short run. Conversely, areas experiencing population decline typically have high rates of unemployment and poor job opportunities.

On the negative side, growth may result in temporary increases in costs for housing and some local goods and services, where the demand grows faster than the supply. Although a moderate level of growth may be beneficial, rapid growth may push up the costs of construction and lead to the sacrifice of some quality in the interest of saving time and getting on to the next job. Rapid growth may also make it difficult to develop careful plans for zoning and the layout of streets and utility lines. In recent years, some of the rapidly growing metropolitan areas have had significant proportions of their populations living in mobile homes or temporary housing.[1]

The effects of population decline on housing and services are also opposite those of growth. Although a small decline tends to reduce the cost of housing to the benefit of residents, a rapid decline often leads to abandonment and neighborhood deterioration. This can result in the concentration of poor people and welfare recipients in areas where declining tax revenues make it difficult to provide the needed public assistance.[2] Population declines also lead to redundancies in services, which may temporarily benefit the purchasers of these services but which eventually lead to some of the providers of services being laid off or forced out of business.

Third, growth (or decline) may result in a change in population composition of an area. Because metropolitan growth is largely due to the difference between inmigration and outmigration, some inferences can be made from knowledge of the characteristics of migrants. In recent decades, migration in the United States has been selective of young adults with above-average education. The only major exception to this rule has been the movement of elderly to a few southern metropolitan areas. This means that areas of net inmigration should have a surplus of young, well-educated persons, while net outmigration areas should have a deficit. It has been argued that growth is self-perpetuating because

---

[1]For example, in the metropolitan areas of Fort Myers–Cape Coral, Sarasota, and Las Vegas, which had growth rates greater than 50 percent in the 1970s, more than 10 percent of households were living in mobile homes in 1980. U.S. Bureau of the Census, *Census of Housing 1980.*

[2]Katherine L. Bradbury, Anthony Downs, and Kenneth A. Small, *Urban Decline and the Future of American Cities* (Washington, DC: The Brookings Institution, 1982).

concentrations of young, well-educated persons are conducive to further economic growth, while a lack of such persons impedes growth.[3]

Compared to the large literature on the determinants of growth, there have been relatively few studies of the consequences of growth or decline. Rust studied several areas that had had population decline or slow growth between 1940 and 1970, and found that these areas had lower average incomes, higher median age of population, and a reluctance of businesses to make investments in the area.[4] However, he also noted that the inhabitants of these declining areas enjoyed lower living costs, less crowding, and probably had more of a stress-free environment than inhabitants of growing areas.

In another study of the consequences of growth, Appelbaum and associates examined urbanized areas with central cities with populations of 50,000 to 400,000, which had grown during the 1960s.[5] They found that growth had little relation to changes in unemployment, to most types of municipal expenditures per capita, or to most measures of health. However, growth was related to increases in per capita income, house values, rent, cirrhosis of the liver, crime rates, and per capita expenses for police. Some of these findings may be distorted by problems in obtaining comparable measures for 1960 and 1970, since the boundaries of urbanized areas change over time.

Alba and Batutis studied the losses experienced by New York state between 1975 and 1980 by comparing inmigrants, outmigrants, and residents selected from the Public Use Microdata Samples of the 1980 census.[6] They found that the outmigrants were younger, better educated, and had higher average incomes than did the resident population. Although some of the net migration loss in the exchange with other states was compensated for by migration from abroad, the foreign immigrants had lower levels of education and income than the outmigrants. These findings are consistent with Muller's finding that migrants to Houston were younger, better educated, and had higher lifetime incomes than did the resident population.[7]

[3]Thomas Muller, "The Declining and Growing Metropolis–A Fiscal Comparison," in G. Sternlieb and James W. Hughes, eds., *Post-Industrial America: Metropolitan Decline and Inter-Regional Job Shifts*, pp. 197–218; and Gordon L. Clark, *Interregional Migration, National Policy, and Social Justice* (Totowa, NJ: Rowman and Allanheld, 1983).

[4]Edgar Rust, *No Growth: Impacts on Metropolitan Areas* (Lexington, MA: Lexington Books, 1975).

[5]Richard P. Appelbaum et al., *The Effects of Urban Growth: A Population Impact Analysis* (New York: Praeger, 1976).

[6]Richard D. Alba and Michael J. Batutis, "Migration's Toll: Lessons from New York State," *American Demographics* (June 1985): 38–42.

[7]Thomas Muller, "Declining and Growing Metropolis."

Method of Analysis

The basic method of analysis used in this chapter involves the comparison of population characteristics at the beginning and end of the decade for metropolitan areas with differing growth rates. If the pattern of change in a particular characteristic varies with the growth rate, it will be assumed that the change in the characteristic is associated with growth. For example, if it is found that housing rents increase more rapidly in growing areas than in declining areas, it will be assumed that growth has a positive effect on rent.

While this method will establish relationships between growth and "consequence" variables, it does not provide solid proof that the change in the consequence variable is a result of growth. The change may be due to some other cause which is also related to growth. For example, population growth may be related to the expansion of business in an area, and the increase in housing rent may be due to the effect of business demand for land on the price of land for residential construction. In each case the causal inferences that are made will rest on arguments about the plausibility of causal mechanisms, which cannot be directly tested with these data.

In order to simplify the analysis and presentation of results, we have grouped metropolitan areas into four categories, according to their growth during the period between the 1970 to 1980 censuses:

Loss = Absolute population decline from 1970 to 1980.
Slow = Growth of less than 10 percent between 1970 and 1980.
Moderate = Growth of 10 to 30 percent between 1970 and 1980.
Rapid = Growth of 30 percent or more between 1970 and 1980.

The dividing line between areas of slow growth and those of moderate growth is approximately equal to the national average growth rate for metropolitan areas between 1970 and 1980, which was 10.3 percent.

Because the composition of migration to retirement areas is very different from the composition of migration to other areas, the 11 Florida areas, which have significant elderly migration, are treated separately in the analysis. All of these retirement areas had either moderate or rapid growth during the 1970s.

The analysis was performed for each consequence variable controlling for both the region of the country and the size of the metropolitan area. To avoid many large tables, only the summary results for all metropolitan areas by category of growth are presented. Where the controls for region and size make a significant difference in the results, the detailed results are discussed in the chapter and the full table is included in Appendix B. It is important to remember that all of the declining areas were located in the North region and that all of the rapidly growing areas are in the South or the West. Thus, it is impossible to completely separate effects of growth and decline from regional effects.

Changes in Population Composition

In this section we shall consider those characteristics, such as race, family structure, and education, which either do not change or change infrequently for individuals. We shall also include age because it changes in a predictable way. Changes in the distribution of these characteristics within a metropolitan area can be viewed as due to three sources: (1) national change in population composition; (2) local deviations from the national trend; and (3) movement of people into and out of the metropolitan area.

Age Structure

Between 1970 and 1980 the average age of the United States population increased by about two years. Within metropolitan areas a similar increase took place—from a mean age of 32.1 years in 1970 to 33.9 years in 1980. This increase was primarily a result of the lower birthrates of the 1970s compared to the three preceding decades, although reductions in mortality and the aging of the large baby-boom cohorts born between 1946 and 1964 also tended to increase the average age.

There was also a significant increase in the elderly population from 9.8 to 11.3 percent for the entire United States population, and from 9.3 to 10.7 percent for the population in metropolitan areas. Declining mortality had more to do with the increase in the elderly population, although the increase in the proportion of elderly would have been much smaller had the fertility rates of the 1950s and early 1960s continued into the 1970s.

Growing areas tend to have younger age distributions than do declining areas. This is because the most important difference in growth components between such areas is migration and young persons predominate in most migration streams. This relationship is shown in Table 5.1 for the 1970–1980 decade. At the end of the decade, the mean age of persons in rapidly growing areas was 32.0, while the mean age in areas of population loss was 35.2. Only part of this difference is accounted for by migration during the decade. At the beginning of the decade there was an inverse relationship between mean age and growth,

TABLE 5.1

Mean Age and Percentage Aged 65 and Over, 1970 and 1980,
for Metropolitan Areas by Growth, 1970–1980

Metropolitan Growth	Mean Age			Percent Aged 65 and Over		
	1970	1980	Change	1970	1980	Change
Loss	33.1	35.2	2.1	10.0	11.7	1.7
Slow	32.0	33.9	1.9	9.2	10.5	1.3
Moderate	31.0	32.7	1.7	8.3	9.5	1.2
Rapid	30.4	32.0	1.6	8.1	8.9	0.8
Retirement Areas	37.5	40.0	2.5	17.2	19.8	2.6
Total	32.1	33.9	1.8	9.3	10.7	1.4

NOTES: Compiled from county data on Summary Tape File 4 for 1970 and 1980 for 304 SMSAs and NECMAs as defined in June 1981.
Slow growth = less than 10 percent for decade; moderate growth = 10 to 30 percent; rapid growth = 30 percent or more.
Retirement Areas include 11 SMSAs in Florida with 10 percent or more of inmigrants 1975–1980 aged 65 or over.

which can be attributed to the effects of previous migration and natural increase.[8] While the mean age increased in all areas during the decade, it increased less in the rapidly growing areas than in other areas, as can be seen by the changes in column 3. The increase was 2.1 years for declining areas, but only 1.6 years for rapidly growing areas. Slowly growing and moderately growing areas had increases between these two values.

Similar results were found for the proportion of persons aged 65 and over. This proportion was inversely related to growth in 1970, and the relationship became stronger in 1980. While the proportion of elderly increased in all areas, the increase was less in the more rapidly growing areas than in the declining and slowly growing areas because of the underrepresentation of elderly in most migration streams.[9] By 1980, 11.7 percent of the population in declining areas were 65 or older in contrast to only 8.9 percent in the rapidly growing areas.

[8]Part of the regional difference in age structure is due to regional differences in natural increase. The average age is the highest in the North, where fertility has been the lowest, and the average age is lowest in the West, where fertility is the highest. Since the western region also has the highest metropolitan growth and the North the lowest, fertility differences account for part of the inverse relationship between growth and mean age.
[9]Persons aged 65 and over accounted for only 5.6 percent of the interstate migrants, although they comprised 11.3 percent of the population in 1980. U.S. Bureau of the Census, *1980 Census of Population, Characteristics of the Population, Detailed Characteristics*, U.S. Summary, 1984, table 259.

The overall effect of growth on average age was the same in all regions of the country, but the higher rates of natural increase in the South and West resulted in lower average ages in most growth categories than in the North (see Appendix Table B.1).

The Florida retirement areas experienced a very different change in age composition. Although persons 55 or older constituted less than 11 percent of the migrants to metropolitan areas in the United States, they accounted for over 29 percent of the migrants to the 11 metropolitan areas in Southern and Central Florida, which we have designated as "retirement areas."[10] All of these areas grew significantly during the decade; nine had growth rates of over 30 percent, qualifying them for the "rapid" growth category, and the remaining two fell in the "moderate" growth category. Because elderly persons and those nearing retirement (aged 55 to 64) accounted for a large percentage of migrants to these areas, the average age of persons in these areas was much higher than in other metropolitan areas; it increased more than in any other growth category. In 1980 the median age in these areas was 40, and the proportion of elderly was approximately double that of other growing metropolitan areas.

The differences in age structures of selected growing and declining areas are further illustrated by the age pyramids shown in Figure 5.1. All of these pyramids show a narrowing at the base, which is due to the national decline in the birthrate since 1964. However, the two growing areas, Denver–Boulder and Houston, have much larger bulges in ages 20 to 35 than do the declining areas. In contrast, Detroit and Philadelphia, which had population declines in the 1970s, have relatively high proportions of their populations in the age groups over age 50. The largest age group in the declining populations is 15 to 19, while in the growing populations, it is 25 to 29. This difference is due primarily to the migration of persons in their 20s from declining to growing areas. The effects of decline on the age structure are particularly pronounced in Pittsburgh, which suffered net outmigration in each decade since 1950. The proportion of Pittsburgh's population in the age groups from 50 to 65 is significantly higher than in the other declining areas.

The final population pyramid in Figure 5.1 is for Tampa–St. Petersburg, a growing retirement area. This age distribution bears some resemblance to that for Pittsburgh. However, because of the large volume of elderly migration to Tampa–St. Petersburg, the second peak in the age distribution occurs in the 65 to 69 age group rather than in the 55 to 59 age group.

[10]U.S. Bureau of the Census, *1980 Census of Population, Gross Migration for Counties: 1975 to 1980,* Supplemental Report 17, 1984.

FIGURE 5.1

Population Pyramids for Selected Metropolitan Areas in 1980

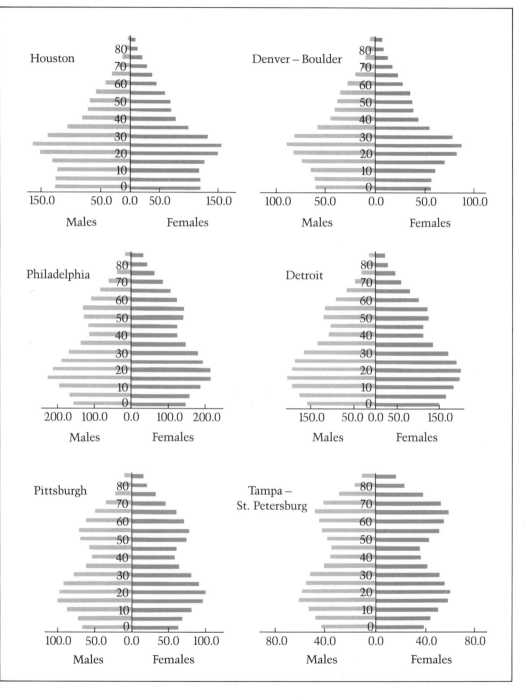

Family Structure

Migration frequently splits households as some members leave and others remain behind. Consequently, migration tends to decrease household sizes in both the areas of origin and the areas of destination. In addition to migration, the 1970s was a period of unusually rapid household fragmentation as the baby-boom cohorts left parental homes to set up new households and the divorce rate increased to an all-time high.[11] For metropolitan households as a whole, the average household size fell from 3.2 in 1970 to 2.8 in 1980, and the proportion of households that contained families decreased from 80.1 percent to 72.6 percent.[12]

In 1970 the proportion of family households was somewhat lower in declining and slowly growing areas than it was in moderate and rapidly growing areas (see Table 5.2). However, the moderate and rapidly growing areas experienced larger decreases in family households than the slowly growing areas, and by 1980 the differences among areas were smaller than they had been at the beginning of the decade. Retirement areas had lower initial proportions of family households, but slower than average decreases in this proportion so that they also became more similar to the average metropolitan area during the decade.

While the typical family is usually envisioned as a husband, wife, and children, less than half of all metropolitan families were of this type in 1970, and this proportion declined to only 41.2 percent in 1980. The remainder of families consisted mainly of married couples without children at home or a single parent with one or more children.

The proportion of families that were "full families," that is, had a husband, wife, and at least one child, was highest in rapidly growing areas and lowest in declining areas and the retirement areas. This proportion decreased most in the declining areas and least in the rapidly growing areas, so that in 1980 there was a greater difference among areas than there had been in 1970.

These results are consistent with the changes in age structure. Since the primary migrants in all streams except those to retirement areas are young adults in the ages of family formation and childbearing, migration tends to reduce the proportion of full families in areas of out-migration and to increase it in areas of inmigration.

[11]See Louise B. Russell, *The Baby Boom Generation and the Economy* (Washington, DC: The Brookings Institution, 1982).

[12]A nonfamily household is either a single-person household or a household that does not contain any persons related by birth, adoption, or marriage. In 1980, 86 percent of all nonfamily households were single-person households.

TABLE 5.2

Percentage of Families and Husband-Wife Families with Children for Metropolitan Areas by Growth, 1970–1980

Metropolitan Growth	Families as a Percent of all Households			Percentage of Families with Husband, Wife, and Child		
	1970	1980	Change	1970	1980	Change
Loss	79.9	72.4	−7.5	47.1	39.0	−8.1
Slow	79.3	72.1	−7.2	49.0	41.6	−7.4
Moderate	81.7	73.8	−7.9	49.8	43.0	−6.8
Rapid	81.0	72.8	−8.2	50.7	44.1	−6.6
Retirement Areas	78.0	71.2	−6.8	37.9	31.0	−6.9
Total	80.1	72.6	−7.5	48.5	41.2	−7.3

NOTE: Family households are those containing two or more persons who are related by birth, marriage, or adoption.

Race and Spanish Origin

Between 1970 and 1980 the proportion of blacks among the population of metropolitan areas increased from 11.6 to 12.6 percent. This increase was primarily the result of a higher rate of natural increase of blacks compared to all other races. However, part of the increase was due to the net migration of blacks toward metropolitan areas and the net migration of whites and others away from metropolitan areas. The proportion of the metropolitan population that was of Spanish origin increased by a considerable amount during the decade, from 5.1 to 7.5 percent. In addition to a higher rate of natural increase, the Spanish origin population also gained from immigration from Mexico, the Caribbean, and other parts of Latin America.

The growth of metropolitan areas was inversely related to the proportion black and the increase in the proportion black in metropolitan areas. The declining areas had the highest proportion black among growth categories in 1970; and these areas experienced the largest increase in the percentage black over the decade (see Table 5.3). The proportion black in the rapidly growing areas in 1970 was only about one-half that of the declining areas, and there was only a slight increase in this percentage over the decade. It appears that the most rapid growth was occurring in areas with relatively low proportions black and that blacks made up only a small proportion of the migrants to these areas. As a consequence, blacks became more heavily concentrated in areas of decline or slow growth by the end of the decade.

The relationship between growth and ethnic concentration was

TABLE 5.3

Black and Spanish Origin Populations, 1970 and 1980, for Metropolitan Areas by Growth, 1970–1980

Metropolitan Growth	Blacks			Spanish Origin		
	1970	1980	Change	1970	1980	Change
Loss	13.0	15.0	2.1	4.4	5.9	1.5
Slow	11.0	12.5	1.5	4.0	6.5	2.5
Moderate	12.8	13.5	0.7	4.3	5.7	1.4
Rapid	6.7	6.8	0.2	11.3	15.4	4.1
Retirement Areas	13.3	12.3	−0.9	8.3	12.1	3.7
Total	11.6	12.6	1.0	5.1	7.5	2.4

very different for persons of Spanish origin. The areas of rapid growth had considerably higher concentrations of persons of Spanish origin in 1970, and these areas experienced the greatest increase in Spanish origin population over the decade. Many of these areas were located in the states just north of the Mexican border, and immigration accounted for a significant proportion of both metropolitan growth and growth of the Spanish origin population.

The changes in racial and ethnic composition were observed in all regions, but there was some variation in the extent of change (see Appendix Table B.2). One result of these changes was a reduction in the difference between northern and southern areas in the proportion black. Southern areas, however, had higher proportions of Spanish origin in 1980 than did northern areas.

Retirement areas, all of which were growing, had relatively high proportions black at the beginning of the decade, but experienced a decrease in proportion black because very few of the inmigrants to these areas were black.[13] On the other hand, the retirement areas experienced an increase in the proportion of Spanish origin, which was almost as high as that for rapidly growing areas. Much of the increase in the Spanish origin population in Florida was due to Cuban immigration. Miami alone received about 91,500 Cuban immigrants between 1970 and 1980, and this accounted for over one-quarter of its growth for the decade.[14]

[13]Between 1975 and 1980, only 5.5 percent of the inmigrants to Florida were black. U.S. Bureau of the Census, *Gross Migration for Counties: 1975 to 1980*, 1980 Census of Population, Supplemental Report 17 (Washington, DC: U.S. Government Printing Office, 1984).

[14]Based on the question on year of immigration in 1980 census. U.S. Bureau of the Census, *1980 Census of Population, Detailed Characteristics, Florida*. The proportion of Cuban immigrants among the inmigrants to Miami was even greater during the 1960s.

118

The direction of change in the retirement areas paralleled that of other growing areas. While the Spanish origin population was concentrated in areas of growth and contributing to this growth through continued immigration and natural increase, the black population was becoming more and more concentrated in areas of decline and slow growth. The implications of these trends for the black population will be discussed at greater length in the next chapter.

Education

If migration is selective of persons of higher than average education, then outmigration would be expected to lower the average level of education in an area and inmigration would be expected to raise it.[15] However, the data in Table 5.4 show very little difference in either the level of education or the change in this level over the decade by growth category. For metropolitan areas as a whole, the mean years of education for persons aged 25 and over increased by about one year. This same increase is observed for each of the growth categories with variations of only 0.1 year, which is equal to the rounding error.

Rapidly growing areas had slightly higher initial levels of education than other areas and they had significantly higher proportions of college graduates, 13.4 percent compared to 11.4 percent for declining areas, and 11.8 percent for slow and moderate growth areas. The rapidly growing areas also experienced a slightly greater increase in the proportion college graduates than other areas. These relationships were very similar in all three regions (see Appendix Table B.3).

One reason why education levels were not greatly affected by migration during the 1970s was the fact that immigration from Mexico and other parts of Latin America made up a significant proportion of the inmigration streams to growing metropolitan areas. Although the migrants from other parts of the United States had above-average education, those from Mexico and Latin America had much lower levels of education.[16]

A more thorough investigation of the relationship of education to

[15]This argument was originally made in Karl E. Taeuber and Alma F. Taeuber, "White Migration and Socioeconomic Differences Between Cities and Suburbs," *American Sociological Review* 29 (1964): 718–729. It was developed further and tested by William H. Frey, "The Changing Impact of White Migration on the Population Compositions of Origin and Destination Metropolitan Areas," *Demography* 16:2 (May 1979): 219–237.

[16]For example, the mean number of years of education of migrants aged 25 and over who moved to Houston from other parts of the United States was 13.5 years compared to 10.9 years for foreign immigrants. The average of all inmigrants was 13.2 years, which was not very different from the native population of Houston. Based on special tabulations from the one percent Public Use Microdata Sample from the 1980 census.

TABLE 5.4

Mean Years of Education and Percent College Graduates for Persons 25 and Over for Metropolitan Areas by Growth, 1970–1980

Metropolitan Growth	Mean Years of Education			Percent College Graduates		
	1970	1980	Change	1970	1980	Chang
Loss	10.8	11.8	1.0	11.4	17.4	6.0
Slow	11.0	12.0	1.0	11.8	18.0	6.2
Moderate	10.7	11.9	1.2	11.8	17.9	6.1
Rapid	11.2	12.3	1.1	13.4	19.7	6.3
Retirement Areas	10.7	11.7	1.0	10.4	15.0	4.6
Total	10.9	11.9	1.0	11.8	17.9	6.1

growth was performed by Clark, using the Public Use Microdata Sample from the 1980 census.[17] By separating natives from migrants and controlling for age, she was able to show that areas of net outmigration experienced a relative loss of highly educated persons while areas of net inmigration experienced a relative gain. The difference in average years of education between migrants and natives was about 1.6 years when age was not controlled, and about 1.0 years when age was controlled.

Wilson has carried out a somewhat similar analysis using samples from the 1940, 1970, and 1980 censuses. He found that the metropolitan areas in the northern regions had a disproportionate decline in the proportion of persons with one or more years of college due to net outmigration. He concludes that "the long-term impact of migration apparently has been to accelerate the rate of convergence of the education levels of the South and the non-South."[18]

Changes in Employment and Income

In the preceding chapter we discussed the interrelations between employment and income and population growth. We observed a very high correlation between growth of population and growth of employment. However, we found that, for the decade of the 1970s, neither

[17]Rebecca Clark, "Composition of Inmigrant and Outmigrant Streams to Metropolitan Areas," M.A. Thesis, Brown University, 1985.

[18]Franklin D. Wilson, "The Impact of Interregional Migration on the Population Composition of Origin/Destination Metropolitan and Nonmetropolitan Areas," working paper 85-32, Center for Demography and Ecology, University of Wisconsin, 1986.

unemployment nor per capita income at the beginning of the decade were very good predictors of growth during the decade. In fact, growth had a negative relationship to income at the beginning of the decade, which was contrary to theories of migration which postulated that migrants should move to areas with higher incomes. In this section, we shall turn the relationships around and look at changes in employment and income as a function of growth during the 1970s. Since employment is the product of the proportion of persons in the labor force and the proportion of these who are employed, we shall consider each of these components separately.

The analysis of changes in employment over time must be undertaken with some care because employment fluctuates with economic conditions. It is important to distinguish short-term fluctuations from longer trends. For the nation as a whole, annual data are available from the Current Population Survey to chart the fluctuations in employment. However, annual data are lacking for the complete set of metropolitan areas for the 1970s, and we are forced to rely on the decennial censuses.[19] The best we can do is to use annual data from the Current Population Survey to indicate where the census date falls in the economic cycle. We have done this by comparing the level of employment in the year of the census with the average level of unemployment for the five years surrounding the census. For the nation as a whole, unemployment was 4.9 percent in 1970, compared to an average of 4.7 percent for 1968–1972. In 1980 unemployment was 7.1 percent compared to a five-year average for 1978–1982 of 7.3 percent.[20] Unemployment in 1970 was 0.2 percent above average and in 1980 it was 0.2 percent below average. Thus, the increase between 1970 and 1980 of 2.2 percent slightly understates the longer term trend toward rising unemployment. If trends in employment and income vary inversely with unemployment, this means that increases in employment and income may be slightly overstated.

This slight difference in the relative points in the economic cycle between 1970 and 1980 will not have a great effect on our analysis, if we can assume that the timing of economic cycles is the same in all types of areas under consideration. If the timing of peaks and dips in

[19]Data on total employment and employment in selected industries are compiled annually for many metropolitan areas by the Bureau of Labor Statistics and published in *Employment, Hours and Earnings, States and Areas* periodically. In 1970 there were 216 areas, not all of which were SMSAs, but these data did not include unemployment for these areas nor was there any breakdown by race.

[20]Annual unemployment rates were obtained from the U.S. Bureau of the Census, *Statistical Abstract of the United States 1984*, table 669.

economic cycles differs from one region to another, or between grow-ing and declining areas, then the effects on our results could be more serious.

Labor Force Participation

The Bureau of the Census defines the labor force as including all persons who are either currently employed or who are unemployed and looking for work. In Table 5.5 we have shown the percentage of all per-sons aged 15 and over who were in the labor force in 1970 and 1980. For metropolitan areas as a whole, there was an increase in the percentage of persons in the labor force from 58.8 percent in 1970 to 63.0 percent in 1980. This was accounted for primarily by a national trend toward in-creased participation of women. Between April 1970 and April 1980 the proportion of women aged 16 and over who were in the civilian labor force increased from 41.6 to 49.8 percent.[21] The increases in participa-tion were particularly large for women aged 20 to 44.

While there were significant changes in age structure between 1970 and 1980, these had little effect on the overall rate of labor force partici-pation. Increases in the proportion of the population in the young-adult years, when participation is high, were offset by increases in the propor-tion aged 65 and over, when participation is very low. If labor force par-ticipation rates at each age had remained the same as they were in 1970, the overall labor force participation rate for persons 15 and over would have been 0.1 percent lower in 1980.

All areas shared in the increase in labor force participation, but not equally. Growing areas experienced larger increases in labor-force parti-cipation than did declining areas, and the amount of increase was greatest for the rapidly growing areas (see Table 5.5).

Part of the increase in labor force participation in growing areas was a result of the changes in age structure. Because growing areas attracted disproportionate numbers of young adults, they gained persons with higher-than-average participation rates. In order to see the effect of age structure on labor force participation, we have calculated the size of the labor force in each area as a percentage of the size that would be ex-pected if each area had the national metropolitan participation rate for each age and sex group (see columns 4 and 5 of Table 5.5). When age structure is taken into account, the variations by type of area become

---

[21]In the same period the proportion of males in the civilian labor force decreased from 76.1 to 74.7 percent. U.S. Bureau of the Census, *1970 Census of Population, Subject Report 6A*, table 1, and *1980 Census of Population, Detailed Characteristics of the Popu-lation*, U.S. Summary, table 272.

TABLE 5.5

Labor Force Participation as a Percentage of Persons Aged 15 and Over for Metropolitan Areas by Growth, 1970–1980

Metropolitan Growth	Percent in Labor Force			Labor Force as Percentage of Expected Labor Force[a]		
	1970	1980	Change	1970	1980	Change
Loss	58.3	61.0	2.7	99.8	98.9	−0.9
Slow	60.1	64.1	4.0	101.6	101.4	−0.2
Moderate	58.8	63.9	5.1	99.3	99.9	0.6
Rapid	57.6	64.4	6.8	97.1	99.3	2.2
Retirement Areas	51.6	54.5	2.9	96.3	97.3	1.0
Total	58.8	63.0	4.2	100.0	100.0	0.0

[a] Expected labor force is the number of persons who would be in the labor force if each metropolitan area had the same labor force participation rates by age and sex as the total metropolitan population.

smaller. In 1980 the difference in the percentages of actual to expected labor force between rapidly growing and declining areas is less than 1 percent (see column 5). However, in 1970 the rapidly growing areas had had participation rates below average while those in declining areas were very close to average, so that the increase between 1970 and 1980 in labor force participation in rapidly growing areas relative to the national rate was 2.2 percent; whereas declining and slowly growing metropolitan areas had declines in their age-adjusted, labor force participation relative to the national rate.

The proportion of persons in the labor force was considerably lower in retirement areas than in any other areas, which is not surprising given the high proportion of elderly in these areas. However, the size of the labor force in these areas was smaller in both 1970 and 1980 than would have been expected based on their age and sex composition. This is probably because some persons aged 55 to 64 moved to these areas upon early retirement. For example, in the Tampa–St. Petersburg area, the participation rate of persons aged 55 to 64 in 1980 was only 42 percent compared to 57 percent nationally.[22] Despite their lower overall participation rate, the retirement areas did experience a growth in labor force participation relative to that expected, which was consistent with their rate of population growth. This increase occurred primarily among younger persons living in these areas.

[22]U.S. Bureau of the Census, *1980 Census of Population, General Social and Economic Characteristics*, U.S. Summary, table 103, and Florida, table 120.

Unemployment

Unemployment is perhaps the most sensitive indicator of current economic conditions in an area. Areas with rapid economic growth frequently have a demand for labor that exceeds the local supply, and leads to low levels of unemployment; while areas of economic decline have workers who have been laid off and new entrants to the labor force who are unable to find jobs. Populations respond to changes in local economic conditions through migration from declining areas to areas of economic growth. If this response were instantaneous, there should be little variation in rates of unemployment from one area to another. However, lags in this response cause unemployment rates to vary among areas.

Unemployment for metropolitan areas increased from 4.3 percent in April 1970 to 6.3 percent in April 1980, a change which was very similar to that for the nation as a whole. Part of this growth was due to changes in the age structure of the population, which increased the proportion of the labor force in the young adult years where unemployment is the highest. Age-standardized rates calculated by Russell indicate that changes in the age structure accounted for a rise of about 0.5 percent in national unemployment between 1970 and 1980.[23]

While all types of areas experienced this increase in unemployment, the increase was much greater in areas of population loss than in areas of rapid growth, as shown in Table 5.6. There was actually a weak positive relationship between unemployment in 1970 and growth in the following decade. The areas that grew rapidly had an average of 5.0 percent unemployment compared to the average of 4.3 percent for all areas. However, in 1980 this situation was reversed, and the highest unemployment rate was found in the areas with population loss. These changes are consistent with the assumption that population growth lags behind economic growth.

Retirement areas had lower unemployment than all other types of areas, and their increase in unemployment was comparable to that of moderately growing areas. The lower unemployment in these areas is related to their older age distributions and the fact that the highest rates of unemployment are found among young persons. The large influx of older persons into these areas had little impact on unemployment since most of these were retired and not looking for work.

Employment by Industry

In the preceding chapter, we discussed the changes in the industrial structure of the United States. Two major trends that were evident in

[23]Louise B. Russell, *The Baby Boom Generation and the Economy*, pp. 51–61.

TABLE 5.6

Percent Unemployed for Metropolitan Areas by Growth, 1970–1980

Metropolitan Growth	Percent Unemployed			Unemployed as Percentage of Expected Unemployed[a]		
	1970	1980	Change	1970	1980	Change
Loss	4.1	7.4	3.3	97.4	116.9	19.6
Low	4.2	6.4	2.3	100.3	103.9	3.6
Moderate	4.4	5.6	1.3	99.6	87.8	−11.8
Rapid	5.0	5.7	0.7	111.7	88.4	−23.3
Retirement Areas	3.7	4.9	1.2	85.1	78.1	−7.0
Total	4.3	6.3	2.0	100.0	100.0	0.0

[a] The expected unemployed is the number of persons who would be unemployed if each metropolitan area had the same unemployment rates by age and sex as the total metropolitan population.

the 1970s were the relative decline of manufacturing and the increase of nodal services, which include wholesale, transportation, communication, finance, and other business services. Between 1970 and 1980, manufacturing employment increased by only 7.7 percent, which was considerably less than the average increase in employment and led to a 4.0 percent decline in the percentage of employed persons who were working in manufacturing (see Table 5.7).

Changes in employment are largely caused by economic factors, which affect the competition among areas and give one area an advantage over another during a particular period of time. Although population change can have an effect on employment by changing the size and composition of the local labor force and the local market for goods and services, we argued in the preceding chapter that the causal relationship was stronger from employment growth to population growth than in the reverse direction. Thus, we should view changes in employment more as "correlates" of growth or decline than as "consequences" of growth or decline. It is important to understand how growing areas differed from declining areas in employment trends if we are to understand the consequences of these changes for income and other factors.

Areas of population decline experienced considerable decline in manufacturing employment. As a group, these areas lost 546,000 manufacturing jobs, or 11.2 percent of the manufacturing jobs that they had in 1970.[24] On the other hand, areas of moderate growth gained 807,000 manufacturing jobs and areas of rapid growth gained 643,000

[24] The losses of northern jobs due to plant closing and relocations are described in Barry Bluestone and Bennett Harrison, *The Deindustrialization of America* (New York: Basic Books, 1982).

TABLE 5.7

Employment in Manufacturing and Nodal Services for Metropolitan Areas by Growth, 1970–1980

Metropolitan Growth	Manufacturing Employment			Manufacturing as Percent of Total Employment		
	1970	1980	Growth	1970	1980	Chang
	(000's)	(000's)				
Loss	4,883	4,337	−11.2	29.4	24.7	−4.8
Slow	6,427	6,597	2.6	28.8	24.7	−4.1
Moderate	3,051	3,858	26.5	22.8	20.6	−2.3
Rapid	983	1,626	65.4	17.3	16.4	−0.9
Retirement Areas	233	352	51.1	14.7	13.4	−1.3
Total	15,577	16,770	7.7	26.2	22.2	−4.0

	Nodal Services Employment[a]			Nodal Services as Percent of Total Employment		
	1970	1980	Growth	1970	1980	Chang
	(000's)	(000's)				
Loss	4,154	4,822	16.1	25.0	27.4	2.4
Slow	5,067	6,777	33.7	22.7	25.4	2.7
Moderate	3,027	4,713	55.7	22.7	25.1	2.5
Rapid	1,295	2,572	98.6	22.8	25.9	3.1
Retirement Areas	399	740	85.5	25.2	28.2	3.0
Total	13,942	19,624	40.8	23.4	26.0	2.6

[a]Nodal services includes wholesale trade, transportation, communication, finance, insurance and re estate and business and repair services, and certain professional services.

manufacturing jobs. Since the declining areas were all located in the North, and most of the moderate and rapidly growing areas were in the South and West, there was considerable regional redistribution of manufacturing during the decade. When the growing areas of the North are combined with the declining areas, the net loss for the region is still 387,000 manufacturing jobs compared to gains of 750,000 and 830,000 in the South and West, respectively. At the end of the decade, areas of growth and decline were more similar in the proportion employed in manufacturing than they were in 1970, and the regions were also more similar in this respect. The distinctive manufacturing centers of the 1950s, such as Cleveland, Detroit, and Pittsburgh, had become less distinctive, while many of the smaller areas, which had been classified as regional trade centers, had added manufacturing and become more diversified.

The growing similarity of the industrial structure in metropolitan areas can also be seen for nodal services, although the variation among areas in the growth of nodal services was not as great as for manufacturing. These services, which are viewed as supportive of economic growth, increased in all types of areas more rapidly than the labor force as a whole (see panel 2 of Table 5.7). The proportion of employed persons in nodal services was highest in both declining areas and retirement areas in 1970, and this remained true in 1980, although the difference between these areas and the others declined somewhat over the decade.

During the 1970s there was considerable regional convergence in industrial structure among regions. While all regions experienced declines in the proportion of their labor force employed in manufacturing, the declines were greater in the North. For example, among metropolitan areas over 1 million, the northern metropolitan areas witnessed a reduction in manufacturing from 28.8 percent in 1970 to 24.3 percent in 1980, while the decrease in southern areas was only from 17.6 to 15.2 percent, and the western areas went from 22.8 to 21.2 percent (see Appendix Table B.5).

Occupational Structure

The arguments about the selectivity of migration and its effects, which were made in relation to education, would seem to apply equally well to the occupational structure of an area. In particular, it would seem reasonable to assume that declining areas lose their best workers as these workers are lured away by growing areas. In Table 5.8 we have shown the change in three groups of skilled workers from 1970 to 1980 by metropolitan growth. Because there was a major revision in the occupational classification scheme between these two censuses, it was necessary to recode the 1980 occupations into 1970 categories for comparison.[25]

The proportion of professionals and managers increased from 24.4 percent in 1970 to 29.1 percent in 1980 for metropolitan areas as a whole. Increases occurred in all areas and the relative growth in professionals and managers was actually greater in declining areas than in rapidly growing areas. While the rapidly growing areas had the highest proportion of professionals and managers in 1970 and continued to have the highest proportion in 1980, the inverse relationship between the

[25]Occupations were regrouped into 1970 categories to the extent possible using the detail available on Summary Tape File 4B for 1980. For some cases, it was necessary to divide a 1980 occupational category into two or more 1970 categories using national averages.

TABLE 5.8

Percentage Employed in Specific Occupations for Metropolitan Areas by Growth, 1970–1980

Metropolitan Growth	Professional or Manager			Clerical or Sales		
	1970	1980	Change	1970	1980	Chang
Loss	24.3	29.5	5.3	28.7	28.5	−0.2
Slow	24.1	28.9	4.8	27.1	27.3	0.2
Moderate	24.1	28.4	4.3	25.7	26.7	1.0
Rapid	26.7	30.6	3.8	26.2	27.0	0.8
Retirement Areas	23.4	28.0	4.6	27.1	28.4	1.3
Total	24.4	29.1	4.7	27.1	27.4	0.3

	Crafts Workers		
	1970	1980	Change
Loss	13.3	9.0	−4.2
Slow	13.9	9.4	−4.5
Moderate	14.1	9.6	−4.5
Rapid	13.7	9.1	−4.7
Retirement Areas	14.6	8.9	−5.7
Total	13.8	9.3	−4.5

NOTE: Occupations defined according to categories used in 1970 census.

change in this proportion and the growth of the area is contrary to the expectation that declining areas would lose disproportionately from their most highly skilled workers. However, it may be that the contraction of businesses leads to layoffs of relatively more blue collar workers than management and professional staff. If this were so, the decrease in the number of blue collar workers would account for the increase in the proportion of professionals and managers among those employed in declining areas.

There were relatively small changes in the proportions of clerical and sales workers by growth rates of metropolitan areas, although these were in the expected direction with relative increase among the moderate and rapid growth areas and little change among the areas with losses or slow growth.

Crafts workers declined in all areas relative to the total labor force. The proportion employed in these occupations fell from 13.8 to 9.3 percent for metropolitan areas as a whole during the 1970s. The relative decline was actually slightly greater in areas of rapid growth than in areas of loss or slow growth, but because of the large differences in the growth of the number of persons in the labor force among these areas, the rapidly growing areas as a group actually had an increase of about 121,000 crafts workers between 1970 and 1980, while declining areas had a loss of about 615,000 crafts workers.

These data contradict the assumption that areas of population decline have had disproportionate losses of their skilled workers. Considering all three groups, professionals and managers, clerical and sales, and crafts workers, areas with population loss have experienced a small increase in the proportion of these workers, while areas of rapid growth have experienced a slight decline. Although there was net migration of professionals and skilled workers from declining areas to growing areas, there was also migration of unskilled workers. In addition, many southern and western metropolitan areas had considerable immigration of low-skilled workers from Mexico and other countries during the 1970s, and this affected the overall distribution of their labor forces.

Income

We have already commented on the fact that the 1970s saw a reversal in the previous positive relationship between initial levels of income and population growth or net migration. This negative relationship is clearly seen in the mean incomes for 1969 by metropolitan growth, which are shown in Table 5.9. While persons in the rapidly growing areas had slightly higher initial incomes than those in areas with moderate growth, persons in both of these area groups had lower incomes than persons in slowly growing areas, and these, in turn, were lower than the incomes of persons in areas of population loss. These results are the same regardless of whether mean family income or per capita income is used.

Population growth had a positive effect on increases in income during the 1970s, as shown in Table 5.9. During the decade the increase in mean family income in metropolitan areas was 107 percent which, when adjusted for the increase in the Consumer Price Index, meant an increase of less than 5 percent in real income.[26] However, the income of families in areas of decline just kept up with the cost of living, while families in areas of moderate and rapid growth had real income gains of 9.7 and 11.6 percent, respectively.

The overall gains in per capita income for the decade were substantially greater than those for family income, amounting to an increase of 136.7 percent for all metropolitan areas and a real income gain of 19.6

[26]The increase in the Consumer Price Index, based on the averages for 1969 and 1979, was 98 percent. U.S. Bureau of the Census, "Money Income of Households, Families, and Persons in the United States, 1983," *Current Population Reports*, P-60, no. 146, 1984, p. 214.

TABLE 5.9

Family and Per Capita Income for Metropolitan Areas by Growth, 1970–1980

Metropolitan Growth	Mean Family Income[a]			Per Capita Income[a]			
	1969	1979	Percent Growth	Real Growth	1969	1979	Percent Growth	Real Growth
Loss	12,670	25,090	98.0	0.0	3,590	8,020	123.4	12.8
Slow	12,180	25,210	107.0	4.5	3,470	8,160	135.2	18.8
Moderate	10,620	23,070	117.2	9.7	2,990	7,520	151.5	27.0
Rapid	11,080	24,490	121.0	11.6	3,120	7,960	155.1	28.9
Retirement Areas	10,590	22,000	107.7	4.9	3,290	7,770	136.2	19.3
Total	11,800	24,430	107.0	4.6	3,350	7,930	136.7	19.6

NOTES: Percent growth is calculated as a percent of 1970 income. Real growth is deflated by growth in the Consumer Price Index (98 percent).

[a]Income in current dollars, rounded to nearest $10.

percent. The differences between the trends for family income and those for personal income are due to two factors. First, the reduction in average family size during the decade meant that the same family income translated into more income per person among those in families. Second, the growth in income for persons who were not in families was greater than that for persons in families.[27]

The average gains in per capita income exceeded the increases in cost of living for all of the growth categories. These gains ranged from about 123 percent in areas of population loss to about 155 percent in areas of rapid growth. In terms of real income these gains were equivalent to 12.8 percent for declining areas and 28.9 percent for rapidly growing areas (see column 8 of Table 5.9).

Since many of the areas with the most rapid growth were in the South and incomes had been lowest in that region in 1970, the positive effect of growth on income resulted in a relative gain for the South and a reduction in the regional differences in income (see Appendix Table B.6). Among SMSAs under 1 million, per capita income in the North had exceeded that in the South by 17 percent in 1970, but by only 8 percent in 1980. This trend toward regional convergence in income is part of a long-term trend from 1929 to the present, which has been studied by Garnick and Friedenberg.[28]

Poverty

The poverty level used in the 1970 and 1980 censuses is set at roughly three times the minimum cost of food needed to provide a nutritionally adequate diet.[29] While this level is adjusted for household composition and is updated annually based on the Consumer Price Index, no adjustment is made for differences in costs among metropolitan areas. The measure has also been criticized because no adjustments are made for taxes or for nonmonetary transfers, such as food stamps and medical benefits.[30] Nevertheless, the proportions of families and persons below the poverty level are useful measures because they provide a rough indicator of income relative to need.

[27]Paul Ryscavage, "Reconciling Divergent Trends in Real Income," *Monthly Labor Review* (July 1986): 24–29.

[28]Daniel H. Garnick and Howard L. Friedenberg, "Accounting for Regional Differences in Per Capita Personal Income Growth, 1929–79," *Survey of Current Business* (Sept. 1982): 24–34.

[29]U.S. Bureau of the Census, *1980 Census of Population, Detailed Characteristics of the Population*, U.S. Summary, Section A: United States, March 1984, Appendix B, pp. 18–20.

[30]Reynolds Farley, *Blacks and Whites: Narrowing the Gap* (Cambridge, MA: Harvard University Press, 1984), pp. 157–167.

Between 1969 and 1979 there was very little change in the proportion of families or persons who were below the official poverty level (see Table 5.10). This appearance of stability was quickly removed by the increases in poverty from 1980 to 1983.[31] However, it can be argued that comparisons to these later years are somewhat misleading because they represent peaks in the economic cycle of unemployment and poverty and that it is more appropriate to compare years that are at equivalent points in the economic cycle. If the year for which census data are collected is compared with the average for the five surrounding years, then both 1969 and 1979 appear to be at equivalent points in the economic cycle of poverty. In 1969 the proportion of persons in poverty was about 0.7 percent below the five-year average, and in 1979 it was 0.6 percent below the five-year average.[32]

While there was little change in poverty for metropolitan areas as a whole between 1969 and 1979, there were significant changes for some metropolitan areas. In 1969 the areas of population decline or slow growth had considerably lower proportions of families and persons in poverty than the areas that grew moderately or rapidly during the following decade, but these areas experienced increases in the proportions in poverty over the decade while the other areas experienced declines in the proportions in poverty. As a result, the proportions in poverty were much more similar at the end of the decade than they were at the beginning.

The changes in poverty were most dramatic for the metropolitan areas of the South with populations of less than 1 million, for which the proportion of families in poverty declined from 14.1 to 10.9 percent (see Appendix Table B.7). Most of these areas were in the moderate growth category and some were in the high growth category. Growth seems to have been particularly beneficial to these areas. Since most of the retirement areas fall in this category, it is significant to note that these areas experienced declines in the proportion in poverty similar to the other southern areas, indicating that the large influx of elderly had not increased the need for assistance to low-income families.

In the West there was little overall change in poverty during the decade although the smaller areas, which had had somewhat higher levels of poverty in 1969, experienced a decrease while the larger areas had a small increase in poverty. In the North both the larger and smaller areas had an increase in poverty due to the decline or slow growth of

---

[31]By 1983 the proportion of persons in poverty had increased to 15.2 percent. U.S. Bureau of the Census, "Characteristics of Population Below the Poverty Level: 1983," *Current Population Reports*, P-60, no. 147 (February 1985).

[32]Ibid.

TABLE 5.10

*Percentage of Families and Persons in Poverty for Metropolitan Areas by Growth,
1970–1980*

Metropolitan Growth	Families Below Poverty Level			Persons Below Poverty Level		
	1970	1980	Change	1970	1980	Change
Loss	7.4	9.2	1.8	9.7	11.5	1.9
Slow	7.5	8.0	0.5	9.8	10.5	0.7
Moderate	11.2	9.3	−1.9	14.0	12.3	−1.7
Rapid	10.3	8.6	−1.7	12.9	11.6	−1.4
Retirement Areas	10.9	8.8	−2.1	14.2	12.1	−2.0
Total	8.7	8.7	0.0	11.2	11.4	0.2

NOTE: Poverty was defined at each census based on a national standard.

most of these areas. In those northern areas where there was more rapid growth, there was also a decline in the proportion in poverty.

Overall, the changes in the proportions in poverty are similar to the changes in income. The growth of southern metropolitan areas during the 1970s improved incomes and reduced poverty in areas that had been worse than the nation on both measures, with the result that the southern metropolitan areas became more similar to the rest of the nation in 1979.

Housing Quality and Costs

Population growth creates a demand for new housing. Since new housing is likely to be more costly than existing housing, growth can be expected to increase the average cost of housing in an area.[33] When growth is moderate, the increased cost may be a reasonable exchange for the better quality of the newer housing. However, rapid growth may lead to excessive demand for housing and this could both increase the cost of housing and lead to sacrifices in quality of construction.

In contrast, slow growth or population decline is likely to mean that most of the available housing in an area is relatively old housing. Although such housing is likely to be cheaper than new housing, it may be of poorer quality if it has been allowed to deteriorate, does not conform to newer building codes or construction standards, or does not

[33]Athena Kottis, "Impact of Migration on Housing in Urban Areas," *Annals of Regional Science* 5:1 (June 1971): 117–124.

take account of changing housing preferences. For example, newer homes tend to have better insulation, more electrical outlets, and more bathrooms than older houses.

It is not possible to obtain measures of all of these aspects of housing quality for all metropolitan areas. However, enough measures are available to enable some conclusions to be drawn about the relationship between population growth and housing. We shall begin by examining trends in homeownership.

Homeownership

Between 1970 and 1980 the proportion of metropolitan households that owned their homes increased slightly from 60.5 to 61.6 percent (see Table 5.11). This is slightly less than the increase from 62.9 to 64.4 percent for the total population.[34] The increase, while not very large, is surprising given the decrease in the proportion of households that were families and the decrease in average housing size. It is also surprising, given the concern over the "crisis" in the affordability of homes during this period.[35] The increase in homeownership was related, in part, to the continuing suburbanization of the population and the fact that a higher proportion of suburban housing was owner-occupied than was central city housing. Another important factor was the increased income available to elderly households, which enabled more of them to remain in their own homes than had been possible in the past, despite the fact that most of these households had only one or two persons.

The increase in homeownership was greatest in areas of population loss or slow growth. Areas with moderate growth experienced hardly any increase in the proportion owning homes, and areas of rapid growth and retirement areas had a decline in the proportion owning homes. This is consistent with our expectations based on the effects of growth on housing supply and upon the age composition of area populations. The growth of population within a fixed geographical area means an increased demand for land. Since rental units typically require less land than owner units, growth should lead to a decrease in the proportion of homeowners and an increase in renters. Conversely, there is much less demand for housing in declining areas, and this enables some households to become homeowners who would not be able to do so in the

---

[34]U.S. Bureau of the Census, *Statistical Abstract of the United States 1985*, p. 735.

[35]Thomas K. Rudel, "Changes in the Access to Homeownership During the 1970s," *Economic Geography* (1985), pp. 37–49. Congressional Budget Office, *Homeownership: The Changing Relationship of Costs and Income and Possible Federal Roles* (Washington, DC: U.S. Government Printing Office, 1977); and Bernard J. Frieden, "The New Housing Cost Problem," *The Public Interest* 49 (1977): 70–78.

Consequences of Growth and Decline

TABLE 5.11

Percentage of Owner-Occupied Housing Units
for Metropolitan Areas by Growth, 1970–1980

Metropolitan Growth	1970	1980	Change
Loss	56.0	57.2	1.1
Slow	60.4	61.8	1.4
Moderate	64.0	64.1	0.1
Rapid	63.0	62.7	−0.3
Retirement Areas	68.2	68.1	−0.2
Total	60.5	61.6	1.1

more competitive markets in growing areas.[36] Furthermore, growing areas have a younger age distribution with a higher proportion of young adults who have not reached the life cycle stages when homeownership predominates, so that there may be less demand for owner-occupied housing in these areas.

Although the changes are in the expected direction, it is important to relate these changes to the variation in the initial levels of homeownership. Declining areas had much lower levels of homeownership in 1970 than did the moderately and rapidly growing areas. Even though homeownership increased in these areas, the level of homeownership in declining areas was 5.5 percent below that in rapidly growing areas in 1980 and 6.9 percent below that in moderately growing areas. Part of the increase in homeownership among the total metropolitan population can be attributed to the movement of people from areas with relatively low levels of homeownership to areas with higher levels of homeownership. The declining areas are dominated by older northern metropolitan areas, such as New York, Cleveland, Detroit, and Philadelphia, which have high population densities and correspondingly lower levels of homeownership than the newer, growing areas of the South and West. For example, Dallas, Denver, Houston, and San Diego all have population densities that are one-third to one-half those of Cleveland, Detroit, and Philadelphia, and less than one-tenth the density of the New York SMSA.[37]

[36]Because the number of households grew more rapidly than the population in the 1970s, many areas with declining populations had either no change or growth in the number of households.

[37]Densities were calculated from populations and land areas of metropolitan areas as defined for the 1980 census. Because SMSAs are constructed from entire counties, many contain rural areas at their periphery. For these SMSAs the density of the SMSA is not always an accurate reflection of density of the urban parts of these areas. One alternative is to use the density of the central cities. These data, which appear in Table 7.1, also show significantly higher densities for the declining areas than for the growing areas.

Thus, during the 1970s the movement of population toward lower-density areas has reduced the overall competition for metropolitan land and has made it easier for households to obtain land for single-family housing. Land is, however, only one of the factors affecting the affordability of housing, and it is important to look at the effect of construction costs and other factors on the actual cost of housing.

Housing Value and Rent

The censuses of 1970 and 1980 asked two questions which provide measures of housing costs. Homeowners were asked to estimate the current value of their homes, while renters were asked for their total monthly rent, which includes utility costs. The value of a house is only a crude indicator of costs because the answer to that question depends upon the householder's knowledge of the local real estate market. If the householder has recently moved in, or lives in a neighborhood with much turnover, he or she may have a fairly accurate estimate of the value of the housing. However, a resident in a stable neighborhood, who has not moved for many years, may not have a very accurate estimate. If there has been considerable inflation, as was the case in the 1970s, residents in stable areas may underestimate the value of their homes.

In addition to the problem of estimating the value of homes, there is a further difficulty in assuming that costs are proportional to value. First, utility rates, mortgage rates, and other operating costs vary considerably from one region of the country to another. Second, since homeownership is an investment, the ultimate costs of owning a home depend upon the resale value. Residents of rapidly growing areas may be able to sell their homes for a greater profit than residents of declining or slowly growing areas because of the greater demand for housing. If this is true, than they can afford to make greater investments in purchasing homes.

The expectation that housing values would increase more in growing areas than in declining areas is clearly supported by the data presented in Table 5.12. The rate of increase in housing values in rapidly growing areas was almost double that in declining areas and considerably above that of areas with slow or moderate growth. The declining areas, which were mainly large northern areas, had the highest housing values in 1970, but they had lower values in 1980 than all areas except for the retirement areas.

Rents, which may be a more accurate reflection of actual housing costs, showed less variation by rate of growth. However, the areas of moderate and rapid growth had considerably higher increases in rent than the areas of slow growth or decline. Rents do not exactly parallel the values of owner-occupied housing. For example, while the declining

136

TABLE 5.12

*Value of Owner-Occupied Units and Rent of Renter-Occupied Units
for Metropolitan Areas by Growth, 1970–1980*

Metropolitan Growth	Value of Owner-Occupied Units			Monthly Rent of Renter Units		
	1970 ($1000's)	1980 ($1,000's)	Growth (percent)	1970 (dollars)	1980 (dollars)	Growth (percent)
Loss	23.3	44.2	89.3	122.2	263.1	115.4
Slow	22.2	51.9	134.1	119.8	262.5	119.1
Moderate	18.6	44.7	140.1	103.4	251.0	142.7
Rapid	20.8	57.3	176.3	114.5	287.0	150.7
Retirement Areas	19.2	39.2	103.8	124.8	277.9	122.7
Total	21.4	48.5	127.1	116.9	263.7	125.6

areas had the highest rents in 1970, except for retirement areas, the declining areas continued to have higher rents than areas with slow or moderate growth in 1980.

Because there is considerable variation in housing costs by both region and size of metropolitan area within the United States, it is important to examine the relationship between growth and housing costs within each region and size category. In both 1970 and 1980, housing values were highest in the West and lowest in the South. Values were also considerably higher in large metropolitan areas than in small areas. For example, in 1980 the average value of owner-occupied homes in large metropolitan areas of the West was $77,500 compared to only $36,300 for small areas in the South.

The increase in housing values was directly proportional to growth in all but one of the region and size categories (see Appendix Table B.8). The exception is the large areas of the West. Among these, the slow growth category contains only two metropolitan areas, Los Angeles and San Francisco. Despite their slow growth, housing values increased by 213 percent over the decade, which is much higher than the national average of 127 percent. While high cost of housing in these two areas may have been a deterrent to further growth, there have also been growth restrictions imposed by suburban communities concerned with the ill effects of continued growth.[38]

While housing values in the West continued to grow at higher than average rates during the 1970s, there was some convergence in values between the North and the South. The average values in small northern

[38]David E. Dowall, *The Suburban Squeeze: Land Conversion and Regulation in the San Francisco Bay Area* (Berkeley: University of California Press, 1984), as cited in Thomas K. Rudel, "Changes in Access to Homeownership During the 1970s."

areas were 18 percent above those in large southern areas in 1970, but only 9 percent above them in 1980. For large areas the values in the South increased sufficiently to put them above northern areas in 1980.

Housing Unit Size and Density

Since housing costs increase with rates of local growth, people in growing areas may have to accept smaller housing units and a greater density of persons per room. This does not appear to have been the case during the 1970s. The average size of housing units in metropolitan areas in the United States increased from 5.27 rooms to 5.65 rooms between 1970 and 1980, and the increase was slightly greater in areas of rapid growth than in areas of loss (see Table 5.13). Although costs of housing were higher in the rapidly growing areas, this did not lead to a reduction in the size of units. To the contrary, the growing areas appear to have benefited from a national trend toward the construction of larger units. For example, between 1970 and 1980 the average size of new single family homes increased from 1500 to 1740 square feet and the proportion of units with two or more bathrooms increased from 48 to 73 percent.[39] These increases in housing unit size are all the more remarkable given the declines in the average household size which occurred during the decade. Since there was more new construction in the rapidly growing areas, the averages for these areas increased more than they did in declining areas.

There is also no evidence that rapid growth resulted in greater crowding within housing units during the 1970s. There is very little variation in the number of persons per room in relation to rate of growth in either 1970 or 1980. In all areas, room crowding declined as the average number of persons per housing unit declined and the average size of unit increased. The decline in persons per room was slightly greater in areas of rapid growth than in areas of decline, which is just the opposite of what was expected. These changes are mainly a result of the larger sizes of newly constructed units because there was virtually no difference in the average household size among areas with different rates of growth.

Quality of Housing

Although the 1970 and 1980 censuses contained several items about housing, there are very few measures that can be used to measure

[39]U.S. Bureau of the Census, *Statistical Abstract of the United States 1985*, table 1303, p. 728.

TABLE 5.13

*Number of Rooms per Unit and Persons per Room for Metropolitan Areas
by Growth, 1970–1980*

Metropolitan Growth	Mean Rooms per Unit			Mean Persons per Room		
	1970	1980	Change	1970	1980	Change
Loss	5.23	5.57	0.34	0.60	0.50	−0.10
Slow	5.27	5.66	0.39	0.60	0.49	−0.11
Moderate	5.36	5.73	0.37	0.61	0.49	−0.11
Rapid	5.25	5.70	0.45	0.62	0.50	−0.12
Retirement Areas	4.90	5.46	0.56	0.58	0.46	−0.12
Total	5.27	5.65	0.38	0.61	0.50	−0.11

the quality of housing. Although earlier censuses had rated housing as dilapidated or sound, this item was found to vary widely from one enumerator to another and, in 1970, it was dropped from the census.[40] Since then, the main measure of housing quality in the census has been whether or not the housing has complete plumbing and kitchen facilities. However, by 1970 only 3.2 percent of metropolitan housing lacked complete plumbing or kitchen facilities and there was not enough variation in this percentage among areas to use this item as a measure of quality.

One measure of quality, which does provide considerable variation among areas, is whether or not the housing unit has air-conditioning. Air-conditioning has been cited as one of the factors that was important for the growth of the southern region in the 1960s and 1970s.[41] In 1950 only a small proportion of southern housing units had air-conditioning. By 1960 this had increased to 18 percent, and between 1970 and 1980 it increased from 63 to 78 percent.[42]

The relationship between the increase in air-conditioning and growth is shown in Table 5.14. In 1970 the areas which grew rapidly during the decade had much higher proportions of housing with air-conditioning than the areas with slow growth. However, the 1970s was a period when air-conditioning became widespread throughout the South, and areas which had relatively low proportions of housing units air-conditioned at the beginning of the decade experienced large in-

[40]U.S. Bureau of the Census, *Twenty Censuses—Population and Housing Questions 1790–1980* (Washington, 1979).

[41]John D. Kasarda, "The Implications of Contemporary Redistribution Trends for National Urban Policy," *Social Science Quarterly* 61:3–4 (December 1980): 373–400.

[42]U.S. Bureau of the Census, *U.S. Census of Housing 1960*, U.S. Summary—States and Small Areas, 1963.

TABLE 5.14

Percentage of Housing Units in the Southern Region
with Air-Conditioning for Metropolitan Areas
by Growth, 1970–1980

Metropolitan Growth	1970	1980	Change
AREAS UNDER ONE MILLION			
Slow	53.7	71.9	18.2
Moderate	57.6	73.9	16.3
Rapid	67.5	79.2	11.7
Retirement Areas	65.7	81.4	15.7
Total	58.3	74.7	16.4
AREAS OF ONE MILLION OR MORE			
Slow	61.1	75.3	14.2
Moderate	72.4	82.2	9.8
Rapid	84.5	90.1	5.6
Retirement Areas	72.4	87.0	14.6
Total	70.4	82.6	12.2
ALL AREAS			
Slow	57.2	73.5	16.3
Moderate	61.6	76.2	14.6
Rapid	74.8	84.0	9.1
Retirement Areas	70.3	85.1	14.8
Total	63.0	77.8	14.8

creases in air-conditioning.[43] As a result, increases in air-conditioning were greatest in the areas with slow growth. These areas still lagged behind the rapidly growing areas in 1980, but the differences were smaller than in 1970. This means that if the availability of air-conditioning was a factor in determining which southern metropolitan areas grew during the 1970s, it should be less of a factor in the 1980s because it was more uniformly available throughout the South.

Additional items on housing quality are available from the Annual Housing Survey for a sample of metropolitan areas, which contains

[43]These differences in the increase in air-conditioning are consistent with a diffusion of an innovation model, whereby the rate of increase is proportional to the proportion of households in an area who have the innovation, multiplied by the proportion who do not have it. In such a model, the most rapid adoption occurs when the proportion having the innovation is 50 percent. By the time that 80 percent have the innovation, the adoption rate is reduced to 64 percent of the maximum.

most of the areas over 1 million. In Table 5.15, we have presented the results of a question that asked all households to rate their neighborhood as a place to live. This provides a summary measure of the residential environment in different metropolitan areas.

In general, the ratings for growing areas are better than those in declining and slowly growing areas. For example, the proportion of owners who rated their neighborhood as excellent increased from 38.5 percent in declining areas to 46.8 percent in rapidly growing areas, while the proportion of renters who gave an excellent rating increased from 18.5 to 24.3 percent. Conversely, the proportions of owners and renters who thought that their neighborhoods were only fair or poor was highest in the declining areas.

There is considerable variation among metropolitan areas in neighborhood ratings, which suggests that these results need to be interpreted with some caution. The six areas with the lowest ratings include three declining areas: New York, Newark, and Detroit, and one from each of the other three growth categories: Los Angeles (slow), New Orleans (moderate), and Houston (rapid). Similarly, the areas with the highest ratings included two slow growing areas: Minneapolis and

TABLE 5.15

*Opinions of Neighborhood by Owners and Renters
in Selected Metropolitan Areas of Over 1 Million
by Rate of Growth*

Rate of Growth 1970–1980	Excellent	Good	Fair or Poor	Total
OWNER'S RATINGS (PERCENTAGE)				
Loss	38.5	46.1	15.4	100.0
Slow	44.4	42.8	12.8	100.0
Moderate	46.3	41.3	12.4	100.0
Rapid	46.8	40.1	13.1	100.0
Total	42.6	43.6	13.8	100.0
RENTER'S RATINGS (PERCENTAGE)				
Loss	18.5	46.5	35.0	100.0
Slow	22.2	47.0	30.8	100.0
Moderate	23.6	48.6	27.8	100.0
Rapid	24.3	49.1	26.6	100.0
Total	21.1	47.1	31.8	100.0

SOURCE: U.S. Bureau of Census, *Annual Housing Surveys, 1978–1981.* Includes 27 metropolitan areas of over 1 million. The questions asked, "How would you rate this neighborhood as a place to live—would you say it is excellent, good, fair, or poor?"

Washington, and two rapidly growing areas: Anaheim and San Diego. Thus, while growth is positively related to subjective ratings of metropolitan neighborhoods, there are clearly other factors that affect these ratings which are not fully understood.

Conclusion

Growth and decline can have many effects on metropolitan areas and their populations. In this chapter we have examined some of these effects and, in many instances, the differences between growing and declining areas were less than had been expected. The 1970s was a period in which some of the preceding growth trends were reversed, so that many of the areas experiencing higher than average growth in the 1970s had not had greater than average growth in earlier decades, and many of the declining areas had been areas of relative growth in the past. In particular, many southern areas, which had lagged behind the rest of the nation both in population growth and in per capita income and other status measures, experienced significant population growth and improvement in status during the 1970s.

For many of the measures studied, the effects of growth were to reduce differences among areas and, because of this, it was important to consider the 1980 measures in relation to the change over the decade. This required constructing measures for 1970 for the metropolitan areas as they were defined in 1980, limiting the number of variables which could be studied.

One of the most noticeable effects of growth and decline is on the age distributions of metropolitan populations. Because migrants tend to be concentrated in the young adult years, the populations in areas of rapid growth are relatively younger than the populations of declining areas. However, during the 1970s there was an exception to this pattern for 11 metropolitan areas in Florida, which attracted significant numbers of elderly migrants with the result that their populations became significantly older relative to those in other metropolitan areas. Although elderly moved to several other metropolitan areas in the United States, it was only in these areas of Florida that they constituted a large enough proportion of the total growth to significantly affect the age distribution of the entire area.

Another consequence of differential rates of migration for different groups was that the proportion of the population of declining areas that was black increased much more than did the proportion black in growing areas. While the proportion black increased in all types of areas because of continued nonmetropolitan to metropolitan migration of blacks and black birthrates, which were higher than white rates, blacks appeared not to participate in the movement from declining areas to growing areas to the same extent that whites did. This observation will be discussed further in the next chapter.

Migration rates also differed by education so that migrants were better educated than nonmigrants. However, this fact seemed to have little impact on changes in educational levels between growing and declining areas because of rapid increases in the proportion of the population with higher levels of education in all areas.

The differences between growth and decline had a much greater impact on employment trends in different metropolitan areas. In declining and slowly growing areas, the proportion of adults participating in the labor force declined and unemployment increased relative to the nation as a whole, while the reverse was the case in more rapidly growing areas. Declining areas suffered significant losses of manufacturing employment, while rapidly growing areas experienced increases in manufacturing. Employment in business services that were not tied directly to local consumption also varied in relation to growth, although all types of areas experienced some employment growth in this expanding sector of the economy. Despite the different employment trends between growing and declining areas, declining areas managed to maintain a relatively high quality labor force, as measured by the proportion employed in professional and managerial occupations. These results suggest that the fears of Bluestone and Harrison and other writers that the northern metropolitan areas were losing their best workers may be unfounded.[44]

There were also clear trends in the relationship between growth and changes in income and poverty. In declining areas the growth in family income barely kept pace with the increase in the cost of living during the decade, while growing areas did significantly better. Declining areas did somewhat better in terms of per capita income because of the reduction in average family size over the decade, but in real terms the gains in per capita income in rapidly growing areas were about double those in declining areas. Poverty increased in declining and slowly growing areas and declined in areas of higher growth. Since many of the rapidly growing areas had had significantly lower incomes and higher proportions in poverty in 1970 than the declining areas, the changes over the decade resulted in a convergence of average incomes and poverty among metropolitan areas.

In housing the main effects of growth were to increase values and rents much more rapidly in areas with moderate or rapid growth than in

[44]Barry Bluestone and Bennett Harrison, *Deindustrialization.*

areas of loss or slow growth. In declining areas outmigration appears to have allowed for a small increase in the proportion of persons who are homeowners, although in 1980 the level of homeownership in these areas still remained lower than the national average. Because migration was in the direction of lower-density metropolitan areas, there was little effect of growth on the number of persons per room in housing units. In subjective terms, residents of growing areas appeared to be more satisfied with their neighborhoods than those in areas of loss or slow growth, although this was not uniformly true for all areas.

In summary, the results presented in this chapter do not point to many ill effects of rapid growth during the 1970s. While housing costs increased, so did incomes, and it is hard to find much evidence that housing quality was adversely affected by rapid growth. Decline, on the other hand, has created some problems. Declining areas have experienced high unemployment, which may be related more to the economic decline that resulted in the population decline than to the population decline per se. However, the exodus of young adults with above-average education and occupational skills has resulted in a growing concentration of elderly, blacks, and persons below the poverty level in these areas. In the next chapter we shall examine the situation of blacks in these metropolitan areas in greater detail.

6

GROWTH
OF THE BLACK POPULATION
IN METROPOLITAN AREAS

I F THE transformation of the total population from rural to urban in the twentieth century was dramatic, the transformation of the black population was spectacular. In 1900 over three-quarters of the black population of the United States lived in rural areas, and all but a very small proportion of the rural blacks lived in the South. By 1960, 73 percent of blacks lived in urban areas and the majority of the urban blacks lived outside the South.[1] Between 1900 and 1980 there were large movements of blacks from the rural South to urban areas in the North. As many as three-quarters of the members of some cohorts of rural southern blacks left the South for other regions, and almost all of these went to urban areas.[2] This migration was strongest between 1940 and 1960 when there was manufacturing growth in the North. Although this movement slowed during the 1960s and 1970s, the concentration of blacks in metropolitan areas continued to increase.

The rapid growth of the black population in metropolitan areas raises several interesting questions which will be explored in this chapter. First, how did the growth of the black metropolitan population in each decade relate to the growth of the population of whites and others? Given the original concentration of blacks in the South, were there

---

[1]Daniel O. Price, *Changing Characteristics of the Negro Population,* U.S. Bureau of the Census (Washington, DC: U.S. Government Printing Office, 1969).
[2]Price, *Changing Characteristics of the Negro Population,* p. 22.

variations among regions in the growth of metropolitan blacks? Did blacks participate in the general trend toward population deconcentration during the 1970s?

A second set of questions relates to the determinants of growth of the black population in specific metropolitan areas. To what extent can the models, which were used to explain net migration and employment growth for the total population, be used to explain black growth in metropolitan areas?

Finally, the chapter will address questions related to the consequences of metropolitan growth and decline for blacks. Given that the black population is more heavily concentrated in areas that declined from 1970 to 1980, how have blacks in these areas fared compared with blacks in growing areas or with whites and others?

It can be argued that blacks played transitional roles in the transformation of the manufacturing sector in response to foreign competition. Faced with increasing competition of manufactured goods from low-wage countries in the 1960s, some American firms responded by hiring blacks and other minorities who were available and willing to work for lower-than-average wages. This encouraged many blacks to move to areas where these firms were located, which were initially the northern metropolitan areas. In the late 1960s and 1970s many of these firms relocated plants in southern metropolitan areas to take advantage of lower wages there, and this created new opportunities for blacks in the South. However, as these steps proved inadequate to meet foreign competition in the 1970s, many manufacturing plants closed or moved operations abroad, and the blacks they had employed were left in declining metropolitan areas.[3] Much of the data presented in this chapter support this description of the black metropolitan experience, but we shall see that this oversimplification ignores trends in black education, black involvement in the service sector, and modest improvements in black income.

Black Growth in Metropolitan Areas

Between 1950 and 1980 the black population in metropolitan areas grew at more than twice the rate of growth of whites and others. Using constant 1980 boundaries, the black metropolitan population increased

[3]This issue is discussed by John D. Kasarda, "Urban Change and Minority Opportunities," in Paul Peterson, ed., *The New Urban Reality* (Washington, DC: The Brookings Institution, 1985); and by Bennett Harrison and Edward Hill, "The Changing Structure of Jobs in Older and Younger Cities," in Benjamin Chinitz, ed., *Central City Economic Development* (Cambridge, MA: Abt Books).

122 percent compared to only 57 percent for whites and persons of other races (see Table 6.1). The increase in the black metropolitan population was strongest in the 1950s and 1960s, when there were absolute declines in the number of blacks in nonmetropolitan areas. In the 1970s, when the rate of total population growth of nonmetropolitan areas exceeded that for metropolitan areas for the first time in the century, the rate of black growth in metropolitan areas declined, but still remained above the rate of growth of blacks in nonmetropolitan areas. Although blacks did not participate in the nonmetropolitan turnaround of the 1970s, their rate of movement from nonmetropolitan to metropolitan areas slowed considerably. Even so, by 1980, over 81 percent of blacks lived in metropolitan areas, compared to about 74 percent of whites and others.

The growth of blacks in metropolitan and nonmetropolitan areas varied considerably by region (see Table 6.2). In the North the black population in metropolitan areas increased at about two times the national rate during the 1960s, implying that there was considerable migration toward northern metropolitan areas, while blacks in nonmetropolitan areas of the North increased at a rate well below the national growth rate. However, in the 1970s the growth of the black population in the North fell below the national average and there was little difference between metropolitan and nonmetropolitan areas.

The trends in the growth of the southern black population were opposite those of the North. In the 1960s, while northern metropolitan areas gained blacks, southern areas grew somewhat less than the national average, implying net outmigration of blacks. However, in the 1970s, southern metropolitan areas grew more rapidly than the national average. Throughout both decades, nonmetropolitan areas of the South experienced outmigration of blacks. In the first of these decades the outmigration was sufficient to cause a considerable decline in the nonmetropolitan black population. Had the black population in southern nonmetropolitan areas grown at the national growth rate of 19.6 percent during the 1960s, there would have been 5.7 million blacks in these areas in 1970 instead of the 4.4 million counted in the census. Roughly 1.4 million blacks left nonmetropolitan areas of the South during the 1960s and most of these went to northern metropolitan areas.[4] Similar calculations for the 1970s indicate that only about 0.5 million blacks left nonmetropolitan areas of the South in the 1970s and that most of these went to southern metropolitan areas.

---

[4]This calculation assumes that the rates of natural increase in metropolitan and nonmetropolitan areas were equal. The estimated migration streams for 1960 to 1970 are consistent with the total interregional streams from 1965 to 1970 which were published in U.S. Bureau of the Census, *1970 Census of Population, General Social and Economic Characteristics*, U.S. Summary, table 131.

TABLE 6.1
Growth of the Total Population and Black Population Within Metropolitan and Nonmetropolitan Areas, 1950–1980
(constant 1980 boundaries)

	Population in Thousands				Percentage Growth		
	1950	1960	1970	1980	1950–1960	1960–1970	1970–1980
TOTAL POPULATION							
Metropolitan	104,842	132,048	154,585	170,493	25.9	17.1	10.3
Nonmetropolitan	46,484	47,276	48,717	56,053	1.7	3.0	15.1
Total	151,326	179,323	203,302	226,546	18.5	13.4	11.4
BLACK POPULATION[a]							
Metropolitan	9,665	13,745	17,858	21,480	42.2	29.9	20.3
Nonmetropolitan	5,381	5,128	4,722	5,015	−4.7	−7.9	6.2
Total	15,045	18,872	22,580	26,495	25.4	19.6	17.3
WHITE AND OTHER POPULATION							
Metropolitan	95,178	118,303	136,727	149,013	24.3	15.6	9.0
Nonmetropolitan	41,103	42,148	43,995	51,038	2.5	4.4	16.0
Total	136,281	160,451	180,722	200,051	17.7	12.6	10.7

[a]1950 black population estimated by multiplying percentage nonwhite in 1950 by percentage of nonwhites in 1960 who were black.

TABLE 6.2

Growth of Black Population, 1960–1980,
in Metropolitan and Nonmetropolitan Areas
by Region (constant 1980 boundaries)

Region and Metropolitan/ Nonmetropolitan	Population in Thousands			Percentage Growth	
	1960	1970	1980	1960–1970	1970–1980
NORTH					
Metropolitan	6,204	8,625	9,866	39.0	14.4
Nonmetropolitan	250	268	306	7.2	14.2
Total	6,454	8,893	10,172	37.8	14.4
SOUTH					
Metropolitan	6,512	7,599	9,420	16.7	24.0
Nonmetropolitan	4,805	4,368	4,630	−9.1	6.0
Total	11,317	11,967	14,050	5.7	17.4
WEST					
Metropolitan	1,029	1,635	2,195	58.9	34.3
Nonmetropolitan	48	57	66	17.7	16.8
Total	1,077	1,691	2,261	57.0	33.7
U.S. TOTAL					
Metropolitan	13,744	17,859	21,481	29.9	20.3
Nonmetropolitan	5,104	4,692	5,002	−8.1	6.6
Total	18,848	22,551	26,483	19.6	17.4

In 1960 less than 6 percent of the total U.S. black population lived in the West region, and over 95 percent of these lived in metropolitan areas. During both the 1960s and the 1970s the black population in metropolitan areas of the West grew much more rapidly than that of the nation as a whole, while the rate of growth of blacks in nonmetropolitan areas of the West approached the national averages. As a result the proportion of all blacks living in the West increased to 8.5 percent by 1980. While they did participate in the general movement of people to the West during this period, blacks were still much more of a minority in the West than in other regions. In 1980 only 6.2 percent of the metropolitan population of the West was black, which is about one-half the average for the rest of the nation.[5]

Although blacks did not participate in the nonmetropolitan turn-

[5]In 1980 the proportion of the metropolitan population that was black was 11.7 percent in the North, 18.7 percent in the South, and 6.2 percent in the West.

TABLE 6.3

Percentage Growth of Black Population, 1970–1980,
by Region and Size of Metropolitan Area in 1980

SMSA Size	Region			U.S. Total
	North	South	West	
Under 250,000	24.3	23.0	50.6	23.7
250–999,999	20.9	21.7	53.3	22.7
1.0–2.9 million	13.7	29.2	62.5	24.5
3.0 million +	12.3	19.3	22.1	14.7
Total	14.4	24.0	34.3	20.3

around of the 1970s, they did share somewhat in the trend toward de-concentration of the metropolitan population. As Table 6.3 shows, the growth of the black population in areas of 3 million or more was less than the growth of smaller areas, and this was true for all three regions. However, for areas below 3 million there was little overall difference in black growth rates, which was in contrast to the trend for the total population toward greater growth rates for smaller areas. Only for the northern areas do the black growth rates decline with size of area in a linear way similar to the total population; even there, the slope of the decline is considerably less than was shown for the total population in Table 3.10. In the South and the West black population growth rates were highest for metropolitan areas ranging in size from 1 to 3 million. Among southern areas in this size range, Atlanta, Fort Lauderdale, Houston, and Miami all experienced a growth in the black population of 35 percent or more between 1970 and 1980. In the West growth rates of black population were even higher, but the initial populations were smaller so that the numerical increases were generally smaller than in the South.[6] A major exception was Los Angeles, which gained 180,000 blacks. In addition, six western cities of over 1 million population had black growth rates in excess of 50 percent: Anaheim, Denver, Riverside–San Bernardino, Sacramento, San Diego, and San Jose.

Unlike earlier decades, when the major sources of black migrants to southern and western metropolitan areas were rural areas of the South, a significant number of migrants to these metropolitan areas in the 1980s came from northern metropolitan regions. The origins of black

[6]In the West there were four metropolitan areas with growth rates exceeding 200 percent (Greeley, CO; Olympia, WA; Provo, UT; and Salem, OR). However, none of these had more than 500 blacks in 1970, so that the black growth was not large either in absolute terms or in relation to the total population of these areas.

migrants to metropolitan areas in each region, which are shown in Table 6.4, indicate that 23 percent of the migrants to southern areas and 30 percent of those to western areas came from northern metropolitan regions. In both regions the largest source of migrants was other metropolitan areas within the same region, and the West also received a significant number of migrants from southern metropolitan areas. However, the southern nonmetropolitan areas, which had been the source of large numbers of black migrants in the past, accounted for only 25 percent of the migration to southern metropolitan areas and 6 percent of the migrants to western metropolitan regions.

Overall, there was a net flow of about 217,800 blacks from the North to the South and West between 1975 and 1980.[7] It is estimated that the net migration from metropolitan areas of the North to metropolitan areas of the South and West was about 192,000 blacks.[8] In addition, the North also lost in its exchange with southern nonmetropolitan areas, in contrast to earlier decades when there had been heavy migration from the rural South to northern cities.

About 10 percent of all black migration came from outside the United States. This included migration from Puerto Rico and other territories, the return of members of the armed forces and other Americans who were abroad in 1975, and immigration from Africa and the Caribbean. These migrants were more likely to go to northern metropolitan areas than to areas of the South or West. Thus, black immigrants and other blacks who were outside the United States in 1975 helped to compensate for some of the outmigration of blacks from the North between 1975 and 1980. Nevertheless, northern metropolitan areas experienced a net outmigration of about 107,000 blacks during this period, while southern areas gained about 297,000 and western areas gained 142,000.

While this regional redistribution of blacks was in the same direction as the redistribution of the total population, the actual rates of redistribution were lower for blacks. The best way to measure this is to look at the change in the regional shares of population between 1970 and 1980. Among the total U.S. population living in metropolitan areas, the proportion living in the North declined from 54.4 to 49.5 percent. However, for blacks the proportion living in northern metropolitan areas declined only from 48.3 to 45.9 percent—about one-half of the decline in the total population of these areas.

In summary, the changes in the black population during the 1970s

[7]From U.S. Bureau of the Census, *1980 Census of Population, General Social and Economic Characteristics*, U.S. Summary, table 214. These data are for the total population, including both metropolitan and nonmetropolitan locations.

[8]These estimates were obtained from special tabulations of the 1 percent Public Use Microdata Sample from the 1980 census.

TABLE 6.4

Origins of Black Migrants to Metropolitan Areas, 1975–1980 (percentage distribution)

Region and Type of Area of Origin	Destination Region		
	North	South	West
North-SMSA	44.5	23.1	30.0
North-Nonmetropolitan	4.6	1.4	2.1
South-SMSA	17.9	35.1	21.2
South-Nonmetropolitan	10.1	24.9	6.1
West-SMSA	5.1	5.8	30.4
West-Nonmetropolitan	0.2	0.4	2.3
United States, other[a]	5.6	5.6	5.3
Foreign, immig.	12.0	3.7	2.8
Total	100.0	100.0	100.0
Number of Migrants	752,000	1,061,600	396,000

[a]Includes migrants from Puerto Rico, U.S. territories, and U.S. citizens returning from abroad. Excludes migrants within the same SMSA.

only partly reflected the changes in the total population. Blacks participated in the shifts of population from the northern region to the South and West, although the proportion of blacks who made such moves was considerably smaller than the proportion of whites and persons of other races. Blacks continued to move from nonmetropolitan to metropolitan areas during a decade when the net flow of the rest of the population was in the opposite direction. Nor did blacks show much of a tendency to move toward smaller metropolitan areas. Although there was some reduction in their growth within metropolitan areas of over 3 million persons, the rate of black population growth in the areas between 1 and 3 million was slightly faster than in smaller areas. In the next section we will seek to explain some of the differences in the growth of black population in metropolitan areas.

Determinants of Black Growth in Metropolitan Areas

There were some significant differences in the patterns of black growth in the 1970s. This suggests that the determinants of black population growth may be different than the determinants of growth of the total population. In addition, since blacks tend to be concentrated in the less-skilled occupations, they respond differently to changes in the economy, particularly to changes in the demand for labor.

During the 1970s there was a relatively rapid shift from manufacturing employment to employment in the service sector. We have already seen that there was net migration out of areas that specialized in manufacturing and into areas specializing in public administration, educational and medical services, and resort and retirement areas. The growth of the black population showed the same trends, but the differences in growth rates among the different types of areas were much smaller than they were for the total population (see Table 6.5). While the growth of the total population in manufacturing areas was a mere 1.7 percent, the growth of the black population was 17.2 percent, which was only 3.1 percent lower than the growth rate for the entire black population in metropolitan areas. The total population in resort areas grew at six times the average for all metropolitan areas, but the black population in these areas grew at a little over three times this average, and less than two times the national metropolitan growth rate for blacks.

In Chapter 4 we tested several models that attempted to explain the growth or decline of metropolitan areas. In Tables 6.6 and 6.7 we have replicated the last of these models using the black population. In Chapter 4 we had used the net migration rate and the rate of employment growth in metropolitan areas as the dependent variables. However, we were unable to calculate reliable black migration rates for each metropolitan area for the 1970–1980 period and have substituted the

TABLE 6.5

*Growth of Total and Black Population in Metropolitan Areas
by Functional Type, 1960–1980
(constant 1980 boundaries)*

Functional Type	Total Population Growth Rate (percent)		Black Population Growth Rate (percent)	
	1960–1970	1970–1980	1960–1970	1970–1980
Nodal Service	17.5	10.7	31.6	19.1
Manufacturing	11.0	1.7	32.0	17.2
Public Administration	27.1	18.9	25.2	28.3
Medical-Education	28.3	25.4	15.7	34.4
Resort-Retirement	61.0	61.6	27.1	36.7
Mixed	21.7	23.3	9.9	22.7
Total	17.1	10.3	29.9	20.3

NOTE: See Table 4.7 for definitions of functional types.

TABLE 6.6

Regression Results for Black Employment Growth
for Metropolitan Areas, 1970–1980[a]
(standardized regression coefficients)

Independent Variables	Region			Total (all areas)
	North	South	West	
Unskilled Earnings	−0.332	−0.040	0.147	−0.110
Log of Density	0.148	0.133	−0.205	0.019
Near Mexico		0.048	0.009	0.087
Percent College	0.078	0.234	0.352	0.219
Percent Manufacturing	−0.131	−0.081	0.370	−0.032
Mean January Temperature	−0.460	0.150	0.324	−0.109
Dummy: South				−0.048
West				0.409
R Squared	0.376	0.171	0.314	0.279
Number of SMSAs	112	92	34	238

[a]Excludes retirement areas in Florida, areas with more than 20 percent of labor force in armed forces, and areas with fewer than 1,000 blacks in 1970.

rate of total black population growth. Although population growth is highly correlated with net migration, it includes natural increase, which may not be as responsive to local economic conditions as is net migration. Nevertheless, these results provide some interesting contrasts to those obtained for the total population.

Before discussing the results, it is important to point out some of the limitations of this analysis. Because the data are aggregated to the level of the metropolitan area, it is possible to misinterpret the relationships that are observed among the variables. This problem was discussed in Chapter 4 and relates to the high level of intercorrelation among predictor variables, which makes it hard to separate the effects of one variable from another. In the analysis of black employment and population growth, we have deliberately used the same predictor variables as were used for the total population in order to facilitate comparison between blacks and the total population. Although more specific variables, such as black wages rather than wages for the total population, might provide better predictors for black employment growth, these variables were not available for all metropolitan areas. In the case of employment growth, we will interpret the predictor vari-

TABLE 6.7

Regression Results for Black Population Growth
for Metropolitan Areas, 1970–1980[a]
(standardized regression coefficients)

Independent Variables	Region			Total (all areas)
	North	South	West	
Unskilled Earnings	−0.018	−0.169	0.137	0.107
Log of Density	−0.155	0.242	−0.057	−0.084
Near Mexico		−0.027	−0.089	−0.009
Percent College	0.642	0.228	0.311	0.481
Percent Manufacturing	0.259	0.032	0.279	0.221
Mean January Temperature	−0.163	0.144	0.363	0.216
Dummy: South				−0.141
West				0.264
R Squared	0.332	0.165	0.346	0.324
Number of SMSAs	112	92	34	238

[a]Excludes retirement areas in Florida, areas with more than 20 percent of labor force in armed forces, and areas with fewer than 1,000 blacks in 1970.

ables in terms of their effect on the supply of jobs; we shall then be testing whether the same factors affect the supply of black jobs as affect the supply of total jobs.

In conducting the analysis, we have eliminated certain metropolitan areas which might distort the results. As in Chapter 4, we have excluded metropolitan areas with a high proportion of elderly migrants and areas with large proportions of the labor force employed in the armed forces. Although the exclusion of military bases is important in terms of our analysis because of the high proportion of blacks in the armed forces, the exclusion of retirement areas is not as necessary because there are relatively few blacks among the elderly moving to retirement areas. However, both exclusions were made so that the units would be comparable to those used in Chapter 4. A third restriction became necessary after examining the distribution of areas by growth rate. Some areas that gained only a few hundred blacks had extremely high black growth rates simply because they had very few blacks in 1970. For example, the growth rate of the black population in Olympia, Washington, was 392 percent, which was due to an increase from 207 to 1,019 persons. To include such cases in the analysis would have meant that a large part of the variation would be accounted for by a few metropolitan areas with extremely small black populations in 1970, and the results would not be very reliable.[9] Therefore, we set an arbitrary minimum of 1,000 blacks in 1970 for an area to be included in the analysis. This resulted in the exclusion of an additional 39 areas.

The relationship between black employment growth and the predictor variables is shown in Table 6.6. This table is similar to Table 4.10 for total employment growth. The levels of explanation are not as high as for the total population, and many of the regression coefficients would not be statistically significant were this a random sample of metropolitan areas.[10] In general, coefficients with absolute values less than 0.1 should be regarded as not very different from zero.

Many of the effects of predictor variables on black employment growth are similar to those for the total population, but there are some exceptions. For the total population there was a negative relationship between earnings of unskilled workers and employment growth and between density and employment growth. These relationships were explained as the outcome of location decisions of manufacturers and other businesses employing relatively unskilled labor to place new plants in areas with relatively low wages and low costs for land, taxes, and local services. This resulted in a shift away from the high-density metropolitan areas where wages and other costs were relatively high to newer, low-density areas with lower wages and costs. Table 6.6 shows that black employment growth also had a negative relationship to unskilled labor earnings. As for total employment, this relationship was observed in both the North and South, but not in the West. However, while black employment grew in higher-density areas in the North and South, for all areas combined there was little relationship between high density and black employment, and in terms of total population high-density areas were negatively correlated with employment growth in all geographic regions.

Why did black employment grow in higher-density areas while total employment declined in these areas? To fully answer this question would require more disaggregated data than those presented here. What we suspect is happening is that in many high-density areas where there was a substantial exodus of whites, businesses remaining in these areas replaced white workers with blacks. Faced with increasing foreign com-

[9]This illustration for Olympia, WA, is based on 100 percent count data. However, the employment and most other census data used in the analysis are based on sample data. The sample data listed about 200 blacks in 1970 compared to 775 in 1980, yielding a growth of 288 percent. The sampling error in this estimate is considerably greater than the differences in growth rates among many major metropolitan areas. Thus, the exclusion of areas with small black populations helps to provide more reliable estimates of growth.

[10]Since the units of analysis include all metropolitan areas with the systematic exclusion of a few types, this is not a random sample and the results are not subject to sampling error.

petition, the replacement of some white workers with blacks would have helped to reduce labor costs because black wages were typically much lower. However, many firms moved away from high-density metropolitan areas to lower-density ones, and since black workers did not follow these firms to the same extent that white workers did, the density relationship is explained mostly by the relatively poorer opportunities for blacks than whites in areas with growing total employment.

There is also a weak relationship between black employment growth and proximity to Mexico. Areas close to Mexico benefited from cheap immigrant labor and this stimulated local economic growth, but blacks did not benefit much from this growth. They received few of the higher-level professional and managerial jobs and suffered from the direct competition of the Mexicans for the low-skilled jobs.

Black employment growth showed the same relationship to the presence of college graduates as was observed for the total population. Areas with high proportions of college graduates are attractive to economic growth because the graduates possess skills that are in demand. The growth that they stimulate appears to benefit blacks as well as others. This is true in all three regions.

The negative effect of manufacturing on total employment growth was much weaker for blacks than for the total population. In the West region, there was a positive relationship between the proportion employed in manufacturing and black employment growth. As argued above, it seems likely that many manufacturing firms hired black workers during the 1970s in an effort to reduce their labor costs. Between 1970 and 1980 black employment in manufacturing increased about twice as fast as total manufacturing employment.[11]

Climate, as measured by average temperature, had a weak positive effect on total employment growth once other factors were controlled. However, for blacks the effect of temperature is negative, indicating that, controlling other factors, there was greater employment growth in colder areas. This effect was entirely due to the North region where black employment growth was greater in relatively colder metropolitan areas, such as Minneapolis–St. Paul and Milwaukee, than it was in relatively warmer areas, such as Philadelphia and New York. The reasons for this probably had more to do with the locations of particular industries that employ blacks than with climate per se.

The growth of the total black population was not entirely parallel to that of employment growth. The correlation between population growth and employment growth was 0.74, which is low enough to allow for considerable difference in the two trends. This difference is due

---

[11]Between the 1970 census and 1980 census, black employment in manufacturing increased by 20.8 percent compared to an increase of 10.5 percent for the total population.

in part to differences among areas in rate of natural increase. However, as we shall see later in the chapter, there are also substantial differences among areas in labor force participation rates of black adults and in the proportion of blacks in the labor force who are employed.

Black population growth had a positive overall relationship to unskilled earnings compared to a negative relationship for employment growth (see Table 6.7). The regional relationships all had the same signs, although the magnitudes were different. The difference was most pronounced in the North, where population growth had virtually no relationship to earnings whereas employment growth had had a substantial negative relationship. This suggests that there may be relatively high black unemployment in northern areas with relatively high wages. When alternative regression models were tested including unemployment as a predictor variable, it was found to have little effect on population growth. It is puzzling why there was not more population movement in response to differences in job opportunities. However, we have used only aggregate measures, and to adequately answer this question would require focusing on the types of work where blacks are most likely to find employment and the factors responsible for the growth of these types of jobs.

The effects of density on population growth are positive in the South, but negative in the North and West. The effects in the South and West are similar to those for employment growth, and it is reasonable to view population growth as a response to employment growth in these regions. In the North, density has a negative effect on population growth, which is opposite to its effect on employment growth, although neither effect is very strong.

Black population growth appears to be occurring in manufacturing areas to a greater extent than is employment growth. This is particularly the case in the North where manufacturing has a positive effect on population and a negative effect on employment.

Finally, the effect of temperature on black population growth is positive in contrast to a negative effect on employment growth. This may be a reflection of higher black birthrates in southern as opposed to northern areas.[12] While temperature had some utility in the models for net migration of the total population as a measure of amenities offered by destination areas, it does not seem to be useful in explaining black population growth.

As a summary measure of the proportion of total variance in

[12]The number of children ever born to black women aged 35 to 44 in 1980 varied by region as follows: Northeast, 2.76; North Central, 3.17; South, 3.22; and West, 2.88. U.S. Bureau of the Census, *1980 Census of Population, General Social and Economic Characteristics*, U.S. Summary, table 214.

growth rates among metropolitan areas, the R Squared figures at the bottom of Tables 6.6 and 6.7 indicate that this set of predictor variables explains only about 28 percent of the variation in employment growth and 32 percent of the variation in population growth among metropolitan areas. Slightly higher proportions of variation are explained within the northern and western regions, but substantially lower proportions are explained in the South. Although these variables help to explain growth, a fuller explanation would appear to require models that are more complex in terms of both the number of variables and the degree of disaggregation. In particular, more attention should be given to measures of job opportunities, income, and other factors specific to the total population.

Consequences of Growth and Decline for Blacks

In the previous chapter we investigated the changes in population characteristics, income, and housing in relation to the rate of population growth. For the total population the changes in most of these variables were not great and, with the exception of housing costs, they favored growing areas. In this section, we shall examine how metropolitan growth or decline affected the black population during the 1970s. We have already seen that blacks were more heavily concentrated in declining areas and areas of slow growth than the total population. This fact alone suggests that blacks may have suffered more from population decline than the population in general. What remains to be seen is whether the experience of blacks in declining areas was similar to that of the total population, or whether blacks suffered more in areas of economic decline than did the rest of the population.

Education

Growth had very little effect on educational levels in metropolitan areas for the total population. Although migrants from northern areas to the South and the West had higher-than-average levels of education, the foreign immigrants to these southern and western areas had considerably less education, so that the total effect of migration on the educational levels at the places of destination was small. However, among blacks, foreign immigrants made up much smaller proportions of the total migration to southern and western metropolitan areas. This factor and other differences between black migration streams and total migration streams suggest that the changes in education of the black population accompanying growth may be different from those of the total population.

Between 1970 and 1980 there was considerable overall improvement in the level of education of the black population (see Table 6.8). The average number of years of education of the black metropolitan population over the age of 25 increased from 9.2 to 10.8 years. This increase of about 1.5 years was greater than the 1.1-year increase for the total metropolitan population. Since the initial levels of education of blacks were lower than those of the total population, the relative increase in education was even greater. By 1980 metropolitan blacks had achieved a level of education that was roughly equivalent to that of the total metropolitan population in 1970. However, the average number of years of school for blacks in 1980 was still 1.1 years lower than that of the total population in 1980.

Increases in black education were greater in areas of moderate or rapid growth than in areas of decline or slow growth. Many of the areas of moderate or rapid growth were in the southern region where levels of education were considerably lower in 1970 than in the rest of the nation. For example, the average number of years of education of blacks in southern metropolitan areas under 1 million in size was only 8.2 years, compared with 9.4 for northern areas, and 9.9 for western areas of the same size (see Appendix C, Table 1). Although the southern areas began the decade with much lower levels of black education, most of these areas experienced growth, which was associated with higher increments to education. Therefore, these areas were closer to the national average in 1980 than in 1970.

The overall improvement in education of the black metropolitan population is also clearly seen in the proportion of high school graduates which increased from 35 percent in 1970 to nearly 55 percent in 1980. This increase was related to the growth of the metropolitan areas, with the change varying from 18.7 percent for declining areas to 24.5

TABLE 6.8

Changes in Educational Levels of Blacks by Metropolitan Growth, 1970–1980 (black population aged 25+)

Metropolitan Growth	Mean Years of Education			Percent High School Graduates		
	1970	1980	Change	1970	1980	Change
Loss	9.6	10.9	1.4	37.5	56.2	18.7
Slow	9.6	11.0	1.4	38.2	57.1	18.9
Moderate	8.5	10.4	1.9	28.4	50.6	22.2
Rapid	9.2	11.1	1.9	35.5	60.0	24.5
Retirement Areas	8.2	9.9	1.8	25.1	45.8	20.7
Total	9.2	10.8	1.5	35.0	54.9	20.0

percent for rapidly growing areas. Since much of the metropolitan growth occurred in southern areas, where the proportion of blacks who were high school graduates was significantly below the national average in 1970, it is not surprising to find that the proportion of high school graduates among the areas with moderate growth was still below the national average, despite an above-average change for the decade.

Similar trends were observed for the proportion of black college graduates (not shown). For metropolitan areas as a whole, the percentage of blacks aged 25 and over who were college graduates increased from 4.7 to 9.1 percent. This near doubling of the proportion of college graduates was observed among all growth categories, although the rapid growth category had the highest percentage of college graduates in both 1970 and 1980. Regional variations in the percentage of college graduates among the black population were nowhere near as great as regional variations in the average number of years of education. For example, the South was far behind the other two regions in average level of black education in 1970, but it exceeded them in the proportion of college graduates and continued to do so in 1980, although the West region was only slightly behind by 1980. The higher proportion of college graduates in the South may be due to the presence of predominantly black colleges in the South which, while helping to maintain the old pattern of racial segregation among schools, may have enabled some blacks to attend college who might not otherwise have done so.

Overall, the increases in black education are much more strongly related to population growth than were the results for the total population. This may be because the gains for the native black population in the South and the West were not diluted by foreign immigration to the same extent that they were for the total population.

Employment of Blacks

Although black education improved considerably during the 1970s and the gap between educational levels of blacks and whites narrowed, the same cannot be said for black employment. While there was a slight increase in the rate of labor force participation of metropolitan blacks during the decade, there was a significant increase in black unemployment. The net result was that a lower proportion of the black population aged 16 and over was employed in 1980 than in 1970.[13]

---

[13]The percentage of blacks aged 16 and over who were employed declined from 55.0 percent in 1970 to 53.1 percent in 1980. See U.S. Bureau of the Census, *1970 Census of Population, General Social and Economic Characteristics of Population*, U.S. Summary; and *1980 Census of Population, Characteristics of Population*, U.S. Summary.

TABLE 6.9

Percentage of Blacks in Metropolitan Areas Who Are in the Labor Force and Percentage Unemployed by Growth Rate, 1970–1980

Metropolitan Growth 1970–1980	Labor Force Participation			Percent Unemployed		
	1970	1980	Change	1970	1980	Change
Loss	58.4	57.9	−0.5	6.9	14.1	7.2
Slow	60.2	60.9	0.7	7.3	12.5	5.2
Moderate	57.2	60.2	3.0	6.4	10.1	3.7
Rapid	59.3	64.7	5.4	6.3	8.4	2.1
Retirement Areas	64.9	64.1	−0.8	4.9	7.7	2.8
Total	59.0	60.2	1.2	6.8	11.8	5.0

In comparing the levels of employment between 1970 and 1980, we need to keep in mind that the results of these comparisons depend on where in the economic cycle the nation is at the time of each census. In the previous chapter we pointed out that the level of unemployment in 1970 was slightly higher than the average for the surrounding five-year period and that the level in 1980 was slightly lower. Since the fluctuations in black unemployment tend to be greater than those in total unemployment,[14] the observed changes for blacks between 1970 and 1980 may understate the long-run changes to a somewhat greater degree than for the total population.

The labor force participation of blacks increased in areas of growth between 1970 and 1980, but declined in areas of population decline and in retirement areas (see Table 6.9). The positive effect of growth on labor force participation for blacks is similar to that observed for the total population in Chapter 5 (see Table 5.5), although the percentage increase for blacks is smaller than that for the total population in all types of areas. This difference is particularly noticeable for the declining and slowly growing areas where the changes in levels of labor force participation for blacks were −0.5 and 0.7 percent, respectively, compared to 2.7 and 4.0 percent for the total population. In terms of labor force participation, the effects of being in areas with below average growth appear to be worse for blacks than others.

The overall change in labor force participation for blacks is the sum of opposing trends for males and females. Between 1970 and 1980 the participation rate for black males in metropolitan areas declined from

---

[14]Between 1970 and 1980 black unemployment fluctuated between 8.2 and 14.8 percent, compared to a range of only 4.5 to 7.8 percent for whites. See U.S. Bureau of Labor Statistics, *Employment and Earnings*, monthly.

71.1 to 67.1 percent while the rate for females increased from 49.1 to 54.5 percent.

Farley gives four possible reasons for the slower-than-average growth in black labor force participation in the 1970s: most of the available jobs for blacks were low-level, dead-end jobs; the increasing availability of welfare and other benefit programs provided alternative means of support; there was increased pressure to treat black employees the same as others, which may have made employers more reluctant to hire blacks who did not have strong credentials; and blacks' residences were concentrated in central cities while job opportunities were increasingly moving to the suburbs.[15] Among these explanations, the last fits with the decline in labor force participation in declining and slowly growing areas, as these tend to be located in the North where there are the greatest disparities between cities and suburbs. This will be seen in the chapters to follow.

When trends in labor force participation are examined by region, it is found that blacks in the western region had somewhat higher levels of participation and a greater increase in participation from 1970 to 1980 than blacks in other regions (see Appendix C, Table 2). This could be due to the larger areas of western cities and the greater equality in economic growth between cities and suburbs in the West. It was also observed among the rapidly growing areas of the South, which were mostly newer areas with relatively large central city areas.

The increase in labor force participation for females was fairly uniform across regions while the decrease for males was much greater in the North than in other regions. For example, among large metropolitan areas of the North there was a 6.1 percent decrease in the participation rate for black males compared to a 3.1 percent decrease in large areas of the South, and a 3.4 percent decrease in large metropolitan areas of the West. While the greater decrease in the North is related to the decline and slow growth of northern areas, it is interesting that the rate of participation of females in these areas increased by 4.5 percent. Thus, the relative change in participation in the North as compared to the other regions is primarily the result of a change in participation of males.

The trends in unemployment, while parallel to those for labor force participation, are even more dramatic. Between 1970 and 1980 the unemployment rate for blacks in metropolitan areas increased from 6.8 to 11.8 percent (see Table 6.9), an increase of 5.0 percent compared to the 2.0 percent increase that was observed for the total population in Chapter 5 (Table 5.6). The seemingly high rate measured in the 1980

[15]Reynolds Farley, *Blacks and Whites: Narrowing the Gap* (Cambridge, MA: Harvard University Press, 1984), pp. 52–55.

census was considerably lower than the average of 14.3 percent measured for the entire year by the Current Population Survey, and rates rose in each succeeding year to 20.6 percent in 1983.[16] In each year since 1977 the black rate of unemployment has been more than double the white rate. Clearly, blacks have suffered much more than whites from shifts in the economy that have affected the demand for labor and the locations of jobs.

The black unemployment rates in 1980 and the changes from 1970 to 1980 were strongly related to the growth of metropolitan areas. Blacks in rapidly growing areas had unemployment rates that were only 2 percent above the average for the total metropolitan population and 3.5 percent higher than the total for rapidly growing areas. In contrast, blacks in declining areas had unemployment rates that were more than double the national average and 6.7 percentage points higher than those for the total population of these areas.

Again, as with labor force participation, there were significant differences among regions even when comparisons were made among metropolitan areas with similar rates of growth. Among areas with slow growth, the unemployment rates for blacks in northern areas were almost as high as in areas of decline where, as in the South and West, they were 3 to 4 percentage points lower (see Appendix Table C.2). It seems likely that these higher rates of employment in northern areas relate to the concentration of blacks in tightly bounded central cities while the few new job opportunities in these areas are to be found on the periphery. This issue will be addressed in greater detail in subsequent chapters.

Black Income

Income can be summarized in a variety of ways and there is no single measure that provides a satisfactory indicator of the changes occurring among blacks in the 1970s. We have chosen two measures, family income and per capita income, which provide somewhat different indications of the changes occurring during the decade. Comparisons of family income between two points in time or between two groups assume that the composition of families, and particularly the number of wage earners per family, remains constant. During the 1970s there was an increase in the proportion of black families with only one adult. This factor alone would have led to a relative decrease in black family income had there been no change in the income of adult family members.

[16]U.S. Bureau of the Census, *Statistical Abstract of the United States 1985*. This rate includes both metropolitan and nonmetropolitan areas.

The same problem occurs in trying to compare black family income with the income of nonblacks. Because a much higher proportion of black families are one-adult families, black family income would be lower even if the incomes of adult family members were equal. [17]

Despite changes in family composition which should have reduced family income, black families in metropolitan areas experienced an increase in income of 113.8 percent between 1969 and 1979. This increase was slightly greater than the 107 percent increase for the total population for the same period (see Table 5.9) and the 98.2 percent increase in the Consumer Price Index. In 1979 black families were still far behind other families in average income, but their relative position had improved somewhat over the decade.

The rate of increase in black family income varied considerably with the rate of growth of the metropolitan area in which they were living (see Table 6.10), ranging from 97 percent in the declining areas to 151 percent in the rapidly growing areas. The slowly growing areas experienced increases in family income close to average while the areas with moderate growth and the retirement areas were above-average. Because family incomes in the areas with moderate and rapid growth and the retirement areas were below average in 1970, the greater increases in income in these areas meant that there was less variation in income among areas in 1980 than there had been in 1970.

The actual increases in family income would probably have been greater had family composition remained the same between 1970 and 1980. Per capita income provides an alternative measure that is independent of the living arrangements of persons. However, since very few children earn incomes, the per capita income is sensitive to the proportion of children in the population. The fact that 28.7 percent of blacks were under age 15 in 1980, compared to only 22.6 percent of the total population, means that there were relatively fewer blacks of working ages to generate income. Per capita income can also be somewhat misleading when used to compare welfare among groups with differing age compositions, since young children require less food, clothing, and other items than do teenagers and adults. Providing that these limitations are kept in mind, per capita income can serve as a useful measure of changes in income during a period of rapid change in living arrangements.

The per capita income of blacks in metropolitan areas rose by 138 percent between 1970 and 1980, which was almost identical to the rise

[17]The effects of family type on income are discussed by Suzanne M. Bianchi and Reynolds Farley in "Racial Differences in Family Living Arrangements and Economic Well-Being: An Analysis of Recent Trends," *Journal of Marriage and the Family*, 41:3 (August 1979): pp. 537–551.

TABLE 6.10

Family and Per Capita Income for Blacks in Metropolitan Areas by Growth, 1969–1979

Metropolitan Growth 1970–1980	Family Income in Dollars[a]				Per Capita Income in Dollars[a]			
	1969	1979	Percent Growth	Real Growth	1969	1979	Percent Growth	Real Growth
Loss	8,410	16,570	97.0	−0.5	2,302	4,986	116.6	9.4
Slow	8,300	17,580	111.8	7.0	2,167	5,167	138.4	20.4
Moderate	6,230	14,840	138.2	20.3	1,547	4,134	167.2	35.0
Rapid	6,760	16,970	151.0	26.8	1,703	4,829	183.6	43.2
Retirement Areas	6,370	14,500	127.6	15.0	1,596	3,980	149.4	26.0
Total	7,680	16,420	113.8	8.0	2,006	4,776	138.1	20.2

NOTE: Percent growth is calculated as a percentage of 1970 income. Real growth is deflated by growth in the Consumer Price Index (98 percent).

[a] Annual income in current dollars, rounded to nearest $10.

of 137 percent for the total population. For both blacks and nonblacks, the rise in per capita income was greater than the rise in family income because of the declining number of persons per family. The fact that the family income of blacks improved somewhat relative to that of all families, while per capita income did not, is probably due to the greater decline in the number of children per family among nonblack families than among black families.

The increase in black per capita income shows a regular relationship to the rate of growth of the metropolitan area, as was the case for family income (see Table 6.10). The percentage increase ranged from 117 percent in declining areas to 184 percent in rapidly growing areas. Again, since the per capita incomes of the moderately and rapidly growing areas were lower than those in the declining and slow growth areas in 1970, the differences in income growth resulted in a convergence of per capita incomes among areas in 1980. Much of this convergence can also be seen between northern and southern areas, since the majority of northern areas experienced decline or slow growth while the southern areas tended to be in the moderate and rapid growth categories. For example, the per capita income of blacks in large northern areas increased by 118 percent during the decade while black income in large southern areas increased by 156 percent (see Appendix C, Table 3). Western areas, which had had higher black incomes in 1970, but relatively few blacks, experienced a 144 percent increase in income, and blacks in these areas continued to have the highest incomes in 1980 of blacks in any of the regions.

Poverty

The proportion of families and persons below the official poverty level is a useful measure because it provides a rough indicator of income relative to need. Between 1969 and 1979 there was a very small decrease in the proportion of black families and black persons who were below the official poverty level (see Table 6.11). While poverty increased considerably after 1979, we argued in Chapter 5 that the reference periods used in the censuses were appropriate points of comparison because they were at equivalent points in the economic cycle.

There was very little change in black poverty for all metropolitan areas between 1969 and 1979, but there was considerable change for many metropolitan areas and this change varied by metropolitan growth. Among declining areas the proportion of black families in poverty increased by 4.5 percent while among rapidly growing areas it decreased by 7.3 percent. Although the proportion in poverty in rapidly

TABLE 6.11

Percentage of Black Families and Individuals Below Poverty Level by Rate of Growth of Metropolitan Area, 1969–1979

Metropolitan Growth 1970–1980	Families Below Poverty			Persons Below Poverty		
	1969	1979	Change	1969	1979	Change
Loss	20.7	25.2	4.5	23.9	27.9	3.9
Slow	22.1	23.4	1.3	25.6	26.2	0.6
Moderate	33.4	26.4	−7.0	37.3	29.8	−7.5
Rapid	28.9	21.6	−7.3	32.2	24.7	−7.5
Retirement Areas	31.9	28.9	−3.0	36.0	32.1	−3.9
Total	25.1	24.8	−0.4	28.8	27.7	−1.0

growing areas was much higher than that in declining areas in 1969, the rapidly growing areas had lower proportions in poverty in 1979, and there was an overall convergence in the proportions in poverty in different metropolitan areas. Similar trends were observed for the proportion of persons living in poverty.

The trends in poverty varied somewhat by region even among areas with similar rates of growth. For example, slowly growing areas in the North experienced an increase in the proportion of blacks in poverty while slowly growing areas in the South experienced either a small decrease (small areas) or no change (large areas), and there was little change for slowly growing areas of the West (see Appendix C, Table 4).

Black Family Status

The income and poverty status of blacks is closely tied to family status. Bianchi and Farley showed that the per capita income of members of husband-wife families was considerably higher than that of female-headed families. Unfortunately, during the 1970s there was an increase in the proportion of black children living in female-headed families and a decrease in the proportion living in husband-wife families.[18] Since family status has important implications for income and poverty, it is important to investigate how location in a growing versus a declining area affects family status.

As shown in Table 6.12, the proportion of black households that were families in 1980 is not too different from the proportion of all

[18]Bianchi and Farley, "Racial Differences in Family Living Arrangements and Economic Well-Being."

TABLE 6.12

Percentage of Families and Husband-Wife Families with Children for Blacks in Metropolitan Areas by Growth, 1970–1980

etropolitan Growth 70–1980	Families as Percentage of Households 1980	Percentage of Families with Husband, Wife, and Child			Percentage of Other Families with Children 1980
		1970	1980	Change	
ss	70.1	39.2	29.5	−9.7	32.2
ɔw	70.9	41.3	31.9	−9.4	30.9
ɔderate	73.8	40.7	35.0	−5.7	26.5
pid	73.3	45.2	39.9	−5.3	24.2
tirement Areas	74.9	42.7	33.9	−8.8	28.9
ɪtal	71.7	40.8	32.7	−8.1	29.6

ɔTE: Family households are those containing two or more persons who are related by birth, marriage, adoption.

households that are families, 71.7 percent compared to the 72.6 percent, which was shown in Table 5.2. However, blacks differ considerably from the rest of the population in the proportion of families that are husband-wife families. In 1970 approximately 40.8 percent of all black families contained a married couple and child in contrast to 48.5 percent of the total population (as shown in Table 5.2). By 1980 this percentage had declined for both blacks and the total population to 32.7 percent and 41.2 percent, respectively. Despite the lower proportion of black families with husband, wife, and child in 1970, the decline in this proportion was greater for blacks than for the total population.

The composition of black families varied significantly by the growth rate of the area in which they resided. Blacks in growing areas had higher initial proportions of husband-wife families with children, and these areas experienced less reduction in that proportion during the 1970s than did declining areas. By 1980 the proportion of black families consisting of a married couple and at least one child was one-third higher in growing areas than in declining areas. Areas with slow and moderate growth had intermediate values, such that the 1980 proportions of black families that had a married couple and one or more children increased regularly with the rate of growth.

At this point one might well argue that the families in growing areas were likely to be younger and to have more children because of the combined effects of higher birthrates in growing areas and higher rates of migration of young adults into these areas. Age structure does explain a small part of this relationship. However, if this were the pri-

169

mary explanation, we would expect to find that the proportion of one-adult families with children was also higher in rapidly growing areas. As shown in the last column of Table 6.12, the reverse is the case. In declining areas 32 percent of the families were "other families with children," compared to 24 percent for rapidly growing areas.

A plausible explanation for these results is that the growth in employment and income which accompanies population growth helps promote family stability among blacks in growing areas. Conversely, the high unemployment rates for blacks in declining areas and rates of income growth lower than the growth in living costs contribute to greater family breakup in these areas. While the poor economic situation of blacks has often been given as an explanation for their high rate of family instability, the results presented here suggest that the growth or decline of the metropolitan area of residence has a considerable impact upon family stability.

Conclusion

The black population in metropolitan areas grew rapidly during the period since World War II. Although much of this growth was due to natural increase, there was also considerable migration from the rural South. The net movement of blacks toward metropolitan areas continued in the 1970s despite the reversal of this stream for the white population. However, the rate of movement toward metropolitan areas slowed during the 1970s, and the major destinations of this movement shifted from large northern areas to smaller metropolitan areas of the South. Throughout the postwar period the black populations in metropolitan areas in the West grew rapidly, but because many of these areas started with extremely small black populations, the numbers of blacks moving to areas in the West was much smaller than the numbers moving to areas in the North and South.

Attempts to explain why some metropolitan areas had higher rates of black employment growth than other areas by using regression equations were only partly successful. These equations showed that many of the factors influencing black employment growth were the same as those influencing total employment growth. In both cases, growth during the 1970s was greater in areas with low wages for unskilled workers, suggesting that the primary force behind employment growth was the decision of firms to locate new plants or relocate old ones in areas where they could minimize wage costs. It was argued that total employment growth was also lower in metropolitan areas with high population density because of higher costs associated with density, but this argument did not apply equally to black employment growth, which was positively related to density once other factors, such as wages, were controlled. There are two possible explanations for this. First, some employers in high-density areas may have substituted black workers for white ones in an effort to reduce labor costs. Second, blacks appear to have been less likely to move to lower-density areas where new employment opportunities were being created. In Chapter 11 we will see that this is also true for the movement from central cities to suburbs.

Black employment growth and black population growth also showed less relation to climate than did white growth. In fact, in the North region the greatest growth was in the colder areas. This finding is consistent with earlier results reported by Greenwood and Gormely for the 1960s and could be interpreted as showing that blacks, because of their lower income levels, are motivated much less by noneconomic considerations than are whites.[19] However, we argued earlier that the relationship of climate to migration was a spurious one, with the exception of elderly persons and those near retirement, and that the observed relationship was due to other factors responsible for growth in the warmer parts of the United States. One of these factors is the availability of cheap immigrant labor in areas near the Mexican border, and blacks do not appear to have benefited much from this immigration.

The difference between being located in a growing versus a declining metropolitan area had significant consequences for blacks. Because metropolitan growth patterns changed during the 1970s to favor smaller southern areas which had relatively low status on many socioeconomic indicators, the effect of growth in the 1970s was often to bring about greater convergence in these indicators among different types of areas.

The educational levels of blacks in metropolitan areas improved significantly during the 1970s by all measures: average years of school completed, the proportion who were high school graduates, and the proportion who were college graduates. On all these measures blacks gained on the white population, and in average years of education they made up about one-half of the difference that existed at the beginning of the decade. Gains in black education were greatest in growing areas of the South which had been considerably behind other areas at the beginning of the decade.

While the education of metropolitan blacks improved during the 1970s, their employment situation did not improve. Unemployment rates at the end of the decade were higher than at the beginning of the decade and there was a strong relationship between black unemployment and the total growth rate of the metropolitan area. In terms of

[19]Michael J. Greenwood and Patrick J. Gormely, "A Comparison of the Determinants of White and Nonwhite Interstate Migration," *Demography* 8 (February 1971):141–155.

both unemployment and labor force participation, blacks in declining areas were considerably worse off than the total population of these areas.

Changes in black income for the decade present a mixed picture. There was a slight improvement in black family income relative to the rate of increase in family income for the total population and relative to the increase in the Consumer Price Index. Because black families tended to have more children than other families, this improvement was not observed for per capita income. There was also little change in black poverty either at the family level or the individual level. However, changes in income and poverty were strongly related to metropolitan growth rates, and because growth rates were higher in southern areas which had had relatively low black income than in higher-income areas of the North, there was considerable convergence in black income and poverty between northern and southern areas.

Finally, it was observed that the overall decline in the proportion of black families with a married couple and one or more children was much greater in areas of population decline than in areas of population growth, and that the increase in one-parent families was greater in declining areas. This change in family stability appears related to the changes in employment opportunities and income in these areas. Economic growth of a metropolitan area appears to help black families to stay together.

In summary, blacks who remained in declining or slowly growing metropolitan areas and those who moved into these areas seemed to have suffered in several ways compared to those who were living in more rapidly growing areas. Yet rates of black movement toward growing areas were less than those of whites and others for the 1970s. Although it appears that blacks might have been better off in 1980 had more of them moved toward growing areas of the South or West, this may not be true. In many of these areas growth was stimulated either by the availability of immigrants who were willing to work for relatively low wages, or by high-skilled industries, such as oil exploration, aerospace research and development, and banking. Because most blacks are still employed in relatively low-skilled jobs, blacks moving to growing areas would face either the competition of immigrants for these jobs or the competition of more highly skilled whites for the other higher-skilled jobs. Black unemployment was lower in areas that grew more rapidly than the national average than in declining and slowly growing areas, yet black per capita income was also lower in these areas. Thus, it is not clear that more blacks would have been better off in 1980 had they moved to growing areas rather than having remained in declining ones.

PART TWO

CITY–SUBURB REDISTRIBUTION WITHIN LARGE METROPOLITAN AREAS

Introduction to Part Two

BEGINNING with this chapter the focus shifts to an evaluation of the *intra*metropolitan central city–suburb redistribution process within the nation's largest metropolitan areas, with particular attention to the post-1970 period. It is during this period that social forces have effected significant changes in race relations, family formation patterns, and the nature of work—all areas that hold implications for city–suburb redistribution. The chapters that follow will examine these societywide changes and the consequences they hold for intrametropolitan shifts in population, households, and employment within both growing and declining metropolitan areas. However, before entering into these analyses directly, we first discuss, in broad strokes, why the post-1970 period might be considered a new era of city–suburb redistribution.

Two Earlier Eras of City–Suburb Redistribution

There is general agreement among students of urban structure that twentieth century forces, which shaped the size and selectivity of population suburbanization in the nation's oldest metropolitan areas prior to

1970, can be distinguished according to two broad eras.[1] The first of these eras is bounded in time roughly by the turn of the century and World War II. It was during this period that suburban hinterlands sustained higher levels of population growth than their central cities—a phenomenon that was facilitated by the widespread adoption of the automobile and other short-distance modes of transportation, which permitted the outward expansion of suburban residences from previously built-up central city core areas. Because suburban-bound movers generally purchased new homes and were also obliged to absorb higher commuting costs than those that located toward the center, these movers ranked significantly higher on income and on other status characteristics than the overall city population. The selectivity was also fostered by a desire on the part of upper-status residents to segregate themselves from more centrally located working class neighborhoods since, for most of this period, a large share of inmigrants to the inner zones of the metropolitan area were either foreign immigrants, rural-to-urban migrants, or poor South-to-North black migrants. Despite higher suburban than city growth during this era, the city population continued to dominate, so that in 1940 the suburbs still housed a minority, albeit typically elite, share of the total metropolitan population.

The second major suburbanization movement, which began in the immediate post–World War II years, was more massive than the first and took place in virtually all large metropolitan areas. The limitations imposed upon housing construction during the war years, high rates of family formation among returning war veterans, increase in the number of middle-class households brought about by the prosperous postwar economy, and continuing migration to metropolitan areas gave rise to a strong demand for new housing. This demand was quickly met by a widespread, heavily government-subsidized construction of new homes, highways, and associated infrastructure in previously undeveloped suburban areas. The sheer magnitude of this suburban population movement caused it to be somewhat less selective in social status than that of the earlier period. However, the strong emphasis on child raising among family-forming couples in the 1950s and 1960s made suburban locations particularly attractive destinations for the large number of husband-wife-with-children families that had formed during this

---

[1]Amos H. Hawley, "Urbanization as Process," in David Street and Associates, eds., *Handbook of Urban Life* (San Francisco: Jossey-Bass Publishers, 1978); R. D. Norton, *City Life-Cycles and American Urban Policy* (New York: Academic Press, 1979); and John F. Long, *Population Deconcentration in the United States*, Special Demographic Analysis, COS–81–5 (Washington, DC: U.S. Government Printing Office, 1981).

period.[2] This suburbanization movement contributed to an "emptying out" of older metropolitan areas' central cities whose pre–World War II populations were still highly concentrated within compact legal boundaries.[3] Moreover, the cumulative effects of a century-long, status-selective suburbanization of the population led to relatively wide city–suburb disparities in measures of residents' income, education, and occupational prestige as the process continued through the 1960s.[4] Thus, the massive post–World War II suburbanization, although somewhat less selective than its predecessor, redistributed a substantial portion of metropolitan activities to the suburbs. By 1970 it was the central city that had come to house the minority and *less* select share of the total population residing in the nation's oldest metropolitan areas.

Throughout both of these eras substantial numbers of blacks had been migrating into large northern metropolitan areas and had been continually segregated from the white population—first within selected neighborhoods and then within central cities of metropolitan areas.[5] The high level of neighborhood and city racial segregation that persisted through the post–World War II period has been attributed, largely, to various forms of institutionalized discrimination.[6] Real estate agents, lending institutions, government agencies, and individual sellers helped to steer white movers into city neighborhoods and suburban communities that were not made available to blacks. As a consequence, only a small minority of the metropolitan black population participated in the suburbanization of the 1950s and 1960s, and their suburban destinations were generally either highly segregated black working class communities that existed prior to metropolitan expansion, or "spillover communities" that came into being when black city ghettos extended themselves into adjacent suburban territory.[7]

[2]Nelson N. Foote, Janet Abu-Lughod, Mary Mix Foley, and Louis Winnick, *Housing Choices and Housing Constraints* (New York: McGraw-Hill, 1960).

[3]John D. Kasarda and George V. Redfearn, "Differential Patterns of City and Suburban Growth in the United States," *Journal of Urban History* 2 (1975):43–66.

[4]Leo F. Schnore, *The Urban Scene* (New York: The Free Press, 1965); and Leo F. Schnore, *Class and Race in Cities and Suburbs* (Chicago: Markham Publishing Company, 1975).

[5]Karl E. Taeuber and Alma F. Taeuber, *Negroes in Cities* .

[6]*Donald Foley, "Institutional and Contextual Factors Affecting the Housing Choices of Minority Residents," in Amos H. Hawley and Vincent P. Rock, eds., Segregation in Residential Areas* (Washington, DC: National Academy of Sciences, 1973).

[7]Reynolds Farley, "The Changing Distribution of Negroes within Metropolitan Areas: The Emergence of Black Suburbs," *American Journal of Sociology* 75 (1970): 512–529; and Harold M. Rose, *Black Suburbanization: Access to Improved Quality of Life or Maintenance of the Status Quo?* (Cambridge, MA: Ballinger Publishing Company, 1976).

The Beginning of a New Era?

Suggestions that the size and selectivity of intrametropolitan population redistribution may have begun to alter significantly in the 1970s are drawn from several societywide demographic and economic trends, namely: (1) noticeable declines in racial status inequality and in housing discrimination; (2) dramatic shifts in the number and types of households; and (3) the adaptation of industrial cities to a postindustrial economy.

Greater black access to suburban housing has begun to occur as a result of social and economic gains achieved by younger segments of the black population and some breakdown in discriminatory housing practices of the past.[8] Noticeable improvements in black income and social status began to take place in the 1960s but did not, by themselves, constitute sufficient conditions for alleviating the residential segregation and city concentration that continued to persist. However, the passage of the 1968 Federal Fair Housing Act and related legislation, which outlawed the most overt forms of racial discrimination in housing sales and construction, seem to have prompted a greater overall receptivity of black inmigrants to suburban residential areas.[9]

Second, changes in lifestyles and living arrangements in the post-1970 period appear to have created a rising demand for centrally located housing among middle-class metropolitan households. New generations of young adults are placing less emphasis on child raising and the traditional familial lifestyle than did adults in the 1950s and 1960s, and women have become more oriented toward work outside the home and following careers.[10] The dramatic post-1970 increase in the number of households, particularly those of unmarried adults and childless couples with good earning potential, has prompted suggestions that these households will depart from their counterparts of earlier decades in their priorities toward intrametropolitan residence locations. Many of these households, it is held, will favor a central location as a viable

---

[8]Thomas Pettigrew, "Racial Change and the Intrametropolitan Distribution of Black Americans," in Arthur P. Solomon, ed., *The Prospective City* (Cambridge, MA: M.I.T. Press, 1980).

[9]Eunice Grier and George Grier, *Black Suburbanization at the Mid–1970s* (Washington, DC: Washington Center for Metropolitan Studies, 1978); and Thomas A. Clark, *Blacks in Suburbs: A National Perspective* (New Brunswick, NJ: Rutgers University Center for Urban Policy Research, 1979).

[10]Andrew J. Cherlin, *Marriage, Divorce, and Remarriage* (Cambridge, MA: Harvard University Press, 1981); and Arland Thornton and Deborah Freedman, eds., "The Changing American Family," *Population Bulletin*, Vol. 38, No. 4 (Washington, DC: Population Reference Bureau, 1983).

long-term residence rather than only as a "staging area" before returning to the suburbs.[11]

The third societywide shift with implications for post-1970 city development draws from the transformation of the nation's industrial structure so as to place greater emphasis on specialized services and nonprofit and government employment. The steady erosion of heavy manufacturing jobs from older urban areas, which became accentuated during the 1960s, forced city decision makers to take stock of their competitive advantages in those sectors of the economy that were growing. In building upon these strategies, many central cities emphasized their roles as diversified-function corporate and specialized service centers, along with the full complement of related production services, specialized retail districts, and recreation and entertainment services, in an effort to reinvigorate the cities' commercial and residential economic bases.[12]

These post-1970 shifts—toward reduced racial discrimination, toward smaller, less family-oriented households, and toward the growth in high-productivity services—constitute fundamental departures from the demographic and economic conditions that fostered the massive and selective suburbanization of the 1945–1970 period. Their effects on the city–suburb redistribution process should serve to moderate postwar central city decline—by providing greater incentives for employers and middle-class residents to locate in the central city and by providing greater opportunities for blacks and other minority groups to reside in any neighborhood or community that they desire.[13]

This is not to suggest that nationwide shifts in race relations, household structure, and the nature of work can overturn decades of selective out-migration and economic disinvestment. Nor are the effects of these developments expected to be uniform across metropolitan areas that differ markedly in their industrial structures, population compositions, and political coalitions. Indeed, a great deal of debate has been directed to the issue of whether or not large declining industrial centers will, in fact, serve a viable economic role in the latter years of

[11]William Alonso, "The Population Factor," in Arthur P. Solomon, ed., *The Prospective City* (Cambridge, MA: M.I.T. Press, 1980).

[12]Thomas J. Black, *The Changing Economic Role of Central Cities* (Washington, DC: Urban Land Institute, 1978); and Thierry J. Noyelle and Thomas M. Stanback, Jr., *The Economic Transformation of American Cities* (Totowa, NJ: Rowman & Allanheld, 1984).

[13]These altered demographic conditions have occurred in concert with a changing political milieu in the late 1970s, wherein local big-city governments have begun to provide an array of incentives for privately initiated central-city economic development. See Susan S. Fainstein, Norman I. Fainstein, Richard Child Hill, Dennis Judd, and Michael Peter Smith, *Restructuring the City: The Political Economy of Urban Redevelopment* (New York: Longman, 1983).

the twentieth century; and experts from several fields differ markedly in their answer to this question.[14]

It *is* being suggested that a new set of societal conditions has begun to operate in the post-1970 period, which will effect changes in the population and industrial patterns that were associated with the second era of suburbanization described above. No longer will racial minorities necessarily be confined to central city residences and all-minority neighborhoods. No longer will low-density suburbs necessarily be the preferred place of residence for most young-adult households. No longer will the majority of white collar workers necessarily reside in suburban communities and commute to central city workplaces. These images of the 1950s and 1960s have begun to change directions since the 1970 census was taken and the chapters in Part Two will describe the nature of this change.

In order to aid in this comparison of metropolitan areas, the next section develops a typology of metropolitan areas which will be employed in the evaluations that follow. The remaining sections of this chapter are devoted to documenting city–suburb population changes as they have evolved since 1950, for the 39 metropolitan areas to be focused upon in these analyses.

A Metropolitan Area Typology

This portion of the monograph will focus exclusively on the 39 metropolitan areas with 1980 populations that exceed 1 million. This group of metropolitan areas includes virtually all of the country's large "problem" cities located in the declining areas of the nation's Midwest and Northeast census regions.[15] Moreover, the 1 million population cri-

---

[14]Views on this topic range from suggestions to reindustrialize decaying central cities and make employers responsible for the consequences of abandoning a community to cries that older industrial cities have outlived their usefulness and that "redundant" city workers should be persuaded to retrain or relocate elsewhere. A more moderate view than the latter promotes scaling down both the size and level of economic activity in these cities so that they can capitalize on their strength as specialized service and cultural-recreation centers. This recommendation also advocates programs to construct low- and moderate-income housing on the periphery of the city to enable the relocating, out of the city, of less-skilled resident workers and to support technical training programs for displaced inner-city workers. See John D. Kasarda, "The Implications of Contemporary Redistribution Trends for National Urban Policy," *Social Science Quarterly* 61 (December 1980):373–400.

[15]Lists of such cities, as compiled by several government agencies and research organizations, are compiled in Robert W. Burchell, David Listokin, George Sternlieb, James W. Hughes, and Stephan C. Casey, "Measuring Urban Distress: A Summary of the Major Urban Hardship Indices and Resource Allocation Systems," in Robert W. Burchell and David Listokin, eds., *Cities Under Stress* (New Brunswick, NJ: Rutgers Center for Urban Policy Research, 1981).

terion insures inclusion of major regional city centers in all parts of the country. While these 39 metropolitan areas are relatively homogeneous with regard to their large size, they differ markedly from each other in development history, population growth, and the geographic characteristics that are important in determining the nature of the city–suburb redistribution process. For this reason we have developed a separate typology for the Part Two analyses of intrametropolitan redistribution which classifies the metropolitan areas on the dimensions of (a) the age of their central cities; (b) recent population growth or decline; and (c) the region of the country in which they are located. We discuss below how each of these dimensions relate to intrametropolitan city–suburb redistribution.[16] We also discuss a fourth metropolitan area characteristic—the metropolitan area's economic function. This characteristic is not formally a part of the typology. However, it also affects the intrametropolitan redistribution process, and will be referred to often in the later analyses.

City age: The age of the metropolitan area's central city, crudely approximated by the census year in which the central city (or largest city in the case of multiple central cities) first achieved a population exceeding 50,000, has proven to be a useful indicator of a metropolitan area's development and internal redistribution history. Large cities that registered such a "birthday" prior to the turn of the century have generally followed common histories of growth, decline, and deconcentration of their populations and economic activities over the course of the twentieth century.[17] The extremely high densities of population that these cities accumulated during the days of early industrialization and

---

[16]These three factors do not represent all of the influences that affect city–suburb redistribution patterns, although they do constitute crude indexes of still other factors, not explicitly mentioned. One of these factors might be termed the "political culture of the central city government." According to Mollenkopf (see John H. Mollenkopf, "Paths Toward the Post–Industrial Service City: The Northeast and the Southwest," in Robert W. Burchell and David Listokin, eds., *Cities Under Stress* (New Brunswick, NJ: Rutgers Center for Urban Policy Research, 1981), most large cities in the South and West have established governmental forms (usually the city-management form) and political coalitions, which have tended to give a strong voice to the cities' business communities and, hence, have promoted strong "pro-growth" policies. This situation differs from that of most northern city governments fraught with the complexities of political conflict among a wider array of interest groups. These northern city governments generally cannot move as directly in enacting growth-oriented legislation. Other influences indexed by one of the three factors in the typology are discussed in the text.

[17]Prior to the year 1900 city density patterns were based on the horse-drawn carriage and electrified street car as modes of local transportation. (See Avery M. Guest, "Urban Growth and Population Densities," *Demography* 10 (1973):53–69.) For further documentation of these patterns, the reader is referred to: Kasarda and Redfearn, 1975, op.cit.; Leo F. Schnore, *The Urban Scene,* and *Class and Race in Cities and Suburbs;* and Amos H. Hawley, *The Changing Shape of Metropolitan America* (Glencoe, IL: The Free Press, 1956).

primitive short-distance transportation gradually became deconcentrated as motor vehicle ownership became more widespread and economic activities became more dispersed. These metropolitan areas exhibited deconcentration of their population (a positive difference between suburban growth and city growth) in every decade since 1920, with the most accentuated deconcentration occurring in the 1950s. Yet the legacy of these areas' settlement patterns is still apparent. Older central cities still tend to exhibit higher density levels and greater city–suburb disparities on population and housing characteristics than do their younger counterparts, which developed chiefly since the advent of the automobile and more dispersed production techniques.

Another factor that has contributed to the wide city–suburb disparities in older areas relates to their inability to annex new territory since the early decades of this century. This represents another legacy that has been attributed to the desire of early suburbanites to incorporate themselves into separate communities—so as to become politically autonomous from the higher taxes, environmental deterioration, and ethnic conflict that characterized industrial cities at the turn of the century.[18] As a consequence, older central cities typically became hemmed in by incorporated suburban communities at a relatively early stage of metropolitan expansion and have become increasingly isolated from the outward redistribution of the metropolitan areas' population and economic activities. Younger central cities, in contrast, have found it easier to annex suburban territory and expand outward along with the population.

Recent growth or decline: Before 1970 virtually all large metropolitan areas registered population growth so that most models of intrametropolitan redistribution assumed, as a given, that the metropolitan area would continue to grow.[19] In this context the important distinction to be noted across metropolitan areas was their relative level of growth; and a great deal of attention focused on redistribution within rapidly growing areas—the unplanned sprawl of their settlements, and the local community's capacity to provide services for ballooning popu-

[18]Norton, *City Life-Cycles*; and Patrick J. Ashton, "The Political Economy of Suburban Development," in William K. Tabb and Larry Sawers, eds., *Marxism and the Metropolis* (New York: Oxford University Press, 1978).

[19]Classic theories of urban expansion, for example, E. W. Burgess, "The Growth of the City: An Introduction to a Research Project," in Robert E. Park, Ernest Burgess, and R. D. McKenzie, eds., *The City* (Chicago: University of Chicago Press, 1925), pp. 47–62; and E. M. Hoover and R. Vernon, *Anatomy of a Metropolis* (Cambridge, MA: Harvard University Press, 1959) are predicated on the assumption of continuous metropolitanwide population growth where less well-off inmigrants are directed to substandard central city housing that filters down through an expansion process, which begins when better-off residents purchase newly constructed housing on the metropolitan periphery.

lations.[20] Beginning with the 1970s, as the earlier chapters have shown, the assumption of positive metropolitanwide population growth no longer applies to a good number of large metropolitan areas, and there exists little historical evidence to guide predictions on how city–suburb redistribution patterns accommodate to negative population growth. It is possible that within the context of the declining metropolitan population, old industrial cities might become more easily transformed into smaller-size specialized service centers, which many experts see to be their future role. In this context, one finds less pressure for residential development on the periphery and greater vacancy, deterioration, and abandonment of substandard city housing. This situation, which now exists in large sections of central cities, creates the potential for central city residential development and restoration, assuming a demand for such housing can be created.

On the other hand, a lack of demand for such centrally located housing would depress the central city's economy and attractiveness for residents and employers even further—while poverty populations will remain anchored in the core. This would lead to selective out-migration and disinvestment from central cities of declining metropolitan areas. A comparative analysis of urban decline in the 1970–1975 period, undertaken by Katharine Bradbury, Anthony Downs, and Kenneth Small, provides support for the latter view. In this study the authors calculate an index of city distress for each city (combining static measures of the city's unemployment rate, violent crime rate, poverty population, old housing, and city–SMSA tax disparity), and an index of city decline (reflecting 1970–1975 changes in similar measures). Among all metropolitan areas studied, both city distress and city decline were found to be greater in areas with large *central city* population losses; and within this group, city stress and decline were most accentuated in the *metropolitan areas* that lost population.[21]

Region: The regional classification locates each metropolitan area in a specific geographic context. This analysis will collapse the four standard census regions into three regions, where the North region will encompass both the Northeast and Midwest census regions, and the South and West regions are defined in accordance with census procedures. This classification distinguishes the northern "Frostbelt" metropolitan areas—older areas which, by and large, either began as or became transformed into major manufacturing areas in the late

---

[20]Real Estate Research Corporation, *Costs of Sprawl* (Washington, DC: U.S. Government Printing Office, 1975).

[21]Katharine L. Bradbury, Anthony Downs, and Kenneth A. Small, *Urban Decline and the Future of American Cities* (Washington, DC: The Brookings Institution, 1982).

nineteenth and early twentieth centuries—from the faster growing South and West "Sunbelt" areas. These two broad categories of areas differ markedly on the dimensions of age, economic function, annexation practices, development history, and city politics.[22] As a result of these differences, South and West cities are generally in a position to retain greater shares of their metropolitan areas' growth in population, and commercial and industrial investment than is the case with their northern counterparts.

The regional typology will also be relevant to the analyses of black–white redistribution in subsequent chapters. The history of black interregional migration, coupled with the distinctly different settlement patterns in northern and southern cities, dictates a separate classification for areas in the South.[23]

Economic function: While not explicitly incorporated into the Part Two metropolitan area typology, the economic function of each metropolitan area will be alluded to in the analyses. Just as a metropolitan area's functional type proved significant for explaining *metropolitan-wide* growth in Part One (Chapter 4), an area's economic function holds additional implications for the city–suburb redistribution process— particularly in areas that are transforming themselves from primarily manufacturing centers to more diversified economic functions.

Past urban scholars have employed various functional classification schemes to distinguish the primary economic activity of metropolitan areas.[24] However, the classification schemes developed by Stanback and Knight (employed in Chapter 4) and by Noyelle and Stanback are particularly appropriate for the present purposes since they are sensitive to the nature of a metropolitan area's service function.[25] Unlike earlier classifications, which follow from the "primary-secondary-tertiary" tri-

[22]While this generalization is valid, for the most part, there exist significant differences among cities within each group in the political dynamics that affected city development and growth in the postwar period. Two comparative analyses of selected cities' experiences are Susan S. Fainstein et al., *Restructuring the City;* and Richard M. Bernard and Bradley R. Rice, eds., *Sunbelt Cities: Politics and Growth Since World War II* (Austin: University of Texas Press, 1983).

[23]Taeuber and Taeuber, *Negroes in the City;* and Horace C. Hamilton, "The Negro Leaves the South," *Demography* 1(1964):273–295.

[24]Earlier classification schemes are discussed in Chauncy D. Harris, "A Functional Classification of Cities in the United States," *Geographical Review* 33 (1943):86–99; Howard J. Nelson, "A Service Classification of American Cities," *Economic Geography* 31, (1955):189–210; Otis Dudley Duncan et al., *Metropolis and Region* (Baltimore: Johns Hopkins Press, 1960); and in Brian J. L. Berry, ed., *City Classification Handbook: Methods and Applications* (New York: Wiley, 1972).

[25]Thomas M. Stanback, Jr. and Richard V. Knight, *The Metropolitan Economy* (New York: Columbia University Press, 1970); and Noyelle and Stanback, *The Economic Transformation of American Cities.*

chonomy of industries, the classification schemes developed by Stanback and his co-authors consider services to be less of a "tertiary" dependent activity than in the past, and suggest a greater role for high-level producer services and the complex of corporate activities. This is because these services, in themselves, can be exported and form the base of an area's industrial structure. While the authors foresee a continued deconcentration of low-level manufacturing production and consumer-oriented services to smaller and peripheral metropolitan areas, they predict an increased *concentration* of high-level services and corporate headquarters in large metropolitan areas which serve as diversified service centers.

We believe that the Noyelle and Stanback scheme, in particular, is relevant for an evaluation of central city growth since the *central cities* of those diversified service center metropolitan areas—which the authors class as "nodal"—should be most likely to prosper during the transformation to a postindustrial economy. The Noyelle and Stanback functional classes most relevant to metropolitan areas in this study are nodal (both national and regional), functional nodal, and manufacturing. Both national and regional nodal areas are considered to be diversified service centers—specializing in the export of headquarters' functions, and producer and distribution services to national and regional hinterlands. It is these high-level service areas which Noyelle and Stanback expect to prosper as other economic functions decentralize down the metropolitan hierarchy. However, because these activities tend to concentrate in central cities, we believe that the central cities of these nodal metropolitan areas hold the best prospects of adapting to a changing national economy.

The functional nodal areas and production areas designated by Noyelle and Stanback have more questionable long-term outlooks than do the regional and national nodal areas—and this carries over to the growth potentials for their central cities. The central cities of functional nodal areas hold somewhat better prospects of surviving as high-level service centers than those of production centers. Although the metropolitan areas of the former type are still heavily grounded in production activities, they have also managed to strengthen their position as corporate and high-level service locations for those industries in which they specialize. The economic survival of these areas' central cities as specialized service centers depends upon the success of those industries within the metropolitan area to which these cities' services are tied. On the other hand, the production center metropolitan areas are primarily engaged in standardized assembly-type production work. These areas have not cultivated specialized service or corporate administrative activities and are most vulnerable to adverse developments affecting their particular industries. The long-term prognosis for the success of their central cities as high-level service centers is not very encouraging.[26]

Classification of Areas

Following the above discussion we classify the 39 metropolitan areas on the basis of two categories of age (Old and Young), two categories of metropolitan area growth (Declining and Nondeclining), and three categories of region (North, South, and West). In this classification, Old metropolitan areas have central cities that achieved populations greater than 50,000 prior to 1900—in the North and South regions, and prior to 1910 in the West region.[27] The definition of Declining metropolitan areas, for this study, includes those which grew by less than one-half over the 1950–1980 period *and* registered negative or negligible metropolitanwide growth over the 1970–1980 decade. All other metropolitan areas are treated as Nondeclining.

Figure 7.1 shows that only six of the possible 12 categories in this typology are used. This is because all of the Declining metropolitan areas also happen to be Old areas that lie in the North region. Also, there exist no Young areas in the North. To simplify the terminology used, therefore, we termed the 13 North Old-and-Declining areas as North-Declining, and characterize the remaining (Nondeclining) areas in all regions on the basis of their region and age status (that is, North-Old, South-Old, West-Old, South-Young, West-Young). The names of the metropolitan areas under each heading are shown with related statistics in Table 7.1 and are located on the map in Figure 7.2.

Of the 13 North-Declining metropolitan areas, the smallest

[26]Other Noyelle and Stanback functional classes that apply to metropolitan areas in this study are: government-education areas, industrial-military areas, resort-retirement areas, and residential areas. These represent more specialized functional types wherein the functions are less directly linked to the city–suburb redistribution process. Of these, the government-education areas are perhaps most closely associated with the sustenance of city economic growth. Noyelle and Stanback consider these areas to be another kind of specialized service center with concentrations of public sector facilities, nonprofit institutions, and universities—growing economic activities which generally require central locations. The remaining area types are considered to be primarily production centers (industrial-military areas), or consumer centers (resort-retirement areas, residential areas). While these types of centers are expected to decline in importance as their metropolitan functions are subject to the vagaries of federal funding and the level of economic prosperity in their immediate regions, the relevance of these functions for the city–suburb redistribution process varies across individual areas.

[27]Portland and Seattle are classed as "Old," even though they did not achieve a 50,000 population until 1900. This decision was made due to the fact that the West Coast cities developed later than those in other regions and because the development and growth histories of Portland and Seattle more closely parallel those of other West-Old areas than West-Young areas.

FIGURE 7.1

Metropolitan Area Typology
for Analysis of City–Suburb Redistribution

	NORTH		SOUTH		WEST	
	OLD	YOUNG	OLD	YOUNG	OLD	YOUNG
DECLINING	13 North – Declining Areas	–	–	–	–	–
NONDECLINING	5 North – Old Areas	–	4 South – Old Areas	6 South – Young Areas	5 West – Old Areas	6 West – Young Areas

1950–1980 growth rates were registered by Pittsburgh (+2.3 percent), New York City (+13.6 percent), and Buffalo (+14.1 percent)—areas that declined by −5.7 percent, −6.5 percent, and −7.9 percent, respectively, in the 1970–1980 decade. These declines for two of the areas are consistent with their functional classifications (shown in column 5), wherein Buffalo represents the only predominantly manufacturing area of the 39, and Pittsburgh is classed as a functional nodal area. The decade decline seems less consistent for New York City's role as a national nodal center. The largest 1970–1980 metropolitan decline was registered for Cleveland, which lost 8 percent of its 1970 population. While Cleveland has been characterized as a regional nodal center, a significant share of its work force is engaged in manufacturing production (see column 6), a factor that contributes to its recent level of decline.

Consistent with their older ages, most of these metropolitan areas have relatively underbounded central cities with high densities (columns 7 and 8). They also tend to have large concentrations of blacks in their cities and (as will be shown in Chapter 9) wide city–suburb disparities on a variety of socioeconomic measures. All of these attributes, as well as the results of the Bradbury, Downs, and Small study (cited above), suggest a rather bleak scenario for the central cities of these areas. A positive sign lies in the fact that 12 of these 13 areas are

TABLE 7.1

Selected Metropolitan Area and Central City Characteristics: 39 Metropolitan Areas[a]

Metropolitan Area Groupings/[b] Metropolitan Areas	Age of Central City[c] (1)	Metropolitan Percent Change 1950–1980 (2)	Metropolitan Percent Change 1970–1980 (3)	1980 Metropolitan Size (millions) (4)	Metropolitan Functional Type[d] (5)	1970 Metropolitan Area Percent Emp. in Mfg. (6)	1980 City Share of Metropolitan Area (7)	1980 City Density (thousands) (8)	1980 Percent City Black (9)
NORTH-DECLINING									
New York	1800	+13.6	−6.5	10.88	Nodal (National)	20.6	65.0	23.4	25.3
Philadelphia	1810	+28.5	−2.2	4.72	Nodal (Regional)	30.9	35.8	12.4	37.8
Boston	1830	+19.5	−1.3	3.66	Nodal (Regional)	25.6	15.4	12.0	22.5
Cincinnati	1850	+37.0	+1.0	1.40	Nodal (Regional)	32.7	27.5	4.9	33.9
St. Louis	1850	+31.6	−2.3	2.36	Nodal (Regional)	28.7	19.2	7.4	45.5
Buffalo	1860	+14.1	−7.9	1.24	Manufacturing	33.4	28.8	8.5	26.7
Chicago	1860	+37.2	+1.8	7.10	Nodal (National)	31.7	42.3	13.1	39.8
Newark	1860	+25.4	−4.5	1.97	Functional Nodal	33.1	16.8	13.7	58.3
Cleveland	1870	+23.9	−8.0	1.90	Nodal (Regional)	35.4	30.2	7.3	43.8
Detroit	1870	+37.3	−1.8	4.35	Functional Nodal	37.4	27.6	8.8	63.0
Milwaukee	1870	+37.8	−0.5	1.40	Functional Nodal	35.1	45.5	6.6	23.1
Pittsburgh	1870	+2.3	−5.7	2.26	Functional Nodal	31.7	18.7	7.7	24.0
Paterson*	1880	+47.6	−4.8	1.29	Functional Nodal	33.1	20.5	11.5	21.8
NORTH-OLD									
Columbus	1880	+71.5	+7.4	1.09	Nodal (Regional)	24.6	51.2	3.1	22.0
Indianapolis	1880	+60.4	+5.0	1.17	Nodal (Regional)	29.2	60.1	2.0	21.8
Kansas City	1880	+53.5	+4.2	1.33	Nodal (Regional)	22.8	33.8	1.4	27.3
Hartford	1890	+61.4	+1.6	1.05	Functional Nodal	33.3	13.0	7.6	33.8
Minneapolis*	1890	+68.8	+7.5	2.11	Nodal (Regional)	24.8	30.3	6.0	6.5
SOUTH-OLD									
Baltimore	1820	+49.2	+5.0	2.17	Nodal (Regional)	25.2	36.2	9.8	54.8
New Orleans	1840	+66.6	+13.4	1.19	Nodal (Regional)	14.1	47.0	2.8	55.3
Washington, D.C.	1860	+99.9	+5.2	3.06	Government-Education	6.5	20.9	10.1	70.2
Atlanta	1890	+134.8	+27.2	2.03	Nodal (Regional)	21.6	20.9	3.2	66.6

TABLE 7.1 (continued)

WEST-OLD									
San Francisco*	1860	+51.2	+4.5	3.25	Nodal (National)	16.7	31.3	10.2	24.1
Denver*	1890	+162.9	+30.8	1.62	Nodal (Regional)	17.0	35.1	4.3	10.6
Los Angeles*	1890	+80.1	+6.2	7.48	Nodal (National)	27.3	44.5	6.5	16.4
Portland	1900	+76.3	+23.4	1.24	Nodal (Regional)	21.0	29.5	3.6	7.7
Seattle	1900	+90.3	+12.8	1.61	Nodal (Regional)	24.2	34.1	3.3	8.6
SOUTH-YOUNG									
San Antonio	1900	+87.7	+20.7	1.07	Industrial-Military	12.3	73.3	3.0	7.3
Dallas*	1910	+144.6	+25.1	2.97	Nodal (Regional)	25.8	43.3	2.2	27.4
Houston	1910	+206.6	+45.3	2.91	Nodal (Regional)	20.4	54.9	2.9	27.6
Tampa*	1920	+265.2	+44.1	1.57	Resort-Retirement	15.8	32.5	3.6	20.5
Miami	1930	+228.4	+28.2	1.63	Nodal (Regional)	14.8	21.3	10.2	25.1
Ft. Lauderdale*	1960	+1113.1	+64.2	1.02	Resort-Retirement	11.8	27.0	5.1	13.6
WEST-YOUNG									
Sacramento	1920	+182.1	+26.2	1.01	Government-Education	9.2	27.2	2.9	13.4
San Diego	1920	+234.4	+37.1	1.86	Industrial-Military	17.5	47.0	2.7	8.9
San Jose	1930	+345.7	+21.6	1.30	Functional Nodal	30.6	48.6	4.0	4.6
Phoenix	1940	+354.9	+55.4	1.51	Nodal (Regional)	20.3	52.3	2.4	4.8
Riverside*	1950	+245.0	+36.8	1.56	Resort-Retirement	17.8	24.2	2.3	8.6
Anaheim*	1960	+793.9	+36.0	1.93	Residential	28.8	28.3	6.3	2.1

SOURCES: U.S. Census of Population, 1970, Vol. I, Part A, *Number of Inhabitants*, Section 1 (U.S. Summary), table 28 (for Age of Central City); Noyelle and Stanback, 1984, Chapter 4 (for Met. Area Functional Type); and machine-readable computer files (for remaining characteristics): *County and City Data Book Consolidated Files*, and *County and City Data Book, 1983 File for Counties, 1947–1977*, and *Cities, 1944–1977* (prepared by the U.S. Bureau of the Census, Washington, DC).

[a] 1980 metropolitan areas with populations greater than 1 million defined as 1980 SMSAs and NECMAs (in New England), except for New York and Paterson–Clifton–Passaic (see Appendix F).

[b] These metropolitan area groupings are based on three categories of region (North, South, West), two categories of age (Old, Young), and two categories of metropolitan growth (Declining, Nondeclining). Thirteen Declining areas are also Old and located in the North, and are placed in the single North-Declining grouping. The remaining 26 areas are all Nondeclining and are sorted into the groupings: North–Old, South–Old, West–Old, South–Young, and West–Young. Further details are provided in the Chapter 7 section "A Metropolitan Area Typology" and Figure 7.1.

[c] Census year when largest central city first achieved a population of 50,000.

[d] Following Thierry J. Noyelle and Thomas M. Stanback, Jr., *The Economic Transformation of American Cities* (Rowman & Allanheld, 1984).

* Largest of multiple central cities (complete metropolitan area names are listed in Appendix F).

FIGURE 7.2

*Map of Large Metropolitan Areas in North, South, and West Regions,
1980*

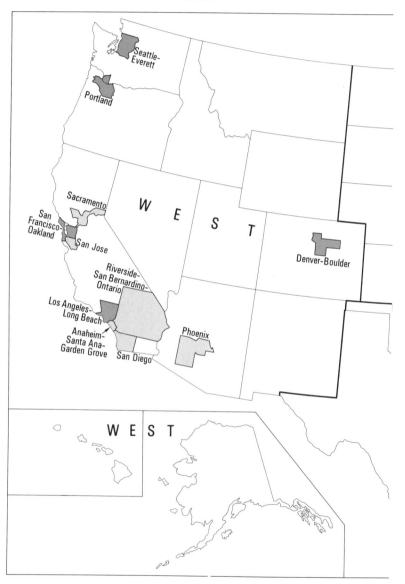

FIGURE 7.2 *(continued)*

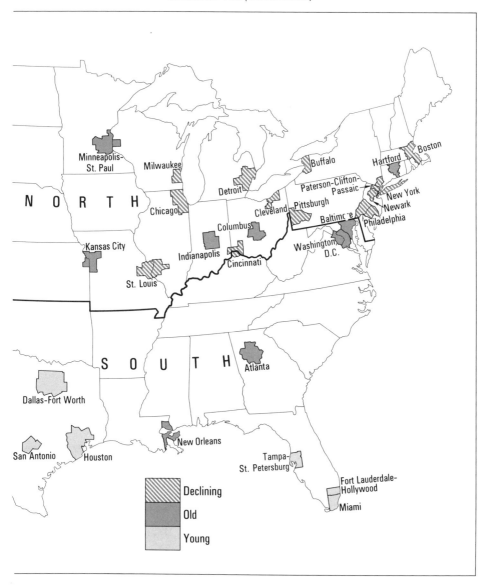

classed as either nodal or functional nodal areas—functional types which, as we have suggested, hold the capacity of sustaining a viable central city economy. However, the functional nodal areas, with a sizable manufacturing component, are the ones for which survival is most open to question.

The remaining 26 Nondeclining metropolitan areas are classed on the basis of their regional location and central city age. Those classed as North-Old actually rank among the newest of the three Old categories. With the exception of Hartford, they are located in the census Midwest region and take on a regional nodal function. Aside from being relatively younger, they contrast with the North-Declining areas by registering slightly smaller manufacturing components in their work force. Also, consistent with their younger ages these central cities have generally larger areas and lower densities than the average North-Declining center. Hartford constitutes the exception among this group. As a functional nodal area with a strong manufacturing component, it registered the lowest 1970–1980 population gain (+1.6 percent) of the North-Old class. It also differs from the others in its internal configuration—displaying a small city area, high population density, and relatively large concentration of blacks. However, as a group, the North-Old areas are in a far better position to sustain a viable city economy than the North-Declining areas—as a consequence of their metropolitan growth, nodal functions, and greater city areas.

The South-Old class areas constitute older, moderately growing areas in a rapidly growing region. These four areas, in fact, diverge in their growth patterns from Baltimore's 49.2 percent to Atlanta's 134.8 percent, over the 1950–1980 period. Yet all four have economic functions which should serve to bolster the central city's prosperity (although Baltimore and Atlanta also hold significant manufacturing activity). The major difference between these areas and those of the North-Old class lies in their internal structure. All four have majority black populations and two (Baltimore and Washington) have underbounded, high-density central cities. These aspects of South-Old areas, in the absence of racial desegregation, might serve to stifle future central city gains.

The West-Old areas, like the South-Old areas, constitute older, relatively well-off areas in a very well-off region. Two of these areas, San Francisco–Oakland and Los Angeles–Long Beach, are national nodal centers. Yet, they are among the slowest growing metropolitan areas of the group. Only Denver–Boulder registers a 30-year growth increase in excess of 100 percent, although Portland's 1970–1980 metropolitan growth rate (+23.4 percent) rivals that of Denver–Boulder (+30.8 percent). Still, all of these centers hold nodal functions; and those that register significant manufacturing employment specialize in newer industries related to aerospace and defense. The central cities of these areas, while more expansive than the typical North-Old and South-Old metropolitan areas, are not as spacious as most of the Young metropolitan areas and display relatively high population densities. Even the sprawling central cities of Los Angeles–Long Beach register high city population densities, and San Francisco's city density is among the highest in the country. Finally, it should be noted that while each of these cities have concentrations of blacks, they have significant concentrations of other minority groups (Hispanics and Asians), which will be elaborated upon in Chapter 8. On balance, these areas' central cities probably stand to fare better than those in any of the other Old or Declining regional groupings. This is a consequence of their favorable metropolitanwide economic functions, moderate population growth, and relatively expansive central city areas.

The 12 cities that comprise classes South-Young and West-Young are an extremely heterogeneous group. One common characteristic, which distinguishes them from the areas discussed above, is their generally high growth level over both the 1950–1980 period and the 1970–1980 period. Except for San Antonio, each of these areas doubled its size over the 1950–1980 period, and several areas increased their 1950 populations by factors of 2, 3, 7, or 11! More recently, over the 1970–1980 decade, these areas grew anywhere from 20.7 percent (for San Antonio) to 64.2 percent (for Ft. Lauderdale–Hollywood).

Another common characteristic, which draws from their very recent development, is their generally expansive city areas and low city population densities. Most of these cities have had little difficulty in annexing suburban territory and, therefore, are able to house larger shares of their metropolitan areas' populations than is the case in older areas. One marked exception to this is Miami, which remains relatively underbounded and registers a population density in excess of 10,000 persons per square mile.

The main source of heterogeneity among these 12 areas pertains to their economic functions. Only 6 of the 12 were classed according to functions that characterize the Old and Declining metropolitan areas, according to the Noyelle and Stanback scheme.[28] These are Dallas–Ft. Worth, Houston, Miami, and Phoenix (regional nodal centers), San Jose (a functional nodal center), and Sacramento (a government-education center). Four of these areas also have significant manufacturing com-

---

[28]Noyelle and Stanback, *The Economic Transformation of American Cities.*

ponents (column 7), but in high-technology industries that have good growth potential.[29] On the basis of their service functions and on the nature of their manufacturing industries, there appears no need to expect a curtailment of growth in these metropolitan areas or their central cities. The remaining areas are involved in more specialized economic functions: industrial-military (San Antonio, San Diego); resort-retirement (Tampa–St. Petersburg, Ft. Lauderdale–Hollywood, Riverside–San Bernardino–Ontario); and residential (Anaheim–Santa Ana–Garden Grove). Although these areas are growing rapidly, it is not apparent how their economic functions will affect the city-suburb redistribution process.

Finally, it should be noted that South-Young cities differ markedly from West-Young cities in one important respect—their central city racial compositions. West-Young cities have the smallest representation of blacks of any of the city groups examined. Some of these cities have large concentrations of Hispanics and Asians, but lacking in all of them is a black presence that characterizes most large cities. Four of the six South-Young cities do show black concentrations in excess of 20 percent of their 1980 populations. Analyses in Chapter 8 will examine the influence these different city racial compositions exert on suburbanization patterns for South-Young and West-Young metropolitan areas.

Discussion

The metropolitan area typology just presented is intended as a framework for evaluating the post-1970 city–suburb redistribution processes in the nation's largest metropolitan areas. In contrast to smaller metropolitan areas (with populations under 1 million), these areas are generally older and have developed sharper central city–suburb growth disparities over time (see Table 7.2). The above discussion has emphasized the particular plight of central cities in North-Declining metropolitan areas, but it has also implied that within this grouping central cities of some areas (nodal centers) might fare well, while the success of other areas' central cities (functional nodal centers) is more questionable. Next worse off are central cities in South-Old areas— moderately growing, nodal, and government centers which are relatively underbounded, black-majority central cities with wide city–suburb disparities in measures of population composition. North-Old metropolitan areas are slightly better off than South-Old areas in terms

[29]John H. Mollenkopf, "Paths Toward the Post-Industrial Service City"; and Amy Glasmeier, Peter Hall, and Ann R. Markusen, "Metropolitan High Technology Industry Growth in the Mid–1970s: Can Everyone Have a Slice of the High Tech Pie?" *Berkeley Planning Journal* 1(1)(Spring 1984):131–142.

TABLE 7.2

Selected Metropolitan Area and Central City Characteristics
for (aggregated) 39 Largest Metropolitan Areas and Other Metropolitan Areas
in North, South, and West Regions

Region/Metropolitan Area Size Class[a]	1980 Metropolitan Size (millions) (1)	Metropolitan Percent Change 1970–1980 (2)	Percent with Old Central Cities (3)	Percent Change 1970–1980	
				Central City (4)	Suburbs (5)
NORTH					
Large Metropolitan Areas	51.3	−2.1	100.0	−12.6	+5.6
Other Metropolitan Areas	33.2	+4.9	15.1	+5.7	+11.9
SOUTH					
Large Metropolitan Areas	19.6	+23.7	40.0	+3.7	+39.2
Other Metropolitan Areas	30.8	+20.1	4.5	+11.4	+28.6
WEST					
Large Metropolitan Areas	24.4	+18.4	45.4	+9.1	+25.0
Other Metropolitan Areas	11.2	+32.7	2.5	+28.7	+36.1

SOURCES: Same as Table 7.1.

[a]"Large Metropolitan Areas" pertain to the 39 1980 metropolitan areas with populations exceeding 1 million. "Other Metropolitan Areas" pertain to all other 1980 metropolitan areas as defined in Appendix F.

of stemming long-term city decline. Most of these serve the role of regional service centers and exhibit fewer city–suburb disparities. Nevertheless, the most successful long-term scenario of all large older central cities would appear to lie with those in West-Old metropolitan areas. These growing areas are national and regional nodal centers, have fairly expansive central cities, and relatively few city–suburb disparities on racial and socioeconomic characteristics. Finally, it is clear that the growth prospects for central cities in the South-Young and West-Young metropolitan areas are strong. It should be instructive to examine the city–suburb redistribution processes in several of these areas that do not serve as nodal centers.

Components of City–Suburb Population Redistribution: 1950–1980

This section documents the demographic components of city and suburb population change within the 39 large metropolitan areas just discussed to provide background for the analyses of selective redistribution patterns in the remaining Part Two chapters. The argument put forth earlier suggests that post-1970 shifts in race relations, household formation patterns, and industrial structure may slow the pace or, perhaps, even reverse the directions of decline and decay in America's large central cities. This reversal may not bring about population gains or even reduced population losses for central cities where the population has been declining for decades. However, it may be influential in effecting an altered city–suburb selectivity of population, households, and employment consistent with a more service-oriented central city function. The discussion of total population change below serves as a point of departure for the later evaluations of these selective redistribution patterns.

Central City and Suburb Population Change, 1950–1980

This section will review postwar population changes in the central cities of the 39 metropolitan areas based on data compiled from the 1950, 1960, 1970, and 1980 Censuses of Population. The review will be placed in the context of the six-category metropolitan area typology presented above. Figure 7.3 plots aggregate metropolitan area and central city growth for each of the six metropolitan area groupings, Figures 7.4 and 7.5 plot similar data for selected individual areas, and Table 7.3 displays 1970–1980 central city and suburb rates of change for all 39

FIGURE 7.3

Population of Metropolitan Areas and Central Cities,
1950, 1960, 1970, 1980: Six Metropolitan Area Groupings

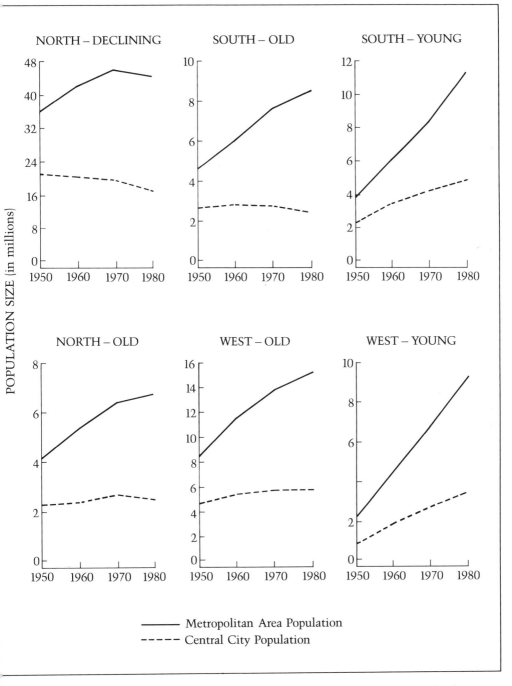

SOURCES: Machine-readable computer files: *County and City Data Book*, Consolidated Files for Counties, 1947–1977, and Cities, 1944–1947; and *County and City Data Book*, 1983 files (prepared by the U.S.
Bureau of the Census, Washington DC).

FIGURE 7.4

Population of Metropolitan Areas and Central Cities,
1950, 1960, 1970, 1980: Six Selected Metropolitan Areas

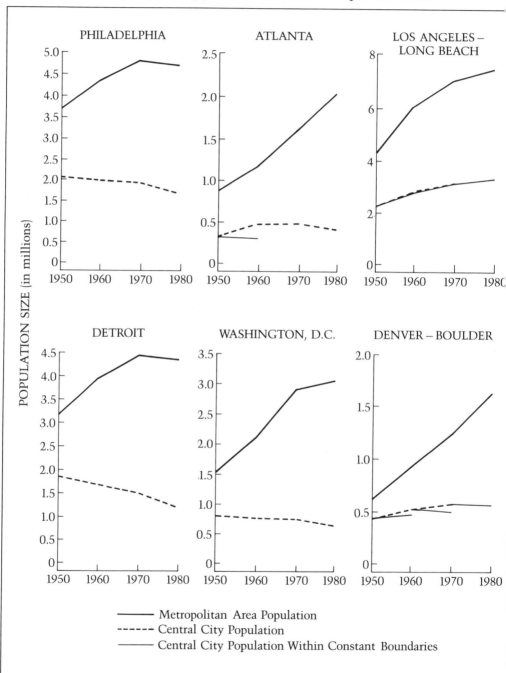

SOURCES: Same as Figure 7.3

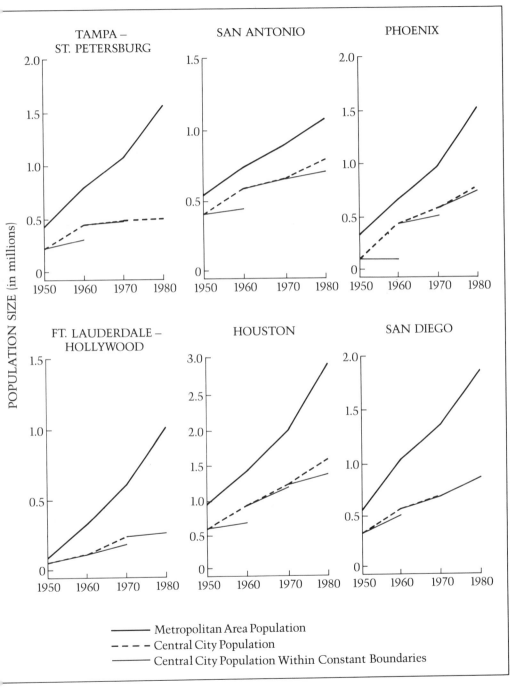

FIGURE 7.5

*Population of Metropolitan Areas and Central Cities,
1950, 1960, 1970, 1980: Six Selected Metropolitan Areas*

POPULATION SIZE (in millions)

TAMPA –
ST. PETERSBURG

SAN ANTONIO

PHOENIX

FT. LAUDERDALE –
HOLLYWOOD

HOUSTON

SAN DIEGO

——— Metropolitan Area Population
- - - - Central City Population
——— Central City Population Within Constant Boundaries

SOURCES: Same as Figure 7.3.

SMSAs. (For further reference, individual metropolitan area and central city 1950–1980 population data for the 39 areas are presented in Appendix E, Tables 7A and 7B.)

North-Declining areas: The upper left panel of Figure 7.3 shows the dominant postwar pattern for North-Declining metropolitan areas— significant growth in the 1950s, slowing growth in the 1960s, and metropolitanwide loss in the 1970s. Paralleling this trend is a dominant central city pattern of loss for all three decades—a pattern that becomes accentuated in the 1970s. Within these dominant patterns there are variations across individual metropolitan areas. These variations are particularly apparent when examining 1970s central city declines, shown in Table 7.3.

New York and Chicago, the two national nodal centers in this group, and Boston and Philadelphia, the East Coast regional nodal centers, sustained levels of city decline that are much more moderated than those of most other North-Declining central cities. This is despite their high density levels and significant metropolitan population declines. In contrast, several functional nodal, regional nodal, and manufacturing metropolitan areas in the country's interior (Detroit, Pittsburgh, St. Louis, Cleveland, and Buffalo) suffered far higher levels of central city loss in the 1970s than did Chicago or the above-mentioned East Coast nodal centers.

The comparison of the growth histories for Philadelphia and Detroit shown in Figure 7.4 illustrates these differences. Both areas displayed comparable rates of metropolitan growth in the 1950s, 1960s, and 1970s (+18.3 percent, +11.1 percent, and −2.2 percent for Philadelphia; +24.6 percent, +12.3 percent, and −1.8 percent for Detroit), and both areas sustained central city losses since 1950. Yet the magnitude of city losses in Detroit had been higher throughout, and particularly so in the 1970s. This Detroit pattern is indicative of those in the other interior metropolitan areas discussed above. It reflects population changes that seem to occur in central cities that are not highly diversified corporate or administrative service centers, or that are heavily dependent on one or more industries. Although Boston, New York, and Chicago displayed similar levels of growth and decline at the metropolitan area level, their central cities were faring much better than those in these interior metropolitan areas.

The four remaining North-Declining metropolitan areas do not conform so clearly to the above patterns. The Midwest metropolitan areas of Cincinnati (a regional nodal center) and Milwaukee (a functional nodal center) displayed 1970–1980 rates of city decline that are more moderated than those of the other interior metropolitan areas.

Both of these areas have relatively lower central city densities and are able to accommodate greater commercial and industrial development within their boundaries. Finally, the two East Coast metropolitan areas, Newark and Paterson–Clifton–Passaic, are functional nodal metropolitan areas that are closely linked with the greater New York metropolitan region. Both of these areas grew considerably during the 1950s and 1960s as the New York region's population began to disperse. Newark's central city declined during all three postwar decades while the Paterson–Clifton–Passaic central cities grew during the 1950s and 1960s and declined at the rate of −6.2 percent during the 1970s.

The data in Table 7.3 show that all North-Declining cities exhibited both central city population losses and positive suburbanization rates (the algebraic difference between suburban percent population change and central city percent population change) during the decade of the 1970s. Indeed, most areas achieved their positive suburbanization rates through levels of central city loss that were greater in absolute value than their levels of suburban gain. (Both the central cities *and* suburbs displayed population losses in four of these metropolitan areas.) This city-loss dominated pattern of suburbanization is characteristic of North-Declining metropolitan areas in the 1970s, reflecting the impact that metropolitanwide population loss can exert in areas that surround older, underbounded central city cores. The remaining metropolitan areas have all shown metropolitanwide population growth in the 1970s although, as shall be seen, their central cities varied greatly in the levels of growth and decline over this decade.

North-Old areas: We turn now to the North-Old areas, where metropolitanwide population growth has tended to diminish over each successive postwar decade. The aggregate city growth patterns shown in Figure 7.3 suggest that their central cities also grew during the 1950s and 1960s, and exhibited losses only in the 1970s. However, this aggregate pattern masks individual area growth patterns and annexation policies. Both the Hartford and Minneapolis–St. Paul metropolitan areas are distinct from the others in this group in that: (1) their cities have not annexed significant territory over the postwar period; and (2) their cities declined in population during all three decades. Hartford, the only functional nodal city of this group, sustained a significant 8.6 percent loss in the 1950s, a more moderate 2.6 percent loss in the 1960s, and an accentuated 13.7 percent loss in the 1970s. Hartford's 1970s city–suburb redistribution process resembles that of the better-off North-Declining areas, showing a fairly significant level of central city loss combined with a small degree of suburban growth.

The Minneapolis–St. Paul area exhibited the second highest metro-

TABLE 7.3

Percent Central City and Suburban Change, 1970–1980:
39 Metropolitan Areas

Met. Area Groupings/ Met. Areas	Percent Change in Population, 1970–1980		Suburbanization Rate (3)
	Central City (1)	Suburbs (2)	
NORTH–DECLINING			
New York	− 10.4	+ 1.9	+ 12.3
Philadelphia	− 13.4	+ 5.4	+ 18.8
Boston	− 12.2	+ 1.0	+ 13.2
Cincinnati	− 15.0	+ 8.8	+ 23.8
St. Louis	− 27.2	+ 6.4	+ 33.6
Buffalo	− 22.7	− 0.2	+ 22.5
Chicago	− 10.8	+ 13.7	+ 24.5
Newark	− 13.8	− 2.3	+ 11.5
Cleveland	− 23.6	+ 0.9	+ 24.5
Detroit	− 20.5	+ 7.8	+ 28.3
Milwaukee	− 11.3	+ 10.8	+ 22.1
Pittsburgh	− 18.5	− 2.2	+ 16.3
Paterson*	− 6.2	− 4.4	+ 1.8
Total	− 13.3	+ 4.3	+ 17.6
NORTH–OLD			
Columbus	+ 4.6	+ 10.6	+ 6.0
Indianapolis	− 4.9	+ 24.4	+ 29.3
Kansas City	− 11.7	+ 14.7	+ 26.4
Hartford	− 13.7	+ 4.3	+ 18.0
Minneapolis*	− 13.9	+ 20.6	+ 34.5
Total	− 7.3	+ 14.6	+ 21.9
SOUTH–OLD			
Baltimore	− 13.1	+ 19.1	+ 32.2
New Orleans	− 6.1	+ 39.0	+ 45.1
Washington, D.C.	− 15.6	+ 12.5	+ 28.1
Atlanta	− 14.1	+ 45.8	+ 59.9
Total	− 12.5	+ 24.1	+ 36.6
WEST–OLD			
San Francisco*	− 5.5	+ 9.9	+ 15.4
Denver*	− 2.1	+ 59.9	+ 62.0
Los Angeles*	+ 5.0	+ 7.2	+ 2.2
Portland	− 3.6	+ 39.7	+ 43.3
Seattle*	− 6.2	+ 26.1	+ 32.3
Total	+ 0.6	+ 16.7	+ 17.3

TABLE 7.3 *(continued)*

let. Area Groupings/ let. Areas	Percent Change in Population, 1970–1980		Suburbanization[a] Rate (3)
	Central City (1)	Suburbs (2)	
OUTH–YOUNG			
San Antonio	+20.1	+22.2	+2.1
Dallas*	+4.2	+47.9	+43.7
Houston	+29.3	+71.1	+41.8
Tampa*	+3.3	+78.1	+74.8
Miami	+3.6	+37.1	+33.5
Ft. Lauderdale*	+11.4	+99.0	+87.6
Total	+14.3	+57.5	+43.2
VEST–YOUNG			
Sacramento	+7.2	+35.0	+27.8
San Diego	+25.5	+49.4	+23.9
San Jose	+36.9	+9.9	−27.0
Phoenix	+35.2	+85.9	+50.7
Riverside*	+21.3	+42.6	+21.3
Anaheim*	+23.2	+41.8	+18.6
Total	+26.9	+41.7	+14.8

SOURCE: Machine-readable computer files: *County and City Data Book,* 1983 file (prepared by the U.S. Bureau of the Census, Washington, DC).

Suburbanization Rate: Suburb Percent Change, column (2), minus Central City Percent Change, column (1).

[a] Largest of multiple central cities.

politan growth (next to Columbus) of all northern areas in 1950–1980, and the greatest rate over the most recent decade. Nevertheless, its central cities have exhibited increased losses over the 1950s, 1960s, and 1970s. The wide 1970s' disparity between this area's city loss (−13.9 percent) and its suburban gain (+20.6 percent) means that Minneapolis–St. Paul's relatively high level of metropolitan growth is becoming increasingly concentrated in its suburbs.

The three remaining North-Old metropolitan areas, Columbus, Indianapolis, and Kansas City, are all regional nodal metropolitan areas. Each of these increased its city's population in both the 1950s and 1960s through a combination of population growth and city annexation. During the 1970s, however, neither Indianapolis nor Kansas City altered their central cities' boundaries significantly, and both registered central city losses. Columbus continued to annex territory in the 1970s (discussed below) and also increased its central city population. Hence, Columbus remains the only North-Old metropolitan area that registers a 1970s' population gain for its central city.

Although most North-Old areas' central cities have displayed accentuated population losses in the 1970s, these losses were, on average, less severe than average losses in North-Declining central cities. Still, the city–suburb redistribution process has occurred more rapidly in these five areas because their relatively higher rates of metropolitan-wide growth became concentrated almost entirely in their suburbs.

South-Old areas: In contrast to these North-Old patterns, the South-Old areas—which sustained higher rates of metropolitan growth—displayed even greater disparities between their central city losses and suburban gains. The latter situation could be expected from our earlier discussion which emphasized the fact that these old, high-density central cities now serve as cores for growing metropolitan areas in the prosperous South region.

The aggregated patterns for South-Old areas (Figure 7.3) show significant metropolitanwide growth in all three postwar decades, although this growth diminished somewhat in the 1970s. The patterns also show aggregate central city growth during the 1950s, followed by increasing city declines in the 1960s and 1970s. The aggregate 1950s central city growth is accounted for largely by Atlanta's extensive city annexation during that period. However, the remaining aggregate patterns represent individual metropolitan trends in broad scope.

Atlanta has grown more rapidly than any of the other South-Old metropolitan areas during the postwar period. The plot in Figure 7.4 shows metropolitan growth rates of +35 percent, +37 percent, and +27 percent, respectively, over the three postwar decades. Despite this growth, the size of Atlanta's central city increased mostly as the result of the extensive annexation of suburban territory in the 1950s.[30] In the absence of this annexation, its 1950–1960 city growth of +47.1 percent would have been a loss of −4.6 percent. Its small 1960–1970 city growth of +1.6 percent was also aided by a modest annexation of territory; and in 1970–1980, when no significant annexation took place, the city lost 14 percent of its population.

New Orleans, like Atlanta, is an older nodal regional center located in the southern heartland, and its metropolitan area has also reaped the gains of the heightened population growth in this region. New Orleans'

---

[30]As an older central city, surrounded by well-entrenched suburban interests, Atlanta's annexation required elaborate political planning and organization which is generally not required in the newer Sunbelt cities (see Bernard and Rice, *Sunbelt Cities*).

central city is somewhat more expansive than Atlanta's—even after the latter's annexation—and has sustained a somewhat smaller population loss in the most recent decade. Nevertheless, this loss (−6.1 percent) is larger than that of the 1960–1970 decade (−5.4 percent), and must be viewed in comparison with the extensive 1970s' gain of +39 percent in New Orleans' suburbs. The rigid boundaries and racial composition of this older central city appear to be contributing to the "city loss–strong suburban gain" pattern in the context of its growing metropolitan area.

The remaining South-Old areas, Washington, D.C. and Baltimore, lie on the East Coast corridor. Yet, in addition to the fact that they are located in the Census Bureau's South region, their racial and socioeconomic population distribution patterns (discussed in Chapters 8 and 9) resemble other southern metropolitan areas. Washington's high metropolitanwide growth can be explained by its role as the national capital. Its 1950s' and 1960s' metropolitan growth rates (illustrated in Figure 7.4) exceeded those for Atlanta, while its 1970s' growth diminished considerably. However, in view of its small fixed central city boundary (the District of Columbia) and its large city concentration of blacks, it is not surprising to observe city population losses over the three postwar decades. Indeed, these losses are moderated by the fact that a large share of Washington's white collar-dominated labor force is employed in city located offices, and by a 1970s' gentrification movement (which will be elaborated upon in later chapters). Baltimore constitutes a more industrialized regional nodal center. Its postwar metropolitanwide growth remains considerably below that of the other South-Old metropolitan areas, though well above those of the East Coast metropolises of Philadelphia, New York, and Boston. Its central city population has declined continuously since 1950, with an accentuated decline in the decade of the 1970s.

As a group, South-Old metropolitan areas sustained 1970s' city losses that rivaled all but the most heavily declining northern metropolitan areas—but in a context of metropolitanwide gain. Clearly, their metropolitan growth is being concentrated in the suburban portions of these areas and, at the same time, their central cities are losing significant shares of their populations.

West-Old areas: The West-Old areas, too, have benefited from comparably high levels of postwar metropolitan growth; yet, as Figure 7.3 shows, their central cities have fared somewhat better. These aggregate postwar trends in West-Old areas camouflage different individual area patterns. The national nodal center of San Francisco–Oakland displays the most distinct pattern—resembling that of the North-Old metropolitan areas in its city–suburb redistribution trend. This is because it surrounds underbounded, high-density central cities more common to older areas in the other regions. San Francisco–Oakland's central city populations declined at -4.5 percent, -2.8 percent, and -5.5 percent, respectively, over the three postwar decades—while the metropolitan area registered growth levels of $+24$ percent, $+17.4$ percent, and $+4.5$ percent. However, these recent city losses may be deceptive because San Francisco, like Washington, D.C., has been the recipient of a significant gentrification-related development during the 1970s.

At the other extreme lies the Los Angeles–Long Beach model of postwar city–suburb redistribution, which combines city annexation and population growth within an extensive low-density central city. The Los Angeles–Long Beach model, to some extent, is evident in the remaining three West-Old areas; but it is more closely adopted by several of the South-Young and West-Young metropolitan areas described later. The Los Angeles–Long Beach metropolitan area grew over all three postwar decades but most significantly in the 1950s (see Figure 7.4). Moreover, its central cities grew through all three decades as well, at rates that were between 60 percent and 80 percent of the metropolitan rate. Most of the Los Angeles–Long Beach expansive central city area was added prior to 1950, but additional annexations over the past three decades have contributed somewhat to recent central city growth.

The remaining three West-Old metropolitan areas, Denver–Boulder, Portland, and Seattle–Everett—all regional nodal centers—exhibited greater rates of 1970–1980 metropolitanwide growth than the national nodal centers of San Francisco–Oakland and Los Angeles–Long Beach. Denver–Boulder registered the greatest metropolitan area growth rates, for this group, over all three postwar decades. Moreover, as Figure 7.4 illustrates, Denver–Boulder's central cities increased their population during the first two of these decades. Much of the early city growth, however, was attributable to annexation rather than population growth within existing territory; and in the 1970s, Denver–Boulder's central cities sustained population losses irrespective of annexation. Like Denver–Boulder, both Seattle–Everett and Portland exhibited significant metropolitanwide growth through the postwar period and the post-1970s. Similarly, their central cities tended to sustain population growth or only modest declines as a result of city annexation and population growth within their relatively low-density areas. In these respects, the West-Old metropolitan areas differ markedly from their counterparts in other regions.

South-Young and West-Young areas: Metropolitan areas in the South-Young and West-Young categories are, for the most part, qualitatively different from the areas reviewed thus far with respect to their development histories and city–suburb redistribution patterns. The extraordinarily high levels of postwar population growth that accrued to each of these metropolitan areas generally occurred in the context of young post-automobile-era central cities that were not encircled by well-entrenched suburban municipal governments. Consequently, both cities and suburbs were able to share in the population growth as these already expansive cities could readily expand their territories by annexing suburban land. Central city boundaries became more alterable; and the city–suburb disparities in growth, density, population, and housing composition, which characterized most old metropolitan areas, are far less evident in these areas.

A comparison of the two right-most plots in Figure 7.3, which display postwar population trends for South-Young and West-Young metropolitan areas, with the other four plots that were reviewed above, underscores broad differences between the younger and older metropolitan areas. To begin with, the younger metropolitan areas grew at markedly higher rates than the older areas during the entire 1950–1980 period and also during the 1970–1980 period. Individual rates of metropolitan growth for the latter period ranged from +20.7 percent for San Antonio to +64.2 percent for Ft. Lauderdale–Hollywood (only Denver–Boulder, Portland, and Atlanta of the older areas lie within this range), and for the four areas of Phoenix, Tampa–St. Petersburg, Houston, and San Diego, the 1970s growth increased significantly over the 1960s growth—a feat not accomplished by any older area.

These plots also demonstrate the stark contrast between Young and Old areas' city–suburb redistribution trends. Each of the 12 Young areas' central cities displayed population growth over all three postwar decades (accomplished only by Columbus and Los Angeles–Long Beach, of the older central cities); and although city growth levels tended to decline somewhat with each succeeding decade, South-Young and West-Young central city growth rates remained remarkably high in the 1970s (shown in Table 7.3). It is clear from the aggregate trend data plotted in Figure 7.3 that in contrast to older central cities, younger central cities comprise larger shares of their metropolitan areas' population and are able to retain these larger (though declining) shares. This is a result of their more expansive initial territory, their ability to annex to that territory, and their continued high levels of population growth.

Individual differences in the city–suburb redistribution process occur even among the 12 Young cities as a result of variations in *their* development histories, economic functions, and annexation practices. The greatest outlier in this regard is the Miami area, where the central city has not expanded its legal boundaries but, instead, shares administrative functions with surrounding communities as part of a comprehensive urban county plan.[31] As a consequence, its legal city population as a share of the metropolitan population is small, its suburbanization rate is relatively high, and its central city growth rate has remained lower than those of other younger cities in the 1950–1980 period. The other Florida areas, Tampa–St. Petersburg and Ft. Lauderdale–Hollywood, also show some of the latter tendencies, although they have annexed considerable central city land in the 1950s and 1960s (see Figure 7.5). The same characterization might also be made for the Sacramento, California, metropolitan area.

The most extreme models of Sunbelt city–suburb redistribution are illustrated by San Antonio, Houston, and Phoenix (shown in Figure 7.5), where city growth, through population increase and annexation, comes much closer to approximating metropolitanwide growth. As a consequence, the city retains a relatively large share of the area's population. The Dallas–Ft. Worth area also followed this pattern through the 1950s and 1960s; however, in the 1970s its central cities annexed only a modest amount of territory and grew by only +4.2 percent for the decade.

The remaining areas, all in California, generally fall somewhere between the experiences of the Florida areas and the Southwest growth centers. The central cities of San Diego (shown in Figure 7.5), Riverside–San Bernardino–Ontario, and Anaheim–Santa Ana–Garden Grove—like their metropolitan areas—grew phenomenally in the 1950s as a result of population growth and extensive territorial annexation. Their central city growth rates, while still among the fastest growing in the country, have tapered off more recently as have their levels of annexation. A special case among this group is San Jose, a high-tech functional nodal center which has a heavy concentration of the electronic computer-applications industry. San Jose's central city grew extensively in the 1950s and 1960s through both population growth and annexation. Yet, already in the 1960s, San Jose's central city registered a growth rate that was significantly greater than its metropolitan growth (without taking annexation into account). Both its metropolitan and central city growth declined in the 1970s. However, the 1960s city–suburb redistribution pattern still holds up with San Jose's central city growing at +36.9 percent—the highest of all cities in this study—and its suburbs growing at only +9.9 percent. The specialized nature and location requirements of this area's employers, coupled with limitations imposed on residential construction by its suburban communities, have contri-

---

[31]A discussion of Miami's comprehensive urban county plan and the metropolitan area's postwar population redistribution patterns can be found in Richard M. Bernard and Bradley R. Rice, *Sunbelt Cities;* and John C. Bollens and Henry J. Schmandt, *The Metropolis* (New York: Harper and Row, 1982), pp. 324–332.

buted to a decidedly atypical city–suburb redistribution process in San Jose.[32]

Summary

A simple summary of the 1970s city–suburb redistribution might be obtained by examining the data in Table 7.3. These data show the rate of city change, the rate of suburb change, and the suburbanization rate for individual metropolitan areas and for the total, or aggregated, population in each class of areas. It is clear that each metropolitan class and, with the exception of San Jose, each individual area continues to display a positive suburbanization rate during the 1970s. It can also be seen that the classes differ fairly systematically in the suburbanization rate levels, and in how city and suburb growth combine to achieve those levels.

Because they are sustaining metropolitanwide population losses in the 1970s, North-Declining areas have the least potential for achieving high rates of suburbanization, and the suburbanization rates they do display are generally city-loss dominated. There is apparently a continued suburbanward movement from these areas' central cities—even in the context of metropolitan decline. This process can obviously not occur indefinitely; and probably will become moderated as many of these central cities take on more specialized service and administrative roles. The South-Old areas come closest to resembling the North-Declining areas in the sense that their older, underbounded central cities are also experiencing high rates of net population loss. Yet, because these areas enjoy a relatively large metropolitanwide growth, and because this growth is concentrated in the suburban ring, South-Old areas exhibit significantly higher suburbanization rates.

North-Old areas, while also growing at the metropolitan level, show city–suburb growth disparities and suburbanization rates that tend to be more moderated than those of North-Declining and South-Old areas and sustain levels of city loss that are less severe than those of the North-Declining areas. However, the lowest levels of 1970s city decline of all old metropolitan areas lie with the West-Old areas. All of their central cities either grow or decline modestly in the 1970–1980 period and their suburbanization rates are dependent on their levels of metropolitanwide growth—which tend to become concentrated primarily in their areas' suburban rings.

[32]Santa Clara County Industry and Housing Management Task Force, *Living Within Our Limits* (San Jose, CA: County–San Jose Environmental Management Agency, November, 1979).

The greatest range of suburbanization rates are displayed among the two classes of young metropolitan areas. Each of these areas received high levels of metropolitan growth, so their suburbanization rates depend on how well or poorly their central cities could share in these gains (and also attract intrametropolitan movers). At one extreme lies San Jose, with a negative suburbanization rate of -27 percent (the combination of a $+9.9$ percent suburban gain and $+36.9$ percent city gain), and at the other lies Ft. Lauderdale–Hollywood, with a positive suburbanization rate of $+87.6$ percent (the combination of a $+99.0$ percent suburban gain and a $+11.4$ percent city gain). One can, nevertheless, point to two constants among these areas: first, all of their central cities gained population in the 1970s; and second, with the exception of San Jose (an admitted anomaly), the suburban rings of each metropolitan area grew faster than their central cities—despite the fact that most of these cities are *not* rigidly bounded high-density settlements with population characteristics that are vastly different from their suburbs. The last observation gives credence to the view that population expansion at the metropolitan periphery is a general concomitant of metropolitan growth, irrespective of city age, region, the level of growth, and the presence or absence of central city disamenities.

Annexation and City Growth

The previous section emphasized the role of annexation as an important means for central cities to increase their populations, particularly in younger metropolitan areas. In the present section, we attempt to quantify the relative contributions of population growth within constant boundaries and the annexation of additional population, for central cities and suburbs. Although extensive annexation introduces complexities into any analysis of demographic change, the "annexation component" should not be regarded simply as a statistical artifact or as a numerical adjustment that has no substantive meaning. Indeed, those city governments that have undertaken extensive annexations are generally eager to acquire population growth in this manner, in order to widen their tax bases and gain a greater share of their metropolitan area's residential and commercial activities. To them, this type of growth is just as important as that sustained through migration and the natural increase of the resident population. It is for this reason that our later analyses of selective population growth and redistribution make no attempt to "adjust" for cross-decade annexations. It is only in the present section that we provide an overview of the role that annexation plays in the city–suburb redistribution process.

Table 7.4 shows the 1980 central city land areas in square miles for the 39 metropolitan areas in this study and indicates what part of those areas, if any, are attributable to annexation over the three postwar decades.[33] The least annexation is shown for the North-Declining and South-Old metropolitan areas which, by virtue of their development before the onset of modern transportation, became hemmed in by a circle of autonomous suburbs and municipalities that became resistant to incorporation with the central city government. Only Milwaukee (which annexed 47 percent of its 1980 area over the 1950–1970 period) and Atlanta (which added 70 percent in the 1950–1960 period) added significantly to their city territories.

Postwar annexation was more prevalent among the "newer" North-Old and West-Old cities. Of the former, Columbus and Kansas City each annexed over 75 percent of their 1980 city territories, and Indianapolis' city consolidation with the surrounding Marion County government in 1969 added territory equivalent to 88 percent of the new city's 1980 territory. The greatest annexations undertaken by the West-Old areas were in Denver–Boulder, Portland, and Seattle–Everett. Their postwar annexations were equivalent to 46 percent, 36 percent, and 27 percent, respectively, of their 1980 territories.

Annexation of central city territory was most prevalent in the South-Young and West-Young metropolitan areas. Eleven of these twelve areas annexed significant territory in both the 1950s and 1960s decades and seven of these did so in all three postwar decades. Aside from Miami (which participates in a comprehensive urban county plan but did not annex to its legal city boundaries), 1950–1980 annexations varied from 34 percent (for Ft. Lauderdale–Hollywood) to 96 percent (for Phoenix) of their respective 1980 territories. In nine of these areas, greater than half of their 1980 territories were annexed over the preceding 30 years. Clearly, part of the widespread annexation of these areas must be attributed to their late development and location in portions of the country that had not been extensively settled. However, also absent from most of their development histories were the immigrant, race, and class conflicts that led to the early incorporation of independent subur-

[33]The authors are grateful to Richard L. Forstall of the U.S. Census Bureau for providing these data, and to Joel C. Miller, also of the Census Bureau, for providing estimates of 1970–1980 city and suburb population change attributable to annexation (for Table 7.5). Additional information on central city annexation is available in Richard L. Forstall, "Annexations and Corporate Changes Since the 1970 Census: With Historical Data on Annexation for Larger Cities for 1900–1970," in *The Municipal Yearbook* (Washington, DC: International City Management Association, 1975), pp. 21–29; and Joel C. Miller and Richard L. Forstall, "Annexations and Corporate Changes, 1970–79 and 1980–83," in *The Municipal Yearbook* (Washington, DC: International City Management Association, 1984), pp. 96–101.

TABLE 7.4

Central City Area and Percent Attributable to Net Change During Decades Between 1950–1980: 39 Metropolitan Areas

Metropolitan Area Groupings/ Metropolitan Areas	1980 Central City Area[a] (1)	Percent of Area Attributable to Net Change[b] over Decades		
		1950–1960 (2)	1960–1970 (3)	1970–1980 (4)
NORTH–DECLINING				
New York	302	−5	*	*
Philadelphia	136	*	*	6
Boston	47	−4	*	*
Cincinnati	78	*	*	*
St. Louis	61	*	*	*
Buffalo	42	5	*	*
Chicago	228	6	*	*
Newark	24	*	*	*
Cleveland	79	*	*	4
Detroit	136	*	*	*
Milwaukee	96	42	5	*
Pittsburgh	55	*	*	*
Paterson*	23	*	*	*
NORTH–OLD				
Columbus	181	26	26	26
Indianapolis	352	4	88	−8
Kansas City	316	16	59	*
Hartford	18	*	*	*
Minneapolis*	107	*	*	*

TABLE 7.4 (continued)

SOUTH–OLD				
Baltimore	80	*	*	*
New Orleans	199	3	–4	*
Washington, D.C.	63	*	*	*
Atlanta	131	70	*	*
WEST–OLD				
San Francisco*	100	*	*	*
Denver*	131	7	22	17
Los Angeles*	515	*	*	*
Portland	103	*	22	14
Seattle*	107	13	20	–6
SOUTH–YOUNG				
San Antonio	263	30	14	30
Dallas*	573	33	14	18
Houston	556	29	20	22
Tampa*	140	36	13	*
Miami	34	*	*	*
Ft. Lauderdale*	55	6	28	*
WEST–YOUNG				
Sacramento	96	29	51	*
San Diego	320	30	38	*
San Jose	158	25	51	14
Phoenix	324	53	19	24
Riverside*	161	7	35	14
Anaheim*	87	54	18	11

SOURCES: Unpublished tabulations provided by the U.S. Bureau of the Census.

[a]Area in square miles of place or places designated as the metropolitan area's central city(s) in 1980.

[b]Changes representing more than 3 percent of 1980 central city area. Total 1970–1980 change includes a residual-error term, reflecting census enumeration corrections, in addition to net migration and natural increase. Source: Richard L. Forstall.

*Largest of multiple central cities.

ban communities around older central cities, and to the more stringent annexation laws that still exist in many northern states.[34] Hence, both logistically and politically, annexation became a more viable process for young areas in the Sunbelt, as is evident from Table 7.4.

The figures in Table 7.5 decompose the total population change for central cities and suburbs of our metropolitan area groupings into population change that occurs within constant beginning-of-decade boundaries ("population growth") and population change that occurs as a result of territorial annexation ("annexation"). Most commonly, when city land is annexed, the city's total population is increased, the suburb's total population is decreased, and the suburbanization rate is diminished. In some cases, as with North-Old city change in 1950–1960, the annexation of city territory leads to a positive change in the city's population—when a negative change would have resulted in the absence of annexation. (Appendix E, Tables E.7C and E.7D show this decomposition for individual cities and suburbs.)

The relevant contributions to central city population change, displayed in the first three columns of Table 7.5, show that the annexation contribution exerts a numerically dominant influence only on West-Young and South-Young city changes in the 1950–1960 period. Yet, when one looks merely for significant contributions of annexation (those contributing to a city change of 3 percent or greater), one finds these to occur in one or more decades for all metropolitan classes except the North-Declining grouping. The significant 1950–1960 annexation contribution to the South-Old areas clearly represents Atlanta's experience (discussed earlier) and the North-Old contributions reflect territory added to Columbus, Kansas City, and Indianapolis. Data in Appendix E, Table E.7C indicate that the 1950–1960 total change in each of these cities' populations was almost entirely dominated by annexation. Moreover, in the latter two areas, their 1960–1970 annexations transformed city losses into gains.

A similar domination of city total growth patterns occurred in the West-Old central cities of Denver–Boulder and Seattle–Everett in 1950–1960, and continued through 1960–1970 in the case of the former area. However, as should be expected, the greatest annexation contributions were made to individual central cities in the South-Young and West-Young areas. In eight of these areas (San Antonio, Dallas–Ft.

[34]This argument is made by R. D. Norton, *City Life-Cycles*, and elaborated upon further in M. N. Danielson, "Differentiation, Segregation, and Political Fragmentation in the American Metropolis," in *Governance and Population*, A. E. Keir Nash, ed. (Washington, DC: U.S. Government Printing Office, 1972). A classification of the degree of difficulty in state annexation laws can be found in Raymond H. Wheeler, "Annexation Law and Annexation Success," *Land Economics* 41 (November 1965):354–360.

TABLE 7.3

Percent Change in Central City and Suburban Populations
Attributable to Population Growth and City Annexation
for Decades Between 1950–1980: Six Metropolitan Area Groupings

Metropolitan Area Groupings/ Components of Change[a]	Percent City Change			Percent Suburb Change		
	1950–1960	1960–1970	1970–1980	1950–1960	1960–1970	1970–1980
NORTH–DECLINING						
Population Growth	−4.0	−4.2	−13.3	+47.8	+22.9	+4.3
Annexation	+0.6	+0.1	0.0	−0.9	−0.1	0.0
Total	−3.4	−4.1	−13.3	+46.9	+22.8	+4.3
NORTH–OLD						
Population Growth	−2.4	−4.1	−7.2	+67.9	+39.1	+14.5
Annexation	+7.3	+16.9	−0.1	−8.9	−13.6	+0.1
Total	+4.9	+12.8	−7.3	+59.0	+25.5	+14.6
SOUTH–OLD						
Population Growth	−0.3	−2.5	−12.5	+75.9	+53.7	+24.1
Annexation	+6.5	+0.1	0.0	−9.0	−0.1	0.0
Total	+6.2	−2.4	−12.5	+65.9	+53.6	+24.1
WEST–OLD						
Population Growth	+11.1	+4.4	+0.4	+68.5	+33.2	+16.9
Annexation	+4.7	+2.3	+0.2	−5.8	−2.0	−0.2
Total	+15.8	+6.7	+0.6	+62.7	+31.2	+16.7
SOUTH–YOUNG						
Population Growth	+17.9	+18.7	+7.4	+126.5	+63.3	+64.7
Annexation	+35.2	+3.8	+6.9	−53.4	−5.1	−7.2
Total	+53.1	+22.5	+14.3	+73.1	+58.2	+57.5
WEST–YOUNG						
Population Growth	+43.3	+27.2	+25.6	+141.8	+68.8	+42.6
Annexation	+77.2	+16.2	+1.3	−50.3	−12.2	−0.9
Total	+120.5	+43.4	+26.9	+91.5	+56.6	+41.7

SOURCE: Census of Population, 1960, vol. I, Characteristics of the Population. A. Number of Inhabitants (States), table 9i; Census of Population, 1970, vol. I, Characteristics of the Population, A. Number of Inhabitants, Section 1, U.S. Summary, table 40; and unpublished 1980 estimates from the U.S. Bureau of the Census.

[a] The Population Growth component pertains to decade population change assuming constant beginning-of-decade central city boundaries. The Annexation component pertains to decade population change within territory annexed over the decade.

215

Worth, Houston, Tampa–St. Petersburg, Sacramento, San Jose, Phoenix, and Anaheim–Santa Ana–Garden Grove) annexation contributed more than half to the 1950–1960 city growth. In 1960–1970, only two central cities were dependent on annexation for more than half of their growth (Sacramento and Riverside–San Bernardino–Ontario); and in 1970–1980 this was the case for both Houston and San Antonio.

Although annexation as a component of central city growth has diminished over time, it still contributed to city growth (or reduced decline) in 12 of the 39 metropolitan areas in the 1970–1980 decade. Moreover, it remains a viable source of selective population gain for central cities in the growing Sunbelt areas.

Net Migration and Natural Increase

The transition from "baby boom" to "baby bust" spanning the 1950s through 1970s decades has, as shown in Chapter 3, led to successively smaller natural increase contributions to population growth in each of the nation's regions and metropolitan areas. In light of this trend, it is important to discern how reduced natural increase is affecting central city growth and decline as well as the city–suburb redistribution process. If older central cities had been declining since 1950, how much of these declines is due to lower net migration—representing an increased tendency for people to avoid living in these cities—and how much of these declines is simply due to lowered natural increase? Indeed, even central cities in younger growing metropolitan areas seem to be increasing at a decreasing rate. How much is this attributable to reduced-level inmigration or, again, simply a lowered natural increase?

To answer these questions, we will refer to the data in Table 7.6, which decomposes total growth into natural increase and net migration for central and suburban county portions of our six metropolitan area groupings.[35] Central counties are those counties that include all or parts of the central cities in our 39 metropolitan areas; suburban counties comprise the remaining portions of the metropolitan areas. Although it would have been preferable to examine these demographic components of change according to central city boundaries, data for births and deaths are not generally available for such areas over the three-decade period. Consequently, we used the cruder central and suburban county definitions because they retain constant boundaries across censuses and

---

[35]As in Chapter 3, the 1970–1980 total population change is not necessarily equal to the algebraic sum of natural increase and net migration. The residual error term reflects census enumeration corrections resulting from differences in coverage between the 1970 and 1980 censuses.

represent geographic units for which births and deaths are routinely compiled.[36]

Before answering the questions posed above, we might first observe that there is a systematic decrease, over time, in the contributions of natural increase for the growth in central counties and suburban counties in large metropolitan areas. This holds true within each broad class of metropolitan areas where population gains due to natural increase tend to diminish by approximately one-third between 1950–1960 and 1960–1970, and by another third between 1960–1970 and 1970–1980. Moreover, a systematic relationship of natural increase levels exists *across* metropolitan area classes, at least within central counties. Highest rates of natural increase are displayed in each period for central counties in the South-Young and West-Young metropolitan areas, lowest rates are always observed for North-Declining areas, and West-Old, South-Old, and North-Old levels lie in between. These differences reflect the younger age structures associated with the higher in-migration to Sunbelt and younger metropolitan areas.

The implications of these systematic patterns can be illustrated by the extreme examples of West-Young and North-Declining central counties. In the former, natural increase contributed to a population increase of +27.2 percent in the 1950s. This contribution was reduced to +9.8 percent in the 1970s. Natural increase augmented North-Declining central counties' population by only +12.6 percent in the 1950s—less than half its contribution in West-Young central counties. In the 1970s this contribution was reduced to +4.3 percent.

Despite the systematic decreases, reduced natural increase does not provide the sole (or even dominant) explanation for lowered central county growth. As the data in Table 7.6 make plain, reduced net migration contributions were primarily responsible for diminished levels of central city growth (or increased decline) in the 1950–1980 periods, although the nature of these contributions varied across metropolitan groupings.

Both North-Declining and South-Old central counties sustained net outmigration for all three postwar decades. However, the most dramatic change in the level of net outmigration occurred with the 1970s—when both areas' central counties suffered an accentuated out-migration. Indeed, the central county net migration levels in each area did not shift markedly between the 1950s and 1960s, leaving reduced natural increase to account for most of the reduced 1960s growth in North-

---

[36]These central county figures will generally overstate actual natural increase and net migration levels for central cities, particularly in older metropolitan areas, because the former will include adjacent suburban communities with younger age distributions. A list of central city counties for these 39 metropolitan areas appears in Appendix F.

TABLE 7.6

Percent Change in Central County and Suburban County Populations Attributable to Net Migration and Natural Increase for Decades Between 1950–1980: Six Metropolitan Area Groupings

Metropolitan Area Groupings/ Components of Change	Percent Central County Change[a]			Percent Suburban County Change[a]		
	1950–1960	1960–1970	1970–1980[b]	1950–1960	1960–1970	1970–1980[b]
NORTH–DECLINING						
Net Migration	−7.1	−7.2	−14.8	+27.8	+11.8	−0.5
Natural Increase	+12.6	+9.0	+4.3	+18.4	+12.0	+5.5
Total	+5.5	+1.8	−9.7	+46.2	+23.8	+5.0
NORTH–OLD						
Net Migration	+7.4	+2.1	−8.4	+20.8	+18.6	+11.2
Natural Increase	+18.6	+13.2	+6.6	+20.1	+15.9	+10.1
Total	+26.0	+15.3	−0.7	+40.8	+34.5	+22.3
SOUTH–OLD						
Net Migration	−12.2	−11.8	−18.9	+44.4	+32.0	+9.3
Natural Increase	+15.5	+10.9	+4.6	+24.7	+19.1	+9.9
Total	+3.3	−0.9	−10.1	+69.1	+51.1	+22.6
WEST–OLD						
Net Migration	+17.1	+4.8	−1.9	+42.5	+26.9	+21.2
Natural Increase	+15.6	+11.1	+7.6	+23.1	+15.2	+9.1
Total	+32.7	+15.9	+5.7	+65.6	+42.1	+30.3
SOUTH–YOUNG						
Net Migration	+43.0	+24.0	+19.2	+0.7	+29.4	+71.1
Natural Increase	+24.0	+13.6	+8.0	+16.7	+9.9	+8.4
Total	+67.0	+37.6	+30.9	+17.4	+39.3	+83.4
WEST–YOUNG						
Net Migration	+77.8	+33.8	+25.4	+32.3	+25.6	+29.3
Natural Increase	+27.2	+17.5	+9.8	+16.8	+12.5	+6.2
Total	+105.0	+51.3	+35.7	+49.1	+38.1	+36.1

SOURCES: Unpublished tabulations provided by the U.S. Bureau of the Census.

[a]Central Counties are listed in Appendix F. Suburbs include other (non-central) counties of metropolitan areas.

[b]Total 1970–1980 change includes a residual-error term, reflecting census enumeration corrections, in addition to net migration and natural

Declining central counties, and 1960s absolute decline in South-Old central counties. Nevertheless, the absolute 1970s population decline observed in both areas' central counties was primarily the result of increased outmigration such that even if both areas observed the high 1950s levels of natural increase during this period, net outmigration levels were still great enough to produce absolute population losses.

At the other extreme lie central counties in the West-Young and South-Young groupings. Their central counties experienced positive net inmigration for all three postwar decades, and the magnitudes of their net migration contributions to city growth were far in excess of the high natural increase contributions already discussed. Nevertheless, the absolute net migration contributions for these "younger" central counties also diminished over time—even more markedly than the reductions in natural increase. Greatest changes in net migration for both area groupings occurred between 1950–1960 and 1960–1970, and the lowered absolute growth registered for the young central counties in the 1960s was primarily a result of reduced net migration contributions. The net migration level diminished further between the 1960s and 1970s, but these changes were more commensurate with the natural increase declines. Bear in mind that the use of central counties as crude indicators for central cities in this analysis of natural increase and net migration may be particularly deceptive in the case of South-Young and West-Young metropolitan areas. High net migration levels observed over these expanded county units may significantly overstate those that occurred within the confines of legal central city boundaries.

The remaining two metropolitan area groupings, North-Old and West-Old, also sustained cross-period reductions in their central counties' net migration, although their trends do not follow either of the two extremes just presented. The net migration contribution of both areas' central counties remained positive in the 1950s and 1960s and turned to net outmigration in the 1970s. Positive 1950s and 1960s net migration in the North-Old counties was relatively small, and its shift to net outmigration in the 1970s was fairly substantial—enough to lead to an absolute population loss in this grouping's central counties. The West-Old central counties' 1950s positive net migration contribution was greater in magnitude than its natural increase contribution; but as in the case of the West-Young and South-Young areas, its contribution declined precipitously for the 1960s—leading to a significant decline in the level of absolute central county gains. The negative net migration contribution in 1970–1980 reflects less of a shift, was relatively small, and combined with a larger positive natural increase contribution to effect a small 1970s central city gain in the West-Old area grouping.

Net migration does indeed contribute to the reduced and negative postwar population gains observed in large central counties—above and beyond the contributions of declining natural increase. In North-Declining and South-Old area central counties the net migration impact is most accentuated in the 1970s, as high levels of net outmigration are evident. The West-Young and South-Young counties' net migration levels, while always positive, declined dramatically between the 1950s and 1960s, and diminished the extraordinarily high growth levels these counties observed in the 1950s. Finally, the North-Old and West-Old net migration trends lie somewhere in between; but in each case, the net migration contribution to central county change diminished for each decade.

Finally, we examine the role that net migration played in contributing to the reduced suburban population growth in most large metropolitan areas over the 1950–1980 period. The earlier postwar years were characterized by a "flight to the suburbs," particularly by family-forming couples in search of a suitable environment for child raising. Suburban population growth during this period, therefore, resulted from high levels of both net migration and natural increase. Since the 1950s this growth has tended to diminish, at least in older metropolitan areas. Is this reduced suburban growth, like reduced city central county growth, a result of *both* lower migration and natural increase?

The Table 7.6 data showing percent suburban county change for the four classes of declining and old metropolitan areas indicate that both reduced net migration *and* natural increase are responsible for these areas' lower suburban county growth in each decade. All four metropolitan area groupings displayed greater net migration than natural increase contributions in the 1950–1960 decade. North-Declining and South-Old suburban counties, in particular, showed over-time declines in net migration to be even more severe than declines in natural increase. In the North-Declining areas the 1960s net migration contribution was already below that of natural increase, and the 1970s net migration was negative. In South-Old areas the net migration contribution declined substantially over each interval and dramatically between 1960–1970 (+ 32.0 percent) and 1970–1980 (+ 9.3 percent). These trends are surprising in light of the high 1970s' net outmigration shown from the central counties of North-Declining and South-Old areas. One might have expected some of these outmigrants to relocate in the suburbs and lead to an increased net migration contribution in the 1970s. Finally, although the suburban county components of South-Young and West-Young areas are extremely crude approximations of the actual suburbs, the data here suggest that in these areas, only, one finds over-time increases in net migration's contribution to suburban population growth.

Migration Stream Contributions

The previous section has suggested that net migration is contributing to reduced population growth in old central cities within both declining and growing metropolitan areas, as well as in younger central cities that lie within metropolitan areas that are growing rapidly. Given these shifts in the migration contribution toward city population decline within large metropolitan areas of all types, it should be instructive to examine the changing inter- and intrametropolitan migration processes that contribute to the total net migration contributions. We ask the question: Are the same or different migration processes affecting city population declines in each of our metropolitan area classes?

To answer this question, it is useful to make a distinction between two different types of migration that affect population change within a metropolitan area's central cities and suburbs. The first type is called "interlabor market migration" and refers generally to long-distance, job-related migration between distinct labor market areas. Metropolitan areas are close approximations of such areas, so that migration streams into and out of a metropolitan area can be considered as interlabor market migration streams. The second type of migration is called "residential mobility" and refers to most short-distance movement that occurs within a labor market. Such movement is generally motivated by life-cycle related changes in consumption preferences or family needs, and occurs more frequently than the first type of migration. All movement within a single metropolitan area (including the city-to-suburb and suburb-to-city movement streams) might be considered residential mobility.[37]

This distinction between the processes of interlabor market migration (referred to as "migration" in the remainder of this section) and intralabor market residential mobility (referred to as "residential mobility") is relevant to examining city–suburb redistribution for the six metropolitan area classes in our typology. One aspect of this typology distinguishes between areas that are declining and those that are growing on a metropolitanwide basis. Because interlabor market migration responds to "pulls" that characterize the entire metropolitan area, growing areas should be experiencing city *and* suburb gains through interlabor market migration while declining areas should be sustaining losses in both parts of the metropolitn area. Residential movers, on the

---

[37]More comprehensive discussions of the rationale underlying these distinctions appear in William H. Frey, "Population Movement and City-Suburb Redistribution: An Analytic Framework," *Demography* (15) (1978):571–578; and William H. Frey, "A Multiregional Population Projection Framework that Incorporates Both Migration and Residential Mobility Streams," *Environment and Planning* (A 15) (1983):1613–1632.

other hand, respond to the relative residential attractiveness of central city and suburban areas within the metropolitan area—irrespective of the metropolitan area's level of attractiveness for migrants beyond its borders. A very strong suburban preference on the part of residential movers may act to counter the population losses resulting from inter-labor market outmigration for a declining area's suburbs—or it may help to augment suburban populations in growing metropolitan areas.

The data in Table 7.7 permit analyses of migration and residential mobility contributions to central city population change, 1965–1970 and 1975–1980, for the six metropolitan area classes in our typology. Because of data constraints, the boundaries employed here correspond to 1970 central city and SMSA definitions for these areas, and they are not strictly comparable to the 1980 metropolitan area boundaries that we have generally adopted.[38] The percentage change measures for the periods 1965–1970 and 1975–1980 are based on the 1970 and 1980 Census questions that asked respondents to indicate their places of residence five years prior to the census.[39] The first three columns of the table pertain to the interlabor market migration streams that connect the central cities with areas outside the metropolitan area where column (3) lists net migration resulting from this exchange. The second three columns pertain to residential mobility streams that connect the central cities with their own suburbs, and column (6) lists net mobility from this exchange. Column (7) lists the contributions of both net migration and net mobility combined.

Let us first evaluate the contributions to city change that are attributable to interlabor market migration in column (3). The results here fall in line, fairly closely, with our typology. Net migration's contribution is consistently negative only for North-Declining central cities and positive, over both periods, for West-Young, South-Young, and West-Old areas. North-Old areas gained slightly through interlabor market migration in 1965–1970 and lost population modestly in 1975–1980. In South-Old central cities, net migration contributed to a +2.2 percent gain in the earlier period, but contributed to a −2.3 percent loss in the later period. As shall be seen below, this reflects the heightened tendency for inmigrants to South-Old areas to reside in the suburbs.

Irrespective of this diversity of net migration patterns across metro-

---

[38]Migration data for the 1965–1970 period pertain exactly to these 1970 SMSA and central city boundaries; those for 1975–1980 pertain to 1970 Equivalent Central City and SMSA definitions, which are obtainable from the 1980 Public Use Microdata computer tape (Sample "A"). These areas very closely approximate 1970 central city and SMSA boundaries and are delineated in Appendix F.

[39]Within each of these periods, allocations were made for individuals who had moved but did not report their residence five years prior to the census, on the basis of those individuals' personal characteristics.

TABLE 7.7

Percent Change in Central City Attributable to Migration Streams with Other Areas
and Residential Mobility Streams Within the Same Metropolitan Area, 1965–1970 and 1975–1980:
Six Metropolitan Area Groupings

Metropolitan Area Groupings[a]/ Period	Migration with Other Areas[b]			Mobility Within Same Metropolitan Area			Net Migration and Mobility (7)
	In-migration (1)	Out-migration (2)	Net Migration (3)	From Suburb (4)	To Suburb (5)	Net Mobility (6)	
NORTH-DECLINING							
1965–1970	+7.5	−9.8	−2.3	+2.7	−9.0	−6.3	−8.6
1975–1980	+8.0	−11.1	−3.1	+2.6	−8.4	−5.8	−8.9
NORTH-OLD							
1965–1970	+14.8	−14.1	+0.7	+5.5	−10.2	−4.7	−4.0
1975–1980	+14.1	−15.6	−1.5	+5.2	−11.6	−6.4	−7.9
SOUTH-OLD							
1965–1970	+13.4	−11.2	+2.2	+3.7	−12.0	−8.3	−6.1
1975–1980	+12.5	−14.8	−2.3	+4.3	−14.9	−10.6	−12.9
WEST-OLD							
1965–1970	+17.9	−15.6	+2.3	+6.5	−11.8	−5.3	−3.0
1975–1980	+19.2	−15.5	+3.7	+6.4	−12.2	−5.8	−2.1
SOUTH-YOUNG							
1965–1970	+19.4	−14.8	+4.6	+4.0	−11.5	−7.5	−2.9
1975–1980	+19.5	−17.6	+1.9	+3.7	−15.0	−11.3	−9.4
WEST-YOUNG							
1965–1970	+22.2	−19.4	+2.8	+5.3	−9.8	−4.5	−1.7
1975–1980	+23.3	−18.2	+5.1	+5.7	−11.8	−6.1	−1.0

SOURCES: Census of Population, 1970, *Subject Reports* PC(2)-2C, Mobility for Metropolitan Areas, tables 15 and 16; and machine-readable computer file: Census of Population and Housing, 1980. Public Use Microdata Samples A and B (prepared by the U.S. Bureau of the Census, Washington, DC).

[a]Defined according to 1970 Central City and SMSA Definitions (1965–1970) and 1970 Equivalent Central City and SMSA Definitions (1975–1980). See Appendix F for definitions.
[b]Includes migration with other metropolitan and nonmetropolitan areas. The immigration column (1) also includes immigrants from abroad.

politan area types, there exists a consistent pattern of city-to-suburb redistribution of intrametropolitan movers, which seems to dominate the combined migration and mobility contributions to population change in all types of cities. It is significant that each of the percent changes in column (6) is negative as a result of the highly imbalanced exchange of mobility streams between an area's central city and its suburbs. Moreover, the negative contribution of net mobility of the city change, shown in column (6), is always larger than the contribution of net migration (either positive or negative) shown in column (3). Consequently, all metropolitan area groupings show a central city total net out-movement (column (7)) as a result of both net migration and net mobility. While the net movement levels shown here are not entirely consistent with the data in Tables 7.5 and 7.6, due to boundary inconsistencies in the areal units used, these data demonstrate the existence of a suburb-directed residential mobility process at work in areas of all metropolitan classes, which effects a substantial city-to-suburb population redistribution irrespective of the levels of metropolitanwide population gain.

Particular notice should be given to the migration and residential mobility shifts in North-Declining central cities. These cities are most dependent on intrametropolitan mobility for their future gains. Moreover, several cities within this grouping are attempting to complete the transition to corporate service and administrative centers to retain a larger and more selective segment of the metropolitan population. While it is clear from column (7) that these cities are losing a significant and increased part of their populations (−8.9 percent) as a result of migration and mobility, only the negative contribution of net migration increased between 1965–1970 and 1975–1980. The contribution of net mobility actually declined slightly over this period, unlike the situation for any other metropolitan area grouping. It remains to be seen (in later chapters) what racial and socioeconomic selectivities underlie the aggregate residential mobility patterns in these metropolitan areas.

The data in Table 7.8 show the migration contributions from the suburbs' perspective and display the percent changes in suburban population attributable to interlabor market migration with areas outside the metropolitan area (columns (1) to (3)), residential mobility with the central city (columns (4) to (6)), and the combination of both types of streams (column (7)). As expected, one finds a disparity in net migration patterns between declining and growing metropolitan area classes. Indeed, the disparity is even wider here than for the central city—such that North-Declining suburbs are losing population through net migration, South-Young and West-Young areas are gaining population at the rates of 11–14 percent, and other areas are gaining at lower levels.

TABLE 7.8

Percent Change in Suburb Attributable to Migration Streams with Other Areas and Residential Mobility Streams Within the Same Metropolitan Area, 1965–1970 and 1975–1980: Six Metropolitan Area Groupings

Metropolitan Area Groupings[a]/ Period	Migration with Other Areas[b]			Mobility Within Same Area			Net Migration and Mobility (7)
	In-migration (1)	Out-migration (2)	Net Migration (3)	From City (4)	To City (5)	Net Mobility (6)	
NORTH–DECLINING							
1965–1970	+9.8	−10.6	−0.8	+7.1	−2.2	+4.9	+4.1
1975–1980	+8.7	−12.8	−4.1	+5.5	−1.7	+3.8	−0.3
NORTH–OLD							
1965–1970	+15.6	−13.0	+2.6	+8.9	−4.8	+4.1	+6.7
1975–1980	+13.4	−13.5	−0.1	+8.2	−3.7	+4.5	+4.4
SOUTH–OLD							
1965–1970	+22.7	−13.8	+8.9	+6.8	−2.1	+4.7	+13.6
1975–1980	+20.1	−16.3	+3.9	+5.9	−1.7	+4.2	+8.1
WEST–OLD							
1965–1970	+18.0	−15.1	+2.9	+8.5	−4.7	+3.8	+6.7
1975–1980	+17.5	−16.7	+0.8	+8.0	−4.2	+3.8	+4.6
SOUTH–YOUNG							
1965–1970	+25.2	−11.5	+13.7	+11.8	−4.1	+7.7	+21.4
1975–1980	+24.4	−11.4	+13.0	+11.4	−2.8	+8.6	+21.6
WEST–YOUNG							
1965–1970	+28.8	−17.3	+11.5	+7.3	−4.0	+3.3	+14.8
1975–1980	+26.7	−15.8	+10.9	+7.1	−3.4	+3.7	+14.6

SOURCES: Same as Table 7.7.

[a]Defined according to 1970 Central City and SMSA Definitions (1965–1970) and 1970 Equivalent Central City and SMSA Definitions (1975–1980). See Appendix F for definitions.

[b]Includes migration with other metropolitan and nonmetropolitan areas. The immigration column (1) also includes immigrants from abroad.

Yet, once again the residential mobility contributions are consistent for all types of areas—positive with only little change across the two periods.[40] These positive net mobility contributions are not always the dominant ones in accounting for the total suburban growth attributed to both net migration and net mobility (column (7)). This is because of the extremely high rates of net inmigration shown in South-Old suburbs in 1965–1970 and in West-Young and South-Young suburbs during both periods. However, in all other types of areas (and in South-Old areas in 1975–1980), a positive net mobility exchange with the central city accounts for most of the movement-induced population growth. This exchange was the only source of such growth in North-Declining areas, and in the 1970s it was not large enough to counter the greater net out-movement attributable to interlabor market migration from North-Declining suburbs to other areas.

While the preceding view of the migration stream data in Tables 7.7 and 7.8 distinguished between interlabor market migration streams and intralabor market residential mobility streams, it was not possible to separate the former streams in these tables into the categories of international immigrants and internal migrants from other parts of the United States. To be sure, the vast number of interlabor market migrants to most metropolitan areas is of the latter type. However, in specific parts of the country, international migrants make a significant impact. The data in Table 7.9 provide a crude indication of this impact for city–suburb redistribution in the six metropolitan area groupings. The number of immigrants are approximated by the number of individuals in the 1970 or 1980 census, who immigrated to the United States over the previous ten years, and the data are presented for central counties and suburban counties. (Data for international emigrants from these counties are not available.)

These data make plain that the effect of immigration is more pronounced in central cities than in suburbs, in the 1980s than in the 1970s, and in West, Southwest, and Northeast cities than in other parts of the country. It is clear that in such cities, the stream of international immigrants contributes significantly to the cities' population gain and, in many cases, serves to counter net losses cities sustained via internal migration.

---

[40]It is not inconsistent to find a cross-period increase in the negative contribution of net mobility for a central city's population and a cross-period decrease in the positive contribution of net mobility for its suburb's population (as is the case for South-Old areas in Tables 7.7 and 7.8). This occurs because the suburban population denominator for this percentage change increases over time (due to all demographic components of change), while the central city denominator either decreases or increases minimally.

TABLE 7.9

Recent Immigrants as Percentage of Population
Central Counties and Suburb Counties,
1970 and 1980: Six Metropolitan Area Groupings[a]

Metropolitan Area Groupings	Central Counties		Suburb Counties	
	1970	1980	1970	1980
North–Declining	2.9	5.9	1.3	2.2
North–Old	0.9	1.8	0.4	0.8
South–Old	1.4	2.7	1.3	2.7
West–Old	4.1	10.0	1.8	3.3
South–Young	3.6	5.5	0.4	1.3
West–Young	2.2	4.8	1.6	3.2
Total	2.9	6.0	1.3	2.3

SOURCES: Machine-readable computer files: Census of Population and Housing, 1970, Fourth Count, Population Summary File Tape; and Census of Population and Housing, 1980, Summary Tape File 3C (prepared by the U.S. Bureau of the Census, Washington, DC).

[a]Immigrants over previous ten years, as reported in 1970 and 1980 Censuses of Population.

Destination Propensity Rates

Another perspective on the city–suburb redistribution process can be gleaned by examining the city and suburban destination choices of recent intrametropolitan movers and inmigrants to the metropolitan area. Although these destination choices represent only part of the entire redistribution process, the destination choices of recent movers and inmigrants are indicative of the relative attractiveness the city and suburbs hold as residential environments for people who are facing the decision of where to locate. If the choices of these movers and inmigrants are more suburban-directed than the city–suburb distribution of all metropolitan residents, this suggests that the suburbs are becoming increasingly attractive and implies that the suburbanization rate might intensify. On the other hand, if these choices are similar or even less suburban-directed than those of the entire residential population, there is a hint that the suburbanization process might be tapering off.

Such comparisons are made for movers and residents of the six metropolitan area classes in Figure 7.6. The *suburb destination propensity rates* for 1975–1980 intrametropolitan movers and inmigrants to metropolitan areas are contrasted with the proportion of the entire

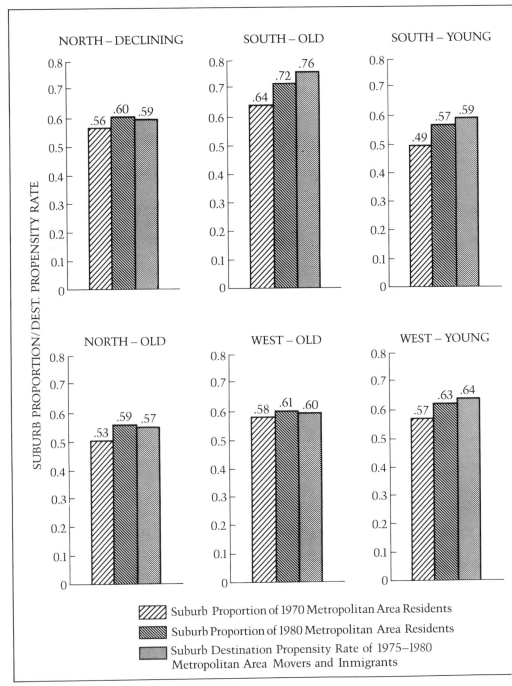

FIGURE 7.6

Suburb Proportion of 1970 and 1980 Metropolitan Area Residents and Suburb Destination Propensity Rates of 1975–1980 Metropolitan Area Movers and Inmigrants: Six Metropolitan Area Groupings

NORTH – DECLINING

SOUTH – OLD

SOUTH – YOUNG

NORTH – OLD

WEST – OLD

WEST – YOUNG

SUBURB PROPORTION/DEST. PROPENSITY RATE

Suburb Proportion of 1970 Metropolitan Area Residents

Suburb Proportion of 1980 Metropolitan Area Residents

Suburb Destination Propensity Rate of 1975–1980 Metropolitan Area Movers and Inmigrants

SOURCES: Same as Table 7.7.

metropolitan resident population that resides in the suburbs for both 1970 and 1980. The suburb destination propensity rate is defined as the proportion of all intrametropolitan movers and inmigrants, over a period, that select suburb destinations. It is considered to be a measure of suburb destination selectivity among those movers and inmigrants who are faced with selecting a city or suburb destination.[41] For each metropolitan area type, the magnitude of the suburb destination propensity rate will be evaluated in relation to the suburban distribution of its entire resident population.

The graphs in Figure 7.6 show clearly that the greatest suburban preference exists within the areas: South-Old, South-Young, and West-Young. This result for South-Old areas is not surprising in light of their older, underbounded central cities. Yet it is noteworthy to find that the suburban distribution of movers and inmigrants (relative to the total resident population) is higher in the newer, lower-density South-Young and West-Young metropolitan areas than in the declining and old areas of the North and West. The fact that North-Declining movers and inmigrants are slightly less well represented in the suburbs than the total resident population, again suggests a potential for arresting city decline. This topic will be taken up in later chapters where the suburb destination propensity rates for movers in different racial and socioeconomic categories will be examined.

To sum up, the foregoing analyses of migration streams and destination propensity rates within the metropolitan area point to the general pervasiveness of city-to-suburb redistribution in large metropolitan areas of all types. Common perception—based on the immediate postwar experience—suggests that this process is most characteristic of older northern industrial metropolitan areas, but the data here indicate almost the opposite. Population losses in Old-Declining central cities are affected, to an increasing extent, by net outmigration to other

---

[41]More explicitly, this measure is defined as:

$$\frac{\text{Intrametropolitan movers and inmigrants, 1975–1980, that select suburban destinations}}{\text{All intrametropolitan movers and inmigrants to the metropolitan area, 1975–1980}}$$

This measure reflects the aggregate destination selections of a metropolitan area's movers and inmigrants—irrespective of the volume of mobility and inmigration. Hence, areas with high levels of residential movement or inmigration should not necessarily show higher or lower levels of suburban destination propensity than areas with low levels of movement and inmigration. Further elaborations and analyses of these rates can be found in William H. Frey, "Mover Destination Selectivity and the Changing Suburbanization of Metropolitan Whites and Blacks," *Demography* (May 1985):223–243.

metropolitan areas and to nonmetropolitan areas, while suburban destinations within the metropolitan area—among recent movers and inmigrants—are actually becoming less popular. It is in the young, fast-growing South and West metropolitan areas that suburbanward redistribution appears to be on the rise, while their cities and suburbs both gain population through interlabor market migration.

City-Suburb Population Change in the Early 1980s

Compilation of postcensal 1980–1984 estimates of city and suburb population change, made available by the Census Bureau, permits some assessment of how well the 1970s redistribution tendencies described in this chapter appear to be continuing through the early 1980s. The 1980–1984 estimates are presented in Table 7.10, along with comparable change measures for the 1970–1980 decade, where both change measures are converted to annual percent changes. (Annual percent changes for the 1950–1960 and 1960–1970 decades, as well, are presented in Appendix E, Table 7E.) Although there is a good deal of similarity between the 1970s and early 1980s patterns, the 1980–1984 estimates indicate a fairly pervasive tendency for central cities to register reduced losses or increased gains in most all of the metropolitan area groupings.

This change is particularly noteworthy for cities in the North-Declining class, where all cities but one (Detroit) appear to be doing better with regard to population growth—serving to reduce the magnitude of their area's suburbanization rates. Particularly noticeable city gains are shown for the East Coast centers, Philadelphia, Boston, and New York (the latter two registering early 1980s central city gains) and for the Midwest regional nodal centers, St. Louis and Cleveland. Whether these new city gains confirm the view that such nodal areas have begun to prosper as advanced service centers remains to be seen. However, the early 1980s' estimates for these North-Declining areas clearly suggest an attenuation of the city loss-dominated suburbanization of the 1970s—yet still within the context of minimal or declining metropolitanwide growth.

While city gains are fairly pervasive across the four Old metropolitan area classes, as well as the North-Declining class, this is less the case for the two younger categories of metropolitan areas. Areas in the South-Young and West-Young classes also appear to be sustaining a reduction in their suburbanization rates from 1980 to 1984—but more as a consequence of reduced suburban gains rather than increased city gains. In this respect they resemble shifts undergone by older areas in the immediate postwar decades.

Although the early 1980s city gains suggested by the postcensal estimates represent a change, basic distinctions in city–suburb redistribution tendencies that were observed in the 1970s still remain across the six metropolitan area categories. In the early 1980s, as in the 1970s, both central cities and suburbs in the North-Declining areas are sustaining low or negative population growth. South-Old areas continue to exhibit high rates of suburbanization; and both the cities and suburbs in the younger South-Young and West-Young classes continue to register high rates of population growth. In the remaining Part Two chapters, the race-, status-, household type-, and worker-selectivity processes underlying these different redistribution tendencies will be evaluated in more detail.

Summary

This chapter is the first of five devoted to the selective population redistribution that has occurred within large metropolitan areas in the post-1970 years. These chapters are concerned with documenting the changing nature of city–suburb redistribution within the nation's largest (one million and over population) metropolitan areas, and its consequences for these areas' central cities. The overriding question in this examination is: Will the social and demographic concomitants of suburbanization and central city change—as observed in the 1970s and beyond—differ significantly from those that characterized the well-known suburbanization surge of the immediate postwar decades?

In the present chapter, we have set the stage for this investigation by offering a typology of metropolitan areas that distinguishes among classes of areas which—by virtue of their development histories—should display somewhat different internal redistribution patterns. Prior to 1970, when virtually all metropolitan areas were growing in population, it would have sufficed to differentiate metropolitan areas on the basis of such factors as the age of their central cities and their regional locations. However, changing economic conditions and urban development shifts in the post-1970 period have given rise to a significant number of metropolitan areas that are sustaining absolute population losses—not only in their central cities—but on a metropolitanwide basis.

Perhaps the most important group of areas in our typology are the 13 which we have classed North-Declining. All located in the North,

TABLE 7.10

Average Annual Percent Change for Central Cities and Suburbs
and Suburbanization Rates for 39 Metropolitan Areas,
1970–1980, and Estimates for 1980–1984

Met. Area Groupings/ Met. Areas	Central City Average Annual % Change		Suburb Average Annual % Change		Annual Suburbanization Rate[a]	
	1970–1980	1980–1984 (est.)	1970–1980	1980–1984 (est.)	1970–1980	1980–1984 (est.)
NORTH-DECLINING						
New York	−1.1	+0.3	+0.2	+0.4	+1.3	+0.1
Philadelphia	−1.4	−0.6	+0.5	+0.8	+1.9	+1.4
Boston	−1.3	+0.3	+0.1	+0.2	+1.4	−0.1
Cincinnati	−1.6	−1.0	+0.9	+0.5	+2.5	+1.5
St. Louis	−3.1	−1.3	+0.6	+0.6	+3.7	+1.9
Buffalo	−2.5	−1.4	0.0	−0.6	+2.5	+0.8
Chicago	−1.1	−0.1	+1.3	+0.8	+2.4	+0.9
Newark	−1.5	−1.2	−0.2	+0.2	+1.3	+1.4
Cleveland	−2.7	−1.2	+0.1	−0.1	+2.8	+1.1
Detroit	−2.3	−2.5	+0.8	−0.4	+3.1	+2.1
Milwaukee	−1.2	−0.6	+1.0	+0.4	+2.2	+1.0
Pittsburgh	−2.0	−1.3	−0.2	−0.4	+1.8	+0.9
Paterson	−0.6	+0.3	−0.5	+0.1	+0.1	−0.2
Total	−1.4	−0.3	+0.4	+0.3	+1.8	+0.6
NORTH-OLD						
Columbus	+0.5	+0.1	+1.0	+1.4	+0.5	+1.3
Indianapolis	−0.5	+0.3	+2.2	+1.0	+2.7	+0.7
Kansas City	−1.2	−0.3	+1.4	+1.2	+2.6	+1.5
Hartford	−1.5	−0.1	+0.4	+0.5	+1.9	+0.6
Minneapolis*	−1.5	−0.7	+1.9	+1.8	+3.4	+2.5

TABLE 7.10 (continued)

SOUTH–OLD						
Baltimore	−1.4	+1.8	−0.7	+1.2	+3.2	+1.9
New Orleans	−0.6	+3.4	+0.1	+1.9	+4.0	+1.8
Washington, D.C.	−1.7	+1.2	−0.6	+1.8	+2.9	+2.4
Atlanta	−1.5	+3.8	+0.1	+3.4	+5.3	+3.3
Total	−1.3	+2.2	−0.4	+2.1	+3.5	+2.5
WEST–OLD						
San Francisco*	−0.6	+0.9	+1.1	+1.3	+1.5	+0.2
Denver*	−0.2	+4.8	+0.6	+3.6	+5.0	+3.0
Los Angeles*	+0.5	+0.7	+1.1	+1.6	+0.2	+0.5
Portland	−0.4	+3.4	0.0	+1.2	+3.8	+1.2
Seattle*	−0.6	+2.3	−0.1	+2.0	+2.9	+2.1
Total	+0.1	+1.6	+0.9	+1.8	+1.5	+0.9
SOUTH–YOUNG						
San Antonio	+1.9	+2.0	+1.8	+4.9	+0.1	+3.1
Dallas*	+0.4	+4.0	+1.9	+4.6	+3.6	+2.7
Houston	+2.6	+5.5	+1.7	+5.9	+2.9	+4.2
Tampa*	+0.3	+5.9	+0.3	+3.7	+5.6	+3.4
Miami	+0.4	+3.2	+1.8	+1.1	+2.8	−0.7
Ft. Lauderdale*	+1.1	+7.1	−0.4	+2.6	+6.0	+3.0
Total	+1.4	+4.7	+1.5	+3.8	+3.3	+2.3
WEST–YOUNG						
Sacramento	+0.7	+3.1	+2.5	+2.6	+2.4	+0.1
San Diego	+2.3	+4.1	+2.3	+2.8	+1.8	+0.5
San Jose	+3.2	+1.0	+2.2	+0.7	−2.2	−1.5
Phoenix	+3.1	+6.4	+2.0	+4.6	+3.3	+2.6
Riverside*	+2.0	+3.6	+2.7	+4.2	+1.6	+1.5
Anaheim*	+2.1	+3.6	+1.9	+1.8	+1.5	−0.1
Total	+2.4	+3.6	+2.2	+2.8	+1.2	+0.6

SOURCE: U.S. Bureau of the Census, Current Population Reports, series P-25, no. 976, Patterns of Metropolitan Areas and County Population Growth: 1980 to 1984; and machine-readable computer files: County and City Data Book Consolidated Files for Counties, 1947–1977, and Cities, 1944–1977; and County and City Data Book, 1983 files (prepared by the U.S. Bureau of the Census, Washington, DC).

[a] Annual Suburbanization Rate: Suburb Average Annual Percent Change minus Central City Average Annual Percent Change.
* Largest of multiple central cities.

with older highly dense central cities and negative or barely positive post-1970 growth, these areas surround the nation's largest "problem" cities. Some of these cities, with largely manufacturing functions, have lost between 20–30 percent of their populations over the 1970–1980 period. Others, which serve as corporate or administrative service centers, sustained city losses close to 10 percent. While civic leaders in all of these cities harbor expectations for city revival and those in the latter corporate headquarter cities have legitimate grounds for anticipating future gains, the nature of city–suburb redistribution within the context of metropolitanwide decline is a relatively new phenomenon and difficult to forecast in the absence of previous historical experience.

The other areas with older central cities, classed as North-Old, South-Old, and West-Old, are growing moderately to rapidly at the metropolitan level. Of these, the South-Old areas display the highest 1970s city decline—at levels which resemble many North-Declining cities. These are complemented by even higher rates of suburban growth. North-Old and West-Old metropolitan areas tend to include more expansive central cities and, therefore, display somewhat more moderate city–suburb redistribution disparities. However, most metropolitan areas in each of these classes display the characteristic "city loss–suburb gain" redistribution pattern which most North-Declining areas experienced in the 1950s and 1960s. It remains to be seen whether or not their race-, status-, and industrial-selectivity patterns also follow suit.

The final two metropolitan area classes, which we have termed South-Young and West-Young, have younger central cities and exist only in the nation's Sunbelt regions. These areas bear little resemblance to the old and declining areas in their past, their present, and probably their future city–suburb redistribution patterns. Their most distinguishing characteristics are their phenomenal metropolitan growth and positive central city growth during each postwar decade, yet these areas differ markedly from each other in their city–suburb growth disparities. Some of this variability across areas draws from city differences in land area. Most of these cities are relatively expansive and have developed within low-density, generously bounded areas, but some have been more successful in annexing territory and, hence, greater shares of their metropolitan areas' growth. Another explanation for this variability lies with the broad array of economic functions represented among these 12 young central cities. Although most older cities served as manufacturing, administrative service, or government centers, only half of these young cities are so classified. The remaining ones serve as resort or retirement centers, military complexes, and other functions—where it is unclear how the central city will share in the entire metropolitan area's growth.

Despite the diversity of historical circumstances, economic conditions, and physical configuration across which these six classes of metropolitan areas vary, there are two aspects of demographic change that appear to affect city–suburb redistribution consistently in all of these areas. The first is the reduced contribution of natural increase. Although growing areas have greater natural increase levels than declining ones, and suburbs generally have higher levels than central cities, we find a reduced postwar contribution of natural increase within each of these area types. This obviously places greater importance on migration in contributing to city, suburb, and metropolitan population gains for all areas in our typology.

The second consistency across areas involves migration and points up an underlying commonality in the city–suburb redistribution process. We find that when total net migration for city and suburbs is decomposed into the interlabor market migration streams with other areas and the intrametropolitan mobility streams between cities and suburbs, the latter exchange is almost always imbalanced in favor of the suburbs and contributes to a greater suburbanization of the metropolitan population. Although this latter exchange of residential mobility streams has long fueled suburbanization in most Old and Declining metropolitan areas, the process is now evident and, in fact, more accentuated in South-Old, South-Young, and West-Young metropolitan areas. Central cities in the latter Sunbelt areas have, in the past, been able to annex population growth on their peripheries and thereby contain widespread suburbanization. But annexation as a component of their city growth has become less prevalent since 1970. It remains to be seen whether or not the suburb-destined migrants within these young Sunbelt metropolitan areas take on the familiar selectivity patterns of the older areas' suburbanization experiences.

The next four chapters will examine the race, status, household and family, and worker and workplace aspects of post-1970 city–suburb redistribution in each metropolitan area class. A main concern in each of these analyses will be the North-Declining metropolitan areas, and the selective redistribution consequences for their central cities as they attempt to adapt to a postindustrial economy. However, recent society-wide demographic shifts in race relations, family formation patterns, and industrial structure have been substantial, and should introduce changes in the nature of intrametropolitan population redistribution within metropolitan areas of all types. The chapters that follow will allow us to assess just how significant these changes are.

8

RACE DIMENSIONS
OF CITY–SUBURB REDISTRIBUTION

Introduction

CHAPTERS 8 and 9 can be regarded as a unit that points up the major dimensions of race and socioeconomic selective population redistribution within the nation's largest metropolitan areas. Just as growth disparities between central cities and suburbs became accentuated in many older metropolitan areas during the immediate postwar decades, the race and status disparities between their cities and suburbs widened. The familiar urban location pattern, which places low-status minority, recent immigrant residents at the city's center and high-status residents on its periphery, was well established in older industrial-based metropolitan areas prior to World War II.[1] However, it was the massive suburbanization that took place in the immediate postwar decades that redistributed much of these areas' middle-class white populations outside of their legal city boundaries and into their surrounding suburban communities over the 1950–1970 period.[2]

---

[1]Literature reviews that document these patterns appear in: R. J. Johnston, *Urban Residential Patterns* (New York: Praeger, 1971); and James R. Pinkerton, "City Suburban Residential Patterns by Social Class: A Review of the Literature," *Urban Affairs Quarterly* 4 (1969):499–519.

[2]See Leo F. Schnore, *The Urban Scene* (New York: The Free Press, 1965); and Reynolds Farley, "Components of Suburban Population Growth," in Barry Schwartz, ed., *The Changing Face of the Suburbs* (Chicago: University of Chicago Press, 1976); and William H. Frey, "Black In-migration, White Flight and the Changing Economic Base of the Central City," *American Journal of Sociology* 85(6) (1980):1396–1417.

Equally important for several large North and South central cities during this time was the *nonparticipation* of blacks in this suburbanization process. The persistence of black residential segregation had remained a notable exception to the experiences of other urban immigrant groups that were able to disperse geographically with increased duration of urban residence.[3] The continued central city confinement of the metropolitan area's black population and the suburbanization of its middle-class whites led to city populations that were disproportionately comprised of blacks and low-income whites and to the associated problems of private disinvestment, reduced public services, environmental deterioration, and crime.

In observing these demographic trends through the 1970 census, urban scholars and policymakers began to express concern that an irreversible cycle of a race- and status-selective movement had been set in place which would cause old and declining central cities to become continually smaller, blacker, and poorer, and also further isolated from their suburban populations.[4] Even more significant than these concerns over the central city's economic development were those that foresaw a crisis in American race relations evolving from the geographic separation of blacks from the broader metropolitan population. The famous conclusion of President Johnson's 1968 National Advisory Commission on Civil Disorders proclaimed that the nation was headed on a course toward "two separate societies," a white society located primarily in the suburbs, and a black society within large central cities.[5]

Speculation regarding the future changes in these demographic patterns was not optimistic. In evaluating 1970 Census results with an eye to these race and redistribution issues, Karl Taeuber wrote:

> The lowered birthrate in the United States and the lowered rate at which whites and blacks are moving into metropolitan areas should sharply reduce population pressure on urban and suburban housing. . . . Reduction of central city densities should occur, and a potential exists for greatly increased black suburbanization. With black populations growing more slowly and with blacks interested in the full spectrum of metropolitan residential neighborhoods, there could be rapid residential desegregation without the population pressures that in

---

[3]Stanley Lieberson, *Ethnic Patterns in American Cities* (New York: Free Press, 1963); and Karl E. Taeuber and Alma F. Taeuber, "The Negro as an Immigrant Group: Recent Trends in Racial and Ethnic Segregation in Chicago," *American Journal of Sociology* 69 (1964):374–382.

[4]See William Gorham and Nathan Glazer, *The Urban Predicament* (Washington, DC: Urban Institute, 1976).

[5]National Advisory Commission on Civil Disorders, *A Report* (Washington, DC: U.S. Government Printing Office, 1968).

the past led so often to immediate resegregation. This pattern could develop, but there is no evidence yet that it will.[6]

Taeuber's reservations were based on the premise that housing discrimination, which prevented blacks from locating into white neighborhoods in the city or suburbs, would probably persist along with the linkages that exist between housing discrimination and discrimination in other realms.

Nevertheless, developments that took place both prior to and during the decade of the 1970s suggest improved prospects for reducing the wide race and status city–suburb disparities that evolved over the 1950–1970 period. First, the enactment of important civil rights legislation of the 1960s, coupled with substantial black gains in income and social status measures over the 1960s and 1970s, have put blacks in a far better position to afford and select suburban residences than has heretofore been possible. Second, a potential increase in the demand for centrally located residences on the part of a growing segment of white middle-class households not engaged in child-rearing has been cultivated by planners and developers in nodal-type central cities with declining populations.

The present chapter, and the one that follows, examine the extent to which the post-1970 city–suburb redistribution processes in the nation's older metropolitan areas have become more integrated and less status-selective than those that characterized the 1950–1970 period. These analyses will also evaluate changes in selective redistribution patterns for younger metropolitan areas where city–suburb growth and status disparities have been less severe. Many of these areas differ from the former areas in the historical development of their minority populations and in community political traditions which determine the nature of status-selective movements within the metropolitan area. The present chapter will be concerned with race and minority group selectivity per se—leaving to Chapter 9 the elaboration of these groups' socioeconomic selectivity patterns. The final section of Chapter 9 summarizes the major findings of both of these chapters.

The next section of this chapter focuses on the new intrametropolitan redistribution tendencies of blacks and nonblacks. It first reviews reasons why these tendencies should differ in the post-1970 period and then evaluates these new tendencies in light of patterns observed in the immediate post–World War II decades. This evaluation is

---

[6]Karl E. Taeuber, "Racial Segregation: The Persisting Dilemma," *Annals of the American Academy of Political and Social Sciences* 422 (1975):87–96.

followed by an examination of the intrametropolitan distribution patterns to "newer" minority groups—Asian-Americans and Hispanics.

Blacks and Nonblacks
Background

The 1945–1970 period has been characterized as an era wherein the demography of race relations became an intrametropolitan concern.[7] During this period the black population, like the white population, experienced increased fertility and extended periods of child-rearing. However, its nonparticipation in the suburbanization process was attributable primarily to racial discrimination which took many forms, including racially motivated site selection and financing on the part of private realtors, lending institutions, and federally sponsored housing programs that operated during this period of greatest suburban construction.[8] Hence, unlike the destinations of white movers, the destinations of black movers were generally constrained to central city locations.

As the 1960s drew on and the urban black population became increasingly northern-born,[9] and closer in socioeconomic status to the white population,[10] one might have expected some reduction in the barriers to interracial residential segregation. However, the evidence from a number of northern cities does not show this to be the case. Residential segregation levels in 1970 were not appreciably lower than those registered in the previous two censuses.[11] The total number of blacks who resided in American suburbs was far lower than that which might be expected on the basis of black income and socioeconomic characteristics.[12] The city and suburb destinations of black and white movers in

[7]Thomas F. Pettigrew, "Racial Change and the Intrametropolitan Distribution of Black Americans," in Arthur P. Solomon, ed., *The Prospective City* (Cambridge, MA: M.I.T. Press, 1980).

[8]Donald Foley, "Institutional and Contextual Factors Affecting the Housing Choices of Minority Residents," in Amos H. Hawley and Vincent P. Rock, eds., *Segregation in Residential Areas* (Washington, DC: National Academy of Sciences, 1973); and K. E. Taeuber, "Racial Segregation."

[9]Karl E. Taeuber and Alma F. Taeuber, "The Changing Character of Negro Migration," *American Journal of Sociology* 60 (1965):429–441.

[10]Reynolds Farley and Albert I. Hermalin, "The 1960s: A Decade of Progress for Blacks," *Demography* 9(3) (1972):353–370.

[11]Thomas L. Van Valey, Wade Clark Roof, and Jerome E. Wilcox, "Trends in Residential Segregation, 1960–1970," *American Journal of Sociology* 82 (1977):826–844.

[12]Albert I. Hermalin and Reynolds Farley, "The Potential for Residential Integration in Cities and Suburbs: Implications for the Busing Controversy," *American Sociological Review* 38 (1973):595–610.

the late 1960s showed the same racial differences as did movers in the 1950s.[13]

Reasons for change: Why then should a greater suburbanization of blacks be expected with the 1970s? First, blacks continued to advance significantly on measures of earnings and educational attainment such that, by the mid-1970s, approximately 40 percent of the black population was considered to be "middle class" (in comparison to about 5 percent in 1940).[14] A good deal of this advancement was accounted for by postwar-born black cohorts that took advantage of educational and employment opportunities made possible by the civil rights movement of the 1950s and 1960s, and the provisions of the Civil Rights Act of 1964.[15] Hence, the black population is in a better position than ever before to afford housing of any type and in any location within the metropolitan area.

Second, fair housing provisions in the Civil Rights Act of 1968 explicitly outlawed racial discrimination in the sale and rental of housing. This legislation not only served to eliminate the most overt forms of housing discrimination but also stimulated local citizens' fair housing efforts. Realtors, renters, and black consumers were alerted to the provisions of this legislation which, therefore, encouraged greater compliance with the law.[16]

Third, a time series of nationwide attitudinal surveys has shown a steady increase in the acceptance by whites of the principle of racial integration. To the question: "If a Negro, with just as much income and education as you have, moved into your block, would it make any difference to you?", a "no" response was given by 85 percent of whites in 1972—as contrasted with 53 percent in 1956 and 35 percent in 1942.[17] Finally, the entire range of consequences emanating from the civil rights movement and associated federal legislation have served to raise the consciousness of whites and blacks in the 1970s to a concern for racial fairness and equity that was not nearly as pervasive in the 1950s and 1960s.

[13]William H. Frey, "Black Movement to the Suburbs: Potentials and Prospects for Metropolitanwide Integration," in Frank D. Bean and W. Parker Frisbie, eds., *The Demography of Racial and Ethnic Groups* (New York: Academic Press, 1978).

[14]Pettigrew, "Racial Change and the Intrametropolitan Distribution of Black Americans," p. 55.

[15]Reynolds Farley, *Blacks and Whites: Narrowing the Gap* (Cambridge, MA: Harvard University Press, 1984).

[16]Thomas A. Clark, *Blacks in Suburbs: A National Perspective* (New Brunswick, NJ: Rutgers University Center for Urban Policy Research, 1979); and Eunice Grier and George Grier, *Black Suburbanization at the Mid–1970s* (Washington, DC: Washington Center for Metropolitan Studies, 1978).

[17]Hermalin and Farley, "The Potential for Residential Integration in Cities and Suburbs."

To be sure, there are counterpoints to be argued in response to each of the points just raised. It has been asserted that: (a) a large number of blacks still reside in poverty households and in an "underclass" stratum which did not benefit greatly from the civil rights movement;[18] (b) the enforcement mechanisms for the federal fair housing laws have remained weak or nonexistent;[19] (c) a widespread acceptance of racial integration in principle is not evident among whites in specific situations;[20] and (d) racial discrimination in housing is still pervasive but has come to exist in more subtle forms.[21] While there is some truth in each of these assertions, it is also true that, beginning with the 1970s, the economic position of blacks has become stronger and the level of racial discrimination in housing weaker than in any previous time. It is for this reason that racial redistribution in the 1970s should begin to depart from the vicious cycle that characterized the immediate postwar decades.

Different metropolitan area contexts: Although the changes just enumerated are significant in scope, their redistribution effects should manifest themselves in different ways across each of our metropolitan area classes. In their landmark study of residential segregation through the 1960 census, Karl and Alma Taeuber demonstrate that the nature of racial change *within* an area is strongly influenced by the *areawide* growth of the black and white populations.[22] For example, they found that the greatest neighborhood racial transition occurred within cities that sustained moderate to strong levels of black citywide population growth, along with low to moderate levels of white citywide growth. On the other hand, in those circumstances when white citywide growth exceeded that for blacks, white to black neighborhood transition was far less common. Clearly, there are other factors in addition to the relative white and black area growth levels that influence the nature of intra-areal transition (such as housing availability, density patterns, placement of political boundaries); yet, the Taeubers' results underscore the significance of these relative growth rates. As they state:

. . . The greater the rate of Negro population growth relative to white population growth . . ., the more likely an increase in proportion

[18]William J. Wilson, *The Declining Significance of Race* (Chicago: University of Chicago Press, 1978).

[19]Clark, *Blacks in Suburbs.*

[20]Reynolds Farley, Howard Schuman, Suzanne Bianchi, Diane Colasanto, and Shirley Hatchett, "Chocolate City, Vanilla Suburbs: Will the Trend Toward Racially Separate Communities Continue?" *Social Science Research* 7 (1978):319–344.

[21]Pettigrew, "Racial Change and the Intrametropolitan Distribution of Black Americans."

[22]Karl E. Taeuber and Alma F. Taeuber, *Negroes in Cities* (Chicago: Aldine, 1965).

Negro neighborhoods, and the faster the rate of racial change. A high growth rate of white population relative to Negro population, on the other hand, is accompanied by declines in the proportion Negro in many neighborhoods and a slow rate of racial change. Any "tipping point" would thus seem to have less to do with levels of racial tolerance of whites than with the levels of supply and demand for housing in areas that will accept Negro residents.[23]

Although our interest here will be in the intrametropolitan redistribution rather than the intracity neighborhood racial transition process, our review will take cognizance of the relative black and nonblack metropolitan areawide growth patterns. (Nonblacks rather than whites will be examined due to inconsistencies between censuses in the definition of the white population.)

The analogy between the Taeubers' study of racial transition across neighborhoods within the city and the present study of city–suburb redistribution within the metropolitan area is most pertinent to the metropolitan areas we have classed as North-Declining. Just as the city-wide white population decline in the 1950s and 1960s provided the context for an expansion of blacks into previously all-white neighborhoods, the metropolitanwide nonblack population decline these areas display in the 1970s should facilitate the black suburbanization process (see Table 8.1).

The metropolitan areas that we have termed South-Old represent a second class of areas wherein racial population redistribution is of interest. Their nonblack and black growth patterns are far different from those that were just reviewed. Like many old southern cities that developed during the nineteenth century, these areas originally housed blacks and whites in separate, although not geographically segregated, housing quarters.[24] As these metropolitan areas began to draw both whites and blacks in the immediate postwar decades, mounting housing pressures within limited space led to high levels of neighborhood racial segregation and city–suburb racial separation through the 1970 census.[25] Yet, unlike the situation in North-Declining areas, the 1970s growth context in South-Old areas is one of significant metropolitan-wide nonblack growth with even higher levels of black growth (Table 8.1). Although the nonblack growth is concentrated entirely in the suburbs—and represents greater competition to black suburbanization than occurs in the North-Declining area context—the levels of black

---

[23]Taeuber and Taeuber, *Negroes in Cities,* p. 4.
[24]Ibid.
[25]Van Valey, Roof, and Wilcox, "Trends in Residential Segregation"; and Frey, "Black Movement to the Suburbs."

TABLE 8.1

Percent Change in Metropolitan Area Population by Race,
1950–1960, 1960–1970, 1970–1980:
Six Metropolitan Area Groupings[a]

Metropolitan Area Groupings/ Race	1950–1960	1960–1970	1970–1980
NORTH-DECLINING			
Nonblack	+13.9	+6.0	−5.7
Black	+52.2	+39.3	+12.1
NORTH-OLD			
Nonblack	+28.1	+18.6	+4.2
Black	+49.3	+36.6	+20.1
SOUTH-OLD			
Nonblack	+29.2	+26.2	+7.2
Black	+37.8	+30.7	+22.1
WEST-OLD			
Nonblack	+34.0	+16.9	+8.6
Black	+89.3	+59.3	+23.9
SOUTH-YOUNG			
Nonblack	+60.7	+37.8	+35.7
Black	+63.5	+37.3	+34.1
WEST-YOUNG			
Nonblack	+102.5	+50.3	+34.6
Black	+122.0	+72.8	+69.5

SOURCES: Same as Figure 8.1, page 249.

[a]These metropolitan area groupings are based on three categories of region (North, South, West), two categories of age (Old, Young), and two categories of metropolitan growth (Declining, Nondeclining). All 13 Declining areas are also Old and located in the North and are placed in the single North-Declining grouping. The remaining 26 areas are all Nondeclining and sorted into the groupings: North-Old, South-Old, West-Old, South-Young, and West-Young. Further details are provided in the Chapter 7 section, "A Metropolitan Area Typology," and Figure 7.1.

metropolitanwide growth relative to nonblack growth have been increasing over time and should exert pressure on city-concentrated blacks toward greater suburbanization.

Metropolitan areas in the South-Young category represent a third class of areas with significant black populations and a high level of city-suburb racial separation. These areas encompass the fast-growing central cities in the "New South"—which grew up largely in the post–Civil War era and house smaller concentrations of blacks than do older southern cities. The significant metropolitan growth characteristic of these cities is that both nonblack and black areawide growth levels are high *and relatively similar to each other.* Hence, blacks will not be able to exert the same pressure on nonblacks for suburban housing that they do in other southern areas. Moreover, as was shown in Chapter 7, the central cities of these areas are fairly expansive and able to accommodate high levels of the metropolitan area's growth within their political boundaries. Clearly, the metropolitanwide growth context in South-Young areas is not particularly conducive to a widespread dispersal of blacks. Black suburbanization is much more likely to occur in North-Declining and South-Old areas with underbounded central cities and where black metropolitanwide population growth exceeds that for nonblacks.

The growth conditions just sketched out for North-Declining, South-Old, and South-Young metropolitan areas constitute three fundamentally different contexts within which intrametropolitan redistribution can occur.[26] The North-Declining context represents the most conducive of the three to both black suburbanization and neighborhood integration since an absolute decline in the areas' nonblack populations creates a softer housing market in the suburbs. The South-Old context is conducive to black suburbanization as high levels of black population growth cannot continue to "pile up" within their already dense, heavily black central cities. However, because of competition with significant nonblack population growth in the suburbs of these areas, the new black suburbanites should be less likely to integrate at the community and neighborhood levels than those in the North-Declining areas. Finally, the South-Young areas' context is least conducive to neighborhood integration and black suburbanization. High levels of nonblack population growth in their central cities and suburbs will create strong competition for housing with incoming blacks.

Although the contexts of black and nonblack metropolitan growth exert a significant influence on the nature of race-selective redistribution within the metropolitan area, they hardly represent the only influence. The inertia of past segregation tendencies holds important sway on future development. Moreover, the existing neighborhood racial segregation and city–suburb racial separation are the products of the collective actions of city and suburb communities, lenders, realtors, developers, and individual buyers and sellers. Most all large metropoli-

[26]The remaining metropolitan area groupings, North-Old, West-Old, and West-Young, have smaller black populations, and metropolitan areas within them vary widely in their city–suburb redistribution patterns. These will be discussed more fully below.

tan areas' suburbs are comprised of a fragmented array of jurisdictions which are carefully stratified on the basis of social status, family type, and race. Many of these communities have both legal and quasilegal mechanisms to control the use of their land or to channel the characteristics of their incoming residents so as to perpetuate this stratified system.[27] There is also a great deal of variation in the degree to which states and local areas encourage the compliance with the provisions of the federal fair housing laws, and many southern states have been particularly deficient in this regard.[28]

Nonetheless, efforts toward alleviating racial discrimination in housing have been more widespread in the 1970s than during any prior period. The overall rise in the status of blacks and the legacy of the civil rights movement should therefore effect a more integrated redistribution of the races in all areas, to a greater or lesser degree.

Black–Nonblack City–Suburb Redistribution

Our examination of city–suburb redistribution patterns in the 39 largest metropolitan areas again focuses on blacks and nonblacks, rather than on blacks and whites, due to the over-time inconsistencies in census definitions of the white population.[29] As our preceding discussion has indicated, we will focus particularly on the post-1970 period in order to determine if black and nonblack patterns have altered significantly as a result of recent societywide developments. Primary attention is given to the three metropolitan area groupings (reviewed earlier) with the greatest concentrations of blacks—North-Declining areas, South-Old areas, and South-Young areas—although data for areas in all classes are presented in text and Appendix E Tables and Figures.

North-Declining areas: Because these areas registered negative metropolitanwide growth in their nonblack populations, along with marked declines in the growth of their black populations in the 1970–1980 decade (shown in Table 8.1), it was anticipated that black suburbanization would become evident in North-Declining metropolitan areas.

[27]Clark, *Blacks in the Suburbs.*

[28]Franklin J. James, Betty L. McCummings, and Eileen A. Tynan, *Minorities in the Sunbelt* (New Brunswick, NJ: Rutgers Center for Urban Policy Research, 1984).

[29]In 1980 nonblack populations for the majority of North-Declining, North-Old, and South-Old metropolitan areas consisted of whites who were not Hispanics. However, Asians and Hispanics comprise significant shares of the nonblack population in several West-Old, South-Young, and West-Young metropolitan areas (refer to Table 8.5). Changes in the historical comparability of the census's white population definition are discussed in "Census of Population and Housing," *User's Guide,* PHC-R1-B, Part B (Glossary) (Washington, DC: U.S. Government Printing Office, 1982).

The suburbanization rate measures in the rightmost three columns of Table 8.2 tend to confirm this expectation. In 1970–1980 the black suburbanization rate had increased markedly from that observed in 1960–1970 or earlier. Indeed, the black population sustained a negative suburbanization rate (greater city percent change than suburb percent change) during the 1950–1960 period—the decade that nonblacks registered their peak postwar suburbanization levels. Hence, the black suburbanization rate has increased over time while the nonblack rate has decreased. The black increase, however, has been most accentuated in the 1970–1980 period—the first decade that it has surpassed the nonblack rate for North-Declining areas as a group. These generalizations can also be made for most individual metropolitan areas in this class (Appendix E, Tables E.8A and E.8B show individual metropolitan area statistics).

The first six columns of Table 8.2 do not directly measure the suburbanization process per se. Rather, they show how the combined impacts of both the suburbanization process and metropolitanwide population change have affected population changes in the central city (columns 1 through 3) or in the suburbs (columns 4 through 6). These data indicate that through all three postwar decades, North-Declining central cities have lost nonblacks and gained blacks. Yet the city gains for both racial groups have become more negative over time. Accentuated nonblack city loss in the 1970s is more closely linked to the metropolitanwide loss of nonblacks than to a shift in the suburbanization process—although there are variations in both processes across individual areas. Black declines in city growth are a result of both decreases in metropolitanwide black growth and an increase in the black suburbanization rate. Together, these trends have contributed to the lower 1970–1980 black rate of growth (+5.1 percent) observed in the North-Declining cities as a group. Appendix Table E.8A data show that 5 of this area's 13 cities registered absolute declines in their black populations over the decade.

North-Declining suburban gains are positive for both races across all three postwar periods. However, nonblack gains taper off significantly in 1970–1980—a result of both the metropolitan decline of nonblacks and the decreased rate of nonblack suburbanization. Black suburban growth benefits from increased suburbanization over the 1960s and 1970s. The high 1960s levels of black percent suburban gain are accentuated, in part, by the small initial black population in the denominator, and these high levels taper off slightly in the 1970s. Yet, due to even greater nonblack declines, black suburban gains dwarf those displayed by nonblacks in the 1970–1980 period (46.1 percent for blacks, compared with 2.5 percent for nonblacks in 1970–1980).

TABLE 8.2

Percent Change in Central City and Suburb Population by Race, 1950–1960, 1960–1970, 1970–1980: Six Metropolitan Area Groupings

Metropolitan Area Groupings/Race	Central City			Suburbs			Suburbanization Rate[a]		
	1950–1960	1960–1970	1970–1980	1950–1960	1960–1970	1970–1980	1950–1960	1960–1970	1970–1980
NORTH-DECLINING									
Nonblack	−11.3	−14.0	−20.4	+47.0	+21.8	+2.5	+58.3	+35.8	+22.9
Black	+54.1	+37.1	+5.1	+42.8	+51.0	+46.1	−11.3	+13.9	+41.0
NORTH-OLD									
Nonblack	+0.0	+9.1	−11.6	+60.2	+25.5	+14.1	+60.2	+16.4	+25.7
Black	+58.4	+38.4	+16.1	+13.0	+26.3	+44.4	−45.4	−12.1	+28.3
SOUTH-OLD									
Nonblack	−10.0	−23.5	−26.3	+72.3	+54.7	+16.7	+82.3	+78.2	+43.0
Black	+43.1	+27.9	−0.7	+19.6	+42.7	+106.8	−23.5	+14.8	+107.5
WEST-OLD									
Nonblack	+10.8	+1.8	−0.8	+61.8	+29.2	+14.7	+51.0	+27.4	+15.5
Black	+87.3	+47.8	+8.9	+95.7	+94.5	+59.1	+8.4	+46.7	+50.2
SOUTH-YOUNG									
Nonblack	+48.8	+18.7	+10.9	+78.0	+61.3	+58.1	+29.2	+42.6	+47.2
Black	+77.2	+40.7	+28.0	+37.5	+29.2	+50.6	−39.7	−11.5	+22.6
WEST-YOUNG									
Nonblack	+118.3	+41.8	+25.5	+92.3	+56.5	+40.6	−26.0	+14.7	+15.1
Black	+182.9	+77.5	+50.9	+51.4	+62.8	+113.3	−131.5	−14.7	+62.4

SOURCES: Same as Figure 8.1, page 249.

[a]Suburbanization Rate: Suburb Percent Change minus Central City Percent Change.

The accentuated suburbanization of blacks and moderated suburbanization of nonblacks shown for North-Declining metropolitan areas should not lead one to conclude that: (1) cities and suburbs are becoming similar to each other in racial composition; or (2) that each North-Declining metropolitan area conforms to the aggregate pattern. The upper left-hand plot in Figure 8.1 provides an overall perspective on black vis-à-vis total population growth trends for North-Declining areas. It reproduces the metropolitan and central city population trends for 1950–1980, shown in Figure 7.2, and superimposes comparable trends for blacks over the same period. The reader can therefore examine trends for the city–suburb or metropolitan populations of blacks, nonblacks, or total residents, by visually isolating relevant sections of the plot. It is apparent that recent shifts toward greater black suburbanization and more moderated nonblack suburbanization have not significantly altered the aggregate city–suburb distribution of the races. Most blacks in North-Declining areas continue to reside in the central city and most nonblacks still reside in the metropolitan suburbs. Still, the increased post-1970 suburbanization of blacks clearly departs from past trends and may well accelerate if the postwar-born cohorts of metropolitan blacks continue to select suburban residences at the same pace.[30]

There are, of course, variations across metropolitan areas in the degree to which the post-1970 trends are displayed. In order to illustrate this, we contrast the experiences of the Philadelphia and Detroit metropolitan areas (displayed in Figure 8.2). When we compared these areas' trends in Chapter 7, we noticed their similar growth trends and attributed the greater city decline in postwar Detroit to this city's less diversified economic base. Yet the patterns observed here for blacks, in the context of total population redistribution, suggest a significant racial dimension to Detroit's heavier city–suburb redistribution.

Both metropolitan areas sustained postwar inmigration of blacks and retained similar metropolitanwide racial compositions in 1970 (blacks comprised 17.5 percent and 17.1 percent, respectively, of the Philadelphia and Detroit metropolitan areas). Also, both areas' metropolitan nonblack populations declined during the 1970–1980 period. Given its higher level of total city decline in the 1960s, one might have expected Detroit rather than Philadelphia to exhibit a greater 1970s rate of black suburbanization in the context of similar levels of metropolitanwide loss. Instead, it is Philadelphia that exhibited the most accentuated black suburbanization. Its black suburbanization rate rose from

[30]William H. Frey, "Lifecourse Migration of Metropolitan Whites and Blacks and the Structure of Demographic Change in Large Central Cities," *American Sociological Review* 49 (December 1984):803–827.

FIGURE 8.1

*Total and Black Population, Metropolitan Areas and Central Cities,
1950, 1960, 1970, 1980: Six Metropolitan Area Groupings*

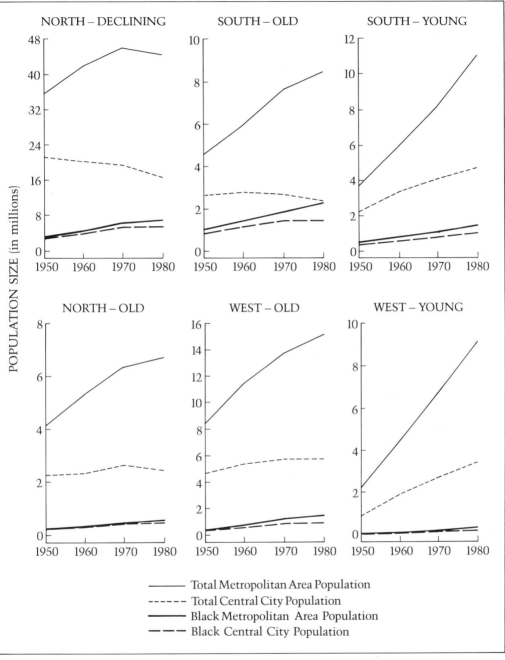

SOURCES: Machine-readable computer files: *County and City Data Book*, Consolidated Files for Counties, 1947–1977, and Cities, 1944–1947; and *County and City Data Book*, 1983 files (prepared by the U.S. Bureau of the Census, Washington DC).

FIGURE 8.2

Total and Black Population, Metropolitan Areas and Central Cities,
1950, 1960, 1970, 1980: Selected Metropolitan Areas

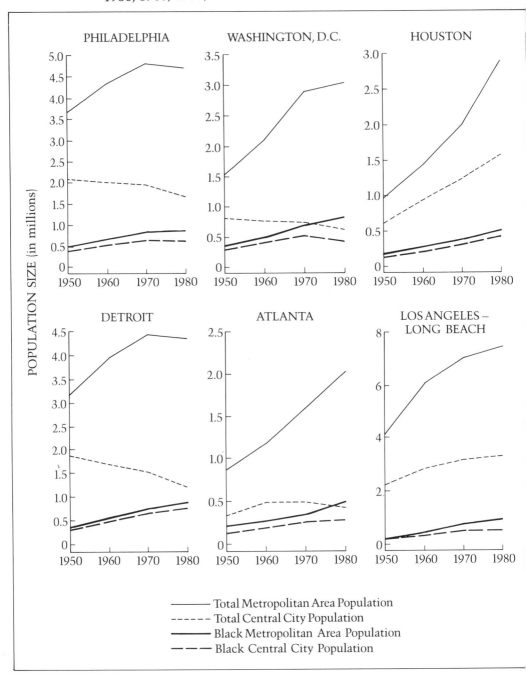

SOURCES: Same as Figure 8.1.

10.9 in the 1960s to 30.3 in the 1970s. Detroit's 1970s suburbanization rate, on the other hand, ranks among the lowest of the North-Declining areas—at 15.9. (Detroit blacks registered negative suburbanization rates during both the 1950s and 1960s.)

The sustained racial selectivity of Detroit's city–suburb redistribution process is most evident for its nonblack population. Detroit's 1970s nonblack suburbanization rate ranked, by far, as the highest of any North-Declining area. At 54.9 it represents less than a 2 percent decline from the area's 56.3 rate in the 1960s (also one of the highest among these areas). In contrast, Philadelphia's 1970s suburbanization rate for nonblacks stands at 22.8—representing a significant decrease from its 34.1 rate in the 1960s. It is clear from this comparison that metropolitanwide black and nonblack growth patterns are not the only factors that condition the racial selectivity of an area's suburbanization process. Aspects of Detroit's development, such as its history of racial violence,[31] the antiblack attitudes of many close-in suburbanites,[32] and the widespread suburbanization of "white" employment opportunities, have served to perpetuate, in Detroit, a race-selective redistribution process to a greater degree than in other areas that are at similar stages of economic and demographic development.

South-Old areas: We now turn to the second metropolitan area grouping with large concentrations of blacks, the South-Old areas. It was anticipated that these areas should also exhibit an increased black suburbanization after 1970, but for different reasons than the North-Declining areas. Here, both black and nonblack metropolitanwide growth rates are high but decreasing. Because nonblacks have been vacating South-Old central cities for several decades and because black rates of metropolitan growth remain high, it was anticipated that blacks would begin spilling over into the suburbs during the 1970s, although still facing stiff competition from nonblacks for suburban housing.

The South-Old suburbanization rates shown in Table 8.2 confirm this expectation. Black suburbanization rates increased rather dramatically over the decade of the 1970s—to a rate of 107.5. When viewed in comparison to the modest 14.8 rate in the 1960s and the negative −23.5 rate in the 1950s, the 1970s looks to be a significant decade for increased suburbanization in the South-Old areas. Not all four of these areas exhibited precisely the same pattern, however. Washington, DC, showed a noticeable shift toward black suburbanization already in the

---

[31]Kathy London, "Geographic Mobility in the Detroit Metropolitan Area," 1983. Unpublished doctoral dissertation, University of Michigan, Ann Arbor.
[32]Farley, Schuman, Bianchi, Colasanto, and Hatchett, "Chocolate City, Vanilla Suburbs."

1960s (see Figure 8.2). High rates of nonblack city loss in the 1950s and 1960s, coupled with continued black inmigration to Washington's underbounded city territory, precipitated black suburbanization a decade earlier than in most other metropolitan areas (Washington's black suburbanization rate shifted from -14.7 in the 1950s to 59.4 in the 1960s). Yet, an even greater rise in the area's black suburbanization (to a rate of 141.6) occurred in the 1970s—as its nonblack metropolitan growth fell off dramatically and made greater way for black outward expansion. During this period Washington's city black population actually declined to an even greater extent than the nonblack population.

Before extrapolating Washington's suburbanization patterns to other areas, however, the reader should be aware that Washington is unique in several respects. First, its small, rigidly bounded central city (the District of Columbia) is largely responsible for its early high level of city–suburb racial separation. It was almost inevitable that the city's black population would eventually spill over into its inner suburbs. Second, as a government center, Washington tends to draw select groups of migrants. Black inmigrants to Washington generally have higher educations and incomes than black inmigrants to other metropolitan areas. This increases their ability to select housing in all parts of the metropolitan area. Finally, because of their proximity to the federal government, the suburban communities of the Washington area received greater pressure, both informal and formal, to comply with the civil rights legislation of the 1960s. A combination of all of these factors helped to facilitate the high 1970s suburbanization rate of blacks in Washington.[33]

During this period, a good deal of popular commentary held up Washington, D.C., as an example of a renewed city renaissance.[34] In fact, although renewed residential development was also observed in other older cities during this period, Washington's experience was relatively unique. In no other older area was the nonblack suburbanization rate decline so accentuated or the reduction of city nonblack population loss so great. Washington's more exaggerated redistribution pattern can be attributed, in part, to the large number of professionals in its labor force who desired to both live and work in a central location. However, it has also been fostered by recent broad shifts in Washington's metropolitanwide demographic growth context, as discussed above.

[33]Grier and Grier, *Black Suburbanization at the Mid-1970s.*
[34]Shirley B. Laska and Daphne Spain, eds., *Back to the City: Issues in Neighborhood Renovation* (New York: Pergamon, 1980); and in John J. Palen and Bruce London, eds., *Gentrification, Displacement, and Neighborhood Revitalization* (Albany: State University of New York Press, 1984).

Atlanta's black suburbanization surge took place in the 1970s (see Figure 8.2). Prior to this decade, both black and nonblack metropolitan-wide growth levels were high (30.3 percent and 38.3 percent, respectively, for the 1960–1970 period); and internally, nonblack growth concentrated in the suburbs leaving greater room for black growth in the city. With the 1970s, Atlanta's metropolitanwide black growth increased to 43.7 percent while its nonblack growth decreased to 22.6 percent. These shifts in relative growth patterns, coupled with societal trends toward reduced discrimination, led to a shift in Atlanta's black suburbanization rate from −21.0 in the 1960s to +123.3 in the 1970s. Baltimore's black suburbanization rate also shifted from negative to positive over this period (from −13.2 to +74.9) in the context of greater black than nonblack metropolitanwide growth. Only New Orleans, of the four South-Old areas, sustained a more modest increase in its black suburbanization rate (from +12.6 in the 1960s to +25.3 in the 1970s), but also under similar black and nonblack metropolitanwide growth conditions.

Each of these old southern metropolitan areas shares a common history of black and white redistribution trends. It appears that their race selectivity has come full circle—from an early pattern where black rural enclaves became displaced by suburbanizing whites, to a "northern" pattern of centralized black ghettos, and, now, toward a pattern of increased black suburbanization.

South-Young areas: The South-Young areas, like the South-Old areas, are sustaining high 1970s levels of black inmigration. Yet these areas contrast markedly with their older counterparts in the race selectivity of their internal redistribution patterns. Because these areas grew up primarily since the Civil War and sustained black inmigration much more recently, they developed neither the large black populations nor the traditional racial settlement characteristics of South-Old metropolitan areas. Moreover, their current growth contexts are also much different. South-Young metropolitan areas sustained 1970s nonblack metropolitanwide growth levels that were either similar to or greater than black levels (Miami being the exception); and due to their low-density development and widespread annexation, South-Young areas' cities have generally shared in their metropolitan areas' nonblack growth. In this context, black metropolitanwide growth is expected to remain confined, largely to central city locations, and only the most select nonblack population is expected to suburbanize.

Both the Figure 8.1 and the Table 8.2 suburbanization rates for South-Young areas support these expectations. The black suburbanization rate was negative during the 1950–1960 and 1960–1970 periods, and shifted to only a moderate positive rate of +22.6 in the 1970–1980 period. Nonblack suburbanization rates are not only positive and higher than black rates over all three periods but, unlike the situation in North-Declining and South-Old areas, these nonblack rates increased with each decade.[35] These data indicate that black suburbanization is clearly less advanced in South-Young areas than in other large areas that represent primary destinations for black inmigration. Even in the 1970s, the nonblack suburban populations of these areas sustain higher rates of growth than their black suburban populations (Table 8.2, column 6).

There are some variations in these South-Young suburbanization trends among individual metropolitan areas. The Houston metropolitan area represents a most extreme case (shown in Figure 8.2); its black population registered a negative suburbanization rate for each of the three postwar decades (−52.9, −42.1, and −17.8, respectively). During both the 1950s and 1960s, Houston's black and nonblack populations sustained high rates of growth that were roughly equivalent to each other. The suburbanization rates for both races were negative in the 1950s as the central city annexed significant suburban territory. In the 1960s racial separation intensified as nonblacks suburbanized at a rate of +37.0 while blacks continued to concentrate with a −42.1 suburbanization rate.

Yet in the 1970s, when racial separation became more moderate in other metropolitan areas, it intensified even further in Houston. This may be conditioned by Houston's metropolitanwide growth context during this decade wherein nonblack growth accelerated at the same time that the black growth tapered off slightly. The high nonblack growth rate in Houston's central city coupled with an increasing nonblack growth in its expanding suburbs provides stiff competition for black suburbanward expansion. Thus, while Houston's nonblack population increased its suburbanization rate from 37.0 in the 1960s to 50.2 in the 1970s, its black suburbanization rate remained negative, signalling a continued concentration of blacks. Black city concentration is less extreme in South-Young areas with more moderated nonblack metropolitan growth rates (i.e., San Antonio), and where nonblack city growth has begun to subside (i.e., Dallas–Ft. Worth). However, in the main, black suburbanization has not yet flourished in South-Young metropolitan areas.

[35]The reader is reminded that most South-Old areas' central cities annexed considerably to their territories over the 1950s and 1960s (see Tables 7.4 and 7.5). This serves to depress black suburbanization rate levels over time, if the annexed territory is comprised primarily of inner suburban land that would be most accessible to blacks.

Other metropolitan area classes: Most metropolitan areas in the North-Old, West-Old, and West-Young classes have not, until recently, served as major destinations for black intermetropolitan migrants (San Francisco–Oakland and Los Angeles–Long Beach constitute the major exceptions to this statement). However, because these areas are becoming more popular destinations for blacks, and their ratios of black to nonblack metropolitanwide growth are high, we might anticipate greater pressure toward black suburbanization in these areas. The suburbanization rates in Table 8.2 and the plots in Figure 8.1 tend to bear out this expectation.

The North-Old areas, which hold highest city concentrations of blacks among these three groupings, shifted from negative black suburbanization rates in the 1950s and 1960s to a positive rate in the 1970s. Nonblack suburbanization rates have been positive throughout and, for the aggregated nonblack population, these rates were overridden by the aggregated black suburbanization rates in the 1970–1980 decade. Individual North-Old areas differ from this aggregate pattern in some respects. For example, Columbus's black suburbanization rate remained negative through all three periods (in part a result of city annexation); Minneapolis–St. Paul's black suburbanization rate rose to a positive level already in the 1960s; and in both Kansas City and Indianapolis, the 1970s nonblack suburbanization rate was not overtaken by the black rate. Nevertheless, all North-Old areas except Columbus showed a pronounced tendency toward increased black suburbanization in the 1970s.

In the West-Old areas, black suburbanization rates have increased dramatically over time. However, the patterns displayed for these, in the aggregate, are heavily influenced by the individual areas of San Francisco–Oakland and Los Angeles–Long Beach. Both of these areas have exhibited either high or increasing rates of black suburbanization and progressive decreases in their rates of nonblack suburbanization, although at somewhat different absolute levels. San Francisco–Oakland's race-selective suburbanization progression resembles many North-Declining areas since it displayed a relatively high 1950s nonblack suburbanization rate of 70.1 and progressed to increasingly lower rates of 40.3 and 18.3, respectively, in the 1960s and 1970s. Over the same period, there was a progression toward greater black suburbanization where, in the 1970s, the suburban population growth of San Francisco–Oakland's black population exceeded that of its nonblack population.

In low-density Los Angeles–Long Beach (shown in Figure 8.2), the overall level of nonblack suburbanization was already moderated in the 1950s. Its nonblack suburbanization rate in that decade was only 43.1 and became further reduced to 10.1 in the 1960s and − 1.7 in the 1970s.

Los Angeles–Long Beach's black suburbanization rate stood well above its nonblack suburbanization rate throughout this period. However, this rate also became moderated over time from 74.1 in the 1950s to 62.1 and 58.3, respectively, in the 1960s and 1970s. However, this race-selective pattern is unique to Los Angeles–Long Beach. The remaining West-Old areas, Denver–Boulder, Portland, and Seattle–Everett showed nonblack and black suburbanization trends that more closely resemble those of San Francisco-Oakland.

The West-Young areas do not really display a characteristic race-selective redistribution pattern. Most of these have very small black populations and, as discussed in Chapter 7, differ quite markedly from each other in their annexation histories and suburbanization practices. Nevertheless, each of these areas is sustaining greater black population growth rates (relative to those of nonblacks) and should exhibit some black suburbanization increases. The aggregate patterns displayed in Figure 8.1 and Table 8.2 clearly indicate such an increase from a strongly negative to a moderately negative black suburbanization in the 1950s and 1960s, to a strongly positive black suburbanization in the 1970s. Over this period nonblack suburbanization evolved much more moderately. Yet, when one compares 1970–1980 black suburbanization rates with nonblack suburbanization rates for individual areas, one finds a great deal of diversity. In Sacramento, San Diego, and Anaheim–Santa Ana–Garden Grove black suburbanization rates greatly overwhelm those for nonblacks; in Phoenix and Riverside–San Bernardino–Ontario black and nonblack levels are relatively similar to each other; and in San Jose black suburbanization rates, like nonblack suburbanization rates, are negative. On the whole, this review of North-Old, West-Old, and West-Young areas suggests that a recent increase in black suburbanization is accompanying the increasing metropolitanwide black inmigration to these areas.

Destination Propensity Rates

The suburb destination propensity rate, introduced in Chapter 7, is defined as the proportion of all intrametropolitan movers and inmigrants over a period that select a suburb (rather than a central city) destination. This rate provides a measure of the suburbs' (vis-à-vis central cities') attractiveness for individuals who are currently faced with the choice of selecting a central-city or suburb destination. Moreover, when compared with the proportion of the entire metropolitan population that resides in the suburbs, it constitutes a simple indicator of future suburbanization trends. For example, if the suburb destination propensity rates for recent movers and inmigrants significantly exceed the suburb proportion of all residents, then suburbanization is likely to intensify. However, if the suburb destination rates lie below the resident populations' suburb proportion, a slow-down in the suburbanization process is signaled.

The analyses here will focus on the 1975–1980 suburb destination propensity rates of blacks and nonblacks and compare them with the 1980 and 1970 suburb proportions of all metropolitan residents of each race (Figure 8.3) for our six metropolitan area groupings.[36] (As in our Chapter 7 analysis of these rates, central cities and metropolitan areas are consistent with 1970 Census SMSA definitions and differ slightly from the 1980-based definitions used elsewhere.) The North-Declining areas' destination propensity rates show contrasting patterns for blacks and nonblacks. The suburb destination propensity rates of 1975–1980 black movers and inmigrants are greater than the suburb proportions of black metropolitan residents in either 1980 or 1970 (.25 versus .22 and .17)—signaling a greater suburban attraction for recent black movers. In contrast, the 1975–1980 suburb destination propensity rates for nonblacks lie slightly *below* the suburb proportions of all 1980 nonblack metropolitan residents (.67 versus .68), suggesting a reduced suburban attraction among recent nonblack movers.

The South-Old destination propensity rates show both black and nonblack mover selectivity to be headed in the same direction—toward greater suburbanization. Indeed, one finds an exceptionally strong suburban attraction (or receptivity) for black movers and inmigrants in 1975–1980 when one compares their recent suburb destination propensity rate with their suburb proportions in 1980 and 1970. Nonblack 1975–1980 movers and inmigrants also reside in the suburbs to a greater extent than all nonblack residents in 1980 and 1970. However, the difference between the 1975–1980 suburb destination propensity rate and the 1980 suburb proportion of all residents is much greater for blacks than for nonblacks (.47 versus .37 for blacks, and .84 versus .83 for nonblacks).

The South-Young areas show a more moderate suburban attraction for both black and nonblack movers in 1975–1980, when one compares recent suburb destination propensity rates with the suburb proportions of all 1980 and 1970 metropolitan residents. While the latter propor-

[36]Analyses of these rates for earlier periods appear in: William H. Frey, "Black Movement to the Suburbs: Potentials and Prospects for Metropolitan-Wide Integration," in Frank D. Bean and W. Parker Frisbie, eds., *The Demography of Racial and Ethnic Groups* (New York: Academic Press, 1978); Kathryn P. Nelson, "Recent Suburbanization of Blacks: How Much, Who and Where?" *Journal of the American Planning Association* (July 1979):287–300; and William H. Frey, "Mover Destination Selectivity and the Changing Suburbanization of Metropolitan Whites and Blacks," *Demography* 22(2) (1985):223–243.

tions increased noticeably between 1970 and 1980 for both races (from .52 to .61 for nonblacks and from .29 to .32 for blacks), their respective suburb destination propensity rates for 1975–1980 showed much smaller increments. This suggests that a more moderate suburbanization of both blacks and nonblacks may be in the offing for these areas.

The black destination propensity patterns shifted in fairly similar ways in each of the three remaining metropolitan area classes. The Figure 8.3 plots for North-Old, West-Old, and West-Young areas show slight suburban attraction for black movers and inmigrants, when compared with 1980 and 1970 black suburb proportions. However, the nonblack destination selectivity patterns do differ across these metropolitan area groupings. Both North-Old and West-Old nonblack 1975–1980 movers and inmigrants show a lesser tendency to reside in a suburban location than 1980 nonblack residents. West-Young areas' nonblack movers and inmigrants are more likely to select suburban destinations than their residents, although the mover-resident difference is not nearly so large as that for South-Young metropolitan areas.

These comparisons, by and large, mirror our earlier analysis of race-selective suburbanization rates. However, the destination propensity rates of recent movers and inmigrants are useful for gauging suburbanization tendencies, because they constitute a direct measure of intrametropolitan destination preferences. The socioeconomic selectivities associated with these rates will be examined further in Chapter 9.

Racial Compositions and Segregation Levels

Our overview of race-selective city–suburb population change, up to this point, has focused on black suburbanization and nonblack suburbanization as separate redistribution processes. However, what is more important for many urban planners and scholars are the implications these processes hold for the racial compositions of central cities, suburbs, and neighborhoods, and the degree to which blacks and nonblacks are residentially segregated across these areas. In this section, therefore, we will examine the effects that recent black and nonblack suburbanization processes have exerted on central city and suburb racial compositions, and on the residential segregation of blacks and nonblacks within the metropolitan area. For ease of exposition we will focus only on the 15 metropolitan areas with the largest 1980 black populations (each in excess of 300,000). The interested reader can find data for all 39 metropolitan areas in Appendix E Tables 8.C and 8.D.

The 1970 and 1980 racial compositions for the 15 areas' central cities and suburbs are shown in Table 8.3. All seven North-Declining

FIGURE 8.3

*Suburb Locations of 1970 and 1980 Metropolitan Area Residents,
and Suburb Destination Propensity Rates of 1975–1980
Metropolitan Area Movers and Inmigrants by Race:
Six Metropolitan Area Groupings[a]*

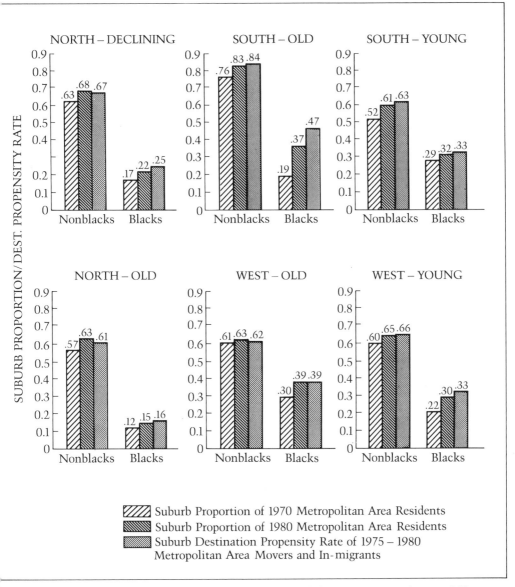

SOURCES: 1970: Census of Population, 1970: Special Census Tabulations. 1980: Machine-readable computer files, Census of Population and Housing, 1980: Public Use Microdata Samples "A" and "B" (prepared the U.S. Bureau of the Census, Washington, DC).

1970 SMSA and Central City Definitions (in 1970) and 1970 Equivalent SMSA and Central City definitions (in 1980).

TABLE 8.3

Percentage of Black Population in Central Cities and Suburbs,
and Index of City–Suburb Dissimilarity, 1970, 1980:
Selected Metropolitan Areas[a]

Metropolitan Area Groupings/ Metropolitan Area	Central Cities		Suburbs		Index of City-Suburb Dissimilarity[b]	
	1970	1980	1970	1980	1970	1980
NORTH-DECLINING						
New York	21.1	25.3	5.8	7.5	24.5	26.3
Philadelphia	33.5	37.8	6.6	8.1	44.8	44.9
St. Louis	40.9	45.5	7.0	10.6	48.9	38.0
Chicago	32.7	39.8	3.4	5.6	50.7	52.0
Newark	54.3	58.3	8.9	13.8	48.0	37.0
Cleveland	38.3	43.8	3.4	7.1	59.7	51.9
Detroit	43.6	63.0	3.4	4.1	63.6	72.5
SOUTH-OLD						
Baltimore	46.4	54.8	6.0	9.0	55.0	55.6
New Orleans	45.0	55.3	12.5	12.6	37.4	48.3
Washington, DC	71.1	70.2	8.4	16.7	64.9	43.9
Atlanta	51.5	66.6	8.4	13.4	54.3	47.5
WEST-OLD						
San Francisco*	20.5	24.1	5.4	6.5	35.9	35.7
Los Angeles*	16.5	16.4	6.3	9.6	25.9	15.2
SOUTH-YOUNG						
Dallas*	23.3	27.4	3.6	3.8	41.1	48.0
Houston	25.7	27.6	9.4	6.7	24.5	34.8

SOURCES: Machine-readable computer files: *County and City Data Book,* 1983 file (prepared by th U.S. Bureau of the Census, Washington, DC).

[a]Figures shown for metropolitan areas with 1980 total populations exceeding 1,000,000 and blac populations exceeding 300,000. As in most other Part Two analyses, metropolitan areas are defined a 1980 SMSAs and NECMAs (in New England) except for New York and Paterson–Clifton–Passaic (se Appendix F).

[b]Represents the percentage of one group that would need to change (city or suburb) residence in order t achieve complete city–suburb residential integration with the other group. A score of 100 indicate complete city–suburb residential segregation; a score of 0 indicates complete city–suburb residentia integration. The computation formula for the two groups, blacks and nonblacks, are as follows:

$$\left[\frac{\text{Nonblack Suburb Population}}{\text{Nonblack Metropolitan Area Population}} - \frac{\text{Black Suburban Population}}{\text{Black Metropolitan Area Population}} \right] \times 100$$

*Largest of multiple central cities (complete metropolitan area names are listed in Appendix F).

areas increased the percentages of their city and suburb black populations, although in each case the city gain was much larger. Detroit, because of its highly race-selective suburbanization patterns (discussed
above), increased its black city percentage by about 20 points—from
43.6 to 63.0 percent; while its suburb gain was inconsequential—from
3.4 to 4.1 percent black. The next largest city gain in black percentage
was Chicago's increase from 32.7 to 39.8 percent, as its suburbs gained
from 3.4 to 5.6 percent. Aside from Detroit, only Newark of the North-
Declining central cities housed a majority black population in 1980 (as
it did in 1970). The remaining city black percentages ranged from 25.3
(New York City) to 45.5 (St. Louis), and the 1970–1980 gains of percentage (aside from those of Detroit and Chicago) ranged from +4 to +5
percent. In contrast, 1980 suburban percentages in these selected North-
Declining metropolitan areas range from 4.1 (Detroit) to 13.8 (Newark)
with 1970–1980 gains in the percentage ranging from +0.7 to +5.1 percent. While 1970–1980 gains in these suburbs' black percentages far
exceed those made in the previous two decades (see Appendix E, Table
8.C), 1970–1980 central city gains were generally larger. Hence, despite
1970s shifts in black and nonblack suburbanization patterns, the 1980
city–suburb racial compositions in heavily black North-Declining
metropolitan areas remain highly imbalanced.

Two of the four South-Old areas' central cities already had black
majority populations in 1970; and in 1980, all four were majority black.
Yet, the area with the largest 1970 black percentage, Washington, DC,
decreased their black percentage slightly over this period—from 71.1 to
70.2—as blacks left the city at a greater rate than nonblacks. At the
same time, Washington's suburbs almost doubled their black percentage—from 8.4 percent in 1970 to 16.7 percent in 1980. The other three
areas, unlike Washington, increased their city black percentages to a
greater extent than their suburban percentages. Atlanta's increase was
highest—from 51.5 to 66.6 percent—although its suburbs also
sustained a significant 5 percent increase. New Orleans's and
Baltimore's city black percentages increased +10.3 and +8.4 percent
respectively, with much smaller increases in their suburban black percentages.

The two West-Old areas, San Francisco–Oakland and Los Angeles–
Long Beach, house much smaller black population shares—metropolitanwide and in their central cities—than the areas discussed above.
(Also, as will be discussed later, both house fairly large Hispanic and
Asian populations.) San Francisco's city black percentage increased
from 20.5 to 24.1 between 1970 and 1980, while its suburban population
black percentage increased from 5.4 to 6.5. Los Angeles–Long Beach,
which has been sustaining strong black suburbanization since the

1950s, already displayed a fairly balanced city–suburb racial distribution in 1970. Between 1970 and 1980 its central city black percentage declined 16.5 to 16.4 while its suburban black percentage gained from 6.3 to 9.6.

Finally, we examine the two South-Young Texas "growth centers," Dallas–Ft. Worth and Houston. Both of these areas registered modest increases in their city black populations between 1970 and 1980. Their suburban black percentages, however, underwent a negligible change in the case of Dallas–Ft. Worth, and a 2.7 decrease in the case of Houston. Suburban black percentage decreases are not unusual in South-Young metropolitan areas (see Appendix Table E.8C). Many of these areas have a history of white displacement of suburban blacks,[37] and most have annexed considerable suburban land to their central city territories. These 1970s patterns, in fact, suggest a moderation of earlier suburban black decreases.

An easier way to summarize the post-1970 shifts in city and suburb racial composition is through the index of city–suburb dissimilarity shown in footnote *b* of Table 8.3. This index measures the percentage of one race (blacks or nonblacks) that would have to shift to the other part of the metropolitan area (city or suburb) in order to be distributed exactly like the other racial group. An index score of 0 indicates total similarity in the two racial groups distributions (the portion of the metropolitan area's black population residing in the suburbs is the same as the portion of the metropolitan area's nonblack population residing in the suburbs), while a score of 100 indicates complete dissimilarity between the two groups (that is, all nonblacks are located in the suburbs and all blacks are located in the central city). The index is not influenced by the metropolitan area's racial composition, so it permits comparisons across metropolitan areas with different racial compositions.

The 1970 beginning-of-decade values for the city–suburb dissimilarity index range from 24.5 (for New York City and Houston) to 64.9 (for Washington, D.C.). Across classes the highest scores tend to be shown for South-Old areas, the lowest for West-Old and South-Young areas— and North-Declining areas tend to fall in between. Yet, despite the trend toward greater post-1970 black suburbanization, 1970–1980 shifts in this index are not uniform across metropolitan areas. The largest decrease in this index is shown for Washington, D.C., which, as the result of recent race selective redistribution patterns, decreased its index by 21 points over the ten-year period. While in 1970, 65 percent of Washington's black population would have had to change residence to

[37]Taeuber and Taeuber, *Negroes in Cities.*

be distributed in the same way as its white population, this percentage dropped to 44 in 1980.

Aside from Washington, D.C., five other areas (St. Louis, Newark, Cleveland, Atlanta, and Los Angeles–Long Beach) display decreases of 7 or more. However, there were also four areas that *increased* their indexes by 7 or more during the decade. These include the South-Young areas, Dallas–Ft. Worth and Houston; the South-Old area of New Orleans; and the North-Declining area of Detroit. As a result of this increase, Detroit's 1980 index of 72.5 lies well above the rest of the areas in this analysis. The remaining five areas displayed smaller index changes (four positive and one negative). While these decreases may not seem to suggest a great reduction in city–suburb racial segregation, they need to be viewed in the context of the strong increases in the city–suburb dissimilarity index that took place between 1950 and 1970. Indeed, the Appendix Table E.8D data reveal that, over this period, 14 of these 15 metropolitan areas sustained increases in the city–suburb dissimilarity index (Los Angeles–Long Beach excepted) where the average increase was +25.

One reason that urban analysts wish to learn how much black suburbanization is taking place draws from the view that black–white racial integration will be more likely to occur across individual neighborhoods as blacks become more suburbanized. We can measure the degree of black–white neighborhood segregation directly by comparing 1970 and 1980 indices of neighborhood dissimilarity for the 15 metropolitan areas.[38] This measure became popularized in Karl and Alma Taeuber's *Negroes in Cities*[39] and is based on a comparison of the distribution of black residents across an area's neighborhoods (census tracts) with the distribution of nonblack residents across the same neighborhoods. As with the index of city–suburb dissimilarity, this index ranges from 0 (where blacks and nonblacks are distributed in the same manner across all neighborhoods) to 100 (where blacks and nonblacks are located in completely separate neighborhoods). The indices of neighborhood dissimilarity that we compare (Table 8.4) were compiled for 1970 by Thomas Van Valey and his colleagues, and for 1980 by Karl Taeuber and his colleagues.[40]

Two points are made clear by looking at these indices of neighbor-

---

[38]A more thorough treatment of neighborhood residential segregation patterns is provided in the 1980 Census monograph on neighborhoods, authored by Michael J. White.

[39]Taeuber and Taeuber, *Negroes in Cities*, p. 235.

[40]Thomas Van Valey, Wade Clark Roof, and Jerome E. Wilcox, "Trends in Residential Segregation: 1960–1970," *American Journal of Sociology* 82 (1977):826–844; and Karl E. Taeuber, Arthur Sakamoto, Jr., Franklin W. Montfort, and Peter A. Massey, "The Trend in Metropolitan Racial Residential Segregation," presented at the 1984 meeting of the Population Association of America, Minneapolis, MN.

TABLE 8.4

Indices of Neighborhood Dissimilarity Between Blacks and Nonblacks for Selected Metropolitan Areas, 1970 and 1980

Metropolitan Area Groupings/ Metropolitan Areas[a]	Indices of Neighborhood Dissimilarity[b]		
	1970	1980	Chan
NORTH-DECLINING			
New York	73.8	72.8	−1
Philadelphia	78.0	77.0	−1.
St. Louis	86.5	81.5	−5.
Chicago	91.2	86.3	−4.
Newark	78.8	78.6	−0.
Cleveland	90.2	87.5	−2.
Detroit	88.9	87.1	−1.
SOUTH-OLD			
Baltimore	81.0	74.1	−6.
New Orleans	74.2	70.4	−3.
Washington, DC	81.7	69.3	−12.
Atlanta	81.7	76.8	−4.
WEST-OLD			
San Francisco*	77.3	68.2	−9.
Los Angeles*	88.5	76.4	−12.
SOUTH-YOUNG			
Dallas*†	86.9	76.2	−10.
Houston	78.4	71.9	−6.

SOURCES: Thomas L. Van Valey, Wade Clark Roof, and Jerome E. Wilcox, "Trends in Resident Segregation: 1960-1970," *American Journal of Sociology* 82(4):826–845; Karl E. Taeuber, Arth Sakamoto, Jr., Franklin W. Montfort, and Peter A. Massey, "The Trend in Metropolitan Rac Residential Segregation." Presented at the 1984 meeting of the Population Association of Americ Minneapolis, MN, May 5, 1984.

[a]Pertains to 1970 SMSA definitions in 1970 and 1980 SMSA definitions in 1980. (The latter differ fro the metropolitan area definitions used elsewhere in this volume for the New York metropolitan area.)
[b]Represents the percent of one group that would need to change neighborhood residence in order achieve complete neighborhood residential integration with the other group. A score of 100 indicat complete neighborhood residential segregation; a score of 0 indicates complete neighborhood residenti integration. The computational formula for the two groups, blacks and nonblacks, is as follows:

$$D = \frac{1}{2}(\text{sum of absolute values of: } B_i/B - N_i/N)$$

where B_i and N_i are the number of blacks and nonblacks, respectively in neighborhood i, and B and N ar the total number of blacks and nonblacks in the entire metropolitan area.

*Largest of multiple central cities.
†In 1970 the Dallas SMSA index was 86.9 and the Fort Worth index was 86.8; in 1980 the Dallas–For Worth SMSA index was 76.2.

hood dissimilarity. First, the 1970 indices of neighborhood dissimilarity show extremely high segregation levels to exist between blacks and nonblacks across neighborhoods. They range from 73.8 (for New York) to 91.2 (for Chicago) so that, in the best case, three out of four blacks would have to change neighborhoods in order to achieve the same metropolitan areawide distribution as nonblacks. The second point to be made is that all of these metropolitan areas have registered declines in neighborhood segregation over the 1970–1980 period. Some of the larger declines are in areas that display 1970–1980 declines in city–suburb segregation, Washington, D.C. (– 12.4), Los Angeles–Long Beach (– 12.1), and St. Louis (– 5.0), suggesting that increased city–suburb integration is not triggering a resegregation within city and suburb neighborhoods. However, other declines in neighborhood dissimilarity occur in areas that registered increases in city–suburb dissimilarity. In these cases, such as Dallas–Ft. Worth and Houston, some of the decline in neighborhood dissimilarity may represent a displacement of blacks by nonblacks in predominantly black neighborhoods.[41]

Overall, however, levels of neighborhood segregation between blacks and nonblacks have not decreased markedly—with 1980 values ranging between dissimilarity indices of 68.2 to 87.5 for the 15 areas in Table 8.4. This raises the question: Why does neighborhood segregation persist in the context of fairly substantial 1970s black suburbanward movement? One answer is provided in a study of large northern suburbs which shows that greatest growth occurred in suburban communities that already had significant black populations, and, as well, high population densities and weak tax bases.[42] Yet, analyses of individual black movers from nationwide, mid-1970s Annual Housing Surveys suggest that breakthroughs in neighborhood racial integration may be in the offing. It was found that roughly 40 percent of blacks who moved to or within the suburbs went to census tracts that were more than 90 percent white, and another 27 percent went to neighborhoods that were between 60 and 90 percent white. Moreover, recent movers to suburbs were more likely to be living in higher-status neighborhoods than the entire black suburban population.[43] Because the destination selections of recent movers serve to signal future redistribution trends, in the aggregate, these Annual Housing Survey findings suggest that more

[41]John R. Logan and Mark Schneider, "Racial Segregation and Racial Change in American Suburbs, 1970–80," *American Journal of Sociology* 89 (1984):874–888.

[42]Logan and Schneider, "Racial Segregation and Racial Change in American Suburbs, 1970–80."

[43]Daphne Spain and Larry H. Long, "Black Movers to the Suburbs: Are They Moving to Predominantly White Neighborhoods?" U.S. Bureau of the Census Special Demographic Analyses, CD8-80-4 (Washington, DC: U.S. Government Printing Office, 1981).

significant reductions in neighborhood racial segregation may well occur in the post-1980 period.

Hispanic- and Asian-Americans

Background

Although a dominant concern of urban analysts and policymakers during the 1950–1970 period focused on the continued city concentration of blacks, increased attention has been given to two other minorities whose metropolitan populations had been growing rapidly—the Hispanics and Asians.[44] Hispanics and Asians have inhabited our largest cities—particularly on the West Coast—since these cities' early development. However, their numbers have increased markedly since 1965. It was in this year that a new national immigration law altered priorities for national origin so that greater numbers of Latin Americans and Asians could enter the United States on a yearly basis.[45] Hence, while Latin Americans and Asians accounted for only 20 percent of all United States immigrants over the period 1940–1960, these two groups represented 42 percent and 39 percent, respectively, of immigrants over the 1975–1979 period.[46] The bulk of this immigration has been directed to a limited number of metropolitan areas and, within these, the phenomenon represents something akin to the turn-of-the-century immigration of Europeans to traditional "melting pot" centers in the nation's North.

These new minorities have their own language and customs and, like earlier Europeans, appear to be assimilating gradually into the mainstream of American life. Yet, their residential location patterns may not necessarily follow the paths of either early European immigrants—who gradually worked their ways out of central city ghettos to become residentially dispersed metropolitanwide—or the recent

[44]Although we include both of these minority groups in our treatment of race-selective redistribution, Hispanics are not considered a racial category according to census definitions. In the 1980 census, residents were asked to identify themselves as having Spanish (Hispanic) origin on the basis of their ancestry. In earlier censuses a variety of techniques were used to identify Hispanic-Americans. Further background on Hispanics can be obtained in Frank Bean and Marta Tienda, *The Hispanic Population of the United States*, The Population of the United States in the 1980s: A Census Monograph Series (New York: Russell Sage Foundation, 1988). A Census Monograph on Asian-Americans is forthcoming.

[45]Leon F. Bouvier, with Henry S. Shryock and Harry W. Henderson, "International Migration: Yesterday, Today, and Tomorrow." *Population Bulletin*, vol. 32, No. 4 (Washington, DC: Population Reference Bureau, Inc., 1977).

[46]Leon F. Bouvier, "Immigration and its Impact on U.S. Society," *Population Trends and Public Policy*, 2 (Washington, DC: Population Reference Bureau, Inc., 1981).

266

experience of blacks who have found it difficult to assimilate geographically.[47] On the one hand, these groups are arriving at a time when civil rights legislation guarantees, at least the legal immigrants among them, fair treatment in the arenas of employment, housing, and education—an advantage most earlier groups did not enjoy. On the other hand many are settling into Sunbelt cities with different development and political histories than the traditional destination areas of immigrants in the North. In some of these cities, racial and ethnic animosities run high and "pro-growth" city governments have traditionally blocked participation of blacks and Hispanics although, in others, the accommodation of these new minority groups has occurred more smoothly.[48]

Of the new minorities, the Hispanic population has drawn the most attention as a result of its large size and significant concentrations in selected areas of the country. Although the Hispanic population actually includes several different Spanish-origin groups, it is the Mexican-American population whose migration and redistribution patterns have aroused greatest concern in the post-1970 period. Through both legal and illegal immigration, this group has grown dramatically—accounting for the largest number of immigrants from a single country over the 1960–1980 period.[49]

The particular fascination with Mexican-Americans stems from two of the group's attributes. First, as a group, they are clearly less well-off in socioeconomic measures than non-Hispanic whites and only slightly better off than black residents in their destination communities.[50] On the basis of their relative income and poverty levels alone, they should be expected to segregate themselves in neighborhoods and communities that are isolated from most middle-class metropolitan residents. In addition, like other "new" ethnic groups before them, they should be expected to concentrate in residential locations to a greater degree than that predicted on the basis of their socioeconomic characteristics.

The second and most distinctive feature of Mexican-Americans is their high level of illegal immigration (estimated in 1979 to be greater than 100,000–500,000 per year).[51] This makes it difficult for destination areas—particularly those close to the Mexican border—to both enumerate their Mexican-American populations and to estimate the future inflow of this group into their communities. It also forces the ille-

---

[47]Lieberson, *Ethnic Patterns in American Cities.*

[48]Bernard and Rice, *Sunbelt Cities.*

[49]Cary Davis, Carl Haub, and JoAnne Willette, "U.S. Hispanics: Changing the Face of America," *Population Bulletin,* vol. 38, no. 3 (Washington, DC: Population Reference Bureau, Inc., 1983).

[50]Ibid.

[51]Ibid.

gal immigrants themselves to maintain a shroud of secrecy, leading perhaps to an even greater ghettoization of first-generation Mexican-Americans than might otherwise be expected.

A few studies that have attempted to monitor housing discrimination against Hispanics in the cities of Phoenix, Houston, Denver, and Dallas suggest that realtors employ the same sorts of discriminatory techniques with Hispanic buyers and renters as they have used with blacks.[52] Statistics on 1970 neighborhood segregation for Hispanics showed them to be moderately segregated from non-Hispanic whites.[53] Yet, further analyses of the 1970 data show that, unlike blacks, Hispanics in these areas became less segregated from whites as they raised their social status and as they increased their length of stay.[54] This suggests that these Hispanics resemble earlier ethnic groups more than blacks, and will tend to disperse geographically as they assimilate.

The second of the two newer minority groups is the Asian-Americans who, even more so than the Hispanics, have increased their size as a result of the changed 1965 immigration law and the consequences of the Indochinese wars. Asian-Americans are sometimes overlooked as a significant minority because of their overall greater socioeconomic status. Also, they represent a numerically smaller share of the American population—1.5 percent in 1980. Yet as with the Hispanic population, Asian-Americans make their most significant contributions numerically to residential change within selected metropolitan areas. During the 1970–1980 period, the Asian population grew from 1.4 to 3.5 million, and it is estimated that approximately 43 percent of the 1980 United States Asian population immigrated during this period. It is projected that the Asian-American population could grow to 9.9 million by the turn of the century, due to the particularly strong immigration of Filipinos, Koreans, and Chinese.[55] The continued rapid immigration of Asian-Americans, therefore, holds the potential for significant growth of this population within both old and new destination metropolitan areas.

We will evaluate below the intrametropolitan distribution patterns

[52]James, McCummings, and Tynan, *Minorities in the Sunbelt.*

[53]Manuel Mariano Lopez, "Patterns of Interethnic Residential Segregation in the Urban Southwest, 1960 and 1970," *Social Science Quarterly* 16 (4):553–563; and Douglas S. Massey "Residential Segregation of Spanish Americans in United States Urbanized Areas," *Demography* 16(4) (1978):553–563.

[54]Massey, "Residential Segregation of Spanish Americans in United States Urbanized Areas;" and Douglas S. Massey, "Effects of Socioeconomic Factors on the Residential Segregation of Black and Spanish Americans in U.S. Urbanized Areas," *American Sociological Review* 44 (December 1979):1015–1022.

[55]Robert W. Gardner, Bryant Robey, and Peter C. Smith, "Asian-Americans: Growth Change and Diversity," *Population Bulletin*, vol. 40, no. 4 (Washington, DC: Population Reference Bureau, Inc., 1985).

...nensions of City–Suburb Redistribution

...erican populations in metropolitan
...l destinations through the 1980
...h of our 39 metropolitan areas
...ics and Asians, and second,
...s are residentially isolate...
...valuation we will ...
...h blacks, ?

...d
...i compare
...i, .ind with non-
...nine, on a comparative
...oup is assimilating geographically.
...e distributed, to a large degree, in
...able to ascertain how their
...ffer from the residential isola-
...ntered in traditional northern

Metropolitan Locations of Hispanic- and Asian-Americans

We can determine the degree to which these other minorities are concentrated in individual metropolitan areas in two ways. One involves identifying which metropolitan areas have the greatest absolute number of these minorities. A second method measures the percentage share of the metropolitan area's total population which these minorities comprise. The data in Table 8.5 allow us to make both types of assessments for Hispanics and Asians in the 39 large metropolitan areas.

On the criterion of absolute numbers we see that the Hispanic population is represented in all areas—from 8,000 in Cincinnati and Columbus to over 2 million in Los Angeles–Long Beach. Furthermore, 17 of the 39 areas meet the more stringent criteria of having 100,000 or more Hispanics. Six areas: Los Angeles–Long Beach, New York, Miami, Chicago, San Antonio, and Houston, house more than 400,000 Hispanics, and seven additional areas (all in California, Texas, and Arizona) have Hispanic populations that number between 200,000 and 400,000.

On the criterion of the percentage Hispanics comprise of the metropolitan population, the largest three areas are: San Antonio (44.9 percent), Miami (35.7 percent), and Los Angeles–Long Beach (27.6 percent) and ten additional areas have Hispanic percentages of between 10 and 20 percent. It is clear that the heaviest concentration of Hispanics lies in the Southwest—areas where Mexican-Americans constitute the most pervasive Hispanic group. Mexican-Americans do not dominate in two major Hispanic concentrations outside the Southwest: New York and Miami. New York's Hispanic population is largely Puerto Rican and Miami's Hispanic population is largely Cuban.

TABLE 8.5

Hispanic, Asian, Black, and White Populations and Percentage of Total Metropolitan Population 39 Metropolitan Areas

Metropolitan Area Groupings/ Metropolitan Areas	Population (in thousands)				Percent of Total	
	Hispanic[a]	Asian	Black	White[b]	Hispanic[a]	Asian
NORTH-DECLINING						
New York	1,568	293	2,073	7,020	14.4	2.
Philadelphia	118	49	883	3,666	2.5	1
Boston	90	43	173	3,351	2.5	1
Cincinnati	8	7	173	1,212	0.6	0
St. Louis	22	14	407	1,911	0.9	0
Buffalo	16	6	115	1,100	1.3	0
Chicago	580	151	1,427	4,943	8.2	2
Newark	133	28	418	1,389	6.8	
Cleveland	26	14	346	1,512	1.4	
Detroit	70	35	889	3,350	1.6	
Milwaukee	35	9	151	1,196	2.5	
Pittsburgh	12	11	176	2,064	0.5	
Paterson*	91	25	92	1,085	7.0	
NORTH-OLD						
Columbus	8	8	134	941	0.8	
Indianapolis	9	6	157	993	0.8	
Kansas City	32	9	172	1,108	2.4	0.7
Hartford	45	6	73	927	4.3	0.6
Minneapolis*	23	25	49	2,000	1.1	1.2

TABLE 8.5 (continued)

SOUTH-OLD							
Baltimore	20	23	556	1,573	0.9	1.1	25.6	72.4
New Orleans	49	14	387	738	4.1	1.2	32.6	62.2
Washington, DC	93	87	854	2,021	3.1	2.8	27.9	66.0
Atlanta	23	13	499	1,494	1.1	0.6	24.6	73.6
WEST-OLD							
San Francisco*	352	336	391	2,168	10.8	10.3	12.0	66.7
Denver*	174	24	78	1,335	10.8	1.5	4.8	82.4
Los Angeles*	2,066	457	943	3,985	27.6	6.1	12.6	53.3
Portland	24	28	34	1,148	1.9	2.2	2.7	92.4
Seattle*	33	68	58	1,433	2.0	4.2	3.6	89.1
SOUTH-YOUNG							
San Antonio	481	9	72	508	44.9	0.8	6.8	47.4
Dallas*	249	29	417	2,268	8.4	1.0	14.0	76.2
Houston	423	55	527	1,895	14.6	1.9	18.1	65.2
Tampa*	80	8	145	1,334	5.1	0.5	9.3	85.0
Miami	580	14	281	756	35.7	0.9	17.3	46.5
Ft. Lauderdale*	40	5	113	860	3.9	0.5	11.1	84.5
WEST-YOUNG							
Sacramento	102	48	61	793	10.0	4.7	6.0	78.2
San Diego	275	95	104	1,382	14.7	5.1	5.6	74.2
San Jose	226	102	43	920	17.5	7.9	3.3	71.0
Phoenix	200	15	48	1,226	13.2	1.0	3.2	81.3
Riverside*	290	27	79	1,147	18.6	1.7	5.1	73.6
Anaheim*	286	93	25	1,516	14.8	4.8	1.3	78.4

SOURCES: Census of Population and Housing, 1980, Summary Tape File 3C (prepared by the U.S. Bureau of the Census, Washington, DC).

[a]The designation Hispanic is not a race category and Hispanics can be classed according to any of the racial categories, including white, black, Asian, or any other racial category. Hence, the percentages in the table's last four columns can sum to greater than 100%.
[b]Non-Hispanic whites.

*Largest of multiple central cities.

The Asian population, being numerically smaller, has less representation in our 39 metropolitan areas. Asians comprise over 100,000 of the populations in only five metropolitan areas: Los Angeles–Long Beach, San Francisco–Oakland, New York, Chicago, and San Jose; and their largest percentage of the population is 10.3 in San Francisco–Oakland. Three other areas have Asian percentages of between 5 and 10 percent. These are San Jose, Los Angeles–Long Beach, and San Diego.

It is clear from Table 8.5 that the "newer" minorities—Hispanics and Asians—are largely confined within three of our metropolitan area groupings: West-Old, South-Young, and West-Young. (New York, Chicago, Newark, and Paterson–Clifton–Passaic are exceptions.) In these areas "minority" populations are generally split among two or three of the groups—Hispanics, Asians, and blacks. San Francisco–Oakland, in fact, has roughly equal percentages of each group, and in several other areas both Hispanics and blacks constitute significant populations. The rest of this section will examine the intrametropolitan residential distributions of these newer minorities in areas that have attracted large numbers of them.

Residential Isolation Within the Metropolitan Area

Earlier in this chapter, we examined two aspects of black–nonblack residential isolation: (1) the degree to which blacks were spatially separated from nonblacks in city–suburb distribution; and (2) the degree to which blacks were segregated from nonblacks on a neighborhood basis. The review that follows will expand upon this examination to evaluate both of these residential isolation dimensions for Hispanics and Asians in areas that contain large concentrations of each group. We will address the questions: How residentially isolated are each of these groups within their metropolitan areas? Do these isolation patterns differ across metropolitan area groupings?[56] The analysis for each group will focus on metropolitan areas that house at least 100,000 of that group's population or in which the group constitutes more than 5 percent of the central city's total population.

We begin by examining the composition of each area's central city and suburb population with regard to Hispanics and Asians (Table 8.6). These data make plain that in most areas, both Hispanics and Asians

---

[56]Redistribution trends across census dates are not undertaken here due to the incomparability of census definitions for Hispanics and, to a lesser extent, Asians, between the 1970 and 1980 censuses. These definition differences are discussed in: John D. Kasarda, "Hispanics and City Change," *American Demographics* (November 1984):24–29; and in Gardner, Robey, and Smith, "Asian-Americans: Growth Change and Diversity."

Percentages of Population Hispanic, Asian, Black, and White in Cities and Suburbs, 1980: Selected Metropolitan Areas[a]

Selected Metropolitan Areas	Percentage Hispanic		Percentage Asian		Percentage Black		Percentage White[b]	
	City	Suburb	City	Suburb	City	Suburb	City	Suburb
NORTH								
New York	19.9	4.2	3.5	1.2	25.3	7.5	52.4	87.1
Philadelphia	3.8	1.8	—	—	37.8	8.1	57.3	89.1
Boston	6.5	1.7	—	—	22.5	1.5	68.3	95.7
Chicago	14.1	3.8	2.5	1.9	39.8	5.6	43.7	88.6
Newark	18.6	4.4	—	—	58.3	13.8	22.8	80.3
Paterson*	22.3	3.1	—	—	21.9	3.3	55.1	91.4
Hartford	20.3	1.9	—	—	33.8	3.0	45.3	94.5
WEST-OLD								
San Francisco*	11.4	10.6	17.4	7.1	24.1	6.5	47.2	75.6
Denver*	16.7	7.5	—	—	10.6	1.7	70.2	89.0
Los Angeles*	26.0	28.9	6.9	5.5	16.4	9.6	50.5	55.6
Seattle*	—	—	7.3	2.7	8.6	1.0	80.4	93.6
SOUTH-YOUNG								
San Antonio	53.7	20.8	—	—	7.3	5.2	38.1	72.8
Dallas*	12.3	5.3	—	—	27.4	3.8	59.0	89.4
Houston	17.6	10.9	—	—	27.6	6.7	52.5	80.6
Tampa*	7.9	3.7	—	—	20.5	3.9	71.1	91.8
Miami	56.0	30.2	—	—	25.1	15.2	19.5	53.8
WEST-YOUNG								
Sacramento	14.1	8.5	8.9	3.1	13.4	3.3	62.8	84.0
San Diego	14.8	14.7	7.0	3.4	8.9	2.7	69.3	78.6
San Jose	22.3	12.9	8.5	7.3	4.6	2.1	64.4	77.3
Phoenix	14.8	11.5	—	—	4.8	1.4	78.1	84.8
Riverside*	21.6	17.6	—	—	8.6	3.9	67.0	75.7
Anaheim*	26.5	10.2	5.5	4.6	—	—	65.1	83.7

SOURCES: Same as Table 8.5.

[a]Figures shown for Hispanics, Asians, or blacks with greater than 100,000 metropolitan population or greater than 5 percent of central city population.

[b]Non-Hispanic whites.

*Largest of multiple central cities.

comprise greater percentages of the central city than suburban populations. Indeed, Hispanics comprise the majority of city populations in
Miami and San Antonio; one-fifth of the city populations in New York,
Paterson–Clifton–Passaic, and Hartford in the North; and one-fifth in
San Jose, Riverside–San Bernardino–Ontario, and Anaheim–Santa
Ana–Garden Grove, all in California. The largest Asian share of a city's
population is 17.4 percent observed in San Francisco–Oakland. In six
other western cities, Asians represent better than 5 percent of the city's
population.

Although the suburban population is generally comprised of a lower
percentage of these groups than the central city, this is not consistently
true. In Los Angeles–Long Beach, Hispanics comprise 28.9 percent of the
suburban population and only 26 percent of the central city population.
In fact, Hispanic percentages in the suburbs of most non-northern metropolitan areas tend to be high relative to central city percentages in these
areas, *and* relative to black suburban percentages. The former is not true
in northern areas where city–suburb Hispanic disparities are large. The
Asian suburban percentage tends to vary across metropolitan areas and
selected areas, such as Los Angeles–Long Beach and San Jose, exhibit
suburban Asian percentages that approach those of their central cities.

A better way to compare the relative degrees of city–suburb separation across minority groups and across metropolitan areas is through
the index of city–suburb dissimilarity. This index was used in the section on blacks and nonblacks in this chapter to review the city–suburb
separation of blacks from nonblacks. It represents the percentage of one
group's population that would need to change areas in order to achieve
the same distribution as the other group. In order to measure city–
suburb separation for Hispanics, Asians, and blacks, we have computed
three city–suburb dissimilarity indices, which represent the dissimilarity of each group's distribution with the distribution of non-Hispanic
whites in the metropolitan area. These are presented in Table 8.7 and
can be used to compare city–suburb separation across the three groups,
and for the same group across areas.

To gain an assessment of how greatly Hispanics are "city-concentrated," we first contrast their dissimilarity indices with those for
blacks. Hispanic city–suburb dissimilarity indices range from 0.2 (for
Los Angeles–Long Beach) to 55.2 (for Hartford), while black values in
the same areas range from 15.6 (for Los Angeles–Long Beach) to 61.5 (for
Boston). These ranges, however, are deceptive because the majority of
Hispanic values lie under 30, while most black index values lie over 30.
Moreover, there are only five instances (where comparisons can be
made) when Hispanic city–suburb separation is more pronounced than
black separation. Three of these instances (New York, Newark, and

TABLE 8.7

Indices of City–Suburb Dissimilarity Comparing Hispanics, Asians, and Blacks with Whites, 1980: Selected Metropolitan Areas[a]

Selected Metropolitan Areas	Indices of City–Suburb Dissimilarity[b]		
	Hispanics/ Whites[c]	Asians/ Whites[c]	Blacks/ Whites[c]
NORTH			
New York	36.9	31.2	33.5
Philadelphia	28.4	—	45.9
Boston	29.0	—	61.5
Chicago	46.5	22.3	57.3
Newark	40.6	—	40.5
Paterson*	51.5	—	49.3
Hartford	55.2	—	56.4
WEST-OLD			
San Francisco*	10.9	30.7	40.6
Denver*	24.6	—	47.6
Los Angeles*	0.2	7.9	15.6
Seattle*	—	27.7	51.1
SOUTH-YOUNG			
San Antonio	28.7	—	20.6
Dallas*	30.4	—	51.1
Houston	22.1	—	39.2
Tampa*	23.1	—	44.7
Miami	24.5	—	22.0
WEST-YOUNG			
Sacramento	16.5	29.8	38.4
San Diego	3.4	20.9	30.3
San Jose	17.9	8.1	23.2
Phoenix	8.3	—	28.6
Riverside*	6.0	—	19.2
Anaheim*	27.2	8.8	—

SOURCES: Same as Table 8.5.

[a]Figures shown for Hispanics or Asians with greater than 100,000 metropolitan population or greater than 5 percent of central city population.
[b]Defined in footnote to Table 8.3.
[c]Non-Hispanic whites.

*Largest of multiple central cities.

Paterson–Clifton–Passaic) occur in the North where Hispanic city–suburb separation is higher, generally; and in the remaining two areas (San Antonio and Miami) black city–suburb separation is unusually low. In each of these five areas, Hispanic dissimilarity is only slightly greater than black dissimilarity. However, in those comparisons where black dissimilarity is greater, the black–Hispanic difference in separation is generally substantial.

Hispanic city–suburb separation also differs markedly by metropolitan area group. Greatest levels of dissimilarity are evident for northern areas where the index values range from 28.4 to 55.2. These higher values might be attributed to the wider city–suburb disparities in status, housing, and other characteristics that exist in northern vis-à-vis Sunbelt areas. They also might be attributable to the prevalence of Puerto Ricans, an economically less well-off Hispanic group in the eastern seaboard metropolitan areas of the North.

A more modest degree of Hispanic city–suburb dissimilarity characterizes the South-Young areas which exhibit dissimilarity indices in the 20s range. However, the lowest levels of Hispanic city–suburb separation are most clearly evident in the West-Old and West-Young areas. With the exceptions of Denver–Boulder and Anaheim–Santa Ana–Garden Grove, the index values in this area grouping range from 0.2 to 17.9. Overall, this comparison of Hispanic dissimilarity indices across metropolitan area groupings indicates that city–suburb separation of Hispanics in Sunbelt areas is lower than in the old and declining areas of the North.

Asian city–suburb separation across the nine areas examined here is somewhat less predictable. While Asians, unlike Hispanics, have superior socioeconomic characteristics to non-Hispanic whites, traditional Asian communities seem to prosper as their populations are replenished with new waves of immigrants. Nevertheless, the Asian–black comparison for the cities considered here shows Asians to be less city-concentrated than blacks in every case. This is barely true in New York where blacks and Asians have similar indices of city–suburb dissimilarity, but Asian–black differences are much more substantial in other areas. Yet the Asian dissimilarity indices do vary widely across metropolitan areas in ways that are not distinctly related to geographic regions. For example, in Los Angeles–Long Beach, Anaheim–Santa Ana–Garden Grove, and San Jose, less than 9 percent of Asians would have to be relocated in order to yield the distribution of non-Hispanic whites, where the percentage rises to 30 or more in New York, San Francisco–Oakland, and Sacramento. If any generalization is to be made about the intrametropolitan variation on this index, it might be that there is some tendency for Asians to be less city-concentrated in Southern California metropolitan areas.

Having determined that both Hispanics and Asians are less city-concentrated than blacks, the question arises: Are Hispanics more city-concentrated than Asians in these metropolitan areas? One might, at first glance, assume this to be true on the basis of Hispanics' lower socioeconomic status. However, the indices in Table 8.7 suggest that the answer is not clear-cut for the eight areas that permit Hispanic–Asian comparisons. Hispanics are more city-concentrated in both northern areas, New York and Chicago but are less city-concentrated than Asians in four of six non-northern areas. Indeed, in three of the latter— San Francisco–Oakland, Sacramento, and San Diego—indices show Asians to be significantly more city-concentrated. The explanation for this "unexpected" pattern might be the greater tendency for Asians to congregate in traditional centrally located settlements, irrespective of their socioeconomic status, while Hispanics are dispersing.

Further assessment of residential isolation can be made by examining segregation across metropolitan neighborhoods. As our review of black isolation bore out, an increased suburbanization of minorities does not necessarily imply integration at the neighborhood level. We now undertake an examination of neighborhood integration patterns for Hispanics, Asians, and blacks in the seven metropolitan areas that house large numbers or proportions of each. These include the North-Declining areas of New York and Chicago, the West-Old areas of San Francisco–Oakland and Los Angeles–Long Beach, and the West-Young areas of Sacramento, San Diego, and San Jose. In order to make this assessment we employ indices of neighborhood dissimilarity that were computed by Mark Langberg and Reynolds Farley.[57] These indices compare each of the three minority groups' distribution patterns with those for the non-Hispanic white population. Index values can be interpreted as the proportion of one group's population (that is, Hispanics, Asians, or blacks) that would have to be relocated in order to achieve the same areal distribution as the other population (that is, non-Hispanic whites).

The data in Table 8.8 show that, for the two northern areas at least, there is a progression across groups—blacks with indices in the 80s, Hispanics with indices in the 60s, and Asians with indices in the 40s. This progression breaks down for non-northern metropolitan areas because Hispanics register lower neighborhood dissimilarity measures (in the 30s, 40s, and 50s)—commensurate with their lower city–suburb dissimilarity measures in non-northern metropolitan areas. Asians, on the other hand, maintain relatively constant (40s) neighborhood dissimilarity indices across areas, except for San Jose. As a result, Asian and Hispanic dissimilarity indices remain closer to each other and further

[57]Mark Langberg and Reynolds Farley, "Residential Segregation of Asian Americans in 1980," *Sociology and Social Research* (October 1985).

TABLE 8.8

Indices of Neighborhood Dissimilarity Comparing Hispanics, Asians,
and Blacks with Whites, 1980: Selected Metropolitan Areas

Metropolitan Areas	Indices of Neighborhood Dissimilarity[a]		
	Hispanics/ Whites[b]	Asians/ Whites[b]	Blacks/ Whites[b]
New York*	65	49	81
Chicago	64	46	88
San Francisco†	41	47	72
Los Angeles†	57	47	81
Sacramento	37	44	56
San Diego	42	46	64
San Jose	46	32	50

SOURCE: Mark Langberg and Reynolds Farley, "Residential Segregation of Asian Americans in 1980," *Sociology and Social Research,* October 1985.

[a]Defined in footnote in Table 8.4.
[b]Non-Hispanic whites.

*Defined as the 1980 census New York SMSA as distinct from the New York metropolitan area definition used elsewhere in this study (see Appendix F).
†Largest of multiple central cities.

from blacks in Los Angeles–Long Beach, San Francisco–Oakland, Sacramento, and San Diego; and in the latter three areas, Hispanics are less residentially segregated than are Asians. San Jose's indices are rather unique since each group's level of segregation appears to be much lower here than in other metropolitan areas.

These neighborhood dissimilarity indices, like those for city–suburb separation, suggest that both Hispanics and Asians are far less racially isolated than blacks. However, because Hispanics are more segregated in northern than Sunbelt areas, the relative segregation levels of Asians and Hispanics vary by region. Hispanics are more segregated than Asians in the North, but there is no consistent pattern in South and West areas with large numbers of each group.

Summary

This chapter is the first of two chapters concerned with evaluating major dimensions of race- and status-selective population redistribution. Our evaluation began by examining post-1970 shifts in the race-selective, city–suburb redistribution of blacks and nonblacks with an eye toward discerning significant differences from 1950s and 1960s redistribution patterns. In assessing these patterns it has become clear that the 1970s constitute a benchmark decade for black suburbanization. Substantial post-1970 increases in black suburbanization rates were observed in metropolitan areas of all classes, although they were particularly strong in North-Declining and South-Old metropolitan areas. Nonblack suburbanization shifts varied across metropolitan area classes. The greatest post-1970 moderation of nonblack suburbanization occurred in North-Declining metropolitan areas. However, this is not to be confused with the "return to the city movement," which was noticeable for only Washington, DC, of the old or declining metropolitan areas examined here. A nonblack suburbanization "slow-down" was evident but less accentuated in the remaining South-Old areas, and in areas of the North-Old and West-Old categories. In the West-Young and, particularly, in the South-Young areas, there was some evidence of a rise in nonblack suburbanization in the 1970–1980 period.

Despite significant post-1970 shifts in the *processes* of black and nonblack suburbanization, their impact on the racial compositions of central cities, suburbs, and neighborhoods was not strongly evident in 1980. Wide disparities still exist in city and suburb racial compositions and high levels of neighborhood residential segregation also continue. Nevertheless, the former disparities (as measured by the index of city–suburb dissimilarity) did not widen in the 1970s as they had in the two immediate postwar decades, and a neighborhood segregation decline, albeit modest, occurred in all metropolitan areas with substantial black populations.

The chapter also examined the city–suburb distribution of Hispanic- and Asian-Americans—two fast-growing minority groups that are particularly heavily concentrated in metropolitan areas of our South-Young, West-Young, and West-Old groupings. Our examination of their city–suburb separation and neighborhood residential segregation showed these groups to be less segregated than blacks in most areas, although there was some variation on their absolute segregation levels. Hispanics tend to be more isolated on both city–suburb separation and neighborhood segregation measures in the few northern metropolitan areas they inhabit in large numbers than in Sunbelt areas, while Asians show fairly consistent neighborhood segregation levels. As a consequence Asians tend to be less isolated than Hispanics in northern areas, but closer to Hispanics than blacks in the Sunbelt.

Our evaluation of these race-selective patterns continues in Chapter 9 where we examine the socioeconomic selectivity dimensions of suburbanization for blacks and nonblacks, as well as for the newer minorities. The final section of Chapter 9 summarizes the major findings of this two-chapter unit.

9

STATUS DIMENSIONS
OF CITY–SUBURB REDISTRIBUTION

Introduction

IN THIS chapter we continue our evaluation of race- and status-selective suburbanization of the population, by placing emphasis on the socioeconomic status dimensions of post-1970 suburbanization. Historically, metropolitan areas have differed markedly in the degree to which they have displayed a city–suburb status gap. In systematic analyses of city–suburb status differences in the 1950s and 1960s, Leo F. Schnore and his collaborators found the characteristic stereotype—low-status residents locating in the city and high-status residents in the suburbs—to exist only in a subset of the nation's largest metropolitan areas.[1] Yet, this characteristic pattern was most evident in precisely those cities that evolved into our greatest "problem" cities as the 1970s decade approached—those encased within old northern metropolises which capitalized on their strengths as industrial centers in the late nineteenth and early twentieth centuries. It was in these cities, during the late 1960s, wherein governments and residents were in the most vulnerable positions due to declining tax bases, disinvestment, the con-

---

[1]Leo F. Schnore, *The Urban Scene* (New York: The Free Press, 1965); and Leo F. Schnore, *Class and Race in Cities and Suburbs* (Chicago: Markham Publishing Company, 1972).

centration of minorities, and selective "white flight."[2] Therefore, much of our attention will be given to these areas in this evaluation of status-selective suburbanization, although other types of areas will be examined as well.

One focus of our evaluation will be to determine if a pervasive and significant moderation of the nonblack population's suburban selectivity occurred since 1970—in light of well-publicized city "gentrification" and revitalization efforts.[3] A complementary focus evaluates the status selectivity associated with the accelerated 1970s black suburbanization, which was documented in the previous chapter. Finally, we examine suburban status selectivity patterns of the newer minorities—Hispanic- and Asian-Americans—in the areas where they comprise significant population concentrations. The concluding section of this chapter summarizes the major findings of both Chapter 8 and 9 evaluations of race- and status-selective suburbanization shifts that took place in the post-1970 period.

Background

The early 1970s status gap within the nation's older industrial areas actually took root at the turn of the century. It was during this period, when improvements in short-distance transportation, coupled with lenient community incorporation laws, gave well-off upper status citizens the opportunity to establish their own residential communities outside the legal limits of the central city and thereby escape the congestion, social conflict, and often corrupt governments that characterized central cities.[4] As yet-to-be assimilated immigrants, rural–urban migrants, and blacks continued to flow into the city center, newer communities evolved on the metropolitan periphery to accommodate the outward dispersal of more affluent city residents. Hence, the metropolitan area developed into a fragmented collection of political jurisdictions that had come to surround the central cities whose boundaries were frozen early in the area's development. Although this process evolved during most of the twentieth century, it was between World War II and 1970 (characterized in Chapter 7 as the "second era" of suburbaniza-

---

[2]Advisory Commission on Intergovernmental Relations, *City Financial Emergencies: The Intergovernmental Dimension* (Washington, DC: U.S. Government Printing Office, 1973); and William H. Frey, "Status Selective White Flight and Central City Population Change: A Comparative Analysis," *Journal of Regional Science* 20(1) (1980):71–89.

[3]Shirley B. Laska and Daphne Spain, eds., *Back to the City: Issues in Neighborhood Renovation* (New York: Pergamon, 1980).

[4]Amos H. Hawley, *Urban Society: An Ecological Approach* (New York: Ronald Press, 1971); and R. D. Norton, *City Life-Cycles and American Urban Policy* (New York: Academic Press, 1979).

tion), when a large share of these areas' white middle-class residents were redistributed into the suburbs, that these central cities became most differentiated from their suburbs with respect to socioeconomic status characteristics of their residents.[5]

In light of this history, why should a post-1970 moderation of this status-selective redistribution be expected? One reason has to do with the changing composition of demand in all metropolitan areas, given society–wide shifts in social, economic, and demographic makeup of households. Although the dominant consumer household in the 1950s and early 1960s consisted of an intact married couple with children, 1970s consumer households are much less oriented toward child-raising. There are larger numbers of professional and career-oriented households, in general, than was the case in the immediate postwar decades and, among these, there are more husband-wife dual-earner households that are not involved in child-rearing. Another type of childless household—that maintained by an elderly person—is also on the rise. Although household and family redistribution implications will be explained more carefully in Chapter 10, it is clear that new housing preferences should be less tied to the types of space and family-raising amenities that made suburban tract housing so attractive right after World War II. Moreover, central cities should be particularly attractive locations to the growing legions of professionals—especially those cities that are cultivating their bases as service and administrative centers.

The second reason for expecting a moderation in selective city out-movement regards the changing supply of housing that could be developed in depopulating cities that serve as "nodal" centers. The occurrence of both central city and metropolitanwide population decline is new to the 1970s and represents a distinct departure from the growth contexts that fostered the peripheral expansion in these areas over most of the twentieth century. Under the condition of metropolitanwide population decline, less pressure is exerted on residential construction at the metropolitan periphery and greater vacancies occur at the city center. This circumstance now appears in the centers of many declining metropolitan areas and creates the opportunity for new city development and restoration.[6] It is conceivable that the demand for such

---

[5]Despite this chapter's focus on the city–suburb status gap, individual suburban communities are also stratified on the basis of their residents' income, occupation, and education status. Aspects of persistence and change in this *intra*suburb stratification process are discussed in: Reynolds Farley, "Suburban Persistence," *American Sociological Review* 29 (1964):38–47; Avery M. Guest, "Suburban Social Status: Persistence or Evolution," *American Sociological Review* 43(2) (1978):251–263; and John R. Logan and Mark Schneider, "The Stratification of Metropolitan Suburbs, 1960–70," *American Sociological Review* 46 (1981):175–186.

development could be generated, in selected cities, by post–1970 socioeconomic and demographic shifts in household composition.

While no one is predicting a wholesale "return to the city" of upper-status suburbanites, the changed post–1970 growth contexts, coupled with a shift in the composition of demand, could bring about some cityward redistribution of white collar, professional, and upper-income residents in central cities that serve nodal functions within our North-Declining metropolitan area grouping.

South-Old metropolitan areas, while not declining in metropolitan population like North-Declining areas, are also ripe for central city development. Their constricted central city boundaries and high concentrations of city blacks promoted a widespread status-selective "white flight" to the suburbs during the 1960s. However, this also exacerbated the filtering-down of central city properties and created the opportunity for further city development. The potential for selective central city counter-suburbanization is most apparent in Washington, DC—a government center with a high proportion of professional downtown workers. Yet, the other South-Old areas are also regional nodal centers and southern suburbanization patterns have traditionally shown some tendency for upper-status whites to locate in the city center.

The metropolitan areas in our North-Old and West-Old metropolitan classes tended to cover large areas, so that their central cities were, historically, less differentiated from their suburbs on socioeconomic and housing characteristics. A notable exception is San Francisco–Oakland, an older national nodal area in the West, with highly dense central cities. Like Washington, DC, this area houses a large share of professional city workers and provides a context amenable to a selective return to the city.

The status-selective patterns just discussed should differ markedly for metropolitan areas in the West-Young and South-Young classes. These areas generally did not evolve during the era of constrained short-distance transportation, nor did they sustain widespread immigration of foreign workers and minorities during their formative years. As a consequence, there was less need for upper-status residents to isolate themselves in independently incorporated suburban enclaves. Central-city governments espoused goals consistent with those of most metropolitan residents so that cities were more able to expand their boun-

---

[6]Neil Smith argues that residential redevelopment in older central cities is a structural product of the land and housing markets. He explains that ". . . The movement of capital to the suburbs along with the continual depreciation of inner city capital eventually produces the rent gap. When this gap grows sufficiently large, rehabilitation can begin to challenge the rates of return available elsewhere and capital flows back." See Neil Smith, "Toward a Theory of Gentrification: A Back to the City Movement, by Capital, Not People," *Journal of the American Planning Association* (October 1979):546.

daries through annexation as the central cities' fringes expanded.[7] Traditionally, these young areas have shown the least status disparities between their city and suburb populations.[8]

Nevertheless, our Chapter 7 results suggested that these areas are beginning to display some of the suburbanization characteristics of older metropolitan areas. For example, the use of annexation as a vehicle for expansion has become less pervasive in the 1970s than in the immediate postwar decades. Moreover, case study observations suggest that these areas' central cities are becoming more distinct from their suburbs with the recent influx of blacks and other minority groups. City governments are becoming less representative of the areawide population's interests as they are becoming more responsive to citybound ethnic and minority concerns, and are increasingly in conflict with suburban communities' objectives.[9] These developments suggest that the city–suburb status gaps may begin to widen in these young Sunbelt metropolitan areas.

Selective Suburbanization of Race and Minority Groups

The observations just made regarding status selectivity in different metropolitan area types apply primarily to the suburbanization of these areas' nonblack populations, since the status selectivity of metropolitan blacks affected overall trends only marginally before 1970. The pre-1970 suburban status selectivity patterns of blacks were often nonexistent in the sense that both high- and low-status blacks were equally restrained from selecting a suburban residence.[10] Moreover, in southern metropolitan areas, suburban blacks tended to be of lower status than city blacks due to the tendency of premetropolitan black enclaves to become surrounded by an expanding metropolitan territory.[11]

If the post-1970 black suburbanization movement is to constitute a bona fide counterpoint to the white suburbanization movement of earlier decades, it should display a heightened tendency toward suburban

[7]Norton, *City Life-Cycles and American Urban Policy.*
[8]Schnore (1972), *Class and Race.*
[9]Richard M. Bernard and Bradley R. Rice, eds., *Sunbelt Cities: Politics and Growth Since World War II* (Austin, TX: University of Texas Press, 1983); and John H. Mollenkopf, "Paths Toward the Post-industrial Service City: The Northeast and the Southwest," in Robert W. Burchill and David Listokin, eds., *Cities Under Stress* (New Brunswick, NJ: Rutgers Center for Urban Policy Research, 1981).
[10]Frey, "Black Movement to the Suburbs"; and William H. Frey, "Mover Destination Selectivity and the Changing Suburbanization of Metropolitan Whites and Blacks," *Demography* 22(2) (1985):223–243.
[11]Reynolds Farley, "The Changing Distribution of Negroes within Metropolitan Areas: The Emergence of Black Suburbs," *American Journal of Sociology* 75 (1970):512–529.

relocation among upper-status blacks, as well as an increased participation of blacks at all status levels. Less desirable from the perspective of declining central cities would be the suburbanization of only upper-status blacks—leaving middle and "underclass" blacks stranded in the central core. If only well-off blacks were able to participate in the movement to the suburbs, then the benefit of suburban location would not be shared by most blacks, and central cities would still retain a large share of the metropolitan area's economically dependent population.

A large part of this chapter's analysis will focus on race-specific patterns of suburban status selectivity in the 1970s of blacks and non-blacks.[12] We will want to determine whether nonblack suburban selectivity patterns have noticeably moderated since the 1970 census was taken and whether a heightened city attractiveness for metropolitan areas' better-off nonblacks can be discerned. With regard to blacks, we wish to determine if the increased post-1970 black suburbanization is strongly status-selective, involving only upper-status blacks, or if it involves broad participation of the black city population. A more moderate status-selective nonblack suburbanization, coupled with a fairly broad-based participation of blacks in this movement, could serve to "narrow" the city–suburb status gap that exists in most older industrial areas, and, at the same time, lead to a greater metropolitanwide residential integration of the races.

Toward the end of this chapter, we turn our attention to the socioeconomic selectivity of Hispanic- and Asian-Americans in metropolitan areas that house large concentrations of these groups. Although our Chapter 8 analysis showed both of these groups to be suburbanizing to some degree, we will evaluate how closely their suburbanization tendencies are related to their income levels and to their duration of residence in the United States. The presence of such relationships would indicate that these groups, like earlier European immigrant groups, are becoming less residentially isolated as the assimilation process progresses.

Before proceeding with our evaluation of black and nonblack redistribution shifts, or our evaluation of Hispanic- and Asian-American selectivity patterns, we first provide an overview of post–World War II trends in the city–suburb status gap for the nation's largest 39 metropolitan areas.

The City–Suburb Status Gap: 1950–1980

An assessment of 1950–1980 shifts in the city–suburb status gap

---

[12]As in Chapter 8, an analysis of 1970–1980 changes in these areas' white populations is precluded because of inconsistent 1970 and 1980 census definitions of the white population.

FIGURE 9.1

Median Adjusted Family Income[a] for Central Cities and Suburbs,
1950, 1960, 1970, 1980: Six Metropolitan Area Groupings[b]

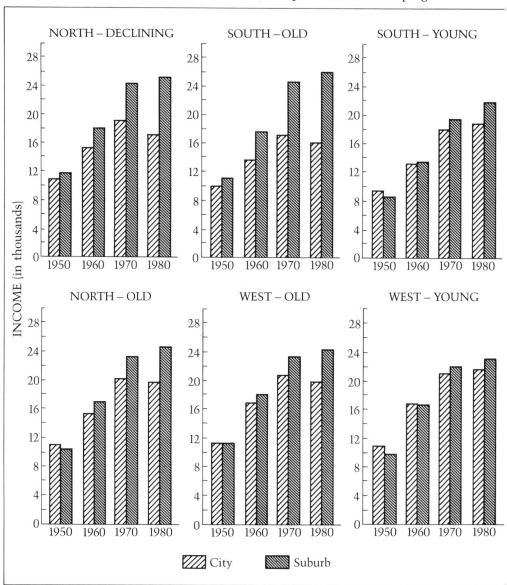

SOURCES: Machine-readable computer files: *County and City Data Book*, Consolidated Files for Cou
ties, 1947–1977, and Cities, 1944–1947; and *County and City Data Book*, 1983 files (prepared by the U.
Bureau of the Census, Washington DC).

[a]In constant 1979 dollars.

[b]These metropolitan area groupings are based on three categories of region (North, South, West), tw
categories of age (Old, Young) and 2 categories of metropolitan growth (Declining, Nondeclining). All
Declining areas are also Old and located in the North, and are placed in the single North-Declining grou
ing. The remaining 26 areas are all Nondeclining and are sorted into the groupings: North-Old, South-O
West-Old, South-Young, and West Young. Further details are provided in the Chapter 7 section, "A Metr
politan Area Typology" and Figure 7.1.

TABLE 9.1

Suburb-to-City Ratio of Median Adjusted Family Income
(in constant 1979 dollars), 1950, 1960, 1970, 1980:
Six Metropolitan Area Groupings

	1950	1960	1970	1980
orth-Declining	1.08	1.19	1.29	1.49
orth-Old	0.97	1.11	1.15	1.25
uth-Old	1.12	1.29	1.45	1.62
est-Old	1.02	1.07	1.13	1.22
uth-Young	0.91	1.01	1.09	1.17
est-Young	0.89	0.99	1.05	1.07

)URCES: Same as Figure 9.1.

can be made from Figure 9.1, where family income, adjusted to constant 1979 levels, is plotted for each of our six metropolitan area groupings. Ratios of suburb to city income for these groupings are presented in Table 9.1, and comparable median income data for the 39 individual metropolitan areas are shown in Appendix E, Table 9.A. These data indicate that the city–suburb status gap increases for all classes of metropolitan areas over the 1970–1980 period and for each individual area, as well. Yet, the magnitude of this gap and its historical trend varies markedly by metropolitan area type.

Both the North-Declining areas and South-Old areas registered discernible gaps already in 1950, and these gaps widened with each succeeding decade. Hence, not only are their gaps widest in 1980, but the 1970–1980 increments to these gaps are greater than over each of the prior decades. Along with the 1970–1980 widening of these gaps in both metropolitan area types, one also finds a 1970–1980 reduction of their central-city income levels. During the 1950s and 1960s North-Declining and South-Old central cities increased their incomes, although to a lesser degree than their suburbs. In the 1970s, city incomes declined.

Within these two groupings differences exist across individual metropolitan areas. The greatest gap in the 1970s belongs to Newark where the suburb–city median income ratio was 1.66 in 1970, and 2.21 in 1980. Aside from Newark, North-Declining areas' ratios ranged from 1.14 to 1.39 in 1970, and from 1.27 to 1.59 in 1980. Among the South-Old areas, Washington, D.C. displays the greatest suburb-to-city median income ratio in 1970 (1.48), and the smallest increment in that ratio in

1980 (to 1.56). The status gap increased more markedly in the remaining South-Old areas—all of which exhibited suburban incomes that were approximately one-third greater than their city incomes in 1970. These suburb-to-city ratios increased in 1980—to 1.68 (for Atlanta), to 1.58 (for Baltimore), and to 1.45 (for New Orleans).

The status gap patterns for North-Old and West-Old metropolitan areas bear some resemblance to those just discussed. These areas also display increases in status disparities over time—with widest gaps registered in 1980. Also, like North-Declining and South-Old areas, their central cities' mean family income declined over the 1970s. There are two distinct differences, however, between these "younger" Old areas and the "more mature" Old areas discussed above. First of all, their status gaps did not become evident until 1960. All but three of these ten areas (Hartford, San Francisco–Oakland, and Los Angeles–Long Beach) exhibited *city* income advantages in 1950, although each of them displayed a suburban income advantage in 1960. Second, their status gaps, even in 1980, were generally more moderate than those in North-Declining and South-Old areas. Aside from Hartford, with a suburb–city median income ratio of 1.75, the 1980 suburb–city ratios for North-Old and West-Old areas ranged from 1.13 to 1.34—approximately the range observed for North-Declining areas in 1960.

We turn now to South-Young and West-Young areas, the most recent of the nation's large metropolitan areas to display city–suburb status gaps. Unlike the four categories of older metropolitan areas, these groupings' central cities increased their median family incomes during *every* postwar decade. Most of the individual areas in these groupings did not display even a modest suburban income advantage until 1970 and many exhibited marked central city advantages in the 1950s.

Miami represents the only one of the 12 that shows a significant suburban income advantage for each census between 1950 and 1980, and an accentuated advantage over the 1970s. Discernible city–suburb gaps in 1970 and 1980 are displayed by the three Texas "growth centers" (San Antonio, Dallas–Ft. Worth, and Houston), and by Anaheim–Santa Ana–Garden Grove. However, the remaining South-Young and West-Young areas showed insignificant status gaps in both 1970 and 1980. In fact, in 1970, four of these seven remaining areas showed higher city than suburb median family incomes and, in 1980, their suburb to city median income ratios ranged from 0.98 to 1.15. Clearly, the areas in the South-Young and West-Young metropolitan groupings have just begun to show evidence of status-selective suburbanization and, of these, only Miami, the three Texas "growth centers," and Anaheim–Santa Ana– Garden Grove have made discernible progress.

Status Selectivity of Blacks and Nonblacks

In this section we examine, separately, the post–1970 status-selective suburbanization patterns of the black and nonblack populations in the nation's largest metropolitan areas. This separate race-specific treatment is necessary because somewhat different selectivity patterns are anticipated for the "majority" nonblack population, which has participated fully in the post–World War II suburbanization surge than for the black population, which remained heavily concentrated in the central city prior to 1970. For reasons discussed earlier, a moderation of status-selective suburbanization for nonblacks may have been set in motion with the 1970s, inside declining and older metropolitan areas that serve as nodal centers. For blacks just entering into the suburbanization process, we wish to determine whether this new redistribution tendency is sharply selective on status or whether it involves the broad participation of blacks at all status levels. This review and its accompanying data will focus on three different dimensions of socioeconomic status that have been examined in previous studies of status-selective suburbanization: family income, occupation, and education.[13] However, most of our discussion will focus on the measure of family income.

Income Selectivity

We begin our evaluation of status selectivity by examining 1970–1980 changes in suburban residence for individuals in families classed according to six broad categories of family income.[14] The plots for this evaluation, shown in Figure 9.2, display the 1970 and 1980 suburb proportions of metropolitan residents for each category. Also displayed are the suburb destination propensity rates of 1975–1980 intrametropolitan movers and metropolitan inmigrants.[15] As in our

---

[13]Studies of status-selective suburbanization that used these measures in earlier periods include: Schnore, *The Urban Scene*; Schnore, *Class and Race in Cities and Suburbs*; and those reviewed in: James R. Pinkerton, "City Suburban Residential Patterns by Social Class: A Review of the Literature," *Urban Affairs Quarterly* 4 (1969):449–519; and R. J. Johnston, *Urban Residential Patterns* (New York: Praeger, 1971).

[14]These income comparisons differ from those reviewed above in that they pertain to individuals in families classed by family income (rather than families classed by family income).

[15]The suburb destination propensity rate, as used here, is defined as the proportion of all 1975–1980 intrametropolitan movers and inmigrants that select a suburb (rather than a central city) destination. See Chapter 7 section on "Destination Propensity Rates" for a further discussion of this measure.

FIGURE 9.2

*Suburb Proportion of 1970 and 1980 Metropolitan Area Residents
and Suburb Destination Propensity Rates of 1975–1980 Metropolitan
Movers and Inmigrants in Families, by Categories of Family Income
and Race:[a] Six Metropolitan Area Groupings[b]*

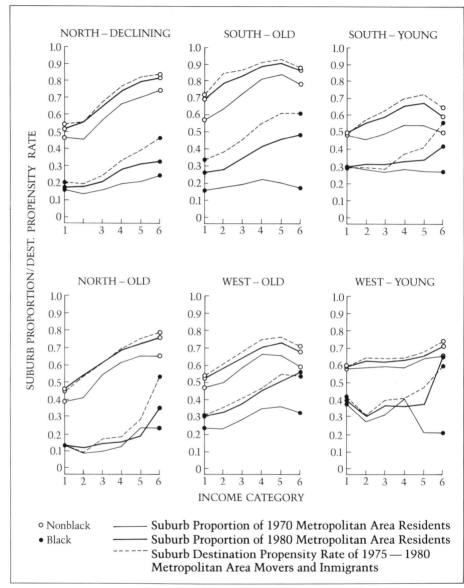

SOURCES: 1970: Census of Population, 1970: Special Census Tabulations 1980: Machine-readable computer files: Census of Population and Housing, 1980, Public Use Microdata Samples "A" and "B" (prepared by the U.S. Bureau of the Census, Washington, DC).

[a]Income Categories: (1979 dollars)

1. Under $6,000		4. $20,000–$29,999	
2. $6,000–$11,999		5. $30,000–$49,999	
3. $12,000–$19,999		6. $50,000 and over	

[b]1970 SMSA and Central City Definitions (in 1970) and 1970 Equivalent SMSA and Central City Definitions (in 1980).

Chapter 7 and 8 analyses, the latter rates—which measure the suburban destination selectivity of recent movers and inmigrants who are faced with either a city or suburb destination alternative—are seen to indicate the direction of post-1980 suburbanization trends.

Metropolitan area groupings—nonblacks: Focusing first on nonblack income selectivity shifts, one can observe a fairly direct relationship between income and suburb proportions among North-Declining area residents in both 1970 and 1980. The 1980 suburb proportions are higher at all income levels and show no evidence of a reduced 1970s suburban selectivity among upper-income residents. If anything, the 1970–1980 increase is slightly greater for individuals with family incomes between $30,000 and $50,000 than those at most lower income levels, and residents in the lowest income level display the smallest 1970–1980 increment in suburb proportion. This trend is further reinforced by the suburb destination propensity rates of 1975–1980 movers and inmigrants, which show higher proportions than all residents at each income level and, particularly so, for those with incomes greater than $30,000 per year.

Before completely dismissing the possibility of an upper-status nonblack "return to the city," perhaps two caveats should be stated. First, much of the "return to the city" speculation evolves from the notion that a significant segment of the postwar-born baby-boom cohorts—with stronger career orientations, few dependents, and high disposable income—will find cities to be more desirable as places of residence than earlier cohorts. Indeed, the popular literature of the early 1980s has coined the term "yuppie" (an acronym for: "young urban professional") to connote the distinct lifestyles and consumer preferences of these individuals.[16] The point is that most yuppies were well under age 35 in 1980 and, while they had more disposable income at their command than members of earlier cohorts at that age, they had not yet reached the peak income years, and are not well represented among the highest income categories in Figure 9.2. It is conceivable that, as these postwar-born cohort members age further and advance into higher income brackets, they may very well remain in the city to a greater degree than their predecessor cohorts, which now dominate these brackets.

A second qualification draws from the exclusion of individuals, not in family households, from this analysis. (Nonfamily households are made up of one or more unrelated individuals.) Nonfamily households, at all income levels, rose dramatically in the 1970s (see Chapter 10), and the most well-off ones were seen as an important "target population"

---

[16]"The Year of the Yuppie," *Newsweek* (December 31, 1984), pp. 14–24.

around which to structure a city's redevelopment. [17] The focus here on individuals in family households, for this evaluation of income selectivity, leaves out any "return to the city" of such persons. This exclusion will not be made in the analyses of occupation and education selectivity below.

The South-Old metropolitan areas represent the second metropolitan class wherein some moderation in nonblack suburban status selectivity was anticipated. The 1970 nonblack residents of these areas exhibit a characteristic "old South" reverse-U-shaped relationship between income and suburban location. Here, the highest income residents are slightly more inclined to locate in the city than those in more moderate income categories, although the lowest income residents are clearly most city-oriented in their locations. During the 1970–1980 period, there was an increase in suburban location at all income levels, but this increase was neither uniform across classes nor was it suggestive of an upper-status "return to the city." The greatest increase in suburban location actually occurred among residents in the two lowest income categories—leading to a flatter U-shaped curve than existed in 1970—a pattern that is further reinforced by 1975–1980 movers and inmigrants. Hence, rather than attracting high-income suburban residents back to the city, South-Old areas are exhibiting a greater suburbanization of their less well-off city residents. The long-term impact of this redistribution might be just as beneficial for the city's tax base and can set the stage for future reinvestment and selective nonblack inmigration to the city.

The 1970s city–suburb status gaps for North-Old and West-Old areas, reviewed earlier, were not nearly as large as the gaps for North-Declining and South-Old areas. Nevertheless, nonblack residents in both of these "newer" Old metropolitan area groupings displayed fairly sharp status selectivity patterns in 1970 and in 1980. North-Old nonblack residents, like the North-Declining residents, show an increasing tendency to locate in the suburbs at higher levels of income. The relationship becomes even more direct in 1980 because, although suburb proportions increased for residents at all income levels, the increase is magnified for the highest income category (and magnified even further among 1975–1980 movers and inmigrants). The income relationship with suburban location in West-Old areas also exhibits sharp gradations but resembles the reverse-U-shape pattern of South-Old areas. Unlike the South-Old case, however, 1970–1980 increases in West-Old non-

---

[17] William H. Frey and Frances E. Kobrin, "Changing Families and Changing Mobility: Their Impact on the Central City," *Demography* 19(3) (1982):261–277.

black suburbanization are not accentuated for low-income groups. Rather, a slightly greater rise is shown for nonblack residents in the highest income category.

The post-1970 nonblack suburban selectivity for the newer Sunbelt metropolitan areas is quite distinct from the four older metropolitan area groupings. For South-Young areas, the 1970s decade represents the virtual beginning of status-selective suburbanization. The Figure 9.2 plot shows that, at the beginning of this decade, the relationship between nonblack residents' income level and their proportions in suburban locations was not very distinct. Residents with family incomes between $12,000 and $50,000 were only slightly more likely to reside in the suburbs than persons in other income categories. Between 1970 and 1980, there was a sharp rise in the suburban location for residents in all but the lowest income category, and this rise was most prominent for persons with incomes between $20,000 and $50,000. As a result of these changes, the 1980 relationship between residents' income and suburban location (and, to an even greater extent, that between 1975–1980 movers' and inmigrants' income and their suburban destination propensity rate) resembles the reverse-U-shape pattern in South-Old areas. In West-Young areas, on the other hand, the relationship between residents' income and suburban location is hardly perceptible in either 1970 or 1980, nor is it implied in the suburban destination propensity rates of 1975–1980 movers and inmigrants.

Metropolitan area groupings—blacks: Just as the 1970s constituted a benchmark decade with regard to the magnitude of black suburbanization, it would also seem to represent a benchmark decade with respect to the status selectivity when the family income measure of status is used. According to Figure 9.2, blacks of all income levels began to participate in the post-1980 black suburbanization movement, and these shifts appear to be most evident in the North-Declining and South-Old metropolitan area groupings.

The 1970–1980 shift for North-Declining metropolitan areas can be observed in Figure 9.2's upper left-hand plot. The fairly modest positive relationship in 1970 between black residents' income and suburbanization was transformed, by 1980, to a sharp one, yet one which increases the participation of blacks at all but the lowest income level in the suburbanization process. The fact that the suburb destination propensity rates of black 1975–1980 movers and inmigrants are both higher and more status-selective than are the locations of all black 1980 residents suggests that this process will continue beyond 1980. The black suburban gains in South-Old areas are even more impressive than those in North-Declining areas. Substantial 1970–1980 rises are observed at all income levels, and these rises are particularly impressive for the highest income categories.

The relatively low level of 1970s black suburbanization, observed earlier for South-Young areas, shows evidence of being an "upper-status"–only black suburbanization in Figure 9.2. The 1970 black suburban proportions in these areas are relatively indifferent to income, and only black residents in the highest income category show a substantial 1970–1980 increase in suburban location. We remarked in the previous chapter that, given the expansive central cities and high 1970s levels of nonblack metropolitan growth in these areas, black suburban participation within them would be more limited than in the other major black destination areas. We see here that not only is the magnitude of black suburbanization more limited in these areas, but that it is also more restricted to high-income black residents. The remaining three metropolitan area groupings are composed, by and large, of individual metropolitan areas with small black populations that tended to diverge widely from the aggregate patterns shown in Figure 9.2. However, the two West-Old metropolitan areas, San Francisco–Oakland and Los Angeles–Long Beach, do have significant black populations, and their selectivity patterns will be discussed below.

The preceding review of black income selectivity for metropolitan area groupings suggests that it is the black population that exhibited the greatest post-1970 change in its income relationship with suburbanization, while nonblack suburbanization, with some exceptions, retained the same income-suburban location relationship observed earlier. The plots in Figure 9.2 also make plain that the 1980 proportion of metropolitan area blacks at all income levels still lies below—and usually well below—the suburb proportion of metropolitan area nonblacks for each metropolitan area grouping. While a significant and pervasive black suburbanization has taken place in the post-1970 period, it has only served to narrow, somewhat, the wide city–suburb racial separation that existed in most large metropolitan areas in 1970.

Individual metropolitan areas: The patterns displayed for metropolitan area groupings serve to characterize the dominant post-1970 redistribution tendencies of areas with common growth and development histories. However, the reader should be aware that each individual area exhibits a distinct pattern which diverges somewhat from that of its metropolitan area grouping. To illustrate this, we present (in Figure 9.3) 1970–1980 selectivity patterns for the individual metropolitan areas of Detroit, Washington, DC, San Francisco–Oakland, and Los Angeles–Long Beach.

FIGURE 9.3

*Suburb Proportion of 1970 and 1980 Metropolitan Area Residents
and Suburb Destination Propensity Rates of 1975–1980 Metropolitan
Movers and Inmigrants in Families, by Categories of Family Income
and Race[a]: Selected Metropolitan Areas[b]*

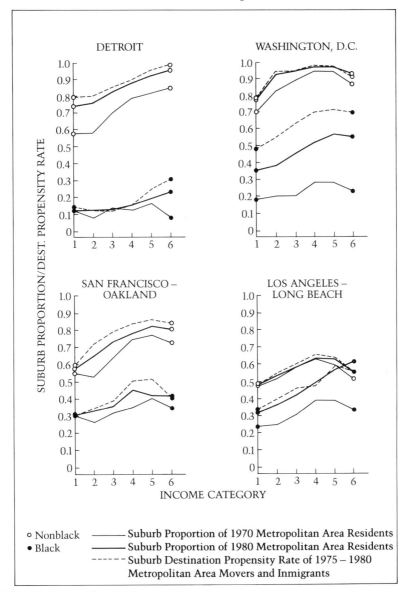

SOURCES: Same as Figure 9.2.

[a]Income Categories:
(1979 dollars)

1. Under $6,000	4. $20,000–$29,999
2. $6,000–$11,999	5. $30,000–$49,999
3. $12,000–$19,999	6. $50,000 and over

[b]1970 SMSA and Central City Definitions (in 1970) and 1970 SMSA and Equivalent Central City Definitions (in 1980).

We remarked in the previous chapter how Detroit's continued high nonblack suburbanization levels, when coupled with its unusually low black suburbanization levels, led to a greater city–suburb racial separation than exists in other North-Declining areas. Figure 9.3 shows that Detroit's nonblack and black status selectivity patterns are also divergent. Although nonblack suburban location increases significantly between 1970 and 1980 at all income levels, the rise is much greater for lower-income categories, leading to a weaker income-suburbanization relationship for Detroit's nonblacks. The black income-suburbanization relationship also remains weak. Hence, as nonblacks of all income levels redistribute themselves into the suburbs, blacks at all income levels remain largely city-bound. Washington, DC's black suburbanization patterns stand in sharp contrast to Detroit's. We display them not because they diverge markedly from other South-Old areas but because they accentuate this metropolitan area grouping's distinct features. What is impressive here is both the magnitude and the increased status selectivity of 1970–1980 black suburbanization in Washington. While Washington's 1970 city–suburb distribution displayed a "Detroit-like" racial separation, a substantial 1970–1980 black suburbanization, coupled with a reduced-level nonblack suburbanization, has lowered this separation somewhat.

As indicated above, the distinctive status-selectivity patterns of San Francisco–Oakland and Los Angeles–Long Beach tend to become camouflaged in the patterns for West-Old areas, so we display them here separately. San Francisco–Oakland's modest nonblack 1970s suburbanization has served to shift a beginning-of-decade, reverse-U-shaped relationship between income and suburban location to a more direct relationship. However, its 1970s black suburbanization has continued the flatter relationship for blacks, such that the suburban locations for blacks at all income levels lie far below those for nonblacks. The latter is not the case for Los Angeles–Long Beach where 1970s black suburbanization is both strong and status-selective. Indeed, 1980 black metropolitan residents in the highest income category resided in the suburbs to a greater extent than nonblack residents in that category. The reader is again reminded that the physical and political configurations of these two metropolitan areas are quite different and that Los Angeles–Long Beach is far less differentiated from its suburbs on a variety of population and housing characteristics. We will return to these two areas again in our discussion of Hispanic- and Asian-Americans.

Suburbanization rates: To complete our overview of income selectivity associated with post-1970–1980 nonblack and black suburbanization, we present, for each metropolitan area grouping, 1970–1980 suburbanization rates for families by broad income categories (see Table 9.2). While the Figure 9.2 plots permitted us to examine static relationships between income and suburban location at both the beginning and end of the decade, these suburbanization rates are more direct measures of the redistribution process at each income level. The suburbanization rates are computed for families, rather than individuals in families, in the broad income categories: under $10,000, $10,000–29,999, and $30,000 and over (in constant 1979 dollars). For the United States population in 1980, most families resided in the middle income category so that the first and third categories represent the "tails" of the distribution. [18]

The suburbanization rates for nonblacks shown in column 3 of Table 9.2 provide a concise summary of income selectivity in the 1970–1980 suburbanization process. The rates for North-Declining areas rise incrementally with higher levels of income. Families in the middle-income category show rates approximately 50 percent higher than those in the lower category (28.5 versus 17.8) and families in the upper-income bracket show rates about 60 percent higher than those in the middle bracket (45.8 versus 28.5). North-Old and West-Old areas also sustained greatest suburbanization rates among their upper-income nonblacks; however, there is less distinction between the rates for their middle- and lower-income categories. The distinguishing feature of 1970s suburbanization within South-Old areas, aside from its large overall magnitude, is the high participation among its low-income nonblacks. This is clearly shown in Table 9.2. Finally, the two younger Sunbelt areas exhibit different post-1970 patterns. South-Young metropolitan areas show very strong suburbanization rate differences across income categories—as 1970–1980 represents their first decade of status-selective suburbanization. West-Young areas, on the other hand, display quite modest income differences in 1970s nonblack suburbanization, although their suburbanization rates do increase at higher income levels.

Black suburbanization rates, in all areas, rise at higher income levels. However in both North-Declining and South-Old areas, one finds already at the lowest income level a significant black suburbanization rate, and distinct increases in the rate at the two higher levels. Our "upper-status-only" characterization of black suburbanization in South-Young areas seems, again, appropriate in describing these areas' suburbanization rates—which increment from 45.8 to 205.6 between their middle- and upper-income categories. A similar characterization

[18]For the reader's reference, Appendix E, Table 9.B shows the 1970 and 1980 percent income distributions for the cities and suburbs of the six metropolitan area groupings.

TABLE 9.2.

Percent Change in City and Suburban Families by Race and Income, 1970–1980: Six Metropolitan Area Groupings

Metropolitan Area Groupings/Family Income (1979 Dollars)	Nonblacks			Blacks		
	Central City Percent Change	Suburb Percent Change	Suburbanization Rate[a]	Central City Percent Change	Suburb Percent Change	Suburbanization Rate[a]
NORTH-DECLINING						
30,000+	−27.3	+18.5	+45.8	+23.8	+137.6	+113.8
10,000–29,999	−30.1	−1.6	+28.5	−12.9	+34.8	+47.7
Under 10,000	+6.2	+24.0	+17.8	+39.8	+69.3	+29.5
NORTH-OLD						
30,000+	−5.2	+42.9	+48.1	+65.5	+156.7	+91.2
10,000–29,999	−18.4	+10.2	+28.6	+6.1	+40.7	+34.6
Under 10,000	+3.6	+27.2	+23.6	+42.4	+56.2	+13.8
SOUTH-OLD						
30,000+	−20.6	+39.2	+59.8	+23.0	+330.3	+307.3
10,000–29,999	−39.0	+8.9	+47.9	−12.4	+123.4	+135.8
Under 10,000	−20.1	+31.1	+51.2	+23.5	+102.9	+79.4
WEST-OLD						
30,000+	−2.5	+35.5	+38.0	+41.0	+156.6	+115.6
10,000–29,999	−14.8	+2.9	+17.7	−7.5	+52.2	+59.7
Under 10,000	+10.9	+29.6	+18.7	+32.3	+86.2	+53.9
SOUTH-YOUNG						
30,000+	+28.0	+121.8	+93.8	+219.1	+424.7	+205.6
10,000–29,999	−1.0	+48.6	+49.6	+22.7	+68.5	+45.8
Under 10,000	+14.4	+42.7	+28.3	+28.4	+40.4	+12.0
WEST-YOUNG						
30,000+	+44.3	+70.9	+26.6	+183.7	+395.7	+212.0
10,000–29,999	+16.4	+34.4	+18.0	+47.0	+135.9	+88.9
Under 10,000	+35.4	+45.0	+9.6	+69.9	+161.4	+91.5

SOURCES: Machine-readable computer files: Census of Population and Housing, 1970, Fourth Count, Population Summary File Tape; and Census of Population and Housing, 1980, Summary Tape File 3C (prepared by the U.S. Bureau of the Census, Washington, DC).

[a]Suburbanization Rate: Suburb Percent Change minus Central City Percent Change.

might also apply to North-Old areas. Lastly, the black populations in the West-Old and West-Young area groupings show relatively high black suburbanization rates for both the low- and medium-income categories, and distinctly greater rates for their high-income categories. There is little doubt, after reviewing these measures, that black suburbanization has become pervasive in all types of areas.

The other statistics in Table 9.2, which underlie the suburbanization rates, are the percent changes in city and suburb families by income category for nonblacks (first and second columns) and blacks (fourth and fifth columns).[19] The city change data for nonblacks provides strong counterevidence to arguments that a selective "return to the city" is taking place. North-Declining central cities have sustained a decline of roughly 30 percent in their nonblack families with incomes greater than $10,000, and an increase of 6 percent among their families with incomes of less than $10,000. Similar patterns of nonblack city change are observed for North-Old and West-Old areas, although the magnitudes of decline are far less. The unique income-selective suburbanization process in South-Old areas results in nonblack city decreases at all income levels. Here, both high- and low-income families exhibit similar 1970–1980 decreases. It is only the South-Young and West-Young areas that show 1970s increases in nonblack city families at the highest income levels; yet these increases are primarily a consequence of large metropolitanwide gains in high-income families.

The measures of black suburb change show, fairly clearly, that substantial black suburbanization has involved all income levels in each metropolitan area class. The high growth rates are sometimes deceptive because they are based on small initial black populations. However, a perusal of aggregate population increases (not shown) indicates black suburban growth to be broad-based across all income categories. Although the income selectivity patterns reviewed here do not suggest a greater city attraction of high income nonblacks, they do document that black suburbanization is both pervasive and broad-based.

---

[19]In interpreting these percentages, the reader should be aware that they represent not only the effects of geographic changes in household location (as well as household births and deaths), but also shifts in household income from one category to another. The latter shifts, for the nation as a whole in 1970–1980, have increased the number of households in the upper- and lower-income categories—to the detriment of the middle-income category. As a result, most areas will exhibit pronounced losses or reduced gains in this income category irrespective of geographic shifts. (For example, the medium-income category registers largest losses in both cities and suburbs for North-Declining areas.) The reader should also keep in mind that city and suburb population increases result not only from city–suburb redistribution but also from metropolitanwide gains and losses. Because interlabor market migration is income-selective, growing areas will accrue greater metropolitanwide gains than slow-growing or declining metropolitan areas in their high-income populations.

Occupation and Education Selectivity

An individual's occupation and education (number of years of schooling completed) are often used as alternative measures of social status. Although they are less directly linked to a consumer's "ability to pay" for housing in a particular area, they constitute additional dimensions of social position or status that have been shown to be relevant to the redistribution process.[20] For example, although high income was not related to city location or a "return to the city" movement, individuals in professional occupations (scattered across several income levels) may constitute a more appropriate "target population" for this movement. It has also been documented that rises in black status have been more evident on occupation and educational status measures than on income.[21] The latter measures, therefore, may be more sensitive to black residents' location patterns than was income. Our review of these measures' relationships to nonblack and black suburban location will be less detailed than our review of the income relationships. Although similar data are provided for the readers' perusal, our discussion will be restricted to highlighting the most important findings and pointing out instances where the two status measures' relationships with suburban location differ from those we have just discussed.

Occupation: Our analysis of occupation relationships, shown in Figure 9.4, pertains to the male civilian labor force, aged 16 and over, and classed by the occupation classification system used in the 1970 census. According to this system, the occupational categories of managers and administrators, professionals and technical workers, sales workers, and clerical workers are considered to be "white collar" workers; those in categories of crafts workers and other less skilled workers (operatives, transport operatives, and nonfarm laborers) are considered to be "blue collar" workers; and service workers and farm workers are not considered to be either white collar or blue collar workers. Figure 9.4 plots residents' 1970 and 1980 suburb proportions and 1975–1980 movers' and inmigrants' suburb destination propensity rates for an abbreviated system of occupational categories. These include the four categories of white collar workers, service workers, crafts workers, and a residual category which shall be referred to as "low-skilled blue collar," although it also includes the small number of farm workers that exist in metropolitan areas.

The relationship between occupation and suburban location for nonblacks is most distinct for North-Declining areas, although it is dis-

---

[20]Johnston, *Urban Residential Patterns.*
[21]Reynolds Farley, *Blacks and Whites: Narrowing the Gap?* (Cambridge, MA: Harvard University Press, 1984).

FIGURE 9.4

*Suburb Proportion of 1970 and 1980 Metropolitan Area Residents and
Suburb Destination Propensity Rates of 1975–1980 Metropolitan Area
Movers and Inmigrants, Employed Civilian Male Workers,
by Occupation and Race: Six Metropolitan Area Groupings[a]*

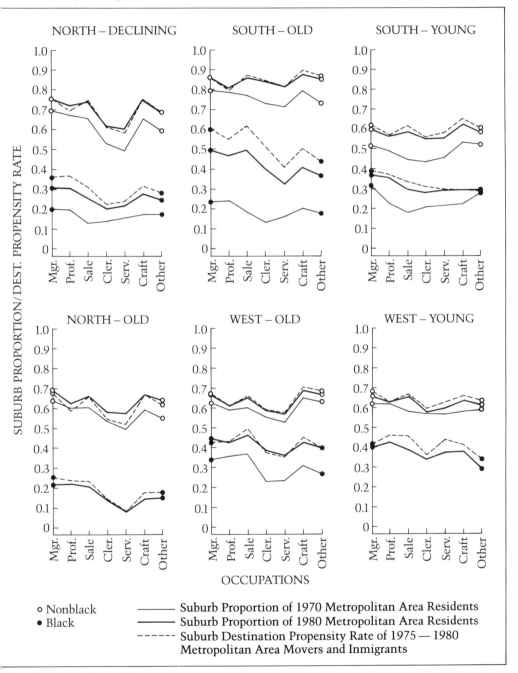

SOURCES: Same as Figure 9.2.

1970 SMSA and Central City Definitions (in 1970) and 1970 Equivalent SMSA and Central City Definitions (in 1980).

cernible for other areas as well. It shows that residents in the three highest status white collar professions exhibit the greatest proportion of suburban residence; that white collar clerical workers and service workers are most centrally located; and that crafts workers and other blue collar workers lie in between. The relationship is consistent with the relative income levels of these broad occupational groups—that is, sales and clerical workers are, on average, less well-paid than crafts workers. It is also consistent with journey-to-work considerations since the central city houses a greater proportion of the metropolitan areas' clerical jobs than those in most other occupations. Yet, for areas outside of the North-Declining metropolitan area grouping, the occupational classification appears to be a less sensitive discriminator of suburban location than was income.

Nevertheless, there are noteworthy shifts in the occupation-suburban location relationship that are particularly evident in North-Declining, North-Old, and South-Old areas. First, professional workers showed a lower tendency to suburbanize than the other broad occupations, including the other categories of white collar workers. Indeed, among all six metropolitan area plots, we see a small "indentation" for professionals in 1980—indicating that professionals are less likely to reside in the suburbs than managers or sales workers. Though hardly compelling, this constitutes some evidence which suggests that a small "return to the city" movement may be in the offing. This discrepancy with the income analysis might be attributed to the fact that many of these professionals are younger and have not yet reached their peak income years. It can also be attributed to the different population universes involved. The income analysis focused on all individuals (including children) residing in families and excluded individuals living in single-person households. The occupation analysis includes male civilian labor force workers residing in all types of households but does not include nonworking dependents of these workers.

The second discernible shift among nonblacks between 1970 and 1980 is an accentuated suburbanization of blue collar workers—both craftsworkers and low-skilled blue collar workers—in North-Declining, North-Old, and South-Old areas. This serves to raise the 1980 suburban proportion of crafts workers above workers in all white collar categories in these metropolitan areas, and further "flattens out" the occupation-suburban location relationship. The suburban shift of these blue collar workers can be generally attributed to the pervasive suburbanward redistribution of manufacturing and other blue collar employment opportunities—providing greater incentive for such workers to relocate their residences outward (this issue is examined further in Chapter 11).

Aside from these more pervasive post-1970 changes, one can see that the South-Old areas' occupational relationship with suburban location has been completely transformed over the 1970–1980 period as a result of an extensive suburban shift of clerical and sales workers. This seems consistent with the South-Old 1970s shifts by income status, which were disproportionately large for the lower income categories. The result of these shifts is an extremely flat occupation-suburban location relationship for 1980 nonblack workers in South-Old areas.

The black suburban location patterns by occupational status, like those for income status, became more selective over the 1970–1980 decade. The greatest shifts toward suburban location are observed for managers and professionals, and for craftsmen and less-skilled blue collar workers—although there are some variations across metropolitan area groupings. Nevertheless, a comparison of the plots in Figure 9.2 with those in Figure 9.4 suggests that income is a more sensitive indicator of black suburban location than is occupation, in the sense that there is greater variation across income categories than occupation categories.

The suburbanization process by occupation status is summarized in Table 9.3 which displays nonblack and black suburbanization rates for white collar workers, service workers, and blue collar workers (including farm workers).[22] The nonblack suburbanization rates (in the third column) for North-Declining, North-Old and South-Old areas, again point up the significance of blue collar suburbanization gains in these areas. In each area these workers registered higher suburbanization rates than white collar workers, and contributed to 1970–1980 losses of city blue collar workers of -32.7, -17.9, and -37.1 percent, respectively, for these three area types. What is also noteworthy with these areas is that their rates of white collar suburbanization are lower than rates of blue collar suburbanization. This provides hope that these older cities might play specialized roles as administrative and corporate decision-making centers. Indeed, individual metropolitan area data show extraordinarily low 1970–1980 white collar suburbanization rates (relative to their blue collar suburbanization rates) for nonblacks in Boston, Washington, DC, San Francisco–Oakland, and Columbus—nodal and government cities that have already established themselves as such specialized centers.

Black suburbanization rates in all area types are greatest for white collar workers. Yet, blue collar suburbanization rates are also substantial in each area grouping, except the South-Young grouping. The suburbanization of blue collar blacks is an important concern because the ex-

---

[22]For the reader's reference, Appendix E, Table 9.C shows the 1970 and 1980 percent occupation distributions for the cities and suburbs of the six metropolitan area groupings.

TABLE 9.3

Percent Change in City and Suburban Employed Civilian Male Workers by Race and Occupation Class, 1970–1980: Six Metropolitan Area Groupings

Metropolitan Area Groupings/ Occupation Class[a]	Nonblacks			Blacks		
	Central City Percent Change	Suburb Percent Change	Suburbanization Rate[b]	Central City Percent Change	Suburb Percent Change	Suburbanization Rate[b]
NORTH-DECLINING						
White collar	−16.7	+14.3	+31.0	+18.7	+109.2	+90.5
Service	−8.8	+31.6	+40.4	+4.7	+51.9	+47.2
Blue collar	−32.7	+1.3	+34.0	−25.6	+22.9	+48.5
NORTH-OLD						
White collar	+2.7	+32.7	+30.0	+50.5	+151.6	+101.1
Service	+14.6	+59.3	+44.7	+32.5	+47.2	+14.7
Blue collar	−17.9	+14.4	+32.3	−6.6	+29.9	+36.5
SOUTH-OLD						
White collar	−12.8	+34.0	+46.8	+11.1	+281.9	+270.8
Service	−6.9	+67.0	+73.9	−1.8	+128.3	+130.1
Blue collar	−37.1	+22.3	+59.4	−21.2	+85.2	+106.4

TABLE 9.3 (continued)

WEST-OLD						
White collar	+12.7	+32.4	+19.7	+50.5	+152.9	+102.4
Service	+26.0	+42.2	+16.2	+1.2	+81.6	+80.4
Blue collar	+3.5	+19.2	+15.7	−8.9	+48.0	+56.9
SOUTH-YOUNG						
White collar	+24.2	+87.4	+63.2	+93.0	+254.5	+161.5
Service	+42.5	+108.4	+65.9	+20.1	+75.7	+55.6
Blue collar	+22.7	+61.2	+38.6	+23.2	+41.3	+18.1
WEST-YOUNG						
White collar	+47.9	+68.4	+20.5	+161.3	+345.4	+184.1
Service	+53.0	+71.2	+18.2	+58.1	+217.1	+159.0
Blue collar	+35.3	+50.7	+15.4	+50.6	+132.2	+81.6

SOURCES: Same as Table 9.2.

[a]Represents conventional 1970 census categories and equivalent 1980 categories, by regrouping 13 broad 1980 categories. Note: Farm workers are included with blue collar workers.

[b]Suburbanization Rate: Suburb Percent Change minus Central City Percent Change.

treme suburbanization of blue collar jobs in the pre-1970 period served to isolate city blacks from employment opportunites. This issue is given closer scrutiny in Chapter 11.

Education: The final status measure to be considered is education, which is operationalized as the level of education completed for persons aged 25 and above. Education is less directly related to residents' current ability to pay or location preference than either their income or occupation status. However, there is an analytic advantage with this measure not associated with the other two in that most individuals retain the same education status after age 25. Any over-time changes in the education-suburban location relationship can therefore be attributed solely to demographic change (geographic shifts, deaths, or births) rather than to shifts in status among the existing population. Another advantage over occupation status is that it does not exclude older persons and other adults not in the labor force. Yet, the restriction to individuals aged 25 and above omits one segment of the population that has been known to prefer a central city residence (young adults aged 15 through 24) and another segment that has traditionally been confined to the suburbs with their parents (children under age 15).[23]

The Figure 9.5 plots that relate education to suburban location for nonblacks in 1970 bear strong similarities to those that relate income to suburban location. However, the education relationships show a narrower range in suburban location levels, such that there is less differentiation in the suburban proportion among the three highest education categories than exists at the highest income categories. At first glance, therefore, one is tempted to conclude that education constitutes a less sensitive measure of the same status dimension than income for explaining suburban location.

However, an examination of 1970–1980 shifts in the education-suburban location relationship uncovers new information not available with the income analysis. It is that in each older metropolitan area grouping, there is a greater increase in the suburbanization of high school graduates and individuals with some college than for college graduates. Although all three categories of 1970 nonblack residents with high school educations or more show fairly similar levels of suburban location, their 1980 counterparts are less likely to reside in the suburbs if they have a college degree. The fact that this pattern is accentuated for 1975–1980 nonblack movers' and inmigrants' suburb destination propensity rates suggests that it is the young adult, more recent college graduates, who are contributing to the pattern. This constitutes more

---

[23]See Frey, "Lifecourse Migration of Metropolitan Whites and Blacks and the Structure of Demographic Change in Large Central Cities."

FIGURE 9.5

*Suburb Proportion of 1970 and 1980 Metropolitan Area Residents and
Suburb Destination Propensity Rates of 1975–80 Metropolitan Area
Movers and Inmigrants, by Education Status[a] and Race:
Six Metropolitan Area Groupings[b]*

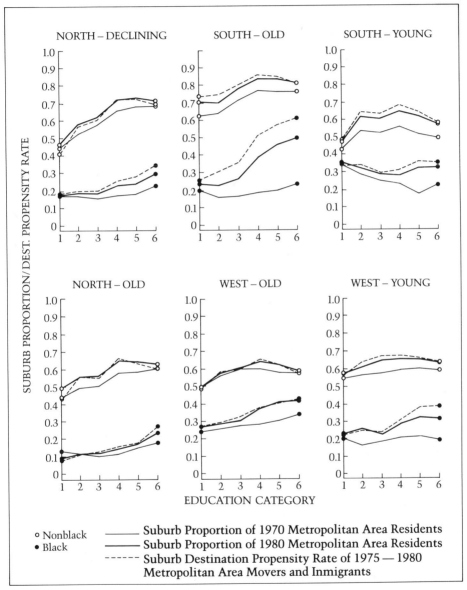

SOURCES: Same as Figure 9.2.

[a]Education Categories:

1. Elem. Grades 0–7   4. High School, 4 yrs
2. Elem. Grade 8   5. College, 1–3 yrs
3. High School, 1–3 yrs 6. College, 4 yrs

[b]1970 SMSA and Central City Definitions (in 1970) and 1970 Equivalent SMSA and Central City Definitions (in 1980).

evidence, albeit small, that a selective "return to the city" may occur with future cohorts of movers. The greater nonblack suburbanization of high school, rather than college, graduates is documented for most metropolitan area groupings in Table 9.4 (third column); and additional data show this pattern to be particularly accentuated in the nodal centers, New York, Boston, San Francisco–Oakland, and Columbus. It is speculative, to be sure, to suggest that this shift in the education relationship signals a return to the city of college graduates. However, these educational status relationships, like those for occupational status, leave open this possibility.

Finally, we observe that education appears to be just as sensitive an indicator of black suburban location as income. Indeed in some area groupings, such as North-Declining areas and South-Old areas, education categories—particularly at the upper levels—do a better job of distinguishing suburban proportions (Figure 9.5) and suburbanization rates (Table 9.4) than do categories of income.[24] This may be attributed to the fact that black advancement in educational status has been more pronounced than their advances in income, so that the differences between black college graduates and black high school graduates may become camouflaged within broad income categories. Regardless of whether one uses income or education status as a measure, it is clear from these data that the suburban status selectivity of blacks has shifted markedly in the decade of the 1970s.

Summary

In this section we have reviewed city–suburb status shifts for nonblacks and blacks over the post-1970 period. Because the results in Chapter 8 showed that nonblack suburbanization had slowed down in North-Declining metropolitan areas in the 1970s, we wondered if this slow-down in the magnitude of suburbanization would be accompanied by a moderation in its status selectivity. After examining income, occupation, and education status relationships with 1970–1980 suburbanization patterns, we must conclude that selectivity has not generally declined. This is most apparent for the family income measure, which has strengthened its relationship with suburban location over the decade. The relationship is significantly modified only in South-Old areas where nonblacks in the lowest income categories have begun to suburbanize at much higher rates, so that southern cities are now sustaining population losses at all income levels rather than only the traditional

[24]For the reader's reference, Appendix E, Table 9.D shows the 1970 and 1980 percent education distributions for the cities and suburbs of the six metropolitan area groupings.

Percent Change in City and Suburban Populations, Aged 25 and Over, by Race and Education Status, 1970–1980: Six Metropolitan Area Groupings

Metropolitan Area Groupings/ Education Status	Nonblacks			Blacks		
	Central City Percent Change	Suburb Percent Change	Suburbanization Rate[a]	Central City Percent Change	Suburb Percent Change	Suburbanization Rate[a]
NORTH-DECLINING						
College graduate	+42.8	+64.1	+21.3	+110.1	+220.9	+110.8
High school graduate	+7.6	+37.7	+30.1	+64.2	+145.2	+81.0
Less than HS graduate	−36.3	−24.1	+12.2	−16.5	−3.5	+13.0
NORTH-OLD						
College graduate	+61.9	+87.4	+25.5	+104.3	+233.3	+129.0
High school graduate	+19.5	+54.7	+35.2	+77.9	+148.0	+70.1
Less than HS graduate	−34.5	−18.7	+15.8	−12.6	−12.6	+0.0
SOUTH-OLD						
College graduate	+42.8	+90.9	+48.1	+71.0	+407.3	+336.3
High school graduate	+5.4	+60.6	+55.2	+59.4	+362.9	+303.5
Less than HS graduate	−44.9	−13.6	+31.3	−15.3	+25.0	+40.3
WEST-OLD						
College graduate	+64.8	+86.0	+21.2	+122.8	+232.0	+109.2
High school graduate	+21.4	+46.9	+25.5	+62.0	+151.2	+89.2
Less than HS graduate	−21.4	−15.0	+6.4	−17.3	+1.8	+19.1
SOUTH-YOUNG						
College graduate	+98.5	+153.4	+54.9	+174.3	+279.7	+105.4
High school graduate	+60.5	+110.4	+49.9	+145.4	+186.8	+41.4
Less than HS graduate	−8.2	+5.9	+14.1	+3.0	−15.7	−18.7
WEST-YOUNG						
College graduate	+102.2	+119.1	+16.9	+256.9	+377.8	+120.9
High school graduate	+64.6	+87.1	+22.5	+151.9	+247.9	+96.0
Less than HS graduate	−4.0	+3.3	+7.3	−5.1	+21.9	+27.0

SOURCES: Same as Table 9.2.

[a]Suburbanization Rate: Suburb Percent Change minus Central City Percent Change.

upper-status "flight." However, some potentially hopeful signs were revealed in our examination of occupation and education selectivity. Capitalizing on their potential strengths as service, administrative, and decision-making centers, we found North-Declining and several other categories of older central cities better able to hold onto their white collar residents than their blue collar residents; and there is a discernible tendency for some of these to attract greater shares of their metropolitan areas' nonblack professionals and college graduates as residents than in the past. In the main, however, status-selective nonblack suburbanization continues to occur in the nation's declining and old metropolitan areas.

A different question pertains to the younger low-density metropolitan areas in the nation's South and West. Have these areas' increased post-1970 suburbanization rates for nonblacks been accompanied by an accentuated status selectivity? The answer to this question varies by area. We found that in our South-Young areas, the 1970–1980 decade represented the beginning of a significant status-selective suburbanization, which was evident with all three socioeconomic status measures, and reflected, in large part, selectivity rises in the Texas "growth centers" (San Antonio, Dallas–Ft. Worth, Houston). West-Young areas showed no such tendency, however. The suburban locations for nonblacks in these areas continues to be relatively indifferent to the broad categories of income, occupation, and education.

Finally, we were interested in learning if the increased magnitude of black suburbanization in the 1970s was accompanied by the traditional "white" suburban selectivity on the three measures of social status. The answer to this question is a resounding "yes." It was found that: (1) black suburbanization in most metropolitan areas involved black residents at all status levels; and (2) black suburbanization increased progressively with increases in black residents' status. One exception to the first generalization is found in South-Young metropolitan areas wherein widespread black suburbanization has not yet taken place. At the other extreme lie South-Old areas which displayed substantial 1970–1980 suburban location shifts at all status levels.

Throughout this section we tended to discuss the selectivity processes of nonblack suburbanization and black suburbanization separately since these have evolved quite differently over time. Yet we wish to emphasize here something that was obvious in each of the status selectivity comparisons undertaken: *the proportion of blacks residing in the suburbs, at all measures of status, lies below (and generally well below) the proportion of nonblacks who reside in the suburbs at all levels of all measures of status.* This is true for all metropolitan area groupings in this study and for practically all individual metropolitan areas. Hence we find that, although black college graduates in North-Declining metropolitan areas increased their suburb proportions from .23 in 1970 to .30 in 1980, these lie well below the .44 suburb proportion displayed for nonblacks with less than seven years of schooling in 1970 (see Figure 9.5). The reality of this statistic, as with others presented in this section, should be plain. It implies that, despite the gains made in the magnitude and selectivity of black suburbanization over the 1970s, a great many more factors, other than their individual socioeconomic status disparities with nonblacks, are responsible for explaining the continued central city concentration of blacks within metropolitan areas.

Status Selectivity of Hispanic- and Asian-Americans

We now turn to the question of how the suburban location of Hispanic- and Asian-Americans is related to rising levels of income, and to greater duration of residence in the United States. Older European ethnic groups tended to disperse outward from the city center as they assimilated into the mainstream of American life. However, these spatial tendencies were generally observed in the older, politically fragmented metropolitan areas of the North, where both economics and the exclusionary practices of suburban communities relegated new, less well-off immigrant groups to central city locations until they had achieved sufficient status and income potential. These newer minority groups have tended to settle in a variety of metropolitan area contexts—many within the less politically fragmented Sunbelt areas. The fact that city–suburb socioeconomic disparities tend to be less accentuated in these areas suggests that income or status may not be as much of a prerequisite to suburban location for minority groups in these areas as in the North.

New York and Chicago

If status or long-term residence are related to suburban location in *any* context for Hispanic- or Asian-Americans, the relationships should be most evident in the northern areas wherein these groups are well represented. Hence, we shall first examine their suburban location patterns in the New York and Chicago metropolitan areas. Status relationships between income and suburban location can be examined in the two left-most plots in Figure 9.6, which show the proportion of residents (in families) living in the suburbs by six income levels for Hispanics, Asians, blacks, and non-Hispanic whites. These plots make

FIGURE 9.6

*Suburb Proportion of Hispanic, Recent Hispanic, Asian, Recent Asian,
and Non-Hispanic White 1980 Metropolitan Residents,[a] by Categories
of Family Income:[b] Selected Metropolitan Areas[c]*

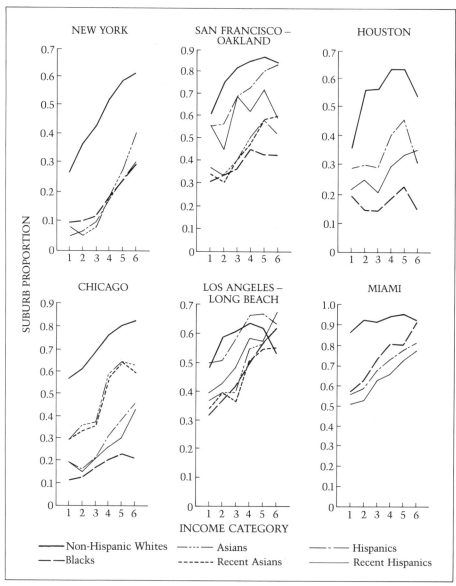

SOURCES: Machine-readable computer files: Census of Population and Housing, 1980,
Public Use Microdata Samples "A" and "B" (prepared by the U.S. Bureau of the Census,
Washington, DC).

[a]Recent Hispanics and Recent Asians are those who were born abroad and immigrated to
the United States since 1965.

[b]Income Categories (1979 dollars):
1. Under $6,000   4. $20,000–$29,999
2. $6,000–$11,999   5. $30,000–$49,999
3. $12,000–$19,999   6. $50,000 and over

[c]1970 Equivalent SMSA and Central City Definitions.

clear that there is a fairly direct relationship between income and suburban location for both Hispanics and Asians in these two North-Declining metropolitan areas. The relationship is slightly more accentuated for Asians than Hispanics in both areas, such that Asians at the highest income levels (those with family income greater than $50,000) are significantly more likely to reside in the suburbs than Hispanics or blacks. Yet, the strengths of the income-suburban location relationships for both immigrant groups (as is evident from their slopes on the plots) are greater than those shown for blacks, particularly in Chicago.

The relative levels of each group's suburban location by income category are noteworthy as well. In both of these areas each group's suburban location at a given income level is well below that shown for the non-Hispanic white population. Yet New York's pattern differs markedly from that of Chicago. In New York there is a vast disparity between the suburban location levels for non-Hispanic whites, on the one hand, and the three minority groups, Asians, Hispanics, and blacks, on the other. In Chicago, Asian and Hispanic suburbanization levels are intermediate between those of non-Hispanic whites, at the one extreme, and blacks at the other. The Chicago pattern for Asians and Hispanics clearly fits the traditional status-suburban location relationship that characterized the distribution of early European immigrant groups.

Our additional question regarding how well duration in the United States will relate to suburban location was also examined in the Chicago metropolitan area. The reader will find two additional lines on the Chicago plot in Figure 9.6 representing the suburban location patterns of recent Asian and recent Hispanic immigrants. These recently arrived residents represent Asians and Hispanics, registered in the 1980 census, who were born abroad but immigrated to the United States since 1965. The plots show that these recent minorities are only slightly less likely to reside in the suburbs at each income level than the total population of their respective ethnic groups. This suggests that, in Chicago, income is somewhat more important than recent immigration status in determining Asians' or Hispanics' suburban location. (Data not shown indicate a similar situation for New York.) However, because recent immigrants of these groups generally have lower incomes than their long-term residents, their residences will be more centrally located.

South and West Metropolitan Areas

Having established that Asians and Hispanics are following stereotypic suburban location relationships with income and recent immigration status in northern metropolitan areas, we turn to observe these relationships in selected Sunbelt areas. San Francisco–Oakland and Los Angeles–Long Beach are two such areas which housed large Asian and Hispanic populations in 1980. Pertinent plots for these areas appear in Figure 9.6. As our Chapter 8 examination pointed up, both of these western areas (although particularly Los Angeles–Long Beach) show less *overall* city–suburb separation for Hispanics, Asians, and blacks than do the typical northern areas; and suburban location patterns *for the population as a whole* are less related to socioeconomic status in these areas as well. Given these facts, we want to determine whether Asians' and Hispanics' socioeconomic status, or recent immigrant status, show any systematic relationship with suburban location in these areas, or whether the city–suburb distribution patterns of these new minorities in West Coast areas are relatively indifferent to traditional assimilation measures.

The plots in Figure 9.6 show that these measures *are* important in determining Asian and Hispanic suburban location in San Francisco–Oakland and Los Angeles–Long Beach. Moreover, recent immigrant status has an even greater effect on Hispanics' suburban location in these areas than it did in Chicago or New York. The slopes between income and suburban location are strongly positive for Hispanics and Asians; and within income categories, recent Hispanic immigrants to both of these areas tend to be much more likely to locate in the city than all Hispanic residents. The latter result provides strong confirmation that the traditional assimilation explanation is relevant to Hispanic location patterns in these areas. This is less the case for recent Asian immigrants to these areas, however. Their suburban location patterns are only slightly more city-concentrated than all Asians, within income levels.

The final two areas we examine, Houston and Miami, are in the South-Young metropolitan area grouping. Because Hispanics constitute the principal nonblack minority in these areas, our examination will focus on this group only. Houston represents one of the Texas "growth centers," which has just begun to exhibit a pattern of status-selective suburbanization in the 1970s, while showing a strong city-concentration of its black population at all status levels. Moreover, the data in the previous chapter's Table 8.7 showed the city–suburb separation of Hispanics in Houston (and in other South-Young areas where central cities have annexed considerable territory) to be somewhat more accentuated than in the two West Coast metropolitan areas just described. Within this context we wish to determine the extent to which rises in socioeconomic status of long-term residents are associated with greater suburban residence among Houston's Hispanic residents.

The plots for Houston show that its Hispanic population lies somewhere in between its black and non-Hispanic white population with regard to suburban access via status selectivity. All three populations exhibit reverse-U-shaped relationships between income and suburban selectivity where individuals with family incomes of between $20,000–$50,000 show greatest suburban locations. Yet variations in suburban location across income levels are much more extreme for non-Hispanic whites than they are for blacks, and lie somewhere in-between for Hispanics. Hence, among individuals making $20,000–$50,000 per year, 64 percent of non-Hispanic whites, 46 percent of Hispanics, and only 23 percent of blacks reside in Houston's suburbs. Clearly, the assimilation model of suburban location also applies to Hispanics in Houston, as it did in the other metropolitan areas we have examined. Further confirmation of this can be seen by observing the suburban locations of recent Hispanics, which lie below those for all Hispanics at most income levels.

Miami's suburban location patterns for non-Hispanic whites, blacks, and Hispanics must be viewed in the context of this area's unique racial and ethnic composition. Less than 20 percent of Miami's city population and just slightly more than half of its suburbs are composed of non-Hispanic whites, while Hispanics and blacks constitute the remainder. The Hispanic population of Miami is largely Cuban and began concentrating heavily in the city since 1959, while the black population continues to expand into highly segregated suburban communities and unincorporated areas.[25] Despite Miami's unique makeup, the city-suburb status selectivity of its blacks, Hispanics, and recent Hispanic immigrants all conform to the expected income-suburban location relationship. Indeed, it is only the "minority" non-Hispanic white population of Miami that does not conform to this pattern. White non-Hispanics at all income levels are highly dispersed within Miami's suburbs.

Discussion

The preceding review of Hispanic- and Asian-American suburban status selectivity, in selected metropolitan areas, suggests that the assimilation process is progressing for these two minorities. Hispanics and Asians in all areas show a consistent income-suburban location relationship although at somewhat different levels. This relationship was always as strong or stronger than that shown for the black population in these areas; and, in some instances (San Francisco–Oakland, Los

[25]Bernard and Rice, *Sunbelt Cities.*

315

Angeles–Long Beach, and Miami), the relationship was more accentuated than that shown for the metropolitan areas' non-Hispanic white population. Finally it was found that, among Hispanics in three of the four Sunbelt areas, suburban location was significantly related to length of residence in the United States, even after income has been taken into account. This review suggests that, although metropolitan areas differ in the extent to which non-Hispanic white suburbanization levels are greater than those for Hispanics and Asians, a positive relationship generally exists between income and suburban location for these two "newer" minority groups.

Summary of Race and Status-Selective Suburbanization

In this chapter and the previous one, we have examined the race and status selectivity of city–suburb redistribution in the context of post-1970 shifts in race relations and suburban preferences. The postwar pattern of black city concentration, coupled with middle-class "white flight," it was thought, might subside during a decade in which greater numbers of blacks entered the middle class, suburban fair housing practices became more pervasive, and white young adult urban residents appeared to be placing greater emphasis on their careers than on parenthood. Of course, these societywide shifts should lead to different redistribution consequences in metropolitan areas with different demographic and economic development histories. For this reason, we have examined race-selective shifts within each of the six metropolitan area groupings, designated in Chapter 7, as well as for selected individual metropolitan areas. We also examined post-1970 status selectivity for blacks, for nonblacks, as well as for the newer minorities—Hispanics and Asians—in an effort to assess the extent to which minority suburbanization has spread across all income and status levels.

Greatest attention in this analysis was given to selectivity shifts in the North-Declining area grouping, which contains most of the "problem" metropolitan areas. Because each of the 13 areas in this grouping sustained metropolitanwide losses in the 1970s for nonblacks, it was felt that conditions were especially ripe for: (1) a dispersal of their previously city-concentrated black populations to a softer suburban housing market; and (2) a selective "return to the city" of well-off nonblacks, attracted to those areas that serve as nodal centers. Our analysis revealed strong support for only the first of these two conjectures. Indeed, we found the 1970s to be a "benchmark" decade for black suburbanization. The magnitude of the 1970–1980 black suburbanization shift outdistanced that shown in any previous postwar decade, and participation in this movement was not limited to only the most well-off segments of the black population.

Evidence supporting any 1970s nonblack "return to the city" in North-Declining metropolitan areas has been meager at best. It is true that the pace of nonblack suburbanization has declined in these areas compared to the 1950s and 1960s. In an environment of metropolitan-wide nonblack decline, most areas' suburbs were sustaining either very modest growth or declines in their nonblack populations. However, the income differentials associated with 1970s nonblack suburbanization served to reinforce the city–suburb status gap that existed at the beginning of the decade. There is *some* suggestion that a select—although not numerically large—nonblack city return might be in the offing among young adult professionals and college graduates. Evidence of this pattern is particularly discernible among the 1975–1980 nonblack movers and inmigrants to these metropolitan areas. Moreover, while North-Declining cities are sustaining losses of nonblack male residents that are employed in all major occupations, these losses are most accentuated for blue collar rather than white collar workers, suggesting that these cities are doing a better job of retaining residents whose skills are most compatible with white collar city jobs.

The South-Old metropolitan area class represents the second metropolitan area grouping that contains distressed and depopulating central cities. While each of the four areas in this class sustained nonblack metropolitanwide gains in the 1970s, their constricted city boundaries coupled with high postwar levels of "white flight" left these areas with wide racial and socioeconomic city–suburb disparities at the time of the 1970 census. In this context, continued high 1970s black migration into these areas could be expected to induce a "spill-over" of blacks into the suburbs. Indeed, the latter has occurred in an even more pervasive manner than was seen in North-Declining areas. Black suburbanward relocation increased dramatically over the 1970–1980 period at all status levels.

The 1970s nonblack suburbanization in South-Old areas tapered off somewhat from earlier levels. Again, it was expected that this would lead to selective nonblack "return to the city" within these areas which—like North-Declining areas—increased their city–suburb status gaps during each postwar decade. The main change in nonblack suburbanization over the 1970–1980 decade in these areas was an increased outward redistribution of less well-off and blue collar whites, serving to "flatten" the relationship between residents' income and suburban location. However, one also finds in these areas the suggestion that young professionals and college graduates who recently moved are less inclined to suburbanize than other nonblack city residents.

The other older metropolitan area groupings, North-Old and West-Old areas, house far fewer blacks than the groupings just reviewed. Yet, these areas are becoming increasingly popular as destinations for black intermetropolitan migrants and, as aggregate groupings, show the increased black suburbanization observed in North-Declining and South-Old areas. The two individual West Coast areas that do house large black populations displayed divergent suburbanization patterns. San Francisco–Oakland's 1970–1980 black suburbanization is a relatively modest one, which has altered neither the magnitude nor the status selectivity of black suburban representation to the extent that this is evident in Los Angeles–Long Beach—where in 1980 high-income blacks are *more* likely to live in the suburbs than high-income nonblacks. The 1970–1980 suburbanization of nonblacks in the North-Old and West-Old groupings, like other older areas, have become more moderated over time. The status selectivity in North-Old areas bears a striking resemblance to that for North-Declining areas, while the status selectivity pattern shown for the aggregated West-Old group has exhibited a smaller shift over time. Yet in neither area grouping is the 1970–1980 city–suburb status gap nearly as large as that observed in the North-Declining and South-Old metropolitan area groupings.

The race and status selectivity observed for the fast-growing Sunbelt metropolitan area groupings contrasts markedly with the patterns just reviewed. For the South-Young areas, the 1970–1980 decade represents the beginning of status-selective suburbanization. Although a small city-suburb status gap existed in these areas prior to 1970, the gap increased significantly over the post-1970 decade due to a nonblack suburban selectivity pattern which resembled that of North-Declining areas in earlier decades. In contrast to this nonblack suburbanization, 1970–1980 black suburbanization in South-Young areas was modest and not pervasive. The black suburbanization that did occur in these areas could be classified as an "upper-status-only" suburbanization. West-Young areas differ strikingly from South-Young areas in post-1970 status selectivity. The 1980 suburban locations of nonblacks in these areas, like their 1970 locations, were relatively indifferent to income or educational attainment levels and varied only marginally by occupation. These areas had relatively few blacks but, like other area groupings, exhibit an increased 1970s black suburbanization. Taken as a whole, however, the 1980 city–suburb status gaps for West-Young metropolitan areas represent the smallest of the six metropolitan area groupings.

Our analysis of black suburbanization in Chapters 8 and 9 has shown a substantial increase in its magnitude across all status levels of blacks, and a selectivity pattern that resembles nonblack suburban selectivity in the 1950s and 1960s. Yet one should not conclude from these analyses that the well-known patterns of city–suburb racial separation and neighborhood racial segregation that characterized Old and Declining metropolitan areas during the immediate postwar decades will soon be coming to an end. This would be confusing redistribution processes with redistribution outcomes. While the process of black suburbanization has increased markedly during the 1970s, this chapter has also shown that (a) the proportion of blacks residing in the suburbs lies well below the nonblack proportion at all status levels for most metropolitan areas; (b) black–nonblack neighborhood segregation indices declined only minimally over the 1970–1980 period in areas with large numbers of blacks; (c) black–nonblack city–suburb separation declined moderately in some areas and increased in others; and (d) blacks are more segregated than Hispanics and Asians in areas that have large numbers of each group. Clearly black–nonblack residential segregation patterns are far from being eliminated. However, the process has begun. It is for this reason that we consider the 1970s to be a "benchmark" decade for black–nonblack residential redistribution.

Our analysis purposely focused on aggregate redistribution patterns for "groupings" of metropolitan areas in order to highlight redistribution patterns that are representative of residents in areas with similar demographic and economic development histories. Although we also pointed up individual metropolitan area patterns, there is a danger in extrapolating too much from an individual area's experience. An analysis of Detroit only, for example, would leave the suggestion that 1970s race- and status-selective redistribution in metropolitan areas has not changed significantly since the 1950s. However, an analysis of Washington, DC, only, would lead one to believe that black suburbanization will be accompanied by a wholesale nonblack "gentrification" movement. The more pervasive situation found in the aggregation of all older "problem" metropolitan areas lies somewhere in between these two extremes. Indeed, we have found significant increases in black suburbanization but only a hint of the selective nonblack "return to the city."

The major trends in race and status selectivity described in Chapters 8 and 9 represent, to some degree, indirect outcomes of other fundamental shifts in society as a whole. One of these shifts pertains to changing household formation and composition patterns entered into by both nonblack and black metropolitan area residents during the 1970s. Another one is linked to the changing composition of employment opportunities in large metropolitan areas. Although we have alluded to these household and employment shifts in evaluating race- and status-selective population changes, the chapters that follow will examine these dimensions of the city–suburb redistribution process in more explicit detail.

10

HOUSEHOLD
AND FAMILY DIMENSIONS
OF CITY–SUBURB REDISTRIBUTION

Introduction

Wɪᴛʜ this chapter we change the focus from the city–suburb redistribution of population to the redistribution of households and families. The post-1970 era has brought with it rather striking societywide shifts in both the magnitudes and compositions of households; some of these shifts hold significant implications for the intrametropolitan redistribution process.[1] First of all, there was a rapid rise in the number of households formed in the post-1970 years. Part of this rise can be attributed to the fact that members of the large post–World War II baby-boom cohorts had, during this period, advanced into peak household formation ages, establishing their own new households and creating parental "empty nests" in their wake. Hence, a shift in the age composition of the nation's population is partially responsible for the larger numbers of households.

Another more important constellation of societywide changes was set in motion during the 1970s and served to increase the number of households even further. These changes arose from the more flexible lifestyles that became possible with lower levels of fertility, greater career opportunities for women, the more widespread acceptance of di-

---

[1]For an insightful discussion which suggests how these shifts might affect the future of urban form, see William Alonso, "The Population Factor and Urban Structure," in Arthur P. Solomon, ed., *The Prospective City: Economy, Population, Energy and Environmental Developments* (Cambridge, MA: MIT Press, 1980).

vorce, the greater pervasiveness of "singles" living among the young and middle-aged, and the greater means to maintain an independent residence among the elderly. This set of changes, which we will designate as "shifts in living arrangement preferences," has led to greater numbers of smaller households, and greater percentages of childless and nonfamily households. Taken together, these changes in "age composition" and "living arrangement preference" have brought about post-1970 rates of household growth that substantially exceeded rates of population growth for the nation as a whole and for individual metropolitan areas. However, it is the second of these two changes that is likely to exert the greatest impact on the city–suburb redistribution process, because it affects the composition of metropolitan households as well as their numbers.

The analyses in this chapter will examine how post-1970 shifts in the number and composition of households have begun to affect the city–suburb redistribution process in the nation's 39 largest metropolitan areas, with particular concern given to the large "problem" areas in the North-Declining and South-Old groupings. On the surface, one might assume that an increase in the number of households formed should serve to counter the effects of widespread population losses which central cities of these metropolitan areas have sustained during the 1970s. The number of households in a city is sometimes viewed to be more important than the number of people in a city for the purposes of assessing its housing market and tax base, or as a general measure of the city's growth.

However, as we shall see in the analyses below, it is important to examine the geographic selectivity associated with each household type rather than the magnitude and redistribution of households per se. Clearly, the strong suburban selectivity among middle-class child-rearing families in the 1950s had a substantial impact on postwar suburbanization. This is obvious from Janet Abu-Lughod and Mary Mix Foley's review of consumer groups' home-buying patterns during this period:

> The family with children, seeking an owned home, represents the major force in the expansion of the suburbs. In the postwar boom era just passed, lack of suitable rental quarters, a prosperous economy, and liberal Federal mortgage insurance for new construction combined to make suburban homeownership feasible for a great many young families of modest income. Even so, the market could hardly have emerged without a widespread preference for the new, single-family-owned home in the suburbs.
>
> In retrospect, then, this particular consumer is seen to have had the most dramatic of effects on the recent development of the metro-

politan pattern. To a great extent, he can be counted responsible, even though innocently so, for the wholesale transformation of open country into the subdivision landscape now encircling most cities.[2]

Of course, the strong impact these family-oriented households' preferences made on suburbanization was facilitated by the fact that such households dominated the *composition* of housing demand during the 1950s. The proportion of the United States population residing in full-family households (husband-wife families with the presence of children) was greater in the 1950s and 1960s than in periods immediately preceding or following.[3] The average woman of marriageable age in the 1950s was more likely to marry, married at an earlier age, began to bear children at an earlier age, bore more children, and registered the longest period of childrearing than was the case for women in any decade since 1910.[4] Hence, the type of housing that was becoming available in the nation's burgeoning suburban stretches in the immediate postwar decades—low-cost, low-density single-family housing—was precisely the type of housing in demand among a household population that placed a strong emphasis on family and childrearing activities.

Recent shifts in the composition of the nation's household population make plain that the strong family orientation and living arrangements, which characterized the 1950s and most of the 1960s, has disintegrated markedly in the decade of the 1970s.[5] Post-1970 household-composition trends reveal continually declining shares of full families with children and more childless-couple families, family households headed by only one adult, and nonfamily households (households comprised of one or more unrelated individuals). Although married-couple families accounted for better than 50 percent of the increase in total households over the 20-year period, 1950–1970, their contribution has dropped to less than 25 percent of the household increase observed over the 1970–1980 decade. Underlying this trend are a series of life course-related changes which represent a de-emphasis of family membership and childrearing in household living arrangements. These

[2]Janet Abu-Lughod and Mary Mix Foley, "Consumer Strategies," in Nelson N. Foote, Janet Abu-Lughod, Mary Mix Foley, and Louis Winnick, eds., *Housing Choices and Housing Constraints, Part Two* (New York: McGraw-Hill, 1960).
[3]George Masnick and Mary Jo Bane, *The Nation's Families: 1960–1980* (Cambridge, MA: Joint Center for Urban Studies of MIT and Harvard, 1980).
[4]Paul C. Glick, "Updating the Family Life Cycle," *Journal of Marriage and the Family* 39 (1977):5–13.
[5]Glick, "Updating the Family Life Cycle"; Frances E. Kobrin, "The Primary Individual and the Family: Changes in Living Arrangements in the United States Since 1940," *Journal of Marriage and the Family* 38 (1976):233–239; Arthur J. Norton, "Family Life Cycle: 1980," *Journal of Marriage and the Family* 45 (1983):267–275; and Arland Thornton and Deborah Freedman, "The Changing American Family," *Population Bulletin* 38(4) (Washington, DC: Population Reference Bureau, 1983).

include: delayed marriage and childbearing, fewer children, greater incidence of divorce, and an increase in the proportion of people who never marry or remain childless.

It is the new diversity of household types and the location preferences associated with each type that hold the potential for changes in the intrametropolitan redistribution process.[6] Some of these changes could benefit declining central cities by augmenting their household populations with small, childless, moderate- to high-income households that can contribute more to the city's economy than they consume. Without children and the need for a detached single-family dwelling unit, a low-density neighborhood, and a high-quality school system, such households, to a greater degree than their full-family counterparts, could well be attracted to the city and its central location advantages of proximity to workplace, transportation, and entertainment. Indeed, it is the large number of nonfamily and childless-couple households, which began forming during the 1970s, that were expected to constitute the target groups for the select return to the city of young urban professionals, discussed in the previous chapter. While the population redistribution patterns analyzed in that chapter did not display evidence of a discernible status-selective "return," they did hint that a more moderate cityward distribution was in the offing. The present chapter will examine more explicitly the household selectivity patterns associated with this process.

There is, however, another post-1970 change in the composition of metropolitan households that holds potential negative consequences for the central city's economy, and may serve to reinforce the "vicious cycle" of race- and status-selective city–suburb redistribution that operated in the 1950s and 1960s. We refer here to the dramatic increase in the number of female-headed family households which is particularly evident among the black population. Of all black household types, female-headed families have benefited least from overall black gains in income and economic well-being.[7] Yet, as a result of trends toward nonmarriage, delayed marriage, and fewer remarriages after divorce among

[6]Although there have been slight modifications, over time, in census definitions of household types (see 1980 Census of Population and Housing, 1982 *User's Guide*, PHC-R1-B, Part B, Glossary) a household is generally regarded as the person or persons who occupy a housing unit, such that the number of households is identical to the number of occupied housing units. A *family household* is a household that contains a family (two or more related individuals), and can be classed by type of family, such as married-couple family. (Family households may also contain subfamilies and unrelated individuals.) A *nonfamily household* consists of a person living alone or with one or more unrelated individuals. The term "full-family household" is not a census definition, but is used here to denote a particular type of family household comprising a married couple living with one or more of their own children under 18.

[7]Reynolds Farley, *Blacks and Whites: Narrowing the Gap?* (Cambridge, MA: Harvard University Press, 1984).

black females, these households have grown by 85 percent during the 1970s, and constitute 29 percent of all black households in 1980.[8] Black female-headed families, by virtue of their large numbers and disadvantaged economic status, are particularly likely to exacerbate the city concentration of the least well-off metropolitan area blacks—irrespective of societywide trends which have led to a greater 1970s suburbanization of blacks overall. While the Chapter 9 analysis indicated that blacks of all socioeconomic categories have participated in the post-1970 black suburbanization movement, it did not take black household composition into explicit account. The examination in this chapter will pay particular attention to city–suburb redistribution patterns of blacks by household type.

The potential consequences, both positive and negative, that changes in the composition of households hold for the city–suburb redistribution process should be most accentuated in "problem" metropolitan areas in our study. These areas, by virtue of their development histories, had shown a strong city–suburb differentiation in their family and household status compositions even prior to World War II. As the selective "white flight" of middle-class, family-forming households continued through the 1950s and 1960s, the cities in these problem areas came to house increasingly disproportionate shares of nonfamily white households and blacks of all household types.[9] These long-standing city–suburb disparities aside, metropolitan areas in both North-Declining and South-Old groupings hold a strong potential for inner-city residential development which can be attractive to the rising numbers of small, nonfamily oriented households. This is especially true among areas that serve as nodal centers (discussed in Chapter 7). In the growing Sunbelt metropolitan area groupings, however, the rising demand for housing, brought about by an increased 1970s household growth, may serve to exacerbate the selective suburbanization of households.

Each of the sections that follows will focus on a particular aspect of household selective city–suburb redistribution. The section on redistribution of households and population will provide an overview of the post-1970 shifts in household growth and redistribution for metropolitan areas in our six area groupings. The section on family and nonfam-

---

[8]Nonblack female-headed families have also risen significantly over this period, yet they constituted only 8.5 percent of all nonblack households in 1980, and registered lower levels of poverty than black female-headed households.

[9]Avery M. Guest, "Patterns of Family Location," *Demography* 9 (1972):159–171; William H. Frey and Frances E. Kobrin, "Changing Families and Changing Mobility: Their Impact on the Central City," *Demography* 19 (1982):261–277; and William H. Frey, "Mover Destination Selectivity and the Changing Suburbanization of Metropolitan Whites and Blacks," *Demography* 22(2) (1985):223–243.

ily households contrasts the redistribution patterns of family and nonfamily households over this period and addresses the question: Are cities more able to retain nonfamily households than family households, in the post-1970 period, as the former are growing more rapidly, metropolitanwide? The section on household type redistribution by race provides a more detailed evaluation of household type redistribution shifts over the 1970–1980 decade, examining nonblack and black patterns separately. In the section on the nonblack "return to the city," we focus specifically on the question: Have the increased numbers of non-black nonfamily households and their geographic selectivity patterns contributed to a household return to the city during the 1970s? It examines the age and household structure of post-1970 nonblack household shifts in North-Declining metropolitan areas and in selected areas that are conducive to such a "return." Finally in the section on the city concentration of poverty, we turn to the redistribution of poor households, in order to determine how shifts in household structure are facilitating either a concentration or deconcentration of metropolitan poverty.

Redistribution of Households and Population

The heightened growth of households relative to population in the post-1970 period is evident for the nation as a whole as well as for individual metropolitan areas. During the 1950s rates of population and household growth were not terribly different from each other—18.5 percent and 21.1 percent, respectively, for the United States as a whole. In the 1960s, as fertility declined somewhat, the country's population growth dipped to 13.4 percent while its household growth only fell to 20.2 percent. The most dramatic shifts, however, took place in the 1970–1980 decade. Continued fertility decline was most responsible for reducing population growth during this period to 11.4 percent, while the growth in the nation's households rose to 27.4 percent—higher than the two previous decades.[10] As indicated above, this 1970s rise in household growth can be attributed to the postwar baby-boom generation "coming of age" and to the tendency for adults at all ages to arrange themselves into larger numbers of smaller households.[11] Hence, this

[10]The statistics cited in this paragraph were obtained in: U.S. Bureau of the Census, *Statistical Abstract*, 1984.

[11]While the latter tendency toward more and smaller households occurred at all ages, it was most prevalent among adults below age 35 (those in the peak household-formation years), and among elderly adults aged 65 and above. See Frances E. Kobrin, "The Fall of Household Size and the Rise of the Primary Individual in the United States," *Demography* 13 (1976):127–138; and Frances E. Kobrin, "Family Extension and the Elderly: Economic, Demographic, and Family Cycle Factors," *Journal of Gerontology* 6 (1981):370–377.

divergence of nationwide population and household growth trends in the 1970s has somewhat different origins. A secular decline in national fertility levels is more responsible for the former, while shifts in living arrangement preferences, coupled with a changing national age composition during this period, are responsible for the latter.[12]

Still another demographic factor—migration—is responsible for affecting both household and population growth in individual metropolitan areas. Yet, migration had a less direct influence on metropolitan area household growth than it had on population growth in the 1970s. This is because the "age composition" and "living arrangement preference" shifts that accounted for the increased nationwide household growth also occurred among the *nonmigrating* adult populations in both growing and declining metropolitan areas. Certainly, metropolitan areas that sustain high population inmigration will exhibit greater levels of household growth than areas that suffer population outmigration. However, household growth is not dependent on population inmigration, and its level is not directly proportional to the level of population inmigration.[13] This can be seen in Table 10.1 and Figure 10.1 which show that, while the ratio of household growth to population growth has increased markedly during the 1970s decade for areas with growing populations, household growth also remains positive for areas that suffered 1970s population losses.[14]

Suburbanization of Households and Population

The relevant question for the city–suburb redistribution process, then, is: To what extent are the central cities of these metropolitan areas benefiting from this post-1970s household growth? This is a particularly crucial question for cities of the declining metropolitan areas, which have sustained significant losses in their populations during the 1970–1980 decade. The answer can be assessed from the suburbaniza-

---

[12]It might be argued that shifts in adult living arrangement preferences and lowered fertility are affected by the same societal influences (see Alonso, "The Population Factor and Urban Structure," p. 37). However, from a demographic accounting point of view, they represent different factors.

[13]This point is underscored in a demographic decomposition analysis of 1970–1980 household growth for the 50 states undertaken by George Masnick, *The Demographic Factor in Household Growth*, Working Paper No. W83-3 (Cambridge, MA: Joint Center for Urban Studies of M.I.T. and Harvard, 1983). Masnick finds that in most inmigration states, migration accounts for less than 50 percent of these states' household growth (the three exceptions are Florida, Arizona, and Nevada); and that in all outmigration states, the negative contributions of outmigration to household growth are counterbalanced by the positive contributions of age composition and of household formation (what we have termed as "shifts in living-arrangement preferences").

[14]A comparison of Appendix E, Table E.10B with Table 7.A shows that these assertions are also true for the 39 individual metropolitan areas.

TABLE 10.1

Percent Change in Households and Population for Metropolitan Area,
1950–1960, 1960–1970, 1970–1980: Six Metropolitan Area Groupings

Metropolitan Area[a] Groupings	1950–1960	1960–1970	1970–1980
NORTH-DECLINING			
Households	+24.0	+14.2	+9.2
Population	+17.2	+9.7	−3.2
NORTH-OLD			
Households	+31.1	+24.1	+22.6
Population	+29.3	+19.8	+5.4
SOUTH-OLD			
Households	+36.3	+36.4	+28.4
Population	+31.2	+27.3	+10.9
WEST-OLD			
Households	+39.4	+23.9	+20.9
Population	+36.6	+19.7	+10.0
SOUTH-YOUNG			
Households	+66.2	+45.0	+54.3
Population	+61.0	+37.8	+35.5
WEST-YOUNG			
Households	+98.2	+59.5	+56.8
Population	+103.0	+50.9	+35.7

SOURCES: Same as Figure 10.1.

[a]These metropolitan area groupings are based on three categories of region (North, South, West), two categories of age (Old, Young), and two categories of metropolitan growth (Declining, Nondeclining). All 13 Declining areas are also Old and located in the North and are placed in the North-Declining grouping. The remaining 26 areas are all Nondeclining and sorted into the groupings: North-Old, South-Old, West-Old, South-Young, and West-Young. Further details are provided in the Chapter 7 section, "A Metropolitan Area Typology," and in Figure 7.1.

tion rates presented in Table 10.2. These rates show that, at least in the 1950s, household suburbanization occurred to a lesser degree than population suburbanization for the North-Declining metropolitan area grouping. Similar results shown for North-Old, South-Old, and West-Old metropolitan areas are consistent with the fact that, during the 1950s, larger childrearing family households were suburbanizing to a greater degree than smaller households.

This household-population suburbanization difference was far less

FIGURE 10.1

Population and Households, Metropolitan Areas and Central Cities, 1950, 1960, 1970, 1980: Six Metropolitan Area Groupings

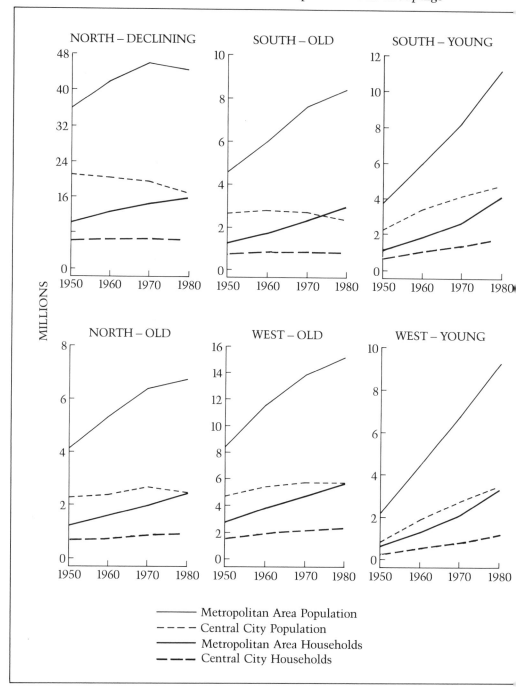

SOURCES: Machine-readable computer files; *County and City Data Book*, Consolidated Files for Counties, 1947–1977, and Cities, 1944–1947; and *County and City Data Book*, 1983 files (prepared by the U.S. Bureau of the Census, Washington, DC).

TABLE 10.2

Percent Change in Households and Population for Central City and Suburbs, 1950–1960, 1960–1970, 1970–1980: Six Metropolitan Area Groupings

Metropolitan Area Groupings	Central City			Suburbs			Suburbanization Rate[a]		
	1950–1960	1960–1970	1970–1980	1950–1960	1960–1970	1970–1980	1950–1960	1960–1970	1970–1980
NORTH-DECLINING									
Households	+7.6	+1.3	−4.2	+49.0	+28.2	+20.8	+41.4	+26.8	+24.9
Population	−3.4	−4.1	−13.3	+46.9	+22.8	+4.3	+50.3	+26.9	+17.6
NORTH-OLD									
Households	+12.2	+18.6	+5.4	+55.8	+29.3	+37.4	+43.6	+10.7	+32.0
Population	+4.9	+12.8	−7.3	+59.0	+25.5	+14.6	+54.1	+12.7	+21.9
SOUTH-OLD									
Households	+14.9	+4.8	−0.2	+68.0	+68.2	+46.5	+53.1	+63.4	+46.6
Population	+6.2	−2.4	−12.5	+65.9	+53.6	+24.1	+59.7	+56.0	+36.5
WEST-OLD									
Households	+24.1	+11.6	+8.6	+60.1	+36.8	+31.5	+35.9	+25.2	+22.9
Population	+15.8	+6.6	+0.6	+62.7	+31.2	+16.7	+46.9	+24.6	+16.1
SOUTH-YOUNG									
Households	+57.9	+29.2	+30.9	+79.4	+67.5	+79.9	+21.5	+38.4	+49.0
Population	+53.1	+22.5	+14.3	+73.1	+58.2	+57.5	+20.0	+35.7	+43.2
WEST-YOUNG									
Households	+113.7	+47.7	+43.2	+87.2	+69.0	+66.3	−26.4	+21.3	+23.1
Population	+120.5	+43.4	+26.9	+91.5	+56.6	+41.7	−29.0	+13.2	+14.8

SOURCES: Same as Figure 10.1.

[a]Suburbanization Rate: Suburb Percent Change minus Central City Percent Change.

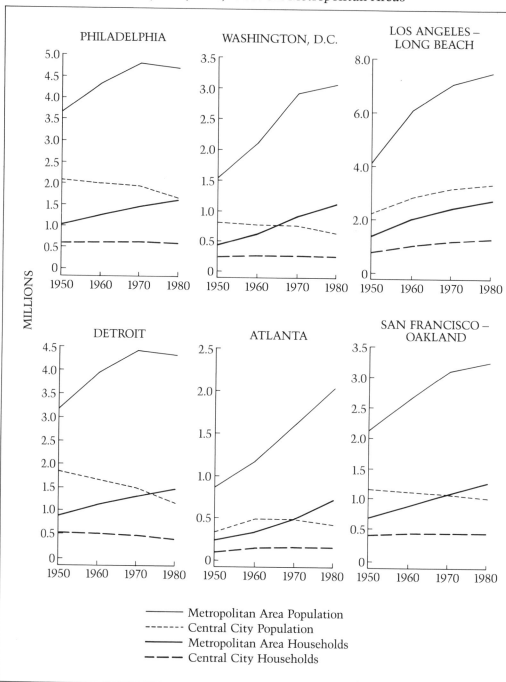

FIGURE 10.2

*Population and Households, Metropolitan Areas and Central Cities,
1950, 1960, 1970, 1980: Six Metropolitan Areas*

PHILADELPHIA

WASHINGTON, D.C.

LOS ANGELES –
LONG BEACH

MILLIONS

DETROIT

ATLANTA

SAN FRANCISCO –
OAKLAND

———— Metropolitan Area Population
------- Central City Population
━━━━ Metropolitan Area Households
━ ━ ━ Central City Households

SOURCES: Same as Figure 10.1.

evident in the 1960s when three of the four Declining and Old metropolitan area groupings show relatively similar suburbanization rates for both households and population, and a fourth—the South-Old grouping—exhibited a higher suburbanization rate for households. Yet in the 1970–1980 decade, when metropolitan household growth levels were substantially higher than metropolitan population growth levels, we find that households were suburbanizing to a *greater* degree than the population in all four metropolitan area groupings. This somewhat unexpected pattern is attributable, in part, to a rise in the number of suburban "empty-nest" households that were created during the 1970s. However, it also suggests that the smaller households formed by young adults during this period found the suburbs to be an attractive location, such that cities are not attracting a disproportionate share of these new households.

Central city household stocks have, nevertheless, benefited from the post-1970 growth in metropolitan households. Although the city's share of the newly forming households had declined from that shown in earlier decades, central cities in all four Declining and Old metropolitan area groupings exhibit higher levels of growth (or lower levels of decline) for households than for populations in the 1970–1980 period. (See Figure 10.1 and the third column of Table 10.2.) North-Declining cities, for example, lost 13.3 percent of their populations during this decade but only 4.2 percent of their households; West-Old cities, as a group, added only 0.6 percent to their population over the 1970s decade and, at the same time, added 8.6 percent to their household stocks. Central city household and population trends for individual metropolitan areas are displayed in Figure 10.2 (and the respective percent change rates for all 39 metropolitan areas can be found in Appendix E, Table 10.B and Appendix E, Table 7.B). These comparisons indicate that central city household stocks within Old and Declining metropolitan areas fare far better than their populations during the 1970–1980 decade.

We turn now to the city–suburb redistribution of households in South-Young and West-Young areas. Both of these growing Sunbelt metropolitan area groupings sustained greater rates of household growth than population growth, metropolitanwide, over the 1970s—at levels that were exceptionally high in comparison to other metropolitan area groupings. Both areas also exhibited greater levels of household suburbanization than population suburbanization during the 1950s and 1960s (see the suburbanization rates in Table 10.2). Yet, because neither of these areas experienced a widespread suburbanization of larger households in the 1950s, their central cities housed relatively similar shares of their metropolitan areas' households and populations in both 1970 and 1980. Each area groupings' central cities *and* suburbs benefited from substantially higher levels of household growth and population growth in the 1970–1980 period.

Person-to-Household Ratios

The divergent post-1970 trends toward declining populations and increasing numbers of households suggest that smaller person-to-household ratios should become pervasive in all areas. For the nation as a whole, the person-to-household ratio has declined significantly over the 1950–1980 period—from 3.4 to 2.8. However, 62 percent of this decline took place over the 1970s decade, as person-to-household ratios were reduced from 3.1 to 2.8. Given what we have observed thus far in this section, we might anticipate that the large city–suburb disparities in person-to-household ratios—arising from the widespread suburbanization of families during the 1950s and 1960s—may have subsided during the 1970s. This should result from the reduced household sizes in all parts of the metropolitan area, as well as from the greater suburbanization of households than population during the 1970s.

The person-to-household ratios shown in Table 10.3 bear out these expectations. While suburb–city disparities for the North-Declining and three Old metropolitan area groupings widened substantially over the 1950–1970 period, these disparities were reduced in the 1970s. The immediate postwar widening of these disparities was primarily the result of reduced city ratios—effected by the suburbanward redistribution (or a greater formation in the suburbs) of the metropolitan area's larger family-building households. In the 1970s suburban person-to-household ratios declined to a greater degree than central city ratios—resulting in a narrower suburb–city person-to-household ratio disparity. For the "Young" areas in the South and West, there has never been a strong city–suburb disparity in person-to-household ratios. Here, secular trends toward smaller household sizes have affected central cities and suburbs in similar ways.

Discussion

In the preceding section we have shown how 1970–1980 shifts in household and population growth and redistribution have begun to diverge from trends observed in the immediate postwar decades. Greater household than population growth, metropolitanwide, has served to cushion the effects of declining population growth on household stocks in large metropolitan areas of all categories. While most of the metropolitan areas in our North-Declining area grouping sustained population losses during the 1970s, all of these areas enjoyed gains in

TABLE 10.3

Person-to-Household Ratios for Cities and Suburbs, 1950, 1960, 1970, 1980: Six Metropolitan Area Groupings

Metropolitan Area Groupings/Ratios Differences in Ratios	1950		1960		1970		1980	
	City	Suburb	City	Suburb	City	Suburb	City	Suburb
NORTH-DECLINING								
Person–Household Ratio (Suburb–City Diff.)	3.4	3.6 (+0.2)	3.1	3.5 (+0.4)	2.9	3.4 (+0.5)	2.6	2.9 (+0.3)
NORTH-OLD								
Person–Household Ratio (Suburb–City Diff.)	3.3	3.5 (+0.2)	3.1	3.6 (+0.5)	2.9	3.5 (+0.6)	2.6	2.9 (+0.3)
SOUTH-OLD								
Person–Household Ratio (Suburb–City Diff.)	3.5	3.8 (+0.3)	3.3	3.7 (+0.4)	3.0	3.4 (+0.4)	2.7	2.9 (+0.2)
WEST-OLD								
Person–Household Ratio (Suburb–City Diff.)	3.0	3.2 (+0.2)	2.8	3.3 (+0.5)	2.7	3.2 (+0.5)	2.5	2.8 (+0.3)
SOUTH-YOUNG								
Person–Household Ratio (Suburb–City Diff.)	3.3	3.5 (+0.2)	3.2	3.4 (+0.2)	3.0	3.2 (+0.2)	2.6	2.8 (+0.2)
WEST-YOUNG								
Person–Household Ratio (Suburb–City Diff.)	3.2	3.4 (+0.2)	3.3	3.5 (+0.2)	3.2	3.3 (+0.1)	2.8	2.8 (0.0)

SOURCES: Same as Figure 10.1.

their numbers of households. Areas that exhibited only moderate population gains during the 1970s exhibited significantly higher levels of household growth. Nevertheless, metropolitan gains in the number of households were disproportionately allocated to the suburbs. The suburbanization of households, in fact, exceeded the suburbanization of population. This suggests that, in contrast to the immediate postwar period, small newly forming households in the 1970s were finding the suburbs to be a more attractive residential location. Although central cities in Old and Declining metropolitan areas continue to exhibit smaller person-to-household ratios than their surrounding suburbs in 1980, the city–suburb disparity has begun to diminish as new cohorts of smaller households find the suburbs more attractive, and more "empty-nest" and elderly "surviving-spouse" households form in the suburbs. Still, the central cities of these areas are able to retain enough of their metropolitan areas' household growth to sustain gains or only modest declines in their household stocks. The household growth "cushion" of the post–1970 period, therefore, has had a beneficial effect on both central cities and suburbs.

Family and Nonfamily Households

While the foregoing discussion focused on the changing magnitude of household growth and its effects on city–suburb redistribution, the next two sections examine the redistribution implications of the changing compositions of households. Perhaps the most significant shift in household composition involves a dramatic increase in nonfamily households comprised of one or more unrelated individuals. The vast majority of such households (86 percent in 1980) consist of only one person living alone. Nonfamily households have increased by 78 percent during the 1970–1980 period and constituted 26 percent of all households at the time the 1980 census was taken. This rise in nonfamily households can be attributed to a greater tendency for individuals to establish their own residences at both ends of the traditional family life cycle.[15] At the beginning end—prior to marriage—young people become increasingly likely to establish separate residences apart from their parents[16]; and at the terminal end—after one marital partner dies—the

[15]Kobrin, "The Primary Individual and the Family"; and Thornton and Freedman, "The Changing American Family."

[16]Since 1970 an increasing number of men and women have been living together as unmarried couples, for the most part prior to marriage and in the young adult ages. Indirect estimates suggest that unmarried couples constituted 2.0 percent of all households, and 7.5 percent of all nonfamily households in 1980, compared with 0.8 percent and 4.3 percent, respectively, in 1970.

surviving spouse is more likely to reside on his or her own than was the case in the past. Delays in marriage, extended life expectancies, and the greater incidence of divorce have led Americans to live increasing portions of their adult lives in nonfamily households.

Our discussion here will examine the implications that the rising numbers of the nonfamily households hold for the intrametropolitan redistribution process. The data in Table 10.4 show that nonfamily households have been growing faster than family households in all metropolitan area groupings during each of the three postwar decades. Yet, these data also make plain that it is the post-1970 rise in nonfamily households that is most responsible for the metropolitanwide house-

TABLE 10.4

Percent Change in Family and Nonfamily Households
for Metropolitan Areas, 1950–1960, 1960–1970, 1970–1980:
Six Metropolitan Area Groupings

Metropolitan Area Groupings/ Household Type	1950–1960	1960–1970	1970–1980
NORTH-DECLINING			
Family	+15.3	+7.7	−1.6
Nonfamily	+110.2	+49.3	+51.2
NORTH-OLD			
Family	+24.1	+18.0	+9.5
Nonfamily	+88.3	+57.0	+75.0
SOUTH-OLD			
Family	+27.3	+28.6	+14.3
Nonfamily	+126.4	+79.9	+85.1
WEST-OLD			
Family	+29.2	+16.9	+8.2
Nonfamily	+93.0	+48.7	+56.2
SOUTH-YOUNG			
Family	+56.2	+37.8	+38.0
Nonfamily	+154.1	+84.4	+120.5
WEST-YOUNG			
Family	+94.1	+51.6	+39.1
Nonfamily	+124.5	+103.0	+129.3

SOURCES: Same as Figure 10.1.

hold growth "cushion" we observed in the previous section. (Indeed, in North-Declining metropolitan areas, nonfamily household growth represents the only such cushion, since these areas sustained losses in their family households over this 1970–1980 period.)

Given the strong metropolitanwide growth of nonfamily households during the 1970s, we raise the question: Have central cities been able to attract a greater share of these new nonfamily households than the family households that were formed during this decade? Historically, nonfamily primary individual households tended to concentrate in central cities, particularly during the peak postwar suburbanization years of the 1950s. Yet this was an era when childrearing was popular among most middle-class Americans, and primary individual households were relatively few, consisting of small numbers of young adult singles, never married individuals of all ages, or surviving widows and widowers. As the nonfamily household becomes more pervasive and accepted as a middle-class living arrangement, suburban municipalities may desire to attract greater numbers of such households into their communities and will work to provide appropriate services, facilities, and housing for these households.

The suburbanization rate data shown in the last three columns of Table 10.5 suggest that the latter may be occurring. During the peak suburbanization decade of the 1950s, nonfamily households actually registered negative suburbanization rates at the same time that family households were suburbanizing at high levels in four of the six metropolitan area groupings. However, the suburbanization rates shown for the 1960s and 1970s indicate an increasing deconcentration of nonfamily households in metropolitan areas of all types. Nonfamily suburbanization rates substantially exceeded family suburbanization rates, and the disparity between the two tended to increase in the 1970–1980 period. (South-Old areas provide an exception as their nonfamily suburbanization rates were greatest in the 1960–1970 decade.) The increased suburbanization of nonfamily households reflects, in large part, a greater tendency for nonfamily households to form in the suburbs.[17] Some of this increase can also be attributed to an increase in suburban surviving-spouse nonfamily households among the elderly.

[17]An analysis of post-1970 nonfamily household suburbanization of nonblacks suggests that their suburbanization is almost entirely a consequence of greater nonfamily household formation in the suburbs, rather than a suburbanward migration of central city nonfamily households. Indeed, the migration of nonfamily households during the 1975–1980 period tended to result in a net gain of such households for central cities, so that, in the absence of migration, suburbs would have exhibited even greater gains in nonfamily households. See Frey, "Mover Destination Selectivity and the Changing Suburbanization of Metropolitan Whites and Blacks," p. 235.

TABLE 10.5

Percent Change in Family and Nonfamily Households for Central City and Suburbs, 1950–1960, 1960–1970, 1970–1980: Six Metropolitan Area Groupings

Metropolitan Area Groupings/ Household Type	Central City			Suburbs			Suburbanization Rate[a]		
	1950–1960	1960–1970	1970–1980	1950–1960	1960–1970	1970–1980	1950–1960	1960–1970	1970–1980
NORTH-DECLINING									
Family	−5.2	−7.0	−16.1	+45.8	+21.7	+9.1	+51.0	+28.7	+25.2
Nonfamily	+122.3	+33.1	+27.7	+86.8	+86.6	+89.8	−35.5	+53.5	+62.1
NORTH-OLD									
Family	−1.1	+11.6	−9.4	+55.8	+23.1	+23.2	+56.9	+11.5	+32.6
Nonfamily	+106.8	+42.5	+44.8	+56.0	+90.5	+127.3	−50.8	+48.0	+82.5
SOUTH-OLD									
Family	+0.7	−4.9	−14.1	+65.0	+57.6	+29.1	+64.3	+62.5	+43.2
Nonfamily	+133.8	+40.0	+33.8	+109.1	+184.0	+151.1	−24.7	+144.0	+117.3
WEST-OLD									
Family	+9.0	+2.7	−5.4	+54.4	+29.4	+17.8	+45.3	+26.7	+23.2
Nonfamily	+88.7	+33.7	+35.3	+102.4	+79.0	+87.6	+13.7	+45.3	+52.3
SOUTH-YOUNG									
Family	+44.5	+21.0	+12.5	+74.9	+60.1	+63.5	+30.4	+39.1	+51.0
Nonfamily	+174.6	+66.7	+92.1	+119.9	+121.2	+165.0	−54.6	+54.6	+72.9
WEST-YOUNG									
Family	+104.3	+40.3	+27.4	+87.0	+60.1	+46.9	−17.3	+19.8	+19.5
Nonfamily	+168.2	+80.5	+97.7	+88.9	+129.2	+158.1	−79.2	+48.7	+60.4

SOURCES: Same as Figure 10.1.

[a]Suburbanization Rate: Suburb Percent Change minus Central City Percent Change.

337

The recent suburbanization increases for nonfamily households have not yet erased the pronounced tendency for cities to house greater shares of their metropolitan area's nonfamily than family households. This is evident in Table 10.6, which shows the number of family and nonfamily households in each metropolitan area grouping at the census years between 1950 and 1980. North-Declining central cities, for example, housed fewer family households than their surrounding suburbs in every census since 1960. Yet, even in 1980—and in spite of recent nonfamily suburbanization rates—these cities housed more nonfamily households than their suburbs. The legacy of the strong 1950s differences in household type redistribution patterns still influences the central city and suburban household compositions in large metropolitan areas. This is apparent, as well, from the Table 10.7 data, which show a persistent suburb–city disparity in the percent of nonfamily households over the period 1950–1980, for metropolitan areas in the North-Declining and three old metropolitan area groupings. Disparities, although less sharp, are also evident in the two "younger" metropolitan area groupings. (Appendix E, Table E.10C provides similar data for individual metropolitan areas.)

How, then, are central city household populations faring as a result of recent redistribution shifts? On the one hand, they are capturing a smaller share of nonfamily households than had been the case in the 1950s, when such households were registering negative suburbanization rates. However, on the other hand, nonfamily households are growing at extremely high levels within all large metropolitan areas, and central cities appear to be capturing enough of this growth to increase their stock of nonfamily households. It is clearly essential for central cities to continue to retain and/or attract large numbers of well-off nonfamily households in order to retain a viable residential and economic base. Such households provided the only source of central city household growth within our declining and old metropolitan area groupings in the 1970s (see Table 10.5); and, even in the South-Young and West-Young central cities, the retention and/or attraction of nonfamily households will be essential for maintaining high levels of household growth. Most large central cities already hold the appropriate housing, services, and amenities for households of this type. This is particularly true of nodal and government service centers, such as Boston, Washington, DC, and San Francisco–Oakland—areas with already large numbers of nonfamily households that both live and work within the city. It remains to be seen how well these and other large central cities will fare in retaining and/or attracting sufficient shares of the nonfamily households that are forming, in increasing numbers, within metropolitan areas.

338

TABLE 10.6

Family and Nonfamily Households for Central Cities and Suburbs, 1950, 1960, 1970, 1980: Six Metropolitan Area Groupings
(in thousands)

Metropolitan Area Groupings	Central City				Suburbs			
	1950	1960	1970	1980	1950	1960	1970	1980
NORTH-DECLINING								
Family Households	5,565	5,273	4,907	4,116	3,760	5,481	6,673	7,282
Nonfamily Households	621	1,381	1,837	2,345	322	602	1,124	2,133
NORTH-OLD								
Family Households	607	601	670	606	483	752	926	1,141
Nonfamily Households	86	177	252	364	49	76	145	331
SOUTH-OLD								
Family Households	671	676	642	552	474	782	1,233	1,592
Nonfamily Households	80	188	263	352	34	71	204	512
WEST-OLD								
Family Households	1,275	1,390	1,428	1,350	1,025	1,582	2,047	2,411
Nonfamily Households	298	563	752	1,018	138	279	499	937
SOUTH-YOUNG								
Family Households	612	885	1,071	1,204	382	669	1,071	1,751
Nonfamily Households	70	193	322	619	42	92	205	545
WEST-YOUNG								
Family Households	235	481	675	860	340	635	1,017	1,493
Nonfamily Households	40	109	196	387	49	94	215	555

SOURCES: Same as Figure 10.1.

339

TABLE 10.7

Percent Nonfamily Households in Cities and Suburbs, 1950, 1960, 1970, 1980: Six Metropolitan Area Groupings

Metropolitan Area Groupings/ Ratios Differences in Ratios	1950		1960		1970		1980	
	City	Suburb	City	Suburb	City	Suburb	City	Suburb
NORTH-DECLINING								
Percent Nonfamily Household (Suburb–City Diff.)	10.0	7.9 (−2.1)	20.8	9.9 (−10.9)	27.2	14.4 (−12.8)	36.3	22.7 (−13.6)
NORTH-OLD								
Percent Nonfamily Household (Suburb–City Diff.)	12.3	9.2 (−3.1)	22.7	9.2 (−13.5)	27.3	13.6 (−13.7)	37.5	22.5 (−15.0)
SOUTH-OLD								
Percent Nonfamily Household (Suburb–City Diff.)	10.7	6.8 (−3.9)	21.7	8.4 (−13.3)	29.0	14.2 (−14.8)	38.9	24.4 (−14.5)
WEST-OLD								
Percent Nonfamily Household (Suburb–City Diff.)	19.0	11.9 (−7.1)	28.8	15.0 (−13.8)	34.5	19.6 (−14.9)	43.0	28.0 (−15.0)
SOUTH-YOUNG								
Percent Nonfamily Household (Suburb–City Diff.)	10.3	9.9 (−0.4)	17.9	12.2 (−5.7)	23.1	16.1 (−7.0)	33.9	23.7 (−10.2)
WEST-YOUNG								
Percent Nonfamily Household (Suburb–City Diff.)	14.7	12.8 (−1.9)	18.4	12.9 (−5.5)	22.5	17.5 (−5.0)	31.1	27.1 (−4.0)

SOURCES: Same as Figure 10.1.

Household Type Redistribution by Race

We provide here a more comprehensive assessment of household selective city–suburb redistribution in the post-1970 period in which we distinguish among different types of family households that have begun to grow in large numbers. We examine household selectivity, separately, for nonblacks and blacks. This is because nonblacks and blacks are distributed somewhat differently among household types and because, as we saw in Chapters 8 and 9, nonblack and black city–suburb redistribution patterns differ strikingly from each other.

What is similar among both nonblacks and blacks during the 1970s is a decrease in the proportion of households that are classified as full families (married-couple households with children under 18). Between 1970 and 1980 the proportion of nonblack households that were full families declined from 41 percent to less than a third (32 percent). Childless-couple families constituted the next largest nonblack household type and comprised about 31 percent of nonblack households at both census dates. The third most prevalent nonblack household type were nonfamily households, which increased their percentage of all nonblack households from 18 percent in 1970 to 26 percent in 1980. Finally, the least prevalent nonblack household type, family households headed by a single adult (which we sometimes abbreviate as "other families"), also increased their share over the 1970s—from 9.2 to 10.6 percent. Although all four household types grew among nonblacks in the 1970–1980 period, the highest growth rates were registered for nonfamily households (79 percent) and for households headed by a single adult (44 percent).

Blacks have historically registered lower proportions of full-family households than have nonblacks. However, like nonblacks, their proportions have declined in the 1970s. The absolute decline of black full-family households over the 1970–1980 decade has reduced their proportions of all black households from 33 to 24 percent—making them the third most prevalent black household type in 1980. The most prevalent black household type is now the family headed by a single adult, which constituted 32 percent of all black households in 1980—up from 25 percent in 1970; and the second most prevalent type is the nonfamily household, which increased its proportion of all black households—from 21 to 28 percent over the decade. Childless-couple families were the least numerous of all black households at both census dates, and their percentage share declined over the 1970s from 20 to 16 percent. Clearly, the greatest gains among black households during the 1970s were made by households headed by a single adult and by nonfamily households. The extremely high growth rates of both household types

(76 percent and 80 percent, respectively) have made each of them more numerous than the two "married-couple" household types among blacks.

The great diversity in household types that has emerged among both nonblacks and blacks during the 1970s represents a striking departure from the 1950s, when full-family households dominated among both races. It also suggests a potential for change in the city–suburb redistribution tendencies of nonblack and black households. We examine, below, the city–suburb redistribution patterns exhibited by each nonblack, and, then, black household type across our six metropolitan area groupings, in order to determine how this more diverse array of households have influenced race-selective redistribution processes.

Nonblack Household City–Suburb Redistribution

To what degree are *non*-full-family households, among nonblacks, distributing themselves between central cities and suburbs? The answer to this question is an important one for those who see both positive and negative consequences accruing to central cities as a result of the proliferation of "nontraditional" households in the 1970s. On the positive side, a greater city attraction and/or retention of nonblack middle-class-childless-couple families and nonfamily households are expected to enhance the city's residential population mix and economic base. On the negative side, a greater retention of nonblack families with a single adult head—predominantly female-headed families with dependent children—are seen to anchor, within the city, a population subgroup characterized by low incomes and higher levels of poverty.

Each of these nontraditional household types have been more prone to reside in the central city than full-family households—particularly since the peak 1950s suburbanization years. This generalization still holds true in 1970 for metropolitan areas in our North-Declining and old metropolitan area groupings. (In North-Declining metropolitan areas, for example, only 30 percent of nonblack full families resided in the central city, while 57 percent of nonblack nonfamily households and 41 percent of both childless-couple families and families with a single adult head resided there.) Nevertheless, the earlier analysis of all nonfamily households (both race groups combined) suggests that such households are suburbanizing faster than all family households—serving to redistribute outward this fast-growing household type. If it is the case that nonblack childless-couple families and nonfamily households are suburbanizing at a greater pace than nonblack full-family households, then cities are at risk of losing their grip on precisely those household types it would be advantageous for them to hold.

The data shown in Table 10.8 and plots displayed in Figure 10.3 permit us to answer the question posed above. The table enables us to compare 1970–1980 suburbanization rates across the four types of non-black households within each metropolitan area grouping. The figure's plots allow us to assess the effects of these suburbanization rates for the central city and suburban nonblack household compositions. (Appendix E, Table E.10D displays the Figure 10.3 data in percentage distribution form.) In these tables and figure, the term "other families" is used to denote families headed by a single adult.

We begin by reviewing the situation for the North-Declining metropolitan area grouping. A comparison of this grouping's household suburbanization rates shows that it is the three nontraditional house-hold types (married couples with no children, other families, and non-family households) that display highest suburbanization rates—all greater than the total nonblack suburbanization rate of 30.1; and that these rates are greatest for the two most desirable household types— nonfamily households and childless-couple families. Only full families are suburbanizing at levels that are lower than the overall rates. [18] Yet, despite the high suburbanization rates exhibited for nonfamily house-holds, North-Declining central cities still register absolute increases in such households—due to their high rates of growth metropolitanwide. These cities are not as fortunate with childless-couple families, how-ever, in that their numbers have decreased by 22.6 percent over the 1970–1980 decade. Relatively high suburbanization rates for households headed by a single adult suggest that they are not being "concentrated" within the central city, although the city shows a slight absolute in-crease in such households. The greatest city household losses are displayed for full-family households. This is not due to a high suburban-ization of these households, however. Because of national declines in the formation of full-family households, discussed above, *both* central cities and suburbs have registered losses in such households; and it is the cities that have lost disproportionately large shares.

In sum, North-Declining central cities registered 1970–1980 de-creases in nonblack households because they bore a disproportionate share of the metropolitan area's decline in full-family households, and because they were unable to capture any of the area's growth in child-

[18] A positive suburbanization rate, when both the city and suburbs are registering de-clines, indicates that suburban declines are less than central city declines and that, as a result of this "loss redistribution," central cities are losing a disproportionate share of the metropolitan area's households.

TABLE 10.8
Percent Change in City and Suburb Households by Race and Household Type, 1970–1980:
Six Metropolitan Area Groupings

Metropolitan Area Groupings/Household Status	Nonblacks			Blacks		
	Central City Percent Change	Suburb Percent Change	Suburb Rate[a]	Central City Percent Change	Suburb Percent Change	Suburb Rate[a]
NORTH-DECLINING						
Married Couple w/Children	−35.2	−11.2	+24.1	−23.5	+35.4	+58.8
Married Couple no Children	−22.6	+26.6	+49.2	−7.1	+36.9	+44.0
Other Family	+1.1	+39.0	+37.9	+51.9	+118.2	+66.3
Nonfamily Household	+17.5	+82.7	+65.2	+50.7	+125.6	+74.9
Total	−11.6	+18.5	+30.1	+18.2	+71.3	+53.1
NORTH-OLD						
Married Couple w/Children	−27.8	+2.2	+30.0	−8.0	+46.8	+54.9
Married Couple no Children	−4.6	+41.9	+46.5	+3.9	+24.8	+20.9
Other Family	+15.2	+64.1	+48.9	+80.8	+124.2	+43.4
Nonfamily Household	+42.2	+117.0	+74.7	+62.7	+116.0	+53.3
Total	+3.1	+34.5	+31.4	+33.2	+72.1	+38.9
SOUTH-OLD						
Married Couple w/Children	−45.3	−0.5	+44.8	−30.8	+108.2	+139.0
Married Couple no Children	−24.7	+45.7	+70.5	−5.2	+106.0	+111.2
Other Family	−17.2	+67.7	+84.8	+48.2	+270.3	+222.1
Nonfamily Household	+17.0	+129.7	+112.7	+53.2	+382.5	+329.4
Total	−14.2	+37.2	+51.5	+15.3	+178.7	+163.4

TABLE 10.8 (continued)

WEST-OLD					
Married Couple w/Children	−20.4	+18.5	−21.5	+39.3	+60.9
Married Couple no Children	−5.8	+33.3	−0.8	+67.8	+68.6
Other Family	+21.9	+37.3	+54.6	+151.5	+96.9
Nonfamily Household	+31.1	+49.6	+54.2	+158.3	+104.1
Total	+6.4	+22.5	+23.8	+92.8	+68.9
SOUTH-YOUNG					
Married Couple w/Children	−8.4	+41.7	+50.1	+9.2	+58.6	+49.4
Married Couple no Children	+16.2	+79.6	+63.4	+21.8	+51.7	+30.0
Other Family	+40.6	+107.2	+66.5	+82.7	+121.2	+38.4
Nonfamily Household	+89.1	+161.3	+72.2	+92.0	+113.9	+21.9
Total	+27.6	+79.5	+52.0	+46.9	+81.5	+34.6
WEST-YOUNG					
Married Couple w/Children	+7.0	+17.6	+10.6	+38.2	+123.5	+85.3
Married Couple no Children	+35.5	+69.7	+34.2	+55.1	+154.2	+99.1
Other Family	+71.9	+97.6	+25.7	+123.3	+327.5	+204.2
Nonfamily Household	+93.5	+149.8	+56.3	+120.7	+304.1	+183.5
Total	+41.5	+64.5	+23.0	+80.2	+197.4	+117.2

SOURCES: Same as Figure 10.3.

[a]Suburbanization Rate: Suburb Percent Change minus Central City Percent Change.

FIGURE 10.3

Nonblack Households by Type for Cities and Suburbs, 1970 and 1980:
Six Metropolitan Area Groupings

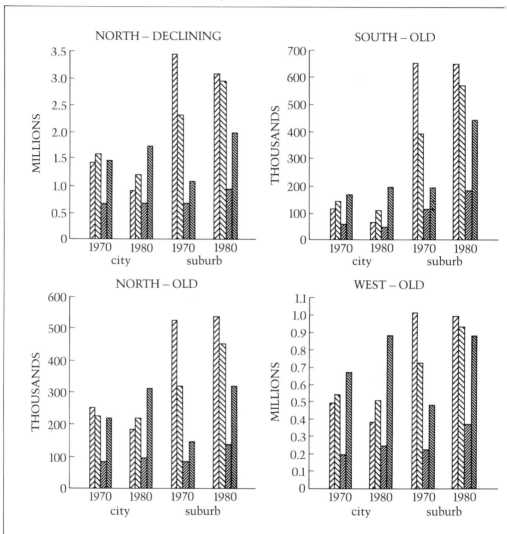

SOURCES: Machine-readable computer files: Census of Population and Housing, 1970, Fourth Count Population Summary Tape File; and Census of Population and Housing, 1980, Summary Tape File 3 (prepared by the U.S. Bureau of the Census, Washington, DC).

less married-couple families. The fact that these cities did not sustain even greater nonblack household losses is due to their ability to attract

FIGURE 10.3 *(continued)*

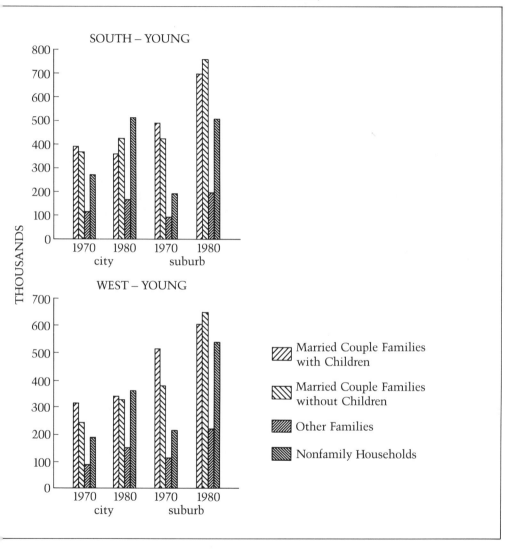

some of the metropolitan area's growth in nonfamily households— even though most of this growth accrued to the suburbs.

The impact these shifts had on North-Declining city and suburb household compositions can be observed in Figure 10.3. In 1970 these cities housed large numbers of full-family, childless-couple family and nonfamily households, and a much smaller number of single-adult-headed family households; while in their suburbs, full-family households clearly predominated along with successively smaller numbers of childless-couple families, nonfamily households, and households headed by a single adult. Quite different city and suburb household compositions are shown in 1980, as a result of the 1970–1980 metropolitanwide and intrametropolitanwide shifts discussed above. Nonfamily households now dominate the nonblack household compositions of North-Declining central cities, and nonblack full-family households still constitute the predominant suburban household type, although there are now almost as many childless-couple families and a significant number of nonfamily households there as well.

The three shifts that brought about these changes—metropolitanwide declines in full-family households, metropolitanwide gains in nonfamily households, and a significant suburbanization of all nontraditional household types—are also evident in the three other old metropolitan area groupings. The greatest losses to central cities in each group are attributable to full-family households, and the greatest city gains are attributable to nonfamily households, despite their high suburbanization rates. Each area also sustains absolute losses for the other desirable household type—childless-couple families—and mixed redistribution tendencies are shown for single-adult-headed households. These redistribution patterns have effected similar outcomes in these areas' city and suburban nonblack household compositions (see Figure 10.3). Nonfamily households dominate the 1980 central city nonblack households in each of these grouping's central cities (this was the case already in 1970 for South-Old and West-Old metropolitan areas), and the suburbs in each area are far less dominated by full-family households than was the case in 1970.

Finally, we turn to the two fastest growing metropolitan area groups—the South-Young and West-Young areas. While these areas have shown much less city–suburb differentiation in physical characteristics and social status than the areas in our older groupings (in Chapters 7 and 9), they show some similarities with the older areas in their household-type suburbanization tendencies (Table 10.8). Within each of these area groupings, it is the nontraditional household types that exhibit the highest 1970–1980 suburbanization rates—suggesting that a "1950s-type"-selective suburbanization of full families is not under way in these new metropolitan areas. These redistribution processes lead to somewhat different outcomes in each area's city and suburb nonblack household composition. In South-Young areas, the 1970–1980 shifts transformed what were relatively similar, full-family-dominated city and suburb nonblack household compositions into 1980 compositions which begin to resemble those of older metropolitan areas. In West-Young areas, 1970 city and suburb nonblack household compositions were also similar to each other; yet, the 1970–1980 shifts changed each part of the metropolitan areas in similar ways. West-Old cities *and* suburbs now house large numbers of nonblack full families, childless-couple families, and nonfamily households with a lesser share of nonblack single-adult-headed households.

To answer the question raised at the outset, the rising numbers of nontraditional nonblack households, evident in the 1970s, have exhibited new city–suburb redistribution patterns. Metropolitan suburbs have begun to gain increasing shares of the nonblack childless-couple families, single-adult-headed families, and nonfamily households that have been growing so rapidly since 1970. At the same time central cities are absorbing a disproportionate share of the metropolitan areas' reduction in nonblack full-family households since 1970. For the time being central cities have been able to retain and attract enough nonblack nonfamily households to avoid dramatic reductions in their household stocks. However, these city gains are related to the large metropolitanwide (and nationwide) growth in such households. If and when this growth tapers off, cities will need to compete even harder with their surrounding suburbs to attract a share of these new, smaller middle-class American households.

Black Household City–Suburb Redistribution

Our Chapter 8 and 9 analyses of black city–suburb population redistribution in the 1970–1980 period found this to be a "benchmark decade" for black suburbanization. Not only did black suburbanization increase markedly during this decade, but the suburbanization involved the participation of blacks in virtually all socioeconomic classes. The issue of broad-based participation will also be the focus of this review of black household type city–suburb redistribution during the 1970–1980 decade. Given the high rates of growth shown for black single-adult-headed families (comprised largely of female-headed families with dependent children) and black nonfamily households, we raise the question: Have black families, headed by single adults, and nonfamily households participated significantly in the post-1970 black suburbanization movement? Black full families and childless-couple households constitute the most economically well-off of all black household types and were the most suburbanized of black households at the beginning of the 1970s decade.[19] A continued black suburbanization that selected primarily from these households would certainly not be "representative" of all black households, given the fact that they are constituting increasingly declining shares of the black household population.

To compare the suburbanization tendencies of black household types during the 1970s, we again refer to Table 10.8 which displays household type specific suburbanization rates for categories of black households in each metropolitan area grouping. An examination of these data reveals that, in four of the six area groupings, single-adult-headed families and nonfamily households display *greater* rates of suburbanization than full families and childless-couple families. (Included in these groupings are the North-Declining areas and South-Old areas—those that house the largest numbers and proportions of blacks.) This constitutes evidence that some suburbanization of these fast-growing black household types is occurring, and that all black household types are participating in the suburbanization movement within those areas that house the largest black populations.

Having stated this, however, we call attention to the fact that suburbanization rate comparisons say more about the redistribution *process* than the redistribution *outcome*. Even large suburbanization rates shown for household types that are initially concentrated in the city will not translate into a large aggregate change in that household type's city–suburb distribution. In spite of the suburbanization rates just reviewed, black nonfamily households and single-adult-headed households are still more city-concentrated than black full families and childless couples in 1980. Nevertheless, the suburbanization rate comparisons indicate the redistribution directions associated with these household types and make clear that the 1970–1980 processes point to an increased suburbanization of black households that are not composed of married couples.

The effects of these 1970–1980 redistribution shifts for central city and suburban black household compositions can be observed in Figure 10.4. (Comparable percent distributions are shown in Appendix E, Table 10.D.) Two aspects of these black household shifts have affected the 1980 city and suburb black household compositions in each metropolitan area grouping. First, the extraordinarily high 1970s growth rates in single-adult-headed families and nonfamily households have led them to dominate the black household compositions of all central cities in 1980. Second, the heightened suburbanization of these two household

---

[19]In North-Declining areas, for example, 18 percent of black full families and 23 percent of black childless-couple families resided in the suburbs. Comparable figures for nonfamily households and single-adult-headed families were 12 percent and 13 percent, respectively.

types during this period had led to a reduced full-family domination of suburban black household compositions. The latter change is particularly noteworthy since, in 1970, the black suburban household compositions, in all metropolitan areas, were extremely atypical of the metropolitan area's black household structure. In each case black full-family households constituted an unusually large share of the suburb's households. The shift to a more mixed suburban household type composition in 1980 is partly the result of the large nationwide growth in black nonfamily and single-adult-headed households during the 1970s. However, it was also facilitated by the suburbanization of these black households during this "benchmark" decade.

The preceding review provides strong evidence that black households of all types participated in the post-1970 black suburbanization movement. The heightened participation of black nonfamily and single-adult-headed households parallels a similar tendency shown for nonblack households of these types during the 1970s. Despite this change in the black redistribution *process,* central cities are still the dominant place of residence for all black households, particularly those that are most susceptible to poverty. Later in this chapter, we focus specifically on the redistribution processes associated with black poor and nonpoor households and their implications for a continued "city concentration" of poverty.

Nonblack "Return to the City"

During the 1970s many urban analysts viewed the widening diversity of household types among metropolitan nonblacks as a potential gain for declining central cities. Indeed, the terms "urban renaissance" and "return to the city" were employed by more hopeful observers.[20] The shift toward greater percentages of nonfamily and childless-couple households, it was thought, might lead to increased city household gains since these households were, in the past, less suburban selective than full-family households. "White collar" administrative and service center cities, such as Boston, Washington, DC, and San Francisco–Oakland, were expected to be the primary beneficiaries of these household composition shifts. We have now shown (in the previous section)

---

[20]Two popular accounts that emphasize this point are: Robert C. Embry, Jr., "Back-to-the-City Movement May Signal the End of Urban Decline," *City, Town and Country* (January 1978):37–38; and Blake Fleetwood, "The New Elite and the Urban Renaissance," *The New York Times Magazine* (January 14, 1979). Several academic papers that allude to this point appear in Shirley Bradway Laska and Daphne Spain, eds., *Back to the City: Issues in Neighborhood Renovation* (New York: Pergamon, 1980).

FIGURE 10.4

Black Households by Type for Cities and Suburbs, 1970 and 1980:
Six Metropolitan Area Groupings

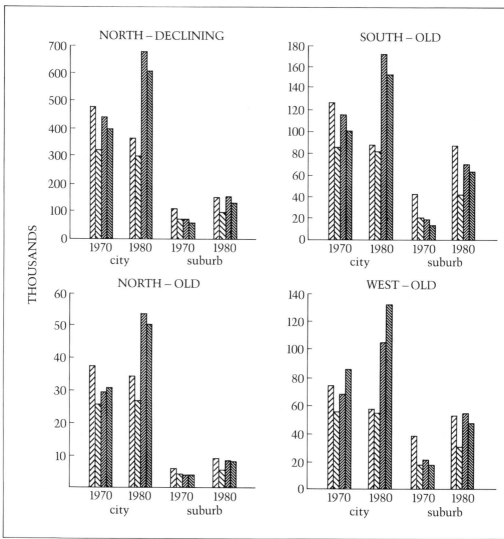

SOURCES: Same as Figure 10.3.

that there is *some* truth to these views. Nonfamily households, if not
childless-couple families, *were* primarily responsible for whatever gains

352

FIGURE 10.4 *(continued)*

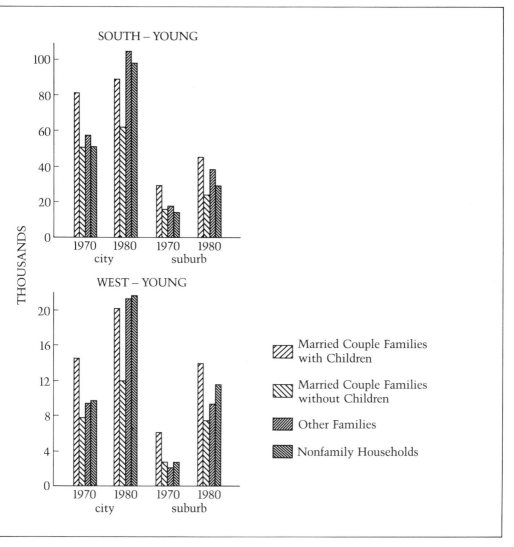

nonblack city household stocks experienced during the 1970–1980 period. However, we also saw that, unlike the situation in the 1950s, nonfamily households exhibited the highest suburbanization rates of any household type. The city gains of nonfamily households among nonblacks were less a consequence of these households preferring to live in the central city than a consequence of the high metropolitan-wide growth rates of these households.

It is unlikely that the high metropolitan growth of nonfamily households will persist indefinitely, particularly if it were tied to the "coming of age" of the large baby-boom cohorts which happened to be passing through their 20s and early 30s during the 1970–1980 decade. If this is the case, and nonfamily household growth for nonblacks falls off as the baby-boom cohorts age, then central cities may be faring much worse than they appeared to be in the 1970s decade. To gain further insights into the sources of nonblack household gains, we shall examine the age structure of this 1970s growth for North-Declining metropolitan areas and for selected individual areas. This will permit us to evaluate the impact of the baby-boom cohorts and speculate further on what post-1970 household composition trends imply for declining central cities.

Impact of Baby-Boom Cohorts

The data in Table 10.9 show the number of 1970 household and 1970–1980 changes (in numbers and percentages) for nonblack households by type and age of head. The most important age category for our purposes is the 25 to 34 age group—since this is the age category that the large baby-boom cohorts began moving into during the 1970–1980 period. The 1970–1980 changes shown for this age group reflect differences in the numbers of households with heads born in 1935–1944 (that is, those aged 25 to 34 in 1970) and those with heads born in 1945–1954 (that is, those aged 25 to 34 in 1980). Indeed, the magnitudes of these changes among those in the 25 to 34 age group reflect the dominant influence that the baby-boom cohorts have exerted on both the central city and suburbs. Within the city, the 25 to 34 age group was the only group that contributed to overall gains in city households (second column), and within the suburbs, the 25 to 34 age group's increase was larger than that of any other 10-year age group (fifth column).

As a result of the large size of the "baby-boom cohorts," the *composition* of these cohorts' new households tends to dominate the composition of *all* new households in the city and suburbs. Thus, as we anticipated, the increase in nonfamily households displayed for metropolitan areas during the 1970–1980 period is attributable, in large measure, to the "coming of age" of large baby-boom cohorts who showed a preference for this particular household type in their late 20s and early 30s. This is confirmed in calculations from Table 10.9 data which show that 64 percent of the total 1970–1980 increase in North-Declining metro-

politan area nonblack households is attributable to nonfamily households in the 25 to 34 age group.

Given their numerical importance, then, how have these baby-
boom nonfamily households distributed themselves across central cities
and suburbs? In order to answer this question, it is helpful to look at the
left-hand plot in Figure 10.5, pertaining to North-Declining metropolitan areas. Shown here are suburb proportions of nonblack household
types in the 25 to 34 age group in 1970—reflecting the experience of the
pre-1945 cohorts, and suburb proportions for 1980—reflecting the experiences of the postwar baby-boom cohorts (the light and dark solid
lines, respectively). It is clear from these plots that at age 25 to 34, the
baby-boom households of *every* type are more suburbanized than the
pre-1945-born cohorts were at the same age. Yet the greatest increases
in suburbanization occurred with nonfamily households. One can verify
this large suburban shift numerically by examining the 1970–1980
household changes in Table 10.9 associated with nonfamily households
in the 25 to 34 age group. The suburbs gained a greater absolute number
of these households than did the city (315,700 versus 205,200) and a
substantially larger percentage change (325 percent versus 113 percent).
Still, because there were so many households of this type, even the cities' smaller share of this gain (205,200) was larger than its combined
gains from all other household types at all other ages over the
1970–1980 period. In future years, when smaller cohorts enter the
"household-forming" category among those aged 25 to 34, the city's
small share of these cohorts' households will reflect far fewer absolute
additions.

A further look at the household type suburbanization proportions
(Figure 10.5) suggests some positive implications for central cities.
Although it is true that nonfamily households in the 25 to 34 age group
increased their suburb proportion significantly between 1970 and 1980,
the suburb proportion of this household type still lies *below* the proportion of all other household types in 1980. This benefits household
growth in North-Declining cities since, still in 1980, the fastest growing
household type in the metropolitan area is the one that tends to be
most concentrated in the city. The suburb destination propensity rates
for 1970–1980 movers and inmigrants to these metropolitan areas
(shown in the dotted lines) also follow this pattern—indicating that recent nonfamily household movers also favor the central city.[21] However, if future cohorts' nonfamily households continue to increase their

---

[21]The suburb destination propensity rate, as used here, is defined as the proportion of
all 1975–1980 intrametropolitan movers and inmigrants who select a suburb (rather than a
central city) destination. See the Chapter 7 section on "Destination Propensity Rates" for
a further discussion of this measure.

TABLE 10.9

1970 Size, 1970–1980 Change and Percent 1970–1980 Change for Nonblacks Households by Type and Age of Head, Central Cities and Suburbs: North-Declining Metropolitan Areas [a]

Household by Age of Head and Type	North-Declining Central Cities			North-Declining Suburbs		
	1970 Size [b]	1970–1980 Change [b]	Percent Change 1970–1980	1970 Size [b]	1970–1980 Change [b]	Percent Change 1970–1980
NONBLACKS						
Head Age Under 25						
Married Couple w/Children	846	−380	−44.9	1,312	−396	−30.2
Married Couple no Children	880	−387	−44.0	1,266	−82	−6.5
Other Family	318	+224	+70.4	229	+205	+89.7
Nonfamily Household	1,175	+460	+39.2	645	+1,289	+199.8
Total	(3,219)	(−83)	(−2.6)	(3,452)	(+1,016)	(+29.4)
Head Age 25–34						
Married Couple w/Children	4,068	−1,009	−24.8	8,997	−178	−2.0
Married Couple no Children	1,364	+183	+13.4	1,894	+1,762	+93.1
Other Family	1,013	+383	+37.8	784	+780	+99.5
Nonfamily Household	1,821	+2,052	112.7	972	+3,157	+324.8
Total	(8,266)	(+1,609)	(+19.5)	(12,647)	(+5,521)	(+43.7)
Head Age 35–44						
Married Couple w/Children	4,369	−1,385	−31.7	11,728	−1,158	−9.9
Married Couple no Children	787	−185	−23.5	1,196	+117	+9.8
Other Family	1,147	+69	+6.1	1,262	+611	+48.4
Nonfamily Household	1,247	+506	+40.6	707	+889	+125.8
Total	(7,550)	(−995)	(−13.2)	(14,893)	(+459)	(+3.1)

TABLE 10.9 (continued)

Head Age 45–64						
Married Couple w/Children	4,674	−2,030	−43.4	10,115	−1,852	−18.3
Married Couple no Children	7,737	−2,365	−30.6	12,076	+2,434	+20.2
Other Family	2,706	−528	−19.5	2,719	+545	+20.0
Nonfamily Household	4,583	−527	−11.5	3,483	+1,022	+29.3
Total	(19,700)	(−5,450)	(−27.7)	(28,393)	(+2,149)	(+7.6)
Head Age 65 +						
Married Couple w/Children	104	−32	−30.4	155	−43	−27.5
Married Couple no Children	5,008	−703	−14.0	5,479	+1,970	+36.0
Other Family	1,527	−186	−12.2	1,352	+288	+21.3
Nonfamily Household	5,869	+189	+3.2	4,344	+2,493	+57.4
Total	(12,508)	(−732)	(−5.9)	(11,330)	(+4,708)	(+41.6)
TOTALS						
Married Couple w/Children	14,061	−4,835	−34.4	32,307	−3,627	−11.2
Married Couple no Children	15,776	−3,457	−21.9	21,911	+6,201	+28.3
Other Family	6,711	−37	−0.6	6,346	+2,430	+38.3
Nonfamily Household	14,695	+2,679	+18.2	10,151	+8,850	+87.2
Total	(51,243)	(−5,650)	(−11.0)	(70,715)	(+13,854)	(+19.6)

SOURCES: Census of Population, 1970: Special Census Tabulations and machine-readable computer file: Census of Population and Housing, 1980 Public Use Microdata Samples "A" and "B" (prepared by the U.S. Bureau of the Census, Washington, DC).

[a] 1970 SMSA and Central City Definitions (in 1970) and 1970 Equivalent SMSA and Central City Definitions (in 1980).

[b] In hundreds.

FIGURE 10.5

Suburb Proportion of 1970 and 1980 Metropolitan Area Households,
and Suburb Destination Propensity Rates of 1975–1980,
Metropolitan Area Mover and Inmigrant Households,
Nonblacks Aged 25–34, by Household Type:
North-Declining and Selected Individual Metropolitan Areas[a]

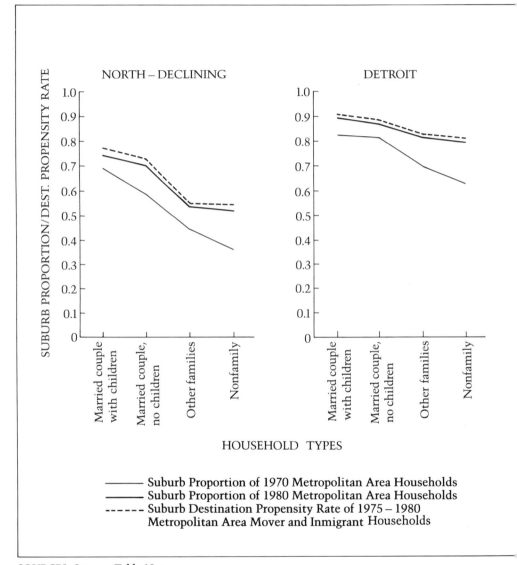

SOURCES: Same as Table 10.g.

[a]1970 SMSA and Central City Definitions (in 1970) and 1970 Equivalent SMSA and Central Ci
Definitions (in 1980).

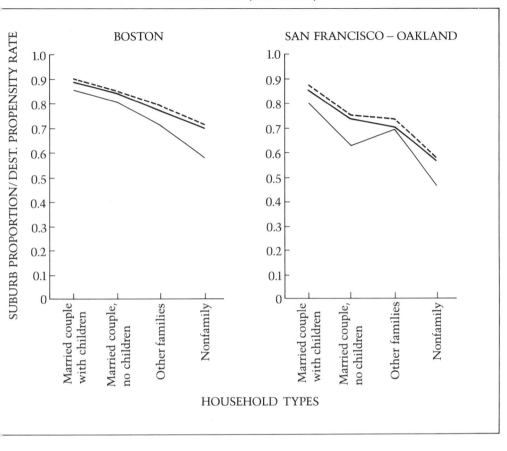

FIGURE 10.5 *(continued)*

BOSTON SAN FRANCISCO – OAKLAND

SUBURB PROPORTION/DEST. PROPENSITY RATE

HOUSEHOLD TYPES

Household types (both panels): Married couple with children; Married couple, no children; Other families; Nonfamily

levels of suburbanization, the present household type difference in suburb proportions may disappear.

The three individual metropolitan areas, for which plots appear in Figure 10.5, represent areas wherein the "baby-boom" nonfamily households, among nonblacks, have suburbanized to different degrees. At the one extreme lies San Francisco–Oakland, where nonblack nonfamily households in the 25 to 34 age group became only slightly more suburbanized during the 1970s—and left intact the household-suburb proportion relationship wherein the metropolitan area nonfamily households are far more centralized than other nonblack household types. At the other extreme lies Detroit, where baby-boom nonfamily households suburbanized significantly, and to a degree where there is little differentiation in the suburb proportions across nonblack household types. The Boston metropolitan area lies in between. Its nonfamily households in the 25 to 34 age group increased their suburb proportions over the 1970–1980 decade, but still display suburb proportions that lie below those of other family types in 1980. San Francisco–Oakland's and Boston's more accentuated household-type differences can be attributed to their largely "white collar" city functions. Detroit, as we have seen in previous chapters, has experienced a rather large scale suburbanization of nonblacks of all social categories over the 1970–1980 period and has long been considered a "blue collar" city.

The impact of these distinctly different 1970–1980 household type shifts is evident when examining the three cities' nonblack household stocks (Table 10.10). San Francisco–Oakland's baby-boom nonfamily households contributed substantially to the city's nonblack household stock—+28,400—which helped to minimize the city's overall nonblack household loss to −6,200.[22] In Boston these households added +14,800 to the city which lost 10,400 nonblack households overall. However, in Detroit, the baby-boom nonfamily households added only +4,400 to the city's nonblack household stock—compensating for less than 4 percent of its overall 122,100 decadewide loss of nonblack households. It can be seen that the continued city attraction of this growing household type made significant differences for the nonblack household stocks in the two former metropolitan areas' central cities—since, in all three metropolitan areas, nonblack nonfamily households in the 25 to 34 age group grew significantly over the decade (by 233 percent, 328 percent, and 221 percent, respectively, in San Francisco–Oakland, Boston, and Detroit).

Discussion

In this section we have pointed up the significance, for depopulating central cities, of attracting the baby-boom cohorts' nonblack nonfamily households during the 1970s. The attraction of such households was an important reason why Old-Declining area central cities sustained gains or only moderate losses in their nonblack household stocks. Yet, in the absence of extensive inmigration from outside the metropolitan area, there is some question as to whether these cities will continue to survive in the same way. First, future cohorts of nonblacks entering their "household-forming" years will be considerably smaller than the postwar baby-boom cohorts. By virtue of their sizes alone, they will provide less potential for city household growth. Second, trends in household selectivity suggest that nonblack nonfamily households are being more attracted to the suburbs than in the past. Many cities, such

[22]Contributing to the central city's nonfamily households is a relatively large homosexual population in the city of San Francisco.

as San Francisco and Washington, DC, will continue to serve as magnets for such households. However, the 1970–1980 trends reviewed here suggest that these cities may be the exceptions. Finally, it should be borne in mind that these nonfamily households still represent a transition, or "staging period," for young adults—although at later ages than in the past. Although the successor cohorts to the baby-boom cohorts are likely to continue to form nonfamily households in their late 20s and even early 30s, most of the single individuals maintaining these households will eventually marry and, perhaps, form full families. Because, even in 1980, young full families and childless-couple families among nonblacks seem to prefer a suburban residence, it is possible that the large numbers of nonblack nonfamily households, momentarily "captured" by central cities, may eventually move out to the suburbs, as they progress along the life course.[23]

What these arguments suggest is that the 1970s nonblack household gains in declining and older areas' central cities could be short-lived, and that a continued flow of young nonfamily households may not follow those of the postwar baby-boom cohorts. The challenge for these cities will be to retain these young households as they enter into the next stage of the less family-oriented life cycle that appears to be evolving in the post-1970 era.

The City Concentration of Poverty

Poverty levels among blacks and nonblacks during the 1970s were appreciably lower than levels observed in the late 1950s and early 1960s.[24] The sharpest declines in poverty, registered over the 1959–1969 period, cut across a wide variety of racial and social categories. Nevertheless, at the beginning of the 1970s decade, the poverty families and unrelated individuals in metropolitan areas were disproportionately concentrated in central cities—serving to reinforce the vicious cycle of selective suburbanward migration. Part of this concentration had to do with the fact that rates of poverty are higher among blacks (approximately three times higher than for nonblacks), who were disproportionately concentrated in the central city. Yet, greater percentages of poor families and unrelated individuals *among both blacks and non-*

---

[23]For an overview of how life course (age-related) migration affects the city–suburb redistribution process, see William H. Frey, "Lifecourse Migration of Metropolitan Whites and Blacks and the Structure of Demographic Change in Large Central Cities," *American Sociological Review* 49 (December 1984):803–827.

[24]For a comprehensive overview of the poverty measure and trends, see William P. O'Hare, "Poverty in America: Trends and New Patterns," *Population Bulletin* 40(3) (Washington, DC: Population Reference Bureau, 1985).

TABLE 10.10

1970 Size, 1970–1980 Change, and Percent 1970–1980 Change in Central City Households for Nonblacks by Age of Head and Household Type: Selected Metropolitan Areas[a]

Household by Race Age of Head, and Type	Detroit			Boston			San Francisco–Oakland		
	1970 (size[b])	1970–1980 (change[b])	Percent Change 1970–1980	1970 (size[b])	1970–1980 (change[b])	Percent Change 1970–1980	1970 (size[b])	1970–1980 (change[b])	Percent Change 1970–1980
NONBLACKS									
Head Age Under 25									
Married Couple w/Children	65	−44	−68.0	28	−19	−67.1	44	−33	−75.5
Married Couple no Children	56	−30	−52.9	41	−21	−52.2	58	−40	−69.7
Other Family	12	+16	+136.7	18	+6	+35.6	23	+2	+9.6
Nonfamily Household	57	+9	+15.1	133	+35	+26.6	164	+2	+1.2
Head Age 25–34									
Married Couple w/Children	239	−115	−47.9	117	−38	−32.3	189	−60	−31.9
Married Couple no Children	47	+9	+20.0	45	+22	+48.4	130	+0	+0.3
Other Family	46	+3	+7.0	32	+21	+65.0	51	+39	+77.3
Nonfamily Household	75	+44	+58.4	105	+148	+141.1	286	+284	+99.2
Head Age 35–44									
Married Couple w/Children	197	−105	−53.3	129	−41	−32.1	182	−26	−14.3
Married Couple no Children	49	−32	−64.9	24	−8	−35.0	62	+2	+3.2
Other Family	61	−26	−43.0	51	−12	−23.1	68	−2	−2.4
Nonfamily Household	76	−22	−29.5	57	+16	+27.7	177	+93	+52.3

TABLE 10.10 (continued)

Head Age 45–64									
Married Couple w/Children	327	−225	−68.7	161	−80	−49.8	224	−74	−33.2
Married Couple no Children	507	−281	−55.5	190	−49	−25.7	432	−114	−26.3
Other Family	148	−66	−44.6	108	−24	−21.9	144	−33	−22.8
Nonfamily Household	280	−84	−30.1	192	−46	−24.0	450	−52	−11.6
Head Age 65 +									
Married Couple w/Children	5	−26	−52.0	4	−2	−50.0	13	−3	−20.0
Married Couple no Children	339	−149	−44.1	160	−38	−24.0	318	−22	−7.0
Other Family	109	−40	−36.9	80	−10	−12.5	96	−16	−16.3
Nonfamily Household	356	−80	−22.4	182	+36	+19.8	509	−9	−1.8
TOTALS									
Married Couple w/Children	833	−491	−58.9	439	−180	−41.0	652	−196	−30.1
Married Couple no Children	998	−483	−48.4	460	−95	−20.7	10,000	−174	−17.4
Other Family	376	−113	−30.0	289	−18	−6.3	382	−8	−2.2
Nonfamily Household	844	−134	−15.9	669	+189	+28.3	1,586	+316	+19.9
Total	3,051	−1,221	−40.0	1,857	−104	−5.6	12,620	−62	−0.5

SOURCES: Same as Table 10.9.

NOTE: Both of these data sources are based on sample tabulations (.01 from the 1970 census and .025 from the 1980 census) and show some inconsistencies with data presented in Table 10.9.

[a] 1970 SMSA and Central City Definitions (in 1970) and 1970 Equivalent SMSA and Central City Definitions (in 1980).
[b] In hundreds.

blacks were concentrated in the city than was the case for the nonpoor families and unrelated individuals of these races. Although this city concentration of poverty is not inconsistent with the city–suburb income selectivity patterns described in Chapter 9, it also reflects the city concentration of female-headed families and unrelated individuals, which are known to have higher levels of poverty than the more "suburban-concentrated" full families and childless-couple families.

Given the overall rise in these more poverty-prone families and individuals during the 1970s, and the trend toward their increased suburbanization, we wish to know: Have poor families and unrelated individuals become less city-concentrated over the decade of the 1970s? This question is most crucial for the black population, given the large growth of its traditionally "city-concentrated" female-headed family households during the decade. These families (comprising most of the black "single-adult-headed families" in the earlier analysis) are, by far, the most poverty-prone households of both racial groups, and their growth during the 1970s has served to halt further declines in overall black poverty levels.[25] Nonblack female-headed family households have also grown during the 1970s and are more poverty-prone than other nonblack households. However, they comprise a much smaller segment of nonblack household stock than is the case for black female-headed households.

In order to address this question, we first compare 1970–1980 suburbanization rates for black and nonblack families and unrelated individuals, by poverty status, in our six metropolitan area groupings (Table 10.11). This permits us to assess poverty/nonpoverty selectivity patterns associated with the 1970s redistribution process. The black comparisons show that, while poor families and unrelated individuals are suburbanizing in five of the six metropolitan area groupings, their suburbanization rates are decidedly lower than those of their black nonpoor counterparts. They are also lower than the suburbanization rates for any of the black household types shown in Table 10.8. In the remaining metropolitan area grouping (North-Old metropolitan areas), black poor families and unrelated individuals registered a negative suburbanization rate during the 1970s, while their nonpoor counterparts exhibited a sizeable positive suburbanization rate.

Of the former five metropolitan area groupings, we find that black

---

[25]Poverty status is determined for families and unrelated individuals (ages 15 and over) rather than for household types. The poverty status of families pertains to only family members of family households. Unrelated individuals can live in nonfamily households (either alone or with other unrelated individuals), in family households, or in noninstitutional group quarters. (See U.S. Census of Population and Housing, 1981, *User's Guide,* PCH80-R1-B, Part B, Glossary.)

poverty suburbanization is barely positive (at a rate less than 6 percent) in North-Declining metropolitan areas—areas that showed a relatively broad-based, status-selective black suburbanization (Chapter 9). In South-Old areas black poor families and unrelated individuals are participating in the suburbanization processes at a rate that exceeds those for both nonblack categories. Yet, there still exists a wide disparity between the suburbanization rates shown for poor blacks and nonpoor blacks. The latter's 204.4 rate represents the greatest suburbanization rate for all metropolitan area groupings and remains consistent with the strong black South-Old suburbanization tendencies observed in other parts of our analysis.

Finally, of older area groupings, West-Old areas display the smallest disparities between black poor and nonpoor black categories; although even here the difference between the rates is fairly substantial. Among the two Young metropolitan area groupings, South-Young areas show the sharpest disparity between poor and nonpoor blacks, such that black poor families and unrelated individuals are barely suburbanizing in these areas. This is consistent with our Chapter 9 evaluation of status-selective suburbanization which showed a strong status disparity for 1970s black suburbanization in these areas.

The foregoing comparison suggests a 1970s redistribution process that is leading to a relative concentration of black poverty in all six metropolitan area groupings. This is further verified in the first three columns of Table 10.12 which show 1970–1980 shifts in the suburban percentages of black poor and black nonpoor families and unrelated individuals, in the aggregate (that is, the outcomes of the redistribution process). The 1970 suburban percentages were not very different for poor blacks and nonpoor blacks due to the low levels of black suburbanization that existed prior to this date. However, as a result of the selective 1970–1980 suburbanization of nonpoor blacks, the differences in these percentages have widened markedly in 1980. The greatest increases and widest disparities are evident for the South-Old and North-Declining metropolitan areas. In the former, the 1980 percentage of black nonpoor families and unrelated individuals residing in the suburbs is 38.8 percent, compared with 21.3 percent for poor blacks (comparable percentages for 1970 were 18.3 and 15.8, respectively). In the latter areas, nonpoor blacks increased their suburban percentage from 16.2 to 23.3 percent between 1970 and 1980, while the suburban percentages of poverty-level blacks increased from 14.2 to only 14.7 percent.

A similar comparison of nonblack 1970s suburbanization rates (Table 10.11) and 1970–1980 shifts in suburban percentages (in Table 10.12) shows that nonblack poor families and unrelated individuals are

TABLE 10.11

1970 Populations and 1970–1980 Percent Change for Families and Unrelated Individuals in Central Cities and Suburbs by Poverty Status and Race: Six Metropolitan Area Groupings

Metropolitan Area Groupings/Race	Central City		Suburbs		Suburbanization Rate[a] 1970–1980
	1970 Population	1970–1980 Percent Change	1970 Population	1970–1980 Percent Change	
NORTH-DECLINING					
Nonblack-Poor	829,023	−1.7	657,752	+2.6	+4.3
Nonblack-Nonpoor	4,645,751	−11.3	7,171,143	+21.8	+33.1
Black-Poor	467,206	+46.0	77,480	+51.9	+5.8
Black-Nonpoor	1,324,590	+10.7	258,366	+72.5	+61.7
NORTH-OLD					
Nonblack-Poor	122,247	+2.8	94,361	+13.9	+11.1
Nonblack-Nonpoor	733,636	+6.1	1,021,666	+39.1	+32.9
Black-Poor	35,680	+39.2	6,935	+13.8	−25.4
Black-Nonpoor	99,349	+34.2	14,463	+89.3	+55.1
SOUTH-OLD					
Nonblack-Poor	84,186	−12.8	111,053	+28.9	+41.7
Nonblack-Nonpoor	451,636	−11.1	1,302,548	+42.1	+53.3
Black-Poor	135,992	+27.6	25,577	+83.8	+56.3
Black-Nonpoor	339,894	+11.2	75,900	+215.7	+204.4

TABLE 10.11 (continued)

WEST-OLD					
Nonblack-Poor	+11.1	314,352	263,631	+27.5	+16.3
Nonblack-Nonpoor	+13.3	1,773,296	2,328,383	+35.3	+22.0
Black-Poor	+33.3	76,830	22,715	+76.0	+42.7
Black-Nonpoor	+28.5	230,421	82,565	+106.2	+77.7
SOUTH-YOUNG					
Nonblack-Poor	+20.9	181,100	153,594	+43.5	+22.6
Nonblack-Nonpoor	+33.5	1,043,723	1,096,789	+89.2	+55.7
Black-Poor	+29.2	84,002	30,560	+34.3	+5.1
Black-Nonpoor	+57.7	177,456	53,522	+108.2	+50.5
WEST-YOUNG					
Nonblack-Poor	+38.0	118,170	153,369	+53.2	+15.2
Nonblack-Nonpoor	+51.5	768,429	1,141,022	+75.0	+23.5
Black-Poor	+57.9	12,710	3,960	+139.5	+81.6
Black-Nonpoor	+101.6	31,900	12,011	+227.3	+125.7

SOURCES: Machine-readable computer files: Census of Population and Housing, 1970; Fourth Count Population Summary Tape and Census of Population and Housing, 1980; Summary Tape File 4B (prepared by the U.S Bureau of the Census, Washington, DC).

[a]Suburbanization Rate: Suburb Percent Change minus Central City Percent Change.

TABLE 10.12
*Percentages in Suburbs of Metropolitan Families and Unrelated Individuals,
1970–1980, and Female-Headed Families, 1980 by Race and Poverty Status:
Six Metropolitan Area Groupings*

Metropolitan Area Groupings/ Race and Poverty Status	Total Families and Unrelated Individuals Suburb Percentages			Female-Headed Families Suburb Percentages
	1970	1980	Diff.	1980
NORTH-DECLINING				
Nonblack-Poor	44.2	45.3	+1.1	41.6
Nonblack-Nonpoor	60.7	67.9	+7.2	62.9
Black-Poor	14.2	14.7	+0.5	14.5
Black-Nonpoor	16.2	23.3	+7.1	20.2
NORTH-OLD				
Nonblack-Poor	43.6	46.1	+2.5	49.6
Nonblack-Nonpoor	58.2	64.6	+6.4	60.4
Black-Poor	16.3	13.7	−2.6	13.3
Black-Nonpoor	12.7	17.0	+4.3	14.1
SOUTH-OLD				
Nonblack-Poor	56.9	66.1	+9.2	72.5
Nonblack-Nonpoor	74.3	82.2	+7.9	80.7
Black-Poor	15.8	21.3	+5.5	20.2
Black-Nonpoor	18.3	38.8	+20.5	33.5
WEST-OLD				
Nonblack-Poor	45.6	49.0	+3.4	57.7
Nonblack-Nonpoor	56.8	61.1	+4.3	61.4
Black-Poor	22.8	28.1	+5.3	29.7
Black-Nonpoor	26.4	36.5	+10.1	36.8
SOUTH-YOUNG				
Nonblack-Poor	45.9	50.2	+4.3	46.7
Nonblack-Nonpoor	51.2	59.8	+8.6	55.8
Black-Poor	26.7	27.4	+0.7	26.1
Black-Nonpoor	23.2	28.5	+5.3	26.4
WEST-YOUNG				
Nonblack-Poor	56.5	59.0	+2.5	58.6
Nonblack-Nonpoor	59.8	63.2	+3.4	60.0
Black-Poor	23.8	32.1	+8.3	28.4
Black-Nonpoor	27.4	37.9	+10.5	30.1

SOURCES: Same as Table 10.11.

also becoming more concentrated in relation to their nonpoor counterparts. In this comparison, poor nonblacks were quite "city-concentrated" already in 1970 (see the first column of Table 10.12), and the poor-nonpoor disparities widened in five of the six metropolitan area groupings over the 1970–1980 period. The greatest increase in this disparity occurred in North-Declining metropolitan areas where nonpoor nonblacks registered a 1970s suburbanization rate of 33.1 as compared to 4.3 percent for their poor counterparts (Table 10.11). As a consequence, the percentage of nonpoor nonblacks residing in the suburbs increased from 60.7 in 1970 to 67.9 in 1980 (Table 10.12); comparable percentages for poor nonblacks were 44.2 percent and 45.3 percent, respectively. Wide 1980 poor-nonpoor disparities in suburban percentages are also shown for South-Old and North-Old metropolitan area groupings (Table 10.12, second column), although all area groupings show disparities.

Clearly, the answer to the question raised above is that poor families and unrelated individuals *have* continued to concentrate in the city relative to their nonpoor counterparts. This is the case for both blacks and nonblacks. Although the household types with the most poverty-prone families and unrelated individuals have suburbanized during the 1970s, the poor families and individuals among them have barely participated in the suburbanization process. This is evident from the fourth column of Table 10.12, which shows 1980 suburban percentages by race and poverty status for female-headed family households—the most poverty-prone household type for both races. Hence, it is likely that increases in poverty-prone households may serve to perpetuate the "city concentration" of poverty. It is also evident from the data reviewed here that the lowest 1980 percentages of suburban residence are associated with black poor families and unrelated individuals—groups that also exhibited extremely low 1970s suburbanization rates. This suggests that the continued high incidence of poverty among black households will contribute to the continued city concentration of poverty in metropolitan areas that house large numbers of blacks.

Summary

During the 1970–1980 decade, the rate of household growth generally exceeded the rate of population growth due to: (1) the "coming of age" of the large postwar baby-boom cohorts, who entered their peak household-formation ages during this decade; and (2) the shift in the composition of America's households, as living arrangement preferences tended to favor smaller childless-couple families, single-adult families, and nonfamily households. This chapter has examined the implications that these post-1970 shifts in the number and composition of households hold for the city–suburb redistribution process. The rise in household growth, in the context of low or declining population growth, provides a "cushion" for the metropolitan areas we have termed declining and old, if one measures an area's growth on the basis of its households or housing units. The fact that small households had, in earlier decades, favored the central city locations has led many observers to assert that this post-1970 surge of small household growth might be particularly beneficial to central cities. Our examination of this and other assertions related to city–suburb household redistribution leads us to conclude that household-type selectivity patterns have changed markedly in the post-1970 decade.

In contrast to the 1950s, when metropolitan populations were suburbanizing at greater rates than their households, and when nonfamily households were centralizing in the context of high levels of family suburbanization, we find almost the opposite to be occurring in the 1970s. Nonfamily households are suburbanizing to a far greater extent than family households in both old and young areas, and the large suburb–city disparity in household size—which arose in older metropolitan areas during the child-oriented 1950s—has begun to narrow. Although central cities still continued to gain in the number of nonfamily households, this gain cannot be attributed to the increased city attraction or retention of such households. It is because the number of nonfamily households is rising in all parts of the metropolitan area. Indeed, even greater numbers of nonfamily households are located in the suburbs because the suburbs are attracting and retaining increasing shares of these households, and because nonfamily suburban households are being created from elderly, married-couple households by the death of a spouse.

We also examined the post-1970 city–suburb redistribution patterns of different types of family and nonfamily households and found that, among both blacks and nonblacks, non-full-family households have become suburbanized to a greater degree than the traditional married-couple-with-children-under-18 households. Over the 1970–1980 decade, declining and old metropolitan areas have sustained metropolitanwide losses in their nonblack, full-family households, and these losses were absorbed primarily by central cities. Central city household stocks have also sustained losses due to the suburbanization of nonblack, childless-couple family households. The only consistent gains in central city, nonblack households were exhibited for nonfamily households and, to a far lesser extent, single-headed, nonblack family households. The suburbs, in contrast, gained large numbers of the new childless-couple family and nonfamily households, and saw many previous full-family households transformed into childless-couple families, as their children departed to establish separate households elsewhere in the metropolitan area. As a consequence of these redistribution tendencies, nonblack central city household stocks are now dominated by nonfamily households, and those of their suburbs are much less dominated by full-family households than was the case in the immediate postwar decades.

Among black households, we wished to determine if the post-1970 rises in suburbanization might have disproportionately selected full-family, black households—the most economically well-off of all black household types. This would have limited the scope of black suburbanization because such households have been decreasing societywide, in the face of rising numbers of black single-adult-headed families and nonfamily households. However, our examination of the data show that 1970s black suburbanization is quite broad-based with regard to household type. Black "nontraditional" households in most metropolitan areas are exhibiting higher suburbanization rates than black full-family households. As a consequence, black suburban household stocks in 1980 were less full-family dominated—and, therefore, less atypical of the metropolitan area black household composition than was the case in 1970.

Finally we examined, in more detail, potential positive and negative dimensions of nontraditional household redistribution for declining central cities. The potential positive dimension draws from the suggestion that small, well-off, nonblack households might "return to the city" during the 1970s and enhance the residential and economic bases of old and declining areas' central cities. We found *some* support for this view in spite of the fact that such households have suburbanized at higher rates than more traditional nonblack households. Central cities in declining and older areas have sustained net gains in nonblack nonfamily households which helped counter the losses of other nonblack household types. However, the primary source of these gains—the tendency of large baby-boom cohorts to form nonfamily households during this period—suggest that it might be short-lived. As smaller-sized cohorts pass into the peak household formation ages, as nonfamily households continue to suburbanize, and as the "baby boomers" themselves shift into childless-couple families and full-family households, central cities may lose this household "cushion." They will need to compete more aggressively with their suburbs to retain greater shares of the family and nonfamily households that have begun to pervade metropolitan areas.

The negative dimension of the post-1970 household and family shifts for old and declining areas' central cities pertains to the rise of poverty-prone families and individuals—particularly female-headed families. Such families have traditionally located in central cities and their growing numbers among both blacks and nonblacks imply a greater "city concentration" of poverty. The data suggest that poor families and unrelated individuals are *not* suburbanizing as quickly as non-poor households, and that black poor households remain the most heavily concentrated in the city. While black female-headed-family households, in general, have shown high suburbanization rates in the 1970s, those in poverty have shown little suburban gains.

In sum, we have found that the greater diversity of household types, which arose during the post-1970 period, has been accompanied by a marked change in household-type selectivity in city–suburb redistribution. Suburbs have clearly become increasingly attractive to new, small, childless, and nonfamily households than was the case in the 1950s and 1960s. In these same suburbs, large numbers of previous full-family households have become transformed "empty-nest" childless-couple households and "surviving-spouse" nonfamily households. However, these shifts only involved the city–suburb redistribution *process* rather than redistribution outcomes. The legacy of the strong child-oriented suburbanization of the immediate postwar decades still dominates the *aggregate* household composition of cities and suburbs in metropolitan areas of the declining and old area groupings, such that strong city–suburb disparities in household size and the prevalence of full-family households still persist in these areas. Yet the new redistribution processes, reflected in both old and young areas, may serve to change these familiar images of city and suburb household compositions fairly soon. Just as the suburbs were successful in attracting the predominant middle-class household type in the 1950s (that is, married-couple families with children under 18), they appear, once again, to be successful in attracting and retaining the new smaller, less child-oriented, middle-class households that have become pervasive since 1970.

11

WORKPLACE
AND RESIDENCE DIMENSIONS
OF CITY–SUBURB REDISTRIBUTION

Introduction

THE RELATIONSHIP between employment and residence location represents yet another dynamic of intrametropolitan redistribution which has begun to shift directions in the post-1970 years. Trends observed through the 1970 census had given rise to the concern that selective population and employment redistribution tendencies—operating in opposite directions over the 1950–1970 period—had created important "mismatches" between the locations of employment opportunities and the locations of the residences of potential workers whose experience and skills were most appropriate for these opportunities.[1] Of particular concern was the increased isolation of low-income city workers and minorities—from both entry-level and well-paying blue collar

---

[1] A thorough empirical analysis of employment and worker redistribution patterns in ten metropolitan areas over the 1940–1970 period appears in: Thomas M. Stanback, Jr. and Richard V. Knight, *Suburbanization and the City* (Monclair, NJ: Allanheld Osmun and Co. Publishers, Inc., 1976). Additional analyses of the mismatch phenomenon appear in: John D. Kasarda, "The Changing Occupational Structure of the American Metropolis: Apropos the Urban Problem," in Barry Schwartz, ed., *The Changing Face of the Suburbs* (Chicago: University of Chicago Press, 1976); Bennett Harrison, *Urban Economic Development: Suburbanization, Minority Opportunity, and the Condition of the Central City* (Washington, DC: The Urban Institute, 1974); Franklin D. Wilson, *Residential Consumption, Economic Opportunity, and Race* (New York: Academic Press, 1979); and Daniel T. Lichter, "Racial Differences in Underemployment in American Cities, *American Journal of Sociology* 93 (4) (1988): 771–792.

manufacturing jobs that had suburbanized, to a significant degree, in the 1950s and early 1960s, and from lower-level white collar and service jobs that tended to follow the suburbanward movement of middle class residents during the immediate postwar decades. This isolation from suburban employment opportunities was particularly debilitating for central city blacks, who were virtually barred from relocating to suburban residences due to the discriminatory housing market of this period, and for whom the costs of city–suburb "reverse" commuting were often prohibitively high.[2]

The other aspect of the mismatch, less detrimental to the workers affected, involved the selective suburbanward residential redistribution of those workers who were most apt to qualify for the "better" white collar professional and managerial jobs still located, to a greater degree, within the central city. As a consequence, suburb–city commuting—a phenomenon not original with the immediate postwar decades— increased dramatically as the massive suburbanization of the middle-class white workers far outdistanced the suburbanward redistribution of those administrative and business service-linked office jobs that tend to function more effectively in a central location. This separation of workplace from residence location represented more of a "voluntary" redistribution on the part of white suburban residents who, because they did not face racial discrimination or financial barriers in the suburban housing market, were in a position to choose a suburban vis-à-vis a city residence. These residents were able to absorb the increased commuting costs in exchange for a more desirable suburban residential environment. The separation of these workers' residences from their workplaces constituted a structural problem for depopulating central cities that were, at once, losing substantial shares of their residential and industrial tax bases. At the same time they were obliged to provide a broad array of services for an expanded "daytime" metropolitanwide population of workers and shoppers, as well as for the special needs of their own less well-off residential populations, who were becoming increasingly isolated from the expanding metropolitanwide economy.[3]

In observing that manufacturing and retail service jobs were suburbanizing at a faster pace than the most prestigious white collar jobs at the same time that minorities and low-income whites still achieved less than full participation in the residential suburbanization process, a number of urban scholars suggested that this widening mismatch

[2]There is some disagreement on how much of central city black unemployment levels can be attributed to the structural dislocation in city–suburb employment opportunities, and how much can be attributed to racially discriminatory hiring policies. See, for example, Harrison, *Urban Economic Development,* Chapter 3; and Stanback and Knight, *Suburbanization and the City,* Chapter 7.

between workplace and residential locations was contributing significantly to the vicious cycle of selective city–suburb redistribution tendencies which became evident in older metropolitan areas, at the time of the 1970 census. These changes, it was felt, would also lead to increasing levels of unemployment among "stranded" low-skilled and unskilled city residents. The solution to these dislocations was seen to lie either with the greater restructuring of the central city's economic opportunities to the characteristics of its residential labor force or, alternatively, by facilitating a greater demographic response to shifts in the metropolitan area's employment redistribution tendencies. [4]

Changing City Employment Opportunities

As indicated in Chapter 7, several societywide economic and demographic shifts have changed the contexts for suburbanization in the post-1970 years from those that shaped suburbanization during most of the 1950s and 1960s. These shifts suggest some alteration in the residence–workplace mismatches that became evident in the late 1960s. One of these shifts involves the nation's industrial structure, which was becoming decidedly more service-oriented in the 1970s and less dependent upon labor-intensive manufacturing. [5] The significance of this industrial transformation for central city economies is linked to the stronger role given to producer services, distributive services, and services in the nonprofit and government sectors—all associated with

[3]In their analysis of city employment and worker resident redistribution patterns over the 1960–1970 period in ten American cities, Stanback and Knight estimate that the percentage of city workers earnings attributable to suburb-to-city commuters increased over the decade from an average of 31.5 percent in 1960 to 48 percent in 1970 (Stanback and Knight, *Suburbanization and the City*, p. 95). Frey's analysis of six large northern cities over the 1955–1970 period demonstrates that reductions in per capita city *resident* income were increasingly attributable to the immobility of these cities' resident black populations. See William H. Frey, "Black In-migration, White Flight and the Changing Economic Base of the Central City," *American Journal of Sociology* 85(6) (1980):1396–1417.

[4]Harrison, *Urban Economic Development.*

[5]In their 1984 study, Noyelle and Stanback provide evidence supporting their claim that the United States economy had undergone a significant shift in employment and value added in the service sector, resulting from the expanding scope of markets, technological improvements in transportation and communication, and the growing importance of producer service firms, government, nonprofit institutions, and large corporations. A large part of this transformation, as they view it, has occurred within the service sector itself. The authors make the case that services are seen less as final products and more so as "inputs" in the production process—in knowledge-based activities like engineering, manufacturing, research and development, and planning. Such activities, they believe, will continue to expand and also benefit from certain economies of agglomeration. See Thierry J. Noyelle and Thomas M. Stanback, Jr., eds., *The Economic Transformation of American Cities* (Totowa, NJ: Rowman and Allanheld, 1984).

administrative decision making, specialized services, and knowledge-based industries that have traditionally shown the greatest tendencies to locate within central cities. The increased importance of high-level producer services and those associated with the complex of corporate activities should lead to a greater concentration of these activities in large metropolitan areas which were classified earlier as "nodal" (see Table 7.1). This would imply a strengthening of their central cities' roles as "exporters" of high-level producer and headquarter services to private sector firms, and as sites for the increasingly expanding non-profit and government sector activities.

The transformation toward a more service-oriented industrial structure signals a greater "white collarization" of the American labor force. [6] Thus, the fastest growing service sectors—those that have traditionally favored city locations—tend to hold greater shares of the "better" white collar jobs.[7] Central cities are also becoming popular sites for what have been termed "gathering service industries." Such industries are associated with the convention and tourism business and are related to entertainment, cultural, and leisure services that cater to the growing, more mobile segments of the population.[8] Hence, central cities—particularly those that developed strong nodal and administrative functions in the past—would appear to be in a strong position to capitalize on post-1970 shifts in the nation's industrial structure to the extent that they can expand the high-level employment opportunities they offer or, at least, avoid a significant reduction in those opportunities.

The negative aspect of this industrial transformation for both central cities and their suburbs involves a precipitous decline in labor-intensive manufacturing employment which has accompanied what is termed the "deindustrialization of America."[9] Although a good deal of manufacturing activity had relocated into suburban areas well before the 1970 census was taken, the post-1970 industrial transformation has involved a substantial phasing out of some production activities as a

---

[6]Thomas M. Stanback, Jr. and Thierry J. Noyelle, *Cities in Transition* (Totowa, NJ: Allanheld, Osmun and Co. Publishers, Inc., 1982).

[7]Stanback and Noyelle *(Cities in Transition)* suggest that the new, more service-oriented industrial structure will bring with it a greater dichotomy between well-paying and poorly paying white collar jobs. Those service sectors that hold the greatest shares of high-paying jobs—distributive services, producer services, nonprofit and government services—are the ones that have traditionally located in cities. The latter point is supported in Stanback and Knight's *(Suburbanization and the City)* analysis of 1970 city–suburb industrial location patterns.

[8]John D. Kasarda, "Urban Change in Minority Opportunities," in Paul Peterson, ed., *The New Urban Reality* (Washington, DC: The Brookings Institution, 1985), pp. 33–67.

[9]Barry Bluestone and Bennett Harrison, *The Deindustrialization of America: Plant Closures, Community Abandonment and the Dismantling of Basic Industry* (New York: Basic Books, 1982).

consequence of technologically induced automation processes, and the filtering-down of others to peripheral areas and producer sites in other countries to take advantage of the lower labor costs in those areas. Hence, there was a sharp decline in the few low-paying manufacturing employment opportunities that still existed in central cities and a significant erosion of the better-paying blue collar manufacturing jobs in the suburbs. These shifts have been most devastating in those large northern metropolitan areas that have been classed as "functional nodal" and "manufacturing" in our metropolitan typology (see Figure 7.1), and are particularly detrimental to the low-skilled central city workers who were already isolated from suburban blue collar employment during the late 1960s.

Changing Residence Locations of Workers

While these post-1970 industrial shifts imply possible gains in the availability of central city employment opportunities to white collar workers and continual losses of opportunities for blue collar workers, two broad demographic shifts that have come to the fore since 1970 suggest a greater relocation of workers' residences that might serve to reduce employment and residence location "mismatches" within the metropolitan area. These shifts were reviewed in earlier chapters although without regard to their effects on residence-workplace dislocations. The first of these—toward greater numbers of smaller, childless, and nonfamily households—could reinforce the growth in the cities' service sector economy by attracting "back to the city" a significant share of these households to residences that are close to both their place of work and to the broader array of cultural amenities that are available in the newly transforming service cities. The second shift is linked to improvements in race relations and black upward mobility, which facilitated a broader participation of blacks in the suburbanization movement and a significant rise in the number of young blacks that have graduated from college and have taken on white collar occupations. Similar tendencies were observed for members of the newer minorities, Hispanics and Asians, as the assimilation process proceeds (see Chapters 8 and 9). These post-1970 developments could serve to alleviate the long-standing isolation of central city blacks from expanding suburban metropolitan employment opportunities.

Our earlier examination of nonblack redistribution tendencies does not provide strong support for the first contention that a significant return of nonblack suburbanites has taken place. We did observe (in Chapter 9) a discernible tendency for nonblack professionals and college graduates—particularly among recent metropolitan movers and in-migrants—to resist the more pervasive suburbanization tendencies shown for other occupations and educational attainment categories; and (in Chapter 10) we found that a significant enough share of baby-boom young adults chose central city locations to reduce the loss levels of North-Declining city populations. It remains to be determined just how closely these slight tendencies toward cityward relocation are linked to the recent shifts in city employment opportunities.

The second demographic shift—regarding the increased geographic and upward mobility of the black population—holds a greater potential for reducing residence–workplace mismatches. The review of black redistribution tendencies in earlier chapters (Chapters 8 and 9) provides broad support for the contention that the 1970s represent a "bench-mark" decade for black suburbanization. Ironically, many of the suburban blue collar employment opportunities, long out of the reach of central city blacks, have begun to dry up during the same decade that blacks began to participate in the suburbanization process. Nevertheless, the educational attainment and skill levels of the black labor force, particularly among young adult blacks, have become considerably up-graded over the course of the three postwar decades.[10] Newly suburbanizing blacks should be able to avail themselves of the broad array of employment opportunities that can be found in the suburbs. They should also engage in the more "voluntary" suburb-to-city variety of commuting, rather than commuting, out of necessity, from suburb to city.

Still, the increased suburbanization of blacks should not be expected to "correct" the structural dislocations associated with central city–suburb residence–workplace mismatches—particularly among the most poverty-prone city residents who are sometimes described as the "urban underclass."[11] Our earlier analysis (Chapter 10) showed that both black and nonblack poverty households participated only minimally in the 1970s suburbanization process—with black poverty households representing the most city-concentrated of all household types. The employment prospects for these residents, still stranded in the city, have become even further impaired by the inter- and intrametropolitan shifts in employment opportunities that took place in the post-1970 years. Coupled with the earlier suburbanization of low-paying retail service jobs, the recent metropolitanwide losses of labor-intensive manufacturing jobs have severely depleted central cities of the

---

[10]John Reid, "Black America in the 1980s," *Population Bulletin*, Vol. 37, No. 4 (Washington, DC: Population Reference Bureau, Inc., 1982); and Reynolds Farley, *Blacks and Whites: Narrowing the Gap?* (Cambridge, MA: Harvard University Press, 1984).

[11]William J. Wilson, *The Declining Significance of Race* (Chicago: University of Chicago Press, 1978).

type of "entry-level" opportunities that they used to provide for minorities and immigrants; and the further transformation of city economies into high-level service centers, along with accompanying gentrification-linked development, can only result in increased levels of unemployment, underemployment, and welfare dependency among the "underclass" element of the city resident population. [12]

Topics To Be Discussed

This chapter will examine the extent to which the worker residence and workplace location relationship has become altered in the post-1970 period as a consequence of shifts in the employment compositions of central cities and their suburbs, and changes in the residential distributions of the metropolitan area's workers. Some broad societal forces—such as the increased service orientation of the economy, a reduced emphasis on childbearing among young adult whites, and the upward social and geographical mobility of the black population—suggest a reduction in the residence–workplace dislocation. However, it is also apparent that the city-concentrated poverty population continues to face an erosion of entry-level employment opportunities. The next section of this chapter also examines the city–suburb redistribution of employment locations for broad economic sectors, in order to determine the magnitude of intrametropolitan employment shifts for our six large metropolitan area groupings. This section is then followed by one that focuses on the demographic response to these employment shifts by examining post-1970 changes in the residence–workplace distributions of metropolitan residents who work within the metropolitan area and the selectivity in these changes for broad occupational and racial subgroups. Also examined are the changing levels of unemployment among city residents in the labor force. Still another section discusses the nature of intrametropolitan commuting flows within the nation's largest metropolitan areas, and the final section summarizes the chapter's major findings.

Central City and Suburb Employment Changes

Although residential suburbanization has generally preceded employment suburbanization in large metropolitan areas, employment opportunities also suburbanized to a significant degree over the 1950–1970

---

[12]This argument is developed in detail in John D. Kasarda, "Urban Change in Minority Opportunities."

period, as technological breakthroughs in production and transportation made suburban sites attractive for manufacturing employment, and retail employment began to follow the extensive suburbanward population movement. In 1970 approximately 47 percent of employed workers in those metropolitan areas that we have classed as North-Declining worked in suburban locations, while 57 percent of the metropolitan area population resided in suburban locations. In this section, we shall examine the extent to which employment has continued to suburbanize in the post-1970 period and the selectivity of this employment suburbanization by broad industrial sectors. Particular attention is given to the North-Declining metropolitan areas in this review since the "problem cities" in this grouping are especially vulnerable to continued post-1970 losses in manufacturing employment. These areas also stand to benefit considerably from a greater central city growth—or retention—of high-level service employment opportunities associated with growing post-1970 industrial sectors.

City Suburb Employment Changes: 1960–1980

The central city and suburban employment locations of workers residing in the metropolitan areas of our six broad area groupings are displayed in Figure 11.1 for years 1960, 1970, and 1980. In the interest of keeping relatively constant boundaries for this time series, given the availability of census place of work data, the 1970 and 1980 employment data pertain to 1970 SMSA and central city definitions, while the 1960 data pertain to 1960 SMSA and central city definitions.[13] It is nevertheless clear from this figure that the suburbanization of employment has continued through the post-1970 period. The North-Declining area central cities continued to lose jobs as their suburbs continued to gain; and while city employment levels continued to increase in South-Old and West-Old metropolitan areas, they became surpassed by suburb

[13]It is not possible to construct this time series on the basis of the 1980-based metropolitan area definitions used in most of the other analyses of city–suburb redistribution, because pre-1980 census place-of-work data are not available in the manner that allows their reaggregation into 1980 boundaries. It is, nevertheless, possible to rearrange 1980 place-of-work data to correspond closely to 1970 central city and SMSA definitions with the "A" Sample of the 1980 Census Public Use Microfile (the 1970-equivalent definitions are discussed in Appendix F). Unfortunately, similar consistency with 1970 definitions cannot be obtained with 1960 place-of-work data. Therefore, the 1960 employment data presented in this chapter are based on 1960 central city and SMSA definitions. (In these comparisons, two central cities in 1970, Long Beach, California, and Everett, Washington, are classed with suburban territory in 1960.) The reader should also be reminded that, as in previous chapters, central city data are not adjusted for annexation of territory (see the section "Annexation and City Growth" in Chapter 7).

FIGURE 11.1

Workers' Employment Location,[a] Central Cities and Suburbs, 1960–1980: Six Metropolitan Area Groupings[b]

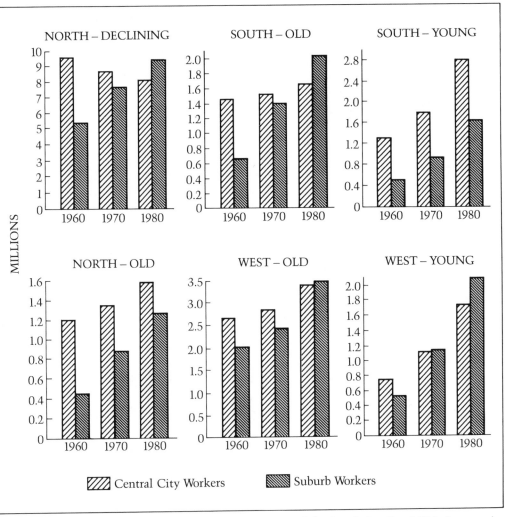

SOURCES: 1960: Census of Population, 1960: *Characteristics of the Population,* Part I (U.S. Summary), Table 302.

1970: Census of Population, 1970: *Characteristics of the Population,* Part I (U.S. Summary), Table 362.

1980: Machine-readable computer file: Census of Population and Housing, 1980, Public Use Microdata Samples "A" and "B" (prepared by the U.S. Bureau of the Census, Washington, DC).

Includes employed workers, at work during census week, for metropolitan area residents who reported workplace (ages 14+ in 1960, ages 16+ in 1970 and 1980).

Defined according to 1960 SMSA and Central City Definitions (1960), 1970 SMSA and Central City Definitions (1970), and 1970 Equivalent SMSA and Central City Definitions (1980).

employment levels over the 1970–1980 decade. By 1980 the West-Young areas increased the suburban employment advantage already displayed in 1970; and only in the North-Old and South-Young groupings did suburban employment levels lie consistently below those shown for their central cities.

The post-1970 suburbanization of employment is perhaps better understood when it is contrasted with suburban residential population redistribution over the period. The data in Table 11.1 show that the 1970 suburban share of employment lies well below that for the residential population in each of the six metropolitan area groupings. However, among the North-Declining and three older groupings, this disparity did not widen significantly and, in fact, declined slightly for North-Declining, South-Old, and West-Old areas. The two younger metropolitan area groupings diverge somewhat from this pattern. In South-Young areas, the change in the suburban share of employment shows up to be quite modest in comparison to the change shown for population. West-Young areas, on the other hand, exhibit a suburban-ward employment shift that is slightly larger than the population shift, although the population continues to remain more dispersed than employment in 1980.

The reduction in the disparity between employment and population shares in many older metropolitan areas implies higher rates of employment suburbanization than of population suburbanization. To examine this matter further we present, in Figure 11.2, plots for 1960–1980 metropolitan area and central city population and employment for six metropolitan areas defined according to constant central city and SMSA boundaries. Five of these areas (all except Washington, DC) exhibited higher rates of employment suburbanization than population suburbanization over the 1970–1980 period, and in three areas (New York, Philadelphia, and San Francisco–Oakland) the disparity between the rates increased since the 1960–1970 period.[14] The plots also point up a 1970s

[14]The suburbanization rates for each metropolitan area are as follows:

	1960–1970		1970–1980	
	Workers	Population	Workers	Population
New York	39.2	25.4	27.3	12.3
Philadelphia	38.5	25.4	38.0	18.8
Chicago	85.2	40.1	41.2	24.5
Detroit	84.0	37.4	42.5	28.3
Washington, DC	114.8	61.1	23.6	28.1
San Francisco–Oakland	21.9	34.7	23.6	15.4

where, for this comparison, New York and Detroit are defined according to 1970 central city and SMSA definitions and the remaining four metropolitan areas are defined according to 1980 SMSA definitions (which do not vary over the 1960–1980 period). None of these areas' central cities sustained significant annexation over the 1960–1980 period.

TABLE 11.1

Metropolitan Area Size, Suburban Share of Population and Employed Workers,[a] 1970 and 1980:
Six Metropolitan Area Groupings[b]

Metropolitan Area Groupings[c]	Metropolitan Area		Percent in Suburbs		
	1970 Size (in thousands)	1970–1980 Percent Change	1970	1980	Difference
NORTH-DECLINING					
Workers	16,290	+7.5	46.8	54.0	+7.2
Population	45,477	−3.5	57.0	61.4	+4.4
NORTH-OLD					
Workers	2,233	+27.4	39.5	44.5	+5.0
Population	6,132	+4.3	55.3	61.0	+5.7
SOUTH-OLD					
Workers	2,888	+26.8	47.7	55.2	+7.5
Population	7,368	+9.1	62.7	70.0	+7.3
WEST-OLD					
Workers	5,249	+30.8	46.3	50.5	+4.2
Population	13,813	+9.8	58.5	62.1	+3.6
SOUTH-YOUNG					
Workers	2,709	+63.9	34.0	36.7	+2.7
Population	7,306	+35.5	46.9	55.4	+8.5
WEST-YOUNG					
Workers	2,263	+69.2	50.3	54.7	+4.4
Population	6,759	+35.7	59.1	61.9	+2.8

SOURCES: 1970 and 1980 workers: Same as Figure 11.1. 1970 and 1980 Population: Machine-readable computer files *County and City Data Book,* Consolidated Files for Counties, 1947–1977, and Cities, 1944–1947: and *County and City Data Book,* 1983 files (prepared by the U.S. Bureau of the Census, Washington, DC).

[a]Includes employed workers, at work during census week, for metropolitan area residents who reported workplace (age 16+).

[b]Defined in 1970 SMSA and Central City Definitions (1970) and in 1970 Equivalent SMSA and Central City Definitions (1980).

[c]These metropolitan area groupings are based on three categories of region (North, South, West), two categories of age (Old, Young), and two categories of metropolitan growth (Declining, Nondeclining). All 13 Declining areas are also Old and located in the North and are placed in the North-Declining grouping. The remaining 26 areas are all Nondeclining and sorted into the groupings: North-Old, South-Old, West-Old, South-Young, and West-Young. Further details are provided in the Chapter 7 section, "A Metropolitan Area Typology," and Figure 7.1.

FIGURE 11.2

*Population and Workers' Employment Location,[a] Metropolitan Areas
and Central Cities, 1960–1980: Six Selected Metropolitan Areas[b]*

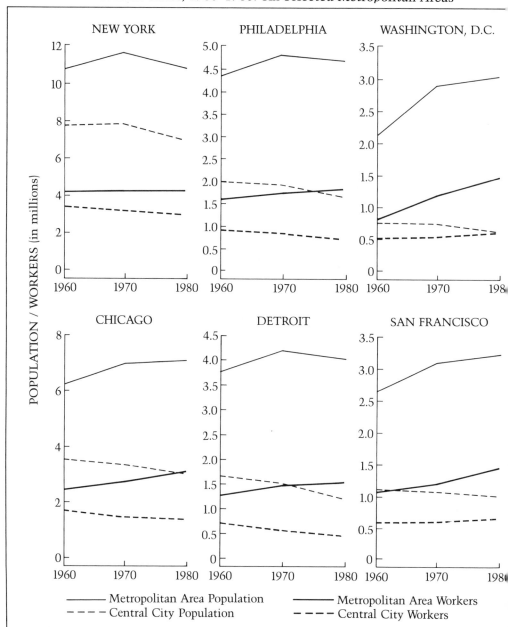

SOURCES: Data for workers: same as Figure 11.1. Data for Population: compiled from machine-readable computer files: *County and City Data Book*, Consolidated Files for Counties 1947–1977, and Cities 1944–1977; and *County and City Data Book*, 1983 file (prepared by the U.S. Bureau of the Census, Washington, DC).

[a]Includes employed workers, at work during census week, for metropolitan area residents who report workplace (ages 14+ in 1960, ages 16+ in 1970 and 1980).

[b]The six metropolitan areas are defined in terms of constant metropolitan area definitions (census SMSA definitions for all areas except New York and Detroit remained constant 1960–1980, New York and Detroit are defined here in terms of 1970 census SMSA definitions 1960–1980). The central cities for each remain the same and have not undergone significant annexation over the 1960–1980 period.

shift that occurs with all metropolitan areas—greater rates of gain in the work force than for the population as a whole. These gains, attributable to the graduation of large baby-boom cohorts into prime labor force ages and to a sharp rise in the labor force participation of women, are responsible for the greater 1970s increases (or reduced decreases) shown for employment vis-à-vis residential population in the cities and suburbs of each metropolitan area. Most of these new jobs were created in various service sector industries, although many involve relatively low-paying occupations.[15]

Manufacturing and Nonmanufacturing Employment

To what extent is the new suburbanization of employment an extension of the substantial pre-1970 suburbanization of manufacturing employment, or to what extent does it involve the suburbanization of other sectors? A broad overview for the six metropolitan area groupings can be gained from the plots shown in Figure 11.3, which display 1960, 1970, and 1980 city and suburb employment levels for manufacturing and other industries. (Percentage distributions based on this figure are presented in Appendix E, Table 11.A.) Again bearing in mind the slightly different 1960 metropolitan definitions, it can be seen that in North-Declining central cities manufacturing employment declined over both the 1960s and 1970s decades. It was during the 1960s that the majority of metropolitan manufacturing jobs—through city job losses and suburban job gains—became relocated into the suburbs. Only with the 1970s did city nonmanufacturing jobs decline, although the number of suburban nonmanufacturing jobs increased significantly during both the 1960s and 1970s. Indeed, the first four columns of Table 11.2 show a slightly higher 1970s rate of nonmanufacturing suburbanization than manufacturing suburbanization for North-Declining metropolitan areas. However, the metropolitanwide loss of manufacturing jobs in these areas, coupled with the continued suburbanization of those that remained, contributed to a substantial erosion of manufacturing employment opportunities within their central cities.

Similar 1960–1980 trends are shown for South-Old areas, although manufacturing constitutes a smaller proportion of their total employment (14 percent in 1970) than in North-Declining areas (27 percent). Here again, suburban manufacturing employment overtook city manufacturing employment in the 1960s, although this did not occur for nonmanufacturing employment until the 1970s. Also, as with North-Declining areas, the 1970 suburbanization rate for nonmanufac-

[15]Stanback and Noyelle, *Cities in Transition.*

FIGURE 11.3

Central City and Suburb Employment Location for Workers in Manufacturing and Other Industries, 1960–1980: Six Metropolitan Area Groupings[a]

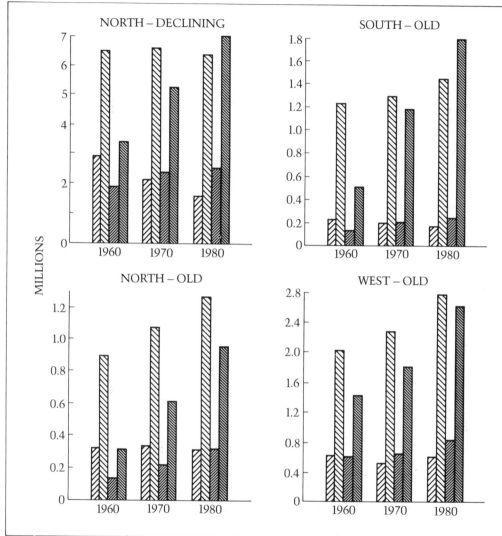

SOURCES: 1960: Census of Population: 1960, *Subject Report* Journey to Work, PL(2) 6B, Table 2.
1970: Census of Population: 1970, *Subject Report* Journey to Work, PL(3) 6D, Table 2.
1980: Machine-readable computer file: Census of Population and Housing, 1980, Public Us Microdata Samples "A" and "B" (prepared by the U.S. Bureau of the Census, Washing ton, DC).

[a]Central city and metropolitan area boundaries, and workers defined as in Figure 11.1.

FIGURE 11.3 *(continued)*

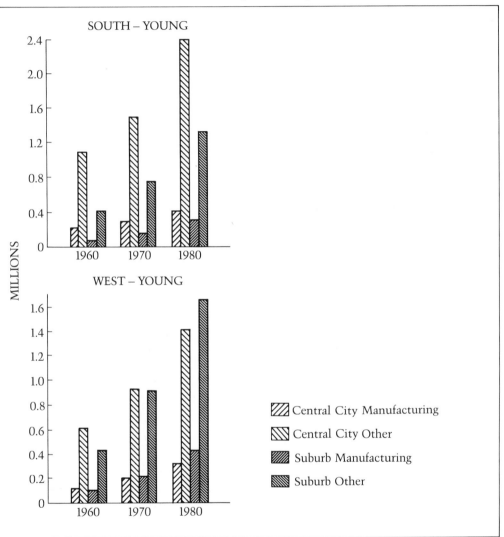

turing employment slightly exceeded that for manufacturing employment; and low (although not negative) metropolitanwide manufacturing growth caused South-Old central cities to sustain losses in their manufacturing jobs over the 1970s decade.

The remaining two older area groupings, North-Old and West-Old, diverged somewhat from the patterns just described, although both have

TABLE 11.2

Percent Change in Metropolitan Area, Central City, and Suburb Employment Location, 1970–1980, and Suburban Share of Employment Location, 1970 and 1980, for Manufacturing and Other Workers[a]. Six Metropolitan Area Groupings[b]

Metropolitan Area Groupings/ Industry Class	1970–1980 Percent Change			Suburbanization Rate[c]	Percent in Suburbs	
	Metropolitan Area	Central City	Suburb		1970	1980
NORTH-DECLINING						
Manufacturing	−8.1	−24.7	+6.9	+31.6	52.5	61.1
Other	+12.3	−3.6	+32.2	+35.8	44.4	52.2
Total	+6.7	−8.8	+24.3	+33.1	46.6	54.4
NORTH-OLD						
Manufacturing	+12.8	−7.1	+43.1	+50.2	39.6	50.2
Other	+31.6	+18.1	+55.4	+37.4	36.4	42.9
Total	+27.0	+12.1	+52.2	+40.1	37.2	44.5
SOUTH-OLD						
Manufacturing	+4.0	−12.8	+20.2	+33.0	50.9	58.8
Other	+30.4	+11.9	+50.7	+38.9	47.7	55.2
Total	+26.7	+8.6	+46.2	+37.6	48.2	55.6
WEST-OLD						
Manufacturing	+22.3	+15.9	+27.4	+11.4	55.6	57.9
Other	+32.0	+21.6	+45.1	+23.5	44.3	48.7
Total	+29.8	+20.5	+40.4	+19.9	46.8	50.6
SOUTH-YOUNG						
Manufacturing	+55.9	+41.0	+82.1	+41.1	36.1	42.2
Other	+64.8	+59.9	+74.5	+14.5	33.7	35.7
Total	+63.3	+56.8	+75.9	+19.0	34.1	36.8
WEST-YOUNG						
Manufacturing	+79.2	+61.2	+95.2	+34.1	52.8	57.5
Other	+65.9	+51.7	+80.1	+28.4	49.8	54.1
Total	+68.3	+53.4	+83.1	+29.7	50.3	54.8

SOURCES: Same as Figure 11.3 for 1970 and 1980.

[a]Includes employed workers, at work during census week, for metropolitan area residents who reported workplace (age 16+)

significant manufacturing sectors (representing 25 percent and 22 percent, respectively, of employed workers in 1970). In some respects, the North-Old city–suburb employment shifts in the 1970s resemble those of North-Declining areas a decade earlier. It was only during the 1970s decade that suburban manufacturing employment overtook city manufacturing employment and, in 1980, city nonmanufacturing employment continues to overshadow that of the suburbs. Table 11.2 data show manufacturing suburbanization to be occurring at a higher rate than nonmanufacturing employment in the 1970s and, as a consequence, North-Old central cities sustained 1970–1980 manufacturing losses. West-Old areas are more consistent with North-Declining and South-Old areas in that their 1970s suburbanization rates are higher for nonmanufacturing rather than manufacturing employment. Metropolitanwide manufacturing growth in these areas remains higher than in any of the other older groupings, and manufacturing suburbanization remains much lower. As a consequence, central cities of these areas have sustained fairly substantial 1970s manufacturing employment gains.

The two young metropolitan area groupings, South-Young and West-Young, differ from the four older groupings in their employment suburbanization tendencies, and also diverge from each other. The distinct feature of these areas is their continued high rates of both manufacturing and nonmanufacturing growth, metropolitanwide, although their manufacturing shares of total employment are relatively low (17 percent and 19 percent, respectively, in 1970). In South-Young areas, as shown in Figure 11.3, both manufacturing and nonmanufacturing employment remained concentrated primarily in central city locations over the 1960–1980 period—although during the 1970s, manufacturing jobs began to suburbanize fairly rapidly. The West-Young areas, in contrast, exhibited greater city–suburb parity in their numbers of manufacturing and nonmanufacturing jobs through 1970. Between 1970 and 1980 a suburbanward redistribution of both sectors occurred. Nevertheless, high rates of employment growth enjoyed by each of these younger metropolitan area groupings have facilitated substantial city and suburb employment growth for each sector, in these areas, in both the 1960s and the 1970s.

The above evaluation of city to suburb employment redistribution indicates that those metropolitan area groupings that contain the most "problem cities"—North-Declining areas and South-Old areas—are exhibiting similar post-1970 redistribution tendencies. First, their rates of employment suburbanization are greater than their rates of population suburbanization. Second, the majority of metropolitan jobs in each area grouping has shifted from the city to the suburbs. Third, their rates of nonmanufacturing employment suburbanization are greater than their rates of manufacturing suburbanization. This third tendency is particularly noteworthy in light of speculation (discussed in the Introduction) that a more service-oriented industrial structure might bolster central city employment prospects. It suggests that further examination be given to the post-1970 suburbanization of specific nonmanufacturing industries.

Service Employment

We therefore examine suburbanization patterns for a more fine-grained classification system in North-Declining areas. The classification of industries, shown in Table 11.3, includes the two "secondary" industries, construction and manufacturing, as well as five industries that represent various categories of services. The most important categories for this review are: producer services, professional services, and public administration—because these are linked to administration and knowledge-based activities that hold the potential for solidifying central city employment bases.[16]

Percent change figures in the middle four columns of Table 11.3 indicate that each of these three industries grew significantly at the metropolitanwide level over the 1970–1980 period. Moreover, they represent the only broad industrial categories to increase within the central city, confirming their significance for city employment gains. Yet despite these city gains, the three industries—particularly producer services—grew at even greater levels in North-Declining suburbs and contributed substantially to the high suburbanization rate shown for nonmanufacturing employment in Table 11.2. The rise of producer services and related industries, therefore, represents an important source of growth to the evolving "service city," but more as a consequence of such cities' already established bases in these industries rather than their ability to attract new growth. (Other data, not shown, confirm similar patterns in South-Old metropolitan areas.) This city-concentration of these industries, as with other nonmanufacturing industries (shown in the last two columns of Table 11.3), is steadily eroding, so that the cities' hold on them vis-à-vis their suburbs would appear to be relative rather than absolute.

___

[16]Producer services as defined here include the broad census categories: finance, insurance and real estate, and business and repair services. It is meant to be a crude indicator (given available census data) of the producer services concept discussed in Noyelle and Stanback, *The Economic Transformation of American Cities,* p. 9.

TABLE 11.3

Metropolitan Area, Central City, and Suburb Employment Location, 1970,
Percent Change in Employment Location, 1970–1980,
and Suburban Share of Employment Location, 1970 and 1980,
for Workers by Industrial Categories: North-Declining Metropolitan Areas[a]

Metropolitan Area Grouping/ Industry Class	1970 Employment Location of Workers (in thousands)			1970–1980 Percent Change			Suburbanization Rate[b]	Percent in Suburbs	
	Metropolitan Area	Central City	Suburbs	Metropolitan Area	Central City	Suburbs		1970	1980
NORTH-DECLINING AREAS									
Construction	747	327	420	−11.2	−23.6	−1.6	+22.0	56.2	62.3
Manufacturing	4,535	2,152	2,382	−8.1	−24.7	+6.9	+31.6	52.5	61.1
Trans., Comm., Pub. Util.	1,348	882	465	−11.1	−21.2	+8.3	+29.5	34.5	42.0
Wholesale/Ret. Trade	3,345	1,675	1,670	+6.0	−19.2	+31.3	+50.5	49.9	61.8
Professional Services	2,902	1,564	1,339	+34.0	+22.9	+47.0	+24.1	46.1	50.6
Producer Services	1,727	1,164	562	+31.0	+7.4	+79.9	+72.5	32.6	44.7
Personal Services	619	328	291	−28.8	−39.4	−16.9	+22.4	47.0	54.9
Public Adm.	824	538	285	+19.7	+9.5	+38.8	+29.3	34.6	40.2
Other	376	130	246	−3.1	−10.7	+1.0	+11.6	65.4	68.1
Total	16,422	8,763	7,659	+6.7	−8.8	+24.3	+33.1	46.6	54.4

SOURCES: Same as Figure 11.3 for 1970 and 1980.

[a]Workers and metropolitan areas defined as in Table 11.2.
[b]Suburbanization Rate: Suburb Percent Change minus Central City Percent Change.

Discussion

The review of central city–suburb employment redistribution, in this section, has pointed up notable post-1970 shifts in both the magnitude and selectivity of change within the metropolitan area groupings that contain the most "problem" cities. In these areas, one finds a continued suburbanization of manufacturing employment, an increasing suburbanization of nonmanufacturing employment, and some central city retention of high-level service employment. Lower levels of metropolitanwide manufacturing growth have led to absolute losses of central city manufacturing jobs, and a good deal of nonmanufacturing employment deconcentrated toward the suburbs. While the city retention of some selected service activities might provide inducement for a limited middle-class "return," the sustained suburbanization of employment, of all types, represents the more pervasive tendency in these areas.

Workplace and Residence Location Changes

The widening worker residence and employment location mismatches, observed at the time of the 1970 census, were brought about by a rise in the largely "voluntary" commuting of city workers, who preferred to reside in the suburbs, and by significant levels of "reverse" city–suburb commuting on the part of city-concentrated minorities, as they became increasingly isolated from expanding suburban employment opportunities. Another type of mismatch involved city residents who, isolated from suburban employment and unable to find appropriate city-located jobs, remained unemployed. The present section examines the extent to which these residence-worker dislocations have become altered, as a consequence of post-1970 shifts in city and suburb employment locations and the societywide demographic shifts that were discussed in the Introduction. The previous section indicated some city employment retention among the growing sectors of professional services, producer services, and public administration—providing, at least, the potential stimulation for a selective cityward redistribution of residents. However, the more pervasive suburbanward relocation of employment opportunities suggests that an increased suburbanward redistribution of black city residents will be necessary to reduce their dislocation.

Overall Residence-Employment Location Shifts

Our review of shifts in workers' residence and workplace locations over the 1970–1980 period will be restricted, due to data constraints, to civilian employed male workers residing in the metropolitan areas of our six broad groupings.[17] The suburban shares of these workers' workplace and residence locations, displayed in Table 11.4, show that workplaces have remained more city-concentrated than residence locations over the 1970–1980 period. Yet, for five of the six metropolitan area groupings, this city-concentration has not increased substantially over the decade. North-Declining and South-Old metropolitan areas exhibited the greatest suburbanward redistribution of both workplace and residence locations, with the latter shifting to a somewhat greater degree. Less accentuated suburbanward redistribution patterns are displayed for North-Old, West-Old, and West-Young groupings. It is only in South-Young metropolitan areas that we observe a markedly greater deconcentration of workers' residences than their workplaces—leading to a wider 1980 than 1970 city concentration of employment in these areas. However, by and large, workplace and residence deconcentration paralleled each other in large metropolitan areas during the decade of the 1970s in a manner that did not increase the city-concentration of employment markedly.

How, then, have residence–workplace dislocations been altered during the post-1970 period? A broad overview can be gained from Table 11.5, which displays shifts in distribution of workplace–residence locations across central cities and suburbs between 1970 and 1980. These comparisons are shown only for the four older metropolitan area groupings because such comparisons for South-Young and West-Young areas during the 1970s would be distorted by their extensive central city annexations. The shifts for North-Declining areas indicate clear reductions in both types of residence–workplace mismatches. That is, there is a reduction in the number of "reverse" city-to-suburb commuters, and a somewhat smaller reduction of "voluntary" commuters. However, the most predominant shifts, in absolute numbers of workers, occurred among same residence–workplace location workers, involving a substantial reduction of city residents who also work in the city, and an almost equally impressive gain in the number of suburban residents who work in the suburbs.

In the aggregate, then, there is no detectable evidence of a "return to the city" movement. In fact, quite the opposite has occurred. The dominant demographic response to the increased number of suburban employment opportunities in these areas appears to have been the

---

[17]Our restriction to civilian males was made to simplify our exposition, and because dates for all of the comparisons in this section were only available for civilian males. This restriction necessitated our leaving out the experience of the growing female labor force. However, a comparison of workplace and residence shifts for all workers, on the one hand, and for civilian males on the other, for our six metropolitan area categories (not shown), showed each group to exhibit similar suburban shares of metropolitan residential and workplace locations in 1970, and similar shifts over the 1970–1980 period.

TABLE 11.4

Metropolitan Area Size and Suburban Share of Workplace
and Residence Locations, Civilian Male Metropolitan Area Residents
Who Work Within the Metropolitan Area,[a] 1970 and 1980:
Six Metropolitan Area Groupings[b]

Metropolitan Area Groupings/ Location	Metropolitan Area		Percent in Suburb		
	1970 Size[c] (in thousands)	1970–1980 Percent Change	1970	1980	Differen.
NORTH-DECLINING					
Workplace	9,154	−3.6	47.5	54.0	+6.5
Residence	9,154	−3.6	57.7	65.6	+7.9
NORTH-OLD					
Workplace	1,245	+14.6	40.2	44.6	+4.4
Residence	1,245	+14.6	55.5	61.2	+5.7
SOUTH-OLD					
Workplace	1,503	+16.4	47.9	55.6	+7.7
Residence	1,503	+16.4	66.4	76.0	+9.6
WEST-OLD					
Workplace	2,951	+15.8	47.2	50.5	+3.3
Residence	2,951	+15.8	58.8	62.4	+3.6
SOUTH-YOUNG					
Workplace	1,474	+48.0	34.6	36.3	+1.7
Residence	1,474	+48.0	46.9	55.1	+8.2
WEST-YOUNG					
Workplace	1,180	+53.1	50.2	54.8	+4.6
Residence	1,180	+53.1	57.3	60.8	+3.5

SOURCES: 1970: Census of Population: 1970; Special census tabulations 1980: Same as Figure 11.1.
[a]Metropolitan residents who both live and work within the metropolitan area, who were employed and at work during census week.
[b]Metropolitan areas defined as in Table 11.2.
[c]Both residence and workplace sizes pertain to the same universe (see footnote a).

suburbanward relocation of individuals who had previously both lived
and worked in the city.[18]

[18]Although this inference would appear to be obvious from the magnitudes of the
1970–1980 decline in the North-Declining city residence-city-worker category (−661,500)
and the increase in the suburb residence-suburb worker category (+586,700), it can only
be made indirectly. The changes in residence-workplace categories, shown in Table 11.5,
indicate only net changes over the period that could result from: shifts across categories,
shifts into and out of the labor force, or in- and outmigration from the metropolitan area.

TABLE 11.5

*Changes in Central City and Suburb Residence–Workplace Categories, 1970–1980,
for Civilian Male Residents Who Work Within the Metropolitan Area[a]:
Selected Metropolitan Area Groupings[b]*

Metropolitan Area Groupings/ Residence–Workplace Category	Residence–Workplace in 1970[c]	Change 1970–1980[c]	Percent Change 1970–1980
NORTH-DECLINING			
City Res.-City Work.	31,866	−6,615	−20.8
City Res.-Sub. Work.	6,819	−1,760	−25.8
Sub. Res.-City Work.	16,183	−819	−5.1
Sub. Res.-Sub. Work.	36,676	+5,867	+16.0
NORTH-OLD			
City Res.-City Work.	4,325	+133	+3.1
City Res.-Sub. Work.	1,218	−139	−11.4
Sub. Res.-City Work.	3,122	+314	+10.1
Sub. Res.-Sub. Work.	3,782	+1,507	+39.8
SOUTH-OLD			
City Res.-City Work.	3,917	−679	−17.3
City Res.-Sub. Work.	1,138	−186	−16.3
Sub. Res.-City Work.	3,907	+622	+15.9
Sub. Res.-Sub. Work.	6,067	+2,701	+44.5
WEST-OLD			
City Res.-City Work.	9,127	+409	+4.5
City Res.-Sub. Work.	3,034	+293	+9.7
Sub. Res.-City Work.	6,451	+919	+14.3
Sub. Res.-Sub. Work.	10,895	+3,054	+28.0

SOURCES: 1970: Census of Population, 1970; special census tabulations 1980; machine-readable computer files: Census of Population and Housing, 1980: Public Use Microdata Samples "A" and "B" prepared by the U.S. Bureau of the Census, Washington, DC).

Metropolitan residents who both live and work within the metropolitan area who were employed and at work during census week.
Metropolitan areas defined as in Table 11.2.
In hundreds.

A similar significant increase in the suburban resident-worker category is evident for South-Old metropolitan areas, although one also finds in these areas an increase in suburb-to-city commuting. Here again there is no detectable "return to the city" movement evident, although the reduction in "reverse" commuters suggests a greater suburbanward accommodation of residences to workplaces among previous city residents.

Of the four groupings examined here, it is only in the North-Old metropolitan areas that a noticeable return to the city movement can be found. While, once again, suburban resident-workers sustained the highest increases over the 1970–1980 period, city workers—both residing in the city and commuting from the suburbs—also exhibited modest gains. Although such gains were evident in West-Old areas, as well, they were overwhelmed by the far larger gains shown for suburban resident-workers in these areas. Nevertheless, both the North-Old and West-Old area groupings show evidence of a reduced-scale reverse commuting over the 1970s. The former grouping registers an absolute decline in city-to-suburb commuters over the 1970–1980 period; while the latter displays an increase that in absolute numbers lies well below the increases shown for the other residence–workplace categories.

A more concise view of the 1970–1980 alterations in residence–workplace distributions is presented in Table 11.6, where several common shifts appear to be occurring among the four older metropolitan area groupings. First, there is an appreciable gain in the share of metropolitan area residents who both live and work in the suburbs. By 1980 this share approached half of all workers residing in North-Declining metropolitan areas and exceeded 50 percent for South-Old areas. Second, there is a significant decline in the share of metropolitan area workers who both live and work within the central city. Finally, we find that the 1970–1980 period heralds a small decline in the share of metropolitan residents who commute between the central city and suburbs. This decline is somewhat more accentuated among reverse commuters than the more voluntary suburb-to-city commuters; and the fact that neither of these commuting stream shares continued to increase during the 1970s is noteworthy. Nevertheless, still in 1980, the stream of suburb-to-city commuters represents a substantial share of the metropolitan worker population in each of the four older area groupings.

While we cannot evaluate the over-time shifts in residence–workplace distributions for the South-Young and West-Young metropolitan areas, their 1980 distributions (shown in Table 11.6) reveal somewhat contrasting patterns. In South-Young areas, where employment is more strongly city-concentrated than workers' residential locations, the greatest share of metropolitan area workers both live and work within the central city and, among those that reside in the suburbs, a fairly high level of commuting is in evidence. This distribution is indicative of the patterns displayed by the now older metropolitan areas during their earlier stages of residential-led suburbanization. The West-Young metropolitan areas have less concentrated employment and residential location distributions than South-Young areas. The majority (43 per-

TABLE 11.6

*Distribution of Residence–Workplace Categories, 1970 and 1980,
and 1970–1980 Difference in Distribution for Civilian Male Residents
Who Work Within the Metropolitan Area: Six Metropolitan Area Groupings*[a]

Metropolitan Area Groupings/ Residence–Workplace Category	Distribution of Residence Workplace		Difference (1980 minus 1970)
	1970	1980	
NORTH-DECLINING			
City Res.-City Work.	34.8	28.6	−6.2
City Res.-Sub. Work.	7.4	5.7	−1.7
Sub. Res.-City Work.	17.7	17.4	−0.3
Sub. Res.-Sub. Work.	40.1	48.2	+8.2
Total	100.0	100.0	
NORTH-OLD			
City Res.-City Work.	34.7	31.3	−3.5
City Res.-Sub. Work.	9.8	7.6	−2.2
Sub. Res.-City Work.	25.1	24.1	−1.0
Sub. Res.-Sub. Work.	30.4	37.1	+6.7
Total	100.0	100.0	
SOUTH-OLD			
City Res.-City Work.	26.1	18.5	−7.5
City Res.-Sub. Work.	7.6	5.4	−2.1
Sub. Res.-City Work.	26.0	25.9	−0.1
Sub. Res.-Sub. Work.	40.4	50.1	+9.8
Total	100.0	100.0	
WEST-OLD			
City Res.-City Work.	30.9	27.9	−3.0
City Res.-Sub. Work.	10.3	9.7	−0.5
Sub. Res.-City Work.	21.9	21.6	−0.3
Sub. Res.-Sub. Work.	36.9	40.8	+3.9
Total	100.0	100.0	
SOUTH-YOUNG			
City Res.-City Work.	—	38.2	—
City Res.-Sub. Work.	—	6.7	—
Sub. Res.-City Work.	—	25.5	—
Sub. Res.-Sub. Work.	—	29.6	—
Total	—	100.0	—
WEST-YOUNG			
City Res.-City Work.	—	27.4	—
City Res.-Sub. Work.	—	11.8	—
Sub. Res.-City Work.	—	17.8	—
Sub. Res.-Sub. Work.	—	43.0	—
Total	—	100.0	—

SOURCES: Same as Table 11.5.

[a] Resident-workers defined as in Table 11.5 and metropolitan areas defined as in Table 11.2.

cent) of their metropolitan workers both live and work in the suburbs and a fairly substantial number of city residents (11 percent) commute to the suburbs.

Occupation-Selective Shifts

In light of the broad suburbanward industrial structure shifts observed previously in this chapter, and our concern with the selective residential responses to these shifts, a more detailed analysis of occupation-selective residence-workplace changes can be made from the data in Table 11.7. Shown here, for North-Declining and South-Old areas—those with the greatest number of "problem cities," are the residence–workplace changes disaggregated by the broad occupation groupings: white collar workers, service workers, and blue collar workers. These data permit us to assess how the suburbanization of nonmanufacturing employment in these areas (observed earlier) has affected white collar residence and employment patterns; and, also, how blue collar employment and residence location patterns have been altered in the context of slow manufacturing growth. The occupation categories pertain to the major occupation categories employed in the 1970 census. The white collar categories include managers and administrators, except those in farming ("managers"); professionals, technical, and kindred workers ("professionals"); sales workers ("sales workers"); and clerical and kindred workers ("clerical workers"). The "service worker" category pertains to service workers, including private households. The two blue collar worker categories consist of: craftsmen and kindred workers ("craftsmen"), and a residual category, which includes operative workers, transport equipment operative workers, and laborers ("other blue collar workers"). The small number of farm workers that exist within metropolitan areas are included in the last category.

The redistribution patterns shown with the Table 11.7 data are not encouraging for older central cities. There appears, indeed, to be a relationship between suburban nonmanufacturing employment gains, and the residence–workplace shifts, observed earlier, for North-Declining metropolitan areas. The Table 11.7 data reveal that the overall 1970–1980 gain in the category "suburb resident-suburb worker" is primarily attributable to the increase in white collar workers. Further, the bulk of the overall 1970–1980 decline in the number of the city residents who also work in the city is accounted for by blue collar workers. Hence, the increased suburbanization of nonmanufacturing employment, in addition to the increasing "white collarization" of the labor force, appears to be associated with most of the suburban gain in

TABLE 11.7

Changes in Central City and Suburb Residence–Workplace Categories, 1970–1980, for Civilian Male Residents Who Work Within the Metropolitan Area, by Occupation: North-Declining and South-Old Metropolitan Area Groupings[a]

Metropolitan Area Groupings/ Residence–Workplace Category	White Collar		Service Workers		Blue Collar[b]	
	Res.-Work in 1970[c]	Change 1970–1980[c]	Res.-Work in 1970[c]	Change 1970–1980[c]	Res.-Work in 1970[c]	Change 1970–1980[c]
NORTH-DECLINING						
City Res.-City Work.	13,708	−1,649	4,327	−409	13,831	−4,557
City Res.-Sub. Work.	2,309	−467	544	−42	3,966	−1,251
Sub. Res.-City Work.	9,484	−296	776	+130	5,923	−652
Sub. Res.-Sub. Work.	16,208	+3,796	2,958	+1,269	17,510	+803
Met. Area (Total)	41,709	+1,384	8,605	+948	41,230	−5,657
SOUTH-OLD						
City Res.-City Work.	1,805	−154	514	−31	1,598	−494
City Res.-Sub. Work.	446	−59	126	−6	566	−120
Sub. Res.-City Work.	2,494	+392	243	+92	1,170	+138
Sub. Res.-Sub. Work.	3,265	+1,482	400	+356	2,402	+864
Met. Area (Total)	8,010	+1,661	1,283	+411	5,736	+388

SOURCES: Same as Table 11.5.

[a]Resident-workers defined as in Table 11.5 and metropolitan areas defined as in Table 11.2.
[b]Includes farm workers.
[c]In hundreds.

workplaces and residences reviewed earlier—and the metropolitanwide decline in blue collar workers is strongly linked with the central cities' decline in workers' residences and workplaces.

Beyond these dominant patterns, it can be seen that the workers of all three occupation groupings share the overall residence–workplace shifts: a decline of city worker-residents, a gain in suburb worker-residents, and (except for suburban resident, city service workers) a reduction in intrametropolitan commuters. As a consequence, North-Declining central cities are sustaining net declines in the workplaces and residences of workers employed in all three occupation groupings.

Similar broad tendencies can be observed for South-Old metropolitan areas in Table 11.7, although the greater metropolitanwide blue collar gains in these areas led to a larger blue collar contribution to the "suburb resident-suburb worker" category than in the North-Declining areas. Also, the South-Old 1970s tendency (observed in Table 11.5) toward absolute increases in suburb-to-city commuting is shared for all three occupation groupings. Nevertheless, as with the North-Declining metropolitan areas, the substantial aggregate growth among workers in the "suburb resident-suburb worker" category is largely accounted for by white collar workers.

The occupation-selective shifts in workplace–residence categories, just reviewed for North-Declining and South-Old areas, indicate an increased suburbanization of both workers' residences and workplaces among all three broad occupational categories. However, to gain a more comprehensive picture of these suburbanization changes using a more refined occupation classification scheme, we present in Figure 11.4 plots which display 1970 and 1980 suburban proportions for all six metropolitan area groupings.

The broad patterns for North-Declining and South-Old areas show that, in both 1970 and 1980, workplace suburban proportions lie below residence proportions for each of the four more detailed white collar occupations (managers, professionals, sales workers, clerical workers), for service workers, and for the two blue collar occupation categories (craftsmen, and other blue collar workers)—and disparities between the workplace and workplace proportions tend to be greatest for white collar occupations. Variations in these tendencies within the broad white and blue collar categories are also evident in the figure. Clerical workers tend to be the most city-concentrated of all white collar workers with regard to residence or workplace. Likewise, craftsmen seem to be the least city-concentrated of all blue collar workers.

The 1970–1980 shifts in suburban proportions are not uniform across occupational categories, however. While suburban proportions of all employment locations increase over time for North-Declining and

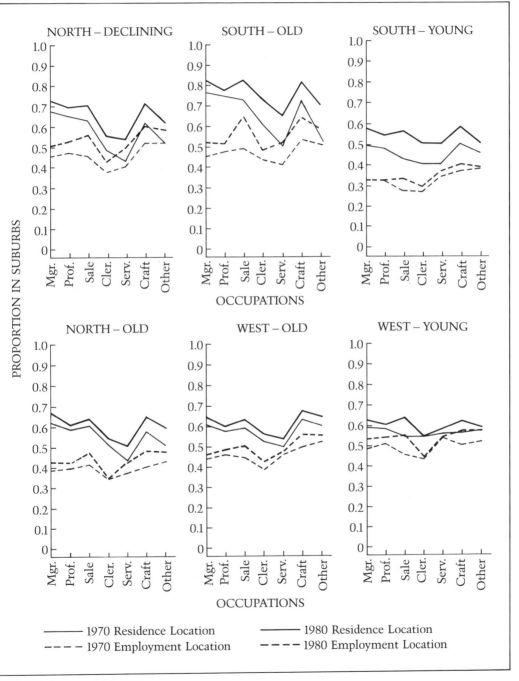

FIGURE 11.4

Residence Location and Employment Location for Civilian Male Residents Who Work Within the Metropolitan Area[a] by Occupation, 1970 and 1980: Six Metropolitan Area Groupings[b]

NORTH – DECLINING

SOUTH – OLD

SOUTH – YOUNG

PROPORTION IN SUBURBS

OCCUPATIONS

NORTH – OLD

WEST – OLD

WEST – YOUNG

OCCUPATIONS

——— 1970 Residence Location   ——— 1980 Residence Location
– – – 1970 Employment Location   – – – 1980 Employment Location

SOURCES: Same as Table 11.5.

[a] Metropolitan residents both living and working within the metropolitan area, who were employed and at work during census week.

[b] Metropolitan areas defined as in Table 11.2.

South-Old metropolitan areas, one finds an accentuated suburbanization for those of sales workers (of the white collar occupations), service workers, and both categories of blue collar workers. Smaller suburban proportion gains are shown for managers, professionals, and clerical workers. These smaller gains are consistent with the more specialized service industry function that many central cities are planning to assume, since each of these three white collar occupations are heavily represented in "the higher-level" producer, nonprofit, and government services.[19] As a result of these shifts, the 1980 suburban proportions differ more sharply across occupations than was the case in 1970, such that managers, professionals, and clerical workers have become more city-concentrated in relation to the other occupations' locations.

The suburb proportions for workers' residence locations increase, as well, for all occupations in North-Declining and South-Old metropolitan area groupings. While these shifts also differ across occupation categories, they tend to moderate—rather than sharpen—the occupational differences in residence locations that existed in 1970. Within white collar occupations, for example, increases in the suburban proportions for sales workers and clerical workers are greater than those for professionals and managers—occupations with the most suburbanized residential locations in 1970. Even greater increases in suburban proportions are shown for service workers and "other" blue collar workers— the occupations that tended to be most city-concentrated in 1970. (The latter shift is attributable, largely, to the substantial reduction of city blue collar jobs over the 1970–1980 period.)

The preceding examination of shifts in North-Declining and South-Old metropolitan areas suggests different tendencies to be operating for worker employment and residence locations. First, the selective suburbanization of employment locations is leading to a greater differentiation between central city and suburb employment opportunities, with a greater (relative) city concentration of high-paying white collar jobs and clerical positions, and an increased suburbanization of other white collar, service worker and blue collar opportunities. Second, the selective suburbanization of workers' residences is leading to less differentiation in the occupational composition of city and suburb resident workers. This is attributable to the large suburbanward shift in the proportion of clerical workers, service workers, and other blue collar workers.

Plots for the North-Old and West-Old metropolitan area groupings in Figure 11.4 show similar, although less accentuated 1970–1980 shifts. In each case, employment opportunities for sales workers and blue collar workers suburbanized to a greater degree than those for

[19]Stanback and Noyelle, *Cities in Transition.*

managers, professionals, and clerical workers. However, shifts in workers' residential locations, again, served to moderate differences in suburban location across occupations. The residence and employment shifts in South-Young areas are distinctly different from those just observed in the four older metropolitan area groupings. In these areas, workers' residence locations suburbanized to a far greater degree than employment opportunities, and the residential suburbanization patterns increased fairly uniformly across all occupations. The shifts in the West-Young areas are also somewhat distinct. Already in 1970 these areas exhibited fairly deconcentrated employment location patterns, and the selective suburbanization opportunities for managers, sales workers, and blue collar workers have led to even smaller employment-residence dislocations across most occupations.

This review of occupation-selective shifts in workers' residence-employment patterns over the 1970s has shown strong suburbanization tendencies to be occurring among both the employment and residence locations of workers in those metropolitan area groupings that contain the most "problem cities." The city losses of jobs and residences are heavily concentrated in blue collar occupations while suburban gains are largely comprised of white collar workers. These shifts can be seen as the result of: an increased suburbanization of nonmanufacturing employment opportunities; the greater "white collarization" of the nation's occupational structure; and a significant decline in manufacturing opportunities, metropolitanwide, but particularly within the central city. Still, despite the white collar dominance of this suburbanward redistribution, the suburban proportion of workplaces and residences of all occupation categories have increased over the 1970–1980 period. These events are leading to an increasing variety of employment opportunities in the suburbs and to a reduced number of jobs (particularly blue collar jobs) in central cities. Yet, embedded within these strong employment suburbanization tendencies, there seems to be emerging a relative city concentration of employment opportunities for higher-paying white collar workers and for clerical workers—thus reinforcing the view that these cities are retaining their specialized economic functions as centers of producer, nonprofit, and government services.

Race-Selective Shifts

Underlying the overall shifts in workers' residence and employment relocations, just reviewed, are shifts in the nature of racial redistribution, which have come to the fore in the post-1970 period. These shifts are particularly relevant to the worker-residence "mismatch" issues raised in the Introduction. One of these mismatches—the isolation of city residents from expanding suburban jobs—is particularly crucial to central city blacks, for whom reverse commuting and unemployment constituted the most popular responses. Greater geographic and occupational mobility of blacks in the post-1970 period could serve to reduce this dislocation, as blacks become better able to adjust their residences to shifts in employment locations. A second mismatch—associated with suburban residents who voluntarily commute to central city jobs—might be alleviated by a selective "return to the city" among less family-oriented, better-off white suburbanites who are employed in city located high-level service occupations. While this latter tendency does not seem to be apparent in the overall shifts reviewed above, a more refined evaluation of how both "mismatches" have been altered over the 1970s can be made by examining race-selective residence–workplace shifts.

Table 11.8 displays 1970–1980 changes in the suburban shares of workers' employment and residence locations for black and nonblack civilian male workers in each of the six metropolitan area groupings. The patterns for nonblacks do not differ markedly from the overall patterns observed earlier showing, for the most part, similar increases in employment and residence location suburban shares over the decade (where, as in the earlier discussion of Table 11.4, the South-Young grouping constitutes an exception). The 1970–1980 shifts for black workers, however, differ markedly for residence and employment locations in a manner that suggests a narrowing of the earlier discussed mismatch.

Unlike the situation for nonblacks, black employment locations in 1970 were less city-concentrated than their residential locations. However, the significant suburbanward redistribution of black residences, coupled with a more moderate, or, in some cases, negative suburban redistribution of workplaces, served to reduce or eliminate these disparities in all six metropolitan area groupings. The two older metropolitan area groupings with the largest number of blacks—North-Declining areas and South-Old areas—displayed suburbanward residential shifts among their black workers that were particularly large in comparison to shifts in black employment locations. In the remainder of this section, we will focus specifically on black and nonblack residence–workplace shifts in these two metropolitan area groupings.

To what extent has the sharp suburbanward residential relocation of blacks served to reduce the "mismatches" between black employment and residence locations? The answer to this question, as revealed in Table 11.9, is somewhat surprising. While the new suburbanward relocation of black workers' residences, as expected, substantially reduces the number of black city residents who commute to suburban employment locations (by 14 percent and 12.8 percent, respectively, in North-Declining and South-Old metropolitan area groupings), it also increases—to an even greater extent—the number of voluntary suburb-to-city commuters among blacks in these metropolitan areas. The latter shift is surprising in light of the substantial suburbanization of metropolitan employment opportunities. Perhaps the new increase in black suburb-to-city commuting represents a transition stage of black suburbanization, wherein blacks who have the means first suburbanize residentially before selecting—or becoming integrated into—suburban located employment opportunities. Nevertheless, blacks also exhibit the dominant nonblack tendencies over the 1970–1980 period, by sustaining losses in the number of workers that both live and work within the city and gains in the number of workers who live and work within the suburbs.

The distributions of black and nonblack metropolitan workers, shown in Table 11.10, provide a more concise assessment of recent alterations in their workplace–residence mismatches. It is clear that, as a result of 1970–1980 shifts, the dominant 1970 tendency for blacks, to both live and work in the central city, has declined in both North-Declining and South-Old metropolitan area groupings. This is particularly evident in the latter areas, where the metropolitan areas' share of such workers declined from 61 percent in 1970 to 44.5 percent in 1980. However, as discussed above, a significant share of black workers, who relocated their residences to the suburbs, still retain central city jobs. The recent suburbanization of blacks has also reduced the number of "reverse" city-to-suburb commuters since 1970, although it has not eliminated them. In 1980, 13.3 percent of North-Declining area workers and 14.6 percent of South-Old area workers still live in the city and commute to the suburbs. These workers account for 43 percent and 34 percent of their respective metropolitan areas' suburban black workers.

Greater insights into the occupation makeup of black workers that shifted workplace and residence locations can be seen in Table 11.11. As with nonblacks, blue collar workers predominate among the 1970–1980 losses of black city residents that either hold city jobs or reverse commute, while white collar workers comprise the bulk of the new suburban residents who also work within the suburbs. This suggests that some blacks, like nonblacks, are increasingly becoming employed in white collar occupations and participate in the greater suburbanization of such employment. However, this response is far less pervasive for blacks than for nonblacks. The data in Table 11.11 suggest that another black response to declining city blue collar employment opportunities involves remaining in the city and taking on lower-level

TABLE 11.8

Metropolitan Area Size and Suburban Share of Workplace and Residence Locations, Nonblack and Black Civilian Male Metropolitan Area Residents Who Work Within the Metropolitan Area, 1970 and 1980: Six Metropolitan Area Groupings[a]

Metropolitan Area Groupings/ Location	Metropolitan Area		Percent in Suburb		
	1970 Size[b]	1970–1980 Percent Change	1970	1980	Difference
NONBLACKS					
NORTH-DECLINING					
Workplace	8,228	−4.2	49.7	56.8	+7.1
Residence	8,228	−4.2	62.4	70.5	+8.1
NORTH-OLD					
Workplace	1,174	+13.8	41.1	46.1	+5.0
Residence	1,174	+13.8	58.1	64.3	+6.2
SOUTH-OLD					
Workplace	1,220	+15.1	51.4	59.8	+8.4
Residence	1,220	+15.1	77.5	84.7	+7.2
WEST-OLD					
Workplace	2,769	+14.9	48.0	51.3	+3.3
Residence	2,769	+14.9	60.8	64.0	+3.2
SOUTH-YOUNG					
Workplace	1,316	+47.9	35.3	37.5	+2.2
Residence	1,316	+47.9	49.4	58.2	+8.8
WEST-YOUNG					
Workplace	1,154	+52.3	50.5	55.2	+4.7
Residence	1,154	+52.3	57.9	61.5	+3.6

white collar or service worker occupations. Finally, it should be noted that while there is clearly a reduction in the reverse commuting on the part of city blue collar blacks—thus serving to alleviate the most important "mismatch" observed in the early 1970s—such commuting still exists and constitutes a significant share of all 1980 blue collar workers in the North-Declining and South-Old area groupings.

The Table 11.11 data again point up a somewhat surprising post–1970 tendency for suburbanizing black residents to retain and commute

TABLE 11.8 *(continued)*

Metropolitan Area Groupings/ Location	Metropolitan Area		Percent in Suburb		
	1970 Size[b]	1970–1980 Percent Change	1970	1980	Difference
BLACKS					
NORTH-DECLINING					
Workplace	926	+1.5	28.5	30.3	+1.8
Residence	926	+1.5	16.7	24.7	+8.0
NORTH-OLD					
Workplace	71	+27.0	25.6	23.3	−2.3
Residence	71	+27.0	12.0	15.1	+3.1
SOUTH-OLD					
Workplace	283	+21.9	33.0	38.5	+5.5
Residence	283	+21.9	18.5	40.9	+22.4
WEST-OLD					
Workplace	181	+31.0	34.9	40.7	+5.8
Residence	181	+31.0	28.6	40.6	+12.0
SOUTH-YOUNG					
Workplace	158	+48.6	28.5	26.4	−2.1
Residence	158	+48.6	26.1	29.2	+3.1
WEST-YOUNG					
Workplace	26	+91.1	39.1	41.1	+2.0
Residence	26	+91.1	29.1	35.0	+5.9

SOURCES: Same as Table 11.5.

[a]Resident-workers defined as in Table 11.5 and metropolitan areas defined as in Table 11.2.
[b]In thousands.

to central city jobs. This tendency occurs for all three broad occupation categories and tends to negate the suggestion that alleviating residence–workplace mismatches constitutes a primary motivation for black suburbanization. Indeed, the plots in Figure 11.5 show that even with increased suburbanization, the suburb proportion of black work-

TABLE 11.9

Changes in Central City and Suburb Residence–Workplace Categories
for Nonblack and Civilian Black Male Metropolitan Area Residents
Who Work Within Metropolitan Areas:
North-Declining and South-Old Metropolitan Area Groupings[a]

Metropolitan Area Groupings/ Residence-Workplace Category	Nonblack			Black		
	Res.-Work in 1970	Change 1970–1980	% Change 1970–1980	Res.-Work in 1970	Change 1970–1980	% Change 1970–1980
NORTH-DECLINING						
City Res.-City Work.	25,603	−6,179	−24.1	6,263	−436	−7.0
City Res.-Sub. Work.	5,364	−1,556	−29.0	1,455	−204	−14.0
Sub. Res.-City Work.	15,820	−1,178	−7.4	363	+359	+99.0
Sub. Res.-Sub. Work.	35,492	+5,450	+15.4	1,184	+418	+35.3
SOUTH-OLD						
City Res.-City Work.	2,188	−485	−22.2	1,729	−194	−11.2
City Res.-Sub. Work.	559	−112	−20.0	579	−74	−12.8
Sub. Res.-City Work.	3,738	+203	+5.4	169	+419	+247.9
Sub. Res.-Sub. Work.	5,711	+2,232	+39.1	356	+469	+131.8

SOURCES: Same as Table 11.5.

[a]Resident-workers defined as in Table 11.5 and metropolitan areas defined as in Table 11.2.

TABLE 11.10

Distribution of Residence–Workplace Categories, 1970 and 1980,
and 1970–1980 Difference in Distribution
for Nonblack and Black Civilian Male Residents
Who Work Within the Metropolitan Areas:
North-Declining and South-Old Metropolitan Area Groupings[a]

Metropolitan Area Groupings/ Race/ Residence–Workplace Category	Distribution of Residence–Workplace		
	1970	1980	Difference (1980 minus 1970)
NORTH-DECLINING			
Nonblack			
City Res.-City Work.	31.1	24.6	−6.5
City Res.-Sub. Work.	6.5	4.8	−1.7
Sub. Res.-City Work.	19.2	18.6	−0.6
Sub. Res.-Sub. Work.	43.2	52.0	+8.8
Total	100.0	100.0	
Black			
City Res.-City Work.	67.6	62.0	−5.6
City Res.-Sub. Work.	15.7	13.3	−2.4
Sub. Res.-City Work.	3.9	7.7	+3.8
Sub. Res.-Sub. Work.	12.8	17.0	+4.2
Total	100.0	100.0	
SOUTH-OLD			
Nonblack			
City Res.-City Work.	17.9	12.1	−5.8
City Res.-Sub. Work.	4.6	3.2	−1.4
Sub. Res.-City Work.	30.6	28.1	−2.5
Sub. Res.-Sub. Work.	46.9	56.6	+9.9
Total	100.0	100.0	
Black			
City Res.-City Work.	61.0	44.5	−16.5
City Res.-Sub. Work.	20.4	14.6	−5.8
Sub. Res.-City Work.	6.0	17.0	+11.0
Sub. Res.-Sub. Work.	12.6	23.9	+11.3
Total	100.0	100.0	

SOURCES: Same as Table 11.5.

[a]Resident-workers defined as in Table 11.5 and metropolitan areas defined as in Table 11.2.

TABLE 11.11

Changes in Central City and Suburb Residence–Workplace Categories, 1970–1980, for Civilian Male Residents Who Work Within the Metropolitan Area, by Occupation and Race: North-Declining and South-Old Metropolitan Area Groupings[a]

Metropolitan Area Groupings/ Residence–Workplace Category	White Collar		Service Workers		Blue Collar[b]	
	Res.-Work. in 1970[c]	Change 1970–1980[c]	Res.-Work. in 1970[c]	Change 1970–1980[c]	Res.-Work. in 1970[c]	Change 1970–1980[c]
NORTH-DECLINING						
Nonblack						
City Res.-City Work.	12,042	-2,115	3,187	-472	10,374	-3,592
City Res.-Sub. Work.	2,082	-517	379	-53	2,903	-986
Sub. Res.-City Work.	9,351	-482	722	+91	5,747	-787
Sub. Res.-Sub. Work.	15,987	+3,531	2,775	+1,163	16,730	+754
Met. Area (Total)	39,462	+417	7,063	+729	35,754	-4,611
Black						
City Res.-City Work.	1,666	+466	1,140	+64	3,457	-965
City Res.-Sub. Work.	227	+50	165	+11	1,063	-265
Sub. Res.-City Work.	133	+186	54	+38	176	+135
Sub. Res.-Sub. Work.	221	+264	183	+105	780	+48
Met. Area (Total)	2,247	+966	1,542	+218	5,476	-1,047
SOUTH-OLD						
Nonblack						
City Res.-City Work.	1,291	-185	180	-17	717	-283
City Res.-Sub. Work.	314	-59	29	+2	216	-55
Sub. Res.-City Work.	2,422	+168	226	+32	1,090	+4
Sub. Res.-Sub. Work.	3,183	+1,277	337	+287	2,191	+669
Met. Area (Total)	7,210	+1,201	772	+304	4,214	+335
Black						
City Res.-City Work.	514	+31	334	-14	881	-211
City Res.-Sub. Work.	132	-1	97	-9	350	-65
Sub. Res.-City Work.	72	+224	17	+61	80	+134
Sub. Res.-Sub. Work.	82	+205	63	+69	211	+195
Met. Area (Total)	800	+459	511	+107	1,522	+53

SOURCES: Same as Table 11.5.

[a] Resident-workers defined as in Table 11.5 and metropolitan areas defined as in Table 11.2.

FIGURE 11.5

*Residence Location and Employment Location
for Civilian Male Residents Who Work Within the Metropolitan Area[a]
by Occupation and Race, 1970 and 1980:
North-Declining and South-Old Metropolitan Area Groupings[b]*

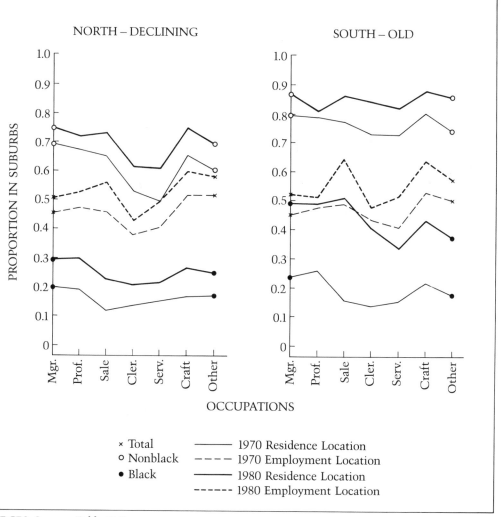

NORTH – DECLINING

SOUTH – OLD

PROPORTION IN SUBURBS

OCCUPATIONS

Mgr. | Prof. | Sale | Cler. | Serv. | Craft | Other

× Total
o Nonblack
• Black

——— 1970 Residence Location
- - - - 1970 Employment Location
——— 1980 Residence Location
------ 1980 Employment Location

SOURCES: Same as Table 11.5.

Metropolitan residents who both live and work within the metropolitan area, who were employed and at work during census week.
Metropolitan areas defined as in Table 11.2.

ers' residences lies below the proportion of metropolitan area jobs available in each occupation in both 1970 and 1980. The tendency for newly suburbanizing blacks to retain city jobs might be attributable to one of several factors: a preference on the part of well-off blacks to reside in the suburbs while retaining their city jobs (including managing their own black-owned businesses in the city); the unsuitability of many newly suburbanizing blacks for suburban jobs; or a subtle discrimination in the hiring practices for more "sheltered" or "protected" union or corporate-based jobs—spanning all occupations—that tend to be located in the suburbs. (To the extent the latter is true, our term "voluntary" does not apply to the new black suburb–city commuting.) It is likely that this tendency among new black suburban residents represents a combination of all of these factors and reflects, as was suggested above, the transitional character of black suburbanization in the 1970s.

Leaving the above tendency aside, the fact that a large number of newly suburbanizing blacks did obtain employment in the suburbs served to reduce, significantly, the residence–workplace mismatch which necessitated a great deal of suburb-to-city reverse commuting in the late 1960s. This is illustrated in the two right-hand plots of Figure 11.6, which show the proportion of suburban workers who resided in the suburbs in 1970 and 1980, by race and occupation, for North-Declining areas and South-Old areas. Also shown are comparable suburb proportions (that is, suburb destination propensity rates) for 1975–1980 movers and inmigrants to the metropolitan area, as a crude indicator of future patterns.[20]

It is, first of all, apparent that the vast majority of suburban non-black workers already resided in the suburbs in 1970, and the proportion of such workers residing in the suburbs increased even further in 1980, and with the 1975–1980 movers and inmigrants. Nevertheless, these plots also make plain that the high level of "reverse" commuting which took place among blacks of all occupation categories in 1970 has been considerably reduced by 1980. This is particularly the case in South-Old areas where the destination propensity rates for 1975–1980 movers and inmigrants in these areas suggest that this trend will continue.

The two left-hand plots in Figure 11.6 illustrate changes, by race and occupation, in the other residence–workplace dislocation—the ten-

---

[20]The suburb destination propensity rate, as used here, is defined as the proportion of all 1975–1980 intrametropolitan movers and inmigrants who select a suburb (rather than a central city) destination. See the Chapter 7 section on "Destination Propensity Rates" for a further discussion of this measure.

dency for workers to reside in the suburbs and commute to the central city. The rising tendency toward black suburb–city commuting is clearly evident here for all occupations in both North-Declining and South-Old areas, and greatest levels occur among workers in the highest status well-paid occupations.

These plots also reveal significant shifts in suburb-to-city commuting that are pertinent to another anticipated 1970s shift—the expected attraction "back to the city" of well-off nonblack residents who are employed in city-located, high-level service industries. The evidence reviewed up until this point has not given much support to this expectation. However, our review of occupation-selective suburbanization in Chapter 9 showed that nonblack professionals in the older metropolitan area groupings exhibited a somewhat more restrained post-1970 suburban shift than did other occupations, suggesting that a modest city retention of white professionals was occurring. The left-hand plots in Figure 11.6 again show this tendency to occur, but specifically among nonblack professionals who work in the central city. They show that, unlike the situation for all other occupations and racial categories of city workers, the nonblack professionals are no more likely to commute from the suburbs in 1980 than in 1970. Moreover, 1975–1980 movers and inmigrants to North-Declining areas, who were professional nonblack city workers, were even less likely to commute from the suburbs. While not too much should be made of this reduced suburbanization tendency on the part of nonblack city professional workers, since it is dwarfed by the continued suburbanization of all other nonblack city and suburb workers, this tendency does represent a departure from previous trends in a direction that is consistent with many older cities' plans to enhance their economic bases as smaller but more specialized service centers.

The preceding review of race-selective shifts in workers' residence and employment locations has underscored significant alterations for the post-1970 period. The previous city concentration of black workers has clearly begun to disperse, as the number of blacks who both reside and work in the suburbs increased considerably over the decade, while the number of city-to-suburb reverse commuters was reduced. Black workers also became employed, to a greater extent, in white collar and service occupations located in both central city and suburban workplaces. Still, another somewhat surprising development which emerged during the 1970s was the strong tendency for new black suburban residents to retain their central city jobs. This suggests that, for some portion of the black population, residential suburbanization is running ahead of their integration into the suburban labor force.

FIGURE 11.6

Proportion Residing in Suburbs of 1970 and 1980 Metropolitan Workers[a]
and Suburb Destination Propensity Rates for Workers
Who Are 1975–1980 Metropolitan Movers and Inmigrants,[b]
by Location of Workplace, Occupation, and Race; Civilian Males:
North-Declining and South-Old Metropolitan Area Groupings[c]

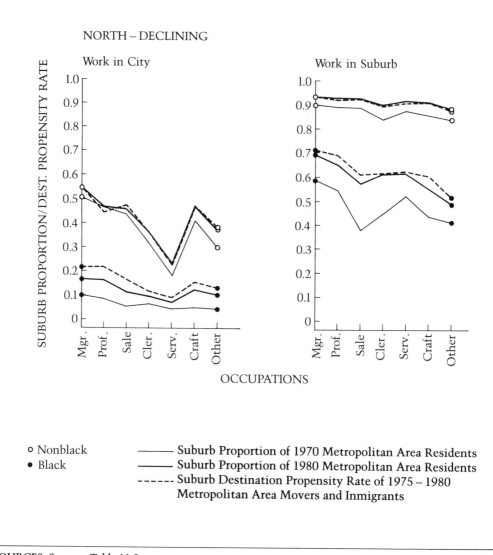

SOURCES: Same as Table 11.5.

[a]Metropolitan residents who both live and work within the metropolitan area, who were employed and at work during census week.

[b]1975–1980 intrametropolitan movers and metropolitan area inmigrants who both live and work within the metropolitan area in 1980 and were employed and at work during census week.

[c]Metropolitan areas as defined in Table 11.2.

FIGURE 11.6 *(continued)*

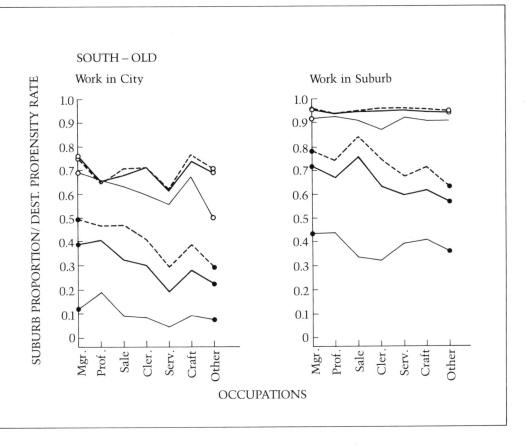

SOUTH – OLD

Increased City Unemployment

While the previous review has demonstrated that large segments of the black population have adapted both geographically and through upward occupational mobility to post-1970 shifts in the metropolitan labor market, it has focused specifically on the residence and employment location shifts of employed workers. Already in 1970, and even more so in 1980, large numbers of central city black and nonblack adults remained underemployed, unemployed, and, in some cases, stayed out of the labor force in response to the out-movement of low-skilled blue collar and other entry-level jobs from many of our "problem cities."[21] Some sense of this can be gained by examining the employ-

---

[21]See Kasarda, "Urban Change in Minority Opportunities," for further documentation of this problem and a discussion of policies directed to alleviate it.

TABLE 11.12

Unemployment Rates for Males in the Labor Force
by Race and Central City–Suburb Residence, 1970 and 1980:
North-Declining and South-Old Metropolitan Areas[a]

Metropolitan Area Grouping	Nonblacks		Blacks	
	1970	1980	1970	198
NORTH-DECLINING				
Central City	3.8	7.3	7.3	17
Suburbs	2.8	5.7	5.8	12
Difference	−1.0	−1.6	−1.5	−4
SOUTH-OLD				
Central City	2.9	5.1	5.5	12
Suburbs	2.3	3.3	4.8	7
Difference	−0.6	−1.8	−0.7	−5

SOURCES: Same as Table 11.5.

[a]Metropolitan area defined as in Table 11.2.

ment rates for the civilian male labor force in cities and suburbs of North-Declining and South-Old metropolitan areas, shown in Table 11.12. These data reveal the extent to which city unemployment rates, and the ratio of city to suburb unemployment rates, have increased over the decade—and particularly so for the black population. Additional data for all of the nation's central cities, compiled by John Kasarda

TABLE 11.13

Unemployment Rates of Central City[a] Males, Aged 16–64,
by Race and Years of School Completed, 1969, 1977, 1982

Schooling	White			Black		
	1969	1977	1982	1969	1977	198
Did not complete high school	4.3	12.2	17.7	6.6	19.8	29.
Completed high school only	1.7	8.0	11.0	4.1	16.2	23.
Attended college 1 year or more	1.6	4.7	4.4	3.7	10.7	16.
All education levels	2.6	7.7	9.5	5.4	16.5	23.

SOURCE: John D. Kasarda, "Urban Change and Minority Opportunities," in Paul E. Peterson, ed., *T New Urban Reality* (Washington, DC: The Brookings Institution, 1985), p. 57.

[a]Central cities of all SMSAs, as identified in U.S. Bureau of the Census *Current Population Survey*, tap 1969, 1977, 1982.

(shown in Table 11.13), indicate that unemployment rates have increased dramatically for black city residents without requisite skills. These measures understate the problem's severity because they do not measure the degree of underemployment, or the extent to which adults are too discouraged to enter the labor force. Nevertheless, these trends make plain that while a large segment of the black population has overcome previous workplace–residence dislocations over the course of the 1970s, other blacks have become even more isolated from appropriate employment opportunities and ill-equipped for those opportunities that lie within close proximity.

Commuting, Public Transportation, and Journey to Work

The continued deconcentration of metropolitan workers' employment and residential locations has significantly altered the character of intrametropolitan commuting. While city-to-suburb commuting still constitutes a sizeable share of all home-to-work travel, we have shown, in the previous section, that a far larger share of metropolitan residents commute to work within the suburbs and that this share has increased substantially over the 1970–1980 period. The shift toward more deconcentrated commuting affects the nature of the commuting process itself. Intrasuburban commuting is much more dependent upon automobile ownership than is commuting into the city, although the degree to which public transportation networks have developed varies widely across metropolitan areas. There is also the question of the time involved in the journey to work. In earlier periods, when suburban residence was synonymous with suburb-to-city commuting, the suburbanite's somewhat longer journey to work was a price that needed to be paid for the advantages of suburban living. To what extent has that changed as a result of the deconcentration of employment opportunities and the more pervasive intrasuburban commuting?

The characteristics of today's more deconcentrated commuting, with respect to dependency on public transportation and length of journey to work, can be assessed with data obtained from the 1980 census. Clearly, the character of commuting will differ not only across the type of commuting stream (that is, within city, suburb to city, city to suburb, within suburb), but also across the six metropolitan area groupings we have identified in this study. The oldest of these metropolitan areas—largely represented in our North-Declining and South-Old area groupings—became established during a period of rather primitive short-distance transportation technology, such that their central city

TABLE 11.14

Percent Central City and Suburb–Workplace Locations for Central City and Suburb Residents Who Work Within Metropolitan Areas,[a] 1980: Six Metropolitan Area Groupings[b]

Metropolitan Area Groupings/ Industry Class	Resident in City 1980 Percent Working in		Resident in Suburbs 198 Percent Working in	
	City	Suburbs	City	Suburb
North-Declining	85.7	14.3	23.2	76.8
North-Old	82.9	17.1	36.9	63.1
South-Old	79.6	20.4	32.5	67.5
West-Old	77.0	23.0	32.3	67.7
South-Young	86.0	14.0	44.3	55.7
West-Young	72.2	27.8	27.6	72.4

SOURCE: Machine-readable computer file: Census of Population and Housing, 1980, Public Us Microdata Samples "A" and "B" (prepared by the U.S. Bureau of the Census, Washington, DC).

[a]Metropolitan residents who both live and work within the metropolitan area, who were employed a at work during census week.
[b]1970 Equivalent SMSA and Central City Definitions.

areas became intensively developed before the onset of widespread automobile usage. Central cities of these areas amassed extremely high population densities and were among the first to develop extensive public transportation systems. Although these older metropolitan areas—like their younger counterparts—exhibited a substantial deconcentration of population and jobs since World War II, their cities still maintain higher population densities, greater concentrations of employment, and more well-developed public infrastructures than the younger areas which became established in periods when more advanced short-distance transportation was available.[22] It is in these older areas that the trend toward deconcentrated, intrasuburban commuting should provide the greatest contrast with other commuting forms.

Despite differences in development histories, the commuting data in Table 11.14 make plain that, in each metropolitan area grouping, the decided majority of working suburban residents are classified as intra-

[22]Support for the latter point is provided in Avery M. Guest, "Urban Growth and Population Densities," *Demography* 10 (1973):53–69. For overviews of the role of transportation in the deconcentration process, see Basil G. Zimmer, "The Urban Centrifugal Drift," in Amos H. Hawley and Vincent P. Rock, eds., *Metropolitan America in Contemporary Perspective* (Beverly Hills, CA: Sage, 1975), pp. 21–91; and Gary A. Tobin, "Suburbanization and the Development of Motor Transportation: Transportation Technology and the Suburbanization Process," in Barry Schwartz, ed., *The Changing Face of the Suburbs* (Chicago: University of Chicago Press, 1976), pp. 95–111.

suburban commuters. These data pertain to the residence and work-place locations of all employed workers (both male and female) who both reside and work within the metropolitan area. Intrasuburb commuting, by this measure, is undertaken by better than three-quarters of working suburban residents in North-Declining areas, better than two-thirds of those in South-Old, West-Old, and West-Young areas, and better than half of working suburbanites in North-Old and South-Young areas. Intrasuburban commuting, therefore, tends to be as prominent in the older metropolitan area groupings as in the younger areas and, as our earlier discussion indicated, it has increased substantially in older areas since 1970.

We now turn to examine the extent to which intrasuburban commuting occurs relatively independently of public transportation networks. The upper panel of Table 11.15, displaying the percentage of workers using public transit in four different commuting streams, provides a fairly straightforward answer. The average use level of public transport among intrasuburban commuters is miniscule (less than 3 percent) in all metropolitan area groupings, irrespective of the exten-

TABLE 11.15

Percent Using Public Transit and Mean Travel Time to Work for Residence–Workplace Categories, 1980: Six Metropolitan Area Groupings [a]

Metropolitan Area Groupings	Reside in City		Reside in Suburbs	
	Work in City	Work in Suburbs	Work in City	Work in Suburbs
PERCENT USING PUBLIC TRANSIT				
North-Declining	42.7	11.4	25.3	2.3
North-Old	11.9	4.8	7.2	0.8
South-Old	30.7	17.1	15.9	2.7
West-Old	18.1	6.9	12.3	2.5
South-Young	6.3	3.7	2.4	1.2
West-Young	3.6	2.7	2.8	1.5
MEAN TRAVEL TIME TO WORK (IN MINUTES)				
North-Declining	30.6	30.6	38.2	18.6
North-Old	18.7	21.8	26.0	15.9
South-Old	24.7	32.3	34.3	21.2
West-Old	21.5	26.9	31.6	18.7
South-Young	21.6	25.6	29.0	18.1
West-Young	17.4	25.7	24.1	16.6

SOURCES: Same as Table 11.3.

[a] 1970 Equivalent SMSA and Central City Definitions.

siveness of their central cities' transport network. Indeed, an examination of individual metropolitan area transport usage among intrasuburban commuters shows use levels rising above 4 percent in only Boston (at 5 percent) and Washington, DC (at 4.4 percent). Both of these are relatively underbounded central cities in which the largely city-based transport networks extend somewhat beyond the legal city boundaries.

Yet, the difference in the use of public transport between suburb-to-city commuters, on the one hand, and intrasuburban commuters on the other, does vary considerably across metropolitan area groupings. A quarter of the suburbanites who commute to the city in North-Declining areas use public transport, as opposed to 2.3 percent who commute within the suburbs. Significant, but less dramatic differences occur for South-Old areas and West-Old areas. These differences, in the availability of public transport for city vis-à-vis suburb employment among working suburban residents, make city employment a much more viable option for those who do not have access to private transportation. This may explain, to some extent, the tendency for newly suburbanizing blacks to retain central city jobs. In the same vein, the low-level of public transportation availability for reverse city-to-suburb commuters represents still another impediment to less well-off city residents in their isolation from suburban employment opportunities.

A final observation regarding dependence on public transportation in large metropolitan areas pertains to the paucity of public transport availability to all commuters within the fast-growing South-Young and West-Young areas. Even within-city commuters for these areas must rely, to a large extent, on their own transportation to get to work. In only 1 of the 12 individual metropolitan areas of these groupings is public transport use as high as 10 percent for intracity commuters (13 percent in Miami). In contrast, only 3 of the 29 older metropolitan areas fall below this level (Paterson–Clifton–Passaic, Columbus, and Indianapolis at 7 percent, 8 percent, and 4 percent, respectively). In light of the substantial population growth sustained by the large Sunbelt areas, and the tendency toward intrasuburban commuting within older metropolitan areas, it is clear that metropolitan workers are becoming ever less dependent on public transportation in their travel from home to work.

We now turn to the question of what the new deconcentrated commuting patterns imply for the length of journey to work. The mean travel times for each commuting stream, shown in the lower panel of Table 11.15, again, suggest a fairly straightforward answer to the question. The journey to work for intrasuburban commuters is uniformly shorter in length than that for the three other commuting streams within each metropolitan area grouping. This is also the case for most individual metropolitan areas displayed in Table 11.16, which shows the mean journey to work for intrasuburban commuters to range between 13 minutes (for Indianapolis) and 22.5 minutes (for Washington, DC). In contrast, the length of journey ranges between 20 and 61 minutes for suburb-to-city commuters, from 20 to 39 minutes for city-to-suburb commuters, and from 13 to 37 minutes for intracity commuters. In every area, intrasuburban commuters spend less time, on the average, commuting to work than suburb-to-city commuters; and in most areas intrasuburban commuters display the lowest average travel time.

Disparities in the length of travel between intrasuburban streams, on the one hand, and the remaining three commuting streams, on the other, tend to be sharper in older metropolitan areas with well-developed transportation networks. New York represents the most extreme situation in this regard where intrasuburban commuters average 19.7 minutes in travel time, while suburb-to-city commuters, city-to-suburb commuters, and intracity commuters average 60.6 minutes, 38.8 minutes, and 36.8 minutes, respectively. Although the disparities observed for other older metropolitan areas are less severe, the directions of difference are similar, so that suburbanites who commute to the city average the longest duration journeys to work in the metropolitan area, and those who commute within the suburbs average the shortest. Both within-city commuters and city-to-suburb reverse commuters lie in between these extremes, although the former commuters tend to exhibit shorter travel times. In newer metropolitan areas, without extensive public transport networks (but well-developed highway systems), disparities in duration times across commuting streams lie within a narrower range. However, in these areas, as well, average travel times are lower for intrasuburban commuters than for suburbanites who commute to the central city.

The preceding review of metropolitan commuting characteristics suggests that with the type of commuting that is emerging within the fast-growing Sunbelt metropolitan areas, and the tendency toward more deconcentrated intrasuburban commuting in older metropolitan areas, the metropolitan workforce is becoming far less dependent on public transportation than has heretofore been known. These new tendencies have brought about greater flexibility in workers' suburban residential locations, as well as shorter travel times in their journeys to work. Although not examined in this chapter, the new flexibility has also facilitated increased commuting into and out of the metropolitan area from expanding residential and employment developments outside the metropolitan boundaries. These patterns, along with those reviewed in earlier sections of this chapter, suggest that the continuing deconcentration of population and employment opportunities are giving rise to a

TABLE 11.16

Mean Travel Time to Work (in minutes) for Residence–Workplace Categories, 1980: 39 Individual Metropolitan Areas[a]

Metropolitan Area Groupings/ Met. Areas[b]	Resident in City 1980 Working in		Resident in Suburbs 198 Working in	
	City	Suburbs	City	Suburl
NORTH-DECLINING				
New York	36.8	38.8	60.6	19.7
Philadelphia	27.9	34.7	38.3	18.1
Boston	23.0	30.0	25.0	17.8
Cincinnati	19.0	24.1	26.8	19.3
St. Louis	20.3	29.4	30.0	19.5
Buffalo	17.9	23.6	25.8	16.0
Chicago	29.7	36.6	46.0	19.7
Newark	21.5	29.9	28.3	17.4
Cleveland	22.4	25.3	30.5	18.0
Detroit	22.4	27.4	31.7	19.7
Milwaukee	18.6	21.0	24.2	14.9
Pittsburgh	21.3	28.2	32.3	18.4
Paterson*	13.1	20.7	20.3	15.9
NORTH-OLD				
Columbus	18.6	19.9	23.8	15.0
Indianapolis	19.5	26.5	31.1	13.0
Kansas City	19.1	22.6	26.5	17.0
Hartford	16.7	21.2	23.0	16.2
Minneapolis*	17.7	21.7	25.8	16.0
SOUTH-OLD				
Baltimore	24.9	31.4	29.9	20.1
New Orleans	23.2	29.7	33.0	19.4
Washington, DC	25.9	35.4	38.0	22.5
Atlanta	24.5	32.0	32.1	20.6

more diffuse and multinodal metropolitan area, which will become increasingly dominated by intrasuburban and exurban commuting patterns.[23] However, these new tendencies will also exert negative consequences on depopulating central cities—which are losing their tax bases

[23]An excellent discussion of this phenomenon can be found in Chapter 4, "The Suburbanization of Economic Activity and the Rise of the Multicentered Metropolis," in Peter O. Muller, *Contemporary Suburban America* (Englewood Cliffs, NJ: Prentice-Hall, 1981).

TABLE 11.16 (continued)

Metropolitan Area Groupings/ Met. Areas[b]	Resident in City 1980 Working in		Resident in Suburbs 1980 Working in	
	City	Suburbs	City	Suburbs
WEST-OLD				
San Francisco*	23.5	29.0	37.5	18.6
Denver*	18.7	22.1	28.5	18.1
Los Angeles*	22.2	27.3	31.2	19.5
Portland	17.3	23.7	28.2	16.4
Seattle*	19.7	28.4	30.4	18.0
SOUTH-YOUNG				
San Antonio	19.9	22.4	22.1	14.0
Dallas*	21.7	25.9	30.0	16.9
Houston	24.3	28.5	35.5	19.2
Tampa*	16.7	23.7	24.2	17.0
Miami	20.2	27.1	26.9	19.5
Ft. Lauderdale*	15.6	20.9	23.6	17.7
WEST-YOUNG				
Sacramento	15.3	21.8	23.6	15.6
San Diego	17.4	24.0	26.0	16.3
San Jose	17.7	28.7	22.2	17.2
Phoenix	19.8	28.3	28.6	17.0
Riverside*	13.2	24.7	20.4	16.1
Anaheim*	15.6	22.2	21.7	17.2

SOURCES: Same as Table 11.3.

Largest of multiple central cities (complete metropolitan area names are listed in Appendix F).

1970 Equivalent SMSA and Central City Definitions.

1980 metropolitan areas with populations greater than 1 million defined as 1980 SMSAs and NECMAs (in New England) except for New York and Paterson–Clifton–Passaic (see Appendix F).

at the same time they are attempting to maintain necessary public transit systems—and on less well-off, "underclass" central city residents, who are becoming increasingly isolated from deconcentrating suburban employment opportunities.[24]

[24]For a review of policy options regarding the role of public transportation in declining central cities, see Kenneth A. Small, "Transportation and Urban Change," in Paul Peterson, ed., *The New Urban Reality* (Washington, DC: The Brookings Institution, 1985), pp. 197–223.

Conclusion

At the outset of this chapter we identified two significant "mismatches," or residence–workplace dislocations, that emerged in large older metropolitan areas in the 1960s and became the source of concern for urban analysts. The first of these pertained to the isolation of less well-off city residents from expanding suburban blue collar, service worker, and lower-paying white collar employment opportunities. This isolation was particularly debilitating for metropolitan area blacks who, during this period, faced both economic and discriminatory barriers to suburban residential relocation. The second mismatch pertained to an expansion of the more traditional suburb-to-city commuting, among largely white middle-class residents, whose numbers proliferated in the suburbs to a far greater extent than did appropriate white collar employment opportunities during the immediate postwar decades. While the first of these mismatches imposed adverse consequences on blacks and less well-off city workers—stranded away from their most appropriate employment opportunities— the second mismatch exacerbated the plight of depopulating central cities, unable to retain as residents, large segments of their daytime middle-class work forces.

In this chapter we have reviewed the post-1970 shifts in the relationships between workers' employment and residence locations with an eye toward evaluating their implications for these mismatches. Several societywide economic and demographic developments, which came to the fore during the 1970s, have altered, somewhat, the conditions that originally shaped these mismatches. Together, these new developments hold the potential for effecting changes in both the distribution of employment opportunities within the metropolitan area, as well as the residential responses of workers to employment opportunities. One such shift involves a change in the nation's industrial structure, leading to even further declines in manufacturing employment and gains in service industry of all kinds—particularly high-level services—such as producer, nonprofit, and government service industries which have traditionally favored central city locations.

The other two post-1970 developments, discussed in earlier chapters, should alter workers' residential responses to the location of employment. The first—the decline of the suburban "familism" life style among more career-oriented young adult whites—should serve to reinforce central cities' transitions toward high-level service centers to the extent that a growing number of these individuals will choose to work and reside within the city. The second such development involves the increased geographic and occupational mobility of the black population that emerged during the 1970s. The fact that a larger number of metropolitan blacks will be able to avail themselves of employment and residential opportunities in all parts of the metropolitan area should serve to relieve a substantial amount of the residence–workplace dislocation that had built up over the 1950–1970 period.

Our examination of post-1970 employment and workers' residence shifts focused, for the most part, on those metropolitan area groupings with the largest number of "problem" central cities (the North-Declining and South-Old metropolitan area groupings) in order to evaluate the extent to which these broad societal shifts have altered worker and workplace distribution patterns that characterized these areas over the immediate postwar decades.

Noteworthy post-1970 shifts in the suburbanization of employment opportunities that occurred within large older metropolitan areas very much reflect broad national industrial structure shifts. In the 1970s nonmanufacturing employment suburbanized at a faster rate than did manufacturing employment, so that suburban areas gained disproportionately from the post-1970 rise in service sector jobs. On the other hand, the 1970s manufacturing job losses in these metropolitan areas were borne, disproportionately, by their central cities. On an aggregate basis, therefore, central cities did not benefit greatly from industrial structure shifts—absorbing most of the metropolitan area's losses in manufacturing employment and receiving little of the area's nonmanufacturing employment gain. Yet central cities are still in a position to build upon their earlier strengths as advanced service centers and have shown 1970 gains (although not disproportionate ones) in professional services, producer services, and public administration. In this respect, national industrial structure shifts are contributing to city employment gains, and facilitating their transformation toward a more specialized economic base.[25]

In the context of these employment changes, the residential relocation tendencies of metropolitan workers have also exhibited post-1970 shifts. The two most dominant shifts in workplace-residence patterns involved: (1) a substantial increase in the number of suburban workers who also reside in the suburbs; and (2) an almost equally large decrease in the number of city workers who also reside in the central city. Less numerically significant was a fairly consistent reduction in the number of "reverse" city-to-suburb commuters; changes in the number of suburb-to-city commuters were less consistent across metropolitan areas. Clearly, the substantial suburban redistribution of employment

---

[25]Evidence from the early 1980s shows that several large northern nodal central cities (for example, Boston, New York, Philadelphia) gained more service jobs than they lost manufacturing jobs.

opportunities in the 1970s has drawn to the suburbs, as residents, workers from all other residence–workplace categories. As a consequence, a larger number of workers reside in the same part of the metropolitan area in which they work (that is, city or suburb) in 1980 than was the case in 1970.

Underlying these broad shifts, however, are race-specific worker residential location changes, which reflect the effects of both the post-1970 black gains and greater career orientations of whites that were discussed earlier. The most significant of these changes is the suburbanward residential redistribution of black workers in all occupational categories. Indeed, the greatest residence–workplace shifts among blacks, as for all workers, involved large losses in the number of city resident-workers and large gains in the number of suburb resident-workers. Blacks also exhibited decreases in the number of reverse commuters and, somewhat unexpectedly, registered gains in the numbers of suburb-to-city commuters among their new suburban residents. Taken as a whole, these residence–workplace changes have served to integrate blacks to a far greater extent than before into the metropolitan area labor market, both residentially and in terms of occupational advancement. Yet there is clearly room for further improvement. The proportion of blacks that reside in the suburbs is substantially below the proportion of metropolitan employment opportunities, for all occupations; the number of black reverse commuters still remains high; and a large and growing number of unemployed "underclass" central city blacks have become even further isolated from appropriate employment opportunities.

As to the potential for a "return to the city" among young adult career-oriented whites, we found little support in the aggregate data, which showed extensive suburbanward relocation of both jobs and residents in the 1970s decade. Still, some selective city retention is suggested by data which indicated that nonblack professionals, who work in the city, were the least likely to increase their suburbanization levels over the 1970–1980 period. If, as the employment analysis implied, central cities are able to retain their competitive advantages with fast-growing advanced service industries—industries that are known to employ disproportionate numbers of professionals—then these data suggest the potential for a down-sized, selective "city return."

The final section of the chapter reviewed the changing character of commuting in both older and younger metropolitan areas. Clearly, the predominant redistribution tendencies for both workers and places of employment are leading to a multinodal suburban development pattern which will, eventually, require all working members of the household to have access to a motor vehicle (that is, through individual ownership or car pooling arrangements). This development tendency allows for far more flexibility in the choice of residential location and provides for shorter average travel time to work. In the context of such deconcentrated development and in light of the changing residence–workplace distributions reviewed in this chapter, it would appear necessary for depopulating central cities to take on more specialized functions in order to remain economically viable. At the same time, their less well-off minority and "underclass" residents will be faced with even more severe residence–employment dislocations than they have known in the past.

SUMMARY

12

CONCLUSION

Changing Contexts of Redistribution

T HE PRECEDING chapters have outlined the most significant redistribution trends that have emerged across metropolitan areas, and for central cities and suburbs within large metropolitan areas over recent decades, placing particular emphasis on the post-1970 period. It has become clear, in these analyses, that the nature of these redistribution processes and the contexts within which they occur have changed markedly during this period. Indeed, the 1970s might be considered a "transition decade" in the history of United States population redistribution. Prior to 1970 and, indeed, for most of the present century, the nation's main redistribution patterns consisted of: (1) a strong westward redistribution of the population at the expense of the Northeast, Midwest, and South regions; (2) a redistribution of metropolitan population "up the hierarchy," such that large metropolitan areas grew faster than small metropolitan areas; (3) a continued growth of all metropolitan areas via nonmetropolitan-to-metropolitan migration; and (4) a suburbanward redistribution of population within metropolitan areas that became particularly accentuated in the immediate post–World War II decades.[1]

[1]Irene B. Taeuber, "The Changing Distribution of the Population of the United States in the 20th Century," in Sara Mills Mazie, ed., *U.S. Commission on Population Growth and the American Future, Reports, Vol. 5, Population Distribution and Policy* (Washington, DC: U.S. Government Printing Office, 1972), pp. 29–107.

431

During the 1970s each of these long-standing redistribution patterns became altered in significant ways. First, the strong westward redistribution became redirected into a strong *southward and westward* redistribution. For the first time, the South gained more from net migration than did the West, and these two Sunbelt regions came to comprise the majority of the nation's population. Second, redistribution across metropolitan areas shifted to a "down the hierarchy" pattern in most parts of the country, such that the country's largest metropolitan areas began to register absolute population losses. Third, during the 1970s nonmetropolitan areas gained population at the expense of metropolitan areas in almost all sections of the country—a phenomenon that was characterized as the "nonmetropolitan turnaround." And fourth, while population continued to suburbanize in most large metropolitan areas, the pace of suburbanization declined from that observed in the immediate postwar period and significant shifts in suburban selectivity began to emerge. Population estimates for the mid-1980s indicate that most of these trends are continuing, although there have been some minor changes.[2]

While each of the shifts of the 1970s is noteworthy, those that altered the relationship between population growth and metropolitan status (the second and third shifts) constitute fundamental departures from urbanization trends observed, historically, in the developed world.[3] In light of the uniqueness and general pervasiveness of these "counterurbanization" patterns in the 1970s, a great deal of attention has been given toward identifying the contexts under which they occurred. Some of these contexts are peculiar to the 1970s decade and can therefore be thought of as "period-specific" influences. Indeed, several period-specific influences have been identified with the surge in nonmetropolitan growth during this decade. The energy shortage, associated with the mid-1970s oil embargo, constitutes one of these since it precipitated an extensive development of extractive industries in several western nonmetropolitan areas. Demographic structural developments, specific to the 1970s, also fueled nonmetropolitan population

[2]Postcensal estimates compiled since 1980 suggest a moderation and, in some parts of the country, a reversal of the "nonmetropolitan turnaround." However, as shall be discussed in the last section of this chapter, these changes do not appear to signal a return to pre-1970 urbanization patterns.

[3]Kingsley Davis, *World Urbanization, 1950–1970: Volume II: Analysis of Trends, Relationships, and Developments* (Berkeley: Institute for International Studies, University of California, 1972); Sidney Goldstein and David F. Sly, eds., *Patterns of Urbanization: Comparative Country Studies*, Vols. I and II (Liège, Belgium: Ordina Editions, 1975); Peter Hall and Dennis Hay, *Growth Centres in the European Urban System* (London: Heinemann, 1980); and United Nations, *Patterns of Urban and Rural Growth*, Population Studies, No. 68 (New York: United Nations, 1981).

growth. It was during this decade that relatively large birth cohorts passed into their retirement ages (those born in the 1910s and 1920s), and into the college enrollment ages (the postwar baby-boom cohorts). These developments, respectively, raised demands for non-metropolitan-located retirement residences, and fostered the expansion of state universities and community colleges that were located, to a large extent, in nonmetropolitan territory.

Period-specific influences have also been identified with population declines sustained by large metropolitan areas during the 1970s. The severe 1974–1975 recession clearly served to reduce the job-generating capacities and, therefore, migrant attraction powers of large metropolitan areas. However, a more fundamental economic shift also occurred during this decade, associated with a general "deindustrialization" of the nation's workforce structure.[4] As a consequence of continued obsolescence in existing industrial infrastructure, rising costs of labor, mounting foreign competition, and a general crisis of profitability, a significant "scaling down" of manufacturing production took place nationwide. This "scaling down" imposed particularly adverse consequences for the economies of large metropolitan areas wherein heavy manufacturing constituted a key economic sector—resulting in substantial reductions in jobs, high rates of unemployment, and selective outmigration to the southern region and to smaller-sized places which became the sites of *some* lower-level production activities.

Yet, it would be a mistake to attribute the 1970s "counterurbanization" tendencies only to period-specific influences which might eventually subside—as energy costs go down, as the demographic structure becomes more stable, and as metropolitan areas, reliant on older "smoke-stack" industries, adjust to deindustrialization-related dislocations. Rather, these new redistribution tendencies reflect, to a considerable degree, more evolutionary shifts in the nation's industrial structure, and in modes of work, travel, and communication which may alter, fairly dramatically, the future character of its settlement system. From this perspective, the 1970s deindustrialization-related reduction in manufacturing employment represents a necessary stage in the long-term transformation of the nation's industrial structure, which is also transforming regional and metropolitan area growth tendencies, in accordance with their capacities to take on new economic functions.

[4]Barry Bluestone and Bennett Harrison, *The Deindustrialization of America: Plant Closings, Community Abandonment and the Dismantling of Basic Industry* (New York: Basic Books, 1982); and Glenn Yago, Hyman Korman, Sen-Yuan Wu, and Michael Schwartz, "Investment and Disinvestment in New York, 1960–80," *The Annals of the American Academy of Political and Social Science* (1984): 28–38.

Just as the nation's early trade centers had to transform their economies into manufacturing centers in order to flourish during the period of rapid industrialization, so, too, will today's metropolitan areas be required to transform their economic functions in an era when advanced services, information processing, and high-tech product development constitute the most significant postindustrial economic bases. At the same time, a broader array of work activities, residential alternatives, and urban amenities will be available outside the confines of metropolitan areas in all regions of the country, due to evolving breakthroughs in transportation, communication, and production technologies.

Long-term trends in population redistribution across the nation's regions and metropolitan areas will likely produce a very different list of "winner" and "loser" areas than existed at the time of the 1980 census, as these areas compete to survive within the context of a rapidly changing economic and technological environment. At the same time, deconcentration of residences and work activities away from large urban areas may increasingly come to characterize settlement patterns within all regions. It is too soon to forecast, with any precision, which metropolitan areas and regions will come to dominate United States settlement patterns in the decades that follow 1980. However, the 1970s must certainly be characterized as a "transition decade" in United States redistribution history, wherein the contexts of regional and metropolitan redistribution have begun to alter appreciably in ways that we do not yet fully comprehend.

The 1970s also represent a transition period for the suburbanization process *within* large metropolitan areas that contrasts sharply with the immediate postwar decades when accelerated suburbanization was pervasive. In the 1970s the pace of suburbanization became reduced for practically all large northern metropolitan areas and most of the older large areas in the Sunbelt. Substantial slowdowns in both central city and suburb growth rates were observed for older northern metropolitan areas with declining metropolitanwide populations in the 1970s—areas that registered some of the greatest suburban population gains in the 1950s and 1960s. Furthermore, 1970s suburbanization in virtually all large metropolitan areas exhibited decidedly different selectivity patterns with respect to race and status population characteristics, househould characteristics, and the relationship between workers' residences and workplaces.

The 1970s transition in the intrametropolitan redistribution process is clearly influenced by the broad economic and technological transformations that are restructuring redistribution patterns across regions and between metropolitan areas. However, even more significant influences on suburbanization patterns follow from changes that impacted upon basic dimensions of social stratification that have occurred during the 1970s—changes in race relations, changes in household and family living arrangement preferences, and changes in the occupational structure of jobs that are generally located in central cities. These changes altered the suburban selectivity patterns of the 1950s and 1960s, when white, middle-class families dominated the suburbanward movement, and led to a sharp city–suburb disparity in race and social class characteristics. Indeed, by the late 1960s, a good deal of concern arose over the possibility that this continued selectivity would lead to two racially separate societies, with blacks dominating the city and whites the suburbs,[5] and to a self-reinforcing city decline.[6]

These selectivity tendencies have become moderated during the 1970s, as blacks, nonfamily households, and professional whites all became more diverse in their central city–suburb redistribution patterns, as the large baby-boom cohorts contributed to central city gains, and as central cities began to assume the roles of advanced service nodes and cultural-entertainment centers in the context of a postindustrial economy. Clearly, the old conditions that fostered city–suburb redistribution patterns in the immediate postwar decades have shifted such that previous selectivity stereotypes no longer apply. While it may be too late to hope for a wholesale "revitalization" of central cities that have sustained several decades of race- and status-selective outmigration, the potential for introducing change, albeit gradually, now exists.

Over the course of this book, we have documented in considerable detail the patterns, determinants, selectivities, and consequences of recent population redistribution to a degree that is only possible with the rich area-based census data at our disposal. When evaluating these patterns, both across regions and metropolitan areas (Chapters 3 through 6), and within large metropolitan areas (Chapters 7 through 11), it becomes apparent that the 1970–1980 redistribution processes—in almost every respect—depart markedly from those observed in previous decades. In the sections that follow, we highlight our major findings with respect to redistribution across metropolitan areas, city–suburb redistribution within metropolitan areas, and the recent redistribution patterns for blacks. In the final section of this chapter, we engage in some speculation as to what the changing redistribution contexts, which emerged in the 1970s, might imply for future growth and decline in the nation's regions, metropolitan areas, and large central cities.

[5]National Advisory Commission on Civil Disorders, *A Report* (Washington, DC: U.S. Government Printing Office, 1968).

[6]Katharine L. Bradbury, Anthony Downs, and Kenneth A. Small, *Urban Decline and the Future of American Cities* (Washington, DC: The Brookings Institution, 1982).

Redistribution Across Metropolitan Areas

As discussed above, the major shifts in post-1970 interregional and intermetropolitan redistribution involved: an accelerated redistribution directed to the South and West regions, with the South sustaining unprecedented gains vis-à-vis all other regions; a new redistribution "down the metropolitan hierarchy," wherein small metropolitan areas grow more rapidly than large ones; and a reversal of the traditional nonmetropolitan-to-metropolitan area exchange. We will review here, briefly, the most important dimensions and demographic components associated with each of these shifts before turning to a discussion of their causes and consequences.

The first change represents a significant regional shift in growth away from the older northern metropolitan areas toward newer metropolitan areas in the South and the West. Although metropolitan areas in the West, such as Los Angeles and San Francisco, have grown relatively rapidly throughout this century, it is only recently that other western areas, such as Anaheim, Phoenix, and San Diego, have achieved national prominence and have accounted for a significant proportion of metropolitan growth. The southern metropolitan areas, which grew slowly prior to 1950, and more rapidly through the 1950s and 1960s, became the leaders in metropolitan growth in the 1970s—receiving over one-half of the total metropolitan growth during this decade. Yet in contrast to the South and West regional patterns, there has been very little growth in the metropolitan populations of the Northeast and Midwest since 1970, and many metropolitan areas in these regions experienced significant population declines.

Most of the differences in metropolitan growth among regions is attributable to net migration. However, a small part of the difference is due to the natural increase which is higher in the West and in the West-South-Central division within the South than in the northern regions. The higher natural increase in these regions is due to both younger age distributions and higher fertility rates. Immigration has also contributed to the shift in metropolitan growth to the South. While the large northern areas that had served as the major destinations of immigrants during the early part of the century—such as New York and Chicago—continued to receive immigrants, the immigration to these areas did not fully compensate for the outmigration from these areas. In contrast, metropolitan areas in the South and West, which had received few immigrants from the earlier waves of European immigration, have received the majority of the newer immigration from Latin America and Asia. Overall, immigration accounted for about one-third of metropolitan growth in the 1970s.

The second major change in metropolitan growth patterns has been a decided shift away from the larger metropolitan areas toward the smaller areas. In all regions except the South, areas with less than 250,000 population grew much more rapidly than large areas during the 1970s. Many of the largest areas in the North, such as New York, Cleveland, and Detroit, suffered significant population declines, and even in the rapidly growing West region, the two largest areas—Los Angeles and San Francisco—experienced such a slow-down in growth that they would have lost population had it not been for the large number of immigrants to these areas. The South has been a major exception with the continued rapid growth of large areas, such as Houston, Ft. Lauderdale, and Tampa. Nevertheless, parts of the South have also experienced the shift in growth to smaller metropolitan areas, with many of the small metropolitan areas in Florida and Texas leading the list of the most rapidly growing areas in the United States. Their growth is offset, however, by the relatively slow growth in Maryland, Delaware, the District of Columbia, Alabama, Louisiana, Kentucky, Mississippi, and West Virginia.

The third major trend in metropolitan growth is the "nonmetropolitan turnaround." When growth is examined within constant boundaries, the 1970s are unique in showing more rapid growth in nonmetropolitan areas than in metropolitan areas. This finding is further supported by data showing that there was net migration from metropolitan areas to nonmetropolitan areas. This "nonmetropolitan turnaround" was primarily a phenomenon of the 1970s, although it has been observed in migration streams for earlier decades in the Northeast. During the 1970s the turnaround was observed for all regions except the South. However, since 1980 there has been little difference between the growth rates of metropolitan and nonmetropolitan areas outside the South, while metropolitan growth has exceeded nonmetropolitan growth in the South.

Although the "nonmetropolitan turnaround" was real in terms of the change in net migration streams between metropolitan and nonmetropolitan areas, the focus of attention upon these phenomena has obscured a basic change in the ways metropolitan areas have been growing in the United States. Prior to 1970 most metropolitan growth was due to growth within fixed metropolitan boundaries, although there was always some growth from the outward expansion of metropolitan areas and the creation of new metropolitan areas. Between 1970 and 1980 about 45 percent of metropolitan growth was due to the territorial expansion and the creation of new areas. The major share of this growth resulted from the creation of 75 new areas between censuses. Had there been no additions to the list of metropolitan areas and no addition of territory to existing metropolitan areas, the proportion of the population living in the metropolitan areas would have declined between 1970 and 1980. This has focused attention on the changes in definitions of metropolitan areas, and whether or not they accurately reflect changes in the pattern of metropolitan settlement, or a response to political pressures from communities wishing to qualify for federal programs that are restricted to metropolitan areas.[7]

The major change in census definitions of metropolitan area units has been the broadening of criteria for the minimum urban core needed to qualify.[8] Starting from an initial requirement of a central city of 50,000 population in 1950, this criteria has been gradually relaxed so that by 1980, the core would be any Urbanized Area of 50,000 or more, providing that the total metropolitan area had at least 100,000 population.[9] This change in criteria is consistent with the extensive suburbanization that has been documented in newer metropolitan areas during the 1970s, and the concept of large multinodal urban settlements that can be maintained without densely settled centers. An example of one of these newer areas is Bradenton, Florida, which had only 30,170 people in its central city, but a surrounding suburban area of over 100,000 and a rapid growth rate. The relaxation of the criteria also allowed areas such as Benton Harbor, Michigan, Cumberland, Maryland, and Sharon, Pennsylvania, to qualify as metropolitan despite little growth during the 1970s. However, the increase in the nation's metropolitan population due to the addition of areas that would not have qualified under earlier definitions is not very large.[10]

The Determinants of Growth and Decline

The trends in growth and decline in metropolitan areas during the 1970s appear to challenge earlier theories of regional growth and in-

---

[7]Calvin L. Beale, "Poughkeepsie's Complaint or Defining Metropolitan Areas," *American Demographics* (January 1984):28–48.

[8]The metropolitan area unit has been given different names in different census years. In the 1950 census, it was termed the Standard Metropolitan Area (SMA) and in the 1960 to 1980 censuses it was termed the Standard Metropolitan Statistical Area (SMSA). Since June 30, 1983, the Census Bureau has defined the primary metropolitan area units to be either Metropolitan Statistical Areas (MSAs), when they are freestanding, and Primary Metropolitan Statistical Areas (PMSAs), when they are adjacent to other metropolitan units. Despite these different names and revisions to their operational definitions, these metropolitan area units remain, fundamentally, the same concept (see Chapter 2 for further discussion of these different definitions).

[9]Areas could also qualify with less than 100,000 population if the central city was 50,000 or more, or if they had achieved metropolitan status under previous definitions. Slightly different rules were used in New England.

[10]Richard Forstall has estimated that, had the 1980 rules been in effect in 1970, there would have been 38 additional metropolitan areas and the total metropolitan population in 1970 would have been about 5.6 million persons larger than reported. Richard L. Forstall, "Is America Becoming More Metropolitan?" *American Demographics* (December 1981):18–22.

terregional migration. While the migration component was most responsible for differences in growth among metropolitan areas, it did not conform to the conventional economic "micro-models" which assume that migrants move from areas with low wages to areas with higher wages. Although migration during the 1950s and 1960s had conformed, at least partly, to the expectations of such models, 1970s net migration was directed, in large measure, toward areas with relatively low wages.

Several authors have sought to explain this shift in net migration in terms of noneconomic motives for migration, observing that migration is positively correlated with temperature.[11] Noneconomic amenities were also used to explain the net migration to metropolitan places and from larger to smaller metropolitan areas.[12] These arguments clearly hold some merit in explaining the significant movement of retired persons to southern states and to Florida, in particular. However, the argument that individuals of labor force age would forego income gains in exchange for better climates was called into question by analyses which employed more refined measures of climate, suggesting that explanations for these unanticipated migration tendencies lay elsewhere.

Our analyses of net migration for the post-1970 period are consistent, in some respects, with descriptions of the regional restructuring patterns led by deindustrialization put forward by several writers.[13] According to this perspective, the 1970s are seen as a period of relative decline in United States manufacturing employment in the face of increased labor costs, foreign competition, and other financial pressures associated with high energy costs, recession, and declining productivity. In response to these pressures, manufacturing plants, largely in the North, were forced to close down or reduce their workforces, and many others relocated production activities to smaller metropolitan areas and

[11]Philip E. Graves, "A Life Cycle Empirical Analysis of Migration and Climate, by Race," *Journal of Urban Economics* 6(1979):135–147; Michael Greenwood and Patrick J. Gormely, "A Comparison of the Determinants of White and Nonwhite Interstate Migration," *Demography* 8(1971):141–155; and Kenneth E. Hinze, *Causal Factors in the Net Migration Flow to Metropolitan Areas of the United States 1960–70* (Chicago: Community and Family Study Center, University of Chicago, 1977).

[12]Richard J. Cebula and Richard K. Vedder, "A Note on Migration, Economic Opportunity and the Quality of Life," *Journal of Regional Science* 13(2)(1973):205–211; and Joe E. Stevens, "The Demand for Public Goods as a Factor in the Nonmetropolitan Migration Turnaround," in David L. Brown and John N. Wardwell, eds., *New Directions in Urban-Rural Migration: The Population Turnaround in Rural America* (New York: Academic Press, 1981), pp. 115–135.

[13]Barry Bluestone and Bennett Harrison, *The Deindustrialization of America*; Glenn Yago, Hyman Korman, Sen-Yuan Wu, and Michael Schwartz, "Investment and Disinvestment in New York, 1960–80"; Manuel Castells, "High Technology, Economic Restructuring, and the Urban-Regional Process in the United States," in Manuel Castells, ed., *High Technology, Space and Society* (Beverly Hills, CA: Sage, 1985); and Thierry J. Noyelle and Thomas M. Stanback, Jr., *The Economic Transformation of American Cities* (Totowa, NJ: Rowman and Allanheld, 1984).

those located in the South where wages were lower. The movement of jobs to areas with lower wages is clearly supported by the data.

Additional factors, which complement the deindustrialization thesis, have been offered to account for the South's attractiveness for industries during the 1970s. It is suggested that two northern metropolitan attributes that attracted manufacturing employment in earlier decades—the availability of skilled labor and the proximity to markets—became less important in the 1970s. The combination of technological change, which reduced skill requirements, and the dramatic increase in levels of education of young workers in the South meant that the relative advantage of the North in terms of skilled labor was far less important in the 1970s than it had been in earlier decades. At the same time, the growth of the interstate highway system and the expansion of regional airlines had the effect of reducing the costs of shipping goods to distant markets; and the increasing population and income in the South meant larger local markets for goods.

Still other factors, associated with the costs of production, have been considered as inducements to industrial growth in the South. One motivation for selecting the South as a location for new plants, it has been suggested, is the lower level of unionization and the "right-to-work" laws for most southern states.[14] This was found to have relatively little effect on migration prior to 1980 but to have some effect in the 1980–1984 period. Related motivations are lower taxes and the more favorable treatment of businesses by many southern communities.[15] Using rather a crude indicator, we were unable to find any significant relationship between taxes and migration once other factors, such as lower wages and lower population density, were taken into account. This does not, however, provide conclusive proof that taxes were not important.

Although it is easy to understand why businesses will want to move to areas with relatively low wages, it may not be obvious that they would be successful in attracting labor to these areas. This success, during the 1970s, was facilitated by two demographic developments which made it possible for businesses to recruit sufficient labor in relatively low-wage areas of the South. The first of these developments was a growth in the number of immigrants to southern metropolitan areas, primarily from Mexico, that provided a source of low-wage labor. In some of the rapidly growing areas of Texas, for example, these immi-

[14]Richard J. Cebula, *Geographic Living-Cost Differentials* (Lexington, MA: Lexington Books, 1983).

[15]Richard J. Cebula, *Geographic Living-Cost Differentials;* and Robert J. Newman, "Industry, Migration and Growth in the South," *Review of Economics and Statistics* 65(1983):76–86.

grants accounted for a significant fraction of all migration in the 1970s.[16]

Second, the entrance of large numbers of young workers into the labor force from the baby-boom cohorts increased unemployment rates in the 1970s, and many of these new workers were willing to work for lower wages than those paid to older workers in the areas of out-migration. The large number of entrants into the labor force meant both an increased supply of native labor in the South and an excess of labor in the North. A large proportion of the workers who moved from the North to the South, during the 1970s, were new entrants to the labor force who did not have the opportunity of earning the average wage of workers who were already employed in the North.

An examination of the incomes of migrants to selected southern metropolitan areas show that they earned at least as much as workers of the same age in northern metropolitan areas of origin, once differences in living costs were taken into account. The observed differences of average wage rates of southern and northern cities were due to differences in the age composition of the labor force and the fact that the southern average included immigrants who typically received lower wages than the migrants from northern areas. Thus, when examined with more disaggregated data, the net movement of labor migrants from North to South was found to fit the economic "micro-model" of migration, while the overall growth patterns were consistent with macro-level deindustrialization distribution shifts.

This explanation holds less well for post-1970 metropolitan area growth in the West. While those areas of the West that grew most in the 1970s were areas with relatively low wages *within* the West region, the average wages in the West were highest of all the regions. Thus, the explanation that businesses were moving to the West from other regions in search of low wages does not apply to the 1970s decade. However, migration estimates for the post-1980 period suggest a slowing migration to the West and, thus, greater conformity to the macro-model.

In summary, it is clear from our analysis of net migration determinants over three decades that aggregate redistribution shifts are affected, to a greater degree than before, by large "footloose" segments of the population (that is, the retired, elderly population); and that, among persons of working age and their employers, traditional migration models have become less applicable. As our analyses have shown, changes in the latter are associated with a period-specific regional re-

[16]For example, in Houston immigrants accounted for 23 percent of the labor migrants from outside the region in 1975–1980, and their wages were only 61 percent of those of migrants from northern metropolitan areas, based on special tabulations from the 1 percent Public Use Microdata Sample of the 1980 Census.

structuring by deindustrialization, wherein jobs and capital were fairly rapidly withdrawn from the North's largest industrial centers at the same time that employment opportunities expanded in the South. However, this interregional redistribution of employment did not constitute simply a rearrangement of the same jobs by employers in their search for lower production costs. This is because a good share of the relatively well-paying northern production jobs were eliminated outright as a consequence of automation, or transferred to other countries where labor costs are lower.

To be sure, the expansion of employment in Sunbelt areas involved *some* growth in low-paying production jobs—although generally less well-paying ones than those lost to the North. However, South and West employment gains were also associated with the expansion of professional and other highly skilled white collar occupations in "home-grown" high-tech industries, energy-related employment, as well as in advanced services. Many of these new redistribution patterns are linked to the long-term economic and industrial transformations that are occurring within all regions of the country, as well as to the increased capacity for workers and employers to relocate in accordance with residential preferences based on both economic and "quality of life" considerations.

Consequences of Growth and Decline

The effect of growth and decline on metropolitan areas is strongly linked to migration selectivity, since migration constitutes the most important demographic component of redistribution across areas in the 1970s. Because migration is selective of the young and better-educated members of the population, it tends to exert a beneficial effect on the population composition of areas of destination and a detrimental effect on areas of origin. To the extent that population growth is associated with economic growth, growing metropolitan areas should be expected to experience increasing levels of employment and income, relative to declining areas. However, there are some costs to growth as well—and it is anticipated that growing areas will experience more rapid rises in living costs, congestion, air pollution, costs of providing infrastructure and related problems. While data constraints preclude an assessment of all potential consequences of growth, our analysis examined changes in population composition, employment, income, and housing that occurred over the course of the 1970s in both growing and declining areas.

The most significant changes in population composition were changes in the age and racial distributions of metropolitan areas. While the United States population as a whole aged considerably during the decade due to the decline in fertility and the decline in mortality at older ages, the mean age and the percentage of elderly rose much more in the areas of population decline and slow growth than in areas of moderate or rapid growth. The increase in the proportion of elderly in declining areas might have risen even higher were it not for the out-movement of elderly from these areas to retirement areas in the South. While the latter movement of the elderly involved fewer numbers of people than the movement of young persons from declining areas, it had a significant impact on the age distribution of the areas of destination, particularly in the small metropolitan areas in Florida.

Blacks, who had historically been concentrated in the rural South, were by 1970 heavily concentrated in metropolitan areas and, during the 1970s decade, their concentration in northern metropolitan areas increased as a result of the higher rates of white outmigration from these areas. In 1970 the areas that experienced subsequent population declines held higher proportions black than the areas of population growth, and the proportion black in the most rapidly growing areas was only about one-half of that of the declining areas. During the decade, the proportion black increased significantly in declining areas while there was very little increase in the proportion black in the rapidly growing areas. However, the rapidly growing areas did show a greater increase in the proportions of their populations that were Hispanics, as immigration constituted an important source of growth in many of these areas. (The changing racial compositions of metropolitan areas will be discussed later in this chapter.)

Surprisingly, there was little relation between the increases in an area's educational level and its growth rates, despite the fact that inter-metropolitan migration is selective of more highly educated persons. There are two explanations for this finding. First, with few exceptions, northern areas that lost migration had initially held higher proportions of persons that completed advanced education levels than did the southern areas which constituted major destinations of migration. Second, many of the southern areas with the highest growth rates received large numbers of immigrants with education levels that lay substantially below those of the internal migrants headed into these areas. Thus, when the education of the immigrants is averaged with the education of the internal migrants, these areas may have gained little or even lost in terms of the overall educational level of their populations.

In like manner, the areas of decline and slow growth did not exhibit disproportionate declines in their proportions of professional and highly skilled workers. In fact, there was a modest increase in the proportion of professionals and managers in the declining areas relative to other areas. Contemporary writers who espouse the deindustrialization thesis are correct in observing that there is a significant loss of skilled blue collar workers in declining metropolitan areas in the North.[17] However, proportional declines in such workers were observed in growing areas as well. The decline in skilled workers is emerging as a national trend, linked to the transformation in the country's industrial structure. Yet, skilled blue collar worker declines were probably more visible in the northern areas where large numbers of workers were laid off from manufacturing plants during this period.

Population growth in the 1970s was highly correlated with economic growth. This meant that not only did the growing areas attract labor force migrants from other areas, but they also experienced significant increases in the labor force participation and employment of their populations. In contrast, the areas of decline or slow growth sustained significant increases in unemployment and much less growth in the proportions of their population who were in the labor force. Northern metropolitan areas which were, on average, below the national average in unemployment in 1970, were considerably above the average in 1980.

Growing areas also experienced much greater increases in family and per capita income than did declining and slowly growing areas. During a decade when the average increase in family income barely kept pace with inflation, families in growing areas experienced real gains in income, while those in declining areas saw losses in purchasing power. Similarly, there were increases in the proportions of family and persons below the poverty level in declining and slowly growing metropolitan areas and declines in poverty in more rapidly growing areas. Because many of the areas with the biggest gains in income and the biggest declines in poverty were southern areas, which had exhibited incomes below and poverty proportions above the national average in 1970, the regional shifts in economic growth resulted in convergence in income and poverty levels among metropolitan areas by 1980.

Earlier, we cited living costs as one of the factors that may have stimulated growth in smaller metropolitan areas, and in the South in general. A major source of variation in living costs among metropolitan areas is the cost of housing. While the South had lower housing costs in 1970, it experienced a much greater increase in these costs in the 1970s, so that by 1980, only the smaller metropolitan areas of the South had lower costs than areas of the same size in the North. Within all regions and size categories, the increase in both rent and the value of owner-occupied housing was positively related to population growth. Thus, if

[17]Barry Bluestone and Bennett Harrison, *The Deindustrialization of America.*

444

living costs are a factor in encouraging people to move to an area, this process appears to be self-limiting due to the increase in living costs accompanying such population shifts.

There are many other costs associated with growth and decline that could not be adequately measured here. Analysis of the incomplete data on air pollution and crime failed to show significant relationships to growth during the 1970s, but there were serious problems with the comparability of these data over time, so that we cannot rule out the possibility that growth may have an effect on these variables. Furthermore, there have been reports that some growing areas have faced acute shortages of water, or foresee future shortages if growth continues.[18] However, we could obtain no systematic measures of water supply for all metropolitan areas or a representative sample of areas.

City–Suburb Redistribution Within Large Metropolitan Areas

Our analysis of intrametropolitan city–suburb redistribution within the largest 39 metropolitan areas—like our intermetropolitan analysis—showed the 1970s decade to diverge significantly from previous periods. Prior to this decade we have identified two earlier eras of suburbanization in the nation's redistribution history. The first of these occurred between the turn of the century and World War II, and was characterized by a highly status-selective suburbanization associated with the initial suburban development that occurred with widespread automobile ownership. The second major suburbanization era took place over the 1945–1970 period and involved a massive suburbanward movement—selective on race and family status but somewhat less selective on socioeconomic status than was the case in the first era. Hence, by the late 1960s, older central cities that bore the brunt of both eras' selective suburbanization tended to house a population that was disproportionately black, low income, and associated with a more diverse array of household types—in comparison with the remainder of the metropolitan area's population.

Our analysis of 1970–1980 city–suburb redistribution patterns in these metropolitan areas was designed to ascertain whether a suburbanization era had begun that could be characterized by a more moderated suburban growth, and less select suburban redistribution patterns. Both

[18]Dale L. Keyes, "Population Redistribution: Implications for Environment Quality and Natural Resource Consumption," in Brian Berry and Lester P. Silverman, *Population Redistribution and Public Policy* (Washington, DC: National Academy of Sciences, 1980), pp. 198–227.

expectations were predicated on the assumption that 1970s societal shifts in race relations, household formation patterns, and location-linked occupational characteristics would serve to loosen the constraints on black suburbanization and increase the attraction of central cities for newly forming middle-class white households.

In evaluating these 1970s changes, we developed a six-category typology of metropolitan areas predictated on the metropolitan areas' age, regional location, and recent growth or decline patterns. The latter criterion proved to be particularly useful since it allowed us to identify 13 "declining" metropolitan areas—all older areas located in the North (and hence classed as North-Declining) which grew by less than 50 percent over the 1950–1980 period and registered negligible or negative growth during the 1970s. Because of their age and regional location, North-Declining areas already registered the greatest city declines and sharpest city–suburb race and status disparities prior to the 1970s decade. However, the new condition of *metropolitanwide* population decline changed the context for intrametropolitan redistribution in these areas. While their central cities sustained even greater losses in the 1970s than in earlier decades, most of these decreases were a consequence of net outmigration losses to other areas rather than to their surrounding suburbs; at the same time, suburban growth in these areas became considerably reduced.

The remaining five categories of areas in our typology all grew moderately to rapidly at the metropolitan level. Of these, the South-Old areas displayed internal redistribution characteristics that came closest to those of the North-Declining areas. North-Old and West-Old metropolitan areas included more expansive central cities and displayed somewhat more moderate city–suburb redistribution disparities. Finally, those areas that we have classed as South-Young and West-Young bore little resemblance to the four previous metropolitan area categories in their city–suburb redistribution patterns. These areas displayed phenomenally high metropolitanwide population growth and, due to their central cities' success in annexing large stretches of territory, their cities grew significantly in population as well.

Two aspects of demographic change occurred fairly consistently across all areas in each class. First, a reduced 1970s contribution of natural increase affected city–suburb redistribution in each area type. While growing areas, with younger age structures, have greater natural increase levels than declining ones, and suburbs generally have higher levels than central cities, all of these levels were reduced during the 1970s decade, placing greater importance on contributions of migration in affecting city–suburb redistribution patterns.

Second, when total net migration for the central cities and suburbs were decomposed into the interlabor market *migration streams* with other areas, and the intrametropolitan *residential mobility streams* between cities and suburbs, the latter exchange is almost always unbalanced in favor of the suburbs and contributes to a greater suburbanization of metropolitan population. The latter process, in fact, became more accentuated with the 1970s in South-Old, South-Young, and West-Young metropolitan areas. Finally, it should be noted that annexation played a significant role in central city population growth, particularly in South-Young and West-Young metropolitan areas, during the 1950–1980 period. However, the contribution of the annexation component became significantly reduced during the 1970s decade.

Race and Status Selectivity

In our analysis of race and status-selective city–suburb redistribution (Chapters 8 and 9), we wished to determine:

1. Whether the 1970s socioeconomic and civil rights gains of blacks—and associated improvements in race relations—precipitated significant increases in black suburbanization.

2. Whether the rise in the number of more career-oriented young adult whites fostered a noticeable white middle-class "city return."

3. Whether the recent influx of the most prominent new minority groups—Hispanics and Asians—are suburbanizing in a manner that is consistent with earlier waves of immigrants.

Our analysis of black city–suburb redistribution patterns suggests that the 1970s constituted a "benchmark" decade for black suburbanization. Substantial increases in black suburbanization rates were observed in most metropolitan areas, although they were particularly strong in North-Declining and South-Old metropolitan areas—those that house the largest numbers of blacks. Furthermore, black suburbanization in the 1970s, unlike that of earlier decades, was accompanied by the traditional "white" status-selective patterns on measures of income, occupation, and years of school completed. Black suburbanization, in most metropolitan areas, involved black residents at all status levels, and black suburbanization increased progressively with increases in black residents' status. Only the South-Young metropolitan areas constituted an exception to these patterns. Here, widespread black suburbanization has not yet taken place, and that which has tended to involve only the upper-status blacks. However, at the other extreme, we found extensive black suburbanization to be occurring in South-Old metropolitan areas, particularly Atlanta and Washington, DC, which involved blacks of all status levels.

Our analysis of nonblack suburbanization of the 1970s did not give widespread support to a pervasive middle-class white "city return" during this decade, though the phenomenon was apparent in selected areas such as Washington, DC. A "slowdown" in nonblack suburbanization, however, was apparent in the North-Declining metropolitan area grouping and, to a lesser extent, in South-Old areas and in areas of the North-Old and West-Old categories. Yet, this slowdown was not generally attributable to the upper-status, city-directed "gentrification" movement that popular media accounts, during the 1970s, tended to emphasize. A very slight tendency toward such redistribution was displayed by professionals and college graduates among the most recent nonblack movers in cities with a large, advanced service economic component, such as New York, Boston, San Francisco–Oakland, and Columbus, leaving open the possibility that a selective "return-to-the-city" movement may be in the offing. However, in the aggregate, traditional status selectivity patterns dominated nonblack suburbanization in most older metropolitan areas. Moreover, in South-Young metropolitan areas, nonblack suburbanization levels increased over the 1970s and status selectivity became more accentuated. This contrasts with nonblack suburbanization in West-Young areas which in the 1970s, as in earlier decades, was relatively indifferent to levels of income, occupation, and education.

An examination of the city–suburb redistribution patterns of the "newer" minority groups—Hispanic- and Asian-Americans—showed them to be particularly strongly concentrated in the South-Young, West-Young, and West-Old metropolitan areas. The city–suburb separation and neighborhood residential segregation levels for both of these groups were lower than those for blacks in most areas, although there was some variation on their absolute segregation levels. Hispanics tended to be more isolated on both city–suburb separation and neighborhood segregation levels in the few northern metropolitan areas they inhabited than was the case in the South and West, while Asians showed fairly consistent neighborhood segregation levels. Asians, therefore, tended to be less isolated than Hispanics in northern areas, but closer to Hispanics than blacks in the Sunbelt. Irrespective of metropolitan area differences, however, our examination of income and recent immigrant-selective suburban location patterns suggested that Hispanics and Asians will tend to disperse to the suburbs as their incomes rise and their length of residence in the United States increases.

Household and Family Selectivity

Underlying the view that central cities might again become more attractive as residential environments was the assumption that the 1970s proliferation of nonfamily and childless-family households— households that had traditionally favored central city locations–might lower the overall appeal of the more "family-oriented" suburbs. In order to investigate this possibility, in Chapter 10 we examined the 1970s suburban redistribution patterns of nonblack and black households by type. In addition, we also wished to determine whether the rise in poor female-headed and other poverty households, which occurred during the 1970s, might be associated with an increased city concentration of poverty.

Our examination of 1970s city–suburb household redistribution patterns leads us to conclude that previous household type selectivity had changed markedly with this decade. Unlike the 1950s, new non-family households are now suburbanizing to a far greater extent than family households in both old and young areas, and—although central cities still continue to gain in the number of nonfamily households— this gain is largely a consequence of the overall growth of such households, rather than the city's continued ability to attract large shares of them. Central cities in the declining and older metropolitan area groupings have sustained net gains in nonblack nonfamily households which helped counter the losses of other nonblack household types. However, the primary sources of this gain were the large baby-boom cohorts. As smaller-sized cohorts pass into the peak household formation ages, as nonfamily households continue to suburbanize, and as the baby boomers themselves shift into childless-couple families and full family (married couple with children under 18) households, the central cities may sustain losses in nonfamily households as well. Nevertheless, the rise of nonfamily households in both the central cities and the suburbs significantly changed the household type compositions in both parts of the metropolitan area. Nonblack central city household stocks are now dominated by nonfamily households, and those of their suburbs are much less dominated by full family households than was the case in the immediate postwar decades. Finally, we found that the 1970s black suburbanization involved households of all types. As a consequence, black suburban household stocks in 1980 were less full family dominated than was the case in the past.

With regard to poor households, however, we found that poor families and unrelated individuals are not suburbanizing as quickly as non-poor households, and that black poor households remain the most heavily concentrated in the city. Although black female-headed households, in general, have shown high suburbanization rates in the 1970s, those in poverty have shown little suburbanization gains.

Worker and Workplace Shifts

An important source of city–suburb separation in the immediate postwar decades was the race-selective worker–workplace "mismatches" which evolved over time. Blacks, unable to relocate into suburban residences, became increasingly isolated from suburbanizing blue collar and lower-level service employment opportunities. At the same time, white collar workers, with city-located jobs, continued to suburbanize and, thus, contribute to a further reduction of the central cities' residential tax base. Central cities, in an attempt to attract back middle-class whites, have begun to consolidate their strengths as advanced service centers. Similarly, blacks have now gained greater residential flexibility. Our analysis of workplace and worker city–suburb redistribution patterns (Chapter 11) examined the scope of recent central city–suburb employment shifts, and accompanying changes in nonblack and black commuting patterns, in order to determine if and how the earlier "mismatches" have been reduced.

An evaluation of employment shifts between central cities and suburbs in declining and old metropolitan area groupings suggests that central cities have not benefited greatly from the national "deindustrialization" tendencies. Cities absorbed most of the metropolitan area's manufacturing employment losses and received little of the area's nonmanufacturing employment gains. Yet, central cities are still in a position to build upon their earlier strengths as advanced service centers, and have shown 1970s gains (although not disproportionate ones in comparison with their suburbs) in professional services, producer services, and public administration. In this respect, national industrial structure shifts are contributing to city employment gains and facilitating their transformation toward a more specialized economic base.

As to the potential for a return to the city among young adult career-oriented nonblacks, we again found little support in the aggregate data; these show an extensive suburbanward relocation of both jobs and residents among nonblacks in the 1970s decade. Still, some selective city retention is suggested by data which indicated that nonblack professionals who worked in the city were the least likely to increase their suburbanization levels over the 1970–1980 period. This suggests that a down-sized, selective "city return" could be possible in some central cities which are able to retain their competitive advantages as advanced service centers. In the main, however, workplace–residence mismatch patterns were reduced largely as a consequence of:

(1) a substantial increase in the number of suburban workers who also reside in the suburbs, and (2) an almost equally large decrease in the number of city workers who also reside in the central city. These shifts occurred among blacks as well—serving to reduce their earlier mismatches significantly. However, large numbers of unemployed blacks remain in the city, unable to find appropriate employment, or to relocate elsewhere.

Black Redistribution in the 1970s

Over the course of this century the redistribution of the black population—across regions, metropolitan areas, and between cities and suburbs—has tended to lag behind that of whites. Yet, there are reasons to believe that this gap may have begun to narrow significantly with the 1970s. Reasons we have cited earlier involve their rise in earnings, educational level, and occupational status—particularly among blacks in the post–World War II baby-boom cohorts. The inequalities between the races have narrowed, somewhat, so that blacks faced less housing and employment discrimination in the 1970s than they did in the 1960s. Finally, the new redistribution patterns, which have emerged among all segments of the population in the 1970s, should permit blacks' early entry into regions, metropolitan areas, and communities—where growth is being spurred by a new regional restructuring of the economy. In this section we review the monograph's major findings regarding blacks in the 1970s in order to answer the question: Is the black-nonblack gap narrowing with respect to redistribution tendencies? Specifically:

1. To what extent are black redistribution patterns across metropolitan areas following those of the total population?

2. Are the determinants of black migration patterns similar to those for the total population?

3. Are blacks experiencing similar consequences as the total population in both growing and declining communities?

4. Are black intrametropolitan city–suburb redistribution patterns in the 1970s leading to significantly reduced neighborhood-and community-level segregation?

Redistribution Across Metropolitan Areas

In each of the decades from 1950 to 1970, the black population in metropolitan areas grew much more rapidly than the nonblack population and, in the 1970s, blacks did not participate in a nonmetropolitan turnaround. In 1980, 81 percent of blacks resided in metropolitan areas, compared to 75 percent of whites and other races. Yet, while blacks continued to move to metropolitan areas in the 1970s, the regional destinations of their moves conformed more closely than previously to those of nonblacks. Historically, and primarily during the 1950s and 1960s, large numbers of blacks moved from nonmetropolitan areas in the South toward metropolitan areas in the North. However, with the 1970s—while the movement out of nonmetropolitan areas of the South continued—most of this movement went to metropolitan areas *in the South*. During the same period southern metropolitan areas gained in their black exchanges with northern metropolitan areas. The West had the highest 1970s rate of black population growth in metropolitan areas, although it started with a much lower proportion of blacks. (In 1970 only about 6 percent of the population in western metropolitan areas was black.) Despite the fact that black movement into growing South and West metropolitan areas during the 1970s increased rapidly, and followed the pattern of nonblacks, blacks were still more heavily concentrated in declining areas than were nonblacks in 1980, leaving blacks greatly underrepresented in the areas of most rapid growth.

Determinants of Intermetropolitan Migration

The determinants of black population growth and black employment growth across metropolitan areas were somewhat different from the determinants of total population and employment growth. Black growth in the 1970s was negatively correlated with wages in the same way as was total population growth—suggesting that the movement of both blacks and nonblacks was influenced by decisions of firms to locate in areas with low wages. However, while the growth of the total population had a negative relationship with the density of metropolitan areas, black growth had a positive relationship to density but did not have the same positive relationship to temperature that was observed for the total population. Hence, while both blacks and nonblacks left northern metropolitan areas for growing areas in the South and West in the 1970s, blacks left these areas at much lower rates and were less likely than nonblacks to go to areas where they would experience competition from large numbers of immigrants.

Consequences of Residing
in Growing and Declining Metropolitan Areas

Metropolitan blacks, in the aggregate, sustained greater gains in education and income than did the total population. These gains were substantial in the smaller metropolitan areas of the South which had shown the lowest levels of education and income for blacks in 1970, resulting in some convergence in education and income among regions and metropolitan size categories. There was also some convergence in rates of labor force participation among blacks in different region and size categories.

Nevertheless, blacks in declining metropolitan areas fared worse than the rest of the population in these areas. They experienced greater declines in labor force participation and much greater increases in unemployment. In 1980, 14 percent of the blacks in declining metropolitan areas were unemployed, compared to only 7 percent of the total population in these areas. The proportion of blacks in poverty also increased significantly in declining metropolitan areas.

The relative concentration of black poverty in southern metropolitan areas, which has been observed in earlier periods, was virtually eliminated by 1980. Though smaller southern areas still had higher rates of black poverty than northern areas, large metropolitan areas of the South had lower levels, and the overall differences between the northern and southern areas were small. If these trends continue, the declining areas of the North will become the major concentrations of black poverty of the future.

Black Suburbanization with Continued Segregation

As indicated earlier, we considered the 1970s to be a "benchmark" decade for black suburbanization, in the sense that blacks at all status levels have finally begun to participate in the suburbanization process. Nevertheless, it should be understood that participation in the *process* is not synonymous with the elimination of aggregate residential segregation patterns that had built up as a result of decades of racially selective redistribution. Strong spatial segregation patterns still exist between central cities and suburbs, across suburban communities, and within central city neighborhoods. While the process of black suburbanization has increased markedly during the 1970s, our analyses have also shown that: (1) the proportion of blacks residing in the suburbs lies well below the nonblack proportion at all status levels for most metropolitan areas; (2) the black-white neighborhood segregation indexes declined only minimally over the 1970–1980 period in areas with large numbers of blacks; (3) the black-nonblack city–suburb separation declined moderately in some areas and increased in others; and (4) blacks are more segregated than Hispanics and Asians in areas that hold large numbers of each group.

Moreover, despite the fact that much of the black worker–residence "mismatch" has been eliminated with the 1970s, it is also the case that: (1) the proportion of blacks who reside in the suburbs is substantially below the proportion of metropolitan employment opportunities therein for all occupations; (2) the number of black "reverse" commuters still remains high; and (3) a large and growing number of unemployed "underclass" central city blacks have become even further isolated from appropriate employment opportunities. Hence, while the new participation of blacks in the suburbanization process constitutes a hopeful sign, it will be decades before the extensive racial segregation of blacks within metropolitan areas becomes eliminated.

Emerging Redistribution Tendencies

At the outset of this chapter, we characterized the 1970s as a transition decade in the history of United States population redistribution patterns. Increased movement to the previously "peripheral" southern region, redistribution down the metropolitan hierarchy, a surge of growth in nonmetropolitan areas, and a moderation of postwar suburban selectivity patterns—all suggest that the long-term social and economic contexts for redistribution had begun to shift. This observation is bolstered by related studies that point up similar post-1970 redistribution tendencies in other developed countries. [19]

In order to illustrate just how greatly the migration patterns—underlying the 1970s interregional and intermetropolitan redistribution—differ from migration patterns that operated during the 1960s, we undertake a population projection "experiment." Using a standard demographic projection methodology, two hypothetical 50-year projections are undertaken—both beginning with the 1980 regional and metropolitan area populations. [20] In the first projection, we apply the ob-

---

[19]Daniel R. Vining, "Migration Between the Core and the Periphery," *Scientific American* 247(6) (1982):45–53; Peter Hall and Dennis Hay, *Growth Centres in the European Urban System* (London: Heinemann, 1980); and L. S. Bourne, R. Sinclair, and K. Dziewonski, eds., *Urbanization and Settlement Systems: International Perspective* (New York: Oxford University Press, 1984).

[20]Each of these projections begins by assuming the existence of an initial population, distributed across the nine areas, and disaggregated into five-year age categories—representing distinct population cohorts born in different five-year periods. Assuming, then, the existence of the 1965–1970 (or 1975–1980) standard age-specific fertility rates, age-specific survival rates, and either 1965–1970 or 1975–1980 age-specific interarea migration stream rates, the projection process proceeds over ten five-year periods (between 1980 and 2030), wherein the members of each cohort's initial population follow the assumed 1965–1970 (or 1975–1980) age-specific migration, fertility, and survival rates as they pass through the life course. These projections, and a more complete discussion of the methodology appear in: William H. Frey, "Migration and Depopulation of the Metropolis: Regional Restructuring or Rural Renaissance?" *American Sociological Review* 52 (April 1987):240–257.

served 1965–1970 interarea migration stream rates to the initial 1980 population, and perpetuate these rates over the entire 1980–2030 projection period. In the second projection, we apply the observed 1975–1980 migration stream rates to the same initial population, and perpetuate these rates over the course of the 50-year projection. Both projections attribute the same fertility and mortality rates to their populations, and are alike in all other respects—except for the migration stream rates that are assumed. The different outcomes of these two projections, therefore, allow us to compare the long-term redistribution consequences of the 1960s (that is, 1965–1970) migration processes with those of the 1970s (that is, 1975–1980) migration processes.

The alternative projections for the nine broad regional and metropolitan area populations are plotted in Figure 12.1 and point up, most vividly, that the 1970s migration patterns—if perpetuated—would lead to far different consequences than the 1960s migration patterns.[21] The greatest difference between the two projections is shown for the large metropolitan areas in the North. (For purposes of these projections, large metropolitan areas pertain to those with 1980 populations of 1 million or greater.) The projection based on the 1960s migration patterns shows these areas to increase their 1980 population by 18 percent (or more than 10 million people), over the 50-year time horizon—while the projections based on the 1970s migration patterns forecasts these areas to lose 12 percent of their 1980 population (or about 7 million people), over the same period. The nonmetropolitan areas in all three regions exhibit higher projected growth when the 1970s migration rates are assumed. South nonmetropolitan areas increase their 1980 population by 47 percent (almost 12 million people), with the 1970s migration rates—as compared to experiencing a 8 percent gain (representing about 2 million people) when the 1960s migration rates are assumed.

---

[21]The regional and metropolitan area groupings used here distinguish between large metropolitan areas, other metropolitan areas, and nonmetropolitan areas on the basis of categories used in the 1980 census. The "large metropolitan area" category includes all aggregated territories of the largest 35 metropolitan areas with 1980 populations of 1 million or greater. Outside of the New England states, these metropolitan areas consist of the 14 Standard Consolidated Statistical Areas (SCSAs), which are combinations of closely related Standard Metropolitan Statistical Areas (SMSAs) and 18 additional free-standing SMSAs with 1980 populations greater than 1 million. Territories for three metropolitan areas that are located in New England (the Boston–Lawrence–Lowell SCSA, the Providence–Fall River SCSA, and the Hartford SMSA) are approximated by county-bounded New England County Metropolitan Areas (NECMAs). "Other metropolitan areas" consist of all other SMSAs outside of New England and SCSAs within New England; and "nonmetropolitan areas" pertain to the residual territory of the country. The regional classification of North, South, and West areas closely approximates census-defined regions. Small discrepancies exist because, in the present analysis, individual metropolitan areas are not allowed to be bisected by regional boundaries. In the case where an individual metropolitan area is bisected by a regional boundary, the entire metropolitan area is assigned to the region wherein most of the metropolitan area's population resides.

FIGURE 12.1

Results of Two Alternative Projections, 1980–2030, for Metropolitan and Nonmetropolitan Populations in North, South, and West Regions that Assume (a) the Perpetuation of Migration Stream Rates Observed in 1965–1970, and (b) the Perpetuation of Migration Stream Rates Observed in 1975–1980

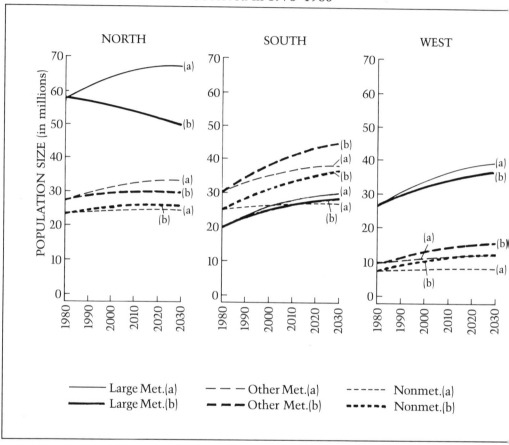

SOURCE: William H. Frey, "Migration and Depopulation of the Metropolis: Regional Restructuring or Rural Renaissance?" *American Sociological Review* 52 (April 1987):240–257.

NOTE: Metropolitan area definitions differ from those used elsewhere in this study (see footnote 21).

These comparisons of the two projections point up the significance of the 1970s cross-regional and metropolitan shifts—toward greater South and West gains, toward greater gains for smaller-sized metropolitan areas, and toward greater gains for nonmetropolitan areas. This is shown in Table 12.1, which displays the year 2030 distribution of the

TABLE 12.1

Percent Distribution of Metropolitan and Nonmetropolitan Populations in North, South, and West Regions in 1980, and Two Alternative Projections for Year 2030, Assuming (a) the Perpetuation of Migration Stream Rates Observed in 1965–1970, and (b) the Perpetuation of Migration Stream Rates Observed in 1975–1980

Percent Distributions by Categories[a]	Actual Year 1980 (1)	Projected to Year 2030		Difference (4)
		Assuming 1965–1970 Rates (2)	Assuming 1975–1980 Rates (3)	
NORTH				
Large Met. Areas	25.4	24.0	17.9	−6.1
Other Met. Areas	12.1	12.0	10.7	−1.3
Nonmet. Areas	10.4	8.9	9.3	+0.4
SOUTH				
Large Met. Areas	8.7	10.7	10.1	−0.6
Other Met. Areas	13.3	13.6	15.8	+2.2
Nonmet. Areas	11.1	9.5	13.1	+3.6
WEST				
Large Met. Areas	11.5	14.0	13.0	−1.0
Other Met. Areas	4.2	4.3	5.6	+1.3
Nonmet. Areas	3.3	2.0	4.5	+1.5
Total	100.0	100.0	100.0	

SOURCE: Same as Figure 12.1.

Metropolitan definitions differ from those used elsewhere in this study (see footnote 21). Large metropolitan areas are those with 1980 populations greater than 1 million.

national population, across regions and area groupings, resulting from each projection. When comparing the resulting 1960s-based distribution (column 2) with the observed initial distribution (column 1), one finds only a slight redistribution toward the South and West regions. Yet, within each of these regions, the 1960s migration rates tend to redistribute population "up the metropolitan hierarchy," such that greatest long-term shifts accrue to the largest Sunbelt metropolitan areas, whereas the nonmetropolitan areas in each of these regions gain least over time. Northern areas' initial share of the national population decrease only slightly over the projection period.

In contrast, the resulting 1970s-based distribution (column 3) leads to a significant southward and westward redistribution of the national population, when compared with the observed 1980 distribution (column 1). Moreover, within both of these Sunbelt regions, small and

457

nonmetropolitan areas gain considerably in their shares of the national population. Finally, the differences between the two projected year 2030 distributions (column 4) underscore, quite clearly, that the 1970s migration rates imply a reversal of the longstanding urbanization tendencies. We wish to make clear that *we are not offering either of these projections as predictions or forecasts of future redistribution patterns in the United States.* We present them only to document how greatly the migration patterns—which underlie the 1970s interregional and intermetropolitan redistribution—depart from those that operated during the 1960s and early decades.[22]

Indeed, there appears to be some moderation in the early 1980s of the redistribution changes observed in the 1970s. However, the 1980s' trends, as discernible from postcensal population estimates, are still more similar to those of the 1970s, than to those of the 1950s and 1960s (see Table 12.2). This is particularly the case for the most dramatic of the 1970s redistribution shifts, which appear to be perpetuated in the early 1980s. The estimated average percent change in large North metropolitan areas over the period 1980–1984, while positive, remains relatively small, and closer in magnitude to 1970s growth levels for these areas, than to the larger 1960s growth levels. At the other extreme, the 1980–1984 estimated growth of South and West nonmetropolitan areas, although somewhat more moderated than that registered over the 1970s, still lies well above the extremely low levels of nonmetropolitan area growth that characterized the pre-1970 period.

While the preceding projections and postcensal population estimates provide some indication of emerging redistribution tendencies, speculations of future patterns are, perhaps, best advanced in light of the changing social and economic contexts that are likely to condition broad redistribution shifts. In the sections that follow, we engage in such speculation with regard to emerging redistribution patterns—across regions and metropolitan areas, and between central cities and suburbs within large metropolitan areas.

Selective Metropolitan Growth and Pervasive Deconcentration

Our examination of migration determinants and redistribution patterns, pertaining to interregional and intermetropolitan shifts during

[22]This comparison of cohort component projections is intended simply as a vehicle for highlighting the different redistribution tendencies associated with the 1965–1970 and 1975–1980 migration processes, upon which each projection is based. For a review of post-1980 regional projections that are used for forecast purposes, see George S. Masnick, *Assessing Population Projections: A Mid-Decade Review,* Working Paper W8G-2 (Cambridge, MA: Joint Center for Housing Studies of M.I.T. and Harvard University, 1986).

TABLE 12.2

Annual Growth Rates for Metropolitan Area Size Classes[a]
in Northeast, Midwest, South, and West Regions,
1950–1960, 1960–1970, 1970–1980, and Estimates for 1980–1984

Regions, Metropolitan Area Size Class	Annual Growth Rates			
	1950–1960	1960–1970	1970–1980	1980–1984 (est.)
NORTHEAST				
1,000,000+	+1.3	+0.9	−0.5	+0.2
250,000–999,999	+1.2	+1.1	+0.4	+0.5
Under 250,000	+1.2	+0.9	+0.7	+0.2
Nonmetropolitan	+1.3	+1.0	+1.2	+0.7
MIDWEST				
1,000,000+	+2.1	+1.2	+0.1	+0.1
250,000–999,999	+2.3	+1.3	+0.4	0.0
Under 250,000	+2.0	+1.2	+0.7	+0.2
Nonmetropolitan	+0.6	+0.4	+0.7	+0.1
SOUTH				
1,000,000+	+3.3	+2.8	+2.1	+2.2
250,000–999,999	+3.2	+1.8	+1.8	+1.8
Under 250,000	+2.8	+1.1	+1.9	+1.7
Nonmetropolitan	+0.3	+0.6	+1.6	+1.2
WEST				
1,000,000+	+4.3	+2.5	+1.7	+1.9
250,000–999,999	+4.4	+2.8	+2.7	+2.2
Under 250,000	+2.8	+2.5	+3.3	+2.2
Nonmetropolitan	+1.8	+1.0	+2.7	+2.0

SOURCES: U.S. Censuses of Population 1950, 1960, 1970, 1980, and U.S. Bureau of the Census, *Current Population Reports*, series P-25, no. 976, *Patterns of Metropolitan Areas and County Population Growth: 1980 to 1984.*

Growth rates are measured within constant boundaries for each period. 1950–1960 rates are measured according to 1960 SMSA and SEA boundaries, 1960–1970 rates according to 1970 SMSA and SEA boundaries, and 1970–1980 and 1980–1984 rates according to 1980 SMSA and NECMA definitions with minor revisions (discussed in Chapter 2 and Appendix F).

the 1970s, underscored the influence of the "deindustrialization" phenomenon, and the associated reduction in manufacturing production employment on redistribution patterns in general, and on the depopulation of older metropolitan areas, in particular. Although to some extent, the deindustrialization phenomenon might be thought of as a "period-specific" occurrence which will exert less severe consequences in the coming decades, it can be viewed alternatively as symptomatic of an even more extensive industrial transformation which will continue to effect a regional restructuring that favors some metropolitan areas and regions at the expense of others.

Several writers taking this view suggest that the rise in advanced services in the areas of finance, law, advertising, and the like are becoming increasingly important "inputs" in the production process, given the ascendency of large multilocational corporations operating in a worldwide market.[23] These "producer services" (in contrast to "consumer services") are seen to foster agglomeration tendencies in those metropolitan areas that house national and regional headquarters for major corporations, banks, and other institutions associated with the complex of corporate activities. Hence, the economic base of such "command and control center" areas lies with their capacity to export advanced services rather than manufacturing goods. Many northern metropolitan areas that sustained deindustrialization-related decline in the 1970s, may well become transformed into advanced service centers, given the initial advantages that many of them—such as New York, Chicago, Boston, and Philadelphia—already possess in corporate complex activities. On the other hand, this transformation may be less painful for upcoming Sunbelt areas with service center advantages—such as Houston, Denver, and Phoenix—which were not subjected to severe manufacturing employment declines. Indeed, the four aforementioned northern metropolitan areas experienced slow estimated growth between 1980–1984, whereas three had declined from 1970–1980. The latter three Sunbelt areas continued to expand, according to the post-1980 estimates.

Advanced service centers are not the only areas that can expect to gain in a postindustrial economy. The growth of new high-technology manufacturing centers such as aerospace or electronics, which began to emerge primarily in the South and West metropolitan areas, can be expected to generate continued agglomeration tendencies in these areas. Many of these industries developed in the Sunbelt as a consequence of federal military expenditures.[24] Other industries took advantage of more favorable labor force characteristics, physical and cultural amenities, and the absence of various scale diseconomies in these lower-

---

[23]Thierry J. Noyelle and Thomas M. Stanback, Jr., *The Economic Transformation of American Cities* (Totowa, NJ: Rowman and Allanheld, 1984); Royce Hanson, ed., *Rethinking Urban Policy: Urban Development in an Advanced Economy* (Washington, DC: National Academy Press, 1983); and Manuel Castells, *High Technology, Space and Society.*

[24]Ann Markusen, Peter Hall, and Amy Glasmeier, *High Tech America: The What, How, Where and Why of the Sunrise Industries* (Winchester, MA: Allen and Unwin, 1986); Ann R. Markusen, and Robin Bloch, "Defensive Cities, Military Spending, High Technology, and Human Settlements," in Manuel Castells, ed., *High Technology, Space and Society,* Urban Affairs Annual Reviews, Vol. 28 (Beverly Hills, CA: Sage, 1985).

density areas.[25] The point is that most of this manufacturing activity is newly developed in these Sunbelt areas and not transplanted from the North. Because it is tied to some of the fastest growing sectors of the economy, it is profitable and, therefore, job-generating. Still other metropolitan areas, specializing in resort and recreation, should also continue to flourish, given the increased disposable income available to a large share of the population and the emergence of large "footloose" population subgroups.

Although the above observations point to a continued metropolitan concentration within areas specializing in selected economic activities, another group of writers have suggested that future redistribution will be characterized by a more pervasive population deconcentration, as foreshadowed by the 1970s "nonmetropolitan turnaround."[26] The emerging deconcentration growth pattern, according to this view, is not simply a consequence of manufacturing production activities that have filtered down from large areas in order to take advantage of lower labor costs. Rather, it is seen to constitute a more pervasive redistribution of the population—embracing all population categories—that is being facilitated by continued improvements in transportation, communication, and production technology. According to this view, long-standing worker and employer preferences toward lower-density residential and workplace locations are becoming less constrained by institutional and technological barriers.

Residents' preferences for low-density, small urban and nonmetropolitan locations are well documented.[27] The rising competition for well-educated, skilled, and professional personnel in new service-based postindustrial industries is expected to motivate firms to relocate into areas that are most attractive to a talented labor force. The new multilocational character of production organizations, along with technologi-

---

[25]R. D. Norton and J. Rees, "The Product Cycle and Spatial Decentralization of American Manufacturing," *Regional Studies* 13 (1979):141–151; John H. Mollenkopf, "Paths Toward the Post-Industrial Service City: The Northeast and the Southwest," in Robert W. Burchell and David Listokin, eds., *Cities Under Stress* (New Brunswick, NJ: Rutgers Center for Urban Policy Research, 1981); and Peter Hall, "The Geography of the Fifth Kondratieff," in Peter Hall and Ann Markusen, eds., *Silicon Landscapes* (Boston: Allen and Unwin, 1985), pp. 1–19.

[26]John M. Wardwell, "Toward a Theory of Urban-Rural Migration in the Developed World," in David L. Brown and John M. Wardwell, eds., *New Directions in Urban-Rural Migration* (New York: Academic Press, 1980), pp. 71–118; John F. Long, *Population Deconcentration in the United States*, Special Demographic Analysis, CDS-81-5 (Washington, DC: U.S. Government Printing Office, 1981); and Franklin D. Wilson, "Urban Ecology: Urbanizations and Systems of Cities," *Annual Review of Sociology* 10 (1984): 283–307.

[27]James J. Zuiches, "Residential Preferences in the United States," in Amos H. Hawley and Sarah Mills Mazie, eds., *Nonmetropolitan America in Transition* (Chapel Hill: University of North Carolina Press, 1981).

cal improvements in communication and extended transportation networks, permit a greater locational flexibility which should precipitate a rapid convergence—across places and regions—in the availability of urban amenities, services, and employment opportunities that were previously constrained to larger metropolitan areas. This more pervasive availability of amenities and services in virtually all parts of the country, it is suggested, will permit both workers and employers to locate in smaller places.

Both the forecasts of continued metropolitan concentration and those of pervasive deconcentration are tied to ongoing economic and technological transformations which should continue to alter, quite markedly, both the nature and locations of production activities. It seems prudent to take the middle ground and suggest that there is merit in both observations.[28] Undoubtedly, a significant number of metropolitan areas will successfully transform their economic bases into productive, employment-generating advanced service or high-technology production centers that will continue to remain viable as the nation's industrial structure changes. By the same token it seems likely that the pervasive 1970s "counterurbanization" tendencies will continue to the extent that energy availability and costs will allow. The forecast of selective metropolitan growth, in the midst of a more pervasive deconcentration of the population, seems a reasonable redistribution scenario that will likely continue to favor the Sunbelt regions—with their "homegrown" industries and vast expanse of high-amenity territory. The largest northern "command and control center" areas, such as New York, Chicago, Boston, and Philadelphia, will probably continue to flourish, and several additional northern areas will become successfully transformed from manufacturing centers to advanced service centers. Some smaller northern areas, such as Nashua and Portsmouth in New Hampshire and Atlantic City, New Jersey, offer particular advantages which may allow them to compete favorably with southern areas. However, it would also appear to be inevitable that many older northern "smokestack industry" areas will not make this transition, and that their populations will continue to diminish.

Specialized Central Cities and Diffuse Suburbanization

The 1970s decade metropolitanwide decline led by deindustrialization also changed the context for central city–suburb redistribution, particularly within large older North metropolitan areas where postwar

---

[28]These two views of future redistribution tendencies are contrasted in William H. Frey, "Migration and Depopulation of the Metropolis."

growth and selective suburbanization led to sharp city–suburb race and status disparities at the decade's beginning. Metropolitanwide population declines, imposed upon areas that we have labeled North-Declining, served to moderate the pace of suburbanization during this decade—as their central cities sustained marked population losses and their suburban populations' gains tapered off considerably from those observed in the immediate postwar period (see Table 12.3). These reduced growth levels, while representing a loss in the *metropolitan area's* economic attractiveness, provide the opportunity for the development and restructuring of the central city's role within the metropolitan area, which is being fostered by post-1970 societywide changes in race relations, living arrangement patterns, and the nature of work.

These three societywide shifts have appreciably altered the constraints and preferences associated with central city–suburb population selectivity—within metropolitan areas of all types—from those that operated in the immediate post–World War II decades. However, the new selectivity processes, permitted by these shifts, are particularly important for central cities of the 13 North-Declining metropolitan areas examined in this study, which have borne the brunt of prolonged race- and status-selective population outmigration and, more recently, significant losses in their share in the metropolitan area's employment opportunities. First, the metropolitanwide dispersal of blacks, which began in earnest during the 1970s, should begin to dispel the "black city–white suburb" image which had heretofore exerted a significant influence on the suburbanward relocation decisions of metropolitan area employers, as well as white middle-class residents.[29]

Second, the greater diversity of household living arrangements, evident during this decade—where a sizeable share of middle-class childless and nonfamily households tended to favor a "close-in" location—represents an increased demand for new city residential development and increments to the city's residential tax base.

Finally, the increased significance of advanced services for the economies of large metropolitan areas should reinforce their central cities' traditional advantages as the locations for such services and complementary industries; and, at the same time, serve to enhance their attractiveness as residential locations for the white collar professionals and upper-level managers employed therein.

It should be understood that these 1970s intrametropolitan selec-

[29]John F. Kain and Joseph J. Persky, "Alternatives to the Guilded Ghetto," *Public Interest* 14 (1969):74–87; William H. Frey, "Central City White Flight: Racial and Nonracial Causes," *American Sociological Review* 44 (June 1979):425–448; and William H. Frey, "Status Selective White Flight and Central City Population Change: A Comparative Analysis," *Journal of Regional Science* 20(1) (1980):71–89.

TABLE 12.3

Average Annual Percent Change for Central Cities
and Suburbs and Suburbanization Rates for Large Metropolitan Areas
in Six Metropolitan Area Groupings,[a] 1950–1960, 1960–1970, 1970–1980,
and Estimates for 1980–1984

Metropolitan Area Groupings/ Central Cities and Suburbs	Average Annual Percent Change			
	1950–1960	1960–1970	1970–1980	1980–1984 (est.)
NORTH-DECLINING				
Central City	−0.3	−0.4	−1.4	−0.3
Suburbs	+3.9	+2.1	+0.4	+0.3
(Suburbanization Rate*)	(+4.2)	(+2.5)	(+1.8)	(+0.6)
NORTH-OLD				
Central City	+0.5	+1.2	−0.8	−0.1
Suburbs	+4.8	+2.3	+1.4	+1.3
(Suburbanization Rate*)	(+4.3)	(+1.1)	(+2.2)	(+1.4)
SOUTH-OLD				
Central City	+0.6	−0.2	−1.3	−0.4
Suburbs	+5.2	+4.4	+2.2	+2.1
(Suburbanization Rate*)	(+4.6)	(+4.6)	(+3.5)	(+2.5)
WEST-OLD				
Central City	+1.5	+0.7	+0.1	+0.9
Suburbs	+5.0	+2.8	+1.6	+1.8
(Suburbanization Rate*)	(+3.5)	(+2.1)	(+1.5)	(+0.9)
SOUTH-YOUNG				
Central City	+4.4	+2.1	+1.4	+1.5
Suburbs	+5.6	+4.7	+4.7	+3.8
(Suburbanization Rate*)	(+1.2)	(+2.6)	(+3.3)	(+2.3)
WEST-YOUNG				
Central City	+8.2	+3.7	+2.4	+2.2
Suburbs	+6.7	+4.6	+3.6	+2.8
(Suburbanization Rate*)	(−1.5)	(+0.9)	(+1.2)	(+0.6)

SOURCE: U.S. Censuses of Population 1950, 1960, 1970, 1980, and U.S. Bureau of the Census, *Current Population Reports*, series P-25, no. 976, *Patterns of Metropolitan Areas and County Population Growth: 1980–1984*.

[a]39 metropolitan areas with 1980 populations greater than 1 million defined in constant 1980 SMSA and NECMA boundaries with minor qualifications (see Appendix F). These areas are the same as those analyzed in Chapters 7 through 11.

*Annual Suburbanization Rate: Suburb Average Annual Percent Change minus Central City Average Annual Percent Change.

tivity shifts constitute changes in redistribution *processes* rather than changes in population and employment compositions, in the aggregate. This is best illustrated in the case of black suburbanization, where we have shown that high levels of city concentration and neighborhood segregation still exist in 1980—in spite of the considerable 1970–1980 rise in black suburbanization. Indeed, it has been demonstrated through alternative population projection "experiments" (such as the one undertaken above) that—even if racial differences in suburban selectivity were completely eliminated—it would take at least 25 years to achieve city–suburb racial balance in the aggregate population, in a typical large northern metropolitan area.[30] Similarly, the city gains in white nonfamily households during the 1970s, which we attributed to the large baby-boom cohorts as they passed through their young adult years, will need to be replicated—and far more decisively—by their smaller-sized successor cohorts, if a viable middle-class residential base is to be established. Finally, the emergence of central cities as foci of advanced services cannot occur within all metropolitan areas but would clearly favor those that we have identified earlier as potential "command and control center" metropolitan areas—those that already possess significant advanced service infrastructures.

What is important with the 1970s shifts in redistribution contexts, however, is the potential for central city redevelopment, which now exists within metropolitan areas that were heretofore faced with a continuing "vicious cycle" of selective outmigration and central city disinvestment. This situation characterized most of the metropolitan areas we have classed as North-Declining and South-Old, as well as selected areas in other metropolitan groupings. Not all of these areas' central cities will recover. But, as a consequence of the changing conditions of race relations, household living arrangements, and metropolitan industrial and occupational structures, some cities will be able to transform their economic and residential bases, and establish themselves as centers of high-level services, culture, and leisure and specialty stores in the broader metropolitan area region.

Yet even these successful central cities will be relegated to playing a far less dominant role in the metropolitan area's economy than was the case in the past. The increasing propensity for metropolitan residents of all races and occupations to both live and work in the suburbs, the proliferation of suburban shopping malls and industrial parks, and the increasing reliance of workers on private automobile ownership in their commuting patterns are leading to a much more dif-

[30]William H. Frey, "Lifecourse Migration of Metropolitan Whites and Blacks and the Structure of Demographic Change in Large Central Cities," *American Sociological Review* 49 (December 1984):803–827.

fuse suburbanization process, within which the central city constitutes only one of a series of workplace, consumption, and recreation nodes. The most successful of the older central cities will be those whose leaders accurately perceive their new roles in this environment, and work effectively toward making the transition. Indeed, the post-1980 estimates, which show reduced central city losses (or increased gains) from 1970s levels for the four older metropolitan area groupings, suggest that such transformations are under way (see Table 12.3).

The negative aspect of the post-1970 redistribution processes—which represents an important obstacle for central city redevelopment—concerns the growth of the largely (although not predominantly) black, "underclass" poverty population which continues to concentrate in the central city. The plight of this underclass population is becoming exacerbated by the ongoing economic transformations within central cities which have already phased out large numbers of "entry-level" blue collar and service jobs and are replacing them with employment opportunities that require more formal education than these residents possess.

Clearly, today's central cities, in their attempts to take on new economic functions and, at the same time, remain fiscally viable, are no longer well positioned to serve the "social upgrading" functions they once provided to new immigrant groups in an earlier era.[31] Nevertheless, the numbers of such individuals are increasing and leading to higher levels of unemployment, nonparticipation in the labor force, and welfare dependency.[32] Unlike most black and nonblack city residents, who are now able to relocate closer to more appropriate suburban employment opportunities, these underclass city residents remain left behind. Although a great deal of public debate has contrasted the relative advantages of providing "place-based" employment and assistance to city underclass residents, as opposed to "people-based" retraining and relocation programs, it seems clear that a reliance on "natural" redistribution forces will exacerbate their plight and lead to an increased race-and-class polarized central city population.[33]

---

[31]John D. Kasarda, "Urban Change and Minority Opportunities," in Paul Peterson, ed., *The New Urban Reality* (Washington, DC: The Brookings Institution, 1985); and R. D. Norton, *City Life-Cycles and American Public Policy* (New York: Academic Press, 1979).

[32]William Julius Wilson and Robert Aponte, "Urban Poverty," *Annual Review of Sociology* 11(1985):231–258.

[33]John D. Kasarda, "The Implications of Contemporary Redistribution Trends for National Urban Policy," *Social Science Quarterly* 61(3, 4) (1980):373–400; and Norman J. Glickman, "Emerging Urban Policies in a Slow-Growth Economy: Conservative Initiatives and Progressive Responses in the U.S," *International Journal of Urban and Regional Research* 5 (1981):492–527.

It is important to emphasize that problems of population decrease, tax-base erosion, and economic isolation from the wider metropolitan area do not characterize the central cities of *all* large metropolitan areas. Indeed, for a number of large metropolitan areas in the Midwest and West (in our North-Old and West-Old categories), central city populations are more diverse, city economies are far more viable, and city–suburb disparities are less sharp than in most of the oldest North and South areas classed in our North-Declining and South-Old categories. In these areas, which are still at an earlier stage of the suburbanization process, the 1970s shifts in race relations, household living arrangements, and occupational structure should make a more significant impact on their future city–suburb development.

It is in the younger areas (that is, in our South-Young and West-Young categories) that the future intrametropolitan development patterns are most unpredictable. Many of these areas evolved around more recently developed, less dense central cities whose boundaries expanded fairly continuously (through annexation) as the cities' hinterlands grew. Most of these cities developed around economic activities other than heavy manufacturing and, prior to their reception of large numbers of Hispanic and Asian immigrants, these areas did not constitute traditional destinations for earlier waves of immigrant groups. These areas, therefore, took on very different initial economic functions, population compositions, and political coalitions than those that fostered the frozen city boundaries, fragmented system of suburban communities, and the disparate socioeconomic ethnic enclaves that evolved within northern metropolitan areas.[34]

As a consequence, the new, fast-growing Sunbelt metropolitan areas differ significantly from older areas and from each other in their levels of city and suburb growth and suburban selectivity on various socioeconomic dimensions, and do not seem to follow any particular model of intrametropolitan redistribution. Nevertheless, it is significant to notice that, during the same decade that older, northern metropolitan areas are displaying a moderation in their suburbanization levels and in their race- and-class-selective redistribution patterns, the young southern metropolitan areas—particularly those with high levels of black and Hispanic immigration—are showing a curtailment in their city annexation patterns, increased levels of white suburbanization, and sharper differences in the status selectivity of white suburbanward movers.

[34]R. D. Norton, *City Life-Cycles and American Public Policy;* and Mollenkopf, "Paths Toward the Post-Industrial Service City."

Transition to What?

We have characterized the 1970s as a "transition decade" of regional and metropolitan growth in the United States—not only because specific redistribution patterns have altered significantly during this decade, but also because broad economic and social contexts for redistribution have changed as well. Although short-term deindustrialization-related shifts accounted for much of the metropolitan losses during this period, a longer-term regional restructuring of the economy has begun to emerge as a consequence of fundamental shifts in the organization of production—from catering to a region- or place-based market to a worldwide market. This has led to the increased emergence of multi-locational corporations, and the ascendency of some large metropolitan areas as advanced-level service centers. Additional metropolitan areas, of all sizes, will specialize in a widening array of lightweight, easily transportable "high tech" manufacturing goods; and still other metropolitan areas will prosper as resort and retirement centers.

At the same time that new technologies and economic priorities have facilitated a greater flexibility of production, they have also brought about a greater flexibility in choice of residential locations. A wide range of employment opportunities, consumer goods, and other "urban" amenities, that have heretofore been confined to the large- and medium-sized cities, are fast becoming available in places of all sizes. Hence, people in the work force now have a far broader array of residential locations to choose from, and a growing number of "footloose" populations in our society can make residential location decisions on the basis of even fewer constraints. Finally, redistribution within metropolitan areas is subject to fewer constraints as the 1970s societywide shifts in race relations, living arrangement preferences, and location-linked occupation structures have begun to moderate the sharp selectivity patterns that characterized post–World War II suburbanization.

The loosening of constraints associated with each of these interregional and intrametropolitan redistribution contexts has led to far more flexible redistribution processes on the parts of employers and residents alike. At the same time, it has led to less predictable population distribution patterns. Our tentative speculation that selective metropolitan growth will emerge along with a more pervasive deconcentration of the population, and that some successful central cities will become specialized, gentrified nodes within an increasingly diffuse multinodal metropolitan complex, is based, largely, on our knowledge of current practices and preferences of production organizations, individual employers, and residents. However, given the loosening of location-based constraints, the future mobility of residents, employers, and capital will be far more responsive to shifts in personal preference, organizational decisions, and economic exigencies than was possible in the past—when the friction of space and more rigid societal norms made the prediction of future population distribution shifts a more straightforward exercise. Hence, with the passage of this "transition decade" and the changing redistribution contexts that have emerged, we will likely never again be able to look as closely to past trends as a guide to future regional and metropolitan redistribution tendencies.

APPENDIX A:
METROPOLITAN GROWTH USING THE
METROPOLITAN STATISTICAL AREAS
DEFINED IN 1983

I N 1983 a major revision in the definition of metropolitan areas was announced by the Office of Management and Budget. These areas were renamed Metropolitan Statistical Areas (MSAs).[1] In addition to redefining the boundaries of existing metropolitan areas to take account of the commuting patterns observed in the 1980 census, there are several changes in the rules for defining metropolitan areas, and a new method of treating contiguous metropolitan areas was developed. As a result of tightening the criteria for the inclusion of outlying counties in metropolitan areas, 51 counties lost metropolitan status. This represented a much greater reclassification than had occurred in either 1963 or 1973 when virtually no counties had been removed from SMSAs. A total of 61 counties were added to metropolitan areas, including those in the three new metropolitan areas that were created in 1983.

Metropolitan areas with over one million population that contained two or more counties were divided into two or more Primary Metropolitan Statistical Areas (PMSAs), if each part met specified criteria for metropolitan status and if local opinion supported such a division. The original metropolitan area then became known as a Consolidated

---

[1] The criteria for these areas were set forth in "The Metropolitan Statistical Area Classification, 1980." Also see Richard L. Forstall and Maria E. Gonzalez, "Twenty Questions—What You Should Know About the New Metropolitan Areas," *American Demographics* (April 1984):22–31, 42–43.

Metropolitan Statistical Area (CMSA), and the components were called Primary Metropolitan Statistical Areas (PMSAs).

The 1983 revision resulted in 253 MSAs which were not part of larger units, plus 19 CMSAs which contained a total of 60 PMSAs.[2] This major revision of the classification system produced relatively small overall effects. The 1980 population classified as metropolitan increased from 170.5 to 172.1 million.[3] This resulted in a slightly higher metropolitan growth rate for the 1970–1980 decade, but it did not alter the basic conclusions about patterns of growth during that decade.

Metropolitan Growth by Different Definitions

To what extent do changes in metropolitan definitions alter the conclusions reached in Chapter 3 about the extent and nature of metropolitan growth? To answer this question, we have calculated metropolitan and nonmetropolitan growth by region for the period 1960 to 1984 according to three different definitions: the definition used in 1970 Census publications; the one used in 1980 publications; and the 1983 MSA definition. Consistent with the analysis presented in this monograph, we have used New England County Metropolitan Areas and have adjusted regional totals so that metropolitan areas are not divided among regions but included within the region with the largest central city.[4]

The choice of definition has an effect on the overall growth rate observed for metropolitan areas. For the 1960–1970 decade this effect is quite small. The average annual growth rate increases only from 1.57 to 1.60 percent in shifting from the 1970 to the 1983 definition. However, for 1970–1980, the increase is from 0.84 to 1.01 percent, and for 1980–1984 it is from 1.02 to 1.11 percent. In all comparisons, the use of 1980 definitions results in a higher growth rate than the use of 1970 definitions, while the use of the 1983 definitions results in an even

[2]These counts and those in the rest of the paragraph are based on using NECMAs rather than MSAs in New England. According to the 1983 classification, there were 15 MSAs, 3 CMSAs, and 17 PMSAs in New England. These are replaced here by 16 NECMAs. Fifteen of the NECMAs are at the level of MSAs, and 1 (Fairfield County, Connecticut) is a PMSA. In 1984, 2 CMSAs, Kansas City and St. Louis, were changed to MSAs as a result of Acts of Congress, and 2 new MSAs, Naples, Florida, and Santa Fe, New Mexico, were created by the Office of Management and Budget.

[3]Using the 1983 classification, the excess of the population of NECMAs over the New England MSAs and PMSAs was only about 350,000. (Personal communication from Richard Forstall.)

[4]The redrawing of regional boundaries to include entire metropolitan areas within the same regions resulted in very little net change in regional populations. For example, as of 1980 the Northeast lost 64,700 to the South, and the Midwest lost 9,500 to the South.

472

higher growth rate. The biggest differences are between the 1970 and 1980 definitions; the differences between the 1980 and 1983 definitions are much smaller. Since the 1980 definitions are used in the monograph, the substitution of 1983 definitions would not significantly alter the conclusions about patterns of growth during the 1970s.

The general increase in metropolitan growth, which is observed in moving from the 1970 to the 1980 definitions, is because existing metropolitan areas grew most rapidly at their peripheries, and some of the area at the periphery was excluded from the 1970 definitions but added to the 1980 or 1983 definitions of metropolitan areas. In the 1983 definitions, growth of 20 percent or more between censuses is one of the criteria for adding adjacent counties to metropolitan areas. [5] In addition, several urban areas that were nonmetropolitan in 1970 became metropolitan areas in 1980, by virtue of rapid growth during the 1970s, which pushed them past the threshold for metropolitan status. [6]

Although some of the nonmetropolitan growth observed in the 1970s was in adjacent counties or small cities, which were subsequently reclassified as metropolitan, the nonmetropolitan turnaround of the 1970s cannot simply be attributed to a lag in the classification of areas. There was substantial growth in nonadjacent counties and counties that were remote from metropolitan areas. [7] As can be seen in Appendix Table A.1, nonmetropolitan growth exceeded metropolitan growth during the 1970s under all three definitions of metropolitan. But the definitions do make a difference when one tries to assess the magnitude of the differences in growth rates. Using constant 1970 boundaries, the nonmetropolitan growth rate is almost double the metropolitan growth rate (94 percent higher). However, if 1980 boundaries are used this difference is reduced to 44 percent, and if the 1983 boundaries are used the nonmetropolitan growth is only 34 percent higher than metropolitan growth.

[5]Federal Committee on Standard Metropolitan Statistical Areas, "The Metropolitan Statistical Area Classification," *Statistical Reporter* (December 1979):35. It should be noted, however, that growth, by itself, is not a sufficient criteria for adding an adjacent county.

[6]This was not the case for all of the 35 new SMSAs that were created in 1980. Several of these new areas had very modest growth rates and qualified for metropolitan status only by virtue of the liberalization of the criteria for metropolitan status. The list of new metropolitan areas includes 9 areas that grew at a less than the average rate for metropolitan areas during 1970–1980.

[7]Larry H. Long and D. DeAre, "Repopulating the Countryside: A 1980 Census Trend," *Science* 217:1111–1116; John F. Long, *Population Deconcentration in the United States*, U.S. Bureau of the Census, Special Demographic Analyses, CDS-81-5 (November 1981), pp. 20–25; D. T. Lichter and G. V. Fuguitt, "The Transition to Nonmetropolitan Population Deconcentration," *Demography* 19 (1982):211–221; and C. J. Tucker, "Changing Patterns of Migration between Metropolitan and Nonmetropolitan Areas in the United States: Recent Evidence," *Demography* 13 (1976):435–443.

APPENDIX TABLE A.1

Metropolitan and Nonmetropolitan Growth by Region, 1960–1984, Using Alternative Definitions of Metropolitan Areas (Average Annual Growth Rate)

Region	Metropolitan Areas			Nonmetropolitan Areas		
	1960–1970	1970–1980	1980–1984	1960–1970	1970–1980	1980–1984
CONSTANT 1970 SMSA DEFINITION						
Northeast	0.92	−0.23	0.19	1.03	1.21	0.71
Midwest	1.23	0.17	0.07	0.35	0.83	0.16
South	2.01	1.79	1.76	0.56	1.91	1.36
West	2.54	1.96	1.84	1.02	2.90	2.01
Total	1.57	0.84	0.96	0.61	1.63	1.04
CONSTANT 1980 SMSA DEFINITION						
Northeast	0.97	−0.15	0.23	0.74	1.19	0.63
Midwest	1.24	0.26	0.09	0.17	0.72	0.13
South	2.00	1.96	1.82	0.18	1.60	1.08
West	2.51	2.06	1.88	0.71	2.71	1.91
Total	1.59	0.98	1.02	0.30	1.41	0.86
CONSTANT 1983 MSA DEFINITION						
Northeast	0.99	−0.10	0.26	0.53	0.94	0.45
Midwest	1.25	0.26	0.09	0.17	0.73	0.11
South	2.00	1.99	1.84	0.12	1.53	1.02
West	2.52	2.06	1.88	0.69	2.69	1.90
Total	1.60	1.01	1.04	0.25	1.35	0.80

NOTES: 1. The 1970 and 1980 SMSA definitions correspond to those used in the 1970 and 1980 censuses, respectively. The 1983 MSA definitions are those published in "Metropolitan Statistical Areas," 1980 Census of Population, Supplementary Report, PC80-S1-18, December 1984.

2. Regional boundaries have been adjusted for metropolitan areas crossing regional boundaries so that the entire metropolitan area is within the region with the largest central city.

3. The average annual rate was calculated from the formula: $P2 = P1(1+r)^t$, where P1 and P2 are the populations at the beginning and end of the period, r is the annual rate of growth, and t is the number of years.

Conclusions about the continuation of the nonmetropolitan turnaround into the 1980s are also affected by the choice of definition. The use of either the 1980 or 1983 definitions shows a return to greater metropolitan than nonmetropolitan growth in the 1980–1984 period. But the use of the 1970 definitions indicates that nonmetropolitan areas are continuing to grow slightly faster in the 1980s. We believe that it is inappropriate to use the 1970 definitions beyond 1980 because they ignore the peripheral growth of many metropolitan areas since the 1970s, as well as the growth of smaller areas to metropolitan status. In Chapter

2 we demonstrated that the 1980 definitions were more appropriate for use in studying change during the 1970s than the 1970 definitions, because the 1970 definitions did not take account of the changes in commuting patterns that occurred between the 1960 and 1970 censuses.[8]

There are also some differences in conclusions about particular regions, depending upon the definition used. However, the biggest differences are between the 1970 and the 1980 definitions and not between the 1980 and the 1983 definitions. Using the 1970 definitions one would conclude that the nonmetropolitan turnaround started in the Northeast during the 1960s, whereas the later definitions show the turnaround in the Northeast only for the 1970s. In this case, we would argue that the 1970 definitions are the appropriate ones to use in studying the 1960s, and that growth was occurring in counties where the urbanized areas were too small to be classified as metropolitan at that time.

Changes in definition also affect whether or not the South is considered to have had a nonmetropolitan turnaround during the 1970s. While nonmetropolitan growth slightly exceeds metropolitan growth using the 1970 definitions, the other two definitions show that southern metropolitan growth is higher than nonmetropolitan.

The results based on any of the three definitions lead to the same conclusions regarding metropolitan and nonmetropolitan growth in the Midwest and the West. They all show that metropolitan growth was substantially higher than nonmetropolitan growth during the 1960s, and that both regions had a significant nonmetropolitan turnaround during the 1970s. While there is convergence in rates during the 1980 to 1984 period, nonmetropolitan growth continued to exceed metropolitan growth in the Northeast, Midwest, and the West, regardless of which definition is used.[9] Thus, for the 1980–1984 period, the return to more rapid metropolitan growth is due entirely to the South, which is the region that experienced the largest numerical growth in both metropolitan and total population. This conclusion does not depend upon which definition of metropolitan areas is used but is most strongly supported by the results based on the most recent definitions, which show the South capturing about one-half of the national metropolitan growth for 1980–1984.

[8]Metropolitan boundaries were not adjusted for commuting patterns observed in the 1970 census until 1973, after most of the census data had been published. The same was true of the 1960 and 1980 censuses.

[9]The differences between metropolitan and nonmetropolitan growth rates for 1980–1984 were very small for the Midwest and West. Estimates for 1985 indicate that metropolitan growth from 1984 to 1985 was sufficiently greater than nonmetropolitan growth to shift the comparison for 1980–1985 in favor of metropolitan areas for these two regions, although the differences are still small. See Richard Forstall, "U.S. Metropolitan/Nonmetropolitan Growth Trends Since 1980," paper presented at Annual Meeting of Association of American Geographers, Minneapolis, May 5, 1986.

Components of Growth for MSAs

The division of metropolitan growth into natural increase and net migration does not vary greatly, whether MSAs or SMSAs are used as units. The rates shown in Appendix Table A.2 using constant 1983 definitions are generally similar to those shown in Tables 3.4, 3.6, and 3.7 in Chapter 3. For 1970–1980 the total growth rates are slightly higher using the 1983 MSAs, except for the New England, West South Central, and Mountain divisions. Metropolitan rates of natural increase are virtually identical for all divisions. Net migration rates are slightly

APPENDIX TABLE A.2

*Components of Growth, 1960–1970 and 1970–1980,
for Metropolitan Statistical Areas as Defined in 1983*

	Percentage of Population at Beginning of Decade					
	1960–1970			1970–1980		
Region and Division	Percent Growth	Natural Increase	Net Migration	Percent Growth	Natural Increase	Net Migration
NORTHEAST	10.3	9.0	1.3	−1.0	3.9	−5.8
New England	13.2	9.9	3.3	2.3	3.9	−2.9
Mid Atlantic	9.5	8.8	0.8	−1.9	3.9	−6.8
MIDWEST	13.2	12.6	0.6	2.6	7.2	−5.6
East N. Central	12.9	12.4	0.4	1.9	7.2	−6.3
West N. Central	14.3	12.9	1.4	5.1	7.4	−3.4
SOUTH	21.9	14.2	7.7	21.7	8.6	9.3
South Atlantic	25.6	13.4	12.2	21.1	6.7	10.6
East S. Central	12.2	13.1	−0.9	14.7	8.3	2.5
West S. Central	21.3	16.1	5.2	26.3	11.8	10.8
WEST	28.2	13.9	14.3	22.7	9.0	12.9
Mountain	34.2	17.4	16.9	41.2	13.5	27.4
Pacific	27.0	13.2	13.8	18.8	8.0	9.9
Total	17.2	12.2	5.0	10.5	7.0	1.9

NOTES:
1. Based on SMSAs and NECMAs as defined by Office of Management and Budget effective June 30 1983.
2. Region and division boundaries were adjusted for MSAs that crossed division boundaries so that the entire MSA was within the division containing the largest of its central cities.
3. Net migration for 1970–1980 has been adjusted for changes in the level of enumeration between the 1970 and 1980 censuses.

higher for the 1983 MSAs, and the differences follow the same pattern as they did for the total growth.

The components of growth for 1960–1970 shown in Appendix Table A.2 are less comparable to those in Chapter 3 because the 1960–1970 components in Chapter 3 were calculated using 1970 definitions. Nevertheless, the differences in results by census division are not large. The growth rates based on the MSAs that were defined in 1983 are equal to or slightly higher than those calculated with the 1970 definitions, except for the South Atlantic, Mountain, and Pacific divisions where the growth is slightly lower using the 1983 MSAs. As was the case for 1970–1980, there is little difference in rates of natural increase. The estimated rates of net migration are higher using the 1983 MSAs, except in the Mountain and Pacific divisions. Overall, the variations among divisions are much larger than the changes due to different definitions, so that the conclusions about geographical differences in growth and its components are not much affected by the definition of metropolitan area that is used.

Growth of MSAs by Size Category

Because the redefinition of metropolitan areas changed the size of many areas, some areas have been moved into different size categories. Nevertheless, the effect of these changes on the observed growth patterns by size and region are relatively small, as can be seen by comparing Appendix Table A.3 and Table 3.10. The overall pattern of growth is the same for 1970–1980—the smaller areas grew at more than twice the rate of the larger areas, on the average. As in Table 3.10, the growth of areas under 250,000 exceeded that of larger areas in all regions except the South, where the variation in growth by size was small. One of the most noticeable differences between Table 3.10 and Appendix Table A.3 was for large northeastern areas, which show a considerably smaller decline under the more recent definitions. This is due to the enlargement of some of these areas to include growing counties on the periphery and the consolidation of some areas, so that some areas that were classified as under 1 million in 1980 were counted as over 1 million using the 1983 definitions.

Table A.3 also shows growth rates for 1980–1984, based on the 1984 population estimates. These show a considerable reduction in the differential between smaller and larger areas. While metropolitan areas as a whole continued to grow at about the same 1 percent per year rate that characterized the 1970s, the larger areas grew more rapidly during 1980–1984 than they had in the 1970s, and the smaller areas grew more

APPENDIX TABLE A.3

Growth of MSAs by Size and Region, 1970–1980 and 1980–1984

Size of MSA or CMSA	Average Annual Percentage Growth				
	Northeast	Midwest	South	West	Tot.
1970–1980					
Under 250,000	0.68	0.71	2.02	3.26	1.6.
250,000–999,999	0.38	0.44	1.93	2.62	1.3.
1 million+	−0.28	0.11	2.03	1.80	0.7.
Total	−0.10	0.26	1.99	2.07	1.0.
1980–1984					
Under 250,000	0.43	0.21	1.75	1.99	1.2.
250,000–999,999	0.32	0.01	1.67	2.25	1.1.
1 million+	0.23	0.09	2.06	1.78	0.9.
Total	0.26	0.09	1.85	1.88	1.0.

SOURCE: Based on Table 8 from U.S. Bureau of the Census, "Patterns of Metropolitan Area and Coun Population Growth: 1980 to 1984," *Current Population Reports*, series P-25, no. 976, October 1985.

slowly, leading to some convergence in rates by size. This convergence occurred in all three regions that had had growth differentials by size for 1970–1980; in the South, the areas over 1 million grew more rapidly in the 1980s than did smaller areas.

Changes in Rankings of Metropolitan Areas

The choice of definition of metropolitan area has relatively little effect on the interpretation of regional patterns of growth, but it has a somewhat greater impact on rankings of individual metropolitan areas. The top 20 CMSAs and MSAs in 1980 are shown in Appendix Table A.4 using the 1983 definitions, along with their rank using the 1980 census definitions. Rank is highly dependent upon whether consolidated areas or Primary Metropolitan Statistical Areas (PMSAs) are used as the units.[10] Because many metropolitan areas that were treated as single units in 1960 and 1970 have been divided into two or more PMSAs in the 1983 classification, it would be confusing to try to rank areas according to size of PMSA. In most cases, the CMSA more nearly approximates

[10]In order to ensure that it would rank as high as possible under all rankings of metropolitan areas, St. Louis had Missouri Senator Danforth attach a rider to an omnibus spending bill in Congress to make St. Louis a single MSA, and do away with the three PMSAs into which it had been divided under the 1983 definition. See "Playing Politics Puts St. Louis in the Top Ten," *The Numbers News*, 4(11) (November 1984).

APPENDIX TABLE A.4

Rank of Metropolitan Statistical Areas in 1980
and Rank of Corresponding SMSA or SCSA in 1980

Rank	Name of Area	1980 Population (in thousands)	Corresponding SMSA or SCSA Rank	Corresponding SMSA or SCSA Population (in thousands)
1	New York–N. New Jersey–Long Island CMSA*	16,605	1	15,796
2	Los Angeles–Anaheim–Riverside CMSA	11,498	2	11,498
3	Chicago–Gary–Lake County CMSA	7,937	3	7,870
4	Philadelphia–Wilmington–Trenton CMSA	5,681	4	5,548
5	San Francisco–Oakland–San Jose CMSA	5,368	5	5,180
6	Detroit–Ann Arbor CMSA	4,753	6	4,618
7	Boston–Lawrence–Salem–. . .NECMA†	3,663	7	3,663
8	Washington, DC MSA	3,251	9	3,061
9	Houston–Galveston–Brazoria CMSA	3,101	8	3,101
10	Dallas–Fort Worth CMSA	2,931	10	2,975
11	Cleveland–Akron–Lorain CMSA	2,834	11	2,834
12	Miami–Fort Lauderdale CMSA	2,644	12	2,644
13	Pittsburgh–Beaver Valley CMSA	2,423	14	2,264
14	St. Louis MSA	2,398	13	2,356
15	Baltimore MSA	2,200	15	2,174
16	Atlanta MSA	2,138	18	2,030
17	Minneapolis–St. Paul MSA	2,137	16	2,114
18	Seattle–Tacoma CMSA	2,093	17	2,093
19	San Diego MSA	1,862	19	1,862
20	Cincinnati–Hamilton CMSA	1,660	20	1,660

SOURCES: 1980 Census of Population, *Characteristics of Population*, vol. 1; 1980 Census of Population, "Metropolitan Statistical Areas," Supplementary Report, PC80-S1-18, December 1984; U.S. Bureau of the Census, "Patterns of Metropolitan Area and County Population Growth: 1980 to 1984," *Current Population Reports*, series P-25, no. 976, October 1985.

*Excludes Connecticut portion to be consistent with the use of NECMAs. With the Connecticut portion, the total population is 17,539,000 for the CMSA and 16,121 for the SCSA.
†The full name is Boston–Lawrence–Salem–Lowell–Brockton NECMA. The corresponding CMSA, which also includes Nashua, New Hampshire, had a population of 3,971,736 in 1980.

the original concept of a metropolitan area, and the use of CMSAs for ranking is consistent with the use of consolidated areas for the 1980 rankings discussed in Chapter 3.

Frequently, the rankings for 1980 are consistent with the rankings of SMSAs and SCSAs, which were shown in Table 3.3. The first seven areas retain the same rank they had using the 1980 census definitions. However, the populations for most areas are slightly different because different outlying counties are included. Using the 1983 definitions, the New York–Northern New Jersey area is about 1.4 million persons larger than the area is using the 1980 definitions because of the addition of Bridgeport and Danbury, Connecticut, and additional counties in New York and New Jersey. Washington, DC, bumped Houston out of eighth place due to redefinition, but this increase in ranking was short-lived because Houston grew faster than Washington, DC, during 1980–1984 and regained eighth position. St. Louis, Minneapolis, and Seattle also dropped slightly in ranking, while Atlanta and Pittsburgh gained, due to redefinition.

Changes in Ranking by Growth or Decline

There are also some changes in the areas that had the greatest growth and decline between 1970 and 1980, as shown in Appendix Table A.5. As in Table 3.11, we have restricted this comparison to areas with over 250,000 population in 1980 to avoid focusing too much attention on changes in small areas. It should be pointed out, however, that 13 out of the 20 most rapidly growing areas in the 1970s had populations under 250,000, whereas only 7 of the 20 areas with the greatest population declines had populations under 250,000.

Both the 1980 definitions and the 1983 definitions show Las Vegas and West Palm Beach to be the leading growth areas, and the rest of the list is the same, with two exceptions. Fort Lauderdale and Santa Rosa, which had appeared on the list using the 1980 definitions, do not appear on the list using the 1983 definitions because they are part of larger consolidated areas which had lower average growth rates. In their place are Tampa–St. Petersburg and Houston–Galveston–Brazoria, which ranked slightly lower on the 1980 list.

The list of areas with the greatest declines differs from that in Table 3.11 primarily due to the use of consolidated areas in Appendix Table A.5, whereas SMSAs were used in Table 3.11. Four areas: Jersey City, Paterson, Newark, and Akron, which appear on the list in Table 3.11, are included in Table A.5 as parts of larger consolidated areas. The other six areas are also on the 1983 list and, in addition, the 1983 list includes four additional areas with declining populations. Thus, the main effect of the change in definitions upon the ranking of declining areas is a result of the consolidation of some of these areas into larger units that were also included on the list of areas with the greatest decline.

The 1980s saw some change in the areas of greatest growth and decline. While Las Vegas and West Palm Beach remained on the list of the ten most rapidly growing areas over 250,000, their growth fell behind

APPENDIX TABLE A.5

The Biggest Gainers and Losers Among MSAs and CMSAs over 250,000 for 1970–1980 and 1980–1984

	BIGGEST GAINERS				
	1970–1980			1980–1984	
ank	Name	Gain in Percent	Rank	Name	Gain in Percent
1	Las Vegas, NV	69.5	1	Fort Myers–Cape Coral, FL	23.2
2	West Palm Beach–Boca Raton, FL	65.3	2	Melbourne–Titusville–Palm Beach, FL	20.7
3	McAllen–Edinburg–Mission, TX	56.0	3	Austin, TX	20.3
4	Phoenix, AZ	55.4	4	West Palm Beach–Boca Raton, FL	20.0
5	Orlando, FL	54.4	5	McAllen–Edinburg–Mission, TX	19.0
6	Daytona Beach, FL	52.7	6	Orlando, FL	17.7
7	Tucson, AZ	51.1	7	Daytona Beach, FL	16.1
8	Austin, TX	48.9	8	Las Vegas, NV	15.8
9	Tampa-St. Petersburg, FL	46.0	9	Houston–Galveston–Brazoria, TX	15.0
10	Houston–Galveston–Brazoria, TX	43.0	10	Stockton, CA	14.8

	BIGGEST LOSERS				
	1970–1980			1980–1984	
ank	Name	Loss in Percent	Rank	Name	Loss in Percent
1	Buffalo–Niagara Falls, NY CMSA	−7.9	1	Duluth, MN-WI	−4.8
2	Utica–Rome, NY	−6.0	2	Detroit–Ann Arbor, MI CMSA	−3.7
3	Cleveland–Akron–Lorain, OH CMSA	−5.5	3	Flint, MI	−3.6
4	Pittsburgh–Beaver Valley, PA CMSA	−5.2	4	Eugene–Springfield, OR	−3.2
5	New York–N. New Jersey–L.I. CMSA	−3.6	5	Buffalo–Niagara Falls, NY CMSA	−3.1
6	Dayton–Springfield, OH	−3.4	6	Peoria, IL	−2.7
7	Springfield, MA	−2.4	7	Youngstown–Warren, OH	−2.5
8	St. Louis, MO	−2.2	8	Saginaw–Bay City–Midland, MI	−2.3
9	Binghamton, NY	−1.8	9	Johnstown, PA	−2.1
10	Philadelphia–Wilm.–Trenton CMSA	−1.2	10	Pittsburgh–Beaver Valley, PA CMSA	−2.1

SOURCES: 1970–1980 from U.S. Bureau of the Census, 1980 Census of Population, "Metropolitan Statistical Areas," Supplementary Report, PC80-S1-18, December 1984. 1980–1984 from U.S. Bureau of the Census, "Patterns of Metropolitan Area and County Population Growth: 1980 to 1984," *Current Population Reports*, series P-25, no. 976, October 1985.

that of Fort Myers, Melbourne, and Austin. As in 1970–1980, Florida and Texas continued to hold most of the areas on the list of the most rapidly growing. Arizona, which had had two cities on the 1970–1980 list, had none on the 1980–1984 list, implying a slowdown of growth of its areas.

The list of the most rapidly declining areas changed considerably from 1970–1980 to 1980–1984. During 1980–1984 the largest declines were in the area from Duluth, Minnesota, to Johnstown, Pennsylvania. Only three of the declining MSAs were in the Northeast region, in contrast to seven for 1970–1980. Only two areas over 250,000 (Buffalo and

Pittsburgh) made the list for both periods, indicating that most areas experiencing significant declines in the 1970s were able to either reverse or reduce these in the 1980s.

Conclusion

The Metropolitan Statistical Areas that were introduced in 1983 represent an improvement over the areas used in tabulating the 1980 census because they were based on the 1980 commuting data, whereas the 1980 commuting data had not been available when the 1980 census was tabulated. The newer definitions also represented an improvement in standardization of criteria and the removal of several exceptions to rules that had existed in prior years. Many also feel that they are preferable because they recognize the decline in importance of the central city by not requiring a densely settled city of 50,000, although there is some debate on this point.

Because much of the data upon which this monograph is based come from the 1980 census, it was necessary for us to use the metropolitan area definitions that the U.S. Bureau of the Census used in tabulating the data. Fortunately, as the brief analysis in the appendix has shown, the results would not have been very different had we been able to use the newer 1983 definitions of metropolitan areas.

APPENDIX B:
SUPPLEMENTAL TABLES
ON CONSEQUENCES OF GROWTH
BY REGION AND SIZE
OF METROPOLITAN AREA

APPENDIX TABLE B.1

Mean Age and Percentage Aged 65 and Over,
1970–1980, by Size of Area, Region, and Growth Rate

Region and Rate of Growth	Mean Age			Percentage Aged 65 +		
	1970	1980	Change	1970	1980	Change
AREAS OF LESS THAN 1 MILLION						
North						
Loss	32.6	34.8	2.2	9.7	11.5	1.8
Slow	32.4	34.3	1.9	9.9	11.4	1.5
Moderate	31.2	32.7	1.5	9.4	10.0	0.7
Total	32.2	34.0	1.8	9.8	11.1	1.4
South						
Slow	31.1	33.3	2.2	8.4	10.2	1.8
Moderate	31.1	32.9	1.8	8.3	9.8	1.4
Rapid	29.6	31.0	1.4	7.8	8.5	0.7
Ret. area	36.9	40.6	3.7	17.0	20.9	3.9
Total	31.3	33.3	2.0	8.7	10.4	1.7
West						
Slow	31.1	33.6	2.5	8.8	10.9	2.1
Moderate	30.9	32.7	1.8	8.3	9.7	1.4
Rapid	30.7	32.0	1.3	8.4	9.2	0.7
Total	30.7	32.3	1.5	8.4	9.4	1.0
AREAS OF 1 MILLION OR MORE						
North						
Loss	33.2	35.2	2.0	10.1	11.8	1.7
Slow	31.7	33.4	1.7	8.9	10.0	1.1
Total	32.8	34.7	1.9	9.8	11.3	1.5
South						
Slow	30.7	33.3	2.6	7.0	8.6	1.6
Moderate	30.3	31.9	1.6	7.5	8.4	0.8
Rapid	29.4	30.3	0.8	6.1	6.1	0.0
Ret. area	37.8	39.7	1.9	17.3	19.3	2.0
Total	31.7	33.7	2.0	9.0	10.4	1.4
West						
Slow	32.9	34.1	1.3	9.4	10.2	0.9
Moderate	31.3	33.4	2.1	8.2	9.4	1.2
Rapid	31.0	33.2	2.2	8.7	9.9	1.2
Total	32.0	33.7	1.7	8.9	10.0	1.0

APPENDIX TABLE B.2

Change in Percentage Black and Spanish Origin, 1970–1980,
by Size of Area, Region, and Growth Rate

Region and Rate of Growth	Percentage Black			Percentage Spanish Origin		
	1970	1980	Change	1970	1980	Change
AREAS OF LESS THAN 1 MILLION						
North						
Loss	7.1	8.2	1.1	2.9	4.3	1.4
Slow	5.3	6.2	0.9	1.7	2.2	0.5
Moderate	2.9	3.3	0.5	1.1	1.4	0.3
Total	5.1	5.9	0.8	1.8	2.3	0.6
South						
Slow	17.3	19.1	1.8	1.4	1.4	−0.1
Moderate	19.2	19.7	0.5	2.5	2.9	0.4
Rapid	12.7	12.4	−0.4	20.1	24.0	4.0
Ret. area	14.2	11.4	−2.8	1.8	3.0	1.2
Total	17.8	18.1	0.2	4.2	5.3	1.2
West						
Slow	1.6	1.6	0.0	16.7	20.8	4.1
Moderate	3.2	3.7	0.5	9.0	13.5	4.5
Rapid	2.2	2.6	0.3	9.1	12.2	3.0
Total	2.6	3.0	0.4	9.3	12.8	3.5
AREAS OF 1 MILLION OR MORE						
North						
Loss	13.7	15.9	2.2	4.6	6.1	1.5
Slow	12.6	14.3	1.7	3.1	4.6	1.5
Total	13.4	15.4	2.0	4.2	5.6	1.5
South						
Slow	24.3	26.9	2.7	1.5	2.2	0.7
Moderate	18.0	18.9	1.0	9.0	11.1	2.0
Rapid	19.5	18.1	−1.3	9.1	14.6	5.4
Ret. area	12.8	12.8	0.0	11.3	16.6	5.3
Total	19.2	19.6	0.5	7.1	10.4	3.3
West						
Slow	10.8	12.4	1.6	12.6	22.5	9.9
Moderate	2.8	3.8	1.0	5.0	7.5	2.5
Rapid	3.4	3.9	0.6	9.9	14.4	4.5
Total	6.9	7.6	0.7	10.2	16.5	6.3

APPENDIX TABLE B.3

Mean Years of Education and Percentage College Graduates
for Persons 25 and Over, 1970–1980, by Size of Area, Region, and Growth Rate

Region and Rate of Growth	Mean Years of Education			Percentage College Graduates		
	1970	1980	Change	1970	1980	Change
AREAS OF LESS THAN 1 MILLION						
North						
Loss	10.6	11.6	1.0	9.0	13.7	4.7
Slow	10.8	11.8	1.0	9.8	15.1	5.3
Moderate	11.1	12.2	1.0	12.6	18.9	6.2
Total	10.8	11.8	1.0	10.2	15.7	5.5
South						
Slow	10.3	11.4	1.0	9.3	13.6	4.3
Moderate	10.3	11.5	1.2	10.3	15.8	5.5
Rapid	10.2	11.4	1.2	12.7	18.4	5.7
Ret. area	11.0	11.8	0.9	11.4	14.7	3.3
Total	10.3	11.5	1.1	10.4	15.6	5.2
West						
Slow	10.9	11.8	0.9	10.0	14.9	5.0
Moderate	11.1	11.9	0.9	12.1	17.2	5.1
Rapid	11.5	12.4	0.9	12.9	18.6	5.7
Total	11.3	12.2	0.9	12.5	18.0	5.5
AREAS OF 1 MILLION OR MORE						
North						
Loss	10.8	11.9	1.1	11.7	17.9	6.2
Slow	11.0	12.1	1.1	12.0	18.7	6.7
Total	10.8	11.9	1.1	11.7	18.1	6.4
South						
Slow	11.3	12.6	1.2	17.7	26.2	8.5
Moderate	10.6	11.9	1.3	12.1	19.2	7.0
Rapid	10.8	12.1	1.3	13.9	22.0	8.1
Ret. area	10.6	11.7	1.0	9.9	15.1	5.2
Total	10.8	12.0	1.2	13.6	20.5	6.9
West						
Slow	11.5	12.2	0.8	14.0	20.9	6.9
Moderate	11.8	12.8	1.0	15.5	22.8	7.3
Rapid	11.6	12.5	0.9	14.1	20.3	6.3
Total	11.6	12.5	0.9	14.3	21.1	6.8

APPENDIX TABLE B.4

*Percentage of Persons 15 and Over in the Labor Force and Percentage Unemployed
for Metropolitan Areas, 1970–1980, by Size of Area, Region, and Growth Rate*

Region and Rate of Growth	Percentage in Labor Force			Percentage Unemployed		
	1970	1980	Change	1970	1980	Change
AREAS OF LESS THAN 1 MILLION						
North						
Loss	58.2	60.4	2.2	4.5	8.2	3.7
Slow	59.3	62.8	3.5	4.0	7.2	3.2
Moderate	59.1	64.2	5.1	4.0	5.9	1.9
Total	59.1	62.7	3.7	4.1	5.3	1.3
South						
Slow	56.4	60.2	3.8	4.4	7.3	2.9
Moderate	57.9	62.5	4.6	3.6	5.5	1.8
Rapid	55.2	61.5	6.3	4.5	5.6	1.1
Ret. area	50.5	51.8	1.3	3.9	4.8	0.9
Total	56.9	61.1	4.3	3.9	5.8	1.9
West						
Slow	58.9	66.8	7.9	6.2	8.0	1.9
Moderate	56.3	61.7	5.4	6.7	7.9	1.2
Rapid	56.7	63.5	6.8	6.1	7.2	1.0
Total	56.5	62.8	6.3	6.4	7.4	1.1
AREAS OF 1 MILLION OR MORE						
North						
Loss	58.3	61.1	2.8	4.1	7.3	3.2
Slow	61.8	66.0	4.2	3.5	6.0	2.5
Total	59.3	62.5	3.3	3.9	6.9	3.0
South						
Slow	62.2	66.8	4.6	3.0	5.1	2.1
Moderate	61.1	66.2	5.1	3.5	4.2	0.7
Rapid	62.1	70.6	8.6	3.0	3.4	0.4
Ret. area	52.1	55.8	3.7	3.6	4.9	1.3
Total	59.7	64.6	4.9	3.3	4.5	1.2
West						
Slow	60.4	65.0	4.6	6.1	5.9	−0.2
Moderate	60.3	66.8	6.5	6.9	6.1	−0.8
Rapid	57.9	64.3	6.4	5.1	5.4	0.3
Total	59.7	65.2	5.5	6.0	5.8	−0.2

APPENDIX TABLE B.5

Employment in Manufacturing and Nodal Services, 1970–1980,
by Size of Area, Region, and Growth Rate (in thousands)

Region and Rate of Growth	Manufacturing Employment			Nodal Services Employment		
	1970	1980	Change	1970	1980	Change
	(000's)			(000's)		
AREAS OF LESS THAN 1 MILLION						
North						
Loss	666.0	581.7	−84.4	325.5	390.3	64.8
Slow	2,831.4	2,854.0	22.6	1,530.8	2,022.1	491.3
Moderate	615.6	743.6	128.0	422.6	649.8	227.3
Total	4,113.1	4,179.3	66.2	2,278.8	3,062.2	783.4
South						
Slow	549.7	566.6	16.9	385.2	525.6	140.4
Moderate	1,428.4	1,739.2	310.8	1,285.7	1,949.6	663.9
Rapid	136.2	235.2	99.0	199.5	387.6	188.1
Ret. area	72.7	109.0	36.3	99.8	199.5	99.6
Total	2,187.0	2,650.0	463.1	1,970.3	3,062.3	1,092.0
West						
Slow	11.7	11.5	−0.2	13.7	20.4	6.7
Moderate	150.1	206.0	55.9	269.2	432.7	163.6
Rapid	224.9	396.6	171.7	367.5	722.4	354.9
Total	386.6	614.0	227.4	650.4	1,175.6	525.2
AREAS OF 1 MILLION OR MORE						
North						
Loss	4,213.7	3,753.3	−460.4	3,821.3	4,421.7	600.4
Slow	1,772.6	1,780.0	7.4	1,519.9	1,991.0	471.1
Total	5,986.2	5,533.2	−453.0	5,341.3	6,412.7	1,071.5
South						
Slow	281.8	264.7	−17.2	484.0	692.2	208.2
Moderate	488.4	605.8	117.4	632.9	1,013.7	380.8
Rapid	163.8	267.6	103.8	209.6	421.9	212.4
Ret. area	160.4	242.9	82.5	298.9	540.1	241.3
Total	1,094.4	1,380.9	286.6	1,625.4	2,668.0	1,042.7
West						
Slow	982.8	1,122.8	140.1	1,140.1	1,535.5	395.4
Moderate	370.2	565.5	195.3	421.8	676.7	255.0
Rapid	456.8	724.4	267.7	514.2	1,030.9	516.7
Total	1,809.7	2,412.8	603.1	2,076.0	3,243.2	1,167.1

APPENDIX TABLE B.6

Annual Family and Per Capita Income for Metropolitan Areas,
1970–1980, by Size of Area, Region, and Growth Rate

Region and Rate of Growth	Family Income (Dollars)			Per Capita Income (Dollars)		
	1970	1980	% Growth	1970	1980	% Growth
	(000's)			(000's)		
AREAS OF LESS THAN 1 MILLION						
North						
Loss	11,400	22,210	94.8	3,210	7,150	122.7
Slow	11,610	23,900	105.9	3,230	7,650	136.8
Moderate	11,110	23,300	109.7	3,040	7,510	147.0
Total	11,490	23,550	105.0	3,190	7,550	136.7
South						
Slow	9,990	21,510	115.3	2,790	6,960	149.5
Moderate	9,610	21,490	123.6	2,720	6,990	157.0
Rapid	9,340	20,910	123.9	2,490	6,500	161.0
Ret. area	10,200	21,580	111.6	3,190	7,710	141.7
Total	9,700	21,430	120.9	2,730	6,970	155.3
West						
Slow	9,658	21,259	120.1	2,670	6,948	160.2
Moderate	10,980	23,410	113.2	3,080	7,620	147.4
Rapid	10,780	23,510	118.1	3,030	7,610	151.2
Total	10,830	23,430	116.3	3,040	7,600	150.0
AREAS OF 1 MILLION OR MORE						
North						
Loss	12,830	25,460	98.4	3,640	8,130	123.4
Slow	12,860	26,540	106.4	3,610	8,440	133.8
Total	12,840	25,780	100.8	3,630	8,220	126.4
South						
Slow	13,540	28,660	111.7	3,840	9,400	144.8
Moderate	11,210	24,210	116.0	3,160	7,770	145.9
Rapid	11,680	28,160	141.1	3,290	9,020	174.2
Ret. area	10,770	22,220	106.3	3,340	7,810	133.8
Total	11,880	25,480	114.5	3,420	8,400	145.6
West						
Slow	12,980	26,640	105.2	3,940	8,860	124.9
Moderate	12,610	26,860	113.0	3,660	9,030	146.7
Rapid	11,900	25,650	115.5	3,420	8,560	150.3
Total	12,580	26,340	109.4	3,730	8,790	135.7

APPENDIX TABLE B.7

Percentage of Families and Individuals in Poverty for Metropolitan Areas,
1970–1980, by Size of Area, Region, and Growth Rate

Region and Rate of Growth	Percentage of Families			Percentage of Individuals		
	1970	1980	Change	1970	1980	Change
AREAS OF LESS THAN 1 MILLION						
North						
Loss	7.0	8.8	1.8	9.1	11.1	2.0
Slow	6.7	7.0	0.3	8.8	9.2	0.4
Moderate	7.2	6.5	− 0.7	9.8	9.8	0.0
Total	6.8	7.1	0.3	9.0	9.6	0.5
South						
Slow	12.7	10.9	− 1.8	15.5	13.9	− 1.7
Moderate	14.1	10.8	− 3.4	17.3	13.9	− 3.3
Rapid	17.6	13.7	− 3.9	21.9	18.4	− 3.5
Ret. area	12.1	8.2	− 3.9	15.4	11.7	− 3.7
Total	14.1	10.9	− 3.1	17.3	14.3	− 3.0
West						
Slow	10.0	9.8	− 0.2	12.6	12.4	− 0.2
Moderate	10.0	9.2	− 0.9	12.5	11.9	− 0.6
Rapid	9.6	8.0	− 1.7	12.0	10.7	− 1.2
Total	9.8	8.5	− 1.3	12.2	11.2	− 1.0
AREAS OF 1 MILLION OR MORE						
North						
Loss	7.5	9.3	1.8	9.7	11.6	1.8
Slow	6.6	7.6	1.1	8.8	10.0	1.2
Total	7.2	8.8	1.6	9.5	11.1	1.6
South						
Slow	7.1	7.4	0.3	9.4	9.7	0.4
Moderate	11.3	10.1	− 1.2	14.2	13.0	− 1.2
Rapid	9.9	7.9	− 2.0	12.6	10.1	− 2.4
Ret. area	10.4	9.1	− 1.3	13.6	12.3	− 1.2
Total	9.7	8.9	− 0.8	12.3	11.6	− 0.8
West						
Slow	7.9	9.5	1.7	10.4	12.3	1.9
Moderate	6.3	6.2	− 0.2	8.6	8.6	0.0
Rapid	7.8	7.1	− 0.7	9.8	9.7	− 0.1
Total	7.5	8.0	0.4	9.8	10.6	0.8

APPENDIX TABLE B.8

Value of Owner-Occupied Units and Rent of Renter-Occupied Units, 1970–1980, by Size of Area, Region, and Growth Rate

egion and ate of rowth	Value in $1,000s, Owners			Monthly Rent in Dollars		
	1970	1980	% Growth	1970	1980	% Growth
REAS OF LESS THAN 1 MILLION						
orth						
Loss	19.3	35.7	85.0	106	226	114.6
Slow	19.3	40.0	107.3	106	241	127.8
Moderate	18.9	39.4	108.5	110	248	125.5
Total	19.2	39.4	105.2	107	240	125.4
ɔuth						
Slow	16.4	35.4	115.9	88	217	145.6
Moderate	16.1	36.0	123.6	89	229	158.0
Rapid	16.2	38.7	138.9	94	241	156.8
Ret. area	18.2	37.3	104.9	105	269	157.4
Total	16.3	36.3	122.7	90	231	156.7
✓est						
Slow	15.3	37.7	146.4	85	204	140.5
Moderate	21.6	59.3	174.5	109	271	149.4
Rapid	20.6	55.8	170.9	110	277	151.2
Total	20.9	56.8	171.8	109	273	150.9
REAS OF 1 MILLION OR MORE						
⅃orth						
Loss	23.9	45.4	90.0	124	267	115.4
Slow	23.8	50.9	113.9	126	254	102.5
Total	23.9	47.1	97.1	124	263	111.9
outh						
Slow	25.1	63.8	154.2	136	289	111.5
Moderate	19.5	46.3	137.4	111	254	129.7
Rapid	17.9	51.3	186.6	113	295	160.2
Ret. area	19.7	40.2	104.1	132	281	113.0
Total	20.9	49.7	137.8	124	276	122.2
⅃est						
Slow	28.8	90.2	213.2	132	300	126.9
Moderate	23.7	70.7	198.3	129	298	131.3
Rapid	23.8	68.7	188.7	126	311	146.8
Total	21.4	48.5	126.6	130	303	132.6

APPENDIX C:
SUPPLEMENTAL TABLES ON ASPECTS OF THE BLACK POPULATION BY REGION AND SIZE OF METROPOLITAN AREA

APPENDIX TABLE C.1

Mean Years of Education and Percentage of High School Graduates
for Blacks 25+, 1970–1980, by Size of Area, Region, and Growth Rate

Region and Rate of Growth	Mean Years of Education			Percentage High School Graduates		
	1970	1980	Change	1970	1980	Change
AREAS OF LESS THAN 1 MILLION						
North						
Loss	9.5	10.9	1.4	36.2	56.0	19.8
Slow	9.4	10.8	1.4	34.6	54.2	19.7
Moderate	9.5	11.2	1.7	36.0	58.2	22.2
Total	9.4	10.8	1.4	35.1	55.1	20.0
South						
Slow	8.3	10.0	1.7	26.2	47.1	20.9
Moderate	8.2	10.1	1.8	26.0	47.1	21.2
Rapid	8.3	10.3	2.0	28.4	51.2	22.8
Ret. area	7.9	9.6	1.7	23.0	41.9	18.9
Total	8.2	10.0	1.8	26.1	47.2	21.2
West						
Slow	10.5	11.3	0.8	50.8	66.2	15.4
Moderate	9.7	11.4	1.7	42.4	66.0	23.6
Rapid	10.0	11.7	1.7	45.0	69.5	24.5
Total	9.9	11.6	1.7	43.8	67.9	24.1
AREAS OF 1 MILLION OR MORE						
North						
Loss	9.6	10.8	1.3	35.1	55.1	20.0
Slow	9.7	10.9	1.2	37.5	56.2	18.6
Total	9.6	11.0	1.4	38.7	55.6	16.9
South						
Slow	9.7	11.2	1.5	38.4	58.3	19.9
Moderate	8.8	10.7	1.9	30.5	54.1	23.6
Rapid	9.2	11.1	1.9	32.8	57.8	25.0
Ret. area	8.3	10.1	1.8	26.2	47.5	21.3
Total	9.2	10.9	1.7	33.5	55.3	21.8
West						
Slow	10.5	11.8	1.3	50.3	68.1	17.8
Moderate	10.4	12.2	1.8	49.9	73.1	23.2
Rapid	10.3	12.0	1.7	48.5	71.4	22.9
Total	10.4	11.8	1.4	50.0	69.2	19.1

APPENDIX TABLE C.2

Percentage of Blacks 16 and Over in the Labor Force and Percentage of Blacks Unemployed, 1970–1980, by Size of Area, Region, and Growth Rate

Region and Rate of Growth	Percentage in Labor Force			Percentage Unemployed		
	1970	1980	Change	1970	1980	Change
AREAS OF LESS THAN 1 MILLION						
North						
Loss	58.5	58.4	−0.1	8.3	16.7	8.4
Slow	60.3	60.9	0.6	7.9	15.4	7.4
Moderate	57.3	60.2	3.0	8.1	13.4	5.3
Total	59.6	60.3	0.7	8.0	15.4	7.3
South						
Slow	55.6	57.5	1.9	7.6	13.1	5.5
Moderate	55.9	59.0	3.1	6.1	10.3	4.2
Rapid	57.6	61.1	3.5	6.6	9.4	2.8
Ret. area	64.0	61.4	−2.5	5.1	7.6	2.5
Total	56.3	59.0	2.7	6.4	10.7	4.3
West						
Slow	52.4	54.3	1.9	8.6	11.9	3.3
Moderate	48.4	55.6	7.1	12.8	13.8	1.0
Rapid	57.3	65.2	7.9	8.2	11.5	3.3
Total	52.9	60.9	8.0	10.2	12.4	2.2
AREAS OF 1 MILLION OR MORE						
North						
Loss	58.4	57.8	−0.6	6.9	14.0	7.1
Slow	59.6	60.0	0.3	6.8	13.8	7.0
Total	58.7	58.4	−0.3	6.8	13.9	7.1
South						
Slow	64.3	64.7	0.4	4.7	9.4	4.6
Moderate	60.9	62.9	2.0	5.9	8.3	2.4
Rapid	62.2	67.9	5.7	5.0	5.9	0.9
Ret. area	65.4	65.2	−0.1	4.8	7.7	2.9
Total	63.0	64.6	1.6	5.2	8.3	3.1
West						
Slow	60.4	60.8	0.4	10.2	10.8	0.6
Moderate	61.2	65.9	4.7	10.9	11.5	0.5
Rapid	57.5	64.5	7.0	7.9	10.1	2.2
Total	60.1	61.9	1.8	10.0	10.8	0.8

APPENDIX TABLE C.3

Annual Family and Per Capita Income for Blacks in Metropolitan Areas, 1970–1980, by Size of Area, Region, and Growth Rate

Region and Rate of Growth	Family Income (Dollars)			Per Capita Income (Dollars)		
	1970	1980	% Growth	1970	1980	% Growth
AREAS OF LESS THAN 1 MILLION						
North						
Loss	8,380	16,160	92.8	2,178	4,802	120.4
Slow	8,180	17,150	109.7	2,042	4,931	141.4
Moderate	8,130	17,732	118.1	2,028	4,869	140.1
Total	8,220	17,020	107.1	2,069	4,899	136.9
South						
Slow	6,170	14,310	131.9	1,502	3,919	161.0
Moderate	5,850	14,260	143.8	1,435	3,889	171.1
Rapid	5,850	14,480	147.5	1,431	3,847	168.9
Ret. area	5,740	13,510	135.4	1,437	3,565	148.1
Total	5,910	14,260	141.3	1,448	3,877	167.7
West						
Slow	7,117	17,726	149.1	1,870	5,194	177.7
Moderate	6,940	15,490	123.2	1,799	4,383	143.6
Rapid	7,680	18,180	136.7	1,936	5,300	173.8
Total	7,310	16,970	132.1	1,868	4,879	161.2
AREAS OF 1 MILLION OR MORE						
North						
Loss	8,420	16,590	97.0	2,310	4,998	116.3
Slow	8,660	17,530	102.4	2,270	5,041	122.1
Total	8,480	16,850	98.7	2,300	5,010	117.9
South						
Slow	9,190	20,050	118.2	2,426	6,010	147.7
Moderate	6,650	15,250	129.3	1,678	4,381	161.1
Rapid	6,800	18,060	165.6	1,729	5,258	204.1
Ret. area	6,680	14,920	123.4	1,678	4,165	148.2
Total	7,680	17,340	125.8	1,982	5,067	155.7
West						
Slow	8,570	18,160	111.9	2,409	5,768	139.4
Moderate	8,910	19,060	113.9	2,350	6,020	156.1
Rapid	7,750	18,110	133.7	2,003	5,360	167.6
Total	8,490	18,250	115.0	2,346	5,721	143.9

APPENDIX TABLE C.4

Percentage of Black Families and Individuals in Poverty for Metropolitan Areas, 1970–1980, by Size of Area, Region, and Growth Rate

Region and Rate of Growth	Percentage of Families			Percentage of Individuals		
	1970	1980	Change	1970	1980	Change
AREAS OF LESS THAN 1 MILLION						
North						
Loss	20.4	25.5	5.2	23.0	28.0	5.1
Slow	21.6	24.7	3.0	24.3	27.0	2.7
Moderate	20.4	21.2	0.8	23.0	24.9	1.9
Total	21.3	24.5	3.2	23.9	27.0	3.1
South						
Slow	34.1	28.6	− 5.6	38.1	32.2	− 5.8
Moderate	36.1	27.3	− 8.7	40.2	31.0	− 9.2
Rapid	37.3	27.1	− 10.2	40.9	31.0	− 9.9
Ret. area	36.7	31.0	− 5.7	41.2	34.9	− 6.3
Total	35.8	27.7	− 8.1	39.9	31.4	− 8.4
West						
Slow	18.5	20.7	2.2	18.7	24.4	5.7
Moderate	26.5	21.8	− 4.7	27.9	24.1	− 3.8
Rapid	20.4	17.6	− 2.8	23.6	21.0	− 2.6
Total	23.4	19.5	− 3.9	25.6	22.4	− 3.2
AREAS OF 1 MILLION OR MORE						
North						
Loss	20.7	25.2	4.5	24.0	27.9	3.9
Slow	20.3	24.9	4.6	24.4	28.1	3.7
Total	20.6	25.1	4.5	24.1	27.9	3.8
South						
Slow	17.7	18.1	0.4	20.9	21.0	0.1
Moderate	30.1	26.1	− 4.0	33.9	29.2	− 4.7
Rapid	26.9	19.7	− 7.3	30.6	22.1	− 8.5
Ret. area	29.5	28.0	− 1.5	33.3	30.9	− 2.5
Total	24.7	22.6	− 2.2	28.3	25.5	− 2.8
West						
Slow	20.3	20.9	0.6	23.2	22.8	− 0.4
Moderate	18.8	19.1	0.3	22.1	21.5	− 0.7
Rapid	22.6	19.0	− 3.5	24.5	21.4	− 3.1
Total	20.5	20.4	− 0.1	23.3	22.4	− 0.9

496

APPENDIX D:
POPULATION GROWTH
AND NET MIGRATION, 1970–1984,
FOR 1980 STANDARD METROPOLITAN
STATISTICAL AREAS
AND NEW ENGLAND COUNTY
METROPOLITAN AREAS

APPENDIX TABLE D.1

FIPS Code	SMSA Name	Population (in thousands)			Growth 1970–1980 (percent)	Net. Mig. 1970–1980 (percent)	Growth 1980–1984 (percent)	Net. Mig. 1980–1984 (percent)
		1970	1980	1984				
40	Abilene, Texas	122.2	139.2	154.3	13.9	2.0	10.9	6.0
80	Akron, Ohio	679.2	660.3	650.1	-2.8	-10.0	-1.6	-3.9
120	Albany, Georgia	96.7	112.4	116.7	16.3	-2.0	3.8	-1.5
160	Albany–Schenectady–Troy, New York	778.0	795.0	801.6	2.2	-2.4	0.8	-0.6
200	Albuquerque, New Mexico	333.3	454.5	484.8	36.4	23.0	6.7	1.6
220	Alexandria, Louisiana	131.7	152.0	156.9	15.4	2.4	3.2	-0.6
240	Allentown–Bethlehem–Easton, Pennsylvania–New Jersey	594.4	635.5	646.7	6.9	3.0	1.8	0.5
280	Altoona, Pennsylvania	135.4	136.6	134.4	0.9	-2.6	-1.6	-2.5
320	Amarillo, Texas	144.4	173.7	190.3	20.3	6.5	9.6	4.7
360	Anaheim–Santa Ana–Garden Grove, California	1,421.2	1,932.7	2,075.8	36.0	24.8	7.4	2.8
380	Anchorage, Alaska	126.4	174.4	226.7	38.0	15.2	30.0	20.5
400	Anderson, Indiana	138.5	139.3	134.1	0.6	-8.0	-3.8	-5.5
405	Anderson, South Carolina	105.5	133.2	138.5	26.3	14.6	4.0	1.7
440	Ann Arbor, Michigan	234.1	264.7	261.4	13.1	1.8	-1.3	-5.2
450	Anniston, Alabama	103.1	119.8	125.7	16.2	3.9	5.0	2.4
460	Appleton–Oshkosh, Wisconsin	276.9	291.4	299.5	5.2	-3.3	2.8	-0.8
480	Asheville, North Carolina	161.1	177.8	182.8	10.4	3.6	2.8	1.9
500	Athens, Georgia	107.7	130.0	136.6	20.7	8.1	5.1	2.0
520	Atlanta, Georgia	1,595.5	2,029.7	2,262.3	27.2	13.2	11.5	7.5
560	Atlantic City, New Jersey	175.0	194.1	201.3	10.9	9.3	3.7	3.0
600	Augusta, Georgia–South Carolina	275.8	327.4	349.0	18.7	5.1	6.6	2.4
640	Austin, Texas	360.5	536.7	645.4	48.9	32.3	20.3	14.7
680	Bakersfield, California	330.2	403.1	462.4	22.1	10.7	14.7	8.6
720	Baltimore, Maryland	2,071.0	2,174.0	2,217.0	5.0	-3.6	2.0	-0.5
733	Bangor, Maine NECMA	125.4	137.0	138.4	9.3	1.8	1.0	-1.5
760	Baton Rouge, Louisiana	375.6	494.2	537.9	31.6	14.9	8.9	3.2
780	Battle Creek, Michigan	180.1	187.3	184.3	4.0	-3.9	-1.6	-4.3
800	Bay City, Michigan	117.3	119.9	117.2	2.2	-7.1	-2.2	-5.3
840	Beaumont–Port Arthur–Orange, Texas	347.6	375.5	391.8	8.0	-3.3	4.3	0.4
860	Bellingham, Washington	82.0	106.7	111.8	30.2	22.7	4.8	1.4
870	Benton Harbor, Michigan	163.9	171.3	163.0	4.5	-4.9	-4.8	-7.5
880	Billings, Montana	87.4	108.0	118.7	23.7	11.8	9.9	5.2

Appendix D

FIPS Code	SMSA Name	Population (in thousands)			Growth 1970–1980 (percent)	Net. Mig. 1970–1980 (percent)	Growth 1980–1984 (percent)	Net. Mig. 1980–1984 (percent)
		1970	1980	1984				
920	Biloxi–Gulfport, Mississippi	160.1	191.9	207.3	19.9	3.6	8.0	3.8
960	Binghamton, New York–Pennsylvania	302.7	301.3	302.9	-0.4	-6.2	0.5	-1.4
1000	Birmingham, Alabama	767.2	847.5	858.2	10.5	0.4	1.3	-1.3
1010	Bismarck, North Dakota	61.0	80.0	86.1	31.1	17.8	7.6	2.3
1020	Bloomington, Indiana	85.2	98.8	100.9	15.9	6.4	2.1	-0.7
1040	Bloomington–Normal, Illinois	104.4	119.1	122.8	14.1	6.0	3.1	-0.2
1080	Boise City, Idaho	112.2	173.0	189.3	54.2	41.2	9.4	4.3
1123	Boston–Lowell–Brockton–Lawrence–Haverhill, Massachusetts NECMA	3,709.6	3,662.8	3,695.3	-1.3	-5.7	0.9	-0.7
1140	Bradenton, Florida	97.1	148.4	169.5	52.9	54.0	14.2	15.0
1150	Bremerton, Washington	101.7	147.2	164.8	44.7	35.8	12.0	7.3
1163	Bridgeport–Stamford–Norwalk–Danbury, Connecticut NECMA	792.8	807.1	816.1	1.8	-3.0	1.1	-0.5
1240	Brownsville–Harlingen–San Benito, Texas	140.4	209.7	241.1	49.4	21.7	15.0	6.7
1260	Bryan–College Station, Texas	58.0	93.6	117.4	61.4	44.8	25.4	19.3
1280	Buffalo, New York	1,349.2	1,242.8	1,204.8	-7.9	-12.2	-3.1	-4.3
1300	Burlington, North Carolina	96.5	99.3	102.2	2.9	-5.6	2.9	1.8
1303	Burlington, Vermont NECMA	99.1	115.5	121.3	16.6	6.2	5.0	1.3
1320	Canton, Ohio	393.8	404.4	404.2	2.7	-4.2	-0.1	-2.3
1350	Casper, Wyoming	51.3	71.9	75.0	40.2	27.7	4.4	-2.8
1360	Cedar Rapids, Iowa	163.2	169.8	169.5	4.0	-5.6	-0.2	-3.5
1400	Champaign–Urbana–Rantoul, Illinois	163.3	168.4	170.3	3.1	-8.2	1.1	-3.0
1440	Charleston–North Charleston, South Carolina	336.0	430.5	472.5	28.1	10.9	9.8	4.3
1480	Charleston, West Virginia	257.1	269.6	266.9	4.8	-4.3	-1.0	-2.8
1520	Charlotte–Gastonia, North Carolina	557.8	637.2	678.2	14.2	1.8	6.4	3.3
1540	Charlottesville, Virginia	89.5	113.6	118.3	26.9	16.9	4.2	1.3
1560	Chattanooga, Tennessee–Georgia	370.9	426.5	422.5	15.0	3.5	-1.0	-3.1
1600	Chicago, Illinois	6,974.8	7,103.6	7,215.9	1.9	-6.2	1.6	-1.9
1620	Chico, California	102.0	143.9	158.5	41.1	38.0	10.2	8.1
1640	Cincinnati, Ohio–Kentucky–Indiana	1,387.2	1,401.5	1,408.0	1.0	-6.5	0.5	-2.6
1660	Clarksville–Hopkinsville, Tennessee–Kentucky	118.9	150.2	152.6	26.3	7.0	1.6	-4.5
1680	Cleveland, Ohio	2,063.7	1,898.8	1,867.0	-8.0	-13.7	-1.7	-3.7
1720	Colorado Springs, Colorado	239.3	317.5	359.6	32.7	15.0	13.3	7.0
1740	Columbia, Missouri	80.9	100.4	106.1	24.0	14.0	5.7	1.9

APPENDIX TABLE D.1 (continued)

FIPS Code	SMSA Name	Population (in thousands)			Growth 1970–1980 (percent)	Net. Mig. 1970–1980 (percent)	Growth 1980–1984 (percent)	Net. Mig. 1980–1984 (percent)
		1970	1980	1984				
1760	Columbia, South Carolina	322.9	410.1	433.3	27.0	12.9	5.7	2.4
1800	Columbus, Georgia–Alabama	238.6	239.2	244.5	0.3	–14.1	2.2	–1.7
1840	Columbus, Ohio	1,017.8	1,093.3	1,124.3	7.4	–2.3	2.8	–0.6
1880	Corpus Christi, Texas	284.8	326.2	361.4	14.5	–4.0	10.8	4.4
1900	Cumberland, Maryland–West Virginia	107.2	107.8	104.5	0.6	–4.8	–3.1	–3.5
1920	Dallas–Fort Worth, Texas	2,377.6	2,974.8	3,402.9	25.1	11.2	14.4	9.3
1950	Danville, Virginia	105.2	111.8	111.2	6.3	–2.1	–0.5	–1.7
1960	Davenport–Rock Island–Moline, Iowa–Illinois	362.6	384.0	380.9	5.9	–2.8	–0.8	–4.3
2000	Dayton, Ohio	852.5	830.1	821.1	–2.6	–11.2	–1.1	–4.1
2020	Daytona Beach, Florida	169.5	258.8	300.3	52.7	52.8	16.1	17.1
2040	Decatur, Illinois	125.0	131.4	128.6	5.1	–2.7	–2.1	–4.4
2080	Denver–Boulder, Colorado	1,239.5	1,620.9	1,794.2	30.8	20.1	10.7	5.8
2120	Des Moines, Iowa	313.6	338.0	347.4	7.8	–1.4	2.8	–0.9
2160	Detroit, Michigan	4,435.1	4,353.4	4,184.8	–1.8	–9.7	–3.9	–6.3
2200	Dubuque, Iowa	90.6	93.7	91.7	3.5	–6.0	–2.2	–5.1
2240	Duluth–Superior, Minnesota–Wisconsin	265.3	266.6	253.8	0.5	–4.1	–4.8	–6.7
2290	Eau Claire, Wisconsin	114.9	130.9	136.1	13.9	6.0	4.0	0.6
2320	El Paso, Texas	359.3	479.9	526.5	33.6	10.2	9.7	2.4
2330	Elkhart, Indiana	126.5	137.3	142.2	8.5	–2.0	3.6	–0.4
2335	Elmira, New York	101.5	97.7	93.5	–3.8	–9.0	–4.3	–6.3
2340	Enid, Oklahoma	56.3	62.8	65.4	11.5	1.3	4.1	–0.3
2360	Erie, Pennsylvania	263.7	279.8	282.1	6.1	–1.9	0.8	–1.8
2400	Eugene–Springfield, Oregon	215.4	275.2	266.4	27.8	18.1	–3.2	–6.7
2440	Evansville, Indiana–Kentucky	285.0	309.4	315.7	8.6	2.9	2.0	–0.5
2520	Fargo–Moorhead, North Dakota–Minnesota	120.3	137.6	143.3	14.4	4.7	4.2	0.1
2560	Fayetteville, North Carolina	212.0	247.2	251.3	16.6	–5.3	1.7	–5.2
2580	Fayetteville–Springdale, Arkansas	127.8	178.6	188.6	39.7	28.7	5.6	2.9
2640	Flint, Michigan	508.7	521.6	502.7	2.5	–8.5	–3.6	–7.3
2650	Florence, Alabama	117.7	135.1	135.7	14.7	4.8	0.5	–1.6
2655	Florence, South Carolina	89.6	110.2	114.0	22.9	8.3	3.5	0.1
2670	Fort Collins, Colorado	89.9	149.2	165.7	65.9	55.1	11.1	6.2
2680	Fort Lauderdale–Hollywood, Florida	620.1	1,018.2	1,093.3	64.2	60.1	7.4	7.3
2700	Fort Myers–Cape Coral, Florida	105.2	205.3	252.9	95.1	89.7	23.2	22.7

FIPS Code	SMSA Name	Population (in thousands)			Growth 1970–1980 (percent)	Net. Mig. 1970–1980 (percent)	Growth 1980–1984 (percent)	Net. Mig. 1980–1984 (percent)
		1970	1980	1984				
2720	Fort Smith, Arkansas–Oklahoma	160.4	203.5	212.9	26.9	15.6	4.6	2.2
2750	Fort Walton Beach, Florida	88.2	109.9	127.5	24.6	5.0	16.0	10.5
2760	Fort Wayne, Indiana	362.0	383.0	376.5	5.8	-4.8	-1.6	-5.3
2840	Fresno, California	413.3	514.6	564.9	24.5	13.1	9.8	4.1
2880	Gadsden, Alabama	94.1	103.1	103.6	9.5	0.0	0.5	-1.0
2900	Gainesville, Florida	104.8	151.3	166.6	44.5	29.8	10.1	5.7
2920	Galveston–Texas City, Texas	169.8	195.9	215.4	15.4	3.0	9.9	5.4
2960	Gary–Hammond–East Chicago, Indiana	633.4	642.8	629.6	1.5	-9.1	-2.1	-5.8
2975	Glens Falls, New York	102.1	109.6	111.6	7.4	1.2	1.8	0.2
2985	Grand Forks, North Dakota–Minnesota	95.5	100.9	102.8	5.7	-6.7	1.8	-3.2
3000	Grand Rapids, Michigan	539.2	601.7	626.4	11.6	1.6	4.1	-0.7
3040	Great Falls, Montana	81.8	80.7	81.8	-1.4	-13.3	1.4	-3.1
3060	Greeley, Colorado	89.3	123.4	131.7	38.2	25.9	6.7	1.5
3080	Green Bay, Wisconsin	158.2	175.3	181.3	10.8	0.1	3.4	-0.5
3120	Greensboro–Winston-Salem–High Point, North Carolina	724.1	827.3	859.2	14.2	3.9	3.9	1.9
3160	Greenville–Spartanburg, South Carolina	473.5	569.1	592.9	20.2	8.3	4.2	1.2
3180	Hagerstown, Maryland	103.8	113.1	112.0	8.9	1.1	-1.0	-2.4
3200	Hamilton–Middletown, Ohio	226.2	258.8	265.5	14.4	4.2	2.6	-0.8
3240	Harrisburg, Pennsylvania	410.5	446.6	458.9	8.8	3.3	2.8	0.7
3283	Hartford–New Britain–Bristol, Connecticut NECMA	1,035.2	1,051.6	1,069.2	1.6	-4.1	1.7	-0.3
3290	Hickory, North Carolina	110.3	130.2	137.4	18.0	5.5	5.5	3.3
3320	Honolulu, Hawaii	630.5	762.2	805.3	20.9	4.6	5.6	-0.3
3360	Houston, Texas	1,999.3	2,905.4	3,350.2	45.3	27.8	15.3	8.6
3400	Huntington–Ashland, West Virginia–Kentucky–Ohio	286.9	311.3	308.3	8.5	-0.7	-1.0	-2.7
3440	Huntsville, Alabama	282.4	308.6	326.0	9.3	-2.9	5.6	2.6
3480	Indianapolis, Indiana	1,111.4	1,166.6	1,194.9	5.0	-4.2	2.4	-0.9
3500	Iowa City, Iowa	72.1	81.7	84.9	13.3	1.5	3.9	-0.6
3520	Jackson, Michigan	143.3	151.5	145.3	5.7	-2.2	-4.1	-6.5
3560	Jackson, Mississippi	258.9	320.4	337.5	23.8	8.4	5.3	1.0
3600	Jacksonville, Florida	621.8	737.5	812.4	18.6	5.6	10.2	6.4
3605	Jacksonville, North Carolina	103.1	112.8	118.6	9.4	-16.6	5.2	-4.3
3620	Janesville–Beloit, Wisconsin	132.0	139.4	138.7	5.7	-2.4	-0.5	-3.5
3640	Jersey City, New Jersey	607.8	557.0	559.9	-8.4	-12.6	0.5	-1.2

APPENDIX TABLE D.1 (continued)

FIPS Code	SMSA Name	Population (in thousands)			Growth 1970–1980 (percent)	Net. Mig. 1970–1980 (percent)	Growth 1980–1984 (percent)	Net. Mig. 1980–1984 (percent)
		1970	1980	1984				
3660	Johnson City–Kingsport–Bristol, Tennessee–Virginia	373.6	433.6	441.9	16.1	6.6	1.9	0.6
3680	Johnstown, Pennsylvania	262.8	264.5	259.0	0.6	-3.9	-2.1	-3.2
3710	Joplin, Missouri	112.8	127.5	131.9	13.0	8.8	3.4	1.7
3720	Kalamazoo–Portage, Michigan	257.7	279.2	281.7	8.3	-0.5	0.9	-2.4
3740	Kankakee, Illinois	97.3	102.9	100.1	5.8	-3.8	-2.8	-6.0
3760	Kansas City, Missouri–Kansas	1,273.9	1,327.1	1,366.0	4.2	-4.2	2.9	-0.5
3800	Kenosha, Wisconsin	117.9	123.1	121.4	4.4	-3.2	-1.4	-4.2
3810	Killeen–Temple, Texas	159.8	214.7	225.7	34.3	7.3	5.1	-3.1
3840	Knoxville, Tennessee	409.4	476.5	491.9	16.4	7.2	3.2	1.3
3850	Kokomo, Indiana	99.8	103.7	101.0	3.9	-6.3	-2.6	-5.4
3870	La Crosse, Wisconsin	80.5	91.1	93.1	13.2	6.7	2.2	-0.7
3880	Lafayette, Louisiana	111.6	150.0	170.1	34.4	16.5	13.4	6.5
3920	Lafayette–West Lafayette, Indiana	109.4	121.7	123.9	11.3	1.3	1.8	-1.6
3960	Lake Charles, Louisiana	145.4	167.2	175.0	15.0	0.4	4.7	-0.9
3980	Lakeland–Winter Haven, Florida	228.5	321.7	354.6	40.8	30.6	10.2	7.7
4000	Lancaster, Pennsylvania	320.1	362.3	381.3	13.2	4.6	5.2	2.1
4040	Lansing–East Lansing, Michigan	424.3	471.6	468.7	11.2	0.0	-0.6	-4.7
4080	Laredo, Texas	72.9	99.3	118.2	36.2	8.9	19.1	10.2
4100	Las Cruces, New Mexico	69.8	96.3	112.2	38.1	21.0	16.5	10.0
4120	Las Vegas, Nevada	273.3	463.1	536.5	69.5	57.2	15.9	11.4
4150	Lawrence, Kansas	57.9	67.6	69.8	16.8	8.0	3.2	-0.7
4200	Lawton, Oklahoma	108.1	112.5	119.4	4.0	-17.2	6.2	-1.3
4243	Lewiston–Auburn, Maine NECMA	91.3	99.7	100.0	9.2	1.9	0.3	-1.7
4280	Lexington–Fayette, Kentucky	266.7	317.6	327.1	19.1	6.2	3.0	0.0
4320	Lima, Ohio	210.1	218.2	215.4	3.9	-5.3	-1.3	-4.8
4360	Lincoln, Nebraska	168.0	192.0	203.0	14.8	5.6	5.2	1.4
4400	Little Rock–North Little Rock, Arkansas	323.3	393.8	406.3	21.8	7.5	3.2	-0.8
4410	Long Branch–Asbury Park, New Jersey	461.8	503.2	525.3	9.0	3.5	4.4	3.1
4420	Longview–Marshall, Texas	120.8	151.8	168.4	25.7	15.1	11.0	7.3
4440	Lorain–Elyria, Ohio	256.8	274.9	271.3	7.0	-4.0	-1.3	-4.7
4480	Los Angeles–Long Beach, California	7,042.0	7,477.5	7,901.2	6.2	-2.6	5.7	1.2
4520	Louisville, Kentucky–Indiana	867.3	906.2	910.0	4.5	-6.5	0.4	-2.2
4600	Lubbock, Texas	179.3	211.7	218.9	18.1	0.7	3.4	-2.2

Appendix D

FIPS Code	SMSA Name	Population (in thousands) 1970	1980	1984	Growth 1970–1980 (percent)	Net. Mig. 1970–1980 (percent)	Growth 1980–1984 (percent)	Net. Mig. 1980–1984 (percent)
4640	Lynchburg, Virginia	134.7	153.3	154.9	13.8	4.6	1.1	−0.5
4680	Macon, Georgia	226.8	253.8	268.4	11.9	−0.8	5.8	2.4
4720	Madison, Wisconsin	290.3	323.5	333.0	11.5	2.2	2.9	−0.6
4763	Manchester–Nashua, New Hampshire NECMA	223.9	276.6	295.2	23.5	15.0	6.7	3.6
4800	Mansfield, Ohio	130.0	131.2	129.1	0.9	−7.6	−1.6	−4.3
4880	McAllen–Pharr–Edinburg, Texas	181.5	283.2	337.1	56.0	25.5	19.0	10.1
4890	Medford, Oregon	94.5	132.5	136.1	40.1	33.7	2.8	0.0
4900	Melbourne–Titusville–Cocoa, Florida	230.0	273.0	329.5	18.7	9.7	20.7	18.8
4920	Memphis, Tennessee–Arkansas–Mississippi	834.1	913.5	934.6	9.5	−3.9	2.3	−1.6
5000	Miami, Florida	1,267.8	1,625.8	1,706.0	28.2	21.9	4.9	2.8
5040	Midland, Texas	65.4	82.6	113.6	26.3	11.1	37.5	29.0
5080	Milwaukee, Wisconsin	1,403.9	1,397.1	1,393.9	−0.5	−7.7	−0.2	−3.4
5120	Minneapolis–St. Paul, Minnesota–Wisconsin	1,965.4	2,113.5	2,206.1	7.5	−1.7	4.4	0.3
5160	Mobile, Alabama	376.7	443.5	465.7	17.8	3.5	5.0	1.0
5170	Modesto, California	194.5	265.9	295.7	36.7	26.7	11.2	6.6
5200	Monroe, Louisiana	115.4	139.2	142.7	20.7	5.2	2.5	−1.7
5240	Montgomery, Alabama	225.9	272.7	284.8	20.7	8.5	4.4	1.1
5280	Muncie, Indiana	129.2	128.6	123.6	−0.5	−8.2	−3.9	−5.8
5320	Muskegon–Norton Shores–Muskegon Heights, Michigan	175.4	179.6	177.7	2.4	−6.3	−1.1	−4.3
5360	Nashville–Davidson, Tennessee	699.3	850.5	890.4	21.6	10.2	4.7	1.7
5403	New Bedford–Fall River, Massachusetts NECMA	444.3	474.6	477.9	6.8	1.5	0.7	−0.9
5460	New Brunswick–Perth Amboy–Sayreville, New Jersey	583.8	595.9	618.4	2.1	−4.8	3.8	1.7
5483	New Haven–West Haven–Waterbury–Meriden, Connecticut NECMA	744.9	761.3	769.6	2.2	−2.6	1.1	−0.5
5523	New London–Norwich, Connecticut NECMA	230.7	238.4	244.6	3.4	−5.1	2.6	−0.4
5560	New Orleans, Louisiana	1,046.5	1,187.1	1,237.3	13.4	0.4	4.2	0.1
5600	New York, New York–New Jersey*	11,632.4	10,880.8	11,030.3	−6.5	−11.4	1.4	−0.4
5640	Newark, New Jersey	2,057.5	1,966.0	1,966.1	−4.5	−9.2	0.0	−1.7
5645	Newark, Ohio	107.8	121.0	124.0	12.2	4.9	2.5	−0.3
5660	Newburgh–Middletown, New York	221.7	259.6	273.5	17.1	9.8	5.4	2.7
5680	Newport News–Hampton, Virginia	333.1	364.4	390.1	9.4	−4.7	7.0	2.7

APPENDIX TABLE D.1 (continued)

FIPS Code	SMSA Name	Population (in thousands)			Growth 1970–1980 (percent)	Net. Mig. 1970–1980 (percent)	Growth 1980–1984 (percent)	Net. Mig. 1980–1984 (percent)
		1970	1980	1984				
5720	Norfolk–Virginia Beach–Portsmouth, Vigrinia–North Carolina	732.6	807.0	884.1	10.2	−3.9	9.6	4.9
5745	Northeast Pennsylvania	621.9	640.4	637.6	3.0	2.3	−0.4	−0.3
5790	Ocala, Florida	69.0	122.5	155.6	77.4	67.6	27.0	25.2
5800	Odessa, Texas	92.7	115.4	144.5	24.5	7.5	25.2	16.9
5880	Oklahoma City, Oklahoma	699.1	834.1	932.1	19.3	6.0	11.8	6.9
5910	Olympia, Washington	76.9	124.3	138.3	61.6	52.3	11.3	7.1
5920	Omaha, Nebraska–Iowa	542.6	569.6	591.9	5.0	−5.9	3.9	−0.4
5960	Orlando, Florida	453.3	700.1	824.1	54.5	42.3	17.7	14.7
5990	Owensboro, Kentucky	79.5	85.9	88.3	8.1	−3.4	2.7	−0.9
6000	Oxnard–Simi Valley–Ventura, California	378.5	529.2	584.7	39.8	27.0	10.5	5.4
6015	Panama City, Florida	75.3	97.7	108.5	29.8	14.6	11.0	7.2
6020	Parkersburg–Marietta, West Virginia–Ohio	148.1	162.8	163.0	9.9	0.2	0.1	−2.1
6025	Pascagoula–Moss Point, Mississippi	88.0	118.0	123.6	34.2	12.8	4.7	−0.4
6040	Paterson–Clifton–Passaic, New Jersey*	1,357.9	1,293.0	1,299.5	−4.8	−8.8	0.5	−0.6
6080	Pensacola, Florida	243.1	289.8	318.7	19.2	3.9	10.0	5.8
6120	Peoria, Illinois	342.0	365.9	355.8	7.0	−2.0	−2.8	−6.0
6140	Petersburg–Colonial Heights–Hopewell, Virginia	128.9	129.3	129.9	12.1	−11.0	0.5	−2.2
6160	Philadelphia, Pennsylvania–New Jersey	4,824.1	4,716.8	4,768.5	−2.2	−7.3	1.1	−0.9
6200	Phoenix, Arizona	971.2	1,509.1	1,714.8	55.4	43.1	13.6	9.1
6240	Pine Bluff, Arkansas	85.3	90.7	90.6	6.3	−5.7	−0.1	−3.5
6280	Pittsburgh, Pennsylvania	2,401.4	2,263.9	2,212.8	−5.7	−8.3	−2.3	−3.0
6323	Pittsfield, Massachusetts NECMA	149.4	145.1	142.4	−2.9	−6.0	−1.9	−2.6
6403	Portland, Maine NECMA	215.4	244.6	253.5	13.6	7.0	3.7	1.3
6440	Portland, Oregon–Washington	1,007.1	1,242.6	1,283.2	23.4	16.3	3.3	−0.1
6453	Portsmouth–Dover–Rochester, New Hampshire–Maine NECMA	321.0	415.4	451.6	29.4	20.4	8.7	5.5
6460	Poughkeepsie, New York	222.3	245.1	253.1	10.2	4.1	3.3	1.5
6483	Providence–Warwick–Pawtucket, Rhode Island NECMA	855.5	865.8	878.2	1.2	−3.0	1.4	0.0
6520	Provo–Orem, Utah	137.8	218.1	240.6	58.3	21.5	10.3	−2.3
6560	Pueblo, Colorado	118.2	126.0	124.9	6.5	−2.4	−0.9	−4.0
6600	Racine, Wisconsin	170.8	173.1	173.8	1.3	−7.1	0.4	−3.1
6640	Raleigh–Durham, North Carolina	419.3	531.2	577.4	26.7	15.2	8.7	5.9

504

FIPS Code	SMSA Name	Population (in thousands)			Growth 1970–1980 (percent)	Net. Mig. 1970–1980 (percent)	Growth 1980–1984 (percent)	Net. Mig. 1980–1984 (percent)
		1970	1980	1984				
6690	Redding, California	77.6	115.7	126.5	49.0	42.0	9.3	6.3
6720	Reno, Nevada	121.1	193.6	211.5	59.9	52.9	9.2	5.5
6740	Richland–Kennewick–Pasco, Washington	93.4	144.5	149.1	54.8	42.0	3.2	-3.4
6760	Richmond, Virginia	547.5	632.0	666.1	12.7	6.3	5.4	2.9
6780	Riverside–San Bernardino–Ontario, California	1,139.1	1,558.2	1,810.9	36.8	28.3	16.2	11.5
6800	Roanoke, Virginia	203.2	224.3	226.7	10.4	2.7	1.1	0.1
6820	Rochester, Minnesota	84.1	92.0	96.2	9.4	-3.1	4.6	-0.7
6840	Rochester, New York	961.5	971.2	989.1	1.0	-5.8	1.8	-0.9
6880	Rockford, Illinois	272.1	279.5	278.8	2.7	-6.6	-0.3	-3.5
6885	Rock Hill, South Carolina	85.2	106.7	114.5	25.2	12.3	7.3	4.3
6920	Sacramento, California	803.8	1,014.0	1,120.7	26.2	17.9	10.5	6.5
6960	Saginaw, Michigan	219.7	228.1	219.1	3.8	-6.8	-3.9	-7.4
6980	St. Cloud, Minnesota	134.6	163.3	171.3	21.3	9.0	4.9	-0.4
7000	St. Joseph, Missouri	98.8	101.9	101.4	3.1	-0.6	-0.5	-2.0
7040	St. Louis, Missouri–Illinois	2,410.9	2,356.5	2,378.0	-2.3	-9.2	0.9	-2.0
7080	Salem, Oregon	186.7	249.9	255.2	33.9	26.4	2.1	-1.3
7120	Salinas–Seaside–Monterey, California	247.4	290.4	319.2	17.4	3.7	9.9	3.5
7140	Salisbury–Concord, North Carolina	164.7	185.1	194.0	12.4	3.7	4.8	3.4
7160	Salt Lake City–Ogden, Utah	705.5	936.3	1054.0	32.7	11.2	12.6	4.0
7200	San Angelo, Texas	71.0	84.8	96.0	19.3	8.5	13.2	8.3
7240	San Antonio, Texas	888.2	1,072.0	1,188.5	20.7	3.8	10.9	5.5
7320	San Diego, California	1,357.9	1,861.8	2,063.9	37.1	27.3	10.9	6.4
7360	San Francisco–Oakland, California	3,109.2	3,250.6	3,413.3	4.6	-1.1	5.0	2.4
7400	San Jose, California	1,065.3	1,295.1	1,371.5	21.6	10.8	5.9	1.2
7480	Santa Barbara–Santa Maria–Lompoc, California	264.3	298.7	322.8	13.0	5.6	8.1	4.7
7485	Santa Cruz, California	123.8	188.1	205.8	52.0	46.9	9.4	5.8
7500	Santa Rosa, California	204.9	299.7	326.3	46.3	40.5	8.9	6.2
7510	Sarasota, Florida	120.4	202.3	237.6	68.0	72.5	17.5	20.1
7520	Savannah, Georgia	208.0	230.7	244.7	10.9	-1.8	6.1	2.1
7600	Seattle–Everett, Washington	1,424.6	1,607.5	1,692.1	12.8	6.5	5.3	2.0
7610	Sharon, Pennsylvania	127.2	128.3	127.1	0.8	-3.7	-0.9	-2.2
7620	Sheboygan, Wisconsin	96.7	100.9	102.1	4.4	-2.0	1.2	-3.5
7640	Sherman–Denison, Texas	83.2	89.8	94.7	7.9	1.4	5.5	3.7

APPENDIX TABLE D.1 (continued)

FIPS Code	SMSA Name	Population (in thousands)			Growth 1970–1980 (percent)	Net. Mig. 1970–1980 (percent)	Growth 1980–1984 (percent)	Net. Mig. 1980–1984 (percent)
		1970	1980	1984				
7680	Shreveport, Louisiana	336.0	376.7	406.3	12.1	-1.6	7.9	3.6
7720	Sioux City, Iowa–Nebraska	116.2	117.5	118.2	1.1	-8.1	0.6	-2.7
7760	Sioux Falls, South Dakota	95.2	109.4	118.1	14.9	4.8	7.9	3.8
7800	South Bend, Indiana	279.8	280.8	280.4	0.3	-6.6	-0.1	-2.7
7840	Spokane, Washington	287.5	341.8	352.9	18.9	10.9	3.2	-0.2
7880	Springfield, Illinois	171.0	187.8	190.2	9.8	3.2	1.3	-1.6
7920	Springfield, Missouri	168.1	207.7	217.2	23.6	15.7	4.6	2.1
7960	Springfield, Ohio	187.6	183.9	181.1	-2.0	-9.2	-1.5	-3.8
8003	Springfield–Chicopee–Holyoke, Massachusetts NECMA	583.0	581.8	583.9	-0.2	-5.0	0.4	-1.3
8050	State College, Pennsylvania	99.3	112.8	114.5	13.6	4.9	1.5	-1.0
8080	Steubenville–Weirton, Ohio–West Virginia	166.4	163.1	157.6	-2.0	-6.9	-3.4	-4.6
8120	Stockton, California	291.1	347.3	398.6	19.3	11.6	14.8	10.1
8160	Syracuse, New York	636.6	643.0	650.5	1.0	-6.2	1.2	-1.5
8200	Tacoma, Washington	412.3	485.6	515.8	17.8	7.7	6.2	1.3
8240	Tallahassee, Florida	109.4	159.5	176.8	45.9	30.6	10.8	6.8
8280	Tampa–St. Petersburg, Florida	1,088.5	1,569.1	1,742.1	44.2	42.0	11.0	11.3
8320	Terre Haute, Indiana	175.1	176.6	173.4	0.8	-2.3	-1.8	-2.9
8360	Texarkana, Texas–Texarkana, Arkansas	113.5	127.0	132.6	11.9	0.9	4.4	1.7
8400	Toledo, Ohio–Michigan	762.7	791.6	781.5	3.8	-4.5	-1.3	-4.1
8440	Topeka, Kansas	180.6	185.4	191.0	2.7	-4.8	3.0	0.1
8480	Trenton, New Jersey	304.1	307.9	313.8	1.2	-4.1	1.9	0.2
8520	Tucson, Arizona	351.7	531.4	594.8	51.1	39.4	11.9	8.0
8560	Tulsa, Oklahoma	549.2	689.4	760.1	25.5	13.8	10.3	6.1
8600	Tuscaloosa, Alabama	116.0	137.5	138.9	18.5	6.3	1.0	-1.8
8640	Tyler, Texas	97.1	128.4	144.6	32.2	20.4	12.7	9.0
8680	Utica–Rome, New York	340.5	320.2	321.4	-6.0	-11.2	0.4	-1.3
8720	Vallejo–Fairfield–Napa, California	251.1	334.4	367.7	33.2	24.0	10.0	5.6
8750	Victoria, Texas	53.8	68.8	74.5	28.0	12.3	8.3	1.9
8760	Vineland–Millville–Bridgeton, New Jersey	121.4	132.9	133.5	9.5	1.2	0.5	-2.0
8780	Visalia–Tulare–Porterville, California	188.3	245.7	272.4	30.5	18.0	10.9	4.7
8800	Waco, Texas	147.6	170.8	182.1	15.7	6.8	6.6	3.6
8840	Washington, DC– Maryland–Virginia	2,910.1	3,060.9	3,218.9	5.2	-7.0	5.2	1.4
8920	Waterloo–Cedar Falls, Iowa	132.9	138.0	137.1	3.8	-5.6	-0.6	-4.2

APPENDIX TABLE D.1 *(continued)*

FIPS Code	SMSA Name	Population (in thousands)			Growth 1970–1980 (percent)	Net. Mig. 1970–1980 (percent)	Growth 1980–1984 (percent)	Net. Mig. 1980–1984 (percent)
		1970	1980	1984				
8940	Wausau, Wisconsin	97.5	111.3	112.7	14.2	4.5	1.3	−2.5
8960	West Palm Beach–Boca Raton, Florida	349.0	576.9	692.2	65.3	61.1	20.0	19.8
9000	Wheeling, West Virginia–Ohio	182.0	185.6	183.2	2.0	−3.5	−1.3	−2.0
9040	Wichita, Kansas	389.4	411.3	428.6	5.6	−4.4	4.2	−0.8
9080	Wichita Falls, Texas	128.6	130.7	136.0	1.6	−10.6	4.1	0.2
9140	Williamsport, Pennsylvania	113.3	118.4	117.1	4.5	−1.6	−1.1	−3.1
9160	Wilmington, Delaware–New Jersey–Maryland	499.5	523.2	539.6	4.8	−5.6	3.1	0.4
9200	Wilmington, North Carolina	107.2	139.2	154.1	29.9	17.4	10.7	8.6
9243	Worcester–Fitchburg–Leominster, Massachusetts NECMA	637.0	646.4	654.0	1.5	−3.5	1.2	−0.6
9260	Yakima, Washington	145.2	172.5	179.5	18.8	9.3	4.1	−0.5
9280	York, Pennsylvania	329.5	381.3	391.4	15.7	8.9	2.7	0.5
9320	Youngstown–Warren, Ohio	537.1	531.3	518.0	−1.1	−7.4	−2.5	−4.3
9340	Yuba City, California	86.7	102.0	109.6	17.7	6.0	7.5	2.6

*Differs from definition used by Bureau of the Census. See Appendix F.

APPENDIX E:
SUPPLEMENTARY TABLES
ON CITY–SUBURB REDISTRIBUTION

APPENDIX TABLE E.7A

Metropolitan Area Size, Central City Size, and City Share of Metropolitan Population, 1950, 1960, 1970, 1980: 39 Metropolitan Areas[a]

Metropolitan Area Groupings/ Metropolitan Areas	Metropolitan Area Size (1000s)				Central City Size (1000s)				City Share of Metropolitan Population			
	1950	1960	1970	1980	1950	1960	1970	1980	1950	1960	1970	1980
NORTH-DECLINING												
New York	9,576	10,726	11,632	10,881	7,892	7,782	7,896	7,072	82.4	72.6	67.9	65.0
Philadelphia	3,671	4,343	4,824	4,717	2,072	2,003	1,950	1,688	56.4	46.1	40.4	35.8
Boston	3,065	3,358	3,710	3,663	801	697	641	563	26.1	20.8	17.3	15.4
Cincinnati	1,023	1,268	1,387	1,401	504	503	454	385	49.3	39.6	32.7	27.5
St. Louis	1,791	2,144	2,411	2,356	857	750	622	453	47.8	35.0	25.8	19.2
Buffalo	1,089	1,307	1,349	1,243	580	533	463	358	53.3	40.8	34.3	28.8
Chicago	5,178	6,221	6,975	7,104	3,621	3,550	3,369	3,005	69.9	57.1	48.3	42.3
Newark	1,568	1,833	2,057	1,966	439	405	382	329	28.0	22.1	18.6	16.7
Cleveland	1,533	1,909	2,064	1,899	915	876	751	574	59.7	45.9	36.4	30.2
Detroit	3,170	3,950	4,435	4,353	1,850	1,670	1,514	1,203	58.3	42.3	34.1	27.6
Milwaukee	1,014	1,279	1,404	1,397	637	741	717	636	62.8	58.0	51.1	45.5
Pittsburgh	2,213	2,405	2,401	2,264	677	604	520	424	30.6	25.1	21.7	18.7
Paterson*	876	1,187	1,358	1,293	262	280	282	265	29.8	23.6	20.8	20.5
NORTH-OLD												
Columbus	637	845	1,018	1,093	376	471	540	565	59.0	55.8	53.1	51.7
Indianapolis	727	944	1,111	1,167	427	476	737	701	58.7	50.4	66.3	60.1
Kansas City	865	1,109	1,274	1,327	457	476	507	448	52.8	42.9	39.8	33.8
Hartford	652	847	1,035	1,052	177	162	158	136	27.2	19.1	15.3	13.0
Minneapolis*	1,252	1,598	1,965	2,114	833	796	744	641	66.5	59.8	37.9	30.3
SOUTH-OLD												
Baltimore	1,457	1,804	2,071	2,174	950	939	906	787	65.2	52.1	43.7	36.2
New Orleans	712	907	1,046	1,187	570	628	593	558	80.1	69.2	56.7	47.0
Washington, DC	1,531	2,109	2,910	3,061	802	764	757	638	52.4	36.2	26.0	20.9
Atlanta	864	1,169	1,596	2,030	331	487	495	425	38.3	41.7	31.0	20.9

APPENDIX TABLE E.7A (continued)

Metropolitan Area Groupings/ Metropolitan Areas	Metropolitan Area Size (1000s)				Central City Size (1000s)				City Share of Metropolitan Population			
	1950	1960	1970	1980	1950	1960	1970	1980	1950	1960	1970	1980
WEST-OLD												
San Francisco*	2,136	2,649	3,109	3,251	1,160	1,108	1,077	1,018	54.3	41.8	34.6	31.3
Denver*	616	935	1,240	1,621	36	532	582	569	70.7	56.9	46.9	35.1
Los Angeles*	4,152	6,039	7,042	7,478	2,221	2,823	3,171	3,328	53.5	46.8	45.0	44.5
Portland	705	822	1,007	1,243	374	373	380	366	53.0	45.3	37.7	29.5
Seattle*	845	1,107	1,425	1,607	501	597	584	548	59.4	54.0	41.0	34.1
SOUTH-YOUNG												
San Antonio	542	736	888	1,072	408	588	654	786	75.3	79.9	73.7	73.3
Dallas*	1,216	1,738	2,378	2,975	713	1,036	1,238	1,289	58.6	59.6	52.1	43.3
Houston	947	1,430	1,999	2,905	596	938	1,234	1,595	62.9	65.6	61.7	54.9
Tampa*	430	809	1,089	1,569	221	456	494	510	51.5	56.4	45.4	32.5
Miami	495	935	1,268	1,626	249	292	335	347	50.4	31.2	26.4	21.3
Ft. Lauderdale*	84	334	620	1,018	51	119	246	275	60.4	35.6	39.7	27.0
WEST-YOUNG												
Sacramento	359	626	804	1,014	138	192	257	276	38.3	30.6	32.0	27.2
San Diego	557	1,033	1,358	1,862	334	573	697	876	60.1	55.5	51.4	47.0
San Jose	291	642	1,065	1,295	95	204	460	629	32.8	31.8	43.2	48.6
Phoenix	332	664	971	1,509	107	439	584	790	32.2	66.2	60.2	52.3
Riverside*	452	810	1,139	1,558	133	223	311	377	29.4	27.5	27.3	24.2
Anaheim*	216	704	1,421	1,933	64	289	513	546	29.5	41.0	31.2	28.3

SOURCES: Machine-readable computer files: *County and City Data Book*, Consolidated File for Counties, 1947–1977, and Cities, 1944–1977; and *County and City Data Book*, 1983 file (prepared by the U.S. Bureau of the Census, Washington, DC).

ª1980 metropolitan areas with populations greater than 1,000,000 defined as 1980 SMSAs and NECMAs (in New England) except for New York and Paterson–Clifton–Passaic (see Appendix F).

*Largest of multiple cities (complete metropolitan area names are listed in Appendix F).

REGIONAL AND METROPOLITAN GROWTH AND DECLINE

APPENDIX TABLE E.7B

Percent Population Change for Metropolitan Areas, Central Cities, and Suburbs, and Suburbanization Rates, 1950–1960, 1960–1970, 1970–1980: 39 Metropolitan Areas[a]

Metropolitan Area Groupings/ Metropolitan Areas	Percent Population Change									Suburbanization Rate[b]		
	Metropolitan Areas			Central Cities			Suburbs					
	1950–1960	1960–1970	1970–1980	1950–1960	1960–1970	1970–1980	1950–1960	1960–1970	1970–1980	1950–1960	1960–1970	1970–1980
NORTH-DECLINING												
New York	+12.0	+8.4	−6.5	−1.4	+1.5	−10.4	+74.8	+26.9	+1.9	+76.2	+25.4	+12.3
Philadelphia	+18.3	+11.1	−2.2	−3.3	−2.6	−13.4	+46.3	+22.8	+5.4	+49.6	+25.4	+18.8
Boston	+9.5	+10.5	−1.3	−13.0	−8.1	−12.2	+17.5	+15.3	+1.0	+30.5	+23.4	+13.2
Cincinnati	+24.0	+9.4	+1.0	−0.3	−9.8	−15.0	+47.5	+21.9	+8.8	+47.8	+31.7	+23.8
St. Louis	+19.7	+12.4	−2.3	−12.5	−17.0	−27.2	+49.2	+28.3	+6.4	+61.7	+45.3	+33.6
Buffalo	+20.0	+3.2	−7.9	−8.2	−13.1	−22.7	+52.1	+14.5	−0.2	+60.3	+27.6	+22.5
Chicago	+20.1	+12.1	+1.8	−1.9	−5.1	−10.8	+71.5	+35.0	+13.7	+73.4	+40.1	+24.5
Newark	+17.0	+12.2	−4.4	−7.6	−5.7	−13.8	+26.5	+17.3	−2.3	+34.1	+23.0	+11.5
Cleveland	+24.6	+8.1	−8.0	−4.2	−14.3	−23.6	+67.3	+27.0	+0.9	+71.5	+41.3	+24.5
Detroit	+24.6	+12.3	−1.8	−9.7	−9.3	−20.5	+72.6	+28.1	+7.8	+82.3	+37.4	+28.3
Milwaukee	+26.1	+9.8	−0.5	+16.3	−3.2	−11.3	+42.6	+27.7	+10.8	+26.3	+30.9	+22.1
Pittsburgh	+8.7	−0.2	−5.7	−10.7	−13.9	−18.5	+17.2	+4.5	−2.2	+27.9	+18.4	+16.3
Paterson*	+35.5	+14.4	−4.8	+6.9	+1.0	−6.2	+47.6	+18.6	−4.4	+40.7	+17.6	+1.8
NORTH-OLD												
Columbus	+32.6	+20.4	+7.4	+25.4	+14.6	+4.6	+43.0	+27.8	+10.6	+17.6	+13.2	+6.0
Indianapolis	+29.9	+17.7	+5.0	+11.5	+54.7	−4.9	+56.1	−20.0	+24.4	+44.6	−74.7	+29.3
Kansas City	+28.2	+14.9	+4.2	+4.1	+6.7	−11.7	+55.2	+21.1	+14.7	+51.1	+14.4	+26.4
Hartford	+30.0	+22.2	+1.6	−8.6	−2.6	−13.7	+44.4	+28.1	+4.3	+53.0	+30.7	+18.0
Minneapolis*	+27.6	+23.0	+7.5	−4.4	−6.5	−13.9	+91.3	+52.3	+20.6	+95.7	+58.8	+34.5
SOUTH-OLD												
Baltimore	+23.8	+14.8	+5.0	−1.1	−3.5	−13.1	+70.4	+34.8	+19.1	+71.5	+38.3	+32.2
New Orleans	+27.3	+15.4	+13.4	+10.0	−5.4	−6.1	+97.0	+62.0	+39.0	+87.0	+67.4	+45.1
Washington, DC	+37.7	+38.0	+5.2	−4.8	−1.0	−15.6	+84.5	+60.1	+12.5	+89.3	+61.1	+28.1
Atlanta	+35.2	+36.5	+27.2	+47.1	+1.6	−14.1	+27.8	+61.5	+45.8	−19.3	+59.9	+59.9

APPENDIX TABLE E.7B (continued)

Metropolitan Area Groupings/Metropolitan Areas	Percent Population Change											
	Metropolitan Areas			Central Cities			Suburbs			Suburbanization Rate[b]		
	1950–1960	1960–1970	1970–1980	1950–1960	1960–1970	1970–1980	1950–1960	1960–1970	1970–1980	1950–1960	1960–1970	1970–1980
WEST-OLD												
San Francisco*	+24.0	+17.4	+4.5	−4.5	−2.8	−5.5	+57.9	+31.9	+9.9	+62.4	+34.7	+15.4
Denver*	+51.6	+32.6	+30.8	+22.0	+9.4	−2.1	+123.2	+63.2	+59.9	+101.2	+53.8	+62.0
Los Angeles*	+45.5	+16.6	+6.2	+27.1	+12.3	+5.0	+66.6	+20.4	+7.2	+39.5	+8.1	+2.2
Portland	+16.6	+22.5	+23.4	−0.3	+2.0	−3.6	+35.6	+39.6	+39.7	+35.9	+37.6	+43.3
Seattle*	+31.1	+28.7	+12.8	+19.1	−2.2	−6.2	+48.6	+64.8	+26.1	+29.5	+67.0	+32.3
SOUTH-YOUNG												
San Antonio	+35.7	+20.7	+20.7	+43.9	+11.3	+20.1	+10.9	+57.8	+22.2	−33.0	+46.5	+2.1
Dallas*	+42.9	+36.8	+25.1	+45.2	+19.5	+4.2	+39.5	+62.4	+47.9	−5.7	+42.9	+43.7
Houston*	+51.0	+39.8	+45.3	+57.4	+31.5	+29.3	+40.1	+55.6	+71.1	−17.3	+24.1	+41.8
Tampa*	+88.3	+34.5	+44.1	+106.1	+8.2	+3.3	+69.5	+68.5	+78.1	−36.6	+60.3	+74.8
Miami	+88.9	+35.6	+28.2	+17.0	+14.8	+3.6	+161.7	+45.0	+37.1	+144.7	+30.2	+33.5
Ft. Lauderdale*	+297.9	+85.7	+64.2	+134.6	+107.3	+11.4	+546.7	+73.7	+99.0	+412.1	−33.6	+87.6
WEST-YOUNG												
Sacramento	+74.0	+28.5	+26.2	+39.3	+34.1	+7.2	+95.5	+26.0	+35.0	+56.2	−8.1	+27.8
San Diego	+85.5	+31.4	+37.1	+71.4	+21.7	+25.5	+106.7	+43.6	+49.4	+35.3	+21.9	+23.9
San Jose	+121.1	+65.9	+21.6	+114.3	+125.2	+36.9	+124.4	+38.2	+9.9	+10.1	−87.0	−27.0
Phoenix	+100.0	+46.4	+55.4	+311.1	+33.0	+35.2	−0.3	+72.5	+85.9	−311.4	+39.5	+50.7
Riverside*	+79.3	+40.7	+36.8	+68.0	+39.6	+21.3	+84.0	+41.1	+42.6	+16.0	+1.5	+21.3
Anaheim*	+225.6	+101.9	+36.0	+352.3	+53.5	+23.2	+172.5	+135.6	+41.8	−179.8	+82.1	+18.6

SOURCES: Machine-readable computer files: *County and City Data Book*, Consolidated File for Counties, 1947–1977, and Cities, 1944–1977; and *County and City Data Book*, 1983 file (prepared by the U.S. Bureau of the Census, Washington, DC).

[a] 1980 metropolitan areas with population greater than 1,000,000 defined as 1980 SMSAs and NECMAs (in New England) except for New York and Paterson–Clifton–Passaic (see Appendix F).

[b] Suburbanization Rate: Suburb Percent Change minus Central City Percent Change.

*Largest of multiple central cities (complete metropolitan area names are listed in Appendix F).

APPENDIX TABLE E.7C

Percent Population Change in Central Cities, Attributable to Population Growth and Annexation, 1950–1960, 1960–1970, 1970–1980: 39 Metropolitan Areas[a]

Metropolitan Area Groupings/ Metropolitan Areas	Percent Population Change in Central Cities								
	1950–1960			1960–1970			1970–1980		
	Growth	Annexation	Total	Growth	Annexation	Total	Growth	Annexation	Total
NORTH-DECLINING									
New York	−1.4	0.0	−1.4	+1.5	0.0	+1.5	−10.4	0.0	−10.4
Philadelphia	−3.3	0.0	−3.3	−2.6	0.0	−2.6	−13.4	0.0	−13.4
Boston	−13.0	0.0	−13.0	−8.1	0.0	−8.1	−12.2	0.0	−12.2
Cincinnati	−1.8	+1.5	−0.3	−10.0	+0.2	−9.8	−15.0	0.0	−15.0
St. Louis	−12.5	0.0	−12.5	−17.0	0.0	−17.0	−27.2	0.0	−27.2
Buffalo	−8.2	0.0	−8.2	−13.1	0.0	−13.1	−22.7	0.0	−22.7
Chicago	−2.1	+0.2	−1.9	−5.2	+0.1	−5.1	−10.8	0.0	−10.8
Newark	−7.6	0.0	−7.6	−5.7	0.0	−5.7	−13.8	0.0	−13.8
Cleveland	−4.2	0.0	−4.2	−14.3	0.0	−14.3	−23.6	0.0	−23.6
Detroit	−9.7	0.0	−9.7	−9.3	0.0	−9.3	−20.5	0.0	−20.5
Milwaukee	−3.1	+19.4	+16.3	−4.2	+1.0	−3.2	−11.3	0.0	−11.3
Pittsburgh	−10.7	0.0	−10.7	−13.9	0.0	−13.9	−18.5	0.0	−18.5
Paterson*	+6.9	0.0	+6.9	+1.0	0.0	+1.0	−6.2	0.0	−6.2
NORTH-OLD									
Columbus	+5.3	+20.1	+25.4	+9.0	+5.6	+14.6	+3.7	+0.9	+4.6
Indianapolis	+0.4	+11.1	+11.5	−9.7	+64.4	+54.7	−3.9	−1.0	−4.9
Kansas City	−5.1	+9.2	+4.1	−8.0	+14.7	+6.7	−11.7	0.0	−11.7
Hartford	−8.6	0.0	−8.6	−2.6	0.0	−2.6	−13.7	0.0	−13.7
Minneapolis*	−4.4	0.0	−4.4	−6.5	.	−6.5	−13.9	0.0	−13.9
SOUTH-OLD									
Baltimore	−1.1	0.0	−1.1	−3.5	0.0	−3.5	−13.1	0.0	−13.1
New Orleans	+10.0	0.0	+10.0	−5.4	0.0	−5.4	−6.1	0.0	−6.1
Washington, DC	−4.8	0.0	−4.8	−1.0	0.0	−1.0	−15.6	0.0	−15.6
Atlanta	−4.6	+51.7	+47.1	+0.9	+0.7	+1.6	−14.1	0.0	−14.1

APPENDIX TABLE E.7C (continued)

Percent Population Change in Central Cities

Metropolitan Area Groupings/ Metropolitan Areas	1950–1960			1960–1970			1970–1980		
	Growth	Annexation	Total	Growth	Annexation	Total	Growth	Annexation	Total
WEST-OLD									
San Francisco*	-4.5	0.0	-4.5	-2.9	+0.1	-2.8	-5.5	0.0	-5.5
Denver*	+9.5	+12.5	+22.0	-4.9	+14.3	+9.4	-2.4	+0.3	-2.1
Los Angeles*	+24.1	+3.0	+27.1	+11.7	+0.6	+12.3	+4.9	+0.1	+5.0
Portland	-3.2	+2.9	-0.3	-2.1	+4.1	+2.0	-5.7	+2.1	-3.6
Seattle*	+2.0	+17.1	+19.1	-4.3	+2.1	-2.2	-6.3	+0.1	-6.2
SOUTH-YOUNG									
San Antonio	+9.7	+34.2	+43.9	+10.9	+0.4	+11.3	+8.5	+11.6	+20.1
Dallas*	+10.3	+34.9	+45.2	+17.3	+2.2	+19.5	+3.6	+0.6	+4.2
Houston	+15.2	+42.0	+57.4	+27.7	+3.8	+31.5	+12.4	+16.9	+29.3
Tampa*	+42.4	+63.7	+106.1	+4.9	+3.3	+8.2	+3.3	0.0	+3.3
Miami	+17.0	0.0	+17.0	+14.8	0.0	+14.8	+3.6	0.0	+3.6
Ft. Lauderdale*	+119.1	+15.5	+134.6	+61.3	+46.0	+107.3	+11.3	+0.1	+11.4
WEST-YOUNG									
Sacramento	+1.0	+38.3	+39.3	+0.8	+33.3	+34.1	+7.2	0.0	+7.2
San Diego	+51.7	+19.7	+71.4	+19.9	+1.6	+21.7	+25.5	0.0	+25.5
San Jose	+10.0	+104.3	+114.3	+86.1	+39.2	+125.2	+38.4	-1.5	+36.9
Phoenix	0.0	+311.2	+311.1	+18.4	+14.6	+33.0	+29.2	+5.8	+35.2
Riverside*	+54.8	+13.2	+68.0	+15.7	+23.9	+39.6	+19.9	+1.2	+21.3
Anaheim*	+188.9	+163.4	+352.3	+39.5	+14.0	+53.5	+22.4	+0.8	+23.2

SOURCES: *Census of Population, 1960,* Vol. I, *Characteristics of the Population.* A. Number of Inhabitants (States), table 9: *Census of Population, 1970,* Vol. I, *Characteristics of the Population,* A. Number of Inhabitants, Section 1 (United States Summary Table 40), and unpublished 1980 estimates from the U.S. Bureau of the Census.

[a] 1980 metropolitan areas with populations greater than 1,000,000 defined as 1980 SMSAs and NECMAs (in New England) except for New York and Paterson–Clifton–Passaic (see Appendix F).

* Largest of multiple central cities (complete metropolitan area names are listed in Appendix F).

APPENDIX TABLE E.7D

Percent Population Change in Suburbs Attributable to Population Growth and Annexation, 1950–1960, 1960–1970, 1970–1980: 39 Metropolitan Areas[a]

Metropolitan Area Groupings/ Metropolitan Areas	Percent Population Change in Suburbs								
	1950–1960			1960–1970			1970–1980		
	Growth	Annexation	Total	Growth	Annexation	Total	Growth	Annexation	Total
NORTH-DECLINING									
New York	+74.8	0.0	+74.8	+26.9	0.0	+26.9	+1.9	0.0	+1.9
Philadelphia	+46.3	0.0	+46.3	+22.8	0.0	+22.8	+5.4	0.0	+5.4
Boston	+17.5	0.0	+17.5	+15.3	0.0	+15.3	+1.0	0.0	+1.0
Cincinnati	+48.9	−1.4	+47.5	+22.0	−0.1	+21.9	+8.8	0.0	+8.8
St. Louis	+49.2	0.0	+49.2	+28.3	0.0	+28.3	+6.4	0.0	+6.4
Buffalo	+52.1	0.0	+52.1	+14.5	0.0	+14.5	−0.2	0.0	−0.2
Chicago	+72.0	−0.5	+71.5	+35.2	−0.2	+35.0	+13.7	0.0	+13.7
Newark	+26.5	0.0	+26.5	+17.3	0.0	+17.3	−2.3	0.0	−2.3
Cleveland	+67.3	0.0	+67.3	+27.0	0.0	+27.0	+0.9	0.0	+0.9
Detroit	+72.6	0.0	+72.6	+28.1	0.0	+28.1	+7.8	0.0	+7.8
Milwaukee	+75.5	−32.9	+42.6	+29.0	−1.3	+27.7	+10.8	0.0	+10.8
Pittsburgh	+17.2	0.0	+17.2	+4.5	0.0	+4.5	−2.2	0.0	−2.2
Paterson*	+47.6	0.0	+47.6	+18.6	0.0	+18.6	−4.4	0.0	−4.4
NORTH-OLD									
Columbus	+71.9	−28.9	+43.0	+34.8	−7.0	+27.8	+11.7	−1.1	+10.6
Indianapolis	+71.9	−15.8	+56.1	+45.5	−65.5	−20.0	+22.4	+2.0	+24.4
Kansas City	+65.5	−10.3	+55.2	+32.1	−11.0	+21.2	+14.7	0.0	+14.7
Hartford	+44.4	0.0	+44.4	+28.1	0.0	+28.1	+4.3	0.0	+4.3
Minneapolis*	91.3	0.0	91.3	+52.3	0.0	+52.3	+20.6	0.0	+20.6
SOUTH-OLD									
Baltimore	+70.4	0.0	+70.4	+34.8	0.0	+34.8	+19.1	0.0	+19.1
New Orleans	+97.0	0.0	+97.0	+62.0	0.0	+62.0	+39.0	0.0	+39.0
Washington, DC	+84.5	0.0	+84.5	+60.1	0.0	+60.1	+12.5	0.0	+12.5
Atlanta	+60.0	−32.2	+27.8	+62.0	−0.5	+61.5	+45.8	0.0	+45.8

APPENDIX TABLE E.7D (continued)

Percent Population Change in Suburbs

Metropolitan Area Groupings/ Metropolitan Areas	1950–1960			1960–1970			1970–1980		
	Growth	Annexation	Total	Growth	Annexation	Total	Growth	Annexation	Total
WEST-OLD									
San Francisco*	+57.9	0.0	+57.9	+31.9	0.0	+31.9	+9.9	0.0	+9.9
Denver*	+153.3	-30.1	+123.2	+82.1	-18.9	+63.2	+60.1	-0.2	+59.9
Los Angeles*	+70.0	-3.4	+66.6	+21.0	-0.6	+20.4	+7.3	-0.1	+7.2
Portland	+39.0	-3.4	+35.6	+43.0	-3.4	+39.6	+41.0	-1.3	+39.7
Seattle*	+73.7	-25.1	+48.6	+67.3	-2.5	+64.8	+26.2	-0.1	+26.1
SOUTH-YOUNG									
San Antonio	+115.1	-104.2	+10.9	+59.4	-1.6	+57.8	+54.8	-32.6	+22.2
Dallas*	+89.1	-49.6	+39.5	+65.5	-3.1	+62.4	+48.5	-0.6	+47.9
Houston	+111.6	-71.5	+40.1	+62.8	-7.2	+55.6	+98.3	-27.2	+71.1
Tampa*	+137.2	-67.7	+69.5	+72.9	-4.4	+68.5	+78.1	0.0	+78.1
Miami	+161.7	0.0	+161.7	+45.0	0.0	+45.0	+37.1	0.0	+37.1
Ft. Lauderdale*	+570.3	-23.6	+546.7	+99.2	-25.5	+73.7	+99.1	-0.1	+99.0
WEST-YOUNG									
Sacramento	+119.3	-23.8	+95.5	+40.7	-14.7	+26.0	+35.0	0.0	+35.0
San Diego	+136.3	-29.6	+106.7	+45.8	-2.2	+43.6	+49.4	0.0	+49.4
San Jose	+175.3	-50.9	+124.4	+56.4	-18.2	+38.2	+8.8	+1.1	+9.9
Phoenix	+147.5	-147.8	-0.3	+101.2	-28.7	+72.5	+94.9	-9.0	+85.9
Riverside*	+89.5	-5.5	+84.0	+50.2	-9.1	+41.1	+43.1	-0.5	+42.6
Anaheim*	+240.9	-68.4	+172.5	+145.3	-9.7	+135.6	+42.2	-0.4	+41.8

SOURCES: *Census of Population, 1960*, Vol. I, *Characteristics of the Population*, A. Number of Inhabitants (States), table 9. *Census of Population, 1970*, Vol. I, *Characteristics of the Population*, A. Number of Inhabitants, Section 1 (United States Summary, Table 40), and unpublished 1980 estimates from the U.S. Bureau of the Census.

[a]1980 metropolitan areas with populations greater than 1,000,000 defined as 1980 SMSAs and NECMAs (in New England) except for New York and Paterson–Clifton–Passaic (see Appendix F).

*Largest of multiple central cities (complete metropolitan area names are listed in Appendix F).

APPENDIX TABLE E.7E

Average Annual Percent Change for Central Cities and Suburbs and Suburbanization Rates: 39 Metropolitan Areas, 1950–1960, 1960–1970, 1970–1980, and Estimates for 1980–1984

Metropolitan Area Groupings/ Metropolitan Areas	Central City Average Annual % Change				Suburb Average Annual % Change				Annual Suburbanization Rate[a]			
	1950–1960	1960–1970	1970–1980	1980–1984 (est.)	1950–1960	1960–1970	1970–1980	1980–1984 (est.)	1950–1960	1960–1970	1970–1980	1980–1984 (est.)
NORTH-DECLINING												
New York	-0.1	+0.1	-1.1	+0.3	+5.7	+2.4	+0.2	+0.4	+5.8	+2.3	+1.3	+0.1
Philadelphia	-0.3	-0.3	-1.4	-0.6	+3.9	+2.1	+0.5	+0.8	+4.2	+2.4	+1.9	+1.4
Boston	-1.4	-0.8	-1.3	+0.3	+1.6	+1.4	+0.1	+0.2	+3.0	+2.2	+1.4	-0.1
Cincinnati	0.0	-1.0	-1.6	-1.0	+4.0	+2.0	+0.9	+0.5	+4.0	+3.0	+2.5	+1.5
St. Louis	-1.3	-1.9	-3.1	-1.3	+4.1	+2.5	+0.6	+0.6	+5.4	+4.4	+3.7	+1.9
Buffalo	-0.9	-1.4	-2.5	-1.4	+4.3	+1.4	0.0	-0.6	+5.2	+2.8	+2.5	+0.8
Chicago	-0.2	-0.5	-1.1	-0.1	+5.5	+3.1	+1.3	+0.8	+5.7	+3.6	+2.4	+0.9
Newark	-0.8	-0.6	-1.5	-1.2	+2.4	+1.6	-0.2	+0.2	+3.2	+2.2	+1.3	+1.4
Cleveland	-0.4	-1.5	-2.7	-1.2	+5.3	+2.4	+0.1	-0.1	+5.7	+3.9	+2.8	+1.1
Detroit	-1.0	-1.0	-2.3	-2.5	+5.6	+2.5	+0.8	-0.4	+6.6	+3.5	+3.1	+2.1
Milwaukee	+1.5	-0.3	-1.2	-0.6	+3.6	+2.5	+1.0	+0.4	+2.1	+2.8	+2.2	+1.0
Pittsburgh	-1.1	-1.5	-2.0	-1.3	+1.6	+0.4	-0.2	-0.4	+2.7	+1.9	+1.8	+0.9
Paterson*	+0.7	+0.1	-0.6	+0.3	+4.0	+1.7	-0.5	+0.1	+3.3	+1.6	+0.1	-0.2
NORTH-OLD												
Columbus	+2.3	+1.4	+0.5	+0.1	+3.6	+2.5	+1.0	+1.4	+1.3	+1.1	+0.5	+1.3
Indianapolis	+1.1	+4.5	-0.5	+0.3	+4.6	-2.2	+2.2	+1.0	+3.5	-6.7	+2.7	+0.7
Kansas City	+0.4	+0.7	-1.2	-0.3	+4.5	+1.9	+1.4	+1.2	+4.1	+1.2	+2.6	+1.5
Hartford	-0.9	-0.3	-1.5	-0.1	+3.7	+2.5	+0.4	+0.5	+4.6	+2.8	+1.9	+0.6
Minneapolis*	-0.5	-0.7	-1.5	-0.7	+6.7	+4.3	+1.9	+1.8	+7.2	+5.0	+3.4	+2.5
SOUTH-OLD												
Baltimore	-0.1	-0.4	-1.4	-0.7	+5.5	+3.0	+1.8	+1.2	+5.6	+3.4	+3.2	+1.9
New Orleans	+1.0	-0.6	-0.6	+0.1	+7.0	+4.9	+3.4	+1.9	+6.0	+5.5	+4.0	+1.8
Washington, DC	-0.5	-0.1	-1.7	-0.6	+6.3	+4.8	+1.2	+1.8	+6.8	+4.9	+2.9	+2.4
Atlanta	+3.9	+0.2	-1.5	+0.1	+2.5	+4.9	+3.8	+3.4	-1.4	+4.7	+5.3	+3.3

APPENDIX TABLE E.7E (continued)

Metropolitan Area Groupings/ Metropolitan Areas	Central City Average Annual % Change				Suburb Average Annual % Change				Annual Suburbanization Rate[a]			
	1950–1960	1960–1970	1970–1980	1980–1984 (est.)	1950–1960	1960–1970	1970–1980	1980–1984 (est.)	1950–1960	1960–1970	1970–1980	1980–1984 (est.)
WEST-OLD												
San Francisco*	−0.5	−0.3	−0.6	+1.1	+4.7	+2.8	+0.9	+1.3	+5.2	+3.1	+1.5	+0.2
Denver*	+2.0	+0.9	−0.2	+0.6	+8.4	+5.0	+4.8	+3.6	+6.4	+4.1	+5.0	+3.0
Los Angeles*	+2.4	+1.2	+0.5	+1.1	+5.2	+1.9	+0.7	+1.6	+2.8	+0.7	+0.2	+0.5
Portland	0.0	+0.2	−0.4	0.0	+3.1	+3.4	+3.4	+1.2	+3.1	+3.2	+3.8	+1.2
Seattle*	+1.8	−0.2	−0.6	−0.1	+4.0	+5.1	+2.3	+2.0	+2.2	+5.3	+2.9	+2.1
SOUTH-YOUNG												
San Antonio	+3.7	+1.1	+1.9	+1.8	+1.0	+4.7	+2.0	+4.9	−2.7	+3.6	+0.1	+3.1
Dallas*	+3.8	+1.8	+0.4	+1.9	+3.4	+5.0	+4.0	+4.6	−0.4	+3.2	+3.6	+2.7
Houston	+4.6	+2.8	+2.6	+1.7	+3.4	+4.5	+5.5	+5.9	−1.2	+1.7	+2.9	+4.2
Tampa*	+7.5	+0.8	+0.3	+0.3	+5.4	+5.4	+5.9	+3.7	−2.1	+4.6	+5.6	+3.4
Miami	+1.6	+1.4	+0.4	+1.8	+10.1	+3.8	+3.2	+1.1	+8.5	+2.4	+2.8	−0.7
Ft. Lauderdale*	+8.9	+7.6	+1.1	−0.4	+20.5	+5.7	+7.1	+2.6	+11.6	−1.9	+6.0	+3.0
WEST-YOUNG												
Sacramento	+3.4	+3.0	+0.7	+2.5	+6.9	+2.3	+3.1	+2.6	+3.5	−0.7	+2.4	+0.1
San Diego	+5.5	+2.0	+2.3	+2.3	+7.5	+3.7	+4.1	+2.8	+2.0	+1.7	+1.8	+0.5
San Jose	+7.9	+8.5	+3.2	+2.2	+8.4	+3.3	+1.0	+0.7	+0.5	−5.2	−2.2	−1.5
Phoenix	+15.2	+2.9	+3.1	+2.0	0.0	+5.6	+6.4	+4.6	−15.2	+2.7	+3.3	+2.6
Riverside*	+5.3	+3.4	+2.0	+2.7	+6.3	+3.5	+3.6	+4.2	+1.0	+0.1	+1.6	+1.5
Anaheim*	+16.3	+4.4	+2.1	+1.9	+10.5	+9.0	+3.6	+1.8	−5.8	+4.6	+1.5	−0.1

SOURCES: U.S. Bureau of the Census, *Current Population Reports*, series P-25, no. 976, *Patterns of Metropolitan Areas and County Population Growth: 1980 to 1984*; and machine-readable computer files: *County and City Data Book*, Consolidated Files for Counties, 1947–1977, and Cities, 1944–1977; and *County and City Data Book*, 1983 files [prepared by the U.S. Bureau of the Census, Washington, DC].

[a] Annual Suburbanization Rate: Suburb Average Annual Percent Change minus Central City Average Annual Percent Change.

*Largest of multiple central cities.

519

APPENDIX TABLE E.8A

Black Percent Population Change for Metropolitan Areas, Central Cities, and Suburbs, and Suburbanization Rates, 1950–1960, 1960–1970, 1970–1980: 39 Metropolitan Areas[a]

Metropolitan Area Groupings/ Metropolitan Areas	Percent Population Change									Suburbanization Rate[b]		
	Metropolitan Areas			Central Cities			Suburbs					
	1950–1960	1960–1970	1970–1980	1950–1960	1960–1970	1970–1980	1950–1960	1960–1970	1970–1980	1950–1960	1960–1970	1970–1980
NORTH-DECLINING												
New York	+49.7	+53.5	+10.0	+45.7	+52.9	+7.3	+90.6	+57.7	+30.3	+44.8	+4.8	+22.9
Philadelphia	+39.7	+25.9	+4.6	+40.6	+23.6	-2.2	+36.6	+34.5	+28.0	-4.0	+10.9	+30.3
Boston	+52.8	+60.1	+27.0	+58.4	+64.7	+21.0	+38.5	+46.6	+46.8	-19.9	-18.1	+25.8
Cincinnati	+34.4	+18.2	+12.3	+38.8	+15.3	+4.3	+16.3	+32.8	+47.1	-22.5	+17.5	+42.9
St. Louis	+36.2	+28.5	+7.2	+39.5	+18.6	-19.0	+28.3	+54.5	+60.6	-11.2	+35.9	+79.6
Buffalo	+86.4	+31.5	+5.7	+93.4	+33.2	+1.3	+53.0	+21.1	+34.9	-40.3	-12.2	+33.6
Chicago	+64.0	+39.1	+16.7	+65.2	+35.5	+8.7	+51.4	+82.9	+90.4	-13.7	+47.4	+81.8
Newark	+67.2	+55.7	+17.5	+84.3	+50.1	-7.4	+46.4	+64.2	+52.2	-37.9	+14.1	+59.6
Cleveland	+68.8	+28.5	+3.8	+69.5	+14.8	-12.7	+51.8	+435.4	+109.0	-17.6	+420.6	+121.7
Detroit	+56.3	+35.1	+17.0	+60.6	+36.8	+14.9	+34.3	+25.2	+30.8	-26.4	-11.6	+15.9
Milwaukee	+184.5	+69.1	+40.8	+186.0	+68.2	+40.4	+118.5	+119.1	+59.0	-67.5	+50.9	+18.6
Pittsburgh	+18.1	+5.5	+3.4	+22.4	+4.1	-3.3	+11.4	+7.9	+14.4	-11.0	+3.8	+17.8
Paterson*	+88.8	+74.3	+22.4	+127.9	+89.3	+18.0	+50.2	+51.9	+30.6	-77.7	-37.4	+12.6
NORTH-OLD												
Columbus	+54.0	+28.5	+24.1	+65.5	+28.6	+25.5	-13.1	+28.5	+8.7	-78.7	-0.1	-16.8
Indianapolis	+52.6	+36.2	+14.2	+53.6	+36.7	+13.7	+25.9	+19.2	+32.1	-27.7	-17.6	+18.4
Kansas City	+33.2	+28.5	+14.1	+49.5	+34.7	+9.1	+5.4	+13.3	+28.3	-44.0	-21.4	+19.2
Hartford	+95.8	+74.1	+23.6	+96.1	+77.7	+4.6	+94.8	+64.5	+79.1	-1.2	-13.2	+74.4
Minneapolis*	+60.1	+55.6	+53.5	+58.3	+51.8	+38.5	+113.9	+141.0	+262.7	+55.7	+89.2	+224.2
SOUTH-OLD												
Baltimore	+39.7	+26.9	+13.3	+44.8	+29.0	+2.5	+17.4	+15.8	+77.4	-27.3	-13.2	+74.9
New Orleans	+33.9	+16.4	+19.8	+28.4	+14.4	+15.3	+73.0	+27.0	+40.6	+44.6	+12.6	+25.3
Washington, DC.	+43.6	+41.8	+18.9	+46.6	+30.7	-16.7	+31.9	+90.1	+125.0	-14.7	+59.4	+141.6
Atlanta	+29.4	+30.3	+43.7	+53.9	+36.6	+11.1	-5.8	+15.5	+134.3	-59.7	-21.0	+123.3

APPENDIX TABLE E.8A (continued)

Metropolitan Area Groupings/ Metropolitan Areas	Metropolitan Areas			Central Cities			Suburbs			Suburbanization Rate[b]		
	1950–1960	1960–1970	1970–1980	1950–1960	1960–1970	1970–1980	1950–1960	1960–1970	1970–1980	1950–1960	1960–1970	1970–1980
WEST-OLD												
San Francisco*	+60.6	+46.4	+18.3	+73.3	+39.8	+11.3	+37.3	+61.6	+32.5	−36.0	+21.8	+21.2
Denver*	+95.3	+59.3	+55.3	+99.3	+56.9	+26.8	+25.9	+126.4	+595.1	−73.4	+69.5	+568.3
Los Angeles*	+110.6	+67.2	+22.9	+96.2	+51.7	+4.3	+170.4	+113.8	+62.5	+74.1	+62.1	+58.3
Portland	+54.9	+37.4	+45.1	+64.3	+36.8	+30.9	−10.2	+44.8	+215.5	−74.4	+8.0	+184.5
Seattle*	+68.3	+45.8	+38.8	+70.5	+41.3	+24.4	+39.0	+120.0	+192.0	−31.5	+78.7	+167.6
SOUTH-YOUNG												
San Antonio	+34.6	+22.1	+20.9	+45.2	+20.6	+14.4	−5.0	+30.7	+54.5	−50.2	+10.1	+40.1
Dallas*	+49.2	+45.1	+26.4	+97.5	+55.6	+22.3	−28.3	−1.4	+55.1	−125.8	−57.0	+32.8
Houston*	+55.5	+37.4	+35.3	+72.2	+47.6	+38.6	+19.3	+5.5	+20.8	−52.9	−42.1	−17.8
Tampa*	+55.4	+22.2	+28.2	+70.1	+23.3	+20.5	+22.4	+18.6	+53.3	−47.6	−4.7	+32.8
Miami	+111.6	+38.4	+47.9	+62.3	+16.3	+14.5	+192.1	+58.3	+70.2	+129.9	+42.0	+55.8
Ft. Lauderdale*	+158.6	+41.5	+46.2	+133.4	+12.1	+53.1	+178.3	+60.9	+43.1	+44.9	+48.8	−10.0
WEST-YOUNG												
Sacramento	+149.1	+85.8	+59.7	+166.1	+125.7	+35.2	+128.4	+29.4	+120.1	−37.7	−96.3	+84.9
San Diego	+130.5	+59.1	+67.2	+130.8	+54.0	+46.3	+128.6	+95.2	+183.5	−2.1	+41.1	+137.2
San Jose	+161.7	+302.8	+136.5	+245.5	+442.1	+160.1	+117.7	+186.9	+99.4	−127.8	−255.1	−60.7
Phoenix	+75.0	+31.0	+44.9	+306.2	+31.3	+36.3	−55.2	+29.2	+88.9	−361.3	−2.2	+52.6
Riverside*	+128.5	+69.7	+56.6	+218.0	+83.6	+40.8	+89.4	+59.5	+69.9	−128.7	−24.2	+29.1
Anaheim*	+296.0	+182.6	+146.9	+256.2	+286.7	+65.6	+348.7	+73.0	+338.1	+92.5	−213.6	+272.5

SOURCES: Machine-readable computer files: *County and City Data Book*, Consolidated File for Counties, 1947–1977, and Cities, 1944–1977; and *County and City Data Book*, 1983 file [prepared by the U.S. Bureau of the Census, Washington, DC].

[a] 1980 metropolitan areas with population greater than 1,000,000 defined as 1980 SMSAs and NECMAs (in New England) except for New York and Paterson–Clifton–Passaic (see Appendix F).

[b] Suburbanization Rate: Suburb Percent Change minus Central City Percent Change.

* Largest of multiple central cities (complete metropolitan area names are listed in Appendix F).

APPENDIX TABLE E.8B

Nonblack Percent Population Change for Metropolitan Areas, Central Cities, and Suburbs, and Suburbanization Rates, 1950–1960, 1960–1970, 1970–1980: 39 Metropolitan Areas[a]

Metropolitan Area Groupings/ Metropolitan Areas	Metropolitan Areas			Central Cities			Suburbs			Suburbanization Rate[b]		
	1950–1960	1960–1970	1970–1980	1950–1960	1960–1970	1970–1980	1950–1960	1960–1970	1970–1980	1950–1960	1960–1970	1970–1980
NORTH-DECLINING												
New York	+8.5	+2.6	−9.6	−6.3	−6.9	−15.2	+74.1	+25.4	+0.2	+80.4	+32.3	+15.4
Philadelphia	+15.1	+8.4	−3.7	−13.1	−12.0	−19.1	+47.0	+22.0	+3.8	+60.1	+34.1	+22.8
Boston	+8.7	+9.2	−2.3	−16.8	−15.3	−18.6	+17.4	+15.1	+0.5	+34.1	+30.4	+19.2
Cincinnati	+22.9	+8.3	−0.4	−7.5	−16.7	−22.3	+48.7	+21.6	+7.6	+56.2	+38.2	+29.9
St. Louis	+17.4	+9.9	−4.0	−23.8	−31.3	−32.9	+50.7	+26.7	+2.3	+74.5	+58.0	+35.2
Buffalo	+17.2	+1.3	−9.1	−15.0	−20.3	−28.8	+52.1	+14.4	−0.7	+67.1	+34.6	+28.1
Chicago	+15.1	+7.7	−1.3	−12.5	−17.2	−20.3	+72.1	+33.8	+11.0	+84.6	+51.0	+31.3
Newark	+12.2	+6.0	−9.0	−26.6	−34.6	−21.3	+25.4	+14.2	−7.6	+52.0	+48.8	+13.7
Cleveland	+19.7	+4.9	−10.3	−18.4	−25.9	−30.3	+67.4	+23.7	−2.9	+85.9	+49.6	+27.4
Detroit	+20.5	+8.5	−5.7	−23.3	−28.1	−47.9	+74.4	+28.2	+7.0	+97.7	+56.3	+54.9
Milwaukee	+22.5	+6.7	−3.9	+10.3	−9.8	−20.2	+42.5	+27.5	+10.7	+32.2	+37.3	+30.8
Pittsburgh	+8.1	−0.6	−6.4	−15.3	−17.6	−22.3	+17.4	+4.3	−2.8	+32.7	+21.9	+19.5
Paterson[*]	+34.0	+12.1	−6.4	+1.4	−8.1	−11.3	+47.5	+17.9	−5.3	+46.1	+26.0	+6.0
NORTH-OLD												
Columbus	+30.6	+19.5	+5.4	+19.7	+11.8	−0.1	+44.7	+27.8	+10.6	+25.1	+15.9	+10.7
Indianapolis	+27.6	+15.4	+3.7	+4.1	+59.4	−9.0	+56.3	−20.3	+24.3	+52.3	−79.7	+33.3
Kansas City	+27.7	+13.3	+2.8	−2.1	+0.7	−17.6	+59.5	+21.5	+13.9	+61.7	+20.8	+31.5
Hartford	+28.2	+20.0	+0.2	−16.6	−17.1	−20.8	+43.9	+27.6	+3.0	+60.5	+44.6	+23.8
Minneapolis[*]	+27.3	+22.6	+6.8	−5.4	−8.0	−16.0	+91.3	+52.3	+20.1	+96.7	+60.3	+36.2
SOUTH-OLD												
Baltimore	+20.1	+11.5	+2.4	−15.4	−20.8	−26.7	+76.4	+36.2	+15.3	+91.8	+57.0	+42.0
New Orleans	+24.6	+14.9	+10.6	+1.4	−17.2	−23.6	+102.3	+68.6	+38.7	+100.9	+85.8	+62.3
Washington, DC	+36.0	+36.8	+0.7	−32.5	−37.9	−13.1	+90.3	+57.8	+2.2	+122.7	+95.7	+15.4
Atlanta	+37.0	+38.3	+22.6	+43.2	−20.2	−40.9	+34.2	+67.5	+37.7	−9.0	+87.7	+78.7

APPENDIX TABLE E.8B (continued)

Metropolitan Area Groupings/ Metropolitan Areas	Percent Population Change									Suburbanization Rate[b]		
	Metropolitan Areas			Central Cities			Suburbs					
	1950–1960	1960–1970	1970–1980	1950–1960	1960–1970	1970–1980	1950–1960	1960–1970	1970–1980	1950–1960	1960–1970	1970–1980
WEST-OLD												
San Francisco*	+21.4	+14.7	+2.9	−11.1	−9.8	−9.8	+59.0	+30.5	+8.6	+70.1	+40.3	+18.3
Denver*	+50.5	+31.7	+29.7	+19.2	+6.5	−4.7	+123.7	+63.0	+57.8	+104.5	+56.5	+62.5
Los Angeles*	+41.8	+12.4	+4.1	+21.2	+6.8	+5.1	+64.2	+16.9	+3.4	+43.1	+10.1	−1.7
Portland	+16.0	+22.2	+22.9	−1.9	+0.4	−5.6	+35.8	+39.6	+39.2	+37.8	+39.2	+44.8
Seattle*	+30.3	+28.2	+12.1	+17.5	−4.2	−8.3	+48.6	+64.6	+25.4	+31.1	+68.8	+33.7
SOUTH-YOUNG												
San Antonio	+35.8	+20.6	+20.7	+43.8	+10.6	+20.6	+11.8	+59.2	+20.9	−32.0	+48.6	+0.2
Dallas*	+42.0	+35.6	+24.9	+37.3	+11.6	−1.4	+48.4	+66.4	+47.6	+11.1	+54.8	+49.0
Houston	+49.9	+40.4	+47.7	+53.5	+26.7	+26.1	+44.1	+63.7	+76.3	−9.3	+37.0	+50.2
Tampa*	+93.6	+36.1	+46.0	+114.3	+5.5	−0.4	+74.0	+71.9	+79.2	−40.3	+66.4	+79.6
Miami	+85.4	+35.1	+24.8	+8.3	+14.4	+0.4	+158.3	+43.3	+32.5	+150.0	+29.0	+32.1
Ft. Lauderdale*	+344.9	+94.4	+66.8	+134.8	+128.6	+6.8	+751.4	+76.1	+108.3	+616.6	−52.5	+101.4
WEST-YOUNG												
Sacramento	+72.3	+26.6	+24.5	+35.0	+28.0	+3.9	+95.0	+25.9	+33.3	+60.0	−2.0	+29.4
San Diego	+84.1	+30.4	+35.7	+68.7	+19.6	+23.8	+106.5	+43.1	+47.4	+37.9	+23.5	+23.6
San Jose	+120.8	+64.2	+19.6	+113.5	+122.0	+33.8	+124.4	+37.3	+8.9	+10.9	−84.7	−24.9
Phoenix	+101.1	+47.0	+55.7	+311.4	+33.1	+35.1	+2.1	+73.3	+85.9	−309.3	+40.2	+50.8
Riverside*	+77.8	+39.6	+35.9	+63.4	+36.9	+19.7	+83.8	+40.5	+41.7	+20.5	+3.6	+22.0
Anaheim*	+225.3	+101.5	+35.2	+353.0	+52.0	+22.6	+172.0	+135.8	+40.9	−181.0	+83.8	+18.3

SOURCES: Machine-readable computer files: *County and City Data Book*, Consolidated File for Counties, 1947–1977, and Cities, 1944–1977; and *County and City Data Book*, 1983 file (prepared by the U.S. Bureau of the Census, Washington, DC).

[a]1980 metropolitan areas with populations greater than 1,000,000 defined as 1980 SMSAs and NECMAs (in New England) except for New York and Paterson–Clifton–Passaic (see Appendix F).

[b]Suburbanization Rate: Suburb Percent Change minus Central City Percent Change.

*Largest of multiple central cities (complete metropolitan area names are listed in Appendix F).

APPENDIX TABLE E.8C

Percentage of Population Black in Central Cities and Suburbs, 1950, 1960, 1970, 1980: 39 Metropolitan Areas[a]

Metropolitan Area Groupings/Metropolitan Areas	Metropolitan Areas				Central Cities				Suburbs			
	1950	1960	1970	1980	1950	1960	1970	1980	1950	1960	1970	1980
NORTH-DECLINING												
New York	8.6	11.4	16.2	19.1	9.5	14.0	21.1	25.3	4.3	4.7	5.8	7.5
Philadelphia	13.1	15.4	17.5	18.7	18.2	26.4	33.5	37.8	6.5	6.1	6.6	8.1
Boston	1.8	2.5	3.7	4.7	5.0	9.1	16.3	22.5	0.7	0.8	1.0	1.5
Cincinnati	9.5	10.3	11.1	12.4	15.5	21.6	27.6	33.9	3.6	2.9	3.1	4.2
St. Louis	12.1	13.8	15.7	17.3	17.9	28.6	40.9	45.5	6.8	5.8	7.0	10.6
Buffalo	4.1	6.3	8.0	9.2	6.3	13.3	20.4	26.7	1.5	1.5	1.6	2.2
Chicago	10.3	14.1	17.5	20.1	13.6	22.9	32.7	39.8	2.8	2.5	3.4	5.6
Newark	8.7	12.5	17.3	21.3	17.1	34.1	54.3	58.3	5.5	6.3	8.9	13.8
Cleveland	10.0	13.6	16.1	18.2	16.2	28.6	38.3	43.8	0.9	0.8	3.4	7.1
Detroit	11.4	14.2	17.1	20.4	16.2	28.9	43.6	63.0	4.5	3.5	3.4	4.1
Milwaukee	2.2	5.0	7.6	10.8	3.4	8.4	14.6	23.1	0.1	0.2	0.3	0.5
Pittsburgh	6.2	6.7	7.1	7.8	12.2	16.7	20.2	24.0	3.5	3.3	3.4	4.0
Paterson*	2.6	3.6	5.5	7.1	4.3	9.3	17.4	21.9	1.9	1.9	2.4	3.3
NORTH-OLD												
Columbus	8.6	10.0	10.6	12.3	12.4	16.4	18.4	22.1	3.1	1.9	1.9	1.8
Indianapolis	9.1	10.7	12.4	13.5	15.0	20.6	18.2	21.8	0.8	0.6	1.0	1.0
Kansas City	10.2	10.6	11.9	13.0	12.2	17.5	22.1	27.3	8.0	5.4	5.1	5.7
Hartford	2.7	4.0	5.7	7.0	7.1	15.3	27.9	33.8	1.0	1.3	1.7	3.0
Minneapolis*	1.0	1.3	1.6	2.3	1.5	2.5	4.0	6.5	0.1	0.1	0.2	0.5
SOUTH-OLD												
Baltimore	19.0	21.4	23.7	25.6	23.7	34.7	46.4	54.8	10.2	7.0	6.0	9.0
New Orleans	29.1	30.6	30.9	32.6	31.9	37.2	45.0	55.3	18.1	15.9	12.5	12.6
Washington, DC	23.0	24.0	24.7	27.9	35.0	53.9	71.1	70.2	9.9	7.0	8.4	16.7
Atlanta	23.8	22.8	21.7	24.6	36.6	38.3	51.5	66.6	15.8	11.7	8.4	13.4

APPENDIX TABLE E.8C *(continued)*

Metropolitan Area Groupings/ Metropolitan Areas	Metropolitan Areas				Central Cities				Suburbs			
	1950	1960	1970	1980	1950	1960	1970	1980	1950	1960	1970	1980
WEST-OLD												
San Francisco*	6.6	8.5	10.6	12.0	7.9	14.2	20.5	24.1	5.1	4.4	5.4	6.5
Denver*	2.6	3.4	4.0	4.8	3.5	5.7	8.2	10.6	0.5	0.3	0.4	1.7
Los Angeles*	5.2	7.6	10.9	12.6	7.9	12.2	16.5	16.4	2.2	3.6	6.3	9.6
Portland	1.5	2.1	2.3	2.7	2.6	4.2	5.6	7.7	0.4	0.3	0.3	0.6
Seattle*	2.0	2.6	2.9	3.6	3.2	4.5	6.5	8.6	0.3	0.3	0.4	1.0
SOUTH-YOUNG												
San Antonio	6.7	6.7	6.7	6.8	7.0	7.1	7.7	7.3	5.8	5.0	4.1	5.2
Dallas*	12.5	13.1	13.9	14.0	13.2	17.9	23.3	27.4	11.6	6.0	3.6	3.8
Houston	19.2	19.8	19.5	18.1	20.9	22.9	25.7	27.6	16.3	13.9	9.4	6.7
Tampa*	13.9	11.5	10.4	9.3	18.7	15.4	17.6	20.5	8.8	6.4	4.5	3.9
Miami	13.1	14.7	15.0	17.3	16.2	22.4	22.7	25.1	10.0	11.2	12.2	15.2
Ft. Lauderdale*	25.2	16.4	12.5	11.1	18.4	18.3	9.9	13.6	35.7	15.4	14.2	10.2
WEST-YOUNG												
Sacramento	2.3	3.3	4.8	6.0	3.3	6.3	10.6	13.4	1.7	2.0	2.0	3.3
San Diego	3.1	3.8	4.6	5.6	4.5	6.0	7.6	8.9	1.0	1.1	1.4	2.7
San Jose	0.6	0.7	1.7	3.3	0.6	1.0	2.4	4.6	0.6	0.6	1.2	2.1
Phoenix	4.3	3.8	3.4	3.2	4.9	4.8	4.7	4.8	4.1	1.8	1.4	1.4
Riverside*	2.9	3.7	4.4	5.1	3.0	5.6	7.4	8.6	2.8	2.9	3.3	3.9
Anaheim*	0.4	0.5	0.7	1.3	0.8	0.6	1.6	2.1	0.3	0.4	0.3	0.9

SOURCES: Machine-readable computer files: *County and City Data Book*, Consolidated File for Counties, 1947–1977, and Cities, 1944–1977; and *County and City Data Book*, 1983 file (prepared by the U.S. Bureau of the Census, Washington, DC).

[a]1980 metropolitan areas with populations greater than 1,000,000 defined as 1980 SMSAs and NECMAs (in New England) except for New York and Paterson–Clifton–Passaic (see Appendix F).

*Largest of multiple central cities (complete metropolitan area names are listed in Appendix F).

APPENDIX TABLE E.8D

City Shares of Black and Nonblack Metropolitan Area Population and Index of City–Suburb Dissimilarity, 1950, 1960, 1970, 1980: 39 Metropolitan Areas[a]

Metropolitan Area Groupings/ Metropolitan Areas	City Share of Metropolitan Areas								Index of City–Suburb Dissimilarity			
	Blacks				Nonblacks							
	1950	1960	1970	1980	1950	1960	1970	1980	1950	1960	1970	1980
NORTH-DECLINING												
New York	91.1	88.7	88.4	86.3	81.6	70.5	63.9	60.0	9.5	18.3	24.5	26.3
Philadelphia	78.3	78.8	77.4	72.3	53.1	40.1	32.6	27.4	25.2	38.7	44.8	44.9
Boston	71.8	74.5	76.6	73.0	25.3	19.4	15.0	12.5	46.5	55.1	61.6	60.5
Cincinnati	80.6	83.2	81.1	75.3	46.0	34.6	26.6	20.8	34.6	48.6	54.5	54.5
St. Louis	70.9	72.6	67.0	50.6	44.7	29.0	18.1	12.7	26.2	43.6	48.9	38.0
Buffalo	82.8	85.9	87.0	83.4	52.0	37.7	29.7	23.2	30.8	48.1	57.3	60.1
Chicago	91.9	92.5	90.1	83.9	67.4	51.2	39.4	31.9	24.5	41.2	50.7	52.0
Newark	54.8	60.4	58.2	45.9	25.4	16.6	10.3	8.9	29.4	43.8	48.0	37.0
Cleveland	96.4	96.7	86.4	72.7	55.6	37.9	26.8	20.8	40.8	58.8	59.7	51.9
Detroit	83.5	85.8	86.9	85.3	55.1	35.1	23.2	12.8	28.4	50.7	63.6	72.5
Milwaukee	97.8	98.3	97.8	97.5	62.1	55.9	47.2	39.2	35.7	42.4	50.5	58.2
Pittsburgh	60.5	62.7	61.9	57.8	28.6	22.4	18.6	15.4	31.9	40.3	43.3	42.4
Paterson*	49.7	60.0	65.1	62.8	29.3	22.2	18.2	17.2	20.4	37.8	46.9	45.6
NORTH-OLD												
Columbus	85.4	91.7	91.7	92.8	56.5	51.8	48.4	45.9	28.9	40.0	43.3	46.9
Indianapolis	96.4	97.0	97.4	97.0	55.0	44.8	61.9	54.3	41.4	52.2	35.5	42.7
Kansas City	63.0	70.7	74.2	70.9	51.7	39.6	35.2	28.2	11.4	31.1	39.0	42.7
Hartford	72.9	73.0	74.5	63.0	26.0	16.9	11.7	9.2	46.9	56.1	62.8	53.8
Minneapolis*	96.8	95.7	93.3	84.2	66.2	49.2	36.9	29.1	30.5	46.4	56.4	55.2
SOUTH-OLD												
Baltimore	81.3	84.3	85.7	77.6	61.4	43.3	30.7	22.0	20.0	41.0	55.0	55.6
New Orleans	87.6	84.0	82.6	79.5	77.0	62.6	45.1	31.2	10.7	21.4	37.4	48.3
Washington, DC	79.6	81.3	74.9	52.5	44.2	22.0	10.0	8.6	35.4	59.3	64.9	43.9
Atlanta	59.0	70.1	73.5	56.8	31.9	33.3	19.2	9.3	27.1	36.8	54.3	47.5

APPENDIX TABLE E.8D (continued)

Metropolitan Area Groupings/ Metropolitan Areas	City Share of Metropolitan Areas								Index of City–Suburb Dissimilarity			
	Blacks				Nonblacks							
	1950	1960	1970	1980	1950	1960	1970	1980	1950	1960	1970	1980
WEST-OLD												
San Francisco*	64.8	69.9	66.7	62.8	53.6	39.2	30.8	27.0	11.2	30.7	35.9	35.7
Denver*	94.5	96.5	95.0	77.5	70.1	55.5	44.9	33.0	24.5	41.0	50.1	44.6
Los Angeles*	80.5	75.0	68.1	57.8	52.0	44.4	42.2	42.6	28.5	30.6	25.9	15.2
Portland	87.4	92.7	92.3	83.3	52.5	44.3	36.4	28.0	35.0	48.4	55.9	55.3
Seattle*	93.1	94.3	91.4	81.9	58.7	52.9	39.5	32.3	34.4	41.4	51.9	49.6
SOUTH-YOUNG												
San Antonio	78.8	85.0	84.0	79.5	75.1	79.5	72.9	72.9	3.7	5.5	11.1	6.6
Dallas*	61.6	81.6	87.5	84.6	58.2	56.3	46.4	36.6	3.4	25.3	41.1	48.0
Houston	68.5	75.8	81.4	83.4	61.6	63.1	56.9	48.6	6.9	12.8	24.5	34.8
Tampa*	69.3	75.8	76.5	71.9	48.7	53.9	41.8	28.5	20.6	21.9	34.8	43.4
Miami	62.0	47.5	40.0	30.9	48.6	28.4	24.0	19.3	13.4	19.2	16.0	11.6
Ft. Lauderdale*	43.9	39.6	31.4	32.9	65.9	34.8	40.9	26.2	22.0	4.8	9.5	6.6
WEST-YOUNG												
Sacramento	54.9	58.6	71.2	60.3	37.9	29.7	30.0	25.1	17.0	28.9	41.2	35.2
San Diego	87.5	87.6	84.8	74.2	59.2	54.2	49.8	45.4	28.3	33.4	35.1	28.8
San Jose	34.4	45.4	61.1	67.2	32.8	31.7	42.9	48.0	1.6	13.7	18.3	19.2
Phoenix	36.0	83.6	83.8	78.9	32.0	65.5	59.3	51.5	4.0	18.1	24.5	27.5
Riverside*	30.4	42.3	45.8	41.2	29.3	27.0	26.5	23.3	1.1	15.4	19.4	17.9
Anaheim*	57.0	51.3	70.2	47.1	29.4	41.0	30.9	28.0	27.6	10.3	39.3	19.1

SOURCES: Machine-readable computer files: *County and City Data Book*, Consolidated File for Counties, 1947–1977, and Cities, 1944–1977; and *County and City Data Book*, 1983 file (prepared by the U.S. Bureau of the Census, Washington, DC).

[a] 1980 metropolitan areas with populations greater than 1,000,000 defined as 1980 SMSAs and NECMAs (in New England) except for New York and Paterson–Clifton–Passaic (see Appendix F).

*Largest of multiple central cities (complete metropolitan area names are listed in Appendix F).

APPENDIX TABLE E.9A

Median Adjusted Family Income (in constant 1979 dollars) for Central Cities and Suburbs, and Suburb-to-City Ratios, 1950, 1960, 1970, 1980: 39 Metropolitan Areas[a]

| Metropolitan Area Groupings/ Metropolitan Areas | Median Adjusted Family Income (100s) | | | | | | | | | | | |
| | Central City | | | | Suburbs | | | | Suburb-to-City Ratio | | | |
	1950	1960	1970	1980	1950	1960	1970	1980	1950	1960	1970	1980
NORTH-DECLINING												
New York	10,748	15,171	19,154	16,818	13,077	19,728	26,570	26,756	1.22	1.30	1.39	1.59
Philadelphia	10,127	14,401	18,536	16,388	11,379	17,462	23,208	23,753	1.12	1.21	1.25	1.45
Boston	9,904	14,314	18,085	16,062	10,663	16,745	23,144	23,289	1.08	1.17	1.28	1.45
Cincinnati	9,712	14,199	17,612	16,800	10,185	16,620	21,621	23,065	1.05	1.17	1.23	1.37
St. Louis	9,770	13,337	16,184	15,265	10,776	16,742	22,172	23,163	1.10	1.26	1.37	1.52
Buffalo	10,367	14,229	17,414	15,432	10,980	17,330	22,249	22,646	1.06	1.22	1.28	1.47
Chicago	12,059	16,782	20,275	18,776	13,318	20,314	26,673	28,046	1.10	1.21	1.32	1.49
Newark	10,023	13,584	15,315	11,989	12,620	19,024	25,455	26,491	1.26	1.40	1.66	2.21
Cleveland	10,764	14,782	18,016	15,991	13,294	19,322	25,011	25,348	1.24	1.31	1.39	1.59
Detroit	12,056	15,116	19,877	17,033	11,946	18,169	25,948	27,151	0.99	1.20	1.31	1.59
Milwaukee	11,584	16,598	20,307	19,738	12,218	18,448	24,707	26,506	1.05	1.11	1.22	1.34
Pittsburgh	10,102	13,960	17,400	17,499	10,261	15,198	19,839	22,175	1.02	1.09	1.14	1.27
Paterson*	11,139	15,268	19,301	17,250	12,846	19,581	26,659	27,307	1.15	1.28	1.38	1.58
NORTH-OLD												
Columbus	11,157	14,899	19,265	18,612	10,282	16,192	21,633	23,062	0.92	1.09	1.12	1.24
Indianapolis	10,837	15,208	21,415	20,715	10,200	16,824	21,027	23,401	0.94	1.11	0.98	1.13
Kansas City	10,367	14,710	19,612	20,034	9,974	16,244	21,859	23,819	0.96	1.10	1.11	1.19
Hartford	10,544	14,919	18,035	14,032	11,498	17,968	24,685	24,526	1.09	1.20	1.37	1.75
Minneapolis*	11,532	16,082	20,198	20,177	10,431	17,347	24,449	26,256	0.90	1.08	1.21	1.30
SOUTH-OLD												
Baltimore	9,983	14,095	17,453	15,721	10,328	16,725	23,291	24,844	1.03	1.19	1.33	1.58
New Orleans	8,435	11,973	14,736	15,003	8,157	14,359	19,695	21,771	0.97	1.20	1.34	1.45
Washington, DC	11,584	14,926	18,962	19,099	14,056	20,291	27,986	29,811	1.21	1.36	1.48	1.56
Atlanta	8,121	12,525	16,629	13,591	8,200	14,463	21,903	22,824	1.01	1.15	1.32	1.68

APPENDIX TABLE E.9A (continued)

Metropolitan Area Groupings/ Metropolitan Areas	Central City				Suburbs				Suburb-to-City Ratio			
	1950	1960	1970	1980	1950	1960	1970	1980	1950	1960	1970	1980
WEST-OLD												
San Francisco*	11,852	16,371	20,176	19,728	12,367	18,814	24,980	26,516	1.04	1.15	1.24	1.34
Denver*	10,788	15,900	19,467	19,901	9,682	16,812	22,722	25,294	0.90	1.06	1.17	1.27
Los Angeles*	10,910	17,073	20,792	19,487	11,501	17,963	22,461	22,367	1.05	1.05	1.08	1.15
Portland	11,337	15,778	19,384	19,501	10,035	15,813	21,439	23,127	0.89	1.00	1.11	1.19
Seattle*	11,919	17,103	21,683	21,813	10,770	17,367	24,174	26,213	0.90	1.02	1.11	1.20
SOUTH-YOUNG												
San Antonio	8,185	11,684	15,309	15,859	8,090	11,920	17,156	20,875	0.99	1.02	1.12	1.32
Dallas*	10,489	14,458	15,344	19,251	8,099	14,052	21,305	23,859	0.77	0.97	1.10	1.24
Houston	10,331	14,700	19,552	21,881	9,962	14,481	21,130	27,231	0.96	0.99	1.08	1.24
Tampa*	7,398	11,168	14,915	15,407	7,081	10,862	15,315	17,062	0.96	0.97	1.03	1.11
Miami	9,157	11,083	14,453	13,355	9,938	14,344	19,617	20,017	1.09	1.29	1.36	1.50
Ft. Lauderdale*	9,200	13,011	19,190	19,521	6,432	12,119	18,566	19,616	0.70	0.93	0.97	1.00
WEST-YOUNG												
Sacramento	12,517	17,393	19,223	18,844	10,566	17,198	21,138	21,758	0.84	0.99	1.10	1.15
San Diego	10,834	16,473	20,116	20,133	10,075	16,095	19,998	20,438	0.93	0.98	0.99	1.02
San Jose	11,306	17,307	23,615	25,598	11,215	19,024	25,382	27,647	0.99	1.10	1.07	1.08
Phoenix	9,739	15,235	19,709	20,365	8,343	13,507	19,214	20,595	0.86	0.89	0.97	1.01
Riverside*	10,163	16,045	19,330	19,735	8,590	14,102	17,970	19,365	0.85	0.88	0.93	0.98
Anaheim*	10,069	17,699	22,217	22,238	10,139	18,129	25,148	27,291	1.01	1.03	1.13	1.23

SOURCES: Machine-readable computer files: *County and City Data Book*, Consolidated Files for Counties, 1947–1977, and Cities, 1944–1977; and *County and City Data Book*, 1983 file (prepared by the U.S. Bureau of the Census, Washington, DC).

a 1980 metropolitan areas with populations greater than 1,000,000 defined as 1980 SMSAs and NECMAs (in New England) except for New York and Paterson–Clifton–Passaic (see Appendix F).

* Largest of multiple central cities (complete metropolitan names are listed in Appendix F).

APPENDIX TABLE E.9B

Percent Distributions of Families by Income for Central Cities and Suburbs, 1970 and 1980, Nonblacks and Blacks: Six Metropolitan Area Groupings

Metropolitan Area Groupings/ Family Income (1979 Dollars)	Nonblacks				Blacks			
	Central City		Suburbs		Central City		Suburbs	
	1970	1980	1970	1980	1970	1980	1970	1980
NORTH-DECLINING								
30,000+	24.5	23.2	34.5	37.9	11.4	13.1	15.0	22.4
10,000–29,999	58.5	53.3	56.5	51.6	57.3	46.3	59.8	50.7
Under 10,000	17.0	23.5	9.1	10.5	31.3	40.6	25.3	26.9
Total	100.0	100.0	100.0	100.0	100.0	100.0	100.0	100.0
(Number in 100s)	(36,692)	(28,161)	(64,317)	(69,244)	(12,374)	(13,332)	(2,415)	(3,839)
NORTH-OLD								
30,000+	23.1	24.9	29.1	34.2	10.4	14.0	13.1	21.0
10,000–29,999	62.2	57.7	61.0	55.4	58.8	50.5	58.2	51.0
Under 10,000	14.8	17.4	9.9	10.4	30.8	35.5	28.7	28.0
Total	100.0	100.0	100.0	100.0	100.0	100.0	100.0	100.0
(Number in 100s)	(5,637)	(4,953)	(9,243)	(11,220)	(932)	(1,150)	(145)	(232)
SOUTH-OLD								
30,000+	27.1	31.1	35.6	40.7	11.3	13.4	13.6	23.8
10,000–29,999	56.3	49.7	55.2	49.4	54.8	46.2	58.8	53.4
Under 10,000	16.6	19.2	9.2	9.9	33.9	40.4	27.6	22.8
Total	100.0	100.0	100.0	100.0	100.0	100.0	100.0	100.0
(Number in 100s)	(3,153)	(2,180)	(11,525)	(14,028)	(3,270)	(3,393)	(802)	(1,971)

APPENDIX TABLE E.9B (continued)

Metropolitan Area Groupings/ Family Income (1979 Dollars)	Nonblacks				Blacks			
	Central City		Suburbs		Central City		Suburbs	
	1970	1980	1970	1980	1970	1980	1970	1980
WEST-OLD								
30,000+	28.7	30.1	30.8	36.0	11.1	14.2	15.7	22.7
10,000–29,999	55.0	50.4	57.5	50.9	56.9	47.5	59.0	50.6
Under 10,000	16.3	19.5	11.7	13.1	32.0	38.3	25.3	26.6
Total	100.0	100.0	100.0	100.0	100.0	100.0	100.0	100.0
(Number in 100s)	(12,298)	(11,427)	(19,673)	(22,839)	(1,980)	(2,191)	(793)	(1,404)
SOUTH-YOUNG								
30,000+	22.9	27.0	22.1	30.0	5.0	11.8	4.9	14.9
10,000–29,999	58.4	53.3	60.5	54.9	55.2	50.2	53.2	51.5
Under 10,000	18.7	19.7	17.3	15.1	39.8	38.0	41.8	33.7
Total	100.0	100.0	100.0	100.0	100.0	100.0	100.0	100.0
(Number in 100s)	(8,808)	(9,559)	(10,087)	(16,520)	(1,898)	(2,559)	(624)	(1,087)
WEST-YOUNG								
30,000+	25.1	28.7	27.9	32.6	9.6	16.2	10.3	18.9
10,000–29,999	59.2	54.6	56.5	52.0	56.9	49.9	59.1	51.5
Under 10,000	15.7	16.8	15.6	15.5	33.5	34.0	30.6	29.6
Total	100.0	100.0	100.0	100.0	100.0	100.0	100.0	100.0
(Number in 100s)	(6,428)	(8,124)	(10,053)	(14,700)	(318)	(533)	(114)	(308)

SOURCES: Machine-readable computer files: Census of Population and Housing, 1970, Fourth Count Population Summary Tape File; and Census of Population and Housing, 1980: Summary Tape File 3C (prepared by the U.S. Bureau of the Census, Washington, DC).

APPENDIX TABLE E.9C

Percent Distribution of Employed Civilian Male Workers by Occupation Class for Central Cities and Suburbs, 1970 and 1980, Nonblacks and Blacks: Six Metropolitan Area Groupings

Metropolitan Area Groupings/ Occupation Class[a]	Nonblacks				Blacks			
	Central City		Suburbs		Central City		Suburbs	
	1970	1980	1970	1980	1970	1980	1970	1980
NORTH-DECLINING								
White Collar	45.2	48.7	48.8	50.8	24.8	32.5	23.8	33.6
Service	11.1	13.1	6.9	8.3	16.7	19.4	15.8	16.2
Blue Collar	43.8	38.2	44.2	40.8	58.5	48.1	60.4	50.2
Total	100.0	100.0	100.0	100.0	100.0	100.0	100.0	100.0
(Number in 100s)	(35,772)	(27,607)	(64,408)	(70,683)	(10,188)	(9,215)	(2,142)	(3,171)
NORTH-OLD								
White Collar	45.8	49.8	46.6	49.2	22.4	29.7	24.7	38.1
Service	8.8	10.6	6.0	7.7	19.4	22.6	16.2	14.7
Blue Collar	45.5	39.6	47.4	43.1	58.1	47.7	59.1	47.2
Total	100.0	100.0	100.0	100.0	100.0	100.0	100.0	100.0
(Number in 100s)	(5,646)	(5,329)	(9,329)	(11,720)	(808)	(920)	(125)	(203)
SOUTH-OLD								
White Collar	56.0	61.8	56.7	57.8	26.3	32.2	24.5	38.9
Service	7.9	9.3	5.8	7.3	18.2	19.7	16.5	15.7
Blue Collar	36.2	28.8	37.5	34.9	55.5	48.1	59.0	45.4
Total	100.0	100.0	100.0	100.0	100.0	100.0	100.0	100.0
(Number in 100s)	(3,190)	(2,516)	(11,290)	(14,849)	(2,949)	(2,678)	(756)	(1,819)

APPENDIX TABLE E.9C (continued)

Metropolitan Area Groupings/ Occupation Class[a]	Nonblacks				Blacks			
	Central City		Suburbs		Central City		Suburbs	
	1970	1980	1970	1980	1970	1980	1970	1980
WEST-OLD								
White Collar	52.0	53.1	47.6	49.5	27.7	38.1	30.0	41.1
Service	9.8	11.1	7.3	8.1	19.9	18.4	15.5	15.2
Blue Collar	38.2	35.8	45.1	42.3	52.4	43.5	54.5	43.7
Total	100.0	100.0	100.0	100.0	100.0	100.0	100.0	100.0
(Number in 100s)	(12,357)	(13,651)	(19,300)	(24,541)	(1,620)	(1,775)	(651)	(1,202)
SOUTH-YOUNG								
White Collar	50.7	50.4	46.1	48.9	17.4	24.9	13.3	26.9
Service	7.5	8.6	6.5	7.7	17.7	15.8	14.8	14.9
Blue Collar	41.8	41.0	47.4	43.4	64.9	59.3	71.9	58.1
Total	100.0	100.0	100.0	100.0	100.0	100.0	100.0	100.0
(Number in 100s)	(8,381)	(10,469)	(8,913)	(15,717)	(1,705)	(2,298)	(569)	(994)
WEST-YOUNG								
White Collar	47.5	49.1	48.9	51.1	26.5	38.2	31.2	44.5
Service	9.4	10.0	8.4	8.9	20.1	17.5	15.9	16.1
Blue Collar	43.1	40.8	42.8	40.0	53.4	44.3	52.9	39.4
Total	100.0	100.0	100.0	100.0	100.0	100.0	100.0	100.0
(Number in 100s)	(5,928)	(8,474)	(8,896)	(14,332)	(234)	(425)	(80)	(251)

SOURCES: Machine-readable computer files: Census of Population and Housing, 1970, Fourth Count Population Summary Tape File; and Census of Population and Housing, 1980: Summary Tape File 3C [prepared by the U.S. Bureau of the Census, Washington, DC].

[a]Represents conventional 1970 census categories and equivalent 1980 census categories by regrouping 13 broad 1980 census categories. Note: Farm Workers are included with Blue Collar.

APPENDIX TABLE E.9D

Percent Distributions of Population, Aged 25 and Over, by Education Status for Central Cities and Suburbs, 1970 and 1980, Nonblacks and Blacks: Six Metropolitan Area Groupings

Metropolitan Area Groupings/ Education Status	Nonblacks				Blacks			
	Central City		Suburbs		Central City		Suburbs	
	1970	1980	1970	1980	1970	1980	1970	1980
NORTH-DECLINING								
College Graduate	10.2	17.3	14.3	20.6	3.7	7.2	5.5	11.3
High School Graduate	36.1	42.0	46.8	53.4	33.5	46.6	34.6	51.6
Less than HS Graduate	53.7	40.7	38.9	26.0	62.8	46.2	59.9	37.1
Total	100.0	100.0	100.0	100.0	100.0	100.0	100.0	100.0
(Number in 100s)	(87,141)	(73,213)	(138,799)	(157,713)	(26,158)	(29,701)	(5,347)	(8,346)
NORTH-OLD								
College Graduate	12.1	20.3	14.0	20.3	4.6	7.7	6.6	14.2
High School Graduate	45.5	50.9	50.5	57.2	34.4	48.9	35.0	52.6
Less than HS Graduate	42.4	28.8	35.5	22.5	61.0	43.4	58.4	33.1
Total	100.0	100.0	100.0	100.0	100.0	100.0	100.0	100.0
(Number in 100s)	(12,553)	(12,128)	(18,929)	(24,352)	(1,967)	(2,414)	(317)	(489)
SOUTH-OLD								
College Graduate	17.3	30.3	18.8	26.9	6.0	9.2	7.5	15.7
High School Graduate	34.9	37.3	44.6	49.4	28.8	40.8	27.7	51.1
Less than HS Graduate	47.9	32.4	36.6	23.7	65.3	49.9	64.8	33.2
Total	100.0	100.0	100.0	100.0	100.0	100.0	100.0	100.0
(Number in 100s)	(8,000)	(6,508)	(23,501)	(31,357)	(7,038)	(7,787)	(1,699)	(4,144)

APPENDIX TABLE E.9D (continued)

Metropolitan Area Groupings/ Education Status	Nonblacks				Blacks			
	Central City		Suburbs		Central City		Suburbs	
	1970	1980	1970	1980	1970	1980	1970	1980
WEST-OLD								
College Graduate	15.7	24.5	14.6	21.5	5.5	10.1	7.5	13.7
High School Graduate	48.0	48.6	51.6	55.6	43.4	55.1	46.3	60.5
Less than HS Graduate	36.3	26.9	33.8	22.8	51.1	34.8	46.2	25.8
Total	100.0	100.0	100.0	100.0	100.0	100.0	100.0	100.0
(Number in 100s)	(29,906)	(31,664)	(41,587)	(52,386)	(4,171)	(5,065)	(1,591)	(2,899)
SOUTH-YOUNG								
College Graduate	13.4	20.7	11.7	18.1	5.0	9.1	4.3	11.8
High School Graduate	39.9	45.9	44.0	53.3	28.3	45.3	22.1	43.1
Less than HS Graduate	46.7	33.4	44.3	28.6	66.7	45.7	73.7	45.1
Total	100.0	100.0	100.0	100.0	100.0	100.0	100.0	100.0
(Number in 100s)	(19,273)	(24,750)	(21,113)	(34,647)	(3,841)	(5,776)	(1,332)	(1,834)
WEST-YOUNG								
College Graduate	13.2	19.1	15.3	21.1	5.5	11.7	7.6	14.9
High School Graduate	49.9	55.4	51.3	57.3	41.1	58.1	46.4	62.2
Less than HS Graduate	36.9	25.4	33.4	21.7	53.4	30.2	46.0	23.0
Total	100.0	100.0	100.0	100.0	100.0	100.0	100.0	100.0
(Number in 100s)	(13,527)	(18,840)	(20,699)	(32,933)	(631)	(1,060)	(249)	(608)

SOURCES: Machine-readable computer files: Census of Population and Housing, 1970, Fourth Count Population Summary Tape File; and Census of Population and Housing, 1980: Summary Tape File 3C (prepared by the U.S. Bureau of the Census, Washington, DC).

APPENDIX TABLE E.10A

Metropolitan Area Size, Central City Size, and City Share of Metropolitan Households, 1950, 1960, 1970, 1980: 39 Metropolitan Areas[a]

Metropolitan Area Groupings/ Metropolitan Areas	Metropolitan Area (1000s)				Central City (1000s)				City Share of Metropolitan Households			
	1950	1960	1970	1980	1950	1960	1970	1980	1950	1960	1970	1980
NORTH-DECLINING												
New York	2,822	3,462	3,892	4,007	2,358	2,655	2,837	2,789	83.6	76.7	72.9	69.6
Philadelphia	1,018	1,267	1,480	1,639	585	616	642	620	57.5	48.6	43.4	37.8
Boston	846	996	1,143	1,297	218	225	218	218	25.8	22.6	19.0	16.8
Cincinnati	310	379	431	499	159	162	160	158	51.2	42.7	37.1	31.6
St. Louis	526	650	750	838	258	249	215	178	49.0	38.3	28.7	21.2
Buffalo	306	387	418	445	165	169	158	141	53.8	43.7	37.8	31.6
Chicago	1,520	1,898	2,182	2,487	1,087	1,157	1,137	1,093	71.5	61.0	52.1	44.0
Newark	440	551	641	677	123	128	121	111	27.9	23.2	18.9	16.4
Cleveland	447	568	650	694	266	270	248	218	59.5	47.5	38.2	31.4
Detroit	872	1,133	1,334	1,509	512	515	498	433	58.8	45.4	37.3	28.7
Milwaukee	289	380	433	501	186	231	237	242	64.4	60.8	54.8	48.3
Pittsburgh	615	710	759	829	191	188	178	166	31.1	26.5	23.4	20.0
Paterson*	258	357	427	454	79	90	95	94	30.5	25.2	22.3	20.7
NORTH-OLD												
Columbus	183	246	314	397	110	142	173	217	60.1	57.8	55.1	54.7
Indianapolis	222	285	347	418	132	150	252	260	59.4	52.6	72.5	62.2
Kansas City	273	353	415	493	148	166	176	175	54.4	47.1	42.5	35.5
Hartford	182	249	318	372	51	55	56	51	28.2	21.9	17.6	13.7
Minneapolis*	365	473	599	762	252	264	265	268	68.9	55.9	44.3	35.2
SOUTH-OLD												
Baltimore	400	505	624	757	269	276	289	281	67.2	54.5	46.3	37.2
New Orleans	205	264	318	418	166	190	191	206	81.1	72.0	60.1	49.3
Washington, DC	421	617	911	1,113	224	252	263	253	53.2	40.9	28.8	22.7
Atlanta	235	332	489	720	93	146	162	163	39.5	44.0	33.2	22.6

APPENDIX TABLE E.10A (continued)

Metropolitan Area Groupings/ Metropolitan Areas	Metropolitan Area(1000s)				Central City(1000s)				City Share of Metropolitan Households			
	1950	1960	1970	1980	1950	1960	1970	1980	1950	1960	1970	1980
WEST-OLD												
San Francisco*	676	885	1,086	1,281	387	426	434	441	57.2	48.1	40.0	34.4
Denver*	188	288	395	609	136	176	206	240	72.4	61.2	52.2	39.4
Los Angeles*	1,371	2,012	2,431	2,730	758	1,001	1,170	1,287	55.3	49.8	48.1	47.1
Portland*	229	269	342	478	127	135	145	159	55.3	50.1	42.4	33.3
Seattle*	272	360	473	618	166	214	225	242	61.1	59.6	47.5	39.1
SOUTH-YOUNG												
San Antonio	143	196	252	349	112	161	191	259	78.5	82.1	75.8	74.1
Dallas*	367	532	752	1,076	221	326	411	499	60.1	61.4	54.6	46.4
Houston	279	419	614	1,027	181	283	393	603	64.9	67.5	64.0	58.7
Tampa*	138	277	400	639	74	159	184	210	53.5	57.3	45.9	32.8
Miami	154	308	428	610	78	108	120	134	50.7	35.0	28.1	22.0
Ft. Lauderdale*	27	109	223	418	17	42	93	118	63.3	38.5	42.0	28.4
WEST-YOUNG												
Sacramento	107	188	256	384	43	67	92	113	40.6	35.5	35.8	29.4
San Diego	169	305	423	670	105	175	227	321	62.0	57.5	53.7	47.9
San Jose	85	185	323	459	30	62	131	210	34.8	33.7	40.5	45.7
Phoenix	96	191	303	545	34	132	186	285	35.5	69.1	61.5	52.3
Riverside*	138	245	362	552	43	70	99	133	30.8	28.7	27.3	24.1
Anaheim*	69	204	436	686	21	83	136	185	30.6	40.6	31.2	27.0

SOURCES: Machine-readable computer files: *County and City Data Book*, Consolidated Files for Counties, 1947–1977, and Cities, 1944–1977; and *County and City Data Book*, 1983 file (prepared by the U.S. Bureau of the Census, Washington, DC).

[a] 1980 metropolitan areas with populations greater than 1,000,000 defined as 1980 SMSAs and NECMAs (in New England) except for New York and Paterson–Clifton–Passaic (see Appendix F).

* Largest of multiple central cities (complete metropolitan area names are listed in Appendix F).

APPENDIX TABLE E.10B

Percent Household Change for Metropolitan Areas, Central Cities, and Suburbs, and Suburbanization Rates, 1950–1960, 1960–1970, 1970–1980: 39 Metropolitan Areas[a]

Metropolitan Area Groupings/ Metropolitan Areas	Percent Household Change									Suburbanization Rate[b]		
	Metropolitan Areas			Central Cities			Suburbs					
	1950–1960	1960–1970	1970–1980	1950–1960	1960–1970	1970–1980	1950–1960	1960–1970	1970–1980	1950–1960	1960–1970	1970–1980
NORTH-DECLINING												
New York	+22.7	+12.4	+3.0	+12.6	+6.9	−1.7	+73.9	+30.7	+15.5	+61.4	+23.9	+17.2
Philadelphia	+24.5	+16.9	+10.8	+5.3	+4.3	−3.5	+50.3	+28.8	+21.7	+45.0	+24.5	+25.1
Boston	+17.7	+14.8	+13.4	+3.0	−3.1	+0.4	+22.8	+20.0	+16.5	+19.8	+23.2	+16.1
Cincinnati	+22.2	+13.6	+15.8	+1.8	−1.2	−1.4	+43.5	+24.7	+25.9	+41.7	+25.9	+27.3
St. Louis	+23.4	+15.4	+11.8	−3.7	−13.3	−17.4	+49.5	+33.2	+23.5	+53.2	+46.6	+40.9
Buffalo	+26.3	+8.2	+6.5	+2.7	−6.6	−10.8	+53.8	+19.7	+17.0	+51.2	+26.3	+27.7
Chicago	+24.9	+15.0	+13.9	+6.5	−1.8	−3.8	+71.1	+41.2	+33.2	+64.6	+43.0	+37.0
Newark	+25.4	+16.3	+5.7	+4.3	−5.3	−8.3	+33.5	+22.8	+9.0	+29.2	+28.1	+17.3
Cleveland	+27.1	+14.4	+6.8	+1.5	−8.0	−12.1	+64.6	+34.7	+18.5	+63.2	+42.7	+30.6
Detroit	+30.0	+17.7	+13.1	+0.5	−3.3	−12.9	+72.0	+35.1	+28.7	+71.6	+38.5	+41.6
Milwaukee	+31.8	+13.8	+15.7	+24.4	+2.6	+2.0	+45.1	+31.1	+32.3	+20.7	+28.5	+30.2
Pittsburgh	+15.5	+6.9	+9.1	−1.3	−5.5	−6.7	+23.1	+11.4	+14.0	+24.5	+16.9	+20.7
Paterson*	+38.1	+19.7	+6.3	+14.0	+5.8	−0.9	+48.7	+24.4	+8.4	+34.7	+18.6	+9.3
NORTH-OLD												
Columbus	+34.6	+27.4	+26.5	+29.4	+21.5	+25.5	+42.5	+35.4	+27.8	+13.2	+13.9	+2.3
Indianapolis	+28.5	+21.8	+20.6	+13.8	+67.8	+3.4	+50.0	−29.3	+66.0	+36.2	−97.1	+62.6
Kansas City	+29.4	+17.7	+18.8	+12.0	+6.3	−0.6	+50.2	+27.9	+33.2	+38.1	+21.7	+33.9
Hartford	+36.8	+27.5	+17.0	+6.3	+2.1	−8.6	+48.7	+34.7	+22.4	+42.5	+32.5	+31.0
Minneapolis*	+29.4	+26.8	+27.2	+5.2	+0.3	+1.1	+83.1	+60.4	+47.9	+77.9	+60.1	+46.9
SOUTH-OLD												
Baltimore	+26.4	+23.4	+21.4	+2.6	+4.9	−2.6	+75.5	+45.6	+42.2	+72.9	+40.7	+44.8
New Orleans	+28.8	+20.8	+31.4	+14.3	+0.8	+7.9	+91.0	+72.1	+66.8	+76.7	+71.3	+59.0
Washington, DC	+46.4	+47.6	+22.2	+12.5	+4.2	−3.6	+85.1	+77.7	+32.7	+72.7	+73.6	+36.2
Atlanta	+41.5	+47.5	+47.1	+57.5	+11.2	+0.2	+31.0	+76.1	+70.3	−26.5	+64.9	+70.1

APPENDIX TABLE E.10B (continued)

Metropolitan Area Groupings/ Metropolitan Areas	Percent Household Change											
	Metropolitan Areas			Central Cities			Suburbs			Suburbanization Rate[b]		
	1950–1960	1960–1970	1970–1980	1950–1960	1960–1970	1970–1980	1950–1960	1960–1970	1970–1980	1950–1960	1960–1970	1970–1980
WEST-OLD												
San Francisco*	+30.9	+22.7	+18.0	+10.1	+1.9	+1.5	+58.6	+42.0	+28.9	+48.5	+40.1	+274
Denver*	+53.6	+37.1	+54.3	+29.8	+16.9	+16.4	+116.1	+68.8	+95.7	+86.2	+51.8	+792
Los Angeles*	+46.7	+20.8	+12.3	+32.1	+16.8	+10.0	+64.8	+24.8	+14.5	+32.6	+8.0	+45
Portland	+17.5	+26.9	+39.8	+6.4	+7.5	+9.6	+31.3	+46.4	+62.1	+24.8	+38.9	+525
Seattle*	+32.2	+31.5	+30.6	+29.0	+4.9	+7.5	+37.3	+70.8	+51.5	+8.3	+65.9	+440
SOUTH-YOUNG												
San Antonio	+37.4	+28.4	+38.9	+43.6	+18.7	+35.8	+14.8	+73.1	+48.5	−28.8	+54.4	+128
Dallas*	+44.8	+41.6	+43.1	+47.8	+25.9	+21.5	+40.2	+66.4	+69.0	−7.6	+40.5	+476
Houston	+50.2	+46.7	+67.2	+56.3	+39.2	+53.2	+39.1	+62.4	+92.1	−17.2	+23.2	+389
Tampa*	+100.9	+44.4	+59.5	+115.0	+15.6	+14.1	+84.5	+83.1	+98.0	−30.6	+67.5	+839
Miami	+99.6	+38.8	+42.5	+37.6	+11.7	+11.3	+163.5	+53.4	+54.7	+126.0	+41.7	+434
Ft. Lauderdale*	+309.3	+104.9	+87.6	+149.0	+123.4	+26.6	+586.4	+93.4	+131.7	+437.4	−30.0	+1051
WEST-YOUNG												
Sacramento	+76.2	+36.2	+50.0	+54.0	+37.6	+23.1	+91.4	+35.5	+65.1	+37.4	−2.1	+420
San Diego	+80.6	+38.5	+58.5	+67.3	+29.4	+41.5	+102.2	+50.8	+78.2	+34.8	+21.4	+368
San Jose	+116.5	+74.5	+42.1	+109.6	+109.7	+60.4	+120.2	+56.7	+29.6	+10.5	−53.0	−308
Phoenix	+98.1	+58.4	+80.0	+285.7	+40.9	+53.0	−5.1	+97.5	+123.1	−290.8	+56.6	+701
Riverside*	+77.5	+47.5	+52.4	+65.1	+40.6	+34.8	+83.0	+50.3	+59.1	+17.9	+9.7	+243
Anaheim*	+193.8	+113.9	+57.4	+298.7	+64.7	+36.1	+151.5	+147.5	+67.0	−138.2	+82.8	+309

SOURCES: Machine-readable computer file: *County and City Data Book*, Consolidated File for Counties, 1947–1977, and Cities, 1944–1977; and *County and City Data Book*, 1983 file (prepared by the U.S. Bureau of the Census, Washington, DC).

[a]1980 metropolitan areas with populations greater than 1,000,000 defined as 1980 SMSAs and NECMAs (in New England) except for New York and Paterson–Clifton–Passaic (see Appendix F).

[b]Suburbanization Rate: Suburb Percent Change minus Central City Percent Change.

*Largest of multiple central cities (complete metropolitan names are listed in Appendix F).

APPENDIX TABLE E.10C

Percent Nonfamily Households for Central Cities, Suburbs, and Suburb–City Differences: 1950, 1960, 1970, 1980: 39 Metropolitan Areas[a]

Metropolitan Groupings/ Metropolitan Areas	Central Cities				Suburbs				Suburb–City Differences			
	1950	1960	1970	1980	1950	1960	1970	1980	1950	1960	1970	1980
NORTH-DECLINING												
New York	+10.4	+21.7	+27.4	+37.0	+8.0	+8.8	+12.3	+18.9	−2.4	−12.8	−15.1	−18.1
Philadelphia	+10.6	+18.7	+25.4	+33.4	+8.1	+9.8	+14.6	+22.5	−2.5	−8.9	−10.8	−10.9
Boston	+11.7	+26.9	+34.7	+46.7	+9.3	+13.2	+18.7	+27.4	−2.4	−13.7	−16.1	−19.3
Cincinnati	+15.2	+22.2	+31.6	+42.5	+9.3	+10.0	+13.2	+20.1	−5.9	−12.1	−16.1	−22.4
St. Louis	+10.3	+22.8	+30.5	+40.0	+8.8	+10.0	+14.3	+22.4	−1.5	−12.8	−18.4	−17.5
Buffalo	+9.3	+19.6	+28.2	+38.0	+8.5	+9.4	+13.9	+22.1	−0.8	−10.1	−16.2	−15.9
Chicago	+11.4	+21.4	+27.3	+35.4	+7.9	+9.1	+13.2	+22.7	−3.5	−12.4	−14.3	−12.7
Newark	+5.9	+18.8	+24.7	+29.4	+6.3	+11.1	+16.2	+23.5	+0.4	−7.7	−14.0	−5.9
Cleveland	+8.5	+18.3	+25.7	+34.8	+7.1	+9.3	+15.1	+24.5	−1.5	−8.9	−8.5	−10.3
Detroit	+5.1	+17.6	+25.2	+33.3	+7.0	+8.6	+12.9	+22.2	+1.9	−9.0	−10.5	−11.0
Milwaukee	+9.7	+18.2	+25.3	+35.0	+8.1	+9.1	+13.4	+21.9	−1.6	−9.1	−12.3	−13.2
Pittsburgh	+9.6	+19.4	+28.4	+38.0	+7.0	+9.8	+15.0	+22.9	−2.6	−9.5	−12.0	−15.1
Paterson*	+8.2	+14.8	+21.3	+27.5	+7.0	+8.6	+13.7	+22.1	−1.2	−6.2	−13.4	−5.4
NORTH-OLD												
Columbus	+13.3	+18.9	+25.7	+37.6	+9.3	+10.1	+13.7	+20.5	−4.0	−8.8	−7.6	−17.1
Indianapolis	+9.5	+19.5	+20.4	+30.4	+9.5	+9.1	+14.1	+19.4	−0.1	−10.4	−12.0	−11.0
Kansas City	+13.5	+24.9	+28.5	+35.9	+10.3	+10.3	+15.0	+23.5	−3.2	−14.6	−6.3	−12.4
Hartford	+10.9	+25.2	+34.2	+40.9	+8.6	+9.9	+14.5	+24.2	−2.3	−15.3	−13.5	−16.6
Minneapolis*	+13.0	+24.7	+32.7	+44.8	+8.5	+7.2	+11.7	+22.4	−4.5	−17.5	−19.8	−22.4
SOUTH-OLD												
Baltimore	+9.9	+16.9	+25.3	+33.3	+8.2	+7.3	+12.0	+21.6	−1.7	−9.6	−21.0	−11.7
New Orleans	+13.1	+19.6	+24.9	+35.6	+9.9	+8.4	+11.7	+21.7	−3.2	−11.3	−13.3	−13.9
Washington, DC	+11.6	+31.1	+37.7	+47.2	+5.3	+9.7	+17.0	+27.9	−6.3	−21.4	−13.2	−19.3
Atlanta	+6.3	+17.5	+26.5	+39.9	+6.6	+7.3	+11.8	+22.3	+0.3	−10.2	−20.7	−17.6

APPENDIX TABLE E.10C (continued)

Metropolitan Groupings/ Metropolitan Areas	Central Cities				Suburbs				Suburb–City Differences			
	1950	1960	1970	1980	1950	1960	1970	1980	1950	1960	1970	1980
WEST-OLD												
San Francisco*	+20.2	+34.4	+41.4	+50.0	+10.9	+14.0	+19.8	+30.8	−9.3	−20.4	−21.6	−19.3
Denver*	+15.3	+24.6	+31.3	+44.9	+9.9	+8.9	+12.4	+24.3	−5.3	−15.7	−18.9	−20.7
Los Angeles*	+19.0	+27.4	+32.7	+39.3	+12.7	+17.0	+22.1	+28.6	−6.3	−10.3	−10.5	−10.8
Portland	+18.4	+27.6	+33.1	+44.2	+11.2	+12.5	+16.3	+26.0	−7.2	−15.1	−16.9	−18.2
Seattle	+19.1	+28.7	+34.5	+46.9	+11.0	+10.9	+14.4	+24.8	−8.1	−17.7	−20.1	−22.1
SOUTH-YOUNG												
San Antonio	+9.9	+14.3	+18.1	+25.3	+5.3	+11.4	+13.0	+17.8	−4.6	−2.9	−5.1	−7.5
Dallas*	+9.3	+16.7	+22.5	+35.2	+9.9	+10.6	+13.1	+20.3	+0.6	−6.0	−9.4	−15.0
Houston	+10.2	+15.7	+21.7	+34.9	+8.8	+9.7	+11.6	+17.4	−1.4	−6.0	−10.1	−17.5
Tampa*	+14.4	+21.3	+27.7	+35.6	+13.9	+14.4	+19.9	+27.3	−0.5	−6.9	−7.8	−8.2
Miami	+9.5	+27.5	+29.7	+35.2	+9.9	+14.8	+20.3	+29.4	+0.4	−12.7	−9.3	−5.8
Ft. Lauderdale*	+12.6	+19.1	+24.6	+38.3	+11.2	+10.7	+16.6	+26.9	−1.4	−8.4	−8.0	−11.3
WEST-YOUNG												
Sacramento	+12.6	+25.1	+28.2	+38.4	+13.8	+11.4	+16.0	+28.0	+1.2	−13.7	−12.2	−10.3
San Diego	+15.2	+21.0	+27.7	+37.3	+10.3	+11.2	+17.0	+26.1	−4.8	−9.8	−10.7	−11.1
San Jose	+14.0	+18.5	+17.8	+25.5	+12.2	+12.1	+19.2	+32.4	−1.8	−6.3	+1.4	+7.0
Phoenix	+17.6	+16.1	+20.9	+29.0	+11.5	+12.2	+15.6	+24.8	−6.1	−3.9	−5.2	−4.2
Riverside*	+14.2	+17.8	+21.8	+27.4	+14.2	+15.7	+18.5	+24.1	+0.0	−2.0	−3.2	−3.3
Anaheim*	+13.6	+11.8	+17.3	+28.0	+14.0	+13.1	+17.2	+28.3	+0.4	+1.3	−0.1	+0.3

SOURCES: Machine-readable computer file: *County and City Data Book*, Consolidated File for Counties, 1947–1977, and Cities, 1944–1977; and *County and City Data Book*, 1983 file (prepared by the U.S. Bureau of the Census, Washington, DC).

[a] 1980 metropolitan areas with populations greater than 1 million defined as 1980 SMSAs and NECMAs (in New England) except for New York and Paterson–Clifton–Passaic (see Appendix F).

*Largest of multiple central cities (complete metropolitan names are listed in Appendix F).

APPENDIX TABLE E.10D

Percent Distribution of Households by Type for Central City and Suburbs, 1970 and 1980, Nonblacks and Blacks: Six Metropolitan Area Groupings

Metropolitan Area Groupings/ Household Types	Nonblack Households				Black Households			
	Central City		Suburbs		Central City		Suburbs	
	1970	1980	1970	1980	1970	1980	1970	1980
NORTH-DECLINING								
Married Couple w/ Children	27.8	20.4	45.8	34.3	29.0	18.8	36.3	28.7
Married Couple w/o Children	30.8	27.0	30.9	33.0	19.5	15.3	22.4	17.9
Other Family	12.9	14.8	8.9	10.4	27.1	34.7	22.7	29.0
Nonfamily Household	28.5	37.9	14.4	22.3	24.4	31.1	18.6	24.5
Total	100.0	100.0	100.0	100.0	100.0	100.0	100.0	100.0
(Number in 100s)	(51,324)	(45,346)	(75,176)	(89,080)	(16,373)	(19,360)	(2,967)	(5,083)
NORTH-OLD								
Married Couple w/ Children	32.4	22.7	48.9	37.2	30.4	21.0	34.4	29.3
Married Couple w/o Children	29.1	26.9	29.6	31.3	20.9	16.3	23.9	17.3
Other Family	10.5	11.7	7.7	9.4	23.9	32.4	20.6	26.8
Nonfamily Household	8.0	38.7	13.7	22.1	24.9	30.4	21.1	26.5
Total	100.0	100.0	100.0	100.0	100.0	100.0	100.0	100.0
(Number in 100s)	(7,831)	(8,073)	(10,712)	(14,407)	(1,240)	(1,652)	(183)	(316)
SOUTH-OLD								
Married Couple w/ Children	3.8	15.2	48.4	35.1	29.6	17.8	44.6	33.3
Married Couple w/o Children	29.7	26.0	29.1	30.9	20.0	16.4	21.3	15.7
Other Family	11.8	11.4	8.2	10.0	27.1	34.8	20.3	27.0
Nonfamily Household	34.7	47.4	14.4	24.1	23.3	31.0	13.9	24.0
Total	100.0	100.0	100.0	100.0	100.0	100.0	100.0	100.0
(Number in 100s)	(4,829)	(4,142)	(13,458)	(18,470)	(4,265)	(4,917)	(931)	(2,595)

APPENDIX TABLE E.10D (continued)

| Metropolitan Area Groupings/ Household Types | Nonblack Households | | | | Black Households | | | |
| | Central City | | Suburbs | | Central City | | Suburbs | |
	1970	1980	1970	1980	1970	1980	1970	1980
WEST-OLD								
Married Couple w/ Children	25.7	19.2	41.2	31.3	26.1	16.5	39.1	28.3
Married Couple w/o Children	28.5	25.2	29.6	29.6	19.4	15.6	19.3	16.8
Other Family	10.6	12.1	9.4	11.6	24.1	30.1	22.4	29.2
Nonfamily Household	35.3	43.5	19.8	27.8	30.4	37.8	19.2	25.8
Total	100.0	100.0	100.0	100.0	100.0	100.0	100.0	100.0
(Number in 100s)	(19,001)	(20,212)	(24,531)	(31,617)	(2,844)	(3,522)	(981)	(1,892)
SOUTH-YOUNG								
Married Couple w/ Children	34.0	24.4	40.7	32.1	33.9	25.2	38.3	33.4
Married Couple w/o Children	32.1	29.2	35.2	35.2	21.1	17.5	20.8	17.4
Other Family	10.3	11.3	7.9	9.1	23.8	29.6	22.9	27.9
Nonfamily Household	23.6	35.0	16.2	23.5	21.2	27.7	18.1	21.3
Total	100.0	100.0	100.0	100.0	100.0	100.0	100.0	100.0
(Number in 100s)	(11,535)	(14,718)	(12,033)	(21,604)	(2,409)	(3,539)	[762]	(1,382)
WEST-YOUNG								
Married Couple w/ Children	38.1	28.8	42.0	30.0	35.0	26.8	44.0	33.1
Married Couple w/o Children	28.9	27.7	31.2	32.2	18.6	16.0	20.5	17.5
Other Family	10.5	12.7	9.2	11.0	22.8	28.3	15.3	22.0
Nonfamily Household	22.5	30.8	17.6	26.8	23.6	28.9	20.1	27.4
Total	100.0	100.0	100.0	100.0	100.0	100.0	100.0	100.0
(Number in 100s)	(8,297)	(11,741)	(12,204)	(20,074)	[416]	[749]	[142]	[424]

SOURCES: Machine-readable computer files: Census of Population and Housing: 1970, Fourth Count Population Summary Tape File; and Census of Population and Housing: 1960, Summary Tape File 3C (prepared by the U.S. Bureau of the Census, Washington, DC).

APPENDIX TABLE E.11A

Percent Distribution of Employed Workers[a] by Industry for Central Cities and Suburbs, 1960, 1970, and 1980: Six Metropolitan Area Groupings[b]

Metropolitan Area Groupings/Industries	Central Cities			Suburbs		
	1960	1970	1980	1960	1970	1980
NORTH-DECLINING						
Manufacturing	31.1	24.6	20.3	35.7	31.1	26.7
Other	68.9	75.4	79.7	64.3	68.9	73.3
Total	100.0	100.0	100.0	100.0	100.0	100.0
(Number in 100s)	(94,314)	(87,633)	(79,958)	(53,185)	(76,592)	(95,214)
NORTH-OLD						
Manufacturing	26.3	23.8	19.7	30.4	26.3	24.8
Other	73.7	76.2	80.3	69.6	73.7	75.2
Total	100.0	100.0	100.0	100.0	100.0	100.0
(Number in 100s)	(12,143)	(14,075)	(15,775)	(4,552)	(8,328)	(12,672)
SOUTH-OLD						
Manufacturing	15.9	13.3	10.7	20.8	14.8	12.2
Other	84.1	86.7	89.3	79.2	85.2	87.8
Total	100.0	100.0	100.0	100.0	100.0	100.0
(Number in 100s)	(14,624)	(14,979)	(16,265)	(6,522)	(13,925)	(20,361)

APPENDIX TABLE E.11A (continued)

Metropolitan Area Groupings/Industries	Central Cities			Suburbs		
	1960	1970	1980	1960	1970	1980
WEST-OLD						
Manufacturing	23.4	18.6	17.9	29.8	26.5	24.0
Other	76.6	81.4	82.1	70.2	73.5	76.0
Total	100.0	100.0	100.0	100.0	100.0	100.0
(Number in 100s)	(26,476)	(27,952)	(33,694)	(20,384)	(24,595)	(34,529)
SOUTH-YOUNG						
Manufacturing	16.8	16.5	14.8	15.3	18.0	18.6
Other	83.2	83.5	85.2	84.7	82.0	81.4
Total	100.0	100.0	100.0	100.0	100.0	100.0
(Number in 100s)	(13,216)	(17,903)	(28,074)	(4,875)	(9,280)	(16,319)
WEST-YOUNG						
Manufacturing	16.8	17.7	18.6	19.4	19.5	20.8
Other	83.2	82.3	81.4	80.6	80.5	79.2
Total	100.0	100.0	100.0	100.0	100.0	100.0
(Number in 100s)	(7,391)	(11,295)	(17,325)	(5,398)	(11,453)	(20,969)

SOURCES: *U.S. Census of Population: 1960, Subject Report PC(2) 6B Journey to Work*, Table 2; *U.S. Census of Population: 1970, Subject Report PC(2) 6D Journey to Work*, Table 2; 1980 Machine-readable computer file: Census of Population and Housing, 1980. Public Use Microdata Samples "A" and "B" (prepared by the U.S. Bureau of the Census, Washington, DC).

[a]Includes employed workers, at work during census week, for metropolitan area residents who reported workplace (ages 14+ in 1960, ages 16+ in 1970 and 1980).

[b]Defined according to 1960 SMSA and central city definitions (1960), 1970 SMSA and central city definitions (1970), and 1970 equivalent SMSA and central city definitions (1980).

APPENDIX F:
BIBLIOGRAPHIC REFERENCES FOR METROPOLITAN AREA AND CENTRAL CITY DEFINITIONS, AND DATA SOURCES USED IN THIS VOLUME

Metropolitan Area and Central City Units

THE METROPOLITAN area and central city units employed in this volume are defined, with some exceptions, in terms of metropolitan area definitions used in the decennial censuses. Listed below are bibliographic citations for Census Bureau reports which delineate these census units in terms of their component counties and cities, as well as the exceptions and revisions to these units that were made for purposes of this study.

Metropolitan Area Units Used in Part One

In the Part One (Chapters 3 through 6) trend analyses, metropolitan areas are defined contemporaneously for the years 1950, 1960, 1970, and 1980. Definitions are based primarily on the census metropolitan area units employed at each census year. Citations of these definitions and an enumeration of exceptions and revisions to these, for purposes of this study, are as follows:

1980 metropolitan area definitions: The 304 1980 metropolitan areas comprise, for the most part, 1980 SMSAs (Standard Metropolitan Statistical Areas) outside of New England, and 1980 NECMAs (New England County Metropolitan Areas) inside New England. County components for 1980 SMSAs and NECMAs are listed in:

U.S. Bureau of the Census, *State and Metropolitan Area Data Book: 1982* (Washington, DC: U.S. Government Printing Office 1982), Table 4.1, Population of Standard Metropolitan Areas with Corresponding Central Cities; and Table 4.2, Population of New England County Metropolitan Areas.

The only exceptions and revisions to these SMSAs and NECMAs for use in this study have to do with the definition of the New York SMSA and the related areas of Nassau–Suffolk, Paterson, Newark, and New Brunswick. First, Nassau and Suffolk counties in New York were combined with the New York SMSA, as they were in 1970 and earlier years. Second, Bergen County, New Jersey, which was transferred to New York in 1973 from the Paterson–Clifton–Passaic area, was kept with the Paterson–Clifton–Passaic area in 1980 to maintain continuity with earlier censuses. These changes do not affect the total metropolitan population in 1980 or their central cities. However, they do result in Paterson–Clifton–Passaic being included in the list of areas over one million and in Nassau–Suffolk being removed from that list.

1970 metropolitan area definitions: The 231 1970 metropolitan areas comprise, for the most part, 1970 SMSAs outside of New England, and 1970 metropolitan SEAs (State Economic Areas) inside New England. County components for 1970 SMSAs and metropolitan SEAs are listed in:

U.S. Bureau of the Census, *Census of Population: 1970*, Vol. I, *Characteristics of the Population*, Part A. *Number of Inhabitants*, Section 1 (Washington, DC: U.S. Government Printing Office, 1972), Table 32, Population of Standard Metropolitan Statistical Areas: 1950 to 1970.

U.S. Bureau of the Census, *Census of Population: 1970, State Economic Areas*, Final Report PC(2)-10B (Washington, DC: U.S. Government Printing Office, 1972), Appendix A–Area Classifications, List of Counties in State Economic Area.

Exceptions and revisions to these SMSAs and metropolitan SEAs for use of this study are as follows:

1. The counties of Middlesex and Somerset in New Jersey, which had been part of the New York–Northeastern New Jersey SMSA in 1950, but were not part of any metropolitan area in 1960 and 1970, were treated as metropolitan in 1970. In accordance with their designations in 1980, Middlesex County was called the New Brunswick SMSA, and Somerset was added to the Newark SMSA.

2. Plymouth County, Massachusetts, was included with the Boston NECMA and was not treated as a separate NECMA, as would have been the case if State Economic Areas had been used. This does not alter the total metropolitan population but treats Brockton as part of Boston, which is consistent with the 1980 definition of the Boston NECMA.

3. Lewiston–Auburn, Maine, was defined as NECMA containing Androscoggin County, although there was no metropolitan SEA for that area in those years. Although Lewiston–Auburn was an SMSA in 1970, there was no corresponding metropolitan SEA because the SMSA lacked a central city of at least 50,000.

1960 metropolitan area definitions: The 203 1960 metropolitan areas comprise, for the most part, 1960 SMSAs outside of New England and 1960 metropolitan SEAs inside New England. County components for 1960 SMSAs and metropolitan SEAs are listed in:

U.S. *Bureau of the Census, U.S. Census of Population: 1960,* Vol. I, *Characteristics of the Population,* Part A, *Number of Inhabitants* (Washington, DC: U.S. Government Printing Office, 1961), Table 31, Population of Standard Metropolitan Statistical Areas and Component Areas in the United States and The Commonwealth of Puerto Rico: 1940 to 1960.

U.S. Bureau of the Census, *U.S. Census of Population: 1960, Selected Area Reports State Economic Areas* (Washington, DC: U.S. Government Printing Office, 1963), Appendix, List of Counties in each State Economic Area.

Exceptions and revisions of these SMSAs and metropolitan SEAs for use in this study are as follows:

1. As in 1970, Middlesex and Somerset counties in New Jersey were treated as metropolitan and included in the New Brunswick and Newark SMSAs, respectively.

2. Plymouth County, Massachusetts, was included with the Boston NECMA and was not treated as a separate NECMA, as would have been the case if State Economic Areas had been used.

3. Lewiston–Auburn, Maine, was defined as NECMA containing Androscoggin County.

1950 metropolitan area definitions: The 165 1950 metropolitan areas comprise, for the most part, 1950 SMAs (Standard Metropolitan Areas) outside of New England, and 1950 metropolitan SEAs inside New England. County components for 1950 SMAs and metropolitan SEAs are listed in:

U.S. Bureau of the Census, *U.S. Census of Population: 1950,* Vol. I., *Number of Inhabitants* (Washington, DC: U.S. Government Printing Office, 1952), Table

26, Population of Standard Metropolitan Areas and Constituent Parts in Continental United States, Hawaii and Puerto Rico: 1950 and 1940.

U.S. Bureau of the Census, *County and City Data Book, 1952* (Washington, DC: U.S. Government Printing Office, 1953), Appendix D, New England State Economic Areas.

Exceptions and revisions of these SMAs and metropolitan SEAs for use in this study are as follows:

1. Honolulu was included as an SMSA to provide continuity with later years, although Hawaii was not a state in 1950.

2. Plymouth County, Massachusetts, was included with the Boston NECMA.

Metropolitan Area and Central City Units Used in Part Two

Most Part Two (Chapters 7 through 11) analyses pertain to the 39 metropolitan areas defined in Part One with 1980 populations greater than one million. The complete names for these 39 areas appear in Appendix Table F.1. The trend analyses in Part Two employ, where possible, 1980 definitions of metropolitan areas and central cities.

1980 metropolitan areas and central cities: The 39 metropolitan areas examined in Part Two chapters correspond exactly to the largest 1980 metropolitan areas employed in Part One (described above)—each with 1980 populations exceeding one million. These 39 areas differ only from 1980 SMSAs and NECMAs (in New England) in the following respects: (1) the 1980 Nassau–Suffolk SMSA was eliminated; (2) the New York metropolitan area differs from the 1980 New York SMSA and consists of the following New York counties: Nassau, Suffolk, Bronx, Kings, New York, Queens, Richmond, Rockland, Westchester, and Putnam; and (3) the Paterson–Clifton–Passaic metropolitan area differs from the 1980 SMSA such that it consists of the New Jersey counties of Bergen and Passaic. The latter change elevates the 1980 population for the Paterson–Clifton–Passaic metropolitan area to greater than one million, so that it is included in the Part Two analyses.

The central cities of these 39 metropolitan areas conform exactly to those of their 1980 SMSA counterparts. Although the New England metropolitan areas of Hartford and Boston are defined in terms of NECMA definitions, their central cities are considered to be the cities of Hartford and Boston, respectively.

1980 central counties: The Chapter 7 analyses of net migration and natural increase components of change pertain to central counties and non-central counties in metropolitan areas. The central counties in this analysis are those which contain all or significant parts of the metropolitan areas' central city(s) population. Appendix Table F-2 lists the counties that were defined as central counties for this part of the analysis.

1970 and "1970 equivalent" SMSAs and central cities: Several trend analyses, involving migration streams, commuting streams, and places of work, present 1970 data in terms of 1970 SMSA and central city boundaries and 1980 data in terms of "1970 Equivalent" SMSA and central city boundaries. (In these particular comparisons, census SMSA units are used both inside and outside of New England.) The actual 1970 central city and SMSA units are defined in terms of county and city components in:

U.S. Bureau of the Census, *Census of Population: 1970,* Vol. I, *Characteristics of the Population,* Part A, *Number of Inhabitants,* Section 1 (Washington, DC: U.S. Government Printing Office 1972), Table 32, Population of Standard Metropolitan Statistical Areas: 1950 to 1970.

The 1970 Equivalent SMSA and central city units, for which selected 1980 data are prepared, represent combinations of County Groups [1] from the "A" and "B" samples of the 1980 Public Use Microsample (PUMS) file. These "Equivalent" units coincide exactly or closely with the actual 1970 SMSA and central city definitions. They represent the closest possible approximations to the 1970 units that can be drawn from the 1980 microsample files. (The reverse transformation of 1970 data according to 1980 metropolitan area and central city boundaries is not possible because the geographic coding scheme for the 1970 census microsample file was inadequate for this purpose.) Of the 39 "1970 Equivalent" SMSAs and central cities, 24 areas are exactly consistent with 1970 central city and SMSA boundaries, another 10 areas are consistent with central city boundaries but differ from SMSA boundaries, and another 4 differ only with respect to central city boundaries. In only one central city and in only four metropolitan areas do the "Equivalent" populations differ from the actual populations by greater than 5 percent. Appendix Table F-3 lists codes for the 1970 PUMS Sample A and B County Groups used to identify the "1970 Equivalent" SMSAs and central cities in these comparisons.

[1]The "County Groups" designated in the 1980 PUMS files are not constrained to county boundaries. Particularly within large metropolitan areas, county groups are composed of combinations of territorial units—including cities, incorporated places, minor civil divisions, etc. They are constrained, however, to circumscribe a territory that contains a residential population of no less than 100,000.

1960 SMSAs and central cities: In a few comparisons involving commuting streams and place of work, we present 1960 data according to actual 1960 census-defined SMSA and central city units. In these particular instances, it was impossible to compile the data consistent with either the 1970 SMSA boundaries or the 1980 metropolitan area boundaries, used elsewhere in Part Two. The 1960 SMSA and central city units are defined in terms of their component counties and central cities in:

U.S. Bureau of the Census, *U.S. Census of Population: 1960*, Vol. I, *Characteristics of the Population*, Part A, *Number of Inhabitants* (Washington, DC: U.S. Government Printing Office, 1961), Table 31: Population of Standard Metropolitan Statistical Areas and Component Areas in the United States and the Commonwealth of Puerto Rico: 1940 to 1960.

Data Sources

Most of the data presented in this volume have been compiled from publicly released census publications and computer files. Listed below are the complete bibliographic citations for these publications or computer files that are referred to as sources in various parts of the monograph.

1980 Census

U.S. Bureau of the Census, *Census of Population: 1980*, Vol. I, *Characteristics of the Population, Chapter A. Number of Inhabitants*, Part I (PC80-1-A) (Washington, DC: U.S. Government Printing Office, 1983).

U.S. Bureau of the Census, Census of Population and Housing, 1980: Summary Tape File 3C [machine-readable data file]. Prepared by the Bureau of the Census [producer and distributor], Washington, DC, 1982.

U.S. Bureau of the Census, Census of Population and Housing, 1980: Summary Tape File 4B [machine-readable data file]. Prepared by the Bureau of the Census [producer and distributor], Washington, DC, 1983.

U.S. Bureau of the Census, Census of Population and Housing, 1980: Public-Use Microdata Samples "A" and "B" [machine-readable data file]. Prepared by the Bureau of the Census [producer and distributor], Washington, DC, 1983.

1970 Census

U.S. Bureau of the Census, *Census of Population: 1970*, Vol. I, *Characteristics of the Population*, Part A. *Number of Inhabitants*, Section 1 (Washington, DC: U.S. Government Printing Office, 1972).

U.S. Bureau of the Census, *Census of Population: 1970, Characteristics of the Population*, Part 1. United States Summary-Section 2 (Washington, DC: U.S. Government Printing Office, 1973).

U.S. Bureau of the Census, *Census of Population: 1970, Subject Reports, Final Report* PC(2)-2C, Mobility for Metropolitan Areas (Washington, DC: U.S. Government Printing Office, 1973.)

U.S. Bureau of the Census, *Census of Population: 1970, Subject Reports, Final Report* PC(2)-6D, Journey to Work (Washington, DC: U.S. Government Printing Office, 1973).

U.S. Bureau of the Census, Census of Population and Housing, 1970: Fourth Count Population Summary Tape [machine-readable data file]. Prepared by the Bureau of the Census, Washington, DC.

1960 Census

U.S. Bureau of the Census, *U.S. Census of Population: 1960*, Vol. I, *Characteristics of the Population*, Part A. *Number of Inhabitants* (Washington, DC: U.S. Government Printing Office, 1961).

U.S. Bureau of the Census, *U.S. Census of Population: 1960*, Vol. I, *Characteristics of the Population*, Part 1. United States Summary (Washington, DC: U.S. Government Printing Office, 1964).

U.S. Bureau of the Census, *U.S. Census of Population: 1960 Subject Reports, Journey to Work*. Final Report PC(2)-6B (Washington, DC: U.S. Government Printing Office, 1963).

1950 Census

U.S. Bureau of the Census, *U.S. Census of Population: 1950*, Vol. I. *Number of Inhabitants* (Washington, DC: U.S. Government Printing Office, 1952).

State and Metropolitan Area Data Book, 1982

U.S. Bureau of the Census, *State and Metropolitan Area Data Book, 1982* (Washington, DC: U.S. Government Printing Office, 1982).

County and City Data Books, 1944–1977; 1983

U.S. Bureau of the Census, *County and City Data Book*, Consolidated File, County Data 1947–1977 [machine-readable data file]. Prepared by the Bureau of the Census [producer and distributor], Washington, DC, 1978.

U.S. Bureau of the Census, *County and City Data Book*, Consolidated File, City Data 1944–1977 [machine-readable data file]. Prepared by the Bureau of the Census [producer and distributor], Washington, DC, 1978.

U.S. Bureau of the Census, *County and City Data Book: 1983*, Files on Tape [machine-readable data file]. Prepared by the Bureau of the Census [producer and distributor], Washington, DC, 1984.

Population Estimates for 1984

U.S. Bureau of the Census, *Current Population Reports*, Series P-25, no. 976, *Patterns of Metropolitan Areas and County Population Growth: 1980 to 1984* (Washington, DC: U.S. Government Printing Office, 1985).

APPENDIX TABLE F.1

List of 1980 Metropolitan Areas with Populations Exceeding 1 Million Examined in Part Two, Chapters 7–11

Metropolitan Areas[a] Listed in Alphabetical Order

Anaheim–Santa Ana–Garden Grove, California
Atlanta, Georgia
Baltimore, Maryland
Boston, Massachusetts
Buffalo, New York
Chicago, Illinois
Cincinnati, Ohio–Kentucky–Indiana
Cleveland, Ohio
Columbus, Ohio
Dallas–Fort Worth, Texas
Denver–Boulder, Colorado
Detroit, Michigan
Fort Lauderdale–Hollywood, Florida
Hartford, Connecticut
Houston, Texas
Indianapolis, Indiana
Kansas City, Missouri–Kansas
Los Angeles–Long Beach, California
Miami, Florida
Milwaukee, Wisconsin
Minneapolis–St. Paul, Minnesota–Wisconsin
New Orleans, Louisiana
New York, New York
Newark, New Jersey
Paterson–Clifton–Passaic, New Jersey
Philadelphia, Pennsylvania–New Jersey
Phoenix, Arizona
Pittsburgh, Pennsylvania
Portland, Oregon–Washington
Riverside–San Bernardino–Ontario, California
Sacramento, California
St. Louis, Missouri–Illinois
San Antonio, Texas
San Diego, California
San Francisco–Oakland, California
San Jose, California
Seattle–Everett, Washington
Tampa–St. Petersburg, Florida
Washington, DC– Maryland–Virginia

[a]These metropolitan areas are defined as 1980 SMSAs and NECMAs (for the Hartford and Boston metropolitan areas), with the exceptions of the New York and Paterson–Clifton–Passaic metropolitan areas. The New York metropolitan area is comprised of Nassau, Suffolk, Bronx, Kings, New York, Putnam, Queens, Richmond, Rockland, and Westchester Counties in New York State. The Paterson–Clifton–Passaic metropolitan area is comprised of Passaic and Bergen Counties in New Jersey.

APPENDIX TABLE F.2

Central Counties of 1980 Metropolitan Areas with Populations Exceeding 1 Million

Metropolitan Area Groupings/ Metropolitan Areas	Central County(s)
NORTH-DECLINING	
New York	Bronx, Kings, New York, Queens, and Richmond Cos., N.Y.
Philadelphia	Philadelphia Co., Pa.
Boston	Suffolk Co., Mass.
Cincinnati	Hamilton Co., Ohio
St. Louis	St. Louis City Co., Mo.
Buffalo	Erie Co., N.Y.
Chicago	Cook Co., Ill.
Newark	Essex Co., N.J.
Cleveland	Cuyahoga Co., Ohio
Detroit	Wayne Co., Mich.
Milwaukee	Milwaukee Co., Wisc.
Pittsburgh	Allegheny Co., Pa.
Paterson*	Passaic Co., N.J.
NORTH-OLD	
Columbus	Franklin Co., Ohio
Indianapolis	Marion Co., Ind.
Kansas City	Clay, Jackson, and Platte Cos., Mo.
Hartford	Hartford Co., Conn.
Minneapolis*	Hennepin and Ramsey Cos., Minn.
SOUTH-OLD	
Baltimore	Baltimore City Co., Md.
New Orleans	Orleans Parish, La.
Washington, DC	District of Columbia
Atlanta	Fulton Co., Ga.
WEST-OLD	
San Francisco*	Alameda and San Francisco Cos., Calif.
Denver*	Denver and Boulder Cos., Colo.
Los Angeles*	Los Angeles Co., Calif.
Portland	Multnomah Co., Oreg.
Seattle*	King and Snohomish Cos., Wash.
SOUTH-YOUNG	
San Antonio	Bexar Co., Tex.
Dallas*	Dallas and Tarrant Cos., Tex.
Houston	Harris Co., Tex.
Tampa*	Hillsborough and Pinellas Cos., Fla.
Miami	Dade Co., Fla.
Ft. Lauderdale*	Broward Co., Fla.
WEST-YOUNG	
Sacramento	Sacramento Co., Calif.
San Diego	San Diego Co., Calif.
San Jose	Santa Clara Co., Calif.
Phoenix	Maricopa Co., Ariz.
Riverside*	Riverside and San Bernardino Cos., Calif.
Anaheim*	Orange Co., Calif.

*Largest of multiple central cities (complete metropolitan area names are listed in Appendix Table F.1).

APPENDIX TABLE F.3

County Group Codes from 1980 PUMS Files
Associated with "1970 Equivalent" Central City and SMSA Definitions

1970 Equivalent SMSA[a]	County Group Codes[b] for Central City(s)	County Group Codes[b] for Rest of SMSA
NORTH-DECLINING		
New York, N.Y.	(A) 36:36–40	(A) 36:41–44
Philadelphia, Pa.–N.J	(A) 42:55	(A) 34:41–48 and 42:56–7?
Boston, Mass.	(A) 25:22	(A) 25:15–21, 23–31
Cincinnati, Ohio–Ky.–Ind.	(A) 39:52	(A) 21:1–2 and 39:53–55
St. Louis, Mo.–Ill.	(A) 29:23	(A) 17:19–22 and 29:24–2(
Buffalo, N.Y.	(A) 36:23	(A) 36:24–25
Chicago, Ill.	(A) 17:32	(A) 17:33–38
Newark, N.J.	(A) 34:13	(A) 34:14–25
Cleveland, Ohio	(A) 39:8	(A) 39:9–17
Detroit, Mich.	(A) 26:36	(A) 26:37–57
Milwaukee, Wisc.	(A) 55:23	(A) 55:24–26
Pittsburgh, Pa.	(A) 42:25	(A) 42:23–24, 26–33
Paterson–Clifton–Passaic, N.J.	(A) 34:1–2	(A) 34:3–9
NORTH-OLD		
Columbus, Ohio	(A) 39:42	(A) 39:43–44
Indianapolis, Ind.	(A) 18:21	(A) 18:22–24
Kansas City, Mo.–Kans.	(A) 29:8	(A) 20:9–10 and 29:9–12
Hartford, Conn.	(A) 9:15	(A) 9:16–19
Minneapolis–St. Paul, Minn.	(A) 27:19	(A) 27:14–18, 20, 22–24
SOUTH-OLD		
Baltimore, Md.	(A) 24:6	(A) 24:4–5, 7–8
New Orleans, La.	(A) 22:21	(A) 22:22–26
Washington, DC,–Md.–Va.	(A) 11:1	(A) 24:9–10 and 51:28–31
Atlanta, Ga.	(A) 13:4	(A) 13:5–9
WEST-OLD		
San Francisco–Oakland, Calif.	(A) 6:14, 16	(A) 6:15, 17–19
Denver, Colo.	(A) 8:6	(A) 8:7–12
Los Angeles–Long Beach, Calif.	(A) 6:40–41	(A) 6:42
Portland, Oreg.–Wash.	(A) 41:2	(A) 41:3–5 and 53:10
Seattle–Everett, Wash.	(B) 53:17	(B) 53:18–19
SOUTH-YOUNG		
San Antonio, Tex.	(A) 48:40	(A) 48:41–42
Dallas, Tex.	(A) 48:13	(A) 48:14–18, 22–24
Houston, Tex.	(A) 48:58	(A) 48:59–64
Tampa–St. Petersburg, Fla.	(A) 12:22, 24	(A) 12:23, 25–26
Miami, Fla.	(A) 12:43	(A) 12:44–53
Ft. Lauderdale–Hollywood, Fla.	(A) 12:36–37	(A) 12:38–42

APPENDIX TABLE F.3 *(continued)*

1970 Equivalent SMSA[a]	County Group Codes[b] for Central City(s)	County Group Codes[b] for Rest of SMSA
WEST-YOUNG		
Sacramento, Calif.	(A) 6:8	(A) 6:9–11
San Diego, Calif.	(A) 6:51	(A) 6:52
San Jose, Calif.	(A) 6:30	(A) 6:31
Phoenix, Ariz.	(A) 4:8	(A) 4:9
San Bernardino–Riverside– Ontario, Calif.	(B) 6:100, 104	(B) 6:101–102, 105
Anaheim–Santa Ana–Garden Grove, Calif.	(A) 6:43–45	(A) 6:46

[a]Names refer to 1970 SMSAs (and central cities) as distinct from the metropolitan area names that are used in the Part Two chapters.

[b]The County Group areas associated with these codes appear in Appendices L and M (for Sample "A" codes) and Appendices N and O (for Sample "B" codes) of *Census of Population and Housing: 1980, Public Use Microdata Samples Technical Documentation*, U.S. Bureau of the Census, 1983. Codes listed show: (sample "A" or "B") State Code: County-Group Code(s).

Bibliography

Alba, Richard D., and Michael J. Batutis "Migration's Toll: Lessons from New York State." *American Demographics* (June 1985):38-42.

Alonso, William "The Population Factor and Urban Structure." In Arthur P. Solomon, ed. *The Prospective City: Economy, Population, Energy and Environmental Developments.* Cambridge, MA: The MIT Press, 1980.

Althaus, Paul H., and Joseph Schachter "Interstate Migration and the New Federalism." *Social Science Quarterly* 64 (1983):35-45.

Beale, Calvin L. "Poughkeepsies's Complaint or Defining Metropolitan Areas." *American Demographics* (January 1984):28-48.

Berry, Brian J. L., and John D. Kasarda *Contemporary Urban Ecology.* New York: Macmillan, 1977.

Bluestone, Barry, and Bennett Harrison *The Deindustrialization of America.* New York: Basic Books, 1982.

Bogue, Donald J. *Population Growth in Standard Metropolitan Areas 1900-1950.* Washington, DC: Housing and Home Finance Agency, 1953.

Boyer, Richard, and David Savageau *Places Rated Almanac.* Chicago: Rand McNally, 1985.

Bradbury, Katharine L.; Anthony Downs; and Kenneth A. Small *Urban Decline and the Future of American Cities.* Washington, DC: The Brookings Institution, 1982.

Brown, David L., and John M. Wardwell, eds. *New Directions in Urban-Rural Migration.* New York: Academic Press, 1980.

Burgess, Ernest W. "The Growth of the City: An Introduction to a Research Project." In Robert E. Park, Ernest Burgess, and R. D. McKenzie, eds. *The City.* Chicago, IL: University of Chicago Press, 1925.

Castells, Manuel "High Technology, Economic Restructuring, and the Urban-Regional Process in the United States." In Manuel Castells, ed. *High Technology, Space and Society.* Beverly Hills, CA: Sage Publications, 1985.

Cebula, Richard J. *Geographic Living-Cost Differentials.* Lexington, MA: Lexington Books, 1983.

Chinitz, Benjamin, ed. *The Declining Northeast: Demographic and Economic Analyses.* New York: Praeger, 1978.

Clark, Gordon L. *Interregional Migration, National Policy, and Social Justice.* Totowa, NJ: Rowman & Allanheld, 1983.

Clark, Thomas A. *Blacks in Suburbs: A National Perspective.* New Brunswick, NJ: Rutgers University Center for Urban Policy Research, 1979.

Duncan, Otis Dudley, and Albert J. Reiss, Jr. *Social Characteristics of Urban and Rural Communities.* New York: Free Press, 1956.

Duncan, Otis Dudley; W.R. Scott; Stanley Lieberson; Beverly Duncan; and Hal Winsborough *Metropolis and Region.* Baltimore: The Johns Hopkins University Press, 1960.

Dunn, Edgar S., Jr. *The Development of the U.S. Urban System.* 2 vols. Washington, DC: Resources for the Future, Inc., 1983.

Fainstein, Susan S.; Norman I. Fainstein; Richard Child Hill; Dennis Judd; and Michael Peter Smith *Restructuring the City: The Political Economy of Urban Redevelopment.* New York: Longman, 1983.

Farley, Reynolds *Blacks and Whites: Narrowing the Gap.* Cambridge, MA: Harvard University Press, 1984.

Farley, Reynolds; Howard Schuman; Suzanne Bianchi; Diane Colasanto; and Shirley Hatchett "Chocolate City, Vanilla Suburbs: Will the Trend Toward Racially Separate Communities Continue?" *Social Science Research* 7 (1978):319-344.

Foote, Nelson N.; Janet Abu-Lughod; Mary Mix Foley; and Louis Winnick *Housing Choices and Housing Constraints.* New York: McGraw-Hill, 1960.

Forstall, Richard L. "Annexations and Corporate Changes Since the 1970 Census: With Historical Data on Annexation for Larger Cities for 1900-1970." In *The Municipal Yearbook.* Washington, DC: International City Management Association, 1975.

Frey, William H. "The Changing Impact of White Migration on the Population Compositions of Origin and Destination Metropolitan Areas." *Demography* 16:2 (May 1979):219-237.

―――"Central City White Flight: Racial and Nonracial Causes." *American Sociological Review* 44 (June 1979):425-448.

――― "Black In-migration, White Flight and the Changing Economic Base of the Central City." *American Journal of Sociology* 85:6 (1980):1396-1417.

――― "Status Selective White Flight and Central City Population Change: A Comparative Analysis." *Journal of Regional Science* 20:1 (1980):71-89.

――― "Lifecourse Migration of Metropolitan Whites and Blacks and the Structure of Demographic Change in Large Central Cities." *American Sociological Review* 49 (December 1984):803-827.

――― "Mover Destination Selectivity and the Changing Suburbanization of Metropolitan Whites and Blacks." *Demography* 22:2 (1985):223-243.

――― "Migration and Depopulation of the Metropolis: Regional Restructuring or Rural Renaissance?" *American Sociological Review* 52 (April 1987):240-257.

Fuguitt, Glenn V., and James J. Zuiches "Residential Preferences and Population Distribution." *Demography* 12:3 (August 1975):491-504.

Gottman, Jean *Megalopolis—The Urbanized Northeastern Seaboard of the United States.* Cambridge, MA: The MIT Press, 1961.

Greenwood, Michael J. "Research on Internal Migration in the United States: A Survey." *Journal of Economic Literature* 3:2 (1975):397-433.

――― *Migration and Economic Growth in the United States.* New York: Academic Press, 1981.

Guest, Avery M. "Patterns of Family Location." *Demography* 9(1972):159-171.

――― "Urban Growth and Population Densities." *Demography* 10 (1973):53-69.

Hall, Peter, and Ann Markusen, eds. *Silicone Landscapes.* Boston, MA: Allen & Unwin, 1985.

Hall, Peter, and Dennis Hay *Growth Centres in the European Urban System.* London: Heinemann, 1980.

Hanson, Royce, ed. *Rethinking Urban Policy: Urban Development in an Advanced Economy.* Washington, DC: National Academy Press, 1983.

Harrison, Bennett, and Edward Hill "The Changing Structure of Jobs in Older and Younger Cities." In Benjamin Chinitz, ed. *Central City Economic Development.* Cambridge, MA: Abt Books, 1979.

Hawley, Amos H. *The Changing Shape of Metropolitan America.* Glencoe, IL: Free Press, 1956.

——— *Urban Society: An Ecological Approach.* New York: Ronald, 1971.

——— "Population Density and the City." *Demography* 9:4 (1972):528.

——— "Urbanization as Process." In David Street and Associates, eds. *Handbook of Urban Life.* San Francisco: Jossey-Bass, 1978.

Hinze, Kenneth E. *Causal Factors in the Net Migration Flow to Metropolitan Areas of the United States 1960-70.* Chicago, IL: Community and Family Study Center, University of Chicago, 1977.

Hoover, Edgar M., and Raymond Vernon *Anatomy of a Metropolis.* Cambridge, MA: Harvard University Press, 1959.

Kasarda, John D. "The Changing Occupational Structure of the American Metropolis: Apropos the Urban Problem." In Barry Schwartz, ed. *The Changing Face of the Suburbs.* Chicago, IL: University of Chicago Press, 1976.

——— "The Implications of Contemporary Redistribution Trends for National Urban Policy." *Social Science Quarterly* 61:3-4 (December 1980):373-400.

——— "Urban Change in Minority Opportunities." In Paul Peterson, ed. *The New Urban Reality.* Washington, DC: The Brookings Institution, 1985.

Kottis, Athena "Impact of Migration on Housing in Urban Areas." *Annals of Regional Science* 5:1 (June 1971):117-124.

Langberg, Mark, and Reynolds Farley "Residential Segregation of Asian Americans in 1980." *Sociology and Social Research* (October 1985).

Laska, Shirley B., and Daphne Spain, eds. *Back to the Cities: Issues in Neighborhood Renovation.* New York: Pergamon Press, 1980.

Lichter, Daniel T., and Glenn V. Fuguitt "The Transition to Nonmetropolitan Population Deconcentration." *Demography* 19 (1982):211-221.

Lieberson, Stanley *Ethnic Patterns in American Cities.* New York: Free Press, 1963.

Liu, Ben-chieh "Differential Net Migration Rates and the Quality of Life." *Review of Economics and Statistics* 57:3 (1975):329-337.

Logan, John R., and Mark Schneider "The Stratification of Metropolitan Suburbs, 1960-70." *American Sociological Review* 46 (1981):175-186.

——— "Racial Segregation and Racial Change in American Suburbs, 1970-80." *American Journal of Sociology* 89 (1984):874-888.

Long, John F. *Population Deconcentration in the United States.* Special Demographic Analysis CDS-81-5. Washington, DC: U.S. Government Printing Office, 1981.

Long, Larry H., and Diane DeAre "Repopulating the Countryside: A 1980 Census Trend." *Science* 217 (1982):1111-1116.

Long, Larry H., and Kristin A. Hansen "Reasons for Interstate Migration." *Current Population Reports* P-23 No. 81. Washington, DC: Bureau of the Census, 1979.

Lowry, Ira S. *Migration and Metropolitan Growth: Two Analytical Models.* San Francisco: Chandler, 1966.

Markusen, Ann R.; Peter Hall; and Amy Glasmeier *High Tech America: The What, How, Where and Why of the Sunrise Industries.* Winchester, MA: Allen & Unwin, 1986.

Massey, Douglas S. "Residential Segregation of Spanish Americans in United States Urbanized Areas." *Demography* 16:4 (1978):553-563.

Mollenkopf, John H. "Paths Toward the Post-industrial Service City: The

Northeast and the Southwest." In Robert W. Burchill and David Listokin, eds. *Cities under Stress.* New Brunswick, NJ: Rutgers Center for Urban Policy Research, 1981.

Moomaw, Ronald L. "Firm Location and City Size: Reduced Productivity Advantages as a Factor in the Decline of Manufacturing in Urban Areas." *Journal of Urban Economics* 17 (1985):73-89.

Morrison, Peter A., and Judith P. Wheeler "Rural Renaissance in America? The Revival of Population Growth in Remote Areas." *Population Bulletin* 31, No. 3, Population Reference Bureau, Inc., Washington, DC.

Mueller, Charles F. *The Economics of Labor Migration—A Behavioral Analysis.* New York: Academic Press, 1982.

Mueller, Eva, and James N. Morgan "Location Decisions of Manufactures." *American Economic Review, Papers and Proceedings* 502 (1962):204-217.

Muller, Thomas "The Declining and Growing Metropolis—A Fiscal Comparison." In George Sternlieb and James W. Hughes *Post-Industrial America: Metropolitan Decline and Inter-Regional Job Shifts.* New Brunswick, NJ: The Center for Urban Policy Research, Rutgers University, 1975.

Nelson, Howard J. "A Service Classification of American Cities." *Economic Geography* 31 (1955):189-210.

Nelson, Kathryn P. *Gentrification and Distressed Cities.* Madison: The University of Wisconsin Press, 1988.

Newman, Robert J. "Industry Migration and Growth in the South." *Review of Economics and Statistics* 65 (1983):76-86.

Norton, R. D. *City Life-Cycles and American Urban Policy.* New York: Academic Press, 1979.

Noyelle, Thierry J., and Thomas M. Stanback, Jr. *The Economic Transformation of American Cities.* Totowa, NJ: Rowman & Allanheld, 1984.

Odeh, Izraeli, and Ah-Loh Lin "Recent Evidence on the Effect of Real Earnings on Net Migration." *Regional Studies* 18 (1984):113- 120.

O'Hare, William P. "Poverty in America: Trends and New Patterns." *Population Bulletin* 40:3 (1985), Population Reference Bureau, Inc., Washington, DC.

Passel, Jeffrey S., and J. Gregory Robinson "Revised Demographic Estimates of the Coverage of the Population by Age, Sex, and Race in the 1980 Census." memorandum, July 8, 1985.

Perry, David C., and Alfred J. Watkins, eds. *The Rise of the Sunbelt Cities.* Beverly Hills, CA: Sage Publications, 1977.

Peterson, Paul E., ed. *The New Urban Reality.* Washington, DC: The Brookings Institution, 1985.

Pettigrew, Thomas "Racial Change and the Intrametropolitan Distribution of Black Americans." In Arthur P. Solomon, ed. *The Prospective City.* Cambridge, MA: The MIT Press, 1980.

Porell, Frank W. "Intermetropolitan Migration and Quality of Life." *Journal of Regional Science* 22 (1982):137-158.

Price, Daniel O. *Changing Characteristics of the Negro Population.* U.S. Bureau of the Census. Washington, DC: U.S. Government Printing Office, 1969.

Rosenwaike, Ira "A Critical Examination of the Designation of Standard Metropolitan Statistical Areas." *Social Forces* 48:3 (1970):322-333.

Rudel, Thomas K. "Changes in the Access to Homeownership during the 1970s." *Economic Geography* (1985):37-49.

Russell, Louise B. *The Baby Boom Generation and the Economy.* Washington, DC: The Brookings Institution, 1982.

Rust, Edgar *No Growth: Impacts on Metropolitan Areas.* Lexington, MA: Lexington Books, 1975.

Ryscavage, Paul "Reconciling Divergent Trends in Real Income." *Monthly Labor Review* (July 1986):24-29.

Sawyers, L., and W. Tabb, eds. *Sunbelt/Snowbelt Urban Development and Regional Restructuring.* New York: Oxford University Press, 1974.

Schnore, Leo F. *The Urban Scene.* New York: Free Press, 1965.

Shryock, Henry S., Jr. *Population Mobility within the United States.* Chicago: Community and Family Studies Center, 1964.

Sjaastad, Larry A. "The Costs and Returns of Human Migration." *Journal of Political Economy* 70 (1962):80-93.

——— "The Relationship between Migration and Income in the United States." *Papers and Proceedings of the Regional Science Association* 6 (1960):37-64.

Sly, David F. "Migration and the Ecological Complex." *American Sociological Review* 37 (1972):615-628.

Smith, Neil "Toward A Theory of Gentrification: A Back to the City Movement, by Capital, Not People." *Journal of the American Planning Association* (October 1979):546.

South, S. J., and D. L. Poston, Jr. "The U.S. Metropolitan System: Regional Change 1950-70." *Urban Affairs Quarterly* 18 (1982):187-206.

Speare, Alden, Jr.; Sidney Goldstein; and William H. Frey *Residential Mobility, Migration and Metropolitan Change.* Cambridge, MA: Ballinger Publishing Co., 1975.

Stanback, Thomas M., Jr., and Richard Knight *The Metropolitan Community (The Metropolitan Economy).* New York: Columbia University Press, 1970.

——— *Suburbanization and the City.* Montclair, NJ: Allanheld, Osmun, 1976.

Stanback, Thomas, Jr., and Thierry J. Noyelle *Cities in Transition.* Totowa, NJ: Allanheld, Osmun, 1982.

Sternlieb, George, and James W. Hughes, eds. *Post-Industrial America: Metropolitan Decline and Inter-Regional Job Shifts.* New Brunswick, NJ: The Center for Urban Policy Research, Rutgers University, 1975.

Stevens, Joe E. "The Demand for Public Goods as a Factor in the Nonmetropolitan Migration Turnaround." In David L. Brown and John N. Wardwell, eds. *New Directions in Urban-Rural Migration: The Population Turnaround in Rural America.* New York: Academic Press, 1981.

Taeuber, Karl E. "Racial Segregation: The Persisting Dilemma." *Annals of the American Academy of Political and Social Sciences* 422 (1975):87-96.

Taeuber, Karl E., and Alma F. Taeuber "White Migration and Socioeconomic Differences Between Cities and Suburbs." *American Sociological Review* 29 (1964):718-729.

——— *Negroes in Cities.* Chicago: Aldine, 1965.

Tobin, Gary A. "Suburbanization and the Development of Motor Transportation: Transportation Technology and the Suburbanization Process." In Barry Schwartz *The Changing Face of the Suburbs.* Chicago: University of Chicago Press, 1976.

Tomaskovic-Devey, Donald, and S. M. Miller "Recapitalization: The Basic Urban Policy of the 1980s." In Norman I. Fainstein and Susan S. Fainstein, eds. *Urban Policy Under Capitalism.* Urban Affairs Annual Reviews 22. Beverly Hills, CA: Sage Publications, 1982.

Tucker, C. J. "Changing Patterns of Migration between Metropolitan and Nonmetropolitan Areas in the United States: Recent Evidence." *Demography* 13 (1976):435-443.

Ullman, Edward "A Theory of Location for Cities." *American Journal of Sociology* 46 (1941):853-864.

Wardwell, John "Toward a Theory of Urban-Rural Migration in the Developed World." In David L. Brown and John M. Wardwell, eds. *New Directions in Urban-Rural Migration: The Population Turnaround in Rural America.* New York: Academic Press, 1980.

Warren, Robert, and Ellen Percy Kraly "The Elusive Exodus, Emigration from the United States." *Population Trends and Public Policy* 8, Population Reference Bureau, 1985.

Warren, Robert, and Jennifer Marks Peck "Foreign-Born Emigration from the United States: 1960 to 1970." *Demography* 17:1 (1980):71- 84.

Webber, Michael J. *Industrial Location.* Beverly Hills, CA: Sage Publications, 1984.

Weinstein, Bernard L., and Firestine, Robert E. *Regional Growth and Decline in the United States.* New York: Praeger, 1978.

Wilson, Franklin D. *Residential Consumption, Economic Opportunity, and Race.* New York: Academic Press, 1979.

—— "Urban Ecology: Urbanization and Systems of Cities." *Annual Review of Sociology* 10 (1984):283-307.

—— "The Impact of Interregional Migration on the Population Composition of Origin/Destination Metropolitan and Nonmetropolitan Areas." Working Paper 85-32, Center for Demography and Ecology, University of Wisconsin, 1986.

Wirth, Louis "Urbanism as a Way of Life." *American Journal of Sociology* 44 (1938):1-24.

Yago, Glenn; Hyman Korman; Sen-Yuan Wu; and Michael Schwartz "Investment and Disinvestment in New York, 1960-80." *The Annals of the American Academy of Political and Social Science* (1984):28-38.

Yeates, Maurice H., and Barry J. Garner *The North American City.* New York: Harper & Row, 1971.

Zimmer, Basil G. "The Urban Centrifugal Drift." In Amos H. Hawley and Vincent P. Rock, eds. *Metropolitan America in Contemporary Perspective.* Beverly Hills, CA: Sage Publications, 1975.

Name Index

Boldface numbers refer to figures and tables.

A

Abu-Lughod, Janet, 177n, 321, 322n
Advisory Commission on
    Intergovernmental Relations, 281n
Alba, Richard D., 110
Alonso, William, 5n, 179n, 320n, 326n
Althaus, Paul H., 100n
Aponte, Robert, 466n
Appelbaum, Richard P., 110
Ashton, Patrick J., 182n

B

Bane, Mary Jo, 322n
Batutis, Michael J., 110
Beale, Calvin L., 8n, 30, 43n, 438n
Beane, Frank, 266n
Bernard, Richard M., 184n, 204n, 208n,
    267n, 284n, 315n
Berry, Brian J. L., 30, 44, 90n, 184n
Bianchi, Suzanne M., 165n, 168, 241n, 251n
Black, Thomas J., 179n
Bloch, Robin, 460n
Bluestone, Barry, 89, 94n, 102, 103n, 125n,
    143, 376n, 433n, 439n, 444n
Bogue, Donald J., 17, 39, **40**, 46n
Bollens, John C., 208n
Bourne, L. S., 454n
Bouvier, Leon F., 266n
Boyer, Richard, 84n
Bradbury, Katharine L., 4n, 109n, 183, 187,
    435n
Briggs, Vernon, Jr., 69n
Brown, David L., 4n
Burchell, Robert W., 180n
Burgess, E. W., 182n

C

Casey, Stephan C., 180n
Castells, Manuel, 4n, 89, 439n, 460n
Cebula, Richard J., 77n, 78, 79n, 84–87, 96,
    99, 439n, 440n
Cherlin, Andrew J., 178n
Chinitz, Benjamin, 4n
Christaller, Walter, 18n
Clark, Gordon L., 10n, 110n
Clark, Rebecca, 120
Clark, Thomas A., 178n, 240n, 241n, 245n
Colasanto, Diane, 241n, 251n
Congressional Budget Office, 134n
Cooley, Charles Horton, 19n
Cowan, Charles, **51**
Cremeans, John E., 94n

D

Danforth, Senator, 478n
Danielson, M. N., 214n
Davis, Cary, 267n
Davis, Kingsley, 432n
DeAre, Diane, 44, 473n
De Jong, Gordon F., 42n
Department of Defense, 9
Dowall, David E., 137n
Downs, Anthony, 4n, 109n, 183, 187, 435n
Duncan, Otis Dudley, 17, 18n, 90n
Dunn, Edgar S., Jr., 91
Dziewonski, K., 454n

E

Embry, Robert C., Jr., 351n

565

Subject Index

Boldface numbers refer to figures and tables.

N